D1409012

# MICROSOFT®

# Office

# 2000

# User Manual

**que®**

# MICROSOFT®

# Office
# 2000
# User Manual

**Simply Written, Inc.**

A Division of Macmillan Computer Publishing, USA
201 West 103rd Street
Indianapolis, IN 46290

# Microsoft® Office 2000 User Manual

Library of Congress Catalog Card Number: 98-88240

International Standard Book Number: 0-7897-1930-4

01   00   99   4   3   2   1

Interpretation of the printing code: The rightmost double-digit number is the year of the book's printing; the rightmost single-digit, the number of the book's printing. For example, a printing code of 98-1 shows that the first printing of the book occurred in 1998.

Composed in Century Old Style by Macmillan Computer Publishing.

Printed in the United States of America.

## Trademarks

**EXECUTIVE EDITOR**
Jim Minatel

**ACQUISITIONS EDITOR**
Jill Byus

**DEVELOPMENT EDITOR**
Jerilynne Sander-Altom

**MANAGING EDITOR**
Tom Hayes

**COPY EDITORS**
Tim Altom
Janice L Beene
Kathy Roche
Jerilynne Sander-Altom

**INDEXER**
Tim Altom

**TECHNICAL EDITORS**
Paul Leininger
Pete Lenges
Mitch Milam

**PRODUCTION & PROOFREADING**
Janice L Beene
Lora Beene

**COVER DESIGNER**
Dan Armstrong

**INTERIOR DESIGNER**
Nathan Clement

# Contents at a Glance

# Table of Contents

# Dedication

To Karen Patrick-Knight, who's made a difference for us, and to our parents (Ruth Altom and Ron and Barbara Arndt) who never quit believing in our abilities.

# About the Authors

Jerilynne Sander is president and founder of Simply Written, Inc. and a co-creator of the Clustar Method™ for doing task-based documentation. She is a senior member of the Society for Technical Communication and has served in both local chapter and international capacities for the Society. She is an Adobe Certified Expert in FrameMaker. She designs templates for clients in both FrameMaker and Microsoft Word, and is an internationally known speaker on creativity and trainer in FrameMaker, technical communication, and the principles of document creation. She lives in Indianapolis with her husband Tim and her son Matthew in a former parsonage.

Tim Altom is vice president of Simply Written, Inc. and a co-creator of the Clustar Method™ for doing task-based documentation. He is a senior member of the Society for Technical Communication and has served in a variety of offices for the Society. He is a frequent speaker at conferences and trains in help file creation and other technical communication topics. He shares the former parsonage with Jerilynne and Matthew.

Janice L Beene is a manager, writer, and researcher for Simply Written, Inc. She is a former U.S. Navy cook, computer programmer, and chess instructor. She is blessed with daughter Lora and Lil' Bit, Tigger and Teddie, her three cats. They share her house in Indianapolis.

Kathy Roche is a contract writer and signing interpreter in Indianapolis. She has three children and a husband, and believes that they're often interchangeable.

Simply Written, Inc. is based in Indianapolis, a place that's within a day's drive of 70% of the U.S. population. The company specializes in highly structured documentation and single source documentation systems for a wide variety of industries.

# Acknowledgments

Thanks go out to the Que editorial team for their irreplaceable help, advice, and patience. A special thanks to Jim Minatel for looking behind the scenes and helping us see how we could use the Clustar Method™ to organize a non task-based book. We've enjoyed the challenge!

Another special thanks to Janice Beene, who has played more roles than you can shake a stick at. She's helped us get this book out the door, even when other folks were dying on the vine. This has truly been a team effort and Janice was an integral part of that team.

Last (but not least), thanks to Mitch Milam for pitching in to do the tech edit—you're a dear!

Thanks to everyone associated with this project—you've helped us look good.

# Who Should Use This Book?

This book is for every Office 2000 user who wants to know intimately what's going on within the software. This version of Office is bigger, more powerful, more flexible, and more confusing than past versions. Even veteran Office users may find features in this book that they didn't dream existed.

This book is for every Office 2000 user, from beginner to expert. Beginners can get started with the simple explanations of features, while experts can always use a reference volume. It's all here, the keyboard shortcuts, the hints, the "gotchas". It's what you should have received with Office 2000, but didn't.

# We'd Like To Hear From You!

Que Corporation has a long-standing reputation for high-quality books and products. To ensure your continued satisfaction, we also understand the importance of customer service and support.

## Tech Support

If you need help with the information in this book or with a CD or disk accompanying the book, please access Macmillan Computer Publishing's online Knowledge Base at **www.superlibrary.com/ general/support**.

Also be sure to visit Que's Web resource center for all the latest information, enhancements, errata, downloads and more. It's located at **www.quecorp.com/**.

## Orders, Catalogs and Customer Service

To order other Que or Macmillan Computer Publishing books, catalogs, or products, please contact our Customer Service Department at 800-428-5331 or fax us at 800-882-8583 (International Fax: 3317-228-4400). Or visit our online bookstore at **www.mcp.com/**.

## Comments and Suggestions

We want you to let us know what you like or dislike most about this book or other Que products. Your comments will help us to continue publishing the best books available on computer topics in today's market.

Que Corporation
201 West 103rd Street, 4B
Indianapolis, IN 46290 USA
Fax: 317-581-4663

*Please be sure to include the book's title and author as well as your name and phone or fax number.* We will carefully review your comments and share them with the author. Please note that due to the high volume of mail we receive, we might not be able to reply to every message.

Thank you for choosing Que!

# First Things First

**In this part**

# About This Book

## In this chapter

# About The Microsoft Office User Guide

Welcome to the *Microsoft Office User Guide.*

We're glad you're here, and we want you to feel comfortable with the information that we've included. We couldn't include everything from the Office 2000 suite; there are features in there that only a tiny fraction of users install, such as Query and NetMeeting. But there's a bunch of information here.

Traditionally, you ran software by taking several steps for each action. Printing a document, for example, could involve learning codes that you had to type into a command line. Opening a document could use a half-dozen steps or more. Using such software was like assembling a bicycle on Christmas morning using the instructions from the box.

Microsoft, however, has pioneered what might be called "stepless" form-centered commands. In Office 2000, for instance, to print something you can simply click a button and pick your options in a dialog box, like filling out a form. In this software universe, "how" you do something is nearly the same thing as "where" you do it. In Office 2000, there isn't a huge need for multi-step instructions, because in many cases the steps are simply "1) Click this button, 2) Fill out the dialog box, 3) Click the OK button."

What matters most in Office 2000 isn't so much knowing steps as it is knowing what all those little controls do in windows and dialog boxes. And Office 2000 has those a'plenty. Almost everything in Office 2000 is done with something you click or type into. Now the trick to Office 2000 is knowing what to click, and when.

That's the premise behind this book, to show you what to click to accomplish a task, and when to click it. There are so many buttons, check boxes, icons, options, features, and other items that even a stepless universe has become confusing. This book is designed to clear away that confusion and show you what you need to know, when you need to know it.

A few notes:

- We actually used, abused, and flat out played with most of the options in Word, Excel, PowerPoint, and Outlook.
- Don't panic if your application looks a little bit different than the screen shots we've included in this book. It doesn't mean that your version of Office 2000 is *wrong*. It's just that Microsoft has made Office 2000 *sooo* customizable that no two Office 2000 installations will look precisely the same. There are lots of ways to customize Office 2000 applications for specific needs. For example, there are applications and add-ins from Microsoft and from other developers that can add buttons or menus, show you odd dialog boxes, and so on. Check with your system administrator or your installation manual for more information.
- We were using Microsoft Windows 98 while we wrote this book. If you're are using another version of Windows some of the menu options and dialog boxes may display a bit differently.

## Structure—The Backbone Of This Book

We've used a very organized structure for this book. It helped keep us on track and it gives you a consistent place to find what you need. This structuring method, developed and trademarked by Simply Written, is called the Clustar Method™. With the Clustar Method, you'll see certain headings used consistently throughout the book and you'll find the same types of information below those headings. We don't mix and match and put information in one place one time and in another place the next.

Figure 1.1 gives you a brief look at how this book is organized and what types of information you'll find throughout this book. The standard headings you'll see are:

- How You Get Here,
- What's In This (Dialog Box, Window, Flyout Menu, Toolbar),
- What's Different, and
- Step-By-Step.

**N O T E**  You won't find every one of these headings used for every topic. But, when they're used, you can count on finding the same type information every time.

**Figure 1.1**    How this book is organized

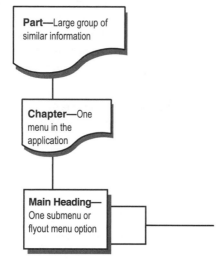

**Introduction**—A brief summary of what the specific menu option does.

**How You Get Here**—At least two different ways you can access the menu option.

**What's In This (Window, Dialog Box, Toolbar, Flyout Menu)**—A picture of the window, dialog box, toolbar, or flyout menu followed by a table with a description of the main options. The callouts in the picture match the numbers in the table.

**What's Different**—A heading that is only used if an option was covered in a chapter describing common options *and* there are some additional options available for a specific application. It follows the same structure as a "What's In This..." heading.

**Step-by-Step**—A series of instructions on how to get a task done. A Step-by-Step doesn't include any of the "why", just the "how".

**Note**—Additional information that might be helpful or get you out of a jam. You may also find some examples if an option was a bit hard to explain.

**Tip**—Tips are usually another way of doing the same thing or another way to use a specific option.

Secondary headings use the same structure as a main heading.

# TechoSpeak—Terms Used In This Book

There are many commonly used terms in Windows applications, and sometimes more than one name for the same thing. One book's "dialog box", for example, may be another book's "message box".

In this book we've tried use the terms you'll find in most other books and manuals. However, this book uses some wording conventions that we've standardized on, and which may not be in other books. We've tried to keep these wording conventions in line with ones that have grown up in the computer community. For instance, when you click the mouse on an item in a menu you've just dropped down, we say that you're "choosing" that item, not "clicking on it" or "selecting it". Call us overly persnickety, but we believe in making a style decision and then sticking to it.

## Windows TechnoSpeak

The following is a list of commonly used Windows terms.

**Table 1.1** Windows terms in this book

| Term | Definition | Sample |
|------|-----------|--------|
| Active | The part of the application or file you have last typed on, placed your cursor on, clicked on, or otherwise caused the part of the window to take and process your commands. Generally, the title bar is colored when the window or part of a window is active or grayed out if inactive. Programmers refer to this as "having the focus" if the object is active. But most of us aren't programmers, so we're using the more descriptive term "active". | |
| Application | The "program" you are using to get your work done, with an example being Microsoft Word. Applications are much more complex than the older "programs" that you might have known in the DOS days, so we have to have a new name for them. | Microsoft Word, Microsoft Excel |
| Button | A control that depresses when clicked. Used for actions that are immediate, such as saving a document. | |
| Checkbox | A control that displays or hides a check in a small square box when clicked. Used to select or deselect options. | Print to file |
| Control | Any device other than a menu in a window or dialog box, used to send a command or text to the application or to specify options. Controls include drop-down lists, checkboxes, buttons, text boxes, and radio buttons. | |

**Table 1.1**   Windows terms in this book, continued

| Term | Definition | Sample |
|---|---|---|
| Dialog Box | A collection of controls, used for taking information from a user and sending it to the application. If you use your imagination a bit, you can see the dialog box holding a "dialog (or conversation)" with you, hence the name. | |
| Drop-down list | A control that displays a list of possible choices when you click on it. This is known to the more technical among us as a "combo box", a name that, while descriptive and accurate, nonetheless sounds like a place where a jazz band sets up to play. | |
| File | Technically, a file is a single, identifiable collection of data. More conventionally, it's a collection of numbers or text that you give a name and save on your computer. | A PowerPoint presentation |
| Flyout Menu | A menu that comes out from a submenu when the main menu doesn't have enough room for additional, subsidiary options. As the number of options in the Office suite has grown, the real estate available for displaying them hasn't. This fact of life has created the need to pack more menu items into the same space, leading Microsoft to use flyout menus. | |
| Icon | An icon is a small picture that standards for an application, a word, or a group of words. The icon "points" to its application or function, so that when you click or double-click on an it, the action "happens". They're supposed to make the commands easier to recognize and use. Although I must admit that I sometimes wonder who came up with the pictures since they don't always make sense to me! | |
| Insertion point | The location where your cursor currently is. Many functions in Office 2000 insert items or perform actions at the insertion point. | I want my mommy! |

**Table 1.1**  Windows terms in this book, continued

| Term | Definition | Sample |
|------|-----------|--------|
| Menu | A list of application actions, commands, or options. The most familiar example is probably the File menu. Menus "unroll" or "drop down" when clicked. Because real estate is getting more dear on the monitor, many menu items are in a second or third "tier" of commands, reached by a subsidiary flyout menu or in a dialog box called onto the screen by a menu item with an ellipsis (...) behind it. Additionally, some menu options have indicators next to them to clue the user that the option is on or off. Other options are used often enough to justify putting a keyboard shortcut next to the menu option, so the user can do the same action more quickly from the keyboard. | File Edit View Insert Format Tools Slide Show Window Help |
| Object | The word "object" has a very technical definition to programmers, but for our purposes here it's anything on the screen that's an identifiable unit, something that moves as one thing, appears as one thing, disappears as one thing. A window is an object. So is a dialog box. | |
| Pane | A subdivision of a window. | Comments From: All Reviewers  Close<br>[EH1]You have a good handle on this subject.<br>[EH2]Please reword this sentence. |
| Radio button | A control with a number of small round areas that show a dark circle inside when clicked. Radio buttons are for selecting *one specific option* from a small number of options, usually all of which are mutually exclusive of one another. Click one radio button and the others are usually deselected. The control takes its name from the old-style round station buttons on car radios. There, too, clicking one button eliminated all the others. | Current page |

**Table 1.1**   Windows terms in this book, continued

| Term | Definition | Sample |
|------|-----------|--------|
| Shortcut menu | The menu that displays when you right-click on an object. There isn't any cue to the user that you can right-click on anything and get a menu, and not all objects have shortcut menus. You just have to know which ones work and which ones don't. The shortcut menu has options that are specific to the object you're right-clicking on. | |
| Submenu | A menu option that is down a level from the main Menu bar. | |
| Tab | So many options, so little space on your screen. Tabs are basically ways to make one dialog box do the work of several, by figuratively placing one tab behind another on screen. The tabs line up like file folder tabs in a drawer, and clicking a particular tab brings that tab forward. | |
| Toolbar | A group of buttons that hang out together. Toolbars group buttons into logical pairings. For example, the Formatting toolbar has buttons that deal exclusively with choosing what your text looks like. Toolbars can often be "undocked" from their positions and made to "float" around on screen. | |

**Table 1.1**  Windows terms in this book, continued

| Term | Definition | Sample |
|---|---|---|
| Text box | A control that you type into. Text boxes are used by applications that need some text from you, the user. For example, a text box might be where you type your name and address prior to printing labels. | Caption: Figure 1 |
| Window | Where the application lives and works on screen. With the Microsoft Windows operating system, almost everything that opens is either a box (such as a dialog box) or a window. Windows are usually persistent, staying on screen and working long hours, unlike dialog boxes, for instance, that open only long enough to talk with you, then disappear. For example, when you start Excel, it opens in its own window. Start another copy of Excel, and it opens in its own window. You can open as many windows as your system can handle. | |

## Actions Technospeak

We assume that you're like any other computer user and you want to use software to take some sort of action. Big actions ("write a letter") break down into smaller ones ("insert clipart"). Most of this book is a description of what happens when you take small actions.

When we tell you to take one of those small actions, we always use exactly the same wording. We don't use the word "type" in one place and "enter text" in another. That's confusing and it's much harder for us to write that way, because frankly we get confused too.

Here's a list of the wording we use in this book for all those little actions.

**N O T E**   The standard mouse setup for windows assumes that your standard mouse clicks are done with the left mouse button, unless otherwise noted in the text. We don't mean to discriminate against southpaws. So, if you've changed your mouse buttons so that they work better for you, you'll need to flip-flop the following descriptions for mouse actions. ▪

**Table 1.2**    Action terms in this book

| Term | What we mean |
| --- | --- |
| Choose | Pick an item or option from a menu. |
| Choose an item that determines | Click your left mouse button on a drop-down list to pick one of the options displayed. |
| Click | Position the cursor over an object and quickly flick the *left* mouse button *once* far enough so that you feel the switch in your mouse go "click". |
| Click to | Click your left mouse button over buttons, radio buttons, icons, and check boxes. |
| Double-click | Position the cursor over an object and quickly flick the *left* mouse button *two times* very quickly, both times being sure to push hard enough to feel the switch in your mouse go "click". |
| Enter | Place your cursor in a text box and type. Note that this isn't anything like pressing the Enter key. See "Press" below. |
| Highlight | Highlighting occurs when text, numbers, or graphics shift color as a result of being clicked or dragged over. The highlighted items can then be manipulated. Office 2000 applications usually offer a number of ways to highlight items on screen. The most common are to click on an item, double-click on one, or hold down the left mouse button and "drag" the cursor over several items. |
| Keyboard | That flat thing with all the keys on it. Usually one per computer. Soon to be obsolete with the advent of voice activation. Where you go to execute keyboard shortcuts. |
| Mouse | The only part of your computer with a truly cute name. The term "mouse" here also includes other types of pointing devices, such as a trackball or a stylus. |
| Point | Do what your mom always told you not to—point to a place on your screen, only using the mouse and cursor. |
| Press | Push down on a specific key. |
| Right-click | Position the cursor over an object and click the *right* mouse button *once*. |
| Triple-click | Position the cursor over something and click the *left* mouse button *three times*. |

## What's With The "Common Options" Chapters?

As we looked through the features, functions, and options in Office 2000, we realized that there were lots of things that were common to three of the four main applications: Word, Excel, and PowerPoint. For example, cut, copy, and paste all work the same way in all the applications. That's when we decided to make a central place to put that kind of information and that was how we came to make a section called *Common Options*.

- If an option is common to Word, Excel, and PowerPoint, it'll be in the "Common Options" section (Part II). There you'll find a screen shot with a description of the common options, tips on using them, and so forth.
- Options specific to an individual application are in that application's part of the manual.

We've included cross-references between the appropriate parts of the manual so that you can easily look up information in the Common Options and in the specific application.

Some options were only common in *two* of the applications. In those cases, we included the information in the appropriate chapter for the specific application.

*...and then there is Outlook. Outlook is such a different beast that it has its own part, with a few references to things that are common.*

# Before You Dive Into Office 2000

## In this chapter

# The Major Parts Of Office 2000 Applications

Office 2000 applications are built of parts, most of which you can manipulate in some way, moving them around, closing them, opening them, resizing them. Sometimes these operations aren't obvious. The major component parts are:

- Windows,
- Dialog Boxes,
- Menus, and
- Toolbars.

# Understanding Windows

As you might suspect from the name, the Microsoft Windows operating system does a lot of creating, using, and closing windows. Applications run in windows. Open a new application and it runs in a new window. Unfortunately, windows aren't perfect mind readers; they don't always land in the right spot on your screen or they get in your way when you're trying to do something else. Fortunately, you can move them around, resize them, hide them, and, in general, customize them to your working environment.

## Parts Of A Window

Figure 2.1 is a sample of a PowerPoint window and Table 2.1 has a description of the options available in most application windows.

**Figure 2.1**   Parts of a window

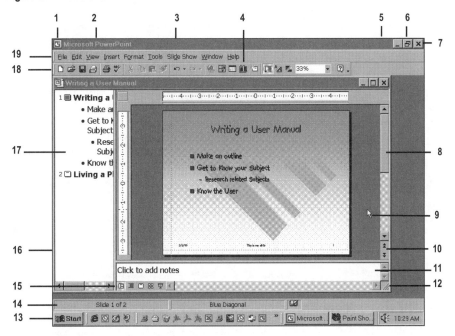

**Table 2.1**   Parts of a window

| Term | Definition |
|------|------------|
| 1   Application icon | The small picture representing the current application. Use this icon to close the application and any open files. You can either: <br> ▪ Click the icon, then choose **Close,** or <br> ▪ Double-click the icon. |
| 2   Application title bar | The colored bar at the top of the application window containing the name of the application and the path for the currently active file. Note that this can be almost any color, depending on how your system is configured. |
| 3   Application window or window | The space onscreen that contains the application you have opened. |
| 4   Icon | A representation of an application or command. |
| 5   Minimize button | The leftmost button of three in the upper right corner, used turn the window into an icon on the Taskbar. |
| 6   Maximize/Restore button | The middle button of three in the upper right corner, used to make the window return to its prior size. |

**Table 2.1**    Parts of a window, continued

| Term | Definition |
|---|---|
| 7  Close/Exit button | The button with an **X**, located in the upper right corner of the application window, document window, dialog box or toolbar. Closes the active window, dialog box or toolbar. |
| 8  Scroll bar | This control takes care of the problem of having too much material to show on screen at one time, by letting you move the viewing area. The scroll bar, usually on the right side of a window, dialog box, or list, or sometimes at the bottom of a window, has an "elevator" for moving the viewing area up or down, right or left, through the current document. The viewing icons are located to the left of the bottom scroll bar. |
| 9  Cursor | What you point to a location, to enter information or click to activate an object. Usually the cursor is an arrow, **I** bar, or flashing line. (For a complete description of the options available, see Table 1.1 on page 7.) You can customize the shape of the cursor, point the arrow in a different direction or change its size |
| 10  Scroll arrows | Small arrows located on a button at either end of a scroll bar that you click to scroll through a document or list with more control. |
| 11  Window Pane | A portion of a window. Each pane has a separate existence within its parent window. This is called Web page view, because most web pages contain at least two panes of information. |
| 12  Window Corner | The lower right corner of an application window, document window, or dialog box that can be dragged with the cursor to make the window bigger or smaller. |
| 13  Taskbar | The bar, normally located at the bottom of your screen, that contain icons, status indicators, and buttons for maneuvering between applications. You can move this bar to any side of your screen you want. |
| 14  Status bar | The bar located directly below the document window that contains information pertaining to the application and file you have active. Indicators like the page/slide number information, num lock, and caps lock indicators are located here. |
| 15  View icons | The icons used to change the way you view the active file. |
| 16  Window Border | The thin gray edge of an application window, document window and dialog box that can be dragged with the cursor to make the window bigger or smaller. |
| 17  Document Window | The space where you enter information in a file in an application. |

**Table 2.1**   Parts of a window, continued

| Term | Definition |
|---|---|
| 18  Toolbar | A group of icons located on a bar that can be placed on the menu bar or moved off the menu bar onto the screen.<br>You can display the list of toolbars available by right-clicking anywhere on a toolbar. The toolbar can also be placed on your menu bar by double-clicking the title bar. Close a toolbar using the **Close/Exit** button. Customize your toolbar by clicking the down pointing arrow, the **Add or Remove buttons** arrow. (For more information, see View ➤ Toolbars on page 64.) |
| 19  Menu bar | The bar directly under the application title bar containing the menus for the application, such as File and Edit. |

**N O T E**   You can't move or resize windows that are maximized (full size). You must make them smaller by minimizing or resizing them first.(For more information, see —Making A Window Fill The Desktop on page 19.) ■

## Step By Step—Resizing A Window

1. If the window is maximized, shrink it.
2. Click and drag on:
   - ■ Any of the edges of the window to move *either* horizontally or vertically, or
   - ■ A corner to move *both* horizontally and vertically at the same time.

## Step By Step—Moving A Window

1. If the window is maximized, shrink it.
2. Click and drag the window's title bar.

   **NOTE**   Click and drag means to you need to press and hold the left mouse button and then move your mouse in the direction where you want the window relocated.

## Step By Step—Making A Window Fill The Desktop

■   To make a window full size (maximize it), click 🗗 .

## Step By Step—Making A Window Into An Icon On The Taskbar

■   To make a window turn into an icon on the Taskbar (minimize it), click ▬ .

# Understanding Dialog Boxes

A dialog box is a collection of controls, used for taking information from you and sending it to the application. If you use your imagination a bit, you can see the dialog box holding a "dialog" with you, hence the name.

## Parts Of A Dialog Box

Figure 2.2 has a sample of a dialog box and Table 2.1 has a description of the options available in most dialog boxes.

**Figure 2.2**   Parts of a dialog box

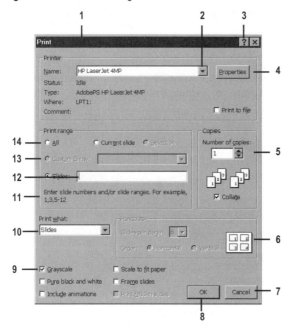

**Table 2.2**   Parts of dialog box

| Term | Definition |
| --- | --- |
| 1   Title bar | The name of the active dialog box or menu option. |
| 2   Arrow | Pulls down a drop-down list from which you can choose from a variety of items. |
| 3   Help icon | A small picture of a question mark (**?**) that displays a description of a highlighted item or the help assistant where you can enter information to get a description of particular part of the application. |
| 4   Button | A control that depresses when clicked. Used for actions that are immediate, such as sending a document to print. |

**Table 2.2** Parts of dialog box, continued

| Term | Definition |
|---|---|
| 5 List | A collection of more than one item. May contain a scroll bar and/or scroll arrows if the list of items is larger than the list area. |
| 6 Sample View area | An area on a dialog box containing a preview of the options you are choosing. |
| 7 Cancel button | Used to cancel from a dialog box without accepting or applying any changes you may have made. |
| 8 OK button | Accepts the action or applies any changes you make. |
| 9 Check box | A control that displays or hides a check in a small square box when clicked. Used to select or deselect options. |
| 10 Drop-down list | A text box with an arrow at the right. When clicked, a list drops down for choosing from among the items. |
| 11 Description area | An area on a dialog box containing some type of description relative to an option. |
| 12 Text box | A box where you can enter text, or that displays text you can edit. |
| 13 Grayed out | An option on a menu or toolbar that is not currently available. Sometimes you need to have a specific part of a document, worksheet, or presentation highlighted to activate an option. |
| 14 Radio button | A control with a number of small round areas that show a dark circle inside when clicked. Used for choosing one specific option from among a small number of options that are mutually exclusive. |

## Step By Step—Filling In A Dialog Box

1. Open the dialog box.
2. Answer the "first question".
   **NOTE**   If you think of a dialog box has having a conversation with you, you can answer the questions one at a time and not forget something.
3. Move down one box or field at a time, answering each question.
4. When everything is filled in, check your answers.
5. Click the **OK** button.

## Understanding Menus

Menus are lists of commands or options that roll down when clicked, then roll back up out of the way. This is both a good thing and a bad thing: it's good because menus are compact, it's bad because you'll often forget under which menu name your desired command is located.

### Parts Of A Menu

Figure 2.2 is a sample of a the different options in a menu (although few menus have *all* of the options available at the same time) and Table 2.1 has a description of the options available in most menus.

**Figure 2.3**   Parts of a menu

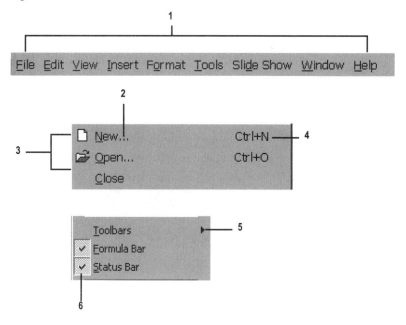

**Table 2.3**   Parts of a menu

| Term | Definition |
| --- | --- |
| 1   Menu name | This is a name that menu gives you a clue as to the menu's purpose and function. |
| 2   Ellipsis indicator | These three dots mean that choosing this option opens a dialog box, rather than executing a command immediately. |
| 3   Options | These are the options that roll down from the menu. To pick one, click on it. |
| 4   Keyboard shortcut | These cryptic notes provide the key sequence you can use if you happen to be a keyboardist instead of a mouser. |

**Table 2.3**   Parts of a menu, continued

| Term | Definition |
| --- | --- |
| 5   Flyout menu indicator | This arrow indictates that there are related options on a flyout menu that you can choose from. |
| 6   Status indicator | This icon shows that the menu option is active or inactive. |

### Step By Step—Choosing A Menu Option

You can choose a menu option by:

- Clicking the main menu item, then choosing the appropriate submenu item, or
- Pressing the **Alt** key, then typing the letter with the underscore (or underline if that's a bit more familiar to you), or
- Pressing the keyboard shortcut, if one is listed.

# Understanding Toolbars

A toolbar is a group of buttons that hang out together. Toolbars group buttons into logical pairings. For example, the Formatting toolbar has buttons that exclusively deal with making your objects look good. Toolbars can often be "undocked" from their positions and made to "float" around on screen. If a toolbar is "attached" (or "docked") to the side of a window, to move it you click and hold while your cursor is over the gray space around the buttons, then drag it away and drop it where you want it. If you pull it to another side of the window, it'll dock there when you release the mouse.

**N O T E**   You can define your own buttons, your own toolbars, and even add buttons to existing toolbar. The possibilities are almost endless. ■

### Parts Of A Toolbar

Figure 2.2 is a sample of a typical toolbar and Table 2.1 has a description of the options available.

**Figure 2.4**   Parts of a toolbar

**Table 2.4**   Parts of a toolbar

| Term | Definition |
|---|---|
| 1   Toolbar title | The name of the toolbar that is currently displayed. This name usually indicates the type of commands available on that toolbar. |
| 2   Icon | The control that, when clicked, performs an action. |
| 3   Surrounding gray space | Separates buttons and gives you a place to click and hold while dragging the toolbar to another location. |
| 4   Close button | Closes the toolbar. To make the toolbar reappear, choose **View ➤ Toolbar ➤ (desired toolbar)**. |

## Step By Step—Moving A Toolbar

1. Display the appropriate toolbar.
2. Click and drag the toolbar's title bar.

    **NOTE**   Click and drag means that you need to press and hold the left mouse button and then move your mouse in the direction where you want the toolbar relocated.

## Step By Step—Resizing A Toolbar

1. Display the appropriate toolbar.
2. Click and drag on the any of the edges of the toolbar to move *either* horizontally or vertically.

**N O T E**   Toolbars resize a bit differently than windows. When you resize a toolbar it either stacks the icons based on how far you've "shrunk" borders of the toolbar or lines the icons up in a nice row if you've expanded the borders. ▪

# Getting Around In Microsoft Office 2000

The whole computer universe is divided into two camps: the mousers and the keyboardists. Mousers prefer to click on everything to take action, while keyboardists like to keep their hands on the keyboard and use keyboard shortcuts.

Windows 98/NT and Office 2000 offer a rich set of control schemes for both. For example, you can make a window come to the front by clicking on it or you can press the **Alt** key and hold it, then the **Tab** key, to step through all of your open applications literally by lifting two fingers.

We've tried to give both mousers and keyboardists their due by listing keyboard shortcuts whenever appropriate, along with the buttons, icons, and menu options. These are all represented this way:

◇ Icons/buttons you click with your mouse

◇ Keys you press on the keyboard

◇ Menu options that you activate by clicking your mouse

As an example, here's the commands you can use to create a new file:

◇ Click      ◇ Press **Alt+F,N** or **Ctrl+N**     ◇ Choose **File ➤ New**

In this example there are three ways for creating a new file.

- In the first action, you just click an icon on the Standard toolbar. That's for mousers.
- Keyboardists can press the key combinations given in the middle.
  This sequence means to press the **Alt** key first, then hold it down as you press the **F** key, then release the **F** key and press the **N** key, releasing the **Alt** key last.

  An even quicker keyboard shortcut is available for this action: just press the **Ctrl** ("Control") key and hold it down as you press the **N** key. Such quickie shortcuts aren't always available, but we note them where they are.

- Those that are new to Office 2000, or who can't remember a million commands (and who can?) may want to use the menus, which is the third option. Whenever a menu name is given, its keyboard equivalent is underlined, meaning that you can always press the **Alt** key and then the keyboard equivalent to activate that menu.

---

**N O T E**    Notice that the Press and Choose options are in bold text. Whenever you see bold text, it's a keyboard or mouse action we're discussing. ▨

## Understanding The Active Desktop

You can choose to have Windows display in classic Windows style or as a series of Web pages. The Web display features is called "Active Desktop". Which one you pick makes the display look and act differently.

For example, when using Active Desktop, you can click once on icons that used to take two clicks to energize. The major benefit to Active Desktop isn't the click count, though, it's the ability to have your desktop act like a browser. Without leaving your desktop, you can check out sports scores or get stock quotes.

---

**T I P**    To switch back and forth from Active Desktop, right-click on the desktop to open the shortcut menu and choose **Active Desktop ➤ View as Web Page.**

Not everybody likes Active Desktop, though, and you'll have to make up your own mind.

# Starting An Application

Generally, there are three main ways to start an application:

- Use the **Start** button on the Taskbar,
- Double-click a file in **Windows Explorer** or on the desktop, or
- Click a **Desktop Shortcut Icon**.

## Step By Step—Using The Start Button On The Taskbar

1. From the Taskbar, click the **Start** button.
2. Choose **Programs** ➤ **<your application>**.

## Step By Step—Using Windows Explorer

1. Open **Windows Explorer.**
2. Display the folder where you stored your file.
3. Open the desired file icon.

   - If you're using the Active Desktop, click the desired file icon.
   - If you're using the standard Windows desktop, double-click the file icon you want to open.

## Step By Step—Using A Desktop Icon

If you already have an icon for the application on your desktop:

- Click it once if you're using Active Desktop, or
- Double-click it if you're using the standard Windows desktop.

## Step By Step—Creating A Desktop Icon

If you don't have such an icon, you can make one by following these steps.

1. Open **Windows Explorer**.
2. Locate the directory with the application you want to create a desktop icon for. This may be the hardest part of this task, because Windows applications are often in scattered places. Consult your installation manual for more information.
3. Right-click on the application icon to open the shortcut menu.
4. From the shortcut menu, choose **Create Shortcut**.
5. Click the shortcut icon that displays and drag it onto the desktop.

## Step By Step—Renaming A Desktop Icon

1. If you want to rename an icon, right-click on the desired icon to open the shortcut menu.
2. From the shortcut menu, choose **Rename**.
3. In the box below the icon, enter the *new name*.
4. Left-click anywhere else on the desktop.

# Creating A New File

As with almost everything in Windows, you can create a new file several different ways. You can open the appropriate application *first*, then create a new file based on an existing file or template. You can even do things the other way around by locating a template file and opening it—bam, you've opened the application and created a blank copy of the template in one step. Here's some of your options.

- Create a new file in Word, Excel, or PowerPoint by clicking the  icon on the Standard toolbar.
- Create a new file in Word, Excel, or PowerPoint by choosing **File ➤ New.**
- Create a new file in Word, Excel, or PowerPoint pressing **Ctrl+N.**
- Create a new file from the **File** menu in Windows Explorer.

### Step By Step—Creating A New File Using An Icon

1. Open the appropriate application.

2. On the Standard toolbar, click 🗋.

**TIP** You don't *have* to save the document right now, but we definitely recommend saving immediately, in case you lose power or have something else equally dreadful happen to you.

- In Word, clicking the 🗋 icon pops open a new Word document, based on the default template named Normal.dot.
- In PowerPoint, you'll get the New Slide dialog box.
- In Excel, clicking the button pops open a new workbook with three blank worksheets.

**NOTE** In all three applications, you can open a new file even if you already have other files open. ▪

## Step By Step—Creating A New File Using A Menu

1. Open the appropriate application.
2. Choose **File ➤ New.**
3. "Answer" the questions in the dialog box.
4. Click the **OK** button.

- In Word, this opens the New dialog box so that you can pick a template. Normal.dot is the default, but there are many others to choose from.
- In PowerPoint, this opens the New Presentation dialog box so that you can either choose a professionally designed presentation master or pick a template with some of the fancy stuff already inserted for you.
- In Excel, you'll get the New dialog box so that you can choose which template you want to use as a starting point.

## Step By Step—Creating A New Document With A Keyboard Shortcut

1. Open the appropriate application.
2. Press **Ctrl+N.**

**N O T E**   This is equivalent to clicking the [ ] icon on the Standard toolbar—you get the default template for the application you're working with. ■

## Step By Step—Creating A New Document In Windows Explorer

One little-used method for creating new documents is to use the File menu in Windows Explorer.

1. Open Windows Explorer.
2. Display the directory where you want the new file stored.
3. Choose **File ➤ New.**
   A flyout menu displays with anywhere from a sparse half-dozen options to enough options to cover the screen from top to bottom. Each document-creation application registered on your computer has a menu item here, including Word, PowerPoint, and Excel.
4. Choose the appropriate application to create your new file.
   When you click, for example, on PowerPoint Presentation, a PowerPoint presentation file is created in the current directory. You can then name it.
5. Enter a name for your new file.
6. Press the **Enter** key.

**N O T E**   To start editing the file, double-click it if you're using the standard Windows desktop or click it if you're using Active Desktop. ■

# Opening Existing Files

As with almost everything in Windows, you can open an existing file several different ways. You can open the appropriate application *first*, then open an existing file by browsing through your directories or using the list of recently opened files. You can even do things the other way around by locating the existing file and opening it—bam, you've opened the application and your file. Here are some of your options.

■ Open an existing file in Word, Excel, or PowerPoint by clicking the 📂 icon on the Standard toolbar.

■ Open an existing file in Word, Excel, or PowerPoint by choosing it from the list of most recently opened files.

■ Open an existing file in Word, Excel, or PowerPoint by choosing **File ➤ Open**.

■ Open an existing file from the Taskbar.
Windows keeps a tally of the last 15 files you worked with, much like Word, Excel, and PowerPoint keep their own tallies.

■ Open an existing file and launch Word, Excel, or PowerPoint by using an icon on the desktop. If a document is one you use often, like a memo that's updated weekly or a spreadsheet that you use every day, you can make a shortcut icon for the document and put it on your desktop. When you click it (with Active Desktop) or double-click it (with the standard Windows desktop), Windows takes a look at the file extension and checks to see if that extension is registered as being attached to Word, Excel, or PowerPoint. If it is, the application is launched and that file is loaded. If the application is already open, the file is opened in the application.

■ Open an existing document and launch Word, Excel, or PowerPoint by clicking or double-clicking on an icon in Windows Explorer.
Sometimes it's convenient to be able to launch an application by clicking on a file icon. Each file type from Word, Excel, and PowerPoint has its own unique icon, letting you instantly spot the type of file you're looking for.

## Step By Step—Opening An Existing Document Using An Icon

1. Open the appropriate application.

2. On the Standard toolbar, click the 📂 icon.

3. Locate the folder where you stored your file.

4. Highlight the desired file.

5. Click the **Open** button.

 **TIP** Once you find the appropriate file, you can double-click it instead of highlighting it and clicking the **Open** button.

## Step By Step—Opening an Existing Document Using The List of Recently Used Files

1. Open the appropriate application.
2. Choose **File**
3. Look at the bottom of the menu.
4. Click the appropriate file.

**TIP** To change how many file names the application "remembers", choose **Tools ➤ Options**, then choose the **General** tab. You should see a Recently used files list option that you can change to fit your needs.

**N O T E** If you've moved the file since that last time you opened it, the application gets all upset and tells you it can't find the file. Don't panic. Just use one of the other options to open the file. ▪

## Step By Step—Opening An Existing Document Using A Menu

1. Open the appropriate application.
2. Choose **File ➤ Open.**
3. "Answer" the questions in the dialog box.
4. Click the **OK** button.

**N O T E** This is the same as clicking the 📂 icon on the Standard toolbar. ▪

## Step By Step—Opening An Existing Document Using The Taskbar

1. Click the **Start** button on the Taskbar.
2. Choose **Documents.**
3. Click the desired file.
   Windows opens the appropriate application and the file at the same time.

**N O T E** The difference between this list and the ones in the Office 2000 applications is that this list includes all of the documents you've worked with, even non-Office ones. ▪

## Step By Step—Opening An Existing Document Using Windows Explorer

1. Open Windows Explorer.
2. Locate the folder where you stored your file.
3. Highlight the desired file.
4. Open the file.
   - Click the file if you're using Active Desktop.
   - Double-click the file if you're using the standard Windows desktop.

---

**N O T E** If the application isn't open, Windows launches it and loads the document in it. If the application is already open, the file is loaded. ▪

---

 It may actually be faster to hunt down a file in Windows Explorer than it is to launch the application and try to find the file using the **Open** dialog box. You can see many more files and directories at one time in Explorer.

## Step By Step—Opening An Existing Document Using An Icon On The Desktop

- Click the icon if you're using Active Desktop.
- Double-click the icon if you're using the standard Windows desktop.

## Step By Step—Putting A File Icon On The Desktop

1. Make sure that you've saved and closed the file.
2. Open Windows Explorer.
   **NOTE** Make sure that Windows Explorer isn't maximized. If it is you won't be able to drag the shortcut out of Explorer and onto the desktop.
3. Locate the folder where you stored your file.
4. Highlight the desired file.
5. Click the right mouse button.
   The shortcut menu displays.
6. Choose **Create Shortcut**.
7. Click on the shortcut that pops into being and hold the mouse button down while dragging the shortcut onto your desktop.

# Saving Documents

It's a good idea to save often. You never know when the electricity will give up the ghost and your last three hours of writing will vanish like a politician's promise. Having said that, however, you may find that Word's files are puzzlingly big if you enable fast saves. Fast saves in Word do just that: the option records only the changes in your document quickly, but at the expense of a bigger file. You can enable fast saves by choosing **Tools ➤ Options Save tab.** Otherwise, you will be saving the full document every time you choose to save.

It's a good idea to save the current document before printing or doing anything else significant to the document. If the Windows system locks up on you, your laboriously concocted document may be lost to the ages.

To save a document, you can:

- Choose **Edit ➤ Save**, or
- Click the 🖫 icon, or
- Press **Ctrl+S**.

---

**N O T E**   If you've previously saved the document, nothing much will happen visually as the document is saved to the drive. If you haven't saved it before, you'll see the Save As dialog box. Type a name for the document and click the Save button. ■

# Closing A File

Okay, so it may seem a bit simplistic, but you do need to know how to close up shop once in a while. Plus, you can get so many files open that the system resigns in protest. And the application is even kind to you if you haven't saved the file recently—it pops up a message that gives you a chance to save the changes you've made, forget the changes you've made, or just forget that you ever told the system to close the file in the first place.

## Step By Step—Closing A File

You can close a file by:

- Choosing **File ➤ Close**, or
- Clicking the ☒ button in the file window's upper right-hand corner, or
- Pressing **Ctrl+F4**, or
- Pressing **Ctrl+W**.

---

**N O T E**   Be sure you have the right ☒ button, however, because just a bit farther out is the application window's ☒ button, which closes the application *and* all open files. If that's what you *want* to do, then by all means close everything that way. ■

# Closing An Application

Now I'm really getting on your nerves, right? Believe me, it's not because I think you don't know anything, I just know how easy it is to get tripped up on this kind of stuff. So here goes. When you close an application, you are actually closing any open files *and* the application itself. As with closing a file, the application reminds you to save your changes.

### Step By Step—Closing An Application

You can close an application by:

- Choosing **File** ➤ **Exit,** or
- Clicking the ☒ button in the application window's upper right-hand corner, or
- Pressing **Alt+F4**.

---

**N O T E**   If you have an open file that hasn't been saved, you'll be prompted to save it before the application closes. ▨

# Getting Help

Office 2000 applications have lots and lots of help: three kinds of help, in fact.

- Office Assistant,
- Standard Help, and
- What's This Help.

### Office Assistant

The first type of help is the new Office Assistant, a figure that prompts you to type your question, whereupon it runs off and checks for an answer. The Office Assistant goes far beyond the paper clip you might have known in the previous Office version. You can now select your figure, for example, and the application automatically performs a sophisticated search. You can enable the Office Assistant or disable it from the shortcut menu.

When Office Assistant is enabled:

- To show the Office Assistant, choose **Help** ➤ **Show Office Assistant**
- To hide the Office Assistant, choose **Help** ➤ **Hide Office Assistant**
- To summon the Office Assistant when it's hidden from view, press **F1**.

### The Standard Help File

The second kind of help is the standard help file. When the Office Assistant is active, you get to the help file by going through Office Assistant and letting Assistant chase down where your answer may be hidden. When Office Assistant is disabled, you get a help file by pressing **F1**.

### What's This Help

The third form of help is called "What's This?" help. It's accessible from the help menu or by pressing **Shift+F1**. The cursor changes into a cursor with a question mark. The application itself is disabled during this time and becomes a mere backdrop for the help system. Click on whatever it is you need help with and "What's This?" help pops up a box with an explanation of that item. You get one item per click, and then the application becomes active again.

## Understanding Templates

Word, Excel, and PowerPoint all feature templates. A template stores the decisions you've already made (or that *somebody* has made) about the file at hand.

- In Word, there's always at least one template attached to a document, a generalized one called "Normal.dot". (The .dot means that the document is a template, not an editable document, which usually has a .doc extension.) Word's templates are the most complex, holding everything from pre-defined font styles to macros and automatically-inserted text. All three come with already-defined templates that you can pick out and use. Or you can define one of your own.
- In PowerPoint and Excel, attaching a template is optional.
  - Excel's template is the simplest, holding only the most rudimentary printing information.
  - PowerPoint's template will hold background colors and graphics, along with slide layout styles and font sizes.

**TIP** A lot of folks don't want to take the time to create a template—they can be a lot of work and take quite a bit of troubleshooting to get them "just right". But I can tell you from long experience that, for repetitive documents, a template is the only way to keep your hair and your sanity.

## Learning More About Macros And Visual Basic

Macros are small programs that are stored with an application and can be written by you, the user, to perform repetitive tasks in a file. The language for these macros has grown in complexity over the years, until today it's known as Visual Basic for Applications (VBA). You can write macros directly in a supplied editor, like a programmer does, or you can record the macro. Either way, you name the macro and save it. Then you can make it run by attaching it to a button that you put on a toolbar. VBA puts incredible power in your hands, if you want it. You could use it to make Word, Excel, or PowerPoint the basis of a whole new application, operated mostly with macros.

Space doesn't permit us to go into macro development here, but we wanted you to know it was available. Even simple macro recording takes some practice, so be prepared to learn something about macros before trying one. Since programming with VBA is beyond the scope of this book, try *Special Edition: Using Visual Basic For Applications* 5, by Paul Sanna (ISBN: 0789709597).

# A Look At The Common Options In Word, Excel, And PowerPoint

**In this part**

# The File Menu, Common Options

## In this chapter

# What Is The File Menu

This menu lists the commands that you'll use to perform actions that affect the entire file, such as saving the document so that you don't lose your work, printing the document, opening additional documents, or reviewing various information about the active file.

If a menu option has an ellipsis (three dots) or an arrow beside it, the application "asks" you for additional information before the action takes place. If the menu doesn't have one of these symbols, the action you choose happens immediately. If the action takes place immediately, you won't see a sample screen in this section.

# File ➤ New

Use this option to create a new file based on an existing template. Templates are the skeleton of your new file and store default settings that control the look of your file (although you can change these settings at any time). For instance, the settings you apply to format the headings in the file are called Styles. The font, style, and size are just a few of the settings you can change to customize the heading format. As you can see, this is just the beginning. The various templates available give you many options to choose from when creating your new file.

## How You Get Here

◇ Click 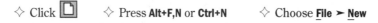    ◇ Press **Alt+F,N** or **Ctrl+N**    ◇ Choose **File ➤ New**

## What's In This Dialog Box

Figure 3.1 is a sample of this dialog box and Table 3.1 has a description of the options that are common to Word, Excel, and PowerPoint.

**Figure 3.1**    The New dialog box

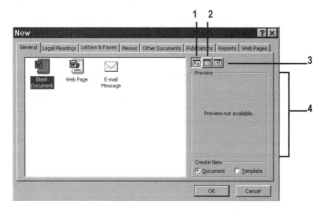

**Table 3.1**   Options in the New dialog box

| # | Option | What you do with it |
|---|--------|---------------------|
| 1 | Large Icon button | Click to display the templates and Wizards as an icons. |
| 2 | List button | Click to display the templates and Wizards as a list of file names. |
| 3 | Details button | Click to display the templates and Wizards with information about the file, such as the file type, size, and when the file was last changed. The file list can also be sorted by clicking on the column headings. |
| 4 | Preview Box | Click to display a preview of the chosen template. |

# File ➤ Open

Use this option to open an existing file that is stored on your local hard drive, a removable drive (such as a diskette or Zip drive), a network drive, an intranet, or the Internet. If your document is stored on your local hard drive, or on a network that you have permission to write to, you can open a file as a copy if you want to create and work on a copy of the document instead of the original. You can also open any document as read-only (which means you can only view the document, not make changes to it).

## How You Get Here

◇ Click       ◇ Press **Alt+F,O** or **Ctrl+O**      ◇ Choose **File** ➤ **Open**

## What's In This Dialog Box

Figure 3.2 is a sample of this dialog box and Table 3.2 has a description of the options that are common to Word, Excel, and PowerPoint.

**Figure 3.2**   The Open dialog box

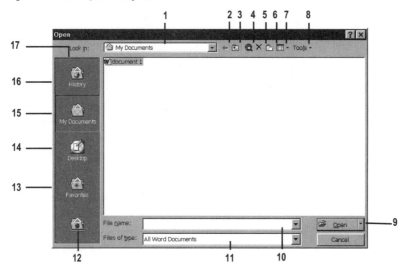

**Table 3.2**   Options in the Open dialog box

| # | Option | What you do with it |
|---|--------|---------------------|
| 1 | Look in drop-down list | Choose an item that determines where the application looks for your files. |
| 2 | My Documents button | Click to display a list of the files stored in the default file folder. |
| 3 | Up One Level button | Click to display the folder that is one level up in the hierarchy. |
| 4 | Search the Web button | Click to open the Web browser so you cansearch the internet for the files you want to open. |
| 5 | Delete button | Click to delete the highlighted item. |
| 6 | New Folder button | Click to create a new folder on the drive or subfolder chosen. |
| 7 | Views drop-down list | Choose an item that determines  what information is displayed about each of your files. |
| 8 | Tools drop-down list | Choose an item that determines which tool you want to use to manipulate your filesdialog box. The options change depending upon the action you're performing. For instance, you can rename a file or you can use the Map Network Drive option to map a new drive for your computer. There are also other options that display when you choose the Save As or Save as Web page menu option. |
| 9 | Open button  Open drop-down list | Click to open the highlighted file. You can also choose the Open drop-down list if you want to open the file in another way (e.g., as a read-only file or as a copy of the original). |

**Table 3.2**  Options in the Open dialog box, continued

| # Option | What you do with it |
|---|---|
| 10 File name text box | Enter the name of the file that you want to open. You can use wildcards and search paths if you are not sure of the exact name or where to find it. |
| 11 Files of type drop-down list | Choose an item that determines what files are displayed in the dialog box. The application then "excludes" files of other types and only displays ones that match the type you've chosen. |
| 12 Web Folders | Click to choose from the files you have created and saved on a Web server. |
| 13 Favorites | Click to choose the shortcut to the file you want to open. You can display various options on opening it by clicking the arrow on the **Open** button. |
| 14 Desktop | Click to display a list of shortcuts. |
| 15 My Documents | Click to display a list of the files stored in the default file folder. |
| 16 History | Click to display a list of most recently opened files. |
| 17 Places bar | The area on the left of the dialog box that contains the list of folders, such as My Documents, that you click to display the desired list of shortcuts and files. |

# File ➤ Close

Use this option to close the active file and save it in the original file folder (you know, that one you used when you *first* saved the file). If the file has not been saved, you'll be asked if you want to save any changes you have made. If you click the **Yes** button so that your most recent changes are saved, the application overwrites the old version of the file.

---

**N O T E**   To save a file with a different name or as a different file type, see File ➤ Save As on page 42. ▪

## How You Get Here

◇ Click

◇ Press **Alt+F,C** or **Ctrl+W**

◇ Choose **File** ➤ **Close**

# File ➤ Save

Use this option to save any changes you've made to a file.

 **TIP** Be sure to save your files frequently (you don't want to lose any of the hard work you've done). A good rule of thumb is to save frequently enough that you can easily recover if the system crashes. For example, if you just wrote a great paragraph or created an awesome formula, save your file immediately after finishing the it. My rule is that I don't go any longer than five minutes without saving, which means I can't lose more than five minutes work! Most of the applications also have an automatic save function that can be set to automatically save your files after a specified amount of time. (For a complete description of the options available, see Table 14.30 on page 250.)

 **N O T E** To save a file under a different name or as different file type, see File ➤ Save As on page 42. ▨

## How You Get Here

◇ Click       ◇ Press **Alt+F,S** or **Ctrl+S**      ◇ Choose **File** ➤ **Save**

# File ➤ Save As

Use this option to save the file for the first time or to save an existing file with a different name or file type.

 **TIP** Be sure you look at where you're storing the file before you click **Save**—don't let "fast fingers" get the better of you. The most frequent reason people can't find a file is because they didn't pay attention to the file folder that was open when they last saved a file.

## How You Get Here

◇ Press **Alt+F,A**      ◇ Choose **File** ➤ **Save As**

## What's In This Dialog Box

Figure 3.3 is a sample of this dialog box, which has the same options as the Open dialog box, except that you now have a **Save** button. See Table 3.2 on page 40 for a complete description of the other options available.

**Figure 3.3** The Save As dialog box

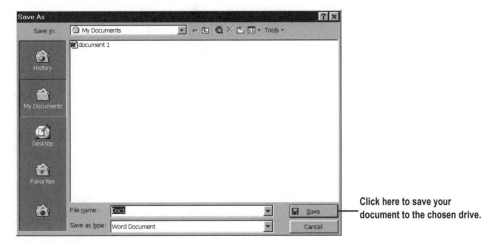

Click here to save your document to the chosen drive.

# File ➤ Save as Web Page

Use this option to save the existing file as a Web page so that you can view it on the Internet or an Intranet using a Web browser. After you save your file as a Web page, the application automatically switches you to Web Layout view, regardless of what view you were in before you saved the file.

## How You Get Here

◇ Press **Alt+F,G**

◇ Choose **File** ➤ **Save as Web Page**

### What's In This Dialog Box

Figure 3.4 is a sample of this dialog box. This dialog box has the same options as the Open dialog box, except that you now have a **Change Title** button. See Table 3.2 on page 40 for a complete description of the other options available.

**Figure 3.4**   The Save As dialog box

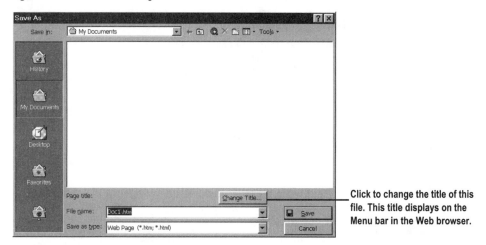

Click to change the title of this file. This title displays on the Menu bar in the Web browser.

# File ➤ Web Page Preview

Use this option to see how a file looks as a Web page. The application opens your Web browser and displays the active file as it would appear if you were viewing the page on the Web.

### How You Get Here

◇ Press **Alt+F,B**          ◇ Choose **File** ➤ **Web Page Preview**

# File ➤ Print

Use this option to create a paper copy of the active file. You can send the file to the default printer or you can choose a new printer, as long as it has already been set up for you.

---

**N O T E**   You can also create an electronic "print" file that you can send to a commercial printer or use to generate a portable document format (PDF) file. ■

### How You Get Here

◇ Click           ◇ Press **Alt+F,P** or **Ctrl+P**          ◇ Choose **File** ➤ **Print**

## What's In This Dialog Box

Figure 3.5 is a sample of this dialog box and Table 3.3 has a description of the options that are common to Word, Excel, and PowerPoint.

**Figure 3.5**   The Print dialog box

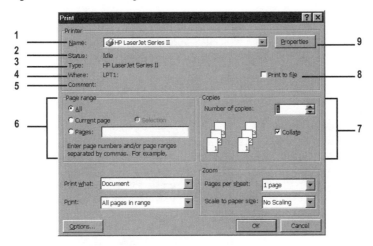

**Table 3.3**   Options in the Print dialog box

| # | Option | What you do with it |
|---|--------|---------------------|
| 1 | Name drop-down list | Choose an item that determines where you want to print the active file. |
| 2 | Status field | View what is going on with the chosen printer, e.g., is it available, ready to print. |
| 3 | Type field | View the name of the printer that has been chosen as the default printer for your system. |
| 4 | Where field | View the printer port ("location") that has been chosen as the default for your system. |
| 5 | Comment field | View notes entered when the printer was installed. |
| 6 | Page range area | Choose an item that determines which pages are actually sent to the printer when you click **OK**. You can also enter a specific page range in the Pages text box. |
| 7 | Copies area | Choose an item that determines how many copies of the file are printed. |
|   |  | Note  Click **Collate** if you want the application to put multiple copies in the correct order for you. If you're only printing one copy, turn this option off to reduce how long it takes to print the file. |

**Table 3.3**   Options in the Print dialog box, continued

| #  | Option                  | What you do with it |
|----|-------------------------|---------------------|
| 8  | Print to file check box | Click to send the active document to an electronic file instead of the chosen printer. |
| 9  | Properties button       | Click to display the Properties dialog box so that you can change Window's printing properties (the printer's "assumptions" of how it should print your document). This doesn't change the printing options for the application itself; click **Options** if you want to customize the settings for the application. |

# File ➤ Send To

Use this option to send your document, spreadsheet, or slide to someone using your email or internet connection. Generally, any of the options in this flyout menu will use your default email connections or the Outlook application to send an email. You fill in the information for the recipient like you would any email address and then you are ready to send it.

You can route documents online by using any 32-bit email program that is compatible with the Messaging Application Programming Interface (MAPI) (such as Microsoft Exchange or Lotus cc:Mail) or by using any 16-bit email program that is compatible with Vendor Independent Messaging (VIM). You don't have to use Microsoft Exchange. If your email program is compatible with MAPI or VIM, the Routing Recipient and Mail Recipient commands display when you choose **File ➤ Send To**. If your e-mail program is not compatible with MAPI or VIM, you can still distribute documents manually by putting the file on a network or on a removable media, such as a diskette. (For more information, see What About Outlook Mail's Forms on page 672.)

## How You Get Here

◇ Press **Alt+F,D**          ◇ Choose **File ➤ Send To**

## What's In This Flyout Menu

Figure 3.6 is a sample of this flyout menu.

**Figure 3.6**   The File ➤ Send To flyout menu

## File ➤ Send To ➤ Mail Recipient

Use this option to send your file as an email message. When you choose this option, the application opens a blank Message form so that you can enter the recipients email address(es) a nd an appropriate description in the Subject text box. Then, when you send it, your compatible email program connects to the server and sends it on its way. (For more information, see A Look At Outlook Mail's Forms on page 673.)

### How You Get Here

✧ Click 🖫          ✧ Press **Alt+F,D,M**          ✧ Choose **File ➤ Send To ➤ Mail Recipient**

## File ➤ Send To ➤ Mail Recipient (as Attachment)

Use this option to include your file with a separate email. When you choose this option you enter all the information for addressing it as well as the message itself. You can see that the file name of your attachment is included in the address area of the window. (For more information, see A Look At Outlook Mail's Forms on page 673.)

### How You Get Here

✧ Press **Alt+F,D,A**          ✧ Choose **File ➤ Send To ➤ Mail Recipient (as Attachment)**

## File ➤ Send to ➤ Routing Recipient

Use this option to send your file to more than one person on a routing slip. Think of this as the electronic version of the note you add to a document that you want several people to review. You know the type: "Bob, please check this out and then pass it on to Mary". You create a list of people that are supposed to review the attachment, add the appropriate notes and tracking information and off goes the file, zipping through the ether, direct to the recipients' email address. When you route a file you can specify whether you want to be notified automatically when the file moves from one person on the list to the next person. When the file has been routed to everyone on the list, you'll need to clear the addresses so you can route other files. (For more information, see A Look At Outlook Mail's Forms on page 673.)

### How You Get Here

✧ Press **Alt+F,D,R**          ✧ Choose **File ➤ Send To ➤ Routing Recipient**

## What's In This Dialog Box

Figure 3.7 is a sample of this dialog box and Table 3.4 has a description of the options that are common to Word, Excel, and PowerPoint.

**Figure 3.7**   The Routing Slip dialog box

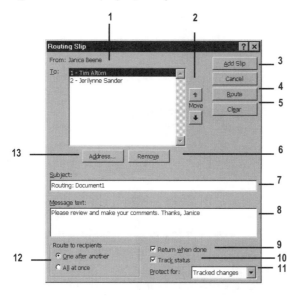

**Table 3.4**   Options in the Routing Slip dialog box

| # | Option | What you do with it |
|---|--------|---------------------|
| 1 | To list | Review the current list of names on the routing slip for this document, workbook, or presentation. |
| 2 | Move button | Click to move the highlighted name in the To: window up or down. |
| 3 | Add Slip button | Click to stores and close this dialog box without sending the routing slip. This lets you work on the file more before you send it. |
| 4 | Route button | Click to attach the routing slip and send the file immediately. |
| 5 | Clear button | Click to remove all the names on the routing list. |
| 6 | Remove button | Click to erase the highlighted name from the list in the To list. |
| 7 | Subject text box | Enter a brief description of what the document is about. |
| 8 | Message text box | Enter a message to the people on the routing list about the attached document. |
| 9 | Return when done check box | Click to have the document returned to you after everyone has reviewed it. |
| 10 | Track status check box | Click to receive an email message when the routed document has been forwarded to another person on the list. |

**Table 3.4** Options in the Routing Slip dialog box, continued

| # | Option | What you do with it |
|---|--------|---------------------|
| 11 | Protect for drop-down list | Choose an item that determines how you want to protect this document. You can choose to retain changes made, protect a distributed form, allow comments but no other changes, or allow changes to the document with no tracking. |
| 12 | Route to recipients radio button | Click to control the order of how the document is received by the people on the routing slip. The document either moves in routing slip order (**One after another**) or is sent to everyone on the list at the same time (**All at once**). |
| 13 | Address button | Click to open the Address Book to look for recipient names. |

## File ➤ Send to ➤ Exchange Folder

Use this option to store the active file in an Exchange or Outlook folder to view, group, categorize, or sort files by properties. (For more information, see What Is The Outlook Mail Application on page 648.)

### How You Get Here

◇ Press **Alt+F,D,E**      ◇ Choose **File** ➤ **Send To** ➤ **Exchange Folder**

## File ➤ Send to ➤ Online Meeting Participant

Use this option to send materials to people in a real-time meeting over the Web using Microsoft NetMeeting.

---

**N O T E**   For more information on NetMeeting try, *Windows 98 Mulitmedia: Lights! Camera! Action!*, by Adam Vujic, (ISBN: 078971857X). ▨

### How You Get Here

◇ Press **Alt+F,D,O**      ◇ Choose **File** ➤ **Send To** ➤ **Online Meeting Participant**

### How You Get Here

# File ➤ Properties

Use this option to review technical information and record technical information about the file.

### How You Get Here

◇ Press **Alt+F,I**      ◇ Choose **File** ➤ **Properties**

## What's In This Dialog Box

Figure 3.8 is a sample of this dialog box and Table 3.5 has a description of the tabs that are common to Word, Excel, and PowerPoint.

**Figure 3.8**    The Document Properties dialog box

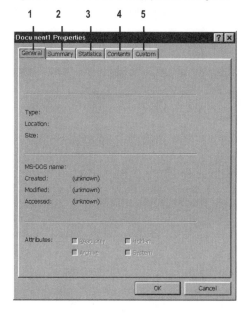

**Table 3.5**    Tabs in the Document Properties dialog box

| # | Tab name | What you do with it |
|---|----------|---------------------|
| 1 | General | Review information about the size, type and location of the file, find out when the file was last changed and used, and look at the MS-DOS file name.<br><br>**Note**   You can't change any of the information displayed in this tab. |
| 2 | Summary | Enter information that you can use to quickly locate this file later. You can also insert this information into the body of your document using fields. (For a complete description of the options available, see Table 3.6 on page 51.) |
| 3 | Statistics | Review information that the application keeps track of for you. (For a complete description of the options available, see Table 3.7 on page 51.)<br><br>**Note**   You can't change any of the information displayed in this tab. |
| 4 | Contents | Review the structural components of the file, e.g., the headings in Word or the names of macros in Excel. |
| 5 | Custom | Create a custom set of properties for the active file. (For a complete description of the options available, see Table 3.8 on page 52.) |

The following tables describe the options for the individual tabs in this dialog box:

- Table 3.6 describes the Summary tab,
- Table 3.7 describes the Statistics tab, and
- Table 3.8 describes the Custom tab.

**Table 3.6**   Options in the Document Properties dialog box Summary tab

| Option | What you do with it |
| --- | --- |
| Title text box | Enter the title of the document. |
| Subject text box | Enter the topic of the document. |
| Author text box | Enter who wrote the document. |
| Manager text box | Enter the name of the writer's supervisor. |
| Company text box | Enter the name of the company that employs the writer or client the document was written for. |
| Category text box | Enter the type of work the document is. |
| Keyword text box | Enter words that can quickly identify the document's subject. |
| Comments text box | Enter your evaluation and judgements about the document. |
| Hyperlink base text box | Enter this document's links to the Web or paths to drives, network servers, or folders in Office. |
| Template information | Read-only information about the document's base template. |
| Save preview picture check box | Store a copy of first page of document to file. |

**Table 3.7**   Options in the Document Properties dialog box Statistics tab

| Option | What you do with it |
| --- | --- |
| Created | Look at when the file was created. |
| Modify | Look at when the file was last changed. |
| Accessed | Look at when the file was last used. |
| Printed | Look at when the file was last printed. |
| Last saved by | Look at the system name of person who last saved the file. |
| Revision number | Look at the number of times the document has been revised. |
| Total editing time | Look at the amount of time changing the document. |
| Statistics | Look at information about the document such as the number of pages, number of paragraphs, and number of words. |

**Table 3.8**    Options in the Document Properties dialog box Custom tab

| Option | What you do with it |
|---|---|
| Name text box | Enter the name of the custom property. |
| Type drop-down list | Choose the type of value given to the property from the list. |
| Value: Field | Enter the text or numeric value assigned to property. |
| Value: Yes radio button | Appears only when Type is "Yes and No". |
| Value: No radio button | Appears only when Type is "Yes and No". |
| Link to Content check box | Choose to link the value to the content of the document. |
| Properties window | Read a list of custom values assigned to the property |

# File ➤ (List of Recently Opened Files)

Use this option to open recently used files, without having to dig through a long list of file folders and drive names to find the file you need.

## How You Get Here

◇ Press **Alt+F,** choose the **number of file in list**      ◇ Choose **File** ➤ **number of file**

# File ➤ Exit

Use this option to close all open files *and* the application that you're using.

---

**N O T E**    If you have made changes in any file you'll be asked if you want to save the changes
when you exit the application. ■

## How You Get Here

◇ Click 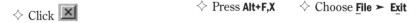      ◇ Press **Alt+F,X**      ◇ Choose **File** ➤ **Exit**

# The Edit Menu, Common Options

## In this chapter

| | | |
|---|---|---|
| ↺ Can't Undo | Ctrl+Z | |
| ↻ Repeat Copy | Ctrl+Y | |
| ✂ Cut | Ctrl+X | |
| 📋 Copy | Ctrl+C | |
| 📋 Paste | Ctrl+V | |
| Paste Special... | | |
| Paste as Hyperlink | | |
| Clear | Del | |
| Select All | Ctrl+A | |
| 🔍 Find... | Ctrl+F | |
| Replace... | Ctrl+H | |
| Go To... | Ctrl+G | |
| Links... | | |
| Object | | |

# What Is The Edit Menu

This menu lists the commands that you'll use to copy information from one place to another, delete information from your file, locate specific words or phrases, change information one instance at a time or throughout the entire file, add links to other documents or locations, and change the look of objects.

If a menu option has an ellipsis (three dots) or an arrow beside it, the application "asks" you for additional information before the action takes place. If the menu doesn't have one of these symbols, the action you choose happens immediately. If the action takes place immediately, you won't see a sample screen in this section.

 **TIP**   Many of the commands on the Edit menu are also available on the shortcut menu. If you like to use your mouse, you can right-click, then choose one of the options displayed. Remember, these menus change based on your cursor location and what is highlighted.

# Edit ➤ Undo

Use this option to change your mind and remove one or more changes made to the active file. You can also undo several actions at once *if* you click the drop-down list to the right of the **Undo** button. Although most actions can be "undone", there are some that can't. If you can't undo an action, the Edit menu displays "Can't undo" instead of "Undo".

**N O T E**   A word of caution: the application won't just let you undo an action in the middle of the Undo list. It "assumes" that you want to undo all actions preceding the one you've chosen. For example, let's say that you've deleted five different paragraphs, then decide that you really didn't want to delete the third paragraph. The application kindly keeps a list of those five actions. You quickly click the drop-down list to the right of the **Undo** button and choose the third action. The application, however, "assumes" that you also want to undo actions one and two. ■

 **TIP**   If you decide you didn't *really* mean to undo an action, choose **Edit ➤ Redo**.

## How You Get Here

◇ Click     ◇ Press **Alt+E,U** or **Ctrl+Z**   ◇ Choose **Edit ➤ Undo**

# Edit ➤ Repeat/Redo

Use this option to either duplicate one or more actions or to change your mind about the last time you chose **Edit ➤ Undo.** You can also repeat/redo several actions at once *if* you click the drop-down list to the right of the Repeat/Redo button. Although most actions can be "repeated" or "redone", there are some that can't. If you can't repeat or redo an action, the Edit menu displays "Can't repeat" or "Can't redo". The name of this menu option changes based on your most recent action.

---

**N O T E**  A word of caution: the application won't just let you choose one action in the middle of the Redo list. It "assumes" that you want to redo all actions preceding the one you've chosen. For example, let's say that you've reinserted three paragraphs using the **Edit ➤ Undo** option. The application kindly keeps a list of those three actions. You quickly click the drop-down list to the right of the Repeat/Redo button and choose the second action. The application, however, "assumes" that you also want to redo action one. ▦

## How You Get Here

◇ Click ▣   ◇ Press **Alt+E,R** or **Ctrl+Y**   ◇ Choose **Edit ➤ Redo** or **Edit ➤ Repeat**

# Edit ➤ Cut

Use this option to completely remove highlighted text or objects from the active file. Items that you cut are stored in an area called the "Clipboard" and can be inserted anywhere, in any open file, regardless of the application.

---

**N O T E**  The Clipboard is cleared once you close the application. ▦

## How You Get Here

◇ Click ✂   ◇ Press **Alt+E,T** or **Ctrl+X**   ◇ Choose **Edit ➤ Cut**

# Edit ➤ Copy

Use this option to leave the highlighted text or objects in their current position **and** store a copy in a temporary storage area called the "Clipboard". Items that you copy can be inserted anywhere, in any open file, regardless of the application.

### How You Get Here

◇ Click     ◇ Press **Alt+E,C** or **Ctrl+C**    ◇ Choose **<u>E</u>dit ➤ <u>C</u>opy**

# Edit ➤ Paste

Use this option to insert text or objects that are stored in the Clipboard at the current cursor position. Items that you've cut or copied can be inserted anywhere, in any open file, regardless of the application.

### How You Get Here

◇ Click     ◇ Press **Alt+P,** or **Ctrl+V**    ◇ Choose **<u>E</u>dit ➤ <u>P</u>aste**

# Edit ➤ Paste Special

Use this option to choose the format of the text or object that you're inserting at the cursor position. This is the option you want to use if you want to link the current file to an external file or if you're copying information between applications and need to control how the information is inserted. For example, you've created a beautiful proposal and want to insert a chart or graph from Excel or a slide from PowerPoint. You also know that this information will change several times before you issue the report. If you choose **Paste ➤ Special**, you can make your changes to the source file and those changes are reflected in your report.

### How You Get Here

◇ Press **Alt+E,S**    ◇ Choose **<u>E</u>dit ➤ <u>P</u>aste <u>S</u>pecial**

## What's In This Dialog Box

Figure 4.1 is a sample of this dialog box and Table 4.1 has a description of the options that are common to Word, Excel, and PowerPoint.

**Figure 4.1**    The Paste Special dialog box

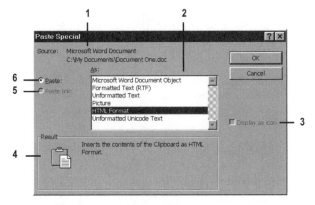

**Table 4.1**    Options in the Paste Special dialog box

| # | Option | What you do with it |
|---|--------|---------------------|
| 1 | Source field | View a description of the text or object you're going to paste. |
| 2 | As list | Choose an item that determines the final format of the text or object you're going to paste. The formats listed vary based on the application you're inserting the information *into*, the application you *copied from*, and *what* you're inserting. |
| 3 | Display as icon check box | Click to display the imported text or object as an icon instead of seeing the "live information". |
| 4 | Result | View a brief description of the option chosen in the As list. |
| 5 | Paste link radio button | Link the file into the document so that the material can be updated |
| 6 | Paste radio button | Copy the file into the document with no link to the original file. |

# Edit ➤ Paste as Hyperlink

Use this option to create a hyperlink for pictures, text, worksheet cells, or a highlighted database object. A hyperlink is an area that is "hot", that is you can click the area so that you automatically jump to a different spot in the current file or in another file.

---

**N O T E**    When you drag text and graphics from one Office program to another one, the application recognizes the location of the information. ■

### How You Get Here

◇ Press **Alt+E,H**          ◇ Choose **Edit ➤ Paste as Hyperlink**

# Edit ➤ Clear

Use this option to permanently delete text or objects from the active file, *without* storing the information in the temporary storage area known as the "Clipboard".

### How You Get Here

◇ Press **Alt+E,A** or **Delete**    ◇ Choose **Edit ➤ Clear**

# Edit ➤ Select All

Use this option to highlight everything in the active file.

### How You Get Here

◇ Press **Alt+E,L** or **Ctrl+A**    ◇ Choose **Edit ➤ Select All**

# Edit ➤ Links

Use this option to open, edit, and maintain the connection ("link") between two files. A link is a way to insert graphics and files into another document so that you can update information if the source is changed.

---

**N O T E**   You can't edit a link until you've inserted one. If you haven't inserted a link, this option is grayed out. ▪

### How You Get Here

◇ Press **Alt+E,K**          ◇ Choose **Edit ➤ Links**

## What's In This Dialog Box

Figure 4.2 is a sample of this dialog box and Table 4.2 has a description of the options that are common to Word, Excel, and PowerPoint.

**Figure 4.2**   The Links dialog box

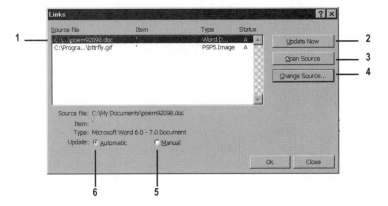

**Table 4.2**   Options in the Links dialog box

| # | Option | What you do with it |
|---|--------|---------------------|
| 1 | Source File list | View the name of the linked file, the type of linked file, and the update method chosen when you inserted the link. |
| 2 | Update Now button | Click to make sure the linked file has the most recent information. |
| 3 | Open Source button | Click to open the linked file in another window and, if necessary, open the appropriate application for the linked file. |
| 4 | Change Source button | Click to change the location of the linked file or to change the link to another file. |
| 5 | Manual radio button | Click to update the linked file when *you* want to update it. |
| 6 | Automatic radio button | Click to update the linked file *every* time you open your file or whenever new information is available. |

# Edit ➤ Object

Use this option to open and edit source files, change the conditions of the links between objects and the files they are linked to, convert objects to different file types, and open them in the appropriate application. When you choose this option, the application "senses" what type of object you've highlighted and changes the menu name to match.

---

**N O T E**   Not all options listed on this flyout menu are available for all object types. ■

## How You Get Here

◇ Press **Alt+E,O**          ◇ Choose **Edit ➤ Object**

## What's In This Flyout Menu

Figure 4.3 is a sample of this flyout menu.

**Figure 4.3**   The Edit ➤ Object flyout menu

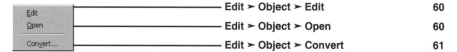

| | |
|---|---|
| Edit ➤ Object ➤ Edit | 60 |
| Edit ➤ Object ➤ Open | 60 |
| Edit ➤ Object ➤ Convert | 61 |

## Edit ➤ Object ➤ Edit

Use this option to open the object in the original application so that you can review it or make changes to it. Once you close the source application, your file is updated.

## How You Get Here

◇ Press **Alt+E,O,E**          ◇ Choose **Edit ➤ Object ➤ Edit**

## Edit ➤ Object ➤ Open

Use this option to open the source application of a linked object, picture, or document.

## How You Get Here

◇ Press **Alt+E,O,O**          ◇ Choose **Edit ➤ Object ➤ Open**

## Edit ➤ Object ➤ Convert

Use this option to change the linked object from one format to another. The options available change based on the type of object you've highlighted before choosing this option.

### How You Get Here

◇ Press **Alt+E,O,V**       ◇ Choose **Edit ➤ Object ➤ Convert**

### What's In This Dialog Box

Figure 4.4 is a sample of this dialog box and Table 4.3 has a description of the options that are common to Word, Excel, and PowerPoint.

**Figure 4.4**   The Convert dialog box

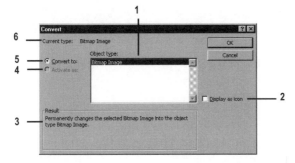

**Table 4.3**   Options in the Convert dialog box

| # | Option | What you do with it |
|---|--------|---------------------|
| 1 | Object type list | Choose an item that determines the new format of the object. |
| 2 | Display as Icon check box | Click to display the object as an icon instead of the full "picture" of the object. |
| 3 | Result field | View a brief description of the highlighted object type. |
| 4 | Activate as radio button | Click to open the object as the type chosen in the Object type list, but to change back to the original type after you edit the object. |
| 5 | Convert to radio button | Click to permanently change the object into the type chosen in the Object type list. |
| 6 | Current Type field | View a definition of the highlighted object. |

# The View Menu, Common Options

## In this chapter

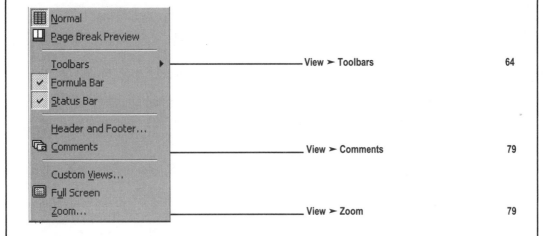

## What Is The View Menu

This menu lists the commands that determine what information is displayed for your application. You can choose how the main part of your file is displayed and what toolbars are visible (or, as is sometimes the case, in your way!); take a look at the information that is consistently used at the top and bottom of your file (the header and footer); display an onscreen ruler (so you can make adjustments visually rather than mathematically); change how big or small your display is (great for tired eyes); and just generally customize what you see on the screen. In most cases, the reason for multiple views is so that you can specialize how you see your work. No single view can encompass everyone's needs; if nothing else, the screen would become too cluttered for use.

If a menu option has an ellipsis (three dots) or an arrow beside it, the application "asks" you for additional information before the action takes place. If the menu doesn't have one of these symbols, the action you select happens immediately. If the action takes place immediately, you won't see a sample screen in this section.

## View ➤ Toolbars

Use this option to choose the toolbars you want displayed while you work. Toolbars are collections of icons (or buttons) and are especially handy when doing work that involves repeated tasks. However, if you open lots of toolbars they'll clutter the screen and you can waste more time than you realize by constantly moving them around as you work.

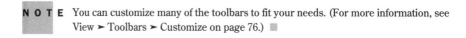

**N O T E**   You can customize many of the toolbars to fit your needs. (For more information, see View ➤ Toolbars ➤ Customize on page 76.) ■

### How You Get Here

◇ Press **Alt+V,T**            ◇ Choose **View ➤ Toolbars**

## What's In This Flyout Menu

Figure 5.1 is a sample of this flyout menu.

**Figure 5.1**   The View ➤ Toolbars flyout menu

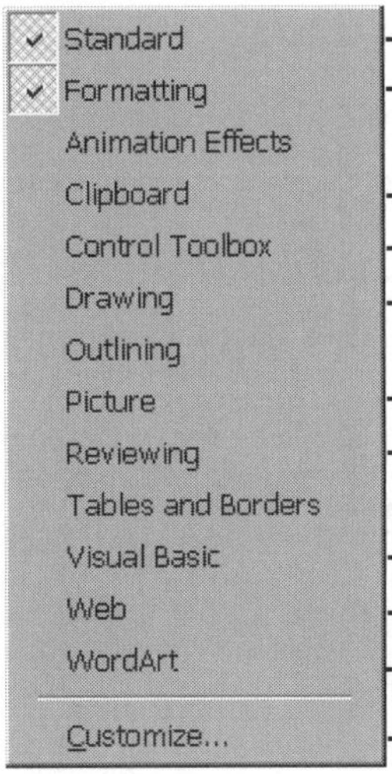

## View ➤ Toolbars ➤ Standard

Use this option to display the Standard toolbar, which has icons for many of your most frequently used options, such as Save, Print, Open, Cut, Paste, and Spellcheck. Although this toolbar displays when you do a standard Office 2000 installation, you can turn it off if you want to see more of your file and less of the icons.

## How You Get Here

◇ Press **Alt+V,T** choose **Standard**   ◇ Choose **View ➤ Toolbars ➤ Standard**

## What's In This Toolbar

Figure 5.2 is a sample of this toolbar and Table 5.1 has a description of the options that are common to Word, Excel, and PowerPoint.

**Figure 5.2**   The Standard toolbar

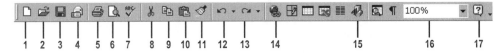

**Table 5.1**   Icons in the Standard toolbar

| #  | Icon | What you do with it |
|----|------|---------------------|
| 1  | New | Click to create a new file based on the default template for your application. |
| 2  | Open | Click to open an existing file. |
| 3  | Save | Click to save the current file using the same file name and file format. |
| 4  | E-mail | Click to open an email dialog box so that you can send the current file as an email message. |
| 5  | Print | Click to print the current file to the default printer. |
| 6  | Print Preview | Click to see what the current file will look like it you print it on the default printer. |
| 7  | Spelling and Grammar | Click to open the Spelling and Grammar dialog box so that you can check the current document for spelling and grammatical errors. |
| 8  | Cut | Click to *remove* the highlighted element and place it on the clipboard. |
| 9  | Copy | Click to *duplicate* the highlighted element *and* place it on the clipboard. |
| 10 | Paste | Click to insert an element from the clipboard into the current file at the current cursor location. |
| 11 | Format Painter | Click to copy the style of one element to another element. Highlight the paragraph or character whose style is to be copied. Click the **Format Painter** icon. Click the element that is to receive the style. |
| 12 | Undo | Click to cancel the last action or click the **Undo** drop-down list to display a list of previous actions that you can cancel. |
| 13 | Redo | Click to reestablish the last undo or click **Redo** drop-down list to display a list of previous actions that you can redo or repeat. |
| 14 | Insert Hyperlink | Click to open the Insert Hyperlink dialog box so that you can create a connection between one position in the active file and another position in the same file or to another file. |
| 15 | Drawing | Click to open the Drawing toolbar so that you can create or edit a drawing. |
| 16 | Zoom | Click to choose how much of the file you can see at one time. The larger the zoom amount, the larger the elements display on your screen. |
| 17 | Help | Click to open the Help dialog box so that you can look something up. |

## View ➤ Toolbars ➤ Formatting

Use this option to display the Formatting toolbar which has icons for the font used for your text, borders that surround an element, and other icons for changing the look of the elements in your file.

■ For information about Word's Formatting toolbar, see The Formatting Toolbar on page 192.
■ For information about Excel's Formatting toolbar, see The Formatting Toolbar on page 338.
■ For information about PowerPoint's Formatting toolbar, see The Formatting Toolbar on page 492.

### How You Get Here

✧ Press **Alt+V,T** choose **Formatting**    ✧ Choose **View** ➤ **Toolbars** ➤ **Formatting**

## View ➤ Toolbars ➤ Clipboard

Use this option to display the Clipboard toolbar, which stores up to twelve copied items. This is very helpful when you have copied items from other applications and want to combine them in one document. If you're working in a non-Office application and have an Office application open, all copied items are added to the Clipboard. However, the Clipboard toolbar is only available in an Office application.

---

**N O T E**   You can't customize this toolbar.  ▥

### How You Get Here

✧ Press **Alt+V,T** choose **Clipboard**    ✧ Choose **View** ➤ **Toolbars** ➤ **Clipboard**

### What's In This Toolbar

Figure 5.3 is a sample of this toolbar and Table 5.2 has a description of the options that are common to Word, Excel, and PowerPoint.

**Figure 5.3**   The Clipboard toolbar

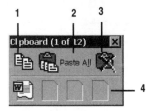

**Table 5.2**   Icons in the Clipboard toolbar

| # | Icon | What you do with it |
|---|------|---------------------|
| 1 | Copy | Click to *duplicate* the highlighted element *and* place it on the clipboard. |
| 2 | Paste All | Click to insert *all* elements from the clipboard into the current file at the current cursor location. |
| 3 | Clear Clipboard | Click to remove all elements from the clipboard. |
| 4 | Clipboard Contents | Click to paste one element at a time into the active file at the current cursor location. You can see what each item is by holding the cursor over it briefly. |

## View ➤ Toolbars ➤ Control Toolbox

Use this option to display the Control Toolbox toolbar so that you create a custom form with ActiveX controls such as radio buttons, text boxes, scroll bars, and other neat stuff that can darn near make your file sing and dance (but that kind of stuff is beyond the scope of this book). These controls are similar to the controls created with a programming language, such as Visual Basic. With an ActiveX control, however, you're actually writing a macro that is stored with the control and it is only available when the file with the control is open.

**N O T E**   These are the same types of controls you can add using the Visual Basic Editor. For more information try, *Special Edition, Using Visual Basic For Applications 5*, by Paul Sanna, (ISBN: 0789709597). ■

## How You Get Here

✧ Press **Alt+V,T** choose **Control Toolbox**      ✧ Choose **View ➤ Toolbars ➤ Control Toolbox**

## What's In This Toolbar

Figure 5.4 is a sample of this toolbar and Table 5.3 has a description of the options that are common to Word, Excel, and PowerPoint.

**Figure 5.4**   The Control Toolbox toolbar

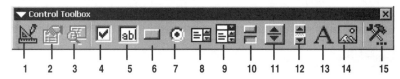

**Table 5.3**   Icons in the Control Toolbox toolbar

| # | Icon | What you do with it |
|---|------|---------------------|
| 1 | Design Mode | Click to turn on the mode that lets you can insert various controls (such as radio buttons or scroll bars) at the current cursor location. |
| 2 | Properties | Click to view or change the behind the scenes workings for the highlighted control element. |
| 3 | View Code | Click to display the Visual Basic editor so you can look at the background information for the highlighted control element. |
| 4 | Check Box | Click to insert a check box control into the current document, at the current cursor location. |
| 5 | Text Box | Click to insert a text box control into the current document, at the current cursor location. |
| 6 | Command Button | Click to insert a command button control into the current document, at the current cursor location. |
| 7 | Option Button | Click to insert an option button control into the current document, at the current cursor location. |
| 8 | List Box | Click to insert a list box control into the current document, at the current cursor location. |
| 9 | Combo Box | Click to insert a combo box control into the current document, at the current cursor location. |
| 10 | Toggle Button | Click to insert a toggle button control into the current document, at the cursor's current location |
| 11 | Spin Button | Click to insert a spin button control into the current document, at the current cursor location. |
| 12 | Scroll Bar | Click to insert a scroll bar next to a list box that contains items that cannot by seen immediately without scrolling through the list. |
| 13 | Label | Click to insert descriptive text for your control. |
| 14 | Image | Click to insert an image control into the current document, at the current cursor location. |
| 15 | More Controls | Click to display a drop-down list of other controls available on the system. |

## View ➤ Toolbars ➤ Drawing

Use this option to display the Drawing toolbar so that you can create your own drawings, insert shapes, add callouts, and apply color to your masterpiece.

## How You Get Here

✧ Click     ✧ Press **Alt+V,T** choose **Drawing**    ✧ Choose **View** ➤ **Toolbars** ➤ **Drawing**

## What's In This Toolbar

Figure 5.5 is a sample of this toolbar and Table 5.4 has a description of the options that are common to Word, Excel, and PowerPoint.

**Figure 5.5**   The Drawing toolbar

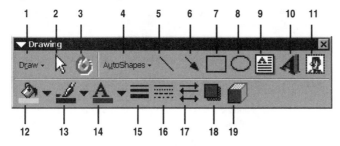

**Table 5.4**   Icons in the Drawing toolbar

| # | Icon | What you do with it |
|---|------|---------------------|
| 1 | Draw drop-down list | Choose an item that determines which drawing command you want to use. |
| 2 | Select Objects | Click to change the cursor to the "select objects mode" so that you can highlight objects you have drawn using your mouse. The cursor changes to this arrow when you move it over the drawn object. |
| 3 | Free Rotate | Click to permit highlighted objects to be rotated to the desired angle. |
| 4 | AutoShapes drop-down list | Choose an item that determines which predefined drawing shape you want to insert in your file. (For more information, see Insert ➤ Picture ➤ AutoShapes on page 86.) |
| 5 | Line | Click to change the cursor to crosshairs so that you can use your cursor to draw a line. |
| 6 | Arrow | Click to change the cursor to crosshairs so that you can use your cursor to draw a line with an arrow on the end. |
| 7 | Rectangle | Click to change the cursor to crosshairs so that you can use your cursor to draw a rectangle or square. |
| 8 | Oval | Click to change the cursor to crosshairs so that you can use your cursor to draw an oval or circle. |
| 9 | Text Box | Click to change the cursor to crosshairs so that you can draw a box to hold descriptive text for your drawing. |
| 10 | Insert WordArt | Click to display the WordArt Gallery so that you can choose a style for your WordArt and insert it into the current document. (For more information, see Insert ➤ Picture ➤ WordArt on page 87.) |
| 11 | Insert Clip Art | Click to display the Insert Clip Art dialog box so that you can choose a piece of clip art to insert at the current cursor position. (For more information, see Insert ➤ Picture ➤ Clip Art on page 84.) |

**Table 5.4**  Icons in the Drawing toolbar, continued

| # Icon | What you do with it |
| --- | --- |
| 12 Fill Color and drop-down list | Click to flood the highlighted drawing object with color. Click the arrow next to the button for a more colors. |
| 13 Line Color and drop-down list | Click to make a highlighted line a specific color. Click the arrow next to the button for a more colors. |
| 14 Font Color and drop-down list | Click to make highlighted text a specific color. Click the arrow next to the button for a more colors. |
| 15 Line Style | Click to apply a specific type of line to any drawing object. |
| 16 Dash Style | Click to apply a variety of dashed lines to any drawing object. |
| 17 Arrow Style | Click to apply a a variety of arrow styles to any drawing object. |
| 18 Shadow | Choose an item that determines what shadow style you want to apply to the highlighted drawing element. <br> **Note**  A drawing element can't have shadowing and 3-D at the same time. |
| 19 3-D | Choose an item that determines what three-dimensional style you want to apply to the highlighted drawing element. <br> **Note**  A drawing element can't have shadowing and 3-D at the same time. |

## View ➤ Toolbars ➤ Picture

Use this option to display the Picture toolbar so that you can insert images into your document and control the way they look. (For more information, see Insert ➤ Picture on page 83.)

### How You Get Here

✧ Press **Alt+V,T** choose **Picture**    ✧ Choose **View ➤ Toolbars ➤ Picture**

### What's In This Toolbar

Figure 5.6 is a sample of this toolbar and Table 5.5 has a description of the options that are common to Word, Excel, and PowerPoint.

**Figure 5.6**  The Picture toolbar

**Table 5.5**    Icons in the Picture toolbar

| # Icon | What you do with it |
|--------|---------------------|
| 1   Insert Picture | Click to display the Insert Picture dialog box. You can insert a copy of an image, linked the image to the original source, or both link and insert a copy at the current cursor location. (For more information, see Insert ➤ Picture on page 186.) |
| 2   Image Control | Choose an item that determines what image control options are applied to the highlighted image. |
| 3   More Contrast | Click to increase the contrast of the highlighted image. |
| 4   Less Contrast | Click to decrease the contrast of the highlighted image. |
| 5   More Brightness | Click to increase the brightness of the highlighted image. |
| 6   Less Brightness | Click to decrease the brightness of the highlighted image. |
| 7   Crop | Click to turn the cursor into a cropping tool for "cutting" the image to fit your needs. |
| 8   Line Style | Click to set the size of a highlighted line. |
| 9   Text Wrapping | Choose an item that determines how the text and image interact. |
| 10  Format Object | Click to display the Format Object dialog box so that you can set or review the properties of the highlighted image. |
| 11  Set Transparent Color | Click to turn the cursor into a color application tool. Click on the color in the image that you want to be transparent. "Transparent" means that the color will be faithfully reproduced in printing, but onscreen it displays as the background color. |
| 12  Reset Picture | Click to restore the image to its original properties. |

## View ➤ Toolbars ➤ Reviewing

Use this option to display the Reviewing toolbar so that you can review existing comments, insert comments, delete existing comments, or accept the changes made to a document. This is a great way keep track of notes, comments, and questions; that way you and other authors can review this information before the text is actually added to the final file. (For more information, see Insert ➤ Comment on page 82 or View ➤ Comments on page 79.)

## How You Get Here

✧ Press **Alt+V,T** choose **Reviewing**    ✧ Choose **View** ➤ **Toolbars** ➤ **Reviewing**

## What's In This Toolbar

Figure 5.7 is a sample of this toolbar and Table 5.6 has a description of the options that are common to Word, Excel, and PowerPoint.

**Figure 5.7**   The Reviewing toolbar

**Table 5.6**   Icons in the Reviewing toolbar

| # | Icon | What you do with it |
|---|------|---------------------|
| 1 | New Comment | Click to insert a new comment at the current cursor position. |
| 2 | Show/Hide Comment | Click to show or hide the comment for the highlighted element. |
| 3 | Previous Comment | Click to step backward to the previous comment. |
| 4 | Next Comment | Click to step forward to the next comment. |
| 5 | Delete Comment | Click to delete the highlighted comment. |
| 6 | Create Microsoft Outlook Task | Click to open the Task dialog box and create a new Outlook task. |
| 7 | Send to Mail Recipient | Click to send the current file as an email attachment. |

## View ➤ Toolbars ➤ Visual Basic

Use this option to display the Visual Basic toolbar so that you can create or edit a macro. Macros are small programs that you use for different purposes. You can create macros that do some of the tedious, repetitive work that you would normally do at the keyboard, one step at a time. In fact, you can create a program for almost any task that you need to perform, which is a great way to ensure accuracy and relieve the boredom of doing the same thing over and over again.

---

**N O T E**   Although the details of programming with Visual Basic are beyond the scope of this book, you might want to try, *Special Edition, Using Visual Basic For Applications 5*, by Paul Sanna, (ISBN: 0789709597). ▦

## How You Get Here

◈ Press **Alt+V,T** choose **Visual Basic**      ◈ Choose **View** ➤ **Toolbars** ➤ **Visual Basic**

## What's In This Toolbar

Figure 5.8 is a sample of this toolbar and Table 5.7 has a description of the options that are common to Word, Excel, and PowerPoint.

**Figure 5.8**    The Visual Basic toolbar

**Table 5.7**    Icons in the Visual Basic toolbar

| # | Icon | What you do with it |
|---|------|---------------------|
| 1 | Run Macro | Click to display the Macros dialog box so that you can choose which existing macro you want to run. |
| 2 | Record Macro | Click to display the Record Macro dialog box so that you can create a new macro. Once you give the macro a name, all your keystrokes, mouse clicks, and other cursor movements are stored under that name. |
| 3 | Security | Click to display the Security dialog box so that you can determine what the application does when it detects unknown macros.  (For more information, see Tools ➤ Macro ➤ Security on page 105.) |
| 4 | Visual Basic Editor | Click to display the Visual Basic Editor. |
| 5 | Controls Toolbox | Click to display the Controls toolbar.  (For more information, see View ➤ Toolbars ➤ Control Toolbox on page 68.) |
| 6 | Design Mode | Click to display the Controls toolbar and place the current window into design mode. (For more information, see View ➤ Toolbars ➤ Control Toolbox on page 68.) |
| 7 | Microsoft Script Editor | Click to display the Script Editor for creating Web scripts. The default language is Microsoft's VBScript, but you can use other languages. |

## View ➤ Toolbars ➤ Web

Use this option to display the Web toolbar so that you can see and use the icons that are used most frequently in a Web Browser.

### How You Get Here

✧ Press **Alt+V,T** choose **Web**      ✧ Choose **View** ➤ **Toolbars** ➤ **Web**

## What's In This Toolbar

Figure 5.9 is a sample of this toolbar and Table 5.8 has a description of the options that are common to Word, Excel, and PowerPoint.

**Figure 5.9**   The Web toolbar

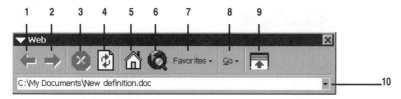

**Table 5.8**   Icons in the Web toolbar

| # | Icon | What you do with it |
|---|------|---------------------|
| 1 | Back | Click to step backward to a previously viewed page in the viewing sequence. |
| 2 | Forward | Click to step forward to a previously viewed page in the viewing sequence. |
| 3 | Stop Current Jump | Click to cancel the current operation. |
| 4 | Refresh Current Page | Click to update and redisplay the current page with any changes. |
| 5 | Start Page | Click to access and display the "home page". |
| 6 | Search the Web | Click to access a Web page with a Web search engine so that you can look for specific information. |
| 7 | Favorites | Choose an item that determines what site you want to visit from a stored list of favorite sites. |
| 8 | Go | Choose an item that determines which navigational command is executed. |
| 9 | Show Only Web Toolbar | Click to hide the other toolbars and make Word look like a Web browser. |
| 10 | Address | Click to display a drop-down list of locations already visited. |

## View ➤ Toolbars ➤ WordArt

Use this option to display the WordArt toolbar so that you can insert and format art items so they look just the way you want them to. This toolbar includes icons for moving and resizing your art objects or changing the way your text is aligned or wrapped around the object. (For more information, see Insert ➤ Picture ➤ WordArt on page 87.)

## How You Get Here

✧ Press **Alt+V,T** choose **WordArt**    ✧ Choose **View** ➤ **Toolbars** ➤ **WordArt**

## What's In This Toolbar

Figure 5.10 is a sample of this toolbar and Table 5.9 has a description of the options that are common to Word, Excel, and PowerPoint.

**Figure 5.10**    The WordArt toolbar

**Table 5.9**    Icons in the WordArt toolbar

| # | Icon | What you do with it |
|---|------|---------------------|
| 1 | Insert WordArt | Click to open the WordArt Gallery dialog box so that you choose the effect you want to apply to the text you type in the Edit Text dialog box. |
| 2 | Edit Text dialog box | Click to open the Edit WordArt Text dialog box so that you can add or change the text you want to apply the effect to. |
| 3 | WordArt Gallery | Click to open the WordArt Gallery dialog box so that you can change the effect for the highlighted text. |
| 4 | Format Object | Click to open the Format WordArt dialog box so that you can change the look of your WordArt element. You can change the fill and line color, add arrows to the end of lines, change the position of the element, and choose the wrapping characteristics for the highlighted element. |
| 5 | WordArt Shape | Click to open a drop-down list of available WordArt shapes that you can use to reshape your text. |
| 6 | Free Rotate | Click to move the shape clockwise or counter clockwise. |
| 7 | WordArt Same Letter Heights | Click to set all of the letters in the highlighted WordArt element to the same vertical height. |
| 8 | WordArt Vertical Text | Click to make the WordArt run from top to bottom or bottom to top on the page. |
| 9 | WordArt Alignment | Choose an item that determines how the text is aligned within the WordArt element. |
| 10 | WordArt Character Spacing | Choose an item that determines the current character spacing option. |

## View ➤ Toolbars ➤ Customize

Use this option to display the Customize window so that you can customize most of the toolbars or menu options.

## How You Get Here

✧ Press **Alt+V,T,C**

✧ Choose **View** ➤ **Toolbars** ➤ **Customize**

## What's In This Dialog Box

Figure 5.11 is a sample of this dialog box and Table 5.10 has a description of the options that are common to Word, Excel, and PowerPoint.

**Figure 5.11** The Customize dialog box

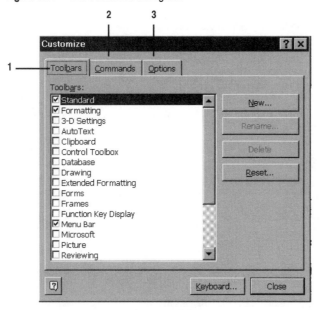

**Table 5.10** Tabs in the Customize dialog box

| # | Tab name | What you do with it |
|---|----------|---------------------|
| 1 | Toolbars | Click to create new toolbars, delete toolbars you've created, or see what toolbars are active. (For a complete description of the options available, see Table 5.11 on page 78.) |
| 2 | Commands | Click to list the available categories of commands and the commands within them. You must display or create a toolbar before you can add new icons to it or to a menu. (For a complete description of the options available, see Table 5.12 on page 78.) |
| 3 | Options | Click to choose various display options for toolbars and menus. (For a complete description of the options available, see Table 5.13 on page 78.) |

The following tables describe the options for the individual tabs in this dialog box:

- Table 5.11 describes the Toolbars tab,
- Table 5.12 describes the Commands tab, and
- Table 5.13 describes the Options tab.

**Table 5.11**   Options in the Customize dialog box Toolbars tab

| Option | What you do with it |
| --- | --- |
| Toolbars area | Click to choose the toolbars you want to modify. When the toolbar is visible, it isn't active, but you can make changes to it. Right-click an icon to display a menu that you can use to modify the highlighted icon. |
| New button | Click to display the New Toolbar dialog box so that you can create a new toolbar. |
| Rename button | Click to display the Rename Toolbar dialog box so that you can rename toolbars you've created. (You can't rename the toolbars included with the application.) |
| Delete button | Click to delete a toolbar you've created. (You can't delete the toolbars included with the application.) |
| Reset button | Click to display the Reset Toolbar dialog box so that you can restore the original settings and buttons for the active file. |
| Keyboard button | Click to display the Customize Keyboard dialog box so that you can create new shortcut keys for system functions such as **File ➤ Close**. |

**Table 5.12**   Options in the Customize dialog box Commands tab

| Option | What you do with it |
| --- | --- |
| Categories area | Choose an item that determines the menu or toolbar you want to change. |
| Commands area | Click to choose the commands you want to change. |
| Description button | Click to display a brief description of the highlighted command. |
| Modify Selection | Click to display a drop-down list of controls for the highlighted command. |
| Keyboard | Click to display the Customize Keyboard dialog box so that you can create new shortcut keys for system functions, such as **File ➤ Close**. |

**Table 5.13**   Options in the Customize dialog box Options tab

| Option | What you do with it |
| --- | --- |
| Personalized Menus and Toolbars area | Choose an item that determines the properties you want to set for your menus and toolbars. |
| Other area | Choose an item that determines how you want to display your menus and toolbars. |
| Menu animations drop-down list | Choose an item that determines the way your menus are animated. |
| Keyboard button | Click to display the Customize Keyboard dialog box so that you can create new shortcut keys for system functions such as **File ➤ Close**. |

# View ➤ Comments

Use this option to view any comments that have been inserted in the current file. This option opens a pane in the current window which has the comment text in it.

---

**N O T E**  Comments in the current document are indicated by yellow highlighting within the text. (For more information, see View ➤ Toolbars ➤ Reviewing on page 72.) ▪

## How You Get Here

❖ Press **Alt+V,C**          ❖ Choose **View ➤ Comments**

# View ➤ Zoom

Use this option to set the size of the display for the current file. You can let the application calculate the size or you can set a precise size that suits your needs.

---

**N O T E**  When you choose a larger number, you see a bigger version of your file, but you can't see as much of the file at one time. You'll spend more time scrolling but your eyes won't be so worn out. ▪

## How You Get Here

❖ Press **Alt+V,Z**          ❖ Choose **View ➤ Zoom**

## What's In This Dialog Box

Figure 5.12 is a sample of this dialog box and Table 5.14 has a description of the options that are common to Word, Excel, and PowerPoint.

**Figure 5.12**   The Zoom dialog box

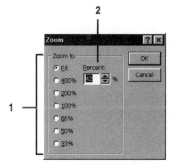

**Table 5.14**    Options in the Zoom dialog box

| # | Option | What you do with it |
|---|--------|---------------------|
| 1 | Zoom to area | Choose an item that determines determines how the information displays on your screen. |
| 2 | Percent area | Enter a specific zoom percentage in the text box or use the arrows to locate the specific zoom percentage you want. |

# The Insert Menu, Common Options

**In** this chapter

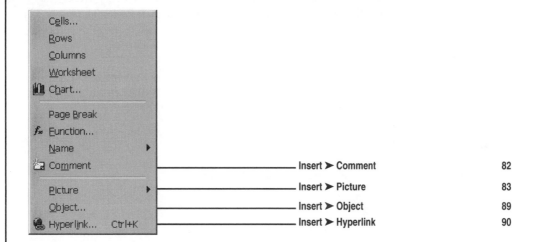

# What Is The Insert Menu

This menu lists the commands that you'll use to add page breaks, page numbers, stored text phrases, comments, pictures, and hyperlinks. Many types of items you want to put in your document are inserted from this menu.

If a menu option has an ellipsis (three dots) or an arrow beside it, the application "asks" you for additional information before the action takes place. If the menu doesn't have one of these symbols, the action you select happens immediately. If the action takes place immediately, you won't see a sample screen in this section.

# Insert ➤ Comment

Use this option to add written or audio notes (if you have a sound card and microphone) to a file that you're editing or reviewing. Be sure you either highlight the text you're making a comment about or click the cursor at the end of the text before you choose this command. Once you insert a comment, the text looks like someone used a highlighting marker over the text, which makes it very easy to see where the comments are. (For more information, see View ➤ Toolbars ➤ Reviewing on page 72 or View ➤ Comments on page 79.)

---

**N O T E**   Several different authors can review the same file and the application keeps track of the comment *and* the name of the person who made the comment. If you place your cursor over a highlighted comment, the reviewer name and comment displays. ▧

## How You Get Here

✧ Press **Alt+I,M**          ✧ Choose **Insert ➤ Comment**

## What's In This Pane

Figure 6.1 is a sample of this pane and Table 6.1 has a description of the options that are common to Word, Excel, and PowerPoint.

**Figure 6.1**   The Comment pane

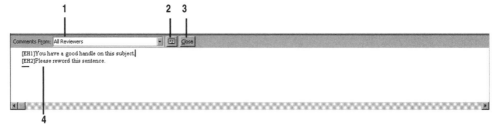

**Table 6.1**   Options in the Comment pane

| # | Option | What you do with it |
|---|--------|---------------------|
| 1 | Comments From drop-down list | Choose an item that determines which reviewer's comments you want to display in the Comments pane. |
| 2 | Insert Sound Object button | Click to record voice comments that are stored with your file. You must have a sound card and a microphone to use this option. |
| 3 | Close button | Click to close this pane and redisplay your file in the currently active view mode. |
| 4 | Comments text box | Enter or edit the text of any comments displayed. This area displays the comments based on which item you choose from the Comments From drop-down list. |

# Insert ➤ Picture

Use this option to insert various types of artwork in your file, including scanned items, the clipart that came with Office 2000, digital pictures, sound clips, and moving pictures. You can embed the artwork (store an actual copy) or create a link to the original file. If you create a link to the original file, you'll always have the latest information, no matter how many times you've edited the original artwork.

---

**N O T E**   Office 2000 accepts most of the popular graphics formats. Some of the formats, however, require a separate filter before you can bring them into your file. These filters are available on your original Office 2000 CD. So, if you don't have the filter you need, you can use the Office 2000 setup program to add them. ■

## How You Get Here

✧ Press **Alt+I,P**          ✧ Choose **Insert ➤ Picture**

## What's In This Flyout Menu

Figure 6.2 is a sample of this flyout menu.

**Figure 6.2**   The Insert ➤ Picture flyout menu

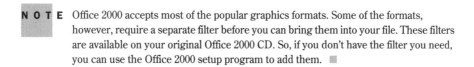

## Insert ➤ Picture ➤ Clip Art

Use this option to add pictures, sounds, or moving images from an electronic clip art library. There are lots of clipart libraries (such as the one included with Office 2000) that have royalty-free items that you can use to enhance your work. For instance, you can insert anything from pictures of animals to weather maps. You can also search the Internet for pictures, sounds, and moving images. The possibilities are almost endless.

---

**N O T E**   You may need your original installation CD to look at, and insert, itemms from the clipart library that ships with Office 2000. ▨

## How You Get Here

✧ Press **Alt+I,P,C**          ✧ Choose **Insert ➤ Picture ➤ Clip Art**

## What's In This Dialog Box

Figure 6.3 is a sample of this dialog box and Table 6.2 has a description of the options that are common to Word, Excel, and PowerPoint.

**Figure 6.3**   The Insert ClipArt dialog box

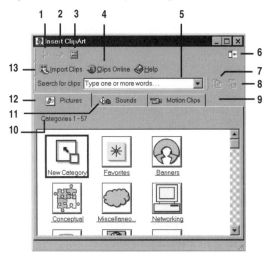

**Table 6.2**   Options in the Insert ClipArt dialog box

| # | Option | What you do with it |
|---|--------|---------------------|
| 1 | Back button | Click to go to the previously viewed item. |
| 2 | Forward button | Click to go to the next viewed item. |

**Table 6.2**   Options in the Insert ClipArt dialog box, continued

| # | Option | What you do with it |
|---|--------|---------------------|
| 3 | All Categories button | Click to view all the catalogs, regardless of what type of clipart is in the catalog. |
| 4 | Clips Online button | Click to access the web for other art to add to your library. |
| 5 | Search for clips drop-down list | Enter a keyword for a quick search for related clips. |
| 6 | Change to Small/Full Window button | Click to make your dialog box smaller or larger. |
| 7 | Copy button | Click to copy the selected image so that you can paste it in your file. |
| 8 | Paste button | Click to paste the selected image in your file at the current cursor position. |
| 9 | Motion Clips tab | Choose an item that determines the animation you want in your document. |
| 10 | Categories list | View which categories of clipart are currently displayed. |
| 11 | Sounds tab | Choose an item that determines which sound you want to insert at the current cursor position. |
| 12 | Pictures tab | Choose an item that determines what picture you want to insert at the current cursor position. |
| 13 | Import Clips button | Click to bring in clips from other sources. |

## Insert ➤ Picture ➤ From File

Use this option to place a picture from another location on your system. The types of files you can use are picture files or various types of graphical mediums. You can link these files so when you make changes to them in the source file they are updated in your document. These can be pictures you created with other tools.

### How You Get Here

✧ Press **Alt+I,P,F**          ✧ Choose **Insert ➤ Picture ➤ From File**

### What's In This Dialog Box

Figure 6.4 is a sample of this dialog box and has a description of the only option that is different from the Open dialog box.

---

**N O T E**   This dialog box is the same basic dialog box displayed when you choose **File ➤ Open**. Select the file location, name, and type, then decide whether you want to insert a copy of the picture in your file or create a link to the source file. (For more information, see File ➤ Open on page 39.) ▪

**Figure 6.4**    The Insert Picture dialog box

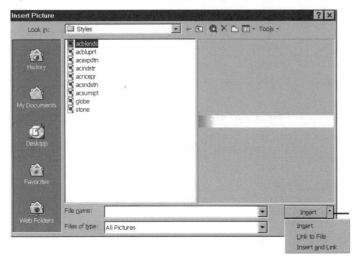

Choose an item that
determines if you want to just
insert, link to a file, or insert
and link.

## Insert ➤ Picture ➤ AutoShapes

Use this option to display the AutoShapes toolbar so that you can add a variety of predefined
graphic elements (such as lines, stars, and arrows) to your file. Once you choose which shape you
want, the cursor becomes a plus sign (+) and can "draw" the shape in your file. Although these
elements predefined, you make them any size you need. Once you've inserted a shape, you can
double-click it and use the Format AutoShape dialog box to change the fill color, the size, and the
position in your file.

### How You Get Here

✧ Press **Alt+I,P,A**          ✧ Choose **Insert ➤ Picture ➤ AutoShapes**

### What's In This Toolbar

Figure 6.5 is a sample of this toolbar and Table 6.3 has a description of the icons that are common
to Word, Excel, and PowerPoint.

**Figure 6.5**    The AutoShapes toolbar

**Table 6.3**   Icons in the AutoShapes toolbar

| # | Icon | What you do with it |
|---|------|---------------------|
| 1 | Lines | Click to pick what type of line you want to draw. Options include everything from a a basic straight line to a tool for freehand drawing. |
| 2 | Basic Shapes | Click to pick what basic shape, (e.g., a square, triangle or rectangle) you want to draw. Options include everything from a square, triangle, or rectangle to a lightening bolt. |
| 3 | Block Arrows | Click to pick what type of two-dimensional arrow you want to draw. Options include everything from your basic arrow to ones with an interesting curve to them. |
| 4 | Flowchart | Click to pick which flowchart shape you want to insert. |
| 5 | Stars and Banners | Click to pick what the type of star or banner you want. Options vary from a scroll-type banner to a starburst. |
| 6 | Callouts | Click to pick what callout style you want to use to enhance that fabulous clipart you inserted. |
| 7 | More AutoShapes | Click to look at the additional shapes available on your system. The More AutoShapes dialog box has many of the same options as the Insert Clip Art dialog box. (For more information, see Insert ➤ Picture ➤ Clip Art on page 84.) |

## Insert ➤ Picture ➤ WordArt

Use this option to create some rather fancy looking type (called "WordArt") for your file. You get to enter the text you want to use and then the application does the fancy work. Once you insert the WordArt you change almost everything about the text—from the size to the colors used to how the main body of your text wraps around the WordArt. The WordArt toolbar displays when you insert a WordArt item. (For more information, see View ➤ Toolbars ➤ WordArt on page 75.)

---

**N O T E**   You can also insert WordArt from the Drawing toolbar. (For more information, see View ➤ Toolbars ➤ Drawing on page 69.) ▥

## How You Get Here

❖ Press **Alt+I,P,W**          ❖ Choose **Insert ➤ Picture ➤ WordArt**

## What's In This Dialog Box

Figure 6.6 is a sample of this dialog box and has a description of the only option available.

**Figure 6.6**    The WordArt Gallery dialog box

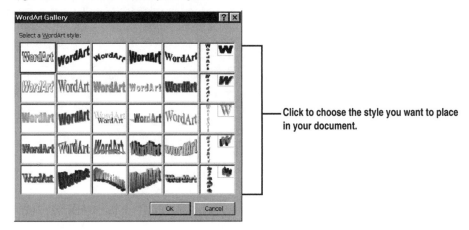

Click to choose the style you want to place in your document.

## Insert ➤ Picture ➤ From Scanner or Camera

Use this option to place a graphic that you're scanning or that you've taken using a digital camera.

---

**N O T E**    If you don't have a scanner connected to your computer you'll be asked if you want to install one. ▪

## How You Get Here

✧ Press **Alt+I,P,S**        ✧ Choose **Insert ➤ Picture ➤ From Scanner or Camera**

## Insert ➤ Picture ➤ Chart

Use this option to insert a chart into your document. You can link a chart to its source file or you can embed it in your document. Linking provides updating whenever the source file is changed. If you embed a chart, then change the source file, you'll have to reimport, or manually update, the file.

## How You Get Here

✧ Press **Alt+I,P,H**        ✧ Choose **Insert ➤ Picture ➤ Chart**

# Insert ➤ Object

Use this option to place items from other applications into your file or to create new items using another application. Inserting an object differs from inserting a file because you create the object with a source application instead of selecting an existing file from your computer system. These items can be embedded in the document or linked to a source.

 **TIP**  This option is primarily for inserting file types that Word doesn't really know how to handle, such as native Portable Document Format (PDF) or Paint Shop Pro (PSP) files. The Insert ➤ File option is primarily for file types that Word already knows about, such as Rich Text Format (RTF) or standard text files created in other applications. (For more information, see Insert ➤ File on page 188.)

## How You Get Here

✧ Press **Alt+I,O**          ✧ Choose **Insert ➤ Object**

## What's In This Dialog Box

Figure 6.7 is a sample of this dialog box and Table 6.4 has a description of the tabs that are common to Word, Excel, and PowerPoint.

**Figure 6.7**   The Object dialog box

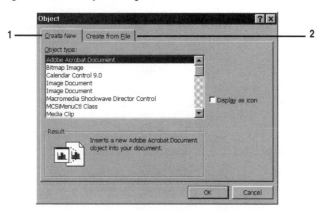

**Table 6.4**   Tabs in the Object dialog box

| # | Tab name | What you do with it |
|---|----------|---------------------|
| 1 | Create New | Click to choose the type of object you want to insert. (For a complete description of the options available, see Table 6.5 on page 90.) |
| 2 | Create from File | Click to choose what, where, and how you want to insert the desired object. (For a complete description of the options available, see Table 6.6 on page 90.) |

The following tables describe the options for the individual tabs in this dialog box:

■    Table 6.5 describes the Create New tab, and
■    Table 6.6 describes the Create from File tab.

**Table 6.5**    Options in the Object dialog box Create New tab

| Option | What you do with it |
| --- | --- |
| Object type list | Click to choose the type of object you want to insert. The application the object was created in opens, then you can choose the file containing the object to insert. |
| Display as icon check box | Click to insert the object as an icon instead of inserting the file's contents. |
| Result area | View a description of what will happen when you insert this object. |

**Table 6.6**    Options in the Object dialog box Create from File tab

| Option | What you do with it |
| --- | --- |
| File name text box | Enter the name of the file containing the desired object. |
| Browse button | Click to locate the desired file containing the object you want to insert. |
| Link to file check box | Click to maintain a link to the source file so that the current file is updated when you change the source file. |
| Display as icon check box | Click to insert the object as an icon instead of inserting the file's contents. |
| Result area | View a description of what will happen when you insert this object. |

# Insert ➤ Hyperlink

Use this option to create a connection between two parts of your file, between the active file and another file, or create a connection between the active file and a website address. Once you've inserted the hyperlink, the text changes color and is underlined and you can click on it to quickly jump to the destination specified. You can use the Web toolbar to work with the hyperlink and you can edit the information stored in the hyperlink after you've inserted it. (For more information, see View ➤ Toolbars ➤ Web on page 74.)

**TIP**    You can also create a screen tip that displays when you place your cursor over the link. If you need to edit the link, select it, then right-click to display the shortcut menu.

## How You Get Here

✧ Click         ✧ Press **Alt+I,I** or **Ctrl+K**    ✧ Choose **Insert ➤ Hyperlink**

## What's In This Dialog Box

Figure 6.8 is a sample of this dialog box and Table 6.7 has a description of the options that are common to Word, Excel, and PowerPoint.

**Figure 6.8** The Insert Hyperlink dialog box

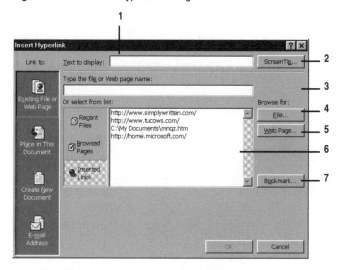

**Table 6.7** Options in the Insert Hyperlink dialog box

| # | Option | What you do with it |
|---|--------|---------------------|
| 1 | Text to display text box | Enter the text you want to link. You can select desired text in your document to link from. |
| 2 | Screen Tip button | Click to enter a description of the link that displays when you place the cursor over the link in the file. |
| 3 | Type the file text box | Enter the file name, the web page name, or a specific location in the active document that you want to link to. |
| 4 | Browse for File button | Click to select the desired file you want to link to. You can display the directories for any drive you have access to. |
| 5 | Browse for Web Page button | Click to choose the name of the web page you want to link to. |

**Table 6.7**   Options in the Insert Hyperlink dialog box, continued

| # | Option | What you do with it |
|---|--------|---------------------|
| 6 | Or select from list | Click to one of the buttons to select a file instead of manually typing a convoluted address that has to be "just right". |
| | | ▪ Click the **Recent Files** icon to display a list of files that have been opened |
| | | ▪ Click the **Browsed Pages** icon to display a list of pages that you've recently viewed |
| | | ▪ Click the **Inserted Links** icon to display a list of the links that are already in the file. |
| 7 | Bookmark button | Click to link to a specific destination that has been already been inserted in the file. (Bookmarks are locations in a file that have been electronically marked so that you can quickly get to a specific spot in the text. They're similar to the piece of paper you insert in a hard copy book to indicate where you quit reading.) |

# The Tools Menu, Common Options

# What Is The Tools Menu

This menu includes options that make using your application easier and more efficient. Some of the more popular tools include spellcheck, AutoCorrect, and macros. This menu also includes options for customizing your application, such as changing the default ("assumed") location for storing files or selecting whether you want the scroll bars to show on your screen.

If a menu option has an ellipsis (three dots) or an arrow beside it, the application "asks" you for additional information before the action takes place. If the menu doesn't have one of these symbols, the action you choose happens immediately. If the action takes place immediately, you won't see a sample screen in this section.

# Tools ➤ Spelling

Use this option to look for words that may be misspelled. The application automatically flags any word it doesn't recognize, even if the word is spelled correctly for your environment For example, a proper name, such as the name of a lake, might be spelled correctly but the application flags it because it isn't in the dictionary. You can select one of the options displayed, skip over the flagged word, add a word to a dictionary so that the word isn't flagged again, or type in your own replacement.

 **TIP**    You can check the spelling of a specific word, sentence, or paragraph by selecting it and choosing **Tools ➤ Spelling**.

You should always visually proofread your document because the application only flags words not found in the standard dictionary. So if you accidentally type 'form" when you should have typed "from," the application doesn't consider it an error and skips over it.

**N O T E**    The dictionary is shared by all the Office 2000 applications, so if you add a word to the dictionary while using Excel, that word isn't flagged in any other Office application. ▮

## How You Get Here

✧ Click       ✧ Press **Alt+T,S** or **F7**      ✧ Choose <u>**Tools**</u> ➤ <u>**Spelling and Grammar**</u>

## What's In This Dialog Box

Figure 7.1 is a sample of this dialog box and Table 7.1 has a description of the options that are common to Word, Excel, and PowerPoint.

**Figure 7.1**    The Spelling dialog box

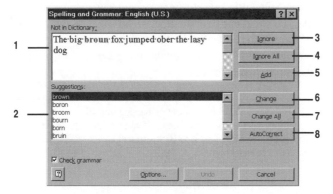

**Table 7.1**    Options in the Spelling dialog box

| # | Option | What you do with it |
|---|--------|---------------------|
| 1 | Not in Dictionary text box | View the words that are spelled incorrectly and highlighted. To correct the spelling you can double-click the word and enter the correct spelling then click the **Change** button. |
| 2 | Suggestions list | Click to choose the correct spelling for the incorrect word then click the **Change** button. You can also double-click the word to accept and change the spelling. |
| 3 | Ignore button | Click to ignore only *this* occurrence of the word. Every other occurrence of the word is flagged as incorrectly spelled. |
| 4 | Ignore All button | Click to ignore *all* occurrences of this word in this document. Future spellchecks of this document, or any other document, will flag the word as being incorrectly spelled. |
| 5 | Add button | Click to add this word to the dictionary so that future spellchecks of this document, or any other document, won't flag the word as being incorrectly spelled. |
| 6 | Change button | Click to accept the highlighted suggestion and replace *this* occurrence of the flagged word with the word highlighted in the Suggestions text box. |
| 7 | Change All button | Click to accept the highlighted suggestion and replace *all* occurrences of the flagged word with the word highlighted in the Suggestions text box. |
| 8 | AutoCorrect button | Click to automatically change the *next* occurrence of the flagged word to the word highlighted in the Suggestions text box. (For more information, see Tools ➤ AutoCorrect on page 96.) |

# Tools ➤ AutoCorrect

Use this option to save time by having the application automatically insert words or phrases when you type an abbreviated, or incorrect, form of the word or phrase. Since the application already has hundreds of entries, the one you need may already be there, or you can add and delete entries as needed. For example, you can have AutoCorrect type your company name when you type your company initials. For example, you could put JL in the Replace box, and then put Jetty, Logan, Campbell, Roche, and Altom in the With box and add it to the dictionary. The next time you need to type out the company name, simply type JL and press the **Space Bar**. The application automatically inserts the full company name for you.

 **TIP**   Autocorrect is wonderful, but it can be obnoxious if you happen to work for a company with initials that are the same as an autocorrect entry. For example, if you work for IHS Environmental, every time you type "IHS", the application changes it to HIS. You will have to delete the IHS/HIS entry so you can easily enter your company name.

## How You Get Here

✧ Press **Alt+T,A**          ✧ Choose **Tools** ➤ **AutoCorrect**

## What's In This Dialog Box

Figure 7.2 is a sample of this dialog box and Table 7.2 has a description of the options that are common to Word, Excel, and PowerPoint.

**Figure 7.2**    The AutoCorrect dialog box

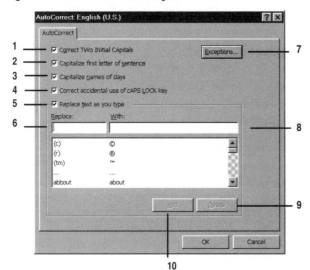

**Table 7.2**  Options in the AutoCorrect dialog box

| # | Option | What you do with it |
|---|--------|---------------------|
| 1 | Correct TWo INitial CApitals check box | Click to automatically replace a second capitalized letter with its lower case counterpart as you type. |
| 2 | Capitalize first letter of sentence check box | Click to automatically capitalize the first letter of a sentence as you type. |
| 3 | Capitalize names of days check box | Click to automatically capitalize the names of days as you type. |
| 4 | Correct accidental use of cAPS LOCK key check box | Click to automatically restore the CAPS unlock when typed text looks like this: sMALL sHIPS or ON OUR MERRY WAY, as you type. |
| 5 | Replace text as you type check box | Click to have corrections automatically applied as you type (see the next option). You should use this option with the AutoCorrect menu option and the Spelling and Grammar tab in the Options dialog box to set up the parameters for correcting text as you type. |
| 6 | Replace text box | Enter the text you want replaced. (Choose an entry in the list if you are editing or deleting an existing entry.) |
| 7 | Exceptions button | Click to store specific abbreviations or spellings that you want ignored by the dictionary. |
| 8 | With text box | Enter the text you want the text in the Replace text box replaced with. |
| 9 | Delete button | Click to delete the Replace/With combination from the dictionary. |
| 10 | Add button | Click to add the Replace/With combination to the dictionary |

# Tools ➤ Online Collaboration

Use this option to conduct a conversation online, similar to making a multiple-party telephone call. You will be collaborating with other people on one file at the same time. Those people who are participating will be able to edit and chat using the server that you specify. As host you will control the meeting, setting up who and how participants will interact during the meeting. In order for someone to join a meeting they all must have access to the same Internet or intranet (an inter-office network) and have Microsoft NetMeeting installed on their computer or network. However, they don't have to have the application you are working from to chat with you or edit your file online. This option works with your default email server and accesses your address book there. (For more information, see What Is The Outlook Mail Application on page 647.)

**N O T E**  This can be pretty complex, especially if you are having a Web discussion. You must first set up a server, then open the presentation you want to have the discussion about, then give the command. Most people would rather email the presentation around for comments rather than have a "live" discussion/collaboration about it. ▪

## How You Get Here

✧ Press **Alt+T,N**          ✧ Choose **Tools** ➤ **O_nline Collaboration**

## What's In This Flyout Menu

Figure 7.3 is a sample of this flyout menu.

**Figure 7.3**   The Tools ➤ Online Collaboration flyout menu

Tools ➤ Online Collaboration ➤ Meet Now          98
Tools ➤ Online Collaboration ➤ Schedule Meeting          99
Tools ➤ Online Collaboration ➤ Web Discussions          100

## Tools ➤ Online Collaboration ➤ Meet Now

Use this option to participate in a real-time Internet meeting. To do this, the application takes you through the following:

■ The Microsoft Netmeeting dialog box—where you establish your name, address, and server information the *first time* you use this option. This dialog box will not display again after you enter this information so if you want to change this information later you have to change it in the Microsoft Netmeeting **Tools** ➤ **Options** ➤ **My Information** tab.

■ The Place a Call dialog box—where you enter or choose participants for the meeting and activate the call.

■ The Online Meeting toolbar—where the meeting controls (call, end meeting, etc.) are displayed.

Once you have entered your information and placed the call the Online Meeting toolbar displays. This toolbar lets you participate in the meeting using the icons displayed. (For a complete description of the options available, see Table 7.4.)

## How You Get Here

✧ Press **Alt+T,N,M**          ✧ Choose **Tools** ➤ **O_nline Collaboration** ➤ **M_eet Now**

## What's In This Dialog Box

Figure 7.4 is a sample of this dialog box and Table 7.3 has a description of the options that are common to Word, Excel, and PowerPoint.

**Figure 7.4**   The Place A Call dialog box

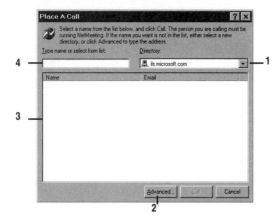

**Table 7.3**   Options in the Place A Call dialog box

| # | Option | What you do with it |
|---|--------|---------------------|
| 1 | Directory drop-down list | Choose an item that determines the server you want to use for the meeting. |
| 2 | Advanced button | Click to enter a new participants name. |
| 3 | Participant list | View or choose the names of the invited or accepted participants. |
| 4 | Type name or text box | Enter the name of the participant you want to call. |

## Tools ➤ Online Collaboration ➤ Schedule Meeting

Use this option to schedule a real-time meeting with others on a designated server. Netmeeting works in conjunction with Outlook when you are scheduling a meeting, so you'll be able to use your existing Contact information. (For more information, see What Is The Calendar on page 680.)

---

**N O T E**   For more information on Microsoft Netmeeting try *Windows 98 Multimedia: Lights! Camera! Action!*, by Adam Vujic, (ISBN: 078971857X). ▪

## How You Get Here

❖ **Alt+T, N, S**      ❖ Choose **Tools** ➤ **Online Collaboration** ➤ **Schedule Meeting**

## Tools ➤ Online Collaboration ➤ Web Discussions

Use this option to display the Microsoft NetMeeting dialog box so that you can establish a real-time link to others on a designated server.

### How You Get Here

✧ Press **Alt+T,N,W**   ✧ Choose **Tools ➤ Online Collaboration ➤ Web Discussions**

### The Online Meeting Toolbar

Use this option to quickly access the commands you need to participate in an online meeting. When you are invited to an online collaboration, and accept the invitation to participate, this toolbar and the file that is the subject of the collaboration displays on your screen.

---

**N O T E**   You must have Microsoft Netmeeting installed on your computer to participate or host an online collaboration meeting. ▪

### What's In This Toolbar

Figure 7.5 is a sample of this toolbar and Table 7.4 has a description of the options that are common to Word, Excel, and PowerPoint.

**Figure 7.5**   The Online Meeting toolbar

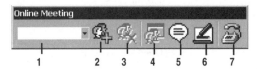

**Table 7.4**   Icons in the Online Meeting toolbar

| # | Icon | What you do with it |
|---|------|---------------------|
| 1 | Participant drop-down list | Choose an item that determines the name of the people you want to participate in the online meeting. |
| 2 | Call Participant | Click to have the application dial the number of the selected person. |
| 3 | Remove Participants | Click to remove selected name from participant list. These participants will not have access to your comments, nor will you have access to theirs. |
| 4 | Allow others to edit | Click to let others edit the file you are collaborating about. |
| 5 | Display Chat Window | Click to display all conversations occurring during the online meeting. |

**Table 7.4** Icons in the Online Meeting toolbar, continued

| # | Icon | What you do with it |
|---|------|---------------------|
| 6 | Display Whiteboard | Click to display the whiteboard where you can enter text, copy, paste, draw shapes or delete objects. If you are a participant you can open the whiteboard using the Microsoft Netmeeting icon on the taskbar. Only the host can open the whiteboard during the meeting from within any Office application. |
| 7 | End Meeting | Click to end the meeting and disconnect the call. |

# Tools ➤ Macro

Use this option to select one of several activities related to macros, such as record, playback, stop, and erase. Macros are a series of steps that you program in a set order and are helpful when you need to perform the same series of steps over and over. In fact, macros are a great way to "replace yourself" at the keyboard when you do the same tasks over and over again. (Never thought you'd be given permission to be lazy, did you?)

**TIP**    Macros can save you a lot of time—if you have a repetitive task that is more than four or five keystrokes, you should create a macro.

## How You Get Here

✧ Press **Alt+T,M**          ✧ Choose **Tools ➤ Macro**

## What's In This Flyout Menu

Figure 7.6 is a sample of this flyout menu.

**Figure 7.6**    The Tools ➤ Macro flyout menu

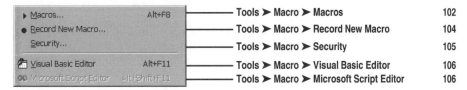

## Step By Step—Creating A Macro

Macros can seem overwhelming, but they don't have to be. It will be helpful to understand all of the macro options once you have actually created and run one. Try the following easy macro:

1. Open Word.
2. Display a blank document.
3. Choose **Tools ➤ Macro ➤ Record New Macro**.
4. In the Macro name text box, type `MyName` (no spaces allowed in the name).
5. Ignore the **Assign macro to Toolbars/Keyboard** buttons.
6. In the Store macro in drop-down list, choose `All documents` (the default).
7. In the Description text box, type a `brief description` of the macro you're recording.
8. Click **OK**.
   The Recording dialog box displays and you're now recording your keystrokes and mouse clicks.
9. Type your Name, Company Name, Address, Phone Number, and Email as you want it to appear in future documents (your cursor can be anywhere).
10. Click **Stop Recording**.
11. Place the cursor where you want your name to appear.
12. Choose **Tools ➤ Macro ➤ Macros**.
13. From the Macro name drop-down list, choose **MyName**.
14. Click **Run**.

Ta Da! Now anytime you need to type in this personal information in any Office 2000 application, you can simply run the macro.

## Tools ➤ Macro ➤ Macros

Use this option to look for the macro that you want to run or to modify an existing macro.

---

**N O T E**   You can create and edit macros using VBA.   ▪

## How You Get Here

✧ Press **Alt+T,M,M**

✧ Choose **Tools ➤ Macro ➤ Macros**

## What's In This Dialog Box

Figure 7.7 is a sample of this dialog box and Table 7.5 has a description of the options that are common to Word, Excel, and PowerPoint.

**Figure 7.7**   The Macro dialog box

**Table 7.5**   Options in the Macro dialog box

| # | Option | What you do with it |
|---|--------|---------------------|
| 1 | Description text box | Enter comments that describe a new macro or view the description of an existing macro. |
| 2 | Macros in drop-down list | Choose an item that determines where the macro is stored or choose a location for a newly created macro. |
| 3 | Macro name text box<br>Macro name drop-down list | Enter the name of the macro you want to run or choose an option from the Macro name drop-down list. |
| 4 | Run button | Click to run the macro you have selected. |
| 5 | Step Into button | Click to run the macro in Visual Basic Editor, one step at a time, pausing at each step. |
| 6 | Edit button | Click to bring up the Visual Basic and the Editing windows so that you can edit the macro using the Visual Basic programming language. |
| 7 | Create button | Click to bring up the Visual Basic and the Create windows so that you can create a macro using the Visual Basic programming language. |
| 8 | Delete button | Click to delete the selected macro currently selected (you will get a warning before it is deleted). |
| 9 | Organizer button | Click to open the Macro Organizer dialog box, which has four tabs. This dialog box is primarily used to copy macros from one document or template to another. |

## Tools ➤ Macro ➤ Record New Macro

Use this option to create a new macro, using steps similar to those used in making a audio or video tape recording (start, pause, stop, play, erase). See above to create a practice macro.

### How You Get Here

✧ Click ⬛    ✧ Press **Alt+T,M,R**    ✧ Choose **Tools ➤ Macro ➤ Record New Macro**

### What's In This Dialog Box

Figure 7.8 is a sample of this dialog box and Table 7.6 has a description of the options that are common to Word, Excel, and PowerPoint.

**Figure 7.8**   The Record Macro dialog box

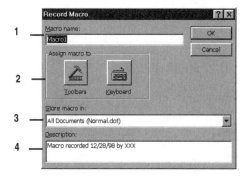

**Table 7.6**   Options in the Record Macro dialog box

| # | Option | What you do with it |
|---|--------|---------------------|
| 1 | Macro name text box | Enter a name for the new macro: no spaces allowed. (If you type an invalid name, a error message displays telling you to rename the macro.) |
| 2 | Assign macro to area | Click to put the macro you're creating on a toolbar of your choice. Click to assign this macro a keyboard shortcut so that you don't have to open the dialog box every time you want to run the macro. |
| 3 | Store macro in drop-down list | Choose an item that determines where you want this macro saved. |
| 4 | Description text box | Enter a description that identifies what the macro does. |

## Tools ➤ Macro ➤ Security

Use this option to have the application let you know when you receive a file from someone else that has macros in it. Since macros may have a virus that would shut your system down, a security level gives you a *little* piece of mind and one more level of protection for your important information.

## How You Get Here

◇ Press **Alt+T,M,S**            ◇ Choose **Tools ➤ Macro ➤ Security**

## What's In This Dialog Box

Figure 7.9 is a sample of this dialog box and Table 7.7 has a description of the options that are common to Word, Excel, and PowerPoint.

**Figure 7.9**    The Security dialog box

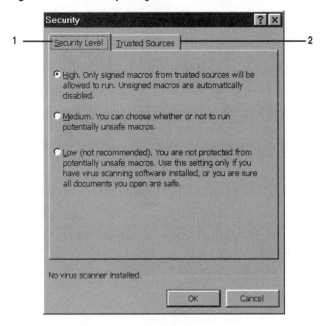

**Table 7.7**    Tabs in the Security dialog box

| # | Option | What you do with it |
|---|--------|---------------------|
| 1 | Security Level | Click to assign a security level that is used to screen documents that you receive from other sources. |
| 2 | Trusted Sources | Click to enter information about sources whose documents are considered safe and whose macros don't need to be identified or disabled. |

### Tools ➤ Macro ➤ Visual Basic Editor

Use this option to create or edit macros using the Visual Basic programming language.

---

**N O T E**   This option isn't for the faint or heart or for those unfamiliar with this language. If you're interesting in learning more about programming with Visual Basic, try *Special Edition: Using VBScript* by Ron Schwarz, (ISBN: 0789708094).

### How You Get Here

✧ Click    ✧ Press **Alt+T,M,V** or **Alt+F11**   ✧ Choose **Tools ➤ Macro ➤ Visual Basic Editor**

### Tools ➤ Macro ➤ Microsoft Script Editor

Use this option to create or edit macros using Microsoft Script Editor programming language.

---

**N O T E**   This option isn't for the faint or heart or for those unfamiliar with this languauge.

### How You Get Here

✧ Click 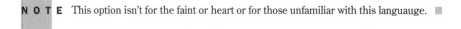   ✧ Press **Alt+T,M,E** or **Alt+Shift+F11**   ✧ Choose **Tools ➤ Macro ➤ Microsoft Script Editor**

# Tools ➤ Add-Ins

Use this option to access or add an application that is not commonly installed with Microsoft Office 2000. These applications provide more specific functions to help you perform your job more efficiently. One example is a specific format for entering dates, so that whether you enter January 1, 2000, or 1/1/00, the text is always displayed as 1 January, 2000.

### How You Get Here

✧ Press **Alt+T,I**   ✧ Choose **Tools ➤ Add-Ins**

# Tools ➤ Customize

Use this option to display the Customize dialog box, where you can customize toolbars, keyboard shortcuts, and menu commands. Customizing allows you to create new tools, shortcuts, and commands, and modify existing ones to better suit your individual needs. (For example, you may want to create a tool to execute a frequently used option that is usually only available using a menu option).

## How You Get Here

✧ Press **Alt+T,C**          ✧ Choose **Tools ➤ Customize**

## What's In This Dialog Box

Figure 7.10 is a sample of this dialog box and Table 7.8 has a description of the options that are common to Word, Excel, and PowerPoint.

**Figure 7.10**   The Customize dialog box

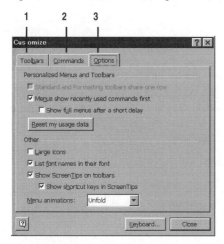

**Table 7.8**   Tabs in the Customize dialog box

| # | Tab name | What you do with it |
|---|----------|---------------------|
| 1 | Toolbars | Click to choose which toolbars you want automatically displayed each time you open the application and create new or customize existing toolbars. (For a complete description of the options available, see Table 7.9 on page 108.) |
| 2 | Commands | Choose or modify categories and commands. (For a complete description of the options available, see Table 7.10 on page 108.) |
| 3 | Options | Personalize menus and toolbars, resize icons, display font name in font style, and customize other options. (For a complete description of the options available, see Table 7.11 on page 108.) |

The following tables describe the options for the individual tabs in this dialog box:

- Table 7.9 describes the Customize Toolbars tab,
- Table 7.10 describes the Commands tab, and
- Table 7.11 describes the Option tab.

**Table 7.9**  Options in the Customize dialog box Toolbars tab

| Option | What you do with it |
| --- | --- |
| Toolbars area | Click to choose the toolbar you want to modify. During modification the toolbar is visible, but it isn't active, so you can make changes to it. Right-click on an icon to display a menu that you can use to modify the highlighted icon. |
| New button | Click to display the New Toolbar dialog box, which has options for creating a new toolbar. |
| Rename button | Click to display the Rename Toolbar dialog box, which lets you rename your custom toolbars. You can't rename the toolbars that come with Outlook. |
| Delete button | Click to delete a toolbar you've created. You can't delete the toolbars that come with Outlook. |
| Reset button | Click to display the Reset Toolbar dialog box, which allows you to restore the original settings and buttons. |
| Keyboard button | Click to display the Customize Keyboard dialog box, which has controls to create new shortcut keys for system functions such as **File ➤ Close**. |

**Table 7.10**  Options in the Customize dialog box Commands tab

| Option | What you do with it |
| --- | --- |
| Categories area | Click to choose the menu or toolbar you want to change. |
| Commands area | Click to choose the commands you want to change. |
| Description button | Click to display a brief description of the highlighted command. |
| Modify Selection drop-down list | Click to display a drop-down list of controls for the highlighted command. |
| Keyboard button | Click to display the Customize Keyboard dialog box, which has controls to create new shortcut keys for system functions, such as **File ➤ Close**. |

**Table 7.11**  Options in the Customize dialog box Options tab

| Option | What you do with it |
| --- | --- |
| Personalized Menus and Toolbars area | Click to choose the properties you want to set for your menus and toolbars. |
| Other area | Click to choose how you want to display your menus and toolbars. |
| Menu animations drop-down list | Choose an item that determines the way your menus are animated. |
| Keyboard button | Click to display the Customize Keyboard dialog box, has controls to create new shortcut keys for system functions such as **File ➤ Close**. |

CHAPTER

8

# The Help Menu, Common Options

| ? Microsoft PowerPoint Help    F1 | Help ➤ Microsoft Help | 110 |
| Show the Office Assistant | Help ➤ Show/Hide Office Assistant | 112 |
| ? What's This?    Shift+F1 | Help ➤ What's This? | 114 |
| Office on the Web | Help ➤ Office on the Web | 114 |
| Detect and Repair... | Help ➤ Detect and Repair | 114 |
| About Microsoft PowerPoint | Help ➤ About Microsoft | 115 |

Microsoft Word Help   F1
Show the Office Assistant
What's This?   Shift+F1
Office on the Web
WordPerfect Help...
Detect and Repair...
About Microsoft Word

——————— Help ➤ WordPerfect Help    116

Microsoft Excel Help   F1
Show the Office Assistant
What's This?   Shift+F1
Office on the Web
Lotus 1-2-3 Help...
Detect and Repair...
About Microsoft Excel

——————— Help ➤ Lotus 1-2-3 Help    117

## What Is The Help Menu

This menu lists the commands you'll use to look up information about the active application and automatically log onto the Internet (if you have a dial-up connection) to review up-to-date information.

If a menu option has an ellipsis (three dots) or an arrow beside it, the application "asks" you for additional information before the action takes place. If the menu doesn't have one of these symbols, the action you choose happens immediately. If the action takes place immediately, you won't see a sample screen in this section.

> **N O T E** Don't panic if the application asks you for the original CD when you choose any of the options on the Help menu. It just means that the Help option wasn't installed when you installed Microsoft Office 2000. All you have to do is insert the original CD and follow the onscreen prompts. Oh, by the way, you'll also need a little patience since it can take a little while to load the Help files. ▩

> **T I P** In Help, a topic can be a broad category (e.g. "Help") or a specific topic within that category (e.g., "Printing a Help Topic"). If you don't want to look through tons of information, try to be as specific as possible when entering topics. Once the application locates your topic, the Contents and Index tabs display all related topics.

# Help ➤ Microsoft Help

Use this option to look up information about a specific topic or to review step-by-step instructions for getting a task done. The only difference between the Help menu for Word, Excel, and PowerPoint is that each one displays the *name* of the active application. In PowerPoint, for example, this option displays as **Help ➤ Microsoft PowerPoint Help.**

## How You Get Here

✦ Click    ✦ Press **Alt+H,H** or **F1**   ✦ Choose **Help ➤ Microsoft Help**

## What's In This Dialog Box

Figure 8.1 is a sample of this dialog box and Table 8.1 has a description of the options that are common to Word, Excel, and PowerPoint.

**Figure 8.1**   The Help dialog box

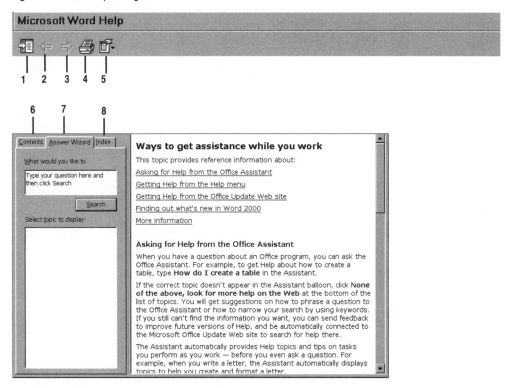

**Table 8.1**   Options in the Help dialog box

| # | Option | What you do with it |
|---|--------|---------------------|
| 1 | Hide/Show Tabs button | Click to hide or show the left pane and maximize the amount of help text you can see on your screen. |
| 2 | Back button | Click to step backward through the topics that you've been reviewing. This option isn't available if you've only looked at one topic. |
| 3 | Forward button | Click to step forward through the topics that you've been reviewing. This option isn't available if you've only looked at one topic or if the current topic only has one page. |
| 4 | Print button | Click to make a hard copy printout of specific help text or an entire topic. **Note** You can't print the left pane. |
| 5 | Options button | Click to choose which options you see on the menu bar. You can also choose from additional options that let you stop a search, go to the first page displayed (home), and reset your Internet options. |

**Table 8.1**    Options in the Help dialog box, continued

| # Option | What you do with it |
|---|---|
| 6   Contents tab | Click to display an electronic Table of Contents organized by topic. Each topic typically has other topics that you can look at—not so very different from a standard book, is it? |
| 7   Answer Wizard tab | Click to display the Answer Wizard so that you can search through all the help topics after you enter an everyday language question instead of trying to think up some keyword that gets you close to what you're looking for. After you enter your question, click the **Search** button. |
| 8   Index tab | Click to display an electronic Index organized alphabetically. You enter a keyword and then the application displays a list of all the topics that match, or are close to, the keyword you entered. |

# Help ➤ Show/Hide Office Assistant

Use this option to display or hide a cute, animated assistant. This assistant can automatically offer tips and advice based on what you're currently doing. To change the character used for the assistant, click the **Options** button and choose the Gallery tab. Click the **Options** tab to set up how the assistant works.

 **TIP**    You can also display the shortcut menu by right-clicking on the animated assistant.

## How You Get Here

✧ Click     ✧ Press **Alt+H,O**    ✧ Choose **Help ➤ Show/Hide the Office Assistant**

## What's In This Dialog Box

Figure 8.2 is a sample of this dialog box and Table 8.2 has a description of the options that are common to Word, Excel, and PowerPoint.

**Figure 8.2**   The Office Assistant dialog box

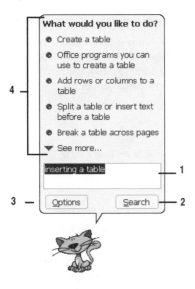

**Table 8.2**   Options in the Office Assistant dialog box

| # | Option | What you do with it |
|---|--------|---------------------|
| 1 | Search text box | Enter the search parameters. |
| 2 | Search button | Click to begin a search after entering the search parameters. |
| 3 | Options button | Click to display the Office Assistant dialog box. This is where you choose the graphic for your assistant and set the options for using the Office Assistant. |
| 4 | What would you like to do area | Choose an item that determines the closest answer to the search result you wanted. |

# Help ➤ What's This?

Use this option to look at information about a specific field or function in a dialog box. When you choose this option the cursor changes and you can click on any option to display a brief description or explanation of what it does.

---

**N O T E**  Don't panic if nothing displays when you position the pointer over an option—some options don't have a description. After reviewing information about a specific option, the pointer may revert back to a standard pointer. If you want to make another "What's This?" selection, make sure you have the question mark/arrow pointer. ■

## How You Get Here

✧ Click     ✧ Press **Alt+H, T** or **Shift+F1** ✧ Choose **Help ➤ What's This?**

# Help ➤ Office on the Web

Use this option to get the latest and greatest information about Office 2000 from Microsoft's website. One caveat—you need to have an Internet account if you want to look at all this great information. When you choose this option the Microsoft Internet Explorer window displays and you'll be connected to the Internet. This site has all sorts of information that you can use in your daily work: the latest fixes for problems, tips and tricks for making your application work the way you want it to, and news about upcoming software releases. You can also sign on to a newsgroup and "talk" to other people that use Office 2000.

## How You Get Here

✧ Press **Alt+H, W**      ✧ Choose **Help ➤ Office on the Web**

# Help ➤ Detect and Repair

Use this option to automatically find and fix any errors in the active application. Any missing files or registry problems will be found and fixed if necessary. This option doesn't change any of your personal documents, worksheets, or presentation. When finished you will be asked whether you want to restart your computer now or wait until later. Either way any changes made to your system's configuration won't happen until you actually restart your computer.

---

**TIP**  Make sure you have saved and closed all open files and applications. Be sure you have your original CD handy since you may be asked to insert it before you can run the program. Try not to run this program when you're under a deadline—it could take a while to run.

## How You Get Here

✧ Press **Alt+H, R**      ✧ Choose **Help ➤ Detect and Repair**

## What's In This Dialog Box

Figure 8.3 is a sample of this dialog box and Table 8.3 has a description of the options that are common to Word, Excel, and PowerPoint.

**Figure 8.3**  The Detect and Repair dialog box

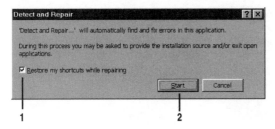

**Table 8.3**  Options in the Detect and Repair dialog box

| # | Option | What you do with it |
|---|--------|---------------------|
| 1 | Restore my shortcuts while repairing radio button | Click to restore the application shortcuts to the **Start** menu. These are the ones that display when you choose the Programs option on the **Start** menu. |
| 2 | Start button | Click to run the program.<br>**Note**  Make sure you have saved and closed all other files and applications. |

# Help ➤ About Microsoft

Use this option to information about the active application such as the version number; copyright, legal, and licensing notices; the user and organization name; the software serial number; and information about your computer and operating system.

## How You Get Here

✧ Press **Alt+H,A**

✧ Choose **Help ➤ About Microsoft**

## What's In This Dialog Box

Figure 8.4 is a sample of this dialog box and Table 8.4 has a description of the options that are common to Word, Excel, and PowerPoint.

**Figure 8.4**    The  About dialog box

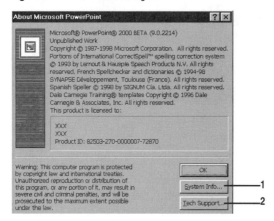

**Table 8.4**    Options in the About dialog box

| # | Option | What you do with it |
| --- | --- | --- |
| 1 | System Info button | Click to view detailed information about your system configuration, installed fonts, graphics filters and other potentially boring information that could help you when things aren't working like you had hoped. |
| 2 | Tech Support button | Click to look up information about how to get technical support when you're in a jam. This dialog box looks like the standard Help dialog box but provides phone numbers and locations where you can talk to someone about your problem. |

# Help ➤ WordPerfect Help

Use this option to find the Word equivalent for an option that you were used to working with in WordPerfect. You can also look at an onscreen demonstration of a specific option.

## How You Get Here

✧ Press **Alt+H,P**          ✧ Choose **Help ➤ WordPerfect Help**

# Help ➤ Lotus 1-2-3 Help

Use this option to find the Excel equivalent for an option that you were used to working with in Lotus 123. You can also look at an onscreen demonstration of a specific option.

## How You Get Here

✧ Press **Alt+H,L**

✧ Choose **Help** ➤ **Lotus 1-2-3 Help**

# A Look At Word

**In this part**

# The Word File Menu

## In this chapter

# What Is The File Menu

This menu lists the commands that you'll use to perform actions that affect the entire file, such as saving the document so that you don't lose your work, printing the document, opening additional documents, or reviewing various information about the active file.

If a menu option has an ellipsis (three dots) or an arrow beside it, the application "asks" you for additional information before the action takes place. If the menu doesn't have one of these symbols, the action you choose happens immediately. If the action takes place immediately, you won't see a sample screen in this section.

# File ➤ New

Use this option to create a new document based on an existing document (called a "template") or to create a new template that you can use to make life easier in the future. There are two basic types of templates, *global* and *document*. The global templates contains elements that are available to all types of files. The document templates contain elements that are only available to that type of file, for instance, a fax template will only be available to files for that purpose. You can choose from a wide variety of existing templates that make creating a document much faster and easier because many of the common formatting decisions have already been made. Or, if you prefer, you can create new templates and store them in the tabs displayed. If you need some help working with a template, or if you're new to creating documents in Word, you can use a Wizard, which walks you through the process of creating a new document one step at a time. (For more information, see File ➤ New on page 38.)

## How You Get Here

✧ Click     ✧ Press **Alt+F,N** or **Ctrl+N**    ✧ Choose **File** ➤ **New**

---

**N O T E**   If you click 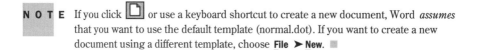 or use a keyboard shortcut to create a new document, Word *assumes* that you want to use the default template (normal.dot). If you want to create a new document using a different template, choose **File** ➤ **New**. ▪

---

**TIP**   If you want to take a quick look at what a template looks like *before* you use the template, click the desired template name then look in the Preview area.

## What's Different

Figure 9.1 is a sample of this dialog box and Table 9.1 has a description of the options that are unique to Word.

**Figure 9.1** The New dialog box

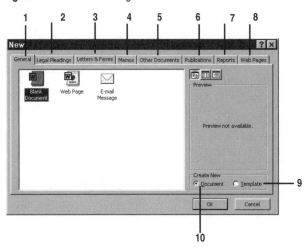

**Table 9.1** Options in the New dialog box

| # | Option | What you do with it |
|---|--------|---------------------|
| 1 | General tab | Double-click the Blank Document icon to create a generic document with the standard settings stored in this template. You can also double-click the Web Page icon to create new web page or double-click the email message icon to create an email message. (For more information, see File ➤ Save as Web Page on page 43 or File ➤ Send To on page 46.) |
| 2 | Legal Pleadings tab | Double-click the Pleading Wizard for step-by-step instructions on how to create a new Legal Pleadings document. |
| 3 | Letters & Faxes tab | Double-click one of the Wizards for step-by-step instructions on how to create a new letter, fax, envelope or mailing label. You can also double-click one of the templates displayed to skip the Wizard and work with a template directly. |
| 4 | Memos tab | Double-click the Memo Wizard for step-by-step instructions on how to create a new memo. You can also double-click one of the templates displayed to skip the Wizard and work with a template directly. |
| 5 | Other Documents tab | Double-click one of the Wizards for step-by-step instructions on how to create a new resume or agenda. You can also double-click one of the templates displayed to skip the wizard and work with a template directly. |
| 6 | Publications tab | Double-click one of the templates displayed to create a professional looking brochure, directory, manual, or thesis. |
| 7 | Reports tab | Double-click one of the templates displayed to create a professional looking report. |

**Table 9.1**    Options in the New dialog box, continued

| #  | Option | What you do with it |
|----|--------|---------------------|
| 8  | Web Pages tab | Double-click the Web Page Wizard for step-by-step instructions on how to create a web page. You can also double-click one of the templates displayed to skip the wizard and work with a template directly. |
| 9  | Template radio button | Click to create your new file as a template that is stored in the corresponding templates folder. |
| 10 | Document radio button | Click to create your new file as a standard Word document. |

# File ➤ Open

Use this option to open an existing file so that you can take a look at what you've done or add more stuff to your masterpiece. (For more information, see File ➤ Open on page 39.)

---

**N O T E**    If you used the **File ➤ Versions** option when you saved your file, you can also open an earlier version of the file with this option. ▪

## How You Get Here

✧ Click 🗁      ✧ Press **Alt+F,O** or **Ctrl+O**      ✧ Choose **File** ➤ **Open**

# File ➤ Close

Use this option to close the active file and save it in the original file folder (you know, that one you used when you *first* saved the file). If the file has not been saved you'll be asked if you want to save any changes you have made. If you click the **Yes** button so that your most recent changes are saved, the application overwrites the old version of the file. (For more information, see File ➤ Close on page 41.)

## How You Get Here

✧ Click ⊠ or Double-click 🗐      ✧ Press **Alt+F,C** or **Ctrl+W**      ✧ Choose **File** ➤ **Close**

# File ➤ Save

Use this option to save any changes you've made to a file. (For more information, see File ➤ Save on page 42.)

 **TIP** Be sure to save your files frequently (you don't want to lose any of the hard work you've done). A good rule of thumb is to save frequently enough that you can easily recover if the system crashes. For example, if you just wrote a great paragraph or created an awesome formula, save your file immediately after finishing the it. My rule is that I don't go any longer than five minutes without saving, which means I can't lose more than five minutes work! Most of the applications also have an automatic save function that can be set to automatically save your files after a specified amount of time.

### How You Get Here

✧ Click   ✧ Press **Alt+F,S** or **Ctrl+S**  ✧ Choose **File** ➤ **Save**

# File ➤ Save As

Use this option to save the file for the first time or to save an existing file with a different name or file type. (For more information, see File ➤ Save As on page 42.)

 **TIP** Be sure you look at where you're storing the file before you click **Save**—don't let "fast fingers" get the better of you. The most frequent reason people can't find a file is because they didn't pay attention to the file folder that was open when they last saved a file.

### How You Get Here

✧ Press **Alt+F,A**  ✧ Choose **File** ➤ **Save As**

# File ➤ Save As Web Page

Use this option to save Word documents as a Web page, ready to be put up on an intranet, the Internet, or be included in a home page. The files are saved in an appropriate file format that can be read by Web browsers.

### How You Get Here

✧ Press **Alt+F,G**  ✧ Choose **File** ➤ **Save as Web Page**

## What's Different

Figure 9.2 is a sample of this dialog box and has a description of the one option that is unique to Word. (For more information, see File ➤ Save as Web Page on page 43.)

**Figure 9.2**    The Save As dialog box

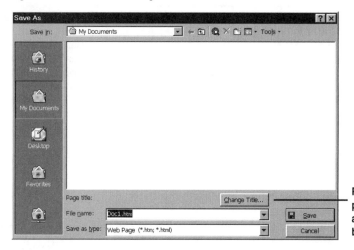

Rename the file for online purposes. The title you type will appear on the web page's title bar.

# File ➤ Versions

Use this option to save different versions of the same document using the same file name. This option creates snapshots of the changes made to a document, which saves disk space because Word only saves the *differences*, not the entire file. Once you've used this option, you can open, review, print, and delete earlier versions.

You can save as many versions of the file at any time you want, have Word automatically save a new version each time you close the document, and save different versions as separate documents so that reviewers can only work with the most current version of the document.

 **TIP**    If you plan to use the Compare Documents option, you must save the versions as separate documents, *then* do the compare.

## How You Get Here

✧ Press **Alt+F,E**          ✧ Choose **File ➤ Versions**

## What's In This Dialog Box

Figure 9.3 is a sample of this dialog box and Table 9.2 has a description of the options available.

**Figure 9.3** The Versions in Document dialog box

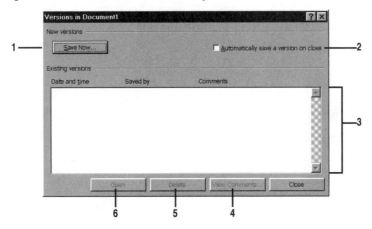

**Table 9.2** Options in the Versions in Document dialog box

| # | Option | What you do with it |
|---|--------|---------------------|
| 1 | Save Now button | Click to save a snapshot of the active document at the current moment in time. |
| 2 | Automatically save a version on close check box | Click to have Word automatically create a new version every time you close the active document. |
| 3 | Existing versions list | Review a list of the currently saved versions of the document. Word notes the date and time the version was created and the name of the author who saved the version. |
| 4 | View Comments button | Click to review the comments written by the author who saved the highlighted version of the document. |
| 5 | Delete button | Click to remove the highlighted version from the file. |
| 6 | Open button | Click to open the highlighted version of the document. |

# File ➤ Web Page Preview

Use this option to see how a file looks as a web page. The application opens your Web browser and displays the active file.

## How You Get Here

✧ Press **Alt+F,B**

✧ Choose **File ➤ Web Page Preview**

# File ➤ Page Setup

Use this option to control how your final document looks, including the overall page size, the amount of white space on the page (margins), the space allowed for text at the top of the page (header) and at the bottom of the page (footer), the paper tray used when you print your document, and whether you use different headers and footers for different types of pages.

## How You Get Here

✧ Press **Alt+F,U**          ✧ Choose **File ➤ Page Setup**

## What's In This Dialog Box

Figure 9.4 is a sample of this dialog box and Table 9.3 has a description of the tabs available.

---

**N O T E**   Each tab has a **Default** button that you can click to set the defaults to the options currently chosen for that tab. ■

**Figure 9.4**   The Page Setup dialog box

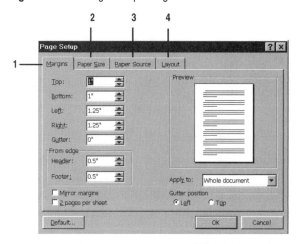

**Table 9.3**   Tabs in the Page Setup dialog box

| # | Tab name | What you do with it |
|---|----------|---------------------|
| 1 | Margins | Click to set the amount of white space on the perimeter of your document. (For a complete description of the options available, see Table 9.4 on page 129.) |
| 2 | Paper Size | Click to set what size paper you're using and which way the paper is oriented (portrait is up-and-down and landscape is left-to-right). (For a complete description of the options available, see Table 9.5 on page 130.) |

**Table 9.3**   Tabs in the Page Setup dialog box, continued

| # Tab name | What you do with it |
|---|---|
| 3   Paper Source | Click to set which printer paper you're using to pull paper from. (For a complete description of the options available, see Table 9.6 on page 130.) |
| 4   Layout | Click to set where new sections should start, the type of headers and footers, line numbering, and page borders. (For a complete description of the options available, see Table 9.7 on page 130.) |

The following tables describe the options for the individual tabs in this dialog box:

- Table 9.4 describes the Margins tab,
- Table 9.5 describes the Paper Size tab,
- Table 9.6 describes the Paper Source tab, and
- Table 9.7 describes the Layout tab.

**Table 9.4**   Options in the Page Setup dialog box Margins tab

| Option | What you do with it |
|---|---|
| Top text box | Enter the amount of white space you want at the top of the page. |
| Bottom text box | Enter the amount of white space you want at the bottom of the page. |
| Left text box | Enter the amount of white space you want on the left side of the page. |
| Right text box | Enter the amount of white space you want on the right side of the page. |
| Gutter text box | Enter the amount of extra space you want on the inside edges of the paper so that you can properly bind two-sided documents. |
| From edge: Header text box | Enter the amount of white space from the top page edge to where the header is inserted. |
| From edge: Footer text box | Enter the amount of white space from the bottom page edge to where the footer is inserted. |
| Mirror margins check box | Click to set margins that are the mirror image of each other if you've used two different values for left and right margins. |
| 2 Pages per sheet check box | Click to print two pages on one sheet so that the page can be folded. |
| Apply to drop-down list | Choose an item that determines which parts of the document the settings apply to. |
| Gutter position: Left radio button | Click to put extra space (a "gutter") on the left side of the page so that text doesn't get obliterated when you bind the document on the left side. |
| Gutter position: Top radio button | Click to put extra space (a "gutter") at the top of the page so that text doesn't get obliterated when you bind the document on the top edge. |

**Table 9.5**   Options in the Page Setup dialog box Paper Size tab

| Option | What you do with it |
| --- | --- |
| Paper size drop-down list | Choose an item that determines the standard paper size for your document. |
| Width text box | Enter a custom paper width. |
| Height text box | Enter a custom paper height. |
| Portrait radio button | Click to orient the text of your document vertically (up-and-down). |
| Landscape radio button | Click to orient the text of your document horizontally (left-to-right). |
| Apply to drop-down list | Choose an item that determines what parts of the document the settings apply to. |

**Table 9.6**   Options in the Page Setup dialog box Paper Source tab

| Option | What you do with it |
| --- | --- |
| First page drop-down list | Choose an item that determines where the printer gets the paper for the first page of your document. |
| Other pages drop-down list | Choose an item that determines where the printer gets the paper for all pages of your document *except* the first page. |
| Apply to drop-down list | Choose an item that determines what parts of the document the settings apply to. |

**Table 9.7**   Options in the Page Setup dialog box Layout tab

| Option | What you do with it |
| --- | --- |
| Section start drop-down list | Choose an item that determines where a new section begins (e.g., at the bottom of the page, on a new page, on an even page, on an odd page). |
| Headers and footers: different odd and even check box | Click to use different text in the headers and footers of even-numbered pages and odd-numbered pages. |
| Headers and footers: different first page check box | Click to use different text in the headers and footers for the first page of a section. |
| Vertical alignment drop-down list | Choose an item that determines how the text is positioned on the page. |
| Suppress endnotes check box | Click to keep endnotes (footnotes that are grouped at the end of a document) from printing. |
| Line Numbers button | Click to turn off line numbering for the highlighted text in the **Apply to** drop-down list. |
| Borders button | Click to choose to set a border around the page. |
| Apply to drop-down list | Choose an item that determines what parts of the document the settings apply to. |

# File ➤ Print Preview

Use this option to see how your document will look *before* you print the document on paper. With this option, you can display full pages or thumbnails (multiple pages of your document in a reduced view) so that you can quickly scan your document for layout errors. You can also make changes to your document and send your document to the printer while in Print Preview mode.

## How You Get Here

✧ Click 🔳    ✧ Press **Alt+F,V**    ✧ Choose **File ➤ Print Preview**

## What's In This Window

Figure 9.5 is a sample of this window and Table 9.8 has a description of the options available.

**Figure 9.5**    The Print Preview window

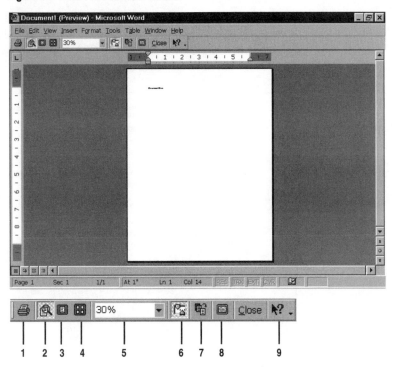

**Table 9.8**    Options in the Print Preview window

| # | Option | What you do with it |
|---|--------|---------------------|
| 1 | Printer button | Click to print the active document. |
| 2 | Preview button | Click to change the cursor into a magnifying glass so that you zoom in on a specific part of your document. |

**Table 9.8**    Options in the Print Preview window, continued

| # | Option | What you do with it |
|---|--------|---------------------|
| 3 | One page button | Click to display a single page. |
| 4 | Multiple pages button | Click to displays multiple pages using a thumbnail view. |
| 5 | Zoom drop-down list | Choose an item that determines how much of the document you can see on your screen at one time. |
| 6 | View ruler button | Click to turn the display of the ruler on and off. |
| 7 | Shrink to fit button | Click to reduce the image so that you can see an entire page of your document. |
| 8 | Full screen button | Click to open a window where only the document page is visible. |
| 9 | Help button | Click to display Word's online help function. |

# File ➤ Print

Use this option to create a paper copy of the active file. You can send the file to the default printer or you can choose a new printer, as long as it has already been set up for you. If you only want to print a few pages in a file you can choose from the Page range area the pages to print.

---

**N O T E**    You can also create an electronic "print" file that you can send to a commercial printer or use to generate a portable document format (PDF) file. ▪

## How You Get Here

✧ Click           ✧ Press **Alt+F,P** or **Ctrl+P**          ✧ Choose **File** ➤ **Print**

## What's Different

Figure 9.6 is a sample of this dialog box and Table 9.9 has a description of the options that are unique to Word. (For more information, see File ➤ Print on page 44.)

**Figure 9.6**   The Print dialog box

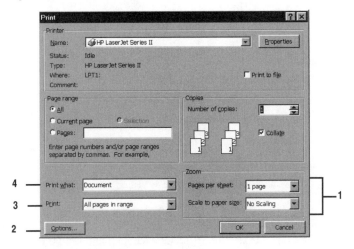

**Table 9.9**   Options in the Print dialog box

| # | Option | What you do with it |
|---|--------|---------------------|
| 1 | Zoom area | Choose an item that determines how many pages you want to print on a sheet of paper and what size paper you are printing on. |
| 2 | Options button | Click to change Word's print settings. |
| 3 | Print drop-down list | Choose an item that determines the range of pages you want to print. For instance, if you want to print all the even numbered pages you can choose them using this drop-down list. |
| 4 | Print what drop-down list | Choose an item that determines exactly what parts of the file you're going to print. For example, you can print the "real" document or you can print just the comments in the file. |

# File ➤ Send To

Use this option to send your document, spreadsheet or slide to someone using your email or Internet connection. Generally, any of the options in this flyout menu will use your default email connections or the Outlook application to send an email message. You fill in the information for the recipient like you would for any other email message and then you're ready to send it. This option and the flyout menu options are completely described in the Common File Menu chapter.

(For more information, see File ➤ Send To on page 46 or What Is The Outlook Mail Application on page 648.)

## How You Get Here

✧ Press **Alt+F,D**            ✧ Choose **File** ➤ **Send To**

## What's Different

Figure 9.7 is a sample of this flyout menu.

**Figure 9.7**    The File ➤ Send To flyout menu

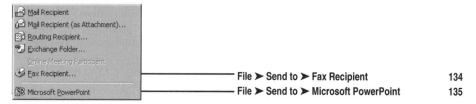

File ➤ Send to ➤ Fax Recipient            134
File ➤ Send to ➤ Microsoft PowerPoint            135

## File ➤ Send to ➤ Fax Recipient

Use this option to open the Fax Wizard (see Figure 9.8 for a sample) and send the active document to a fax machine. Since the Fax Wizard walks you through the process one step at a time, we didn't include step-by-step instructions in this document.

---

**N O T E**    You must have access to fax software to use this option. Microsoft Office ships with Microsoft Fax or you may use another fax software, such as Winfax Pro, to fax your documents directly from Word.

## How You Get Here

✧ Press **Alt+F,D,F**            ✧ Choose **File** ➤ **Send To** ➤ **Fax Recipient**

### What's In This Dialog Box

Figure 9.8 is a sample of this dialog box and has a description of the options available.

**Figure 9.8**   The Fax Wizard dialog box

Choose the
action you want
and click it to
start the wizard.

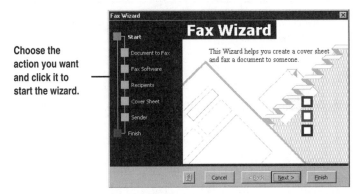

## File ➤ Send to ➤ Microsoft PowerPoint

Use this option to copy the active document from Word to PowerPoint so that you can create a
new presentation. PowerPoint uses the structure of the document as a rough basis for the created
presentation. You can then edit the presentation to fit your needs.

### How You Get Here

✧ Press **Alt+F,D,P**      ✧ Choose **File ➤ Send To ➤ Microsoft PowerPoint**

# File ➤ Properties

Use this option to review technical information and record technical information about the active
file. (For more information, see File ➤ Properties on page 49.)

### How You Get Here

✧ Press **Alt+F,I**      ✧ Choose **File ➤ Properties**

# File ➤ (List of Recently Opened Files)

Use this option to open recently used files, without having to dig through a long list of file folders
and drive names to find the file you need.

### How You Get Here

✧ Press **Alt+F,** choose the **number of file in list**   ✧ Choose **File ➤ number of file**

# File ➤ Exit

Use this option to close all open files *and* the application that you're using.

---

**N O T E**   If you have made changes in any file you'll be asked if you want to save the changes when you exit the application. ▪

## How You Get Here

✧ Click ☒ or Double-click 🗎          ✧ Press **Alt+F,X**      ✧ Choose **File** ➤ **Exit**

# The Word Edit Menu

## In this chapter

## What Is The Edit Menu

This menu lists the commands that you'll use to copy information from one place to another, delete information from your file, locate specific words or phrases, change information one instance at a time or throughout the entire file, add links to other documents or locations, and change the look of objects.

If a menu option has an ellipsis (three dots) or an arrow beside it, the application "asks" you for additional information before the action takes place. If the menu doesn't have one of these symbols, the action you choose happens immediately. If the action takes place immediately, you won't see a sample screen in this section.

 Many of the commands on the Edit menu are also available on the shortcut menu. If you like to use your mouse, you can right-click, then choose one of the options displayed. Remember, these menus change based on your cursor location and what is highlighted.

## Edit ➤ Undo

Use this option to change your mind and remove one or more changes made to the active file. You can also undo several actions at once *if* you click the drop-down list to the right of the **Undo** button. Although most actions can be "undone", there are some that can't. If you can't undo an action, the Edit menu displays "Can't undo" instead of "Undo".

**N O T E**   A word of caution: the application won't just let you undo an action in the middle of the Undo list. It "assumes" that you want to undo all actions preceding the one you've chosen. For example, let's say that you've deleted five different paragraphs, then decide that you really didn't want to delete the third paragraph. The application kindly keeps a list of those five actions. You quickly click the drop-down list to the right of the **Undo** button and choose the third action. The application, however, "assumes" that you also want to undo actions one and two. ▪

 If you decide you didn't *really* mean to undo an action, choose **Edit ➤ Redo**.

### How You Get Here

✧ Click ↻   ✧ Press **Alt+E,U** or **Ctrl+Z**   ✧ Choose **Edit ➤ Undo**

# Edit ➤ Repeat/Redo

Use this option to either duplicate one or more actions or to change your mind about the last time you chose **Edit ➤ Undo.** You can also repeat/redo several actions at once *if* you click the drop-down list to the right of the Repeat/Redo button. Although most actions can be "repeated" or "redone", there are some that can't. If you can't repeat or redo an action, the Edit menu displays "Can't repeat" or "Can't redo". The name of this menu option changes based on your most recent action.

---

**N O T E**   A word of caution: the application won't just let you choose one action in the middle of the Redo list. It "assumes" that you want to redo all actions preceding the one you've chosen. For example, let's say that you've reinserted three paragraphs using the **Edit ➤ Undo** option. The application kindly keeps a list of those three actions. You quickly click the drop-down list to the right of the Repeat/Redo button and choose the second action. The application, however, "assumes" that you also want to redo action one. ▪

### How You Get Here

✦ Click [▭]      ✦ Press **Alt+E,R** or **Ctrl+Y**     ✦ Choose **Edit ➤ Redo** or **Edit ➤ Repeat**

# Edit ➤ Cut

Use this option to completely remove highlighted text or objects from the active file. Items that you cut are stored in an area called the "Clipboard" and can be inserted anywhere, in any open file, regardless of the application.

---

**N O T E**   The Clipboard is cleared once you close the application. ▪

### How You Get Here

✦ Click [▭]      ✦ Press **Alt+E,T** or **Ctrl+X**     ✦ Choose **Edit ➤ Cut**

# Edit ➤ Copy

Use this option to leave the highlighted text or objects in their current position **and** store a copy in a temporary storage area called the "Clipboard". Items that you copy can be inserted anywhere, in any open file, regardless of the application.

### How You Get Here

✦ Click [▭]      ✦ Press **Alt+E,C** or **Ctrl+C**     ✦ Choose **Edit ➤ Copy**

# Edit ➤ Paste

Use this option to insert text or objects that are stored in the Clipboard at the current cursor position. Items that you've cut or copied can be inserted anywhere, in any open file, regardless of the application.

## How You Get Here

✦ Click 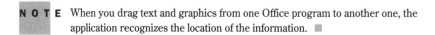     ✦ Press **Alt+P**, or **Ctrl+V**     ✦ Choose **Edit ➤ Paste**

# Edit ➤ Paste Special

Use this option to choose the format of the text or object that you're inserting at the cursor position. This is the option you want to use if you want to link the current file to an external file or if you're copying information between applications and need to control how the information is inserted. For example, you've created a beautiful proposal and want to insert a chart or graph from Excel or a slide from PowerPoint. You also know that this information will change several times before you issue the report. If you choose Paste ➤ Special, you can make your changes to the source file and those changes are reflected in your report. (For more information, see Edit ➤ Paste Special on page 56.)

## How You Get Here

✦ Press **Alt+E,S**          ✦ Choose **Edit ➤ Paste Special**

# Edit ➤ Paste as Hyperlink

Use this option to create a hyperlink for pictures, text, worksheet cells, or a highlighted database object. A hyperlink is an area that is "hot", that is you can click the area so that you automatically jump to a different spot in the current file or in another file.

---

**N O T E**   When you drag text and graphics from one Office program to another one, the application recognizes the location of the information. ▪

## How You Get Here

✦ Press **Alt+E,H**          ✦ Choose **Edit ➤ Paste as Hyperlink**

# Edit ➤ Clear

Use this option to permanently delete text or objects from the active file, *without* storing the information in the temporary storage area known as the "Clipboard".

### How You Get Here

✧ Press **Alt+E,A** or **Delete**    ✧ Choose **Edit** ➤ **Clear**

# Edit ➤ Select All

Use this option to highlight everything in the active file.

### How You Get Here

✧ Press **Alt+E,L** or **Ctrl+A**    ✧ Choose **Edit** ➤ **Select All**

# Edit ➤ Find

Use this option to find text or formats in the active document.

### How You Get Here

✧ Click 🔍    ✧ Press **Alt+E,F** or **Ctrl+F**    ✧ Choose **Edit** ➤ **Find**

### What's In This Dialog Box

Figure 10.1 is a sample of this dialog box and Table 10.1 has a description of the tabs available.

**Figure 10.1**   The Find and Replace dialog box

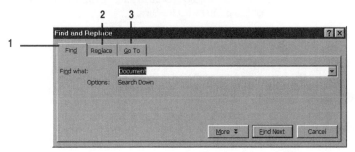

**Table 10.1**   Tabs in the Find and Replace dialog box

| # | Tab name | What you do with it |
|---|----------|---------------------|
| 1 | Find | Click to display the Find dialog box so that you can enter the text or formats you want to locate. (For a complete description of the options available, see Table 10.2 on page 142.) |
| 2 | Replace | Click to display the Replace dialog box so that you can enter the text or formats you want to replace. (For more information, see Edit ➤ Replace on page 143.) |
| 3 | Go To | Click to display the Go To dialog box so that you can move to a specific location in the document. (For more information, see Edit ➤ Go To on page 144.) |

The following tables describe the options for the individual tabs in this dialog box:

- Table 10.2 describes the Find tab,
- Table 10.3 describes the Replace tab, and
- Table 10.4 describes the Go To tab.

**Table 10.2**   Options in the Find and Replace dialog box Find tab

| Option | What you do with it |
|--------|---------------------|
| Find what text box | Enter the text you want to look for. |
| More button | Click to display the lower half of the dialog box so that you can choose from additional options. |
| Less button | Click to close the lower half of the dialog box. |
| Find next button | Click to begin the search or go to the next occurrence of the information entered in the Find what text box. |
| Search drop-down list | Choose an item that determines how much, or in what direction, Word looks for the information in the Find what text box. |
| Match case check box | Click to locate *only* text that matches the same pattern of upper-case and lower-case letters entered in the Find what text box. |
| Find whole words only check box | Click to *only* find the text in the Find what text box if it is a entire word, not part of another word. |
| Use wildcards check box | Click to use special characters, such as an asterisk (*) or question mark (?) to find special patterns of text, even if you don't know the entire text string. |
| Sounds like check box | Click to search using a phonetic spelling of your target text. |
| Find all word forms check box | Click to replace all forms of the text in the Find what text box with the appropriate form of the text entered in the Replace with text box. Make sure you use the same part of speech (e.g., nouns or verbs). |
| Format button | Choose an item that determines the specific format (or formats) used when you do your search. You can, for example, search for all bolded words or a specific Paragraph Style. You can search just for formats or do a search for both text and formats. |

**Table 10.2**   Options in the Find and Replace dialog box Find tab, continued

| Option | What you do with it |
| --- | --- |
| Special button | Choose an item that determines which special characters you want to search for. For example, you can look for paragraph markers or text markers. |
| No formatting button | Click to clear all the formatting from the Find what option. |

# Edit ➤ Replace

Use this option to change one or more occurrences of the text entered in the Find dialog box to the text entered in the Replace dialog box.

 **TIP**   This is a *really* efficient way to change information quickly and efficiently. For example, you've got the great proposal all done when, OOPS, the boss says he forgot to tell you that the customer's company name changed. But...the boss still wants that proposal done in five minutes!

## How You Get Here

✧ Press **Alt+E,E** or **Ctrl+H**   ✧ Choose **Edit ➤ Replace**

## What's In This Dialog Box

Figure 10.2 is a sample of this dialog box and Table 10.3 has a description of the options available.

**N O T E**   Many of the options in the Replace dialog box are the same as the Find dialog box. (For a complete description of the options available, see Table 10.2 on page 142.) ■

**Figure 10.2**   The Find and Replace dialog box

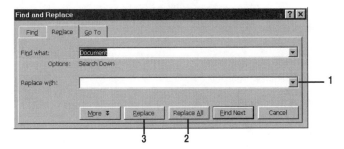

**Table 10.3**    Options in the Find and Replace dialog box

| # | Option | What you do with it |
|---|--------|---------------------|
| 1 | Replace with text box | Enter the text you want to change to. |
| 2 | Replace All button | Click to change **all** instances of the text entered in the Find text box to the text entered in the Replace with text box.<br>**Be careful**—this is also known as *search and destroy*. If you aren't careful, you could end up with a real mess. It's usually better to click the **Replace** button to make sure you've got everything just right. |
| 3 | Replace button | Click to change the currently highlighted text with the text entered in the Replace with text box. |

# Edit ➤ Go To

Use this option to move quickly from one part of your file to another part.

## How You Get Here

❖ Press **Alt+E,G** or **Ctrl+G**    ❖ Choose **Edit** ➤ **Go To**

## What's In This Dialog Box

Figure 10.3 is a sample of this dialog box and Table 10.4 has a description of the options available.

**Figure 10.3**    The Find and Replace dialog box

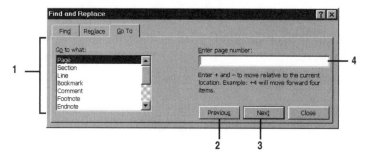

**Table 10.4**    Options in the Find and Replace dialog box

| # | Option | What you do with it |
|---|--------|---------------------|
| 1 | Go to what list | Choose an item that determines which type of element you jump to. |
| 2 | Previous button | Click to move the cursor to the previous element of the type chosen in the Go to what list. |
| 3 | Next button | Click to move the cursor to the next element of the type chosen in the Go to what list. |
| 4 | Enter text box | Enter the appropriate number or text to move to. |

# Edit ➤ Links

Use this option to open, edit, and maintain the connection ("link") between two files. A link is a way to insert graphics and files into another document so that you can update information if the source is changed.

---

 **N O T E**   You can't edit a link until you've inserted one. If you haven't inserted a link, this option is grayed out. ■

## How You Get Here

✧ Press **Alt+E,K**          ✧ Choose **Edit ➤ Links**

## What's Different

Figure 10.4 is a sample of this dialog box and Table 10.5 has a description of options that are unique to Word. (For more information, see Edit ➤ Links on page 58.)

**Figure 10.4**   The Links dialog box

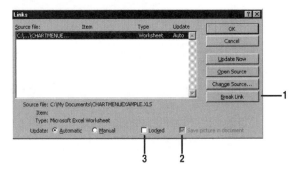

**Table 10.5**   Options in the Links dialog box

| # | Option | What you do with it |
|---|--------|---------------------|
| 1 | Break Link button | Click to eliminate the link between the two files. This option leaves the text or object so that you can continue working with it. |
| 2 | Save picture in document check box | Click to make sure you can edit a graphic in the file where you've inserted a link. Turn off this option if you only want to store a *link* to the graphic instead of a copy of the graphic. (This reduces the size of your file.) |
| 3 | Locked check box | Click to keep the application from automatically updating the linked file. If you turn on this option, **Update Now** isn't available. |

# Edit ➤ Object

Use this option to open and edit source files, change the conditions of the links between objects and the files they are linked to, convert objects to different file types, and open them in the appropriate application. When you choose this option, the application "senses" what type of object you've highlighted and changes the menu name to match. (Remember, not all options listed on this flyout menu are available for all object types.)

---

**N O T E**   Word, Excel, and PowerPoint have the same options on the flyout menu. (For more information, see Edit ➤ Object on page 60.) ■

## How You Get Here

❖ Press **Alt+E,O**          ❖ Choose **Edit ➤ Object**

# The Word View Menu

## In this chapter

# What Is The View Menu

This menu lists the commands that determine what information is displayed for your application. You can choose how the main part of your file is displayed and what toolbars are visible (or, as is sometimes the case, in your way!); take a look at the information that is consistently used at the top and bottom of your file (the header and footer); display an onscreen ruler (so you can make adjustments visually rather than mathematically); change how big or small your display is (great for tired eyes); and just generally customize what you see on the screen. In most cases, the reason for multiple views is so that you can specialize how you see your work. No single view can encompass everyone's needs; if nothing else, the screen would become too cluttered for use.

If a menu option has an ellipsis (three dots) or an arrow beside it, the application "asks" you for additional information before the action takes place. If the menu doesn't have one of these symbols, the action you choose happens immediately. If the action takes place immediately, you won't see a sample screen in this section.

# View ➤ Normal

Use this option to set the overall document view to Normal mode, which is the most basic way of displaying a document—the "plain vanilla" view, if you will. One way to quickly identify Normal view is that it shows the document as if it was one long page, with its pages connected at their top and bottom edges. Normal view makes no pretense of showing you how your document will look when you print it: tables don't necessarily break in the right places, graphics may not display right or at all, and you don't see the information at the top and bottom of the page. The advantage? It's fast. You can get through the document quickly and you can focus on the text instead of the formatting.

## How You Get Here

✧ Click    ✧ Press **Alt+V,N**   ✧ Choose **View** ➤ **Normal**

# View ➤ Web Layout

Use this option to set the overall document view to Web Layout mode so that you can see what your file will look like when you display it in a Web browser. The document seems to be one continuous page, and tables and other elements behave as they might in a browser.

## How You Get Here

✧ Click 🖟   ✧ Press **Alt+V,W**   ✧ Choose **View** ➤ **Web Layout**

# View ➤ Print Layout

Use this option to see what the document will look like when you actually print it to the default printer. You can see the actual "pages", see what tables will look like, and see how the page looks with the header and footer information displayed.

 **N O T E**  This is a great way to save trees, but it takes a little longer to scroll through the pages when you're in this view. You can use the Zoom tool to look at specific areas of the document and then print the document from this view. ■

## How You Get Here

✧ Click     ✧ Press **Alt+V,P**        ✧ Choose <u>View</u> ➤ <u>P</u>rint Layout

# View ➤ Outline

Use this option to set the overall document view to outline mode, which highlights the drop-down list document's structure, rather than its visual appearance. In outline view, the screen shows the document as a hierarchy of headings and body text. A heading's place in the document's hierarchy is determined by the style you assign; for example, the style "heading 1" is at the top level. Outline view is popular for people who like to create a "shell" document with headings, then return later to fill in the explanation or text for a specific topic.

 **N O T E**  When you choose this option, Word automatically opens the Outlining toolbar for you. However, this toolbar isn't listed when you choose **View ➤ Toolbars** unless you've looked at your document in Outline view *at least once* during the current session. Once you close Word, this toolbar disappears again. (For more information, see The Outlining Toolbar on page 150.) ■

 **T I P**  Make sure you apply Word's heading styles (e.g., Heading 1) to the titles and headings in your document. If you don't use these styles, Word assumes that you want to show everything and there is no way to just show the main headings when you choose **View ➤ Outline**.

## How You Get Here

✧ Click     ✧ Press **Alt+V,O**        ✧ Choose <u>View</u> ➤ <u>O</u>utline

# The Outlining Toolbar

Use this option to display the Outlining Toolbar so that you can move the items on your outline around without seeing all that messy formatting stuff.

## What's In This Toolbar

Figure 11.1 is a sample of this toolbar and Table 11.1 has a description of the icons available.

**Figure 11.1**   The Outlining toolbar

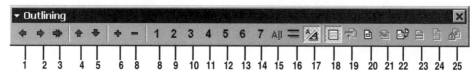

**Table 11.1**   Icons in the Outlining toolbar

| #  | Icon               | What you do with it                                                                                                                                                                                                                                                          |
|----|--------------------|---------------------------------------------------------------------------------------------------------------------------------------------------------------------------------------------------------------------------------------------------------------------------------|
| 1  | Promote            | Click to move the text where the cursor is positioned one level higher in the heading hierarchy. The level in the hierarchy is determined by what level is currently assigned to the text. For example, if you promote a second level heading, that text becomes a first level heading. |
| 2  | Demote             | Click to move the text where the cursor is positioned one level lower in the heading hierarchy. The level in the hierarchy is determined by what level is currently assigned to the text. For example, if you demote a first level heading, that text becomes a second level heading. |
| 3  | Demote to Body Text | Click to change the text where the cursor is positioned from a heading to standard body.                                                                                                                                                                                       |
| 4  | Move Up            | Click to move the text where the cursor is positioned up one level in the text order. For example, if you move the first body text paragraph below a heading up, that text becomes the last item below the previous heading.                                                     |
| 5  | Move Down          | Click to move the text where the cursor is positioned down one level in the text order. For example, if you move a heading down, that text moves to the next position in the text order.                                                                                          |
| 6  | Expand             | Click to show everything in the paragraph where the cursor is positioned.                                                                                                                                                                                                      |
| 7  | Collapse           | Click to show only the highest heading level for the paragraph where the cursor is positioned.                                                                                                                                                                                 |
| 8  | Show Heading 1     | Click to show only paragraphs that have the Heading 1 style applied.                                                                                                                                                                                                           |
| 9  | Show Heading 2     | Click to show only paragraphs that have the Heading 1 and Heading 2 styles applied.                                                                                                                                                                                            |
| 10 | Show Heading 3     | Click to show only paragraphs that have the Heading 1—Heading 3 styles applied.                                                                                                                                                                                                |
| 11 | Show Heading 4     | Click to show only paragraphs that have the Heading 1—Heading 4 styles applied.                                                                                                                                                                                                |

**Table 11.1**   Icons in the Outlining toolbar, continued

| # | Icon | What you do with it |
|---|------|---------------------|
| 12 | Show Heading 5 | Click to show only paragraphs that have the Heading 1—Heading 5 styles applied. |
| 13 | Show Heading 6 | Click to show only paragraphs that have the Heading 1—Heading 6 styles applied. |
| 14 | Show Heading 7 | Click to show only paragraphs that have the Heading 1—Heading 7 styles applied. |
| 15 | Show All Headings | Click to show all heading styles for the document (Heading 1—Heading 9). |
| 16 | Show First Line Only | Click to show the headings and *just* the first line of text below the heading. An ellipsis (three dots) indicates that there are more lines that you can't see. |
| 17 | Show Formatting | Click to show or hide graphics and formatting that are used when you print your presentation or view the presentation on a computer. |
| | | **Note**  The default outline view doesn't show all the fancy formatting which means it also displays information more quickly as you scroll through your presentation. |
| 18 | Master Document View | Click to switch between the Outline view and the Master Document view. |
| | | **Note**  Master Documents are used to organize and maintain long or complex documents, such as books. With this feature, you can store parts (called "subdocuments") of your book in a separate files and then work with multiple files to insert cross-references, create a Table of Contents, or print all the files at one time. |
| 19 | Collapse Subdocuments | Click to hide the text of a subdocument and only display the file name. |
| 20 | Create Subdocument | Click to divide a long document into individual files using a heading style as the "dividing" mark. For example, if your current cursor position is in text with the Heading 2 style, Word breaks the file into a subdocument every time it detects text with a Heading 2 style. |
| 21 | Remove Subdocument | Click to convert the currently highlighted subdocument from a separate file to text that is stored in the master document. |
| 22 | Insert Subdocument | Click to display the Insert Subdocument dialog box so that you can choose which file you want to insert. |
| | | **Note**  The Insert Subdocument dialog box is very similar to the Open dialog box. |
| 23 | Merge Subdocument | Click to combine two or more subdocuments into one document. |
| | | **Note**  You must highlight a minimum of two subdocuments before clicking this icon. |
| 24 | Split Subdocument | Click to divide a subdocument into multiple subdocuments at the current cursor position. |
| 25 | Lock Document | Click to make sure that no one can makes changes to the master document. Click again when you're ready to make changes. |

# View ➤ Toolbars

Use this option to choose the toolbars you want displayed while you work. Toolbars are collections of icons (or buttons) and are especially handy when doing work that involves repeated tasks. However, if you open lots of toolbars they'll clutter the screen and you can waste more time than you realize by constantly moving them around as you work.

---

**N O T E**   You can customize many of the toolbars to fit your needs.  (For more information, see View ➤ Toolbars ➤ Customize on page 76.)   ▣

## How You Get Here

✧ Press **Alt+V,T**               ✧ Choose **View ➤ Toolbars**

## What's In This Flyout Menu

Figure 11.2 is a sample of this flyout menu.

**Figure 11.2**   The View ➤ Toolbars flyout menu

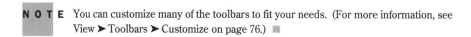

| Menu item | Reference | Page |
|---|---|---|
| ✓ Standard | View ➤ Toolbars ➤ Standard | 153 |
| Formatting | View ➤ Toolbars ➤ Formatting | 154 |
| AutoText | View ➤ Toolbars ➤ AutoText | 154 |
| Clipboard | View ➤ Toolbars ➤ Clipboard | 155 |
| Control Toolbox | View ➤ Toolbars ➤ Control Toolbox | 155 |
| Database | View ➤ Toolbars ➤ Database | 155 |
| Drawing | View ➤ Toolbars ➤ Drawing | 156 |
| Forms | View ➤ Toolbars ➤ Forms | 157 |
| Frames | View ➤ Toolbars ➤ Frames | 158 |
| Picture | View ➤ Toolbars ➤ Picture | 158 |
| Reviewing | View ➤ Toolbars ➤ Reviewing | 158 |
| Tables and Borders | View ➤ Toolbars ➤ Tables and Borders | 159 |
| Visual Basic | View ➤ Toolbars ➤ Visual Basic | 160 |
| Web | View ➤ Toolbars ➤ Web | 160 |
| Web Tools | View ➤ Toolbars ➤ Web Tools | 160 |
| WordArt | View ➤ Toolbars ➤ WordArt | 162 |
| Customize... | View ➤ Toolbars ➤ Customize | 162 |

## View ➤ Toolbars ➤ Standard

Use this option to display the Standard toolbar, which has icons for many of your most frequently used options, such as Save, Print, Open, Cut, Paste, and Spellcheck. Although this toolbar displays when you do a standard Office 2000 installation, you can turn it off if you want to see more of your file and less of the icons.

### How You Get Here

❖ Press **Alt+V,T** choose **Standard**    ❖ Choose **View ➤ Toolbars ➤ Standard**

### What's Different

Figure 11.3 is a sample of this toolbar and Table 11.2 has a description of the icons that are unique to Word. (For more information, see View ➤ Toolbars ➤ Standard on page 65.)

**Figure 11.3**   The Standard toolbar

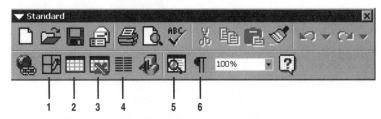

**Table 11.2**   Icons in the Standard toolbar

| # | Icon | What you do with it |
|---|------|---------------------|
| 1 | Tables and Borders | Click to display the Tables and Borders toolbar and switch the view to Print Preview. (For more information, see The Tables and Borders Toolbar on page 252.) |
| 2 | Insert Table | Click to display another pane so that you can define the size of the table you want to insert at the current cursor position. (For more information, see Table ➤ Insert on page 254.) |
| 3 | Insert Microsoft Excel Worksheet | Click to display another pane so that you can define the size of the Excel spreadsheet you want to insert at the cursor position. Once you've inserted the spreadsheet, it looks a little bit like a typical Word table, but it has the standard editing and data entry functions that you find on an Excel spreadsheet. |
| 4 | Columns | Click to display another pane so that you can define the number of text columns you have in the active document. |

**Table 11.2**    Icons in the Standard toolbar, continued

| # | Icon | What you do with it |
| --- | --- | --- |
| 5 | Document Map | Click to display a Document Map pane on the left side of your document. This pane displays the headings of your document, based on the heading styles you've applied. Once this information is displayed, you can quickly review the structure of your document and jump to specific topics in the active document. |
| 6 | Show/Hide Markers | Click to turn on and off the nonprinting markers (e.g., paragraph return markers and tab markers) in your text. |

## View ➤ Toolbars ➤ Formatting

Use this option to display the Formatting toolbar which has icons for the font used for your text, borders that surround an element, and other icons for changing the look of the elements in your file. (For more information, see The Formatting Toolbar on page 192.)

### How You Get Here

✧ Press **Alt+V,T** choose **Formatting**    ✧ Choose **View ➤ Toolbars ➤ Formatting**

## View ➤ Toolbars ➤ AutoText

Use this option to display the AutoText toolbar so that you can insert prestored text at the current cursor position in your document. For instance, in a header you can choose to insert the path and filename of your document or you can create an AutoText entry for that signature you have to type umpteen times a day. (For more information, see The AutoText Toolbar on page 172.)

### How You Get Here

✧ Press **Alt+V,T** choose **AutoText**    ✧ Choose **View ➤ Toolbars ➤ AutoText**

## View ➤ Toolbars ➤ Clipboard

Use this option to display the Clipboard toolbar, which stores up to twelve copied items. This is very helpful when you have copied items from other applications and want to combine them in one document. If you're working in a non-Office application and have an Office application open, all copied items are added to the Clipboard. However, the Clipboard toolbar is only available in an Office application. (For more information, see View ➤ Toolbars ➤ Clipboard on page 67.)

**N O T E**   You can't customize this toolbar. ■

### How You Get Here

❖ Press **Alt+V,T** choose **Clipboard**   ❖ Choose **View** ➤ **Toolbars** ➤ **Clipboard**

## View ➤ Toolbars ➤ Control Toolbox

Use this option to display the Control Toolbox toolbar so that you create a custom form with ActiveX controls such as radio buttons, text boxes, scroll bars, and other neat stuff that can darn near make your file sing and dance (but that kind of stuff is beyond the scope of this book). These controls are similar to the controls created with a programming language, such as Visual Basic. With an ActiveX control, however, you're actually writing a macro that is stored with the control and it is only available when the file with the control is open. (For more information, see View ➤ Toolbars ➤ Control Toolbox on page 68.)

**N O T E**   These are the same types of controls you can add using the Visual Basic Editor. For more information try *Special Edition: Using Visual Basic For Applications 5* by Paul Sanna, (ISBN: 0789709597). ■

### How You Get Here

❖ Press **Alt+V,T** choose **Control Toolbox**   ❖ Choose **View** ➤ **Toolbars** ➤ **Control Toolbox**

## View ➤ Toolbars ➤ Database

Use this option to display the Database toolbar so that you can insert data from another source into your Word document (such as an Access database file). The data can be automatically updated if you have changed the source files by pressing the **F9** key. You can also make changes directly to the records in your document and those changes are made in the original database file.

### How You Get Here

❖ Press **Alt+V,T** choose **Database**   ❖ Choose **View** ➤ **Toolbars** ➤ **Database**

## What's In This Toolbar

Figure 11.4 is a sample of this toolbar and Table 11.3 has a description of the icons available.

**Figure 11.4**    The Database toolbar

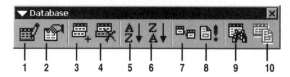

**Table 11.3**    Icons in the Database toolbar

| # | Icon | What you do with it |
|---|------|---------------------|
| 1 | Data Form | Click to display the Data Form dialog box so that you can create and edit data in an existing table in the current document. |
| 2 | Manage Fields | Click to display the Manage Fields dialog box so that you can add, remove, and rename fields in an existing table in the current document. |
| 3 | Add New Record | Click to add another record to the end of the table where the cursor is currently positioned. |
| 4 | Delete Record | Click to delete the highlighted record. |
| 5 | Sort Ascending | Click to sort the data in the column where the cursor is currently positioned, from the bottom of the column to the top of the column. |
| 6 | Sort Descending | Click to sort the data in the column where the cursor is currently positioned, from the top of the column to the bottom of the column. |
| 7 | Insert Database | Click to import data from another source. This option displays the Database dialog box which is similar to the Mail Merge dialog box. (For more information, see Tools ➤ Merge Documents on page 236.) |
| 8 | Update Field | Click to make sure that current field has the most recent value from the source file. |
| 9 | Find Record | Click to display the Find in Field dialog box so that you can search for the contents of named fields. |
| 10 | Mail Merge Main Document | Click to use the current document as a source database for another type of document. You can create documents such as form letters, address labels, or membership directories using this option. |

## View ➤ Toolbars ➤ Drawing

Use this option to display the Drawing toolbar so that you can create your own drawings, insert shapes, add callouts, and apply color to your masterpiece. (For more information, see View ➤ Toolbars ➤ Drawing on page 69.)

## How You Get Here

✧ Click           ✧ Press **Alt+V,T** choose **Drawing**   ✧ Choose **View** ➤ **Toolbars** ➤ **Drawing**

# View ➤ Toolbars ➤ Forms

Use this option to display the Forms toolbar so that you can create a document with "empty" places to fill in information at a later date (think "IRS"). For instance, you can use a form as a questionnaire with blank spaces for answers or you can use this toolbar along with the Database toolbar to create forms to use on the Web.

## How You Get Here

✧ Press **Alt+V,T** choose **Forms**     ✧ Choose **View** ➤ **Toolbars** ➤ **Forms**

## What's In This Toolbar

Figure 11.5 is a sample of this toolbar and Table 11.4 has a description of the icons available.

**Figure 11.5**   The Forms toolbar

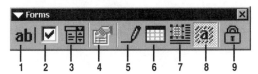

**Table 11.4**   Icons in the Forms toolbar

| # | Icon | What you do with it |
|---|------|---------------------|
| 1 | Text Form Field | Click to insert a fill-in field at the current cursor location. This gives your forms user a specific location to enter the required information. You can control what type of information is allowed in the field (e.g., limiting the entry to valid dates) and insert a default value so that the forms user doesn't have to do anything if the value is correct. |
| 2 | Check Box Form Field | Click to insert a check box next to an independent element that you choose or clear. You can also use this option to insert a check box next to each element in a group of choices where the forms user can choose more than one option. |
| 3 | Drop-Down Form Field | Click to insert a drop-down list so that your forms user can pick from a list of available options rather than having to type in a response. If needed, your forms user can scroll through the list to see additional choices. |
| 4 | Form Field Options | Click to set and review the options for the highlighted form field. |
| 5 | Draw Table | Click to use a "pencil" to draw the cells for a table and display the Tables and Borders toolbar. (For more information, see The Tables and Borders Toolbar on page 252.) |
| 6 | Insert Table | Click to display a drop-down list for defining a table to be inserted at the cursor position. (For more information, see Table ➤ Insert on page 254.) |
| 7 | Insert Frame | Click to insert a container that can be used to hold other information or to rearrange information in unusual ways. |

**Table 11.4**   Icons in the Forms toolbar, continued

| # | Icon | What you do with it |
|---|------|---------------------|
| 8 | Form Field Shading | Click to add or remove the gray background covering fields that you've inserted in the current document. |
| 9 | Protect Form | Click to let your forms user to enter information into the designated areas *without* changing the form's layout and standard elements. When you're ready to make changes to the form, turn off the protection, make your changes, and turn the protection back on. |

## View ➤ Toolbars ➤ Frames

Use this option to display the Frames toolbar so that you can organize information on a Web page. (For more information, see Format ➤ Frames on page 214 or The Frames Toolbar on page 215.)

### How You Get Here

✧ Press **Alt+V,T** choose **Frames**      ✧ Choose **View** ➤ **Toolbars** ➤ **Frames**

## View ➤ Toolbars ➤ Picture

Use this option to display the Picture toolbar so that you can insert images into your document and control the way they look. (For more information, see Insert ➤ Picture on page 83 or View ➤ Toolbars ➤ Picture on page 71.)

### How You Get Here

✧ Press **Alt+V,T** choose **Picture**      ✧ Choose **View** ➤ **Toolbars** ➤ **Picture**

## View ➤ Toolbars ➤ Reviewing

Use this option to display the Reviewing toolbar so that you can review existing comments, insert comments, delete existing comments, or accept the changes made to a document. This is a great way keep track of notes, comments, and questions; that way you and other authors can review this information before the text is actually added to the final file. (For more information, see Insert ➤ Comment on page 82 or View ➤ Comments on page 79.)

### How You Get Here

✧ Press **Alt+V,T** choose **Reviewing**   ✧ Choose **View** ➤ **Toolbars** ➤ **Reviewing**

## What's Different

Figure 11.6 is a sample of this toolbar and Table 11.5 has a description of the icons that are unique to Word. (For more information, see View ➤ Toolbars ➤ Reviewing on page 72.)

**Figure 11.6** The Reviewing toolbar

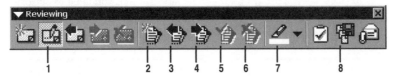

**Table 11.5** Icons in the Reviewing toolbar

| # | Icon | What you do with it |
|---|------|---------------------|
| 1 | Edit Comment | Click to display the Comment pane at the bottom of the current window so that you can review or change the text of a comment. You can't insert a new comment while this pane is open. |
| 2 | Track Changes | Click to begin tracking changes while you're editing the document. If you want to customize how your changes are tracked, use the **Tools ➤ Track Changes** option. (For more information, see Tools ➤ Track Changes on page 233.) |
| 3 | Previous Change | Click to step through each change in the current document, in reverse order. |
| 4 | Next Change | Click to step through each change in the current document, in order. |
| 5 | Accept Change | Click to eliminate the editing indicators and make the changes permanent. |
| 6 | Reject Change | Click to return the highlighted change to its original state. |
| 7 | Highlight<br>Highlight drop-down list | Click to turn the cursor into a highlighter so that you can emphasize specific elements (kind of like an "electronic" yellow highlighter pen). Click the Highlight drop-down list to change the highlighter color. |
| 8 | Save Version | Click to display the Save Version dialog box so that you can enter comments about the current version of the document. |

## View ➤ Toolbars ➤ Tables and Borders

Use this option to display the Tables and Borders toolbar so that you can insert tables and change the way tables and borders look in your file. (For more information, see The Tables and Borders Toolbar on page 252.)

## How You Get Here.

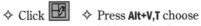

✧ Click 🔲  ✧ Press **Alt+V,T** choose **Tables and Borders**  ✧ Choose **View ➤ Toolbars ➤ Tables and Borders**

## View ➤ Toolbars ➤ Visual Basic

Use this option to display the Visual Basic toolbar so that you can create a new program such as a macro. Macros are small programs that you use for different purposes. You can create macros that do some of the tedious, repetitive work that you would normally do at the keyboard, one step at a time. In fact, you can create a program for almost any task that you need to perform, which is a great way to ensure accuracy and relieve the boredom of doing the same thing over and over again. (For more information, see View ➤ Toolbars ➤ Visual Basic on page 73.)

**N O T E**   Although the details of programming with Visual Basic are beyond the scope of this book, you might want to try *Special Edition: Using Visual Basic For Applications 5* by Paul Sanna, (ISBN: 0789709597). ▓

## How You Get Here

❖ Press **Alt+V,T** choose **Visual Basic**     ❖ Choose **View ➤ Toolbars ➤ Visual Basic**

## View ➤ Toolbars ➤ Web

Use this option to display the Web toolbar so that you can see and use the icons that are used most frequently in a Web Browser. (For more information, see View ➤ Toolbars ➤ Web on page 74.)

## How You Get Here

❖ Press **Alt+V,T** choose **Web**     ❖ Choose **View ➤ Toolbars ➤ Web**

## View ➤ Toolbars ➤ Web Tools

Use this option to display the Web Tools toolbar, which looks uncannily similar to the Controls toolbar and which lets you do the same basic stuff, except that you're creating controls for Web pages. Now you can create a custom Web page with ActiveX controls such as radio buttons, text boxes, scroll bars, and other neat stuff that can darn near make your file sing and dance (but that kind of stuff is beyond the scope of this book).

**N O T E**   These are the same types of controls you can add using the Visual Basic Editor. For more information try *Special Edition: Using Visual Basic For Applications 5* by Paul Sanna, (ISBN: 0789709597). ▓

## How You Get Here

❖ Press **Alt+V,T** choose **Web Tools**   ❖ Choose **View ➤ Toolbars ➤ Web Tools**

## What's In This Toolbar

Figure 11.7 is a sample of this toolbar and Table 11.6 has a description of the icons available.

**Figure 11.7** The Web Tools toolbar

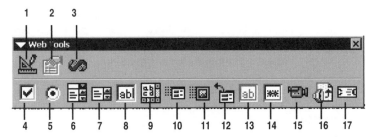

**Table 11.6** Icons in the Web Tools toolbar

| # | Icon | What you do with it |
|---|------|---------------------|
| 1 | Design Mode | Click to turn on the mode that lets you insert various controls (such as radio buttons or scroll bars) at the current cursor location. |
| 2 | Properties | Click to view or change the behind the scenes workings for the highlighted control element. |
| 3 | Microsoft Script Editor | Click to open the Microsoft Script Editor dialog box so that you can create Web scripts. The default scripting language is Microsoft's VBScript, although other languages can be used. |
| 4 | Checkbox | Click to insert a check box control into the current document, at the current cursor location. |
| 5 | Option Button | Click to insert an option button control into the current document, at the current cursor location. |
| 6 | Dropdown box | Click to insert a drop-down box into the current document, at the current cursor location. |
| 7 | List Box | Click to insert a list box into the current document, at the current cursor location. |
| 8 | Textbox | Click to insert a text box control into the current document, at the current cursor location. |
| 9 | Text Area | Click to insert a text area into the current document, at the current cursor location. |
| 10 | Submit | Click to insert a submit button into the current document, at the current cursor location. |
| 11 | Submit with Image | Click to display the Insert Picture dialog box and insert both the highlighted image and a submit button, at the current cursor location. |
| 12 | Reset | Click to insert a reset button into the current document, at the current cursor location. |
| 13 | Hidden | Click to insert a hidden text field into the current document, at the current cursor location. |

**Table 11.6**   Icons in the Web Tools toolbar, continued

| # | Icon | What you do with it |
|---|------|---------------------|
| 14 | Password | Click to insert a password field into the current document, at the current cursor location. |
| 15 | Movie | Click to insert a movie into the current document, at the current cursor location. |
| 16 | Sound | Click to insert a sound into the current document, at the current cursor location. |
| 17 | Scrolling Text | Click to insert a scrolling text box into the current document, at the current cursor location. |

## View ➤ Toolbars ➤ WordArt

Use this option to display the WordArt toolbar so that you can insert and format art items so they look just the way you want them to. This toolbar includes icons for moving and resizing your art objects or changing the way your text is aligned or wrapped around the object. (For more information, see Insert ➤ Picture ➤ WordArt on page 87.)

### How You Get Here

◇ Press **Alt+V,T** choose **WordArt**   ◇ Choose <u>V</u>iew ➤ <u>T</u>oolbars ➤ **WordArt**

### What's Different

Figure 11.8 is a sample of this toolbar, plus a description of the only icon that is unique to Word. (For more information, see View ➤ Toolbars ➤ WordArt on page 75.)

**Figure 11.8**   The WordArt toolbar

Text Wrap: Click to control how text is stationed around the WordArt.

## View ➤ Toolbars ➤ Customize

Use this option to display the Customize window so that you can customize most of the toolbars or menu options. (For more information, see View ➤ Toolbars ➤ Customize on page 76.)

### How You Get Here

◇ Press **Alt+V,T,C**   ◇ Choose <u>V</u>iew ➤ <u>T</u>oolbars ➤ <u>C</u>ustomize

# View ➤ Ruler

Use this option to show or hide a nonprinting ruler at the top of your application window. This option toggles (switches back and forth) and indicates the current state (in case you can't tell from looking at the ruler on screen) with a check mark next to the menu item. The ruler displays the position of elements within the current document, including graphics and tabs.

## How You Get Here

✧ Press **Alt+V,R**     ✧ Choose **View** ➤ **Ruler**

# View ➤ Document Map

Use this option to split the current document window into two panes: the left pane displays the headings of your document and the right pane displays the main text of your document. You can choose to display a few or all levels of headings and move quickly around a document. When you click on a heading in the document map, Word highlights the heading and jumps to the corresponding page, displaying that heading in the right hand pane.

## How You Get Here

✧ Click 📖     ✧ Press **Alt+V,D**     ✧ Choose **View** ➤ **Document Map**

# View ➤ Header and Footer

Use this option to display the current document's headers and footers, as well as the Headers and Footers toolbar. The current view switches to Print Layout if you aren't already there and hides the body of text. The items that you insert here show up on every page of the document.

---

**N O T E**    If you are already in the Print Layout View, you can double-click the inactive header or footer area to display this toolbar. When you're finished, close this toolbar by double-clicking anywhere on the page outside of the header or footer area or click the **Close** button. ▓

## How You Get Here

✧ Press **Alt+V,H**     ✧ Choose **View** ➤ **Header and Footer**

# The Header And Footer Toolbar

Use this option to add, change, or review the information printed at the top or bottom of every page in your document.

## What's In This Toolbar

Figure 11.9 is a sample of this toolbar and Table 11.7 has a description of the icons available.

**Figure 11.9**    The Header and Footer toolbar

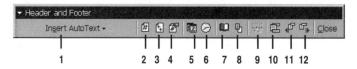

**Table 11.7**    Icons in the Header and Footer toolbar

| # | Icon | What you do with it |
|---|------|---------------------|
| 1 | Insert AutoText | Choose an item that determines what AutoText entry to insert at the current cursor current location. |
| 2 | Insert Page Number | Click to insert a field that displays the page number of the current page. |
| 3 | Insert Number of Pages | Click to insert a field that displays the total number of pages in the current document. |
| 4 | Format Page Number | Click to open the Page Number Format dialog box so that you can add, change, or view how the page number displays. |
| 5 | Insert Date | Click to insert a field that displays the current date. |
| 6 | Insert Time | Click to insert a field that displays the current time. |
| 7 | Page Setup | Click to display the Page Setup dialog box so that you can set such page characteristics as margins and paper size, as well as setting the options for your section breaks. (For more information, see File ➤ Page Setup on page 128.) |
| 8 | Show/Hide Document Text | Click to show or hide the document text while working in the header or footer. |
| 9 | Same as Previous | Click to make the header or footer in the current section have the same characteristics as the header or footer in the previous section. |
| 10 | Switch Between Header and Footer | Click to move the cursor back and forth between the header and the footer. |
| 11 | Show Previous button | Click to move the cursor to the header or footer for the previous section. |
| 12 | Show Next button | Click to move the cursor to the header or footer for the next section. |

# View ➤ Footnotes

Use this option to step through footnotes that have already been inserted into the document. Unlike some other options in the view menu, this one does not shift to a different mode. Rather, with each click on the option you move from one footnote to the next. If there are no footnotes inserted, this menu item is grayed out. (For more information, see Insert ➤ Footnote on page 178.)

### How You Get Here

✧ Press **Alt+V,F**          ✧ Choose **View ➤ Footnotes**

# View ➤ Comments

Use this option to view any comments that have been inserted in the current file. This option opens a pane in the current window which has the comment text in it. (For more information, see View ➤ Toolbars ➤ Reviewing on page 158.)

---

**N O T E**   Comments are indicated by yellow highlighting within the text.  ▮

### How You Get Here

✧ Press **Alt+V,C**          ✧ Choose **View ➤ Comments**

# View ➤ Full Screen

Use this option to make the current document take up the full "real estate" of the screen. In the process, toolbars and other controls disappear. Secondary panes, such as the comments pane, remain visible.

### How You Get Here

✧ Press **Alt+V,U**          ✧ Choose **View ➤ Full Screen**

### What's In This Dialog Box

Figure 11.10 is a sample of this dialog box and includes a description of the only option available.

**Figure 11.10**   The Full Screen dialog box

 Click to return to the previous view.

# View ➤ Zoom

Use this option to set the size of the display for the current file. You can let the application calculate the size or you can set a precise size that suits your needs.

---

**N O T E**    When you choose a larger number, you see a bigger version of your file, but you can't see as much of the file at one time. You'll spend more time scrolling but your eyes won't be so worn out. ▪

## How You Get Here

✧ Press **Alt+V,Z**          ✧ Choose **View ➤ Zoom**

## What's Different

Figure 11.11 is a sample of this dialog box and Table 11.8 has a description of the options that are unique to Word. (For more information, see View ➤ Zoom on page 79.)

**Figure 11.11**    The Zoom dialog box

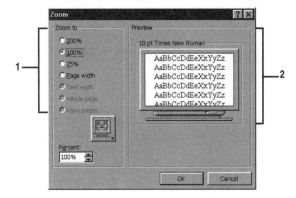

**Table 11.8**    Options in the Zoom dialog box

| # | Option | What you do with it |
|---|--------|---------------------|
| 1 | Zoom to area | Choose an item that determines the zoom size. You can zoom in at a percentage of the current zoom size, by a specific amount of the page you want to see or by entering a specific view percentage. If you choose **Many Pages**, you can click the Many Pages drop-down list to determine which way you want to display the pages. |
| 2 | Preview area | View a sample of what the text will look like if you choose the specified zoom percentage. |

# The Word Insert Menu

# What Is The Insert Menu

This menu lists the commands that you'll use to add page breaks, page numbers, stored text phrases, comments, pictures, and hyperlinks. Many types of items you want to put in your document are inserted from this menu.

If a menu option has an ellipsis (three dots) or an arrow beside it, the application "asks" you for additional information before the action takes place. If the menu doesn't have one of these symbols, the action you choose happens immediately. If the action takes place immediately, you won't see a sample screen in this section.

# Insert ➤ Break

Use this option to force text to move to the next page or column instead of letting Word make that decision for you. You can force information to the next column, the next page, or create a new section that has different properties than the previous one. Section breaks are typically used to change properties such as page width, page numbering, or what information is stored in the header—the information at the top of every page— or the footer—the information at the bottom of every page. (For more information, see File ➤ Page Setup on page 128.)

## How You Get Here

✧ Press **Alt+I,B**          ✧ Choose **Insert** ➤ **Break**

## What's In This Dialog Box

Figure 12.1 is a sample of this dialog box and Table 12.1 has a description of the options available.

**Figure 12.1**    The Break dialog box

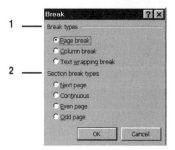

**Table 12.1**   Options in the Break dialog box

| # | Option | What you do with it |
|---|--------|---------------------|
| 1 | Break types area | Choose an item that determines the type of break you want to use in your document. Word inserts a break from *the current position* forward, so make sure you don't have your cursor in the middle of a line. |
| 2 | Section break types area | Choose an item that determines what type of section break you want to insert and how you want Word to handle the next page in the document. |

# Insert ➤ Page Numbers

Use this option to add page numbers to your document, control where the numbers are placed, and pick what number is used to start the numbering sequence.

## How You Get Here

✧ Press **Alt+I,U**          ✧ Choose **Insert ➤ Page Numbers**

## What's In This Dialog Box

Figure 12.2 is a sample of this dialog box and Table 12.2 has a description of the options available.

**Figure 12.2**   The Page Numbers dialog box

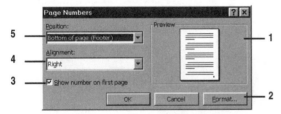

**Table 12.2**   Options in the Page Numbers dialog box

| # | Option | What you do with it |
|---|--------|---------------------|
| 1 | Preview area | View the page number position and alignment before you apply the settings in this dialog box. |
| 2 | Format button | Click to display the Page Number Format dialog box so that you can choose what the page numbers look like and what numbering is used to start the numbering sequence. |
| 3 | Show number on first page check box | Click to make sure that the first page of the file has a page number. Turn this option off if you don't want to insert a page number on the first page. (The page *is* included in the number sequence, it just isn't printed on the page.) |
| 4 | Alignment drop-down list | Choose an item that determines where the page numbers should line up. |
| 5 | Position drop-down list | Choose an item that determines whether you want the page numbers at the top of the page or at the bottom of the page. |

# Insert ➤ Date and Time

Use this option to place the current date, the current time, or the current date *and* time at the current cursor position. You can choose several different formats and automatically update this information every time you open the file.

---

**N O T E**   You can insert this information in the body of your file or insert in the header or footer so that it displays on every page. ▣

---

**TIP**   If you want to have the application update this information every time you open the file, be sure to click the **Update automatically** check box. Be careful with this one—it really does update the date every time you open the file, not just when you make changes to the file.

## How You Get Here

✧ Press **Alt+I,T**          ✧ Choose **Insert ➤ Date and Time**

## What's In This Dialog Box

Figure 12.3 is a sample of this dialog box and Table 12.3 has a description of the options available.

**Figure 12.3**   The Date and Time dialog box

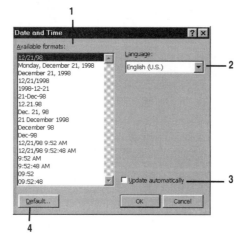

**Table 12.3** Options in the Date and Time dialog box

| # | Option | What you do with it |
|---|--------|---------------------|
| 1 | Available formats list | Choose an item that determines what the date/time will look like when you insert it in your document. |
| 2 | Language drop-down list | Choose an item that determines what language is applied to the date/time when you insert it in your document. The default language is the one you've set up for Word. |
| 3 | Update automatically check box | Click to choose to whether you want Word to update the date and time *every* time you open the document. |
| 4 | Default button | Click to store the currently highlighted format as the new formatting style . |

# Insert ➤ AutoText

Use this option to place predefined text into your document. This is a handy way to store frequently used phrases, tables, and other information that you don't want to proofread over and over again. Although Word comes with quite a few AutoText entries, you can also create, define, or rename entries.

**TIP** You can drag this flyout menu off the Insert menu and it becomes the AutoText toolbar.  (For more information, see The AutoText Toolbar on page 172.)

## How You Get Here

✧ Press **Alt+I,A**          ✧ Choose **Insert ➤ AutoText**

## What's In This Flyout Menu

Figure 12.1 is a sample of this flyout menu.

**Figure 12.4**    The Insert ➤ AutoText flyout menu

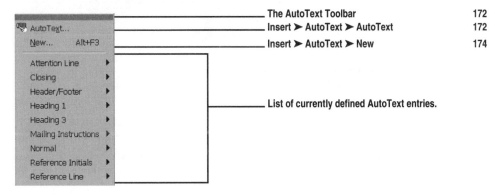

List of currently defined AutoText entries.

## The AutoText Toolbar

Use this option to drag the flyout menu off the Insert menu so that it changes to the AutoText toolbar. You can use this toolbar to format your AutoText entries or display the AutoText tab on the AutoCorrect dialog box where you can choose the specific type of text you want to insert into your document.

### How You Get Here

✧ Press **Alt+I,A** choose and drag **menu bar**
or
Press **Alt+V,T** choose **AutoText**

✧ Choose **Insert ➤ AutoText ➤ menu bar**
or
Choose **View ➤ Toolbars ➤ AutoText**

### What's In This Toolbar

Figure 12.5 is a sample of this toolbar and Table 12.4 has a description of the icons available.

**Figure 12.5**   The AutoText toolbar

**Table 12.4**   Icons in the AutoText toolbar

| # | Icon | What you do with it |
|---|------|---------------------|
| 1 | Autotext | Click to open the AutoText dialog box so you can add, delete, preview, and edit AutoText entries.  (For more information, see Insert ➤ AutoText ➤ AutoText on page 172.) |
| 2 | All Entries | Click to open a drop-down list of currently defined AutoText entries. You can either review what's available or choose which entry you want to insert at the current text position. If a specific type of entry has more than one option available, you can look at the definition of each one. |
| 3 | New | Click to create a new AutoText entry from the currently highlighted text. If you haven't highlighted any text this option is inactive. |

## Insert ➤ AutoText ➤ AutoText

Use this option to create or customize text for use as an AutoText entry. You can preview the entry and can choose templates that have other entries that you can use in the active document.

### How You Get Here

✧ Press **Alt+I,A,X**

✧ Choose **Insert ➤ AutoText ➤ AutoText**

## What's In This Dialog Box

Figure 12.6 is a sample of this dialog box and Table 12.5 has a description of the options available.

**Figure 12.6**   The AutoCorrect dialog box AutoText tab

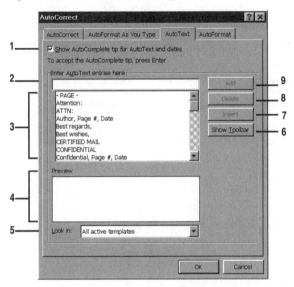

**Table 12.5**   Options in the AutoCorrect dialog box AutoText tab

| # | Option | What you do with it |
|---|--------|---------------------|
| 1 | Show AutoComplete tip check box | Click to display the complete text of the AutoText entry when you type something in your text that is a close match to an existing AutoText entry. When Word displays the tip, you can press the **Enter** key or **F3** to accept the entry and Word types the rest of the information for you. If you don't want the suggestion Word is displaying, just continue typing the information into your document. |
| 2 | Enter AutoText entries here text box | Enter a name for a new AutoText entry or rename the highlighted AutoText entry. When you choose an entry from the AutoText entries list, the name of that entry displays in this text box. |
| 3 | AutoText entries list | Choose an item that determines which AutoText text you want to insert, delete, or modify. |
| 4 | Preview area | View the text of the highlighted AutoText entry. |
| 5 | Look in drop-down list | Choose an item that determines where you can find the desired AutoText entries you want in your document. You can choose entries from templates placed in the Windows\Application Data\Microsoft\Templates folder on your system. |
| 6 | Show Toolbar button | Click to display the AutoText toolbar. (For more information, see The AutoText Toolbar on page 172.) |
| 7 | Insert button | Click to place the highlighted entry at the current cursor position. |

**Table 12.5**   Options in the AutoCorrect dialog box AutoText tab, continued

| # | Option | What you do with it |
|---|--------|---------------------|
| 8 | Delete button | Click to remove an existing AutoText entry from the list. |
| 9 | Add button | Click to add a new AutoText entry to the list and give it the name displayed in the Enter AutoText entries here text box. |

## Insert ➤ AutoText ➤ New

Use this option to create a new AutoText entry that stores the highlighted text.

**N O T E**   You can use this option to quickly create an AutoText entry from the text highlighted, but you can also change the name of the entry or remove it.  (For more information, see Insert ➤ AutoText ➤ AutoText on page 172.)  ■

### How You Get Here

◈ Press **Alt+I,A,N** or **Alt+F3**      ◈ Choose **Insert ➤ AutoText ➤ New**

### What's In This Dialog Box

Figure 12.7 is a sample of this dialog box and has a description of the only option available.

**Figure 12.7**   The Create AutoText dialog box

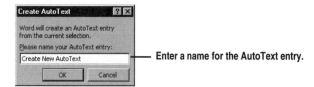

—— **Enter a name for the AutoText entry.**

# Insert ➤ Field

Use this option to place special types of coded information at the current position. This "coded information" is called a field and there are a bunch of different categories that you can insert into your document. Once you've inserted a field the information is automatically updated as it changes. In fact, you may have already used a field. If you've used the **Insert ➤ Date and Time** option, you've used a field. There, that's not so bad, is it?

### How You Get Here

◈ Press **Alt+I,F**      ◈ Choose **Insert ➤ Field**

## What's In This Dialog Box

Figure 12.8 is a sample of this dialog box and Table 12.6 has a description of the options available.

**Figure 12.8**   The Field dialog box

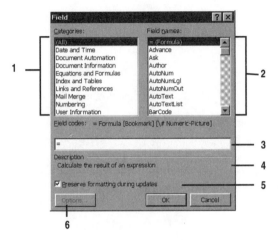

**Table 12.6**   Options in the Field dialog box

| # | Option | What you do with it |
|---|--------|---------------------|
| 1 | Categories list | Choose an item that determines which major group (called a "category") of fields you want to work with. |
| 2 | Field names list | Choose an item that determines which type of information you want to insert at the current cursor position. The options available change based on which Category you choose. And, when you actually click the **OK** button, Word inserts the *value for the field*, not the field name. |
| 3 | Field codes text box | View the field syntax of the currently highlighted field name. You can enter the codes by typing them in this text box or click the **Options** button to choose special formatting information. |
| 4 | Description area | View a brief summary of the highlighted field names and what it will do when you insert the field at the current cursor position. |
| 5 | Preserve formatting check box | Click to make sure that the field keeps the original formatting applied to the *field value* once it's inserted at the current cursor position. |
| 6 | Options button | Click to display the Field Options dialog box so that you can apply more formatting options to the field value (not the field name). For instance, you can apply uppercase formatting or choose from the list of styles stored in your document, such as Heading 1. |

# Insert ➤ Symbol

Use this option to place special characters, such as a trademark or copyright symbol, in your document. When the Symbol dialog box displays, you can change the font or assign a keyboard shortcut sequence if you think you'll use a symbol frequently.

## How You Get Here

✦ Press **Alt+I,S**            ✦ Choose **Insert ➤ Symbol**

## What's In This Dialog Box

Figure 12.9 is a sample of this dialog box and Table 12.7 has a description of the tabs available.

---

**N O T E**    The AutoCorrect button and the Shortcut Key button display on each tab in this dialog box. The AutoCorrect button displays the AutoCorrect dialog box. (For more information, see Tools ➤ AutoCorrect on page 232.) The Shortcut key button displays the Customize Keyboard dialog box where you can assign a keyboard shortcut sequence to the highlighted character or symbol. (For more information, see Tools ➤ Customize on page 245.)  ▪

**Figure 12.9**    The Symbol dialog box

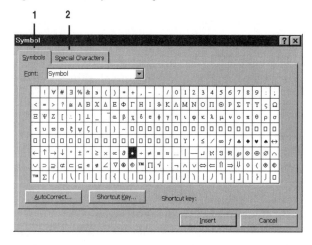

**Table 12.7** Tabs in the Symbol dialog box

| # | Tab name | What you do with it |
|---|----------|---------------------|
| 1 | Symbols | Choose an item that determines which symbol you want to use. (For a complete description of the options available, see Table 12.8 on page 177.) |
| 2 | Special Characters | Choose an item that determines the character you want to use. (For a complete description of the options available, see Table 12.9 on page 177.) |

The following tables describe the options for the individual tabs in this dialog box:

- Table 12.8 describes the Symbols tab, and
- Table 12.9 describes the Special Characters tab.

**Table 12.8** Options in the Symbol dialog box Symbols tab

| Option | What you do with it |
|--------|---------------------|
| Font drop-down list | Choose an item that determines which font has the symbol or letter you want to insert. |
| Symbols list | View the symbols or letters available for the font you've chosen. Click to highlight a specific symbol or letter. To insert the highlighted character at the current cursor position, double-click it or click the **Insert** button. |
| Shortcut key area | View the shortcut key assigned to the highlighted symbol or letter, if one is currently assigned. |

**Table 12.9** Options in the Symbol dialog box Special Characters tab

| Option | What you do with it |
|--------|---------------------|
| Character area | Click to choose the which character you want to insert. To insert the highlighted character at the current cursor position, double-click it or click the **Insert** button. |
| Shortcut key area | View the keyboard shortcut key assigned to the currently highlighted character. |

# Insert ➤ Comment

Use this option to add written or audio notes (if you have a sound card and microphone) to a file that you're editing or reviewing. Be sure you either highlight the text you're making a comment about or click the cursor at the end of the text *before* you choose this command. Once you insert a comment, the text looks like someone used a highlighting marker over the text, which makes it very easy to see where the comments are. (For more information, see View ➤ Toolbars ➤ Reviewing on page 72 or View ➤ Comments on page 79.)

---

**N O T E**   Several different authors can review the same file and the application keeps track of the comment *and* the name of the person who made the comment. If you place your cursor over a highlighted comment, the reviewer name and comment displays. ▪

## How You Get Here

✧ Press **Alt+I,M**          ✧ Choose **Insert ➤ Comment**

# Insert ➤ Footnote

Use this option to place either footnotes (additional explanations inserted at the bottom of the appropriate page) or endnotes (additional explanations inserted at the end of your document) in your document. You can choose how the notes are marked (with numbers, letters, or special symbols), where they're placed, what number is used for the first note, and whether the numbering starts over for each new page, or whether the notes are numbered sequentially throughout the document.

---

**N O T E**   Once you insert a footnote, Word positions the cursor in the appropriate area so that you can type the text of the footnote or endnote. ▪

## How You Get Here

✧ Press **Alt+I,N**          ✧ Choose **Insert ➤ Footnote**

## What's In This Dialog Box

Figure 12.10 is a sample of this dialog box and Table 12.10 has a description of the options available.

**Figure 12.10**   The Footnote and Endnote dialog box

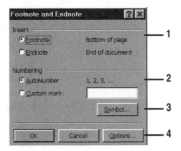

**Table 12.10**   Options in the Footnote and Endnote dialog box

| # | Option | What you do with it |
|---|--------|---------------------|
| 1 | Insert area | Choose an item that determines whether the note entered is inserted at the bottom of the current page or at the end of the document. |
| 2 | Numbering area | Choose an item that determines whether you want to use standard numbers or special characters. |
| 3 | Symbol button | Click to display the Symbol dialog box so that you can choose the type of mark you want for the note. (For a complete description of the options available, see Table 12.8 on page 177.) |
| 4 | Options button | Click to display the Footnote Options dialog box so that you can choose where, how, and what type of note you want to place in your document. |

# Insert ➤ Caption

Use this option to automatically number figures (these are typically graphics that you've inserted), tables, and equations. If you're adding several items to your document, you can have Word automatically insert a caption when you insert specified items. You can choose how the captions are marked (with numbers, letters, or Roman numerals), what text precedes the number, what number is used for the first caption, and whether you want to include a chapter number when the caption is inserted.

## How You Get Here

✧ Press **Alt+I,C**         ✧ Choose **Insert ➤ Caption**

## What's In This Dialog Box

Figure 12.11 is a sample of this dialog box and Table 12.11 has a description of the options available.

**Figure 12.11**    The Caption dialog box

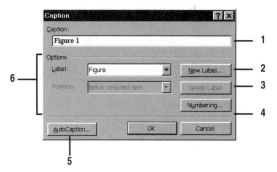

**Table 12.11**    Options in the Caption dialog box

| # | Option | What you do with it |
|---|--------|---------------------|
| 1 | Caption text box | View the caption label. You can enter a caption title but you cannot type over the label. |
| 2 | New Label button | Click to create a new label type. Once you've created a new label type, you can choose it from the Label drop-down list. The text entered in this text box precedes the caption number when you insert the caption |
| 3 | Delete Label button | Click to delete the highlighted label. You can only delete labels that you've created, not the default labels included with Word. |
| 4 | Numbering button | Click to display the Caption Numbering dialog box so that you can customize the numbering format you use for your captions. You can choose the numbering style and whether you want to include the chapter numbering as part of the caption. |
| 5 | AutoCaption button | Click to display the AutoCaption dialog box so that you can have Word automatically add a caption when you insert specific items in your document. |
| 6 | Options area | Choose an item that determines which label you want for the caption and where the caption displays. |

# Insert ➤ Cross-reference

Use this option to place text that refers you to another place in the current document or in another document. You've seen a bunch of these in this book—(For more information, see Insert ➤ AutoText on page 171.). You can display the text of the cross-reference, the page number where the information is located or paragraph numbers (if you're numbering your paragraphs). You can also create a hypertext link (a link that you can click and Word automatically takes you to the source of the cross-reference.

**N O T E**   The Web toolbar displays when you click an existing cross-reference. (For more information, see View ➤ Toolbars ➤ Web on page 160.) ▓

## How You Get Here

◆ Press **Alt+I,R**

◆ Choose **Insert ➤ Cross-reference**

## What's In This Dialog Box

Figure 12.12 is a sample of this dialog box and Table 12.12 has a description of the options available.

**Figure 12.12**   The Cross-reference dialog box

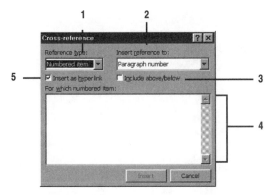

**Table 12.12**   Options in the Cross-reference dialog box

| # | Option | What you do with it |
|---|--------|---------------------|
| 1 | Reference type drop-down list | Choose an item that determines what type of information contains the *source* of the information to reference. |
| 2 | Insert reference to drop-down list | Choose an item that determines what part of the source text you want to display at the current cursor position as a reference. For instance, you could choose to display only a figure title or a table title and the page where it is located. |

**Table 12.12**    Options in the Cross-reference dialog box, continued

| # | Option | What you do with it |
|---|--------|---------------------|
| 3 | Include above/below check box | Click to choose a location to place in the cross-reference relative to the figure or table you are referencing. For instance, if the figure is above the cross-reference you may want it to say *See Figure 4, above.* This option is only available for certain options and is based on what you've chosen in the Reference type drop-down list. |
| 4 | For which list | Choose an item that determines the specific source of the text you want to reference. This list displays the first few words of each entry that matches the type chosen in the Reference type drop-down list. |
| 5 | Insert as hyperlink check box | Click to make the reference a hot link to the source item so that once you insert the link you can click on it and automatically jump to the source of the cross-reference. |

# Insert ➤ Index and Tables

Use this option to create that nasty stuff called "front matter" or "back matter". This is the stuff that you typically see at the front or back of a book or long document (things like a Table of Contents, an Index, a List of Figures or a List of Tables). You know, that stuff that makes it easier to find what you're looking for? Another handy option is commonly used for legal documents—you can use the Table of Authorities option to create a list of citations, rulings, etc.

## How You Get Here

❖ Press **Alt+I,D**              ❖ Choose **Insert ➤ Index and Tables**

## What's In This Dialog Box

Figure 12.13 is a sample of this dialog box and Table 12.13 has a description of the tabs available.

**Figure 12.13**   The Index and Tables dialog box

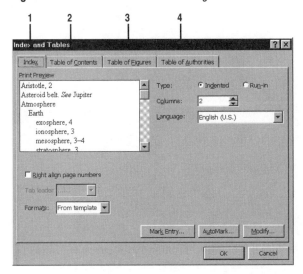

**Table 12.13**   Tabs in the Index and Tables dialog box

| # | Tab name | What you do with it |
|---|----------|---------------------|
| 1 | Index | Click to choose how you want your entries to display when you create an alphabetical list of topics. (For a complete description of the options available, see Table 12.14 on page 184.) |
| 2 | Table of Contents | Click to choose how you want your headings to display when you create a Table of Contents-style listing. (For a complete description of the options available, see Table 12.15 on page 184.) |
| 3 | Table of Figures | Click to choose how you want the items (tables, graphics, or figures) to display when you create a list of these items. (For a complete description of the options available, see Table 12.16 on page 185.) |
| 4 | Table of Authorities | Click to choose what and how the items are to display when you create this type of list. (For a complete description of the options available, see Table 12.17 on page 186.) |

The following tables describe the options for the individual tabs in this dialog box:

- Table 12.14 describes the Index tab,
- Table 12.15 describes the Table of Contents tab,
- Table 12.16 describes the Table of Figures tab, and
- Table 12.17 describes the Table of Authorities tab.

**Table 12.14**   Options in the Index and Tables dialog box Index tab

| Option | What you do with it |
| --- | --- |
| Print Preview list | View what your entries will look like if you apply the currently chosen settings. |
| Type area | Click to define the way secondary level index entries display. |
| Columns list | Click to choose the number of columns you want when the index is created. |
| Language list | Click to choose the language you want to have the index display in. The default language was set when you installed Office 2000. |
| Right align numbers check box | Click to make sure the page numbers line up on the right side instead of the left. This means that the page numbers will line up properly even if you have both single-digit and multiple-digit numbers in your list. |
| Tab leader drop-down list | Click to choose what character (if any) is inserted in the space between the text and page number. |
| Formats drop-down list | Click to choose what your index will look like when it's created. You can click each option and take a look at the effects of your choice *before* you commit to anything. |
| Mark entry button | Click to display the Mark Entry dialog box so that you can apply specific formatting to an index entry or insert the specific category for the index text. This dialog box stays open so that you can mark several entries at one time. |
| AutoMark button | Click to automate marking text for indexes by using a file you have set up previously as an index file. This file is called a concordance. You set up the concordance first with all your index entries you want to use to automate indexing. |
| Modify button | Click to display the Style dialog box so that you can change the look of a specific level of index entry. You can't change the name of the style, only what it looks like when that level is inserted in your index. (For more information, see Format ➤ Style on page 217.) |

**Table 12.15**   Options in the Index and Tables dialog box Table of Contents tab

| Option | What you do with it |
| --- | --- |
| Print Preview list | View what your entries will look like if you apply the currently chosen settings. |
| Web Preview list | View what your entries will look like if you display the Table of Contents as a Web page. |
| Show page numbers check box | Click to display the page numbers when you insert the Table of Contents. |
| Right align page numbers check box | Click to make sure the page numbers line up on the right side instead of the left. This means that the page numbers will line up properly even if you have both single-digit and multiple-digit numbers in your list. |
| Tab leader drop-down list | Click to choose what character (if any) is inserted in the space between the text and page number. |

**Table 12.15**   Options in the Index and Tables dialog box Table of Contents tab, continued

| Option | What you do with it |
| --- | --- |
| Formats drop-down list | Click to choose what your Table of Contents will look like when it's created. You can click each option and take a look at the effects of your choice *before* you commit to anything. |
| Show levels list | Enter or choose how many heading levels you want to include when you create the Table of Contents. |
| Options button | Click to choose which styles you want to include in the Table of Contents. |
| Modify button | Click to display the Style dialog box so that you can change the look of a specific level of text in your Table of Contents. You can't change the name of the style, only what it looks like when that level is inserted in your Table of Contents. (For more information, see Format ➤ Style on page 217.) |

**Table 12.16**   Options in the Index and Tables dialog box Table of Figures tab

| Option | What you do with it |
| --- | --- |
| Print Preview list | View what your entries will look like if you apply the currently chosen settings. |
| Web Preview list | View what your entries will look like if you display this type of list as a Web page. |
| Show page numbers check box | Click to display the page numbers when you create this type of list . |
| Right align page numbers check box | Click to make sure the page numbers line up on the right side instead of the left. This means that the page numbers will line up properly even if you have both single-digit and multiple-digit numbers in your list. |
| Tab leader drop-down list | Click to choose what character (if any) is inserted in the space between the text and page number. |
| Formats drop-down list | Click to choose what the highlighted type of list will look like when it's created. You can click each option and take a look at the effects of your choice *before* you commit to anything. |
| Caption label list | Click to choose which caption types you want to include when your list is created. |
| Include label and numbers check box | Click to display the title and number when your list is created. |
| Options button | Click to choose the paragraph styles you want to include in the Table of Figures. |
| Modify button | Click to display the Style dialog box so that you can change the look of a specific level of text in your list. You can't change the name of the style, only what it looks like when that level is inserted in the list. (For more information, see Format ➤ Style on page 217.) |

**Table 12.17**   Options in the Index and Tables dialog box Table of Authorities tab

| Option | What you do with it |
|---|---|
| Print Preview list | View what your entries will look like if you apply the currently chosen settings. |
| Web Preview list | View what your entries will look like if you display this type of list as a Web page. |
| Use passim check box | Click to replace more than five page numbers to one authority with the word "passim". |
| Keep original formatting check box | Click to retain the formatting of the original citation instead of changing it when it's added as a Table of Authorities entry. |
| Tab leader drop-down list | Click to choose what character (if any) is inserted in the space between the text and page number. |
| Formats drop-down list | Click to choose what the Table of Authorities will look like when it's created. You can click each option and take a look at the effects of your choice *before* you commit to anything. |
| Mark Citation button | Click to mark and choose a category for the citations you want to include in the Table of Authorities. |
| Modify button | Click to display the Style dialog box so that you can change the look of a specific level of text in your Table of Authorities. You can't change the name of the style, only what it looks like when that level is inserted in your Table of Contents. (For more information, see Format ➤ Style on page 217.) |

# Insert ➤ Picture

Use this option to insert various types of artwork in your file, including scanned items, the clipart that came with Office 2000, digital pictures, sound clips, and moving pictures. You can embed the artwork (store an actual copy) or create a link to the original file. If you create a link to the original file, you'll always have the latest information, no matter how many times you've edited the original artwork. Office 2000 accepts most of the popular graphics formats. Some of the formats, however, require a separate filter before you can bring them into your file. These filters are available on your original Office 2000 CD. So, if you don't have the filter you need, you can use the Office 2000 setup program to add them.

**N O T E**   Word, Excel, and PowerPoint have the same options on the flyout menu. (For more information, see Insert ➤ Picture on page 83.) ▪

## How You Get Here

✧ Press **Alt+I,P**          ✧ Choose **Insert ➤ Picture**

# Insert ➤ Text Box

Use this option to draw a box around the currently highlighted text or insert a new text box if no text is currently highlighted. If no text is highlighted, the cursor changes to a plus (+) and you can draw the text box by dragging your mouse across the document. Once you've inserted a text box, you change change the properties by displaying the shortcut menu and choosing **Edit Text Box.**

**N O T E**  You can also link a series of text boxes so that the text automatically moves to the next linked box as the amount of text expands. ▓

## How You Get Here

✧ Press **Alt+I,X**          ✧ Choose **Insert ➤ Text Box**

## What's In This Toolbar

Figure 12.14 is a sample of this toolbar and Table 12.18 has a description of the icons available.

**Figure 12.14**  The Text Box toolbar

**Table 12.18**  Icons in the Text Box toolbar

| # | Icon | What you do with it |
|---|------|---------------------|
| 1 | Create Text Box Link | Click to create links between multiple text boxes (this option "assumes" that you're going to click the next text box that you want to link). |
| 2 | Break Forward Link | Click to disconnect the link between the currently highlighted text box and the next one. |
| 3 | Previous Text Box | Click to move to the text box prior to the currently highlighted one. |
| 4 | Next Text Box | Click to move to the text box following the currently highlighted one. |
| 5 | Change Text Direction | Click to rotate the text in a different direction, |

# Insert ➤ File

Use this option to place the contents of another file in your document. If you want to maintain the source file separately you can link the inserted file to the source. This makes maintenance less complicated—make your changes in one place and your work is done in two places! For instance, suppose you are preparing an annual report and need information from another file, just insert it with links and if the source information is changed your report will still be up to date.

## How You Get Here

✧ Press **Alt+I,L**                ✧ Choose **Insert ➤ File**

## What's In This Dialog Box

Figure 12.15 is a sample of this dialog box and Table 12.19 has a description of the options available. This dialog box is the same basic dialog box displayed when you choose **File ➤ Open**. Choose the file location, name, and type, then decide whether you want to insert a copy of the file in your the active document or create a link to the source file. (For more information, see File ➤ Open on page 39.)

**Figure 12.15**   The Insert File dialog box

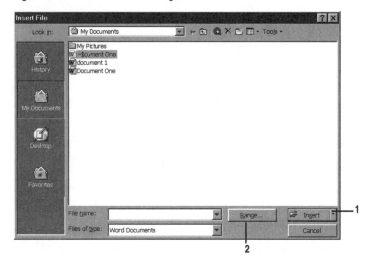

**Table 12.19**   Options in the Insert File dialog box

| # | Option | What you do with it |
|---|--------|---------------------|
| 1 | Insert button | Click to place the highlighted file in your document. You can link the file to its source file for easy updating. |
| 2 | Range button | Click to display the Set Range dialog box so that you can insert cells from a worksheet or a choose bookmark name. |

# Insert ➤ Object

Use this option to place items from other applications into your file or to create new items using another application. Inserting an object differs from inserting a file because you create the object with a source application instead of using an existing file. These items can be embedded in the document or linked to a source. (For more information, see Insert ➤ Object on page 89.)

 **TIP** This option is primarily for inserting file types that Word doesn't really know how to handle, such as native portable document format (PDF) or Paint Shop Pro (PSP) files. The Insert ➤ File option is primarily for file types that Word already knows about, such as Rich Text Format (RTF) or standard text files created in other applications. (For more information, see Insert ➤ File on page 188.)

## How You Get Here

✧ Press **Alt+I,O**          ✧ Choose **Insert ➤ Object**

# Insert ➤ Bookmark

Use this option to mark a location for future reference, very much like you insert a slip a paper to mark the spot in the book you're reading. The nice part is that you can have numerous bookmarks with a name you choose and you can create a cross-reference to the bookmark. (For more information, see Insert ➤ Cross-reference on page 181.)

 **TIP** To quickly jump to an existing bookmark, press **Ctrl+G or** choose **Edit ➤ Go to**. (For more information, see Edit ➤ Go To on page 144.)

## How You Get Here

✧ Press **Alt+I,K**          ✧ Choose **Insert ➤ Bookmark**

## What's In This Dialog Box

Figure 12.16 is a sample of this dialog box and Table 12.20 has a description of the options available.

**Figure 12.16**   The Bookmark dialog box

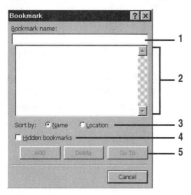

**Table 12.20**   Options in the Bookmark dialog box

| # | Option | What you do with it |
|---|--------|---------------------|
| 1 | Bookmark name text box | Enter the bookmark name for the location where you cursor is located. |
| 2 | Bookmark name list | View the bookmarks currently available in your document or choose an existing bookmark so you can delete it or jump to it. |
| 3 | Sort by area | Click to arrange the bookmark list sequentially by location in the file or alphabetically. Results are displayed in the Bookmark name list. |
| 4 | Hidden bookmarks check box | Click to display special hidden bookmarks that are created by Word, such as the ones for cross-references. |
| 5 | Go To button | Click to move to the location of the highlighted bookmark. |

# Insert ➤ Hyperlink

Use this option to create a connection between two parts of your file, between the active file and another file, or create a connection between the active file and a website address. Once you've inserted the hyperlink, the text changes color and is underlined and you can click on it to quickly jump to the destination specified. You can use the Web toolbar to work with the hyperlink and you can edit the information stored in the hyperlink after you've inserted it. (For more information, see View ➤ Toolbars ➤ Web on page 74 or  Insert ➤ Hyperlink on page 90.)

## How You Get Here

✧ Click       ✧ Press **Alt+I,I** or **Ctrl+K**      ✧ Choose **Insert ➤ Hyperlink**

# The Word Format Menu

## In this chapter

# What Is The Format Menu

This menu lists the commands that you'll use to change the "look" of your file. You can choose the typeface for your text (the typeface for this text is Century Old Style), define bullets or numbering, set tab markers, choose the spacing and alignment for your paragraph (or paragraph styles), and, in general, tweak the look of your file. Generally, any type of style you want to apply to the text can be set somewhere within this menu.

If a menu option has an ellipsis (three dots) or an arrow beside it, the application "asks" you for additional information before the action takes place. If the menu doesn't have one of these symbols, the action you choose happens immediately. If the action takes place immediately, you won't see a sample screen in this section.

---

**N O T E**   Most of the options for this menu are located on the Formatting toolbar for this application. ■

# The Formatting Toolbar

Use this option to quickly perform the formatting tasks in your file. The options described here are the default icons that appear on the toolbar. You can, however, customize this toolbar so that it has all the icons for the tasks you perform most frequently. If you want to apply other formatting options not appearing on this toolbar see the related topic in this chapter for more information.

## How You Get Here

✧ Press **Alt+V,T** choose **Formatting**    ✧ Choose **View ➤ Toolbars ➤ Formatting**

## What's In This Toolbar

Figure 13.1 is a sample of this toolbar and Table 13.1 has a description of the icons available.

**Figure 13.1**   The Formatting toolbar

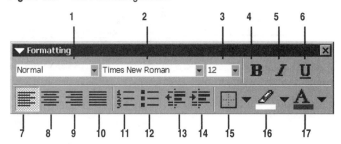

**Table 13.1**   Icons in the Formatting toolbar

| #  | Icon | What you do with it |
|----|------|---------------------|
| 1  | Style | Click to choose the style you want to apply. You can either select a paragraph style, which applies to the entire paragraph where the cursor is positioned or a character style, which only applies to the selected text. |
| 2  | Font | Click to choose the typeface you want to apply to the selected text. |
| 3  | Font Size | Click to choose the size you want to apply to the selected text. |
| 4  | Bold | Click to make the selected text darker than the standard font. |
| 5  | Italic | Click to make the selected text "lean" to the right. |
| 6  | Underline | Click to apply a line under the selected text. |
| 7  | Align Left | Click to align the text lines on the left side. |
| 8  | Center | Click to align the text lines around a center point. |
| 9  | Align Right | Click to align the text lines on the right side. |
| 10 | Justify | Click to align both the right and left sides of the text between the margins. |
| 11 | Numbering | Click to sequentially number the selected text. |
| 12 | Bullets | Click to apply bullets to the selected text. |
| 13 | Decrease Indent | Click to make the space between the text and the margins smaller. You can press **Shift+Tab** to decrease the indent. |
| 14 | Increase Indent | Click to make the space between the text and the margins larger. You can also press **Tab** to increase indents. |
| 15 | Outside Border | Click to display a drop-down menu different border styles. This menu also displays as a toolbar by clicking and dragging the menu bar off the Formatting toolbar. <br>(For more information, see Format ➤ Borders and Shading on page 202.) |
| 16 | Highlight | Click to apply a light colored background to the selected text. |
| 17 | Font Color | Click to apply a color to the selected text. |

# Formatting Keyboard Shortcuts

The following table lists many of the keyboard shortcuts you can use to quickly format selected text.

 **TIP**   If an effect has already been applied, you can press **Ctrl+Spacebar** to return the formatting to the default value set for the paragraph style.

To see a description of the formatting applied to your text, press **Shift+F1** and click on the text. Once you've looked at the description, press **Esc.**

**Table 13.2**   Keyboard shortcuts for formatting your text

| To do this | Press this |
| --- | --- |
| **Change Alignment** | |
| Left | **Ctrl+L** |
| Center | **Ctrl+E** |
| Justify | **Ctrl+J** |
| Right | **Ctrl+R** |
| **Apply font effects** | |
| Bold | **Ctrl+B** |
| Change the font size | **Ctrl+Shift+P**, then **Up or Down arrow** Press **Enter** when the right size displays |
| Change the typeface | **Ctrl+Shift+F**, then **Up or Down arrow** Press **Enter** when the right size displays |
| Double underline | **Ctrl+Shift+D** |
| Hidden text | **Ctrl+Shift+H** |
| Italics | **Ctrl+I** |
| Subscript | **Ctrl+=** |
| Superscript | **Ctrl+Shift+=** |
| Symbol font | **Ctrl+Shift+Q** |
| Underline | **Ctrl+U** |
| **Change case** | |
| Change case (cycle through uppercase, title case and lowercase) | **Shift+F3** |
| Small caps | **Ctrl+Shift+K** |
| Uppercase | **Ctrl+Shift+A** |
| **Increase/decrease font size** | |
| Decrease the font size in preset increments | **Ctrl+Shift+<** |
| Decrease the font size 1 point at a time | **Ctrl+[** |

**Table 13.2**   Keyboard shortcuts for formatting your text, continued

| To do this | Press this |
| --- | --- |
| Increase the font size in preset increments | **Ctrl+Shift+>** |
| Increase the font size 1 point at a time | **Ctrl+]** |
| **Change indents** | |
| Decrease the left indent | **Ctrl+Shift+M** |
| Hanging indent (indent all but the first line to a preset amount) | **Ctrl+T** |
| Increase the left indent (Move all lines of the paragraph in by a preset amount) | **Ctrl+M** |
| Indent only the first line | **Ctrl+M**, then **Ctrl+Shift+T** |
| Reduce hanging indent | **Ctrl+Shift+T** |
| **Change spacing** | |
| Add/remove one line space before the current paragraph | **Ctrl+0** |
| Double-space lines | **Ctrl+2** |
| 1.5-space lines | **Ctrl+5** |
| Single-space lines | **Ctrl+1** |

# Format ➤ Font

Use this option to define how you want your text to display and print, including the typeface, size and weight plus a variety of special effects such as superscript, subscript, and shadowing. You can also determine how close or far apart your characters are and whether characters are animated (have movement).

## How You Get Here

✧ Press **Alt+O,F** or **Ctrl+D**   ✧ Choose **Format ➤ Font**

## What's In This Dialog Box

Figure 13.2 is a sample of this dialog box and Table 13.3 has a description of the tabs available.

---

**N O T E**   The Preview area and the Default button appear on each tab in this window. You can view the options in the preview area before you apply them. If you want to apply the selected options to the default template (Normal.dot) click **Default**. Make sure you really want to do this before you click the **Yes** button. ■

**Figure 13.2**   The Font dialog box

**Table 13.3**   Tabs in the Font dialog box

| # | Tab name | What you do with it |
|---|----------|---------------------|
| 1 | Font | Choose the kind of typeface, size and other characteristics you need to make your document look the way you want.  (For a complete description of the options available, see Table 13.4 on page 197.) |
| 2 | Character Spacing | Choose the spacing between the characters in your text. For instance, whether you can expand the characters so they will have a distance of 1 point between them. (For a complete description of the options available, see Table 13.5 on page 197.) |
| 3 | Text Effects | Choose an item that determines the kind of special effect you want. This places an effect that moves around or on the selected text or object. For instance, the Black Marching Ants effect surrounds text with a crawling black dashed outline. |

The following tables describe the options for the individual tabs in this dialog box:

■   Table 13.4 describes the Font tab, and

■   Table 13.5 describes the Character Spacing tab.

**Table 13.4**   Options in the Font dialog box Font tab

| Option | What you do with it |
|---|---|
| Font list | Choose an item that determines the typeface you want. |
| Font style list | Choose an item that determines the way the font looks. |
| Size list | Choose or enter a point size for the font. |
| Font Color drop-down list | Choose an item that determines the color of the font. |
| Underline style drop-down list | Choose an item that determines the style of underline you want for the highlighted text. |
| Underline color drop-down list | Choose an item that determines the color for the underline. |
| Effects area check boxes | Choose an item that determines the effect you want to apply. |

**Table 13.5**   Options in the Font dialog box Character Spacing tab

| Option | What you do with it |
|---|---|
| Scale drop-down list | Choose an item that determines the scale for selected character(s). |
| Spacing drop-down list | Choose an item that determines whether character(s) display normally, expanded or condensed. |
| Spacing by: text box | Choose an item that determines how much you want to expand or condense your text. You can enter a specific amount or use the arrows to choose a preset amount. |
| Position drop-down list | Choose an item that determines where the character(s) are placed on a line. |
| Position by: text box | Choose an item that determines how high or low you want to place the characters on the line. You can enter a specific amount or use the arrows to choose a preset amount. |
| Kerning for fonts check box | Click to place the characters to fit properly together, based on the information stored in the specific font you've chosen. |
| Points and above text box | Choose an item that determines when the application applies the kerning rules stored in the font you've chosen. You can enter a specific amount or use the arrows to choose a preset amount. |

# Format ➤ Paragraph

Use this option to establish the parameters for the selected paragraph or paragraph style. Options include the alignment, the spacing between lines, the spacing around paragraphs, the indents, standard page breaks, how many lines must stay together, and whether the selected paragraph must stay with the next paragraph.

> **T I P**    If a value has already been applied, you can press **Ctrl+Q** to return the formatting to the default value set for the paragraph style.

## How You Get Here

✧ Press **Alt+O,P**          ✧ Choose **Format ➤ Paragraph**

## What's In This Dialog Box

Figure 13.3 is a sample of this dialog box and Table 13.6 has a description of the tabs available.

> **N O T E**    The Preview area and the Tabs button display on all tabs. View the paragraph with the options you have chosen in the Preview area. The Tabs button displays the Tabs window. See Format ➤ Tabs for more information. ■

**Figure 13.3**    The Paragraph dialog box

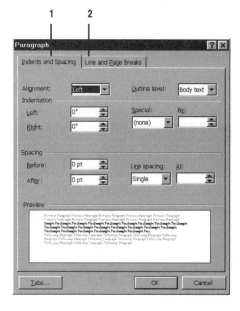

**Table 13.6**   Tabs in the Paragraph dialog box

| # | Tab name | What you do with it |
|---|----------|---------------------|
| 1 | Indents and Spacing | Choose an item that determines the spacing, alignment, and indentation for a paragraph or paragraph style. (For a complete description of the options available, see Table 13.7 on page 199.) |
| 2 | Line and Page Breaks | Choose an item that determines how Word breaks lines and paragraphs when it does pagination.  (For a complete description of the options available, see Table 13.8 on page 199.) |

The following tables describe the options for the individual tabs in this dialog box:

- Table 13.7 describes the Indents and Spacing tab, and
- Table 13.8 describes the Line and Page Breaks tab.

**Table 13.7**   Options in the Paragraph dialog box Indents and Spacing tab

| Option | What you do with it |
|--------|---------------------|
| Alignment drop-down list | Choose an item that determines where the paragraph lines up. For instance, you center the text between the margins. |
| Outline level drop-down list | Choose an item that determines what style of outline you want to apply to the selected text. (For more information, see View ➤ Outline on page 149 or The Outlining Toolbar on page 150.) |
| Indentation area | Choose an item that determines how far from the side of the page the paragraph is placed. |
| Spacing area | Choose an item that determines the amount of white space before and after a paragraph. You can also specify the amount of line spacing (space *between* the lines) for the paragraph. |

**Table 13.8**   Options in the Paragraph dialog box Line and Page Breaks tab

| Option | What you do with it |
|--------|---------------------|
| Pagination area | Choose an item that determines how you want the document to break between paragraphs. |
| Suppress line number check box | Click to prevent line numbering from appearing next to the selected paragraph(s). This option only applies if you've turned on the line numbering option. (For more information, see File ➤ Page Setup on page 128.) |
| Don't hyphenate check box | Click to prevent Word from breaking words in the selected paragraph(s). |

# Format ➤ Bullets and Numbering

Use this option to format a list of items in your document. You can choose different numbering styles and bullet characters to customize the look of your lists.

---

**N O T E**   You can choose this option *before* you start typing or you can type the list (making sure you press **Enter** after each line) and then apply the bullets or numbers.   ▓

## How You Get Here

✧ Click ▦ or ▦          ✧ Press **Alt+O,N**   ✧ Choose **Format ➤ Bullets and Numbering**

## What's In This Dialog Box

Figure 13.4 is a sample of this dialog box and Table 13.9 has a description of the tabs available.

---

**N O T E**   The Customize and Reset buttons display on each tab page. Click **Customize** to change how the bullets or numbers display. Click **Reset** to restore the default options.   ▓

**Figure 13.4**   The Bullets and Numbering dialog box

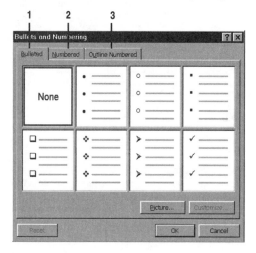

**Table 13.9**  Tabs in the Bullets and Numbering dialog box

| # | Tab name | What you do with it |
|---|----------|---------------------|
| 1 | Bulleted | Choose an item that determines what bullet character is used for the paragraph(s). (For a complete description of the options available, see Table 13.10 on page 201.) |
| 2 | Numbered | Choose an item that determines how your paragraph(s) are numbered. (For a complete description of the options available, see Table 13.11 on page 201.) |
| 3 | Outline Numbered | Choose an item that determines the outline style for your outline. (For a complete description of the options available, see Table 13.11 on page 201.) |

The following tables describe the options for the individual tabs in this dialog box:

■ Table 13.10 describes the Bulleted tab, and
■ Table 13.11 describes the Numbered tab and the Outline Numbered tab.

**Table 13.10**  Options in the Bullets and Numbering dialog box Bulleted tab

| Option | What you do with it |
|--------|---------------------|
| Bullet format buttons | Click to choose the desired type of bullet format. |
| Picture button | Click to display the Picture bullets window so that you can use a graphic element that is stored in another file as a bullet character for your list. You can also insert a bullet character that is animated. (For more information, see Insert ➤ Picture on page 186.) |

**Table 13.11**  Options in the Bullets and Numbering dialog box Numbered and Outline Numbered tabs

| Option | What you do with it |
|--------|---------------------|
| Restart Numbering radio button | Click to restart the numbering for the selected paragraph(s) at 1. For instance, if you have a alpha list you can start each list with the letter (a). |
| Continue previous list radio button | Click to start the numbering for the selected paragraphs(s) with the next consecutive letter or number. For instance, if your previous list ended with the number 5 the current list will start at 6. |

# Format ➤ Borders and Shading

Use this option to apply lines to paragraphs, table cells, or the page or add a tint to a paragraph or table cell. You can choose different styles of lines, different colors, or different line widths and apply them to any (or all) sides of the selected area. If you're building a Web page, you can import a line picture graphic using the Horizontal Lines button. If you want to see what the new formats will look like before you apply them, use the Preview area.

**TIP**   To quickly apply a border style use the Borders icon on the Formatting toolbar.

## How You Get Here

✧ Click       ✧ Press **Alt+O,B**           ✧ Choose **Format ➤ Borders and Shading**

## What's In This Dialog Box

Figure 13.5 is a sample of this dialog box and Table 13.12 has a description of the tabs available.

**NOTE**   The Preview area, Apply to drop-down list, Horizontal Line, and Show Toolbar buttons appear on each tab in this window. Use the Apply to drop-down list to determine what you are going to apply the borders to. Show Toolbar displays the Tables and Borders Toolbar. (For more information, see Table ➤ Draw Table on page 252.) The Options button is available on two of the tabs. Use it to display the Border and Shading Options window so you can define how much space you want between the text and the borders on all sides.

**Figure 13.5**   The Borders and Shading dialog box

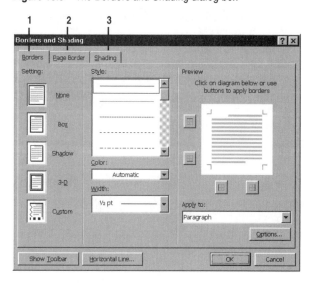

**Table 13.12**   Tabs in the Borders and Shading dialog box

| # | Tab name | What you do with it |
|---|----------|---------------------|
| 1 | Borders | Choose an item that determines how you want borders to appear around selected text. (For a complete description of the options available, see Table 13.13 on page 203.) |
| 2 | Page Border | Choose an item that determines how you want borders to appear around a page. (For a complete description of the options available, see Table 13.14 on page 203.) |
| 3 | Shading | Choose an item that determines the type and color of the shading you want to apply. (For a complete description of the options available, see Table 13.15 on page 204.) |

The following tables describe the options for the individual tabs in this dialog box:

■   Table 13.13 describes the Borders tab,

■   Table 13.14 describes the Page Border tab, and

■   Table 13.15 describes the Shading tab.

**Table 13.13**   Options in the Borders and Shading dialog box Borders tab

| Option | What you do with it |
|--------|---------------------|
| Setting area | Click to choose the type of preset format you want to apply to selected text or choose the Custom option to create a customized format. |
| Style list | Click to choose the look of the border. |
| Color drop-down list | Click to choose the color for the border. |
| Width drop-down list | Click to choose how wide your border will be. |

**Table 13.14**   Options in the Borders and Shading dialog box Page Border tab

| Option | What you do with it |
|--------|---------------------|
| Setting area | Click to choose the type of preset format you want to apply to the page or choose the Custom option to create a customized format. |
| Style list | Click to choose the look of the border. |
| Color drop-down list | Click to choose the color for the border. |
| Width drop-down list | Click to choose how wide your border will be. |
| Art drop-down list | Click to choose one of the preset graphics for your page border (if you've chosen the Custom option). |

**Table 13.15**   Options in the Borders and Shading dialog box Shading tab

| Option | What you do with it |
| --- | --- |
| Fill area | Click to choose the color you want to apply. |
| More colors button | Click to display the Colors window so that you can define custom colors for your shading. |
| Patterns area | Click to choose the style and color of the pattern for a shaded area. |

# Format ➤ Columns

Use this option to set the number and width of columns and the spacing between them.

**N O T E**   If you want to create columns for an entire document or a section, make sure you don't have any text selected when you choose this option. ■

## How You Get Here

✧ Press **Alt+O,C**          ✧ Choose **Format ➤ Columns**

## What's In This Dialog Box

Figure 13.6 is a sample of this dialog box and Table 13.16 has a description of the options available.

**Figure 13.6**   The Columns dialog box

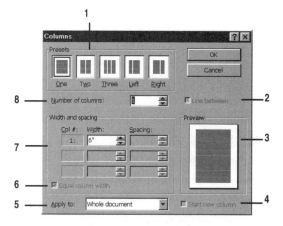

**Table 13.16**   Options in the Columns dialog box

| # | Option | What you do with it |
| --- | --- | --- |
| 1 | Presets area | Click to choose a preset number of columns. |
| 2 | Line between check box | Click to add a vertical line between each column. |

**Table 13.16**   Options in the Columns dialog box, continued

| # | Option | What you do with it |
|---|--------|---------------------|
| 3 | Preview area | View your settings before you apply them. |
| 4 | Start new column check box | Click to move text to the next column. This moves the text that follows the current cursor position. |
| 5 | Apply to drop-down list | Click to choose what area of the document should have columns. |
| 6 | Equal column width check box | Click to make all the columns the same width. |
| 7 | Width and Spacing area | Click to customize how wide you want the columns and how much space you want between them. |
| 8 | Number of columns list | Click to choose how many columns you want. You can enter a specific number of columns or use the arrows to choose a preset number. |

# Format ➤ Tabs

Use this option to set the location of the tabs for your paragraph (or paragraph style) and to set the alignment for the tab. You can also add leaders (characters that fill up the space between the end of the text and the tab marker) so that you can create a traditionally formatted index or table of contents (or even create signature lines for your document).

**N O T E**   You can set tabs "mathematically" by choosing the Format ➤ Tabs option or "visually" by using the ruler to move the tab markers where you need them. ▧

   To remove a tab "visually", make sure the ruler is displayed and drag the tab marker into the document.

## How You Get Here

✧ Press **Alt+O,T**          ✧ Choose **Format ➤ Tabs**

## What's In This Dialog Box

Figure 13.7 is a sample of this dialog box and Table 13.17 has a description of the options available.

**Figure 13.7**   The Tabs dialog box

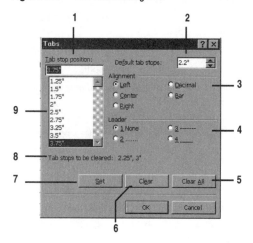

**Table 13.17**   Options in the Tabs dialog box

| # | Tab name | What you do with it |
|---|----------|---------------------|
| 1 | Tab stop position text box | Enter the number for where you want to place the tab stop. You can use any type of measurement for a tab stop (e.g., points, picas or inches). You can also select the value for an existing tab stop and change the value for it. |
| 2 | Default tab stops list | Choose an item that determines how frequently Word inserts a tab stop. |
| 3 | Alignment area | Choose an item that determines how you want the text to line up when you press the **Tab** key. |
| 4 | Leader area | Choose an item that determines what type of symbol/punctuation you want to precede the tab stop. |
| 5 | Clear All button | Click to remove all the tab stops in the tab list. |
| 6 | Clear button | Click to remove the selected tab stop from the tab list. You must select the tab stop from the tab list before you click this button. |
| 7 | Set button | Click to set a tab stop. You must click the OK button for the tab stops to be saved and applied in your document. |
| 8 | Tab stops to be cleared field | View the list of tab stops you have selected to be cleared. |
| 9 | Tab list | View the tab stops you have set. You can select tab stops from this list to be cleared or applied or to change its measurement. |

# Format ➤ Drop Cap

Use this option to make the first letter of a paragraph larger than the other characters. You can choose the typeface, specify the spacing between the drop cap and other text, and choose how many lines you want the letter to extend.

## How You Get Here

✧ Press **Alt+O,D**       ✧ Choose **Format ➤ Drop Cap**

## What's In This Dialog Box

Figure 13.8 is a sample of this dialog box and Table 13.18 has a description of the options available.

**Figure 13.8**   The Drop Cap dialog box

**Table 13.18**   Options in the Drop Cap dialog box

| # Option | What you do with it |
|---|---|
| 1 Position area | Click to choose how you want the drop cap positioned in the text. If you choose **None**, the options area isn't available. |
| 2 Font drop-down list | Click to choose the font for the drop cap. |
| 3 Lines to drop list | Click to choose how many lines the drop cap will extend down. |
| 4 Distance from text list | Click to choose the spacing you want between drop cap and the remaining text in the paragraph. |

# Format ➤ Text Direction

Use this option to rotate text in a table cell, text box, or frame. You can rotate text either right or left at a 90 degree angle.

## How You Get Here

✧ Press **Alt+O,X**       ✧ Choose **Format ➤ Text Direction**

### What's In This Dialog Box

Figure 13.9 is a sample of this dialog box and Table 13.19 has a description of the options available.

**Figure 13.9**   The Text Direction dialog box

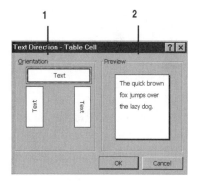

**Table 13.19**   Options in the Text Direction dialog box

| # | Option | What you do with it |
|---|--------|---------------------|
| 1 | Orientation area | Click to choose the direction for the text. |
| 2 | Preview area | View your settings before you apply them. |

# Format ➤ Change Case

Use this option to change the capitalization of the highlighted letters in your file.

### How You Get Here

✧ Press **Alt+O,E**          ✧ Choose **Format ➤ Change Case**

### What's In This Dialog Box

Figure 13.10 is a sample of this dialog box and Table 13.20 has a description of the options available.

**Figure 13.10**   The Change Case dialog box

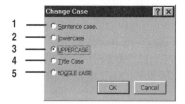

**Table 13.20**   Options in the Change Case dialog box

| # | Option | What you do with it |
|---|--------|---------------------|
| 1 | Sentence case radio button | Click to capitalize the first letter in the first word in a sentence. |
| 2 | lowercase radio button | Click to eliminate all capitalization in the selected text. |
| 3 | UPPERCASE radio button | Click to make *all* letters in the selected text capitalized. |
| 4 | Title Case radio button | Click to capitalize the first letter of each word in the selected text. |
| 5 | tOGGLE cASE radio button | Click to reverse the capitalization of each word in the selected text. If the text is currently capitalized, it switches to lowercase and vice versa. |

# Format ➤ Background

Use this option to set up the background color or pattern for online viewing or for a Web page. You can specify colors, gradients, patterns, and textures using this option. Graphic pictures can also be used for the background. Special effects are useful to make a web page look more professional. This option only displays the chosen background if you are in the Web layout view.

 **TIP**   If you don't specify a color you'll end up with the default color specified by your Web browser.

## How You Get Here

✧ Press **Alt+O,K**          ✧ Choose **Format ➤ Background**

## What's In This Flyout Menu

Figure 13.11 is a sample of this flyout menu.

**Figure 13.11**   The Format ➤ Background flyout menu

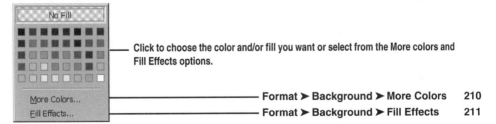

Click to choose the color and/or fill you want or select from the More colors and Fill Effects options.

Format ➤ Background ➤ More Colors      210
Format ➤ Background ➤ Fill Effects      211

## Format ➤ Background ➤ More Colors

Use this option to display the Colors window so that you can choose standard or customized colors for your document. In the Custom tab you can click the color chart to choose a color or you can enter a number for intensity, brightness, and the amount of red, green and blue in the color.

### How You Get Here

✧ Press **Alt+O,K,M**     ✧ Choose **Format ➤ Background ➤ More Colors**

### What's In This Dialog Box

Figure 13.12 is a sample of this dialog box and Table 13.21 has a description of the tabs available.

---

**N O T E**   Both tabs in the Colors window contain a Colors area and a New/Current preview area. Choose a color in the colors area; use the Preview area to look at samples of the new and current colors. ▪

**Figure 13.12**   The Colors dialog box

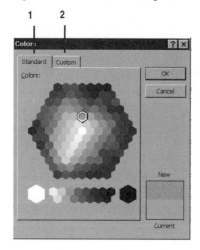

**Table 13.21**   Tabs in the Colors dialog box

| # | Tab name | What you do with it |
|---|----------|---------------------|
| 1 | Standard | Click to choose the desired color. |
| 2 | Custom | Click to create customized colors. (For a complete description of the options available, see Table 13.22 on page 211.) |

**Table 13.22**   Options in the Colors dialog box Custom tab

| Option | What you do with it |
|---|---|
| Slider arrow | Click to drag the arrow to adjust the luminosity of the selected color. |
| Hue list | Click to choose the actual color. |
| Sat list | Click to choose the intensity of the color. |
| Lum list | Click to choose the brightness of the color. |
| Red list | Click to adjust the amount of red in the selected color. |
| Green list | Click to adjust the amount of green in the selected color. |
| Blue list | Click to adjust the amount of blue in the selected color. |

## Format ➤ Background ➤ Fill Effects

Use this option to apply special effects to a highlighted object, such as textures, pictures, patterns, or gradients.

### How You Get Here

✧ Press **Alt+O,K,F**   ✧ Choose **Format ➤ Background ➤ Fill Effects**

### What's In This Dialog Box

Figure 13.13 is a sample of this dialog box and Table 13.23 has a description of the tabs available. The Sample area displays on all tab windows. You can preview the fill effects in this area.

**Figure 13.13**   The Fill Effects dialog box

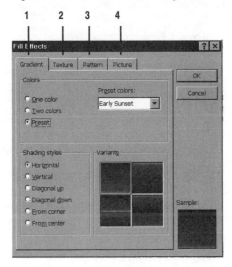

**Table 13.23**   Tabs in the Fill Effects dialog box

| # | Tab name | What you do with it |
|---|----------|---------------------|
| 1 | Gradient | Choose an item that determines the shading for the selected object. (For a complete description of the options available, see Table 13.24 on page 212.) |
| 2 | Texture | Choose an item that determines the look of the fill. You can choose marble or other effects for your background. (For a complete description of the options available, see Table 13.25 on page 212.) |
| 3 | Pattern | Choose an item that determines a preset look for the fill. You can specify foreground and background colors for the pattern. (For a complete description of the options available, see Table 13.26 on page 212.) |
| 4 | Picture | Choose a graphic to insert for the fill. The graphic will completely fill the object. (For a complete description of the options available, see Table 13.27 on page 213.) |

The following tables describe the options for the individual tabs in this dialog box:

- Table 13.24 describes the Gradient tab,
- Table 13.25 describes the Texture tab,
- Table 13.26 describes the Pattern tab, and
- Table 13.27 describes the Picture tab.

**Table 13.24**   Options in the Fill Effects dialog box Gradient tab

| Option | What you do with it |
|--------|---------------------|
| Colors area | Click to choose the colors. You can set different color combinations or use a preset color. |
| Shading styles area | Click to choose the direction for the colors to display. |
| Variants area | View the selected color scheme. |

**Table 13.25**   Options in the Fill Effects dialog box Texture tab

| Option | What you do with it |
|--------|---------------------|
| Texture area | Click to choose a preset texture. |
| Other Texture button | Click to display the Select Textures dialog box so that you can choose which picture you want to use for your textured background. |

**Table 13.26**   Options in the Fill Effects dialog box Pattern tab

| Option | What you do with it |
|--------|---------------------|
| Pattern area | Click to choose the desired pattern. |
| Foreground drop-down list | Click to choose a color for the pattern foreground. |
| Background drop-down list | Click to choose a color for the pattern background. |

**Table 13.27**  Options in the Fill Effects dialog box Picture tab

| Option | What you do with it |
| --- | --- |
| Picture area | View the selected picture. |
| Select Picture button | Click to display the Select Picture window so that you can choose a picture to insert as the background. |

# Format ➤ Theme

Use this option to set up the look of a document. This is different from a template because it uses color, fonts, and other graphic elements. It doesn't use the things you set in a template such as any macros or autotext entries. Themes are used to customize things like heading styles and bullets.

## How You Get Here

✧ Press **Alt+O,H**      ✧ Choose **Format ➤ Theme**

## What's In This Dialog Box

Figure 13.14 is a sample of this dialog box and Table 13.28 has a description of the options available.

**Figure 13.14**  The Theme dialog box

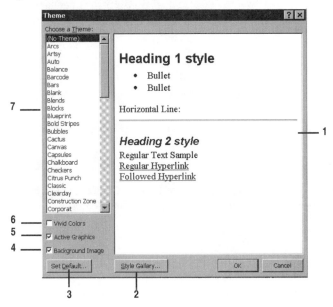

**Table 13.28** Options in the Theme dialog box

| # | Option | What you do with it |
|---|---|---|
| 1 | Theme preview area | View the theme before you apply it to your document. |
| 2 | Style Gallery button | Click to display the Style Gallery window, where you choose from an assortment of preset styles to apply your document. |
| 3 | Set Default button | Click to set or remove the default theme for your document. |
| 4 | Background Image check box | Click to apply a background to the theme. |
| 5 | Active Graphics check box | Click to animate graphics for a Web page. |
| 6 | Vivid Colors check box | Click to apply brighter colors to the theme. |
| 7 | Choose a Theme list | Click to choose from the list of themes. |

# Format ➤ Frames

Use this option to organize information once you've saved your document as a Web page. If you want to display several different pages of information in your Web page, use frames to create them. You can create frames for a Table of Contents, footers, and text on a page. Use the Frames toolbar to insert or delete frames or to define the properties for the selected frame. Once you create a frame the Format ➤ Frames flyout menu also displays the same options that are on the Frames toolbar. (For more information, see The Frames Toolbar on page 215 or File ➤ Save as Web Page on page 43.)

## How You Get Here

- ✧ Press **Alt+O,R**
- ✧ Choose **Format ➤ Frames**

## What's In This Flyout Menu

Figure 13.15 is a sample of this flyout menu.

**Figure 13.15** Format ➤ Frames flyout menu

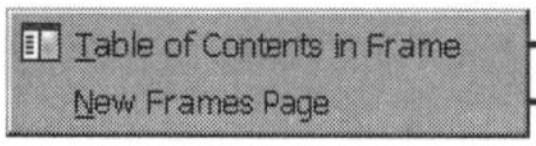


**Format ➤ Frames ➤ Table of Contents in Frame** 215
**Format ➤ Frames ➤ New Frames Page** 215

## Format ➤ Frames ➤ Table of Contents in Frame

Use this option to create a Table of Contents for your Web page. Word will ask you if you want to save your document as a frame page if you haven't already and after you click **OK**, the new frame displays on the left of the active window. This frame contains the headings from your document, which become active links that you can click to take you to that heading.

> **N O T E**  Make sure that you have defined all your headings before you choose this option. If you are missing a heading, you can update the Table of Contents. Right-click in the Table of Contents and choose the **Update field** option. ■

### How You Get Here

✧ Press **Alt+O,R,T**  ✧ Choose **Format ➤ Frames ➤ Table of Contents in Frame**

## Format ➤ Frames ➤ New Frames Page

Use this option to save your document as a frame for use in a Web page. Word automatically saves the document as a frame page and displays the Frames toolbar.

### How You Get Here

✧ Press **Alt+O,R,N**  ✧ Choose **Format ➤ Frames ➤ New Frames Page**

### The Frames Toolbar

Use this option to format the frames that you insert on your Web page.

### What's In This Toolbar

Figure 13.16 is a sample of this toolbar and Table 13.29 has a description of the icons available.

**Figure 13.16**   The Frames toolbar

**Table 13.29**   Icons in the Frames toolbar

| # | Icon | What you do with it |
|---|------|---------------------|
| 1 | Table of Contents in Frame | Click to add a frame containing the headings in your document. By clicking on a heading you can jump to the page in your document where that heading is located. |
| 2 | New Frame Left | Click to add a frame to the left of the selected frame. |
| 3 | New Frame Right | Click to add a frame to the right of the selected frame. |

**Table 13.29**    Icons in the Frames toolbar, continued

| # | Icon | What you do with it |
|---|------|---------------------|
| 4 | New Frame Above | Click to add a frame above the selected frame. |
| 5 | New Frame Below | Click to add a frame below the selected frame. |
| 6 | Delete Frame | Click to delete the selected frame. |
| 7 | Frame Properties | Click to display the Frame Properties window so that you can define the name, border size, and color of the frame. |

# Format ➤ AutoFormat

Use this option to have Word evaluate your document and automatically apply formatting to specific elements in the document.

---

**N O T E**    You may want to check the AutoCorrect AutoFormat tab for the preset changes you will be making. (For more information, see Tools ➤ AutoCorrect on page 96.)  ▨

---

    If you don't want to review your choices, press **Alt+Ctrl+K.**

## How You Get Here

✧ Press **Alt+O,A**              ✧ Choose **Format ➤ AutoFormat**

## What's In This Dialog Box

Figure 13.17 is a sample of this dialog box and Table 13.30 has a description of the options available.

**Figure 13.17**    The AutoFormat dialog box

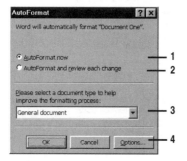

**Table 13.30**   Options in the AutoFormat dialog box

| # | Option | What you do with it |
|---|--------|---------------------|
| 1 | AutoFormat now radio button | Click to automatically format a document without prompting you to review each change. |
| 2 | AutoFormat and review each change radio button | Click to automatically format a document, but give you a chance to decide if you want to make the change. |
| 3 | Please select a document type drop-down list | Click to choose the type of document you want to use as a "model" for automatically formatting your document. |
| 4 | Options button | Click to display the AutoFormat tab of the AutoCorrect window. (For a complete description of the options available, see Table 14.20 on page 246.) |

# Format ➤ Style

Use this option to create or apply a predetermined set of formats to a paragraph or character. Styles help you consistently format your document—you make all the decisions about what a specific element (such as a heading or bulleted list) should look like *once*, then you store that definition in a style. When you're ready to format a specific element, you apply the style and off you go. Now everything can look consistent without you having to remember what you did the last time! You can define new styles, redefine Word's standard styles, or just use the styles that are stored with your template. You can also copy styles between documents.

## How You Get Here

✧ Press **Alt+O,S**          ✧ Choose **Format** ➤ **Style**

## What's In This Dialog Box

Figure 13.18 is a sample of this dialog box and Table 13.31 has a description of the options available.

**Figure 13.18**    The Style dialog box

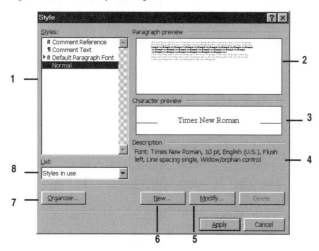

**Table 13.31**    Options in the Style dialog box

| # | Option | What you do with it |
|---|--------|---------------------|
| 1 | Styles list | Click to choose the paragraph or character style you want to apply or modify. The styles with a paragraph symbol are paragraph styles and the character styles have an **a** beside them. |
| 2 | Paragraph preview area | View what the current paragraph will look like if you apply the selected *paragraph style*. |
| 3 | Character preview area | View what the current text will look like if you apply the selected *character style*. |
| 4 | Description area | Lists the font, size of the characters, and other characteristics for the selected style. |
| 5 | Modify button | Click to change the characteristics of the selected style. This displays the Modify Style window where you choose the items you want to change. |
| 6 | New button | Click to add a customized style to your document. |
| 7 | Organizer button | Click to copy a style from another document or template into your active document. |
| 8 | List drop-down list | Click to choose the type of styles available to use. The defaults are All styles, Styles in use and User-defined. |

# Format ➤ AutoShape/Picture/Object/Text Box

Use this option to customize inserted graphics, shapes, or text boxes. The menu option displayed is specific to the action. For instance, if you highlight text, the menu option displays **Insert Textbox**.

**N O T E**   This menu option is active *only* if you have highlighted a graphic or text. (For more information, see Insert ➤ Picture on page 83.) ▪

## How You Get Here

✧ Press **Alt+O,F** or
   Press **Alt+O,I** or
   Press **Alt+O,O**

✧ Choose **Format ➤ AutoShape** or
   Choose **Format ➤ Picture** or
   Choose **Format ➤ Object** or
   Choose **Format ➤ Text Box** or
   Choose **Format ➤ Insert Text Box**

## What's In This Dialog Box

Figure 13.19 is a sample of this dialog box and Table 13.32 has a description of the tabs available.

**N O T E**   On the Web tab you enter a description of the selected text in the Alternative text area. This text displays while the Web page is loading. ▪

**Figure 13.19**   The Format AutoShape dialog box

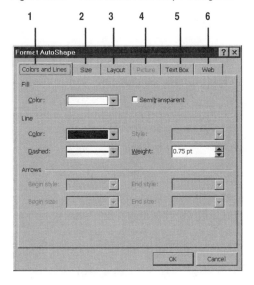

**Table 13.32**   Tabs in the Format AutoShape dialog box

| # | Tab name | What you do with it |
|---|----------|---------------------|
| 1 | Colors and Lines | Choose an item that determines how you want the colors and lines to display. (For a complete description of the options available, see Table 13.33 on page 220.) |
| 2 | Size | Choose an item that determines the width and height of the selected item. (For a complete description of the options available, see Table 13.34 on page 220.) |
| 3 | Layout | Choose an item that determines where you want the selected item in relation to the text of your document. (For a complete description of the options available, see Table 13.35 on page 221.) |
| 4 | Picture | Choose an item that determines how you will control the way a picture displays. (For a complete description of the options available, see Table 13.36 on page 221.) |
| 5 | Text Box | Choose an item that determines the spacing of the text from the edge of the frame. (For a complete description of the options available, see Table 13.37 on page 221.)<br><br>**Note**   This tab is available when you have either a text box or a callout highlighted. |
| 6 | Web | Choose an item that determines the text that will display while a graphic is loading on a web page. |

The following tables describe the options for the individual tabs in this dialog box:

- Table 13.33 describes the Colors and Lines tab,
- Table 13.34 describes the Size tab,
- Table 13.35 describes the Layout tab,
- Table 13.36 describes the Picture tab, and
- Table 13.37 describes the Text Box tab.

**Table 13.33**   Options in the Format AutoShape dialog box Colors and Lines tab

| Option | What you do with it |
|--------|---------------------|
| Fill area | Click to choose the color that fills the inside of a picture. |
| Lines area | Click to choose the color and type of line style for your document. |
| Arrows area | Click to choose the type of arrow style for your document. |

**Table 13.34**   Options in the Format AutoShape dialog box Size tab

| Option | What you do with it |
|--------|---------------------|
| Size and rotate area | Click to choose the width and height of the picture or text box. You can also rotate a picture by degrees. |
| Scale area | Click to size a picture by a percentage value of its original size. |

**Table 13.34**   Options in the Format AutoShape dialog box Size tab, continued

| Option | What you do with it |
| --- | --- |
| Original size area | View the height and width of the picture as it was originally created. |
| Reset button | Click to return the selected picture to its original size. |

**Table 13.35**   Options in the Format AutoShape dialog box Layout tab

| Option | What you do with it |
| --- | --- |
| Wrapping style area | Click to choose the way text will move around a picture. |
| Horizontal alignment area | Click to choose where the picture will set. |
| Advanced button | Click to choose from more specific layout options. |

**Table 13.36**   Options in the Format AutoShape dialog box Picture tab

| Option | What you do with it |
| --- | --- |
| Crop from area | Click to cut the picture size down to the desired size. |
| Image control area | Click to set the color and related settings for the picture. |
| Reset button | Click to change the settings to how they were originally. |

**Table 13.37**   Options in the Format AutoShape dialog box Text Box tab

| Option | What you do with it |
| --- | --- |
| Internal margin area | Click to define the margin size *inside* the highlighted text box. |
| Format Callout button | Click to change the style of the callout. |
| Convert to Frame button | Click to change the highlighted text box into a frame. |

# The Word Tools Menu

## In this chapter

# What Is The Tools Menu

This menu includes options that make using your application easier and more efficient. Some of the more popular tools include spellcheck, AutoCorrect, and macros. This menu also includes options for customizing your application, such as changing the default ("assumed") location for storing files or selecting whether you want the scroll bars to show on your screen.

If a menu option has an ellipsis (three dots) or an arrow beside it, the application "asks" you for additional information before the action takes place. If the menu doesn't have one of these symbols, the action you choose happens immediately. If the action takes place immediately, you won't see a sample screen in this section.

# Tools ➤ Spelling and Grammar

Use this option to display the Spelling and Grammar dialog box, which identifies words and grammatical structures not acceptable to the Word dictionary. Word displays the most complex dialog box of the three applications. One key difference is the addition of a grammar check, and the ability to customize it. A grammar check sounds fairly straightforward, but there are actually several different styles of grammar (casual, business, formal), and there may be times when you don't want any grammar style (when documenting any of Mark Twain's writings, or the poetry of e.e. cummings, for example). Word gives you the ability to customize which grammar elements to check for and which to ignore. You can establish several distinct styles; you only need to remember to apply the right one before you start the check.

**TIP** You should always visually proof read your document, because the grammar check may not accurately identify the error. For example, if instead of typing "from which" you type "form which," the grammar check identifies "which" as being the incorrect pronoun for "form," and suggests you replace "which" with "that."

## How You Get Here

✧ Click     ✧ Press **Alt+T,S** or **F7**    ✧ Choose **Tools ➤ Spelling and Grammar**

## What's Different

Figure 14.1 is a sample of this dialog box and Table 14.1 has a description of options that are unique to Word.

**Figure 14.1** The Spelling and Grammar dialog box

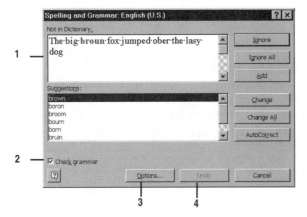

**Table 14.1** Options in the Spelling and Grammar dialog box

| # | Option | What you do with it |
|---|--------|---------------------|
| 1 | Grammatical flag area | View the text that Word considers "grammatically" incorrect. This description of this area changes to reflect each highlighted error. This text is replaced by "Not in Dictionary" when the grammar check box is unchecked (see below). |
| 2 | Check Grammar check box | Click to check the grammar in your document. |
| 3 | Options button | Click to display the Spelling and Grammar dialog box. This is where you set the parameters for how Word checks the spelling and grammar in your document. (For a complete description of the options available, see Table 14.28 on page 250.) |
| 4 | Undo button | Click to revert the last change made by the spelling and grammar function . |

# Tools ➤ Language

Use this option to display a flyout menu with three options: Set Language, Thesaurus, and Hyphenation. The language option lets you take advantage of the thesaurus, as well as establish guidelines for hyphenation, and determines which language is being used. The most commonly used of the three is the Thesaurus.

## How You Get Here

✧ Press **Alt+T,L**          ✧ Choose **Tools ➤ Language**

## What's In This Flyout Menu

Figure 14.2 is a sample of this flyout menu.

**Figure 14.2**    The Tools ➤ Language flyout menu

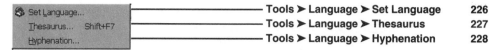

## Tools ➤ Language ➤ Set Language

Use this option to  determine which language is used for the spell check, when the document contains more than one language. When a document contains more than one language, foreign words and grammar may appear as errors. You must select the text containing the other language to mark it so the dictionary for that language is used to check the grammar and spelling.

---

**N O T E**    When setting a language to something other than the default language, Word may display a dialog box asking you to install the multi-language pack. Word does not load all dictionaries by default, in the interest of saving space on your hard drive. Insert your CD and install the desired language packs on your computer system.  ■

## How You Get Here

✧ Press **Alt+T,L,L**            ✧ Choose **Tools ➤ Language ➤ Set Language**

## What's In This Dialog Box

Figure 14.3 is a sample of this dialog box and Table 14.2 has a description of the options available.

**Figure 14.3**    The Language dialog box

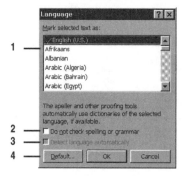

**Table 14.2** Options in the Language dialog box

| # | Option | What you do with it |
|---|--------|---------------------|
| 1 | Mark selected text as text box/listing | Click to choose only one of the listed languages. You cannot enter an unlisted language, and you cannot enter more than one language. |
| 2 | Do not check spelling or grammar check box | Click to ignore highlighted sections when doing a spellcheck or a grammar check. If no section is highlighted, this option applies to the entire document. |
| 3 | Detect Language automatically check box | Click to automatically check the document for more than one language and use the appropriate dictionary. |
| 4 | Default button | Click to change the default language for all language options. If you wish to change the default language, you may need to install the Office 2000 multi-language pack. |

## Tools ➤ Language ➤ Thesaurus

Use this option to display the Thesaurus dialog box so that you can search for a synonym or antonym. A thesaurus is helpful when you need to find a different way of saying the same thing, to avoid sounding repetitive.

**N O T E** You can either highlight a word or phrase, then open the thesaurus or you can open the thesaurus and type in a word or phrase. ▪

**T I P** Some words, like "hot" also produce an antonym. The antonym is always the last word in the Replace With list and has the word antonym in brackets next to the word. This is helpful when you can't think of the word you need, but you can think of acceptable opposites. For example, if you are trying to think of a word that doesn't mean "bold". The antonym "cowardly" comes up in the list. Not every word has antonyms.

## How You Get Here

❖ Press **Alt+T,L,T** or **Shift+F7**    ❖ Choose **Tools ➤ Language ➤ Thesaurus**

## What's In This Dialog Box

Figure 14.4 is a sample of this dialog box and Table 14.3 has a description of the options available.

**Figure 14.4**   The Thesaurus dialog box

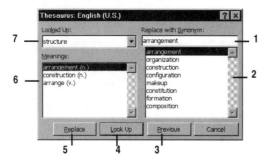

**Table 14.3**   Options in the Thesaurus dialog box

| # | Option | What you do with it |
|---|--------|---------------------|
| 1 | Replace with related word/ synonym text box | View the words you can choose from to replace the selected word. |
| 2 | Replace with related list | Click to choose the word to replace the original selected word. |
| 3 | Previous button | Click to display the last word you looked up, as well as the meanings and synonyms. |
| 4 | Look Up button | Click to begin the search for related words. |
| 5 | Replace button | Click to replace the selected word with the word in the Replace with text box. |
| 6 | Alphabetical/Meanings list | Click to choose the appropriate meaning for the word (i.e. "have" can either mean "need", or "possess"). |
| 7 | Looked up text box | View the selected word or phrase or the word or phrase you typed in the Replace text box. |

## Tools ➤ Language ➤ Hyphenation

Use this option to  display the Hyphenation dialog box, so you can choose how Word hyphenates your entire document. You can decide how many letters are required before Word inserts a hyphen and how many consecutive lines end in a hyphen. If you want to have the control over the hyphenation you can choose the manual settings. The options you select determine the smoothness of the right margin—the more hyphens you have, the more flush the right margin appears, and the less hyphens you have, the more ragged the right margin appears. For the best "look" and the most readability, don't let Word put more than two hyphens in a row.

## How You Get Here

✧ Press **Alt+T,L,H**          ✧ Choose **Tools** ➤ **Language** ➤ **Hyphenation**

## What's In This Dialog Box

Figure 14.5 is a sample of this dialog box and Table 14.4 has a description of the options available.

**Figure 14.5**   The Hyphenation dialog box

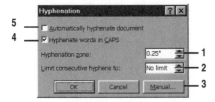

**Table 14.4**   Options in the Hyphenation dialog box

| # | Option | What you do with it |
|---|--------|---------------------|
| 1 | Hyphenation zone text box | Enter the length from the right margin that Word uses to determine where it should hyphenate your text. |
| 2 | Limit consecutive hyphens to: text box | Enter the maximum number of consecutive lines that can end with a hyphen. You can manually enter a number or select from the drop-down list by clicking on the arrow. |
| 3 | Manual button | Click to start a rehyphenating the document with the current hyphenation settings. |
| 4 | Hyphenate words in CAPS check box | Click to have Word include words in CAPS when hyphenating document. Most people leave this unchecked, because words in CAPS typically aren't hyphenated. |
| 5 | Automatically hyphenate document check box | Click to have Word hyphenate words as you type. |

# Tools ➤ Word Count

Use this option to have Word count the number of words in your active document. This option also counts characters, lines, paragraphs, and pages for you, which is helpful if you're writing papers with minimum/maximum word or page counts. By the way, Word counts all punctuation marks as characters and they're included in the character count.

 **TIP**   If you highlight text before using this option, Word only checks the highlighted text, not the entire document.

## How You Get Here

✧ Press **Alt+T,W**                    ✧ Choose **Tools** ➤ **Word Count**

## What's In This Dialog Box

Figure 14.6 is a sample of this dialog box. The only option available is the **Include footnotes and endnotes** check box. Choose this option if you want Word to check the body of the document as well as footnotes and endnotes.

**Figure 14.6**    The Word Count dialog box

# Tools ➤ AutoSummarize

Use this option to  create a document which pulls the main ideas of the text (as it appears to the Word editor) into a separate document or to place this text at the beginning or end of the document. Word uses style headings and grammar to pick out these main ideas, which may or may not accurately reflect the document's main theme, so be sure you review the review this summary before you save it.

---

**N O T E**    This feature works best when you've applied Word's heading styles (e.g., Heading 1, Heading 2). The first time you choose this option, Word may display a dialog box asking if you would like to install this feature so you might want to have your Office 2000 CDs available. ■

## How You Get Here

✧ Press **Alt+T,U**          ✧ Choose **Tools ➤ AutoSummarize**

## What's In This Dialog Box

Figure 14.7 is a sample of this dialog box and Table 14.5 has a description of the options available.

**Figure 14.7** The AutoSummarize dialog box

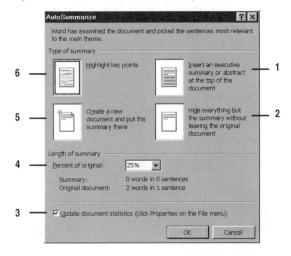

**Table 14.5** Options in the AutoSummarize dialog box

| # | Option | What you do with it |
|---|--------|---------------------|
| 1 | Insert an executive summary button | Click to place the summary at the top of the original document where it can be edited, but it isn't linked to the original document (edits don't affect the original document). |
| 2 | Hide everything but button | Click to display only the summary text and hide all of the other text. |
| 3 | Update document statistics check box | Click to automatically update the properties dialog box (**File ➤ Properties**) with the new keywords and summary highlighted in this dialog box. |
| 4 | Percent of original text box | Enter the maximum percentage of the original you want the summary to be. |
| 5 | Create a new document and put summary there button | Click to create a new document with only the summary text. This document can be edited, and is not linked to the original document (edits will not affect the original document). |
| 6 | Highlight key points button | Click to highlight key points in color, and fade other text into light gray. |

# Tools ➤ AutoCorrect

Use this option to display the AutoCorrect dialog box, where you can add text to correct or replace frequently (mis)typed words. For example, you can tell Word to replace "doucment" with "document" if you always mistype this word. AutoCorrect can also automatically replace certain abbreviated keystrokes with the extended version. For example, you can tell Word to automatically replace "AKA" with "also known as" each time you type those letters.

## How You Get Here

❖ Press **Alt+T,A**          ❖ Choose **Tools** ➤ **AutoCorrect**

## What's Different

Figure 14.8 is a sample of this dialog box and Table 14.6 has a description of the options in this tab. (For more information, see Tools ➤ AutoCorrect on page 96.)

**Figure 14.8**   The AutoCorrect dialog box

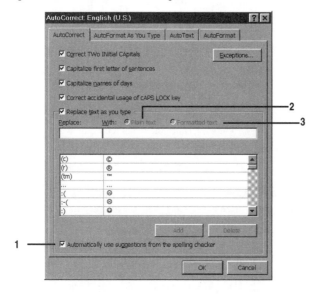

**Table 14.6**   Options in the AutoCorrect dialog box AutoCorrect tab

| # | Option | What you do with it |
|---|--------|---------------------|
| 1 | Automatically use suggestions check box | Click to use the spell checker's replacement suggestions automatically as you type. |
| 2 | Plain text radio button | Click to replace the selected text without formatting. |
| 3 | Formatted text radio button | Click to keep the formatting on the highlighted text. |

# Tools ➤ Track Changes

Use this option to display a flyout menu containing the three options: Highlight Changes, Accept or Reject Changes, and Compare Documents. This option lets you make changes to an original document and then see exactly where these changes were made (they appear in a different color of your choice), who made these changes and when (a yellow hover box indicates the computer profile name and date the changes were made. Several editors can work on the same document, with each editor having a different profile, each represented with a different color text. This is helpful when you're editing a co-workers report. Your co-worker can see exactly what you've done and accept or reject your edits as appropriate.

 **TIP**    You must choose this option *before* you start making changes or the changes aren't marked.

## How You Get Here

✧ Press **Alt+T,T**          ✧ Choose **Tools ➤ Track Changes**

## What's In This Flyout Menu

Figure 14.9 is a sample of this flyout menu.

**Figure 14.9**    The Tools ➤ Track Changes flyout menu

## Tools ➤ Track Changes ➤ Highlight Changes

Use this option to specify where changes are going to be highlighted. You can choose to highlight changes on the screen, in the printed document or in both places. When changes are highlighted you can also choose the color and style of the highlight. For instance, you may want to place a double underline beneath the text and make the text red for easy visibility.

**N O T E**   You need a color printer to print tracked changes. ■

## How You Get Here

✧ Press **Alt+T,T,H**          ✧ Choose **Tools ➤ Track Changes ➤ Highlight Changes**

## What's In This Dialog Box

Figure 14.10 is a sample of this dialog box and Table 14.7 has a description of the options available.

**Figure 14.10**   The Highlight Changes dialog box

**Table 14.7**   Options in the Highlight Changes dialog box

| # | Option | What you do with it |
|---|--------|---------------------|
| 1 | Track changes while editing check box | Click to mark changes by reviewer name while editing the document. |
| 2 | Highlight changes on screen check box | Click to see the changes highlighted on the screen as you review the document. |
| 3 | Highlight changes in print check box | Click to have changes highlighted on the printed document (you must have more than one color option on your printer). |
| 4 | Options button | Click to display the Options dialog box, where you can customize the color and presentation of the highlighted changes. (For a complete description of the options available, see Table 14.22 on page 248.) |

## Tools ➤ Track Changes ➤ Accept or Reject Changes

Use this option to search an edited document for changes and review each one to accept or reject it in the revised document. This process converts edited text into "real" text, which no longer appears highlighted.

### How You Get Here

✧ Press **Alt+T,T,A**      ✧ Choose **Tools ➤ Track Changes ➤ Accept or Reject Changes**

## What's In This Dialog Box

Figure 14.11 is a sample of this dialog box and Table 14.8 has a description of the options available.

**Figure 14.11**   The Accept or Reject Changes dialog box

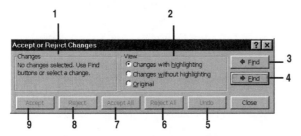

**Table 14.8**   Options in the Accept or Reject Changes dialog box

| # | Option | What you do with it |
|---|--------|---------------------|
| 1 | Changes area | View to the changes made to the original document. |
| 2 | View area | Choose an item that determines what you'll see in the changed document.<br>■ Choose **Changes with highlighting** to view the changed document with your changes highlighted.<br>■ Choose **Changes without highlighting** to see what the document will look like if you accept all the changes made.<br>■ Choose **Original** to see what the document will look like if you *don't* accept the changes you made. |
| 3 | Find previous button | Click to review the last tracked change. |
| 4 | Find next button | Click to review the next tracked change. |
| 5 | Undo button | Click to undo the action on the previous tracked change. |
| 6 | Reject All button | Click to *reject* all tracked changes in the document, revert to the original document and remove all highlighting from the document. |
| 7 | Accept All button | Click to *accept* all tracked changes in the document and remove all highlighting from the document. |
| 8 | Reject button | Click to reject the tracked change, and revert to original text (highlighting is removed). |
| 9 | Accept button | Click to accept the selected change and remove the highlighting. |

### Tools ➤ Track Changes ➤ Compare Documents

Use this option to compare two different documents and see what changes were made. From this dialog box, you select a file to open (the original document), then compare it to the current document. This is helpful when you are not certain whether or not the editing is beneficial and you want to look at both documents so you can decide what you want to do.

### How You Get Here

✧ Press **Alt+T,T,C**            ✧ Choose **Tools ➤ Track Changes ➤ Compare Documents**

## Tools ➤ Merge Documents

Use this option to merge the tracked changes from the active document into a document selected from the Select File to Merge dialog box. (Use this option when you want to keep a copy of the original—just in case.) You can make changes to a *copy* of the original, review the changes and accept or reject them, *then* merge the changes into the original document.

---

 **NOTE**    If you're going to make your changes to a copy, make sure that the copy you're working from wasn't created using the Windows ➤ New Window option. That option creates a duplicate window, not a duplicate document. Which means that changes you make or track in the new window are actually made or tracked in the original. You should create a second document using File ➤ Save As, as described in Figure 3.3 on page 43. ■

### How You Get Here

✧ Press **Alt+T,D**            ✧ Choose **Tools ➤ Merge Documents**

## Tools ➤ Protect/Unprotect Document

Use this option to password-protect your document and keep unauthorized users from making changes to it. When you protect a document you, or authorized users, must use a password to access the document and choose **Unprotect Document** before you can make any changes. This is helpful when you have several people sharing a computer, sharing a file, or working together on a particular project, and you want to be sure that only authorized folks can make changes.

### How You Get Here

✧ Press **Alt+T,P**            ■    Choose **Tools ➤ Protect Document/Unprotect Document**

## What's In This Dialog Box

Figure 14.12 is a sample of this dialog box and Table 14.9 has a description of the options available.

**Figure 14.12**   The Protect Document dialog box

**Table 14.9**   Options in the Protect Document dialog box

| # | Option | What you do with it |
|---|--------|---------------------|
| 1 | Tracked changes radio button | Select to protect the tracked changes from being altered or rejected by unauthorized users. |
| 2 | Comments radio button | Select to protect comments from being changed by unauthorized users. Unauthorized users may still add their own comments. |
| 3 | Forms radio button | Select to protect text, except those in form fields or unprotected sections, from being changed by unauthorized users. |
| 4 | Password text box | Enter a password assigned to authorized users. Only those entering the correct password can enable or disabled protections. |
| 5 | Sections button | Click to open the Sections dialog box, where you can select the specific sections you want to protect (or unprotect). You can only use this option if your document is broken up into sections using the **Insert ➤ Break ➤ Section** option. |

# Tools ➤ Online Collaboration

Use this option to conduct a conversation online, similar to making a multiple-party telephone call. You will be collaborating with other people on one file at the same time. Those people who are participating will be able to edit and chat using the server that you specify. As host you will control the meeting, setting up who and how participants will interact during the meeting. In order for someone to join a meeting they all must have access to the same Internet or intranet (an inter-office network) and have Microsoft NetMeeting installed on their computer or network. However, they don't have to have the application you are working from to chat with you or edit your file online. This option works with your default email server and accesses your address book there. (For more information, see What Is The Outlook Mail Application on page 647.)

---

> **N O T E**    This can be pretty complex, especially if you are having a Web discussion. You must first set up a server, then open the presentation you want to have the discussion about, then give the command. Most people would rather email the presentation around for comments rather than have a "live" discussion/collaboration about it. ▪

## How You Get Here

✧ Press **Alt+T,N**        ✧ Choose **Tools** ➤ **Online Collaboration**

# Tools ➤ Mail Merge

Use this option to create form letters, mailing labels, and other documents that accepts merged text. The dialog box provides a step-by-step (1, 2, 3) approach to creating these documents. This feature is helpful for those who need to create a few form letters but don't have a separate program to do this task.

## How You Get Here

✧ Press **Alt+T,R**        ✧ Choose **Tools** ➤ **Mail Merge**

## What's In This Dialog Box

Figure 14.13 is a sample of this dialog box and Table 14.10 has a description of the options available.

**Figure 14.13**    The Mail Merge Helper dialog box

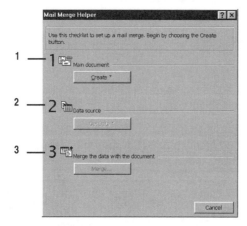

**Table 14.10**   Options in the Mail Merge Helper dialog box

| # | Option | What you do with it |
|---|--------|---------------------|
| 1 | Create button | Click to display a drop-down list from which you select the type of document you wish to create. |
| 2 | Get Data button | Click to create a new data source or select an existing data source (such as an address database created in Access). |
| 3 | Merge button | Click to run the merge. |

# Tools ➤ Envelopes and Labels

Use this option to create envelopes and labels with return and delivery addresses and take much of the guesswork out of sizing and positioning addresses correctly.

## How You Get Here

✧ Click 🖾    ✧ Press **Alt+T,E**    ✧ Choose **Tools ➤ Envelopes and Labels**

## What's In This Dialog Box

Figure 14.14 is a sample of this dialog box and Table 14.11 has a description of the tabs available.

**Figure 14.14**   The Envelopes and Labels dialog box

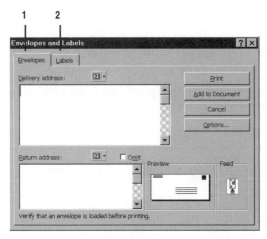

**Table 14.11** Tabs in the Envelopes and Labels dialog box

| # Option | What you do with it |
| --- | --- |
| 1 Envelopes | Determine return and delivery address, envelope orientation for printer, etc. (For a complete description of the options available, see Table 14.12 on page 240.) |
| 2 Labels | Choose an item that determines the addresses you want to print on the labels. (For a complete description of the options available, see Table 14.13 on page 240.) |

The following tables describe the options for the individual tabs in this dialog box:

- Table 14.12 describes the Envelopes tab, and
- Table 14.13 describes the Labels tab.

**Table 14.12** Options in the Envelopes and Labels dialog box Envelopes tab

| Option | What you do with it |
| --- | --- |
| Delivery address list | Enter the address to print on the envelopes. |
| Address book icon | Click to choose the address from your address book. |
| Add to Document button | Click to add the address to the top of your document so it will print when you print your document. |
| Options button | Choose an item that determines the settings for printing your envelopes. |
| Return address list | Enter the return address to print on the envelopes. |
| Omit check box | Click to omit a return address on the envelope. |
| Preview area | View the envelope with the settings for the addresses. |
| Feed preview area | View the direction you have set for the envelopes to feed into your printer. Double-click this area to set the feed direction. |

**Table 14.13** Options in the Envelopes and Labels dialog box Labels tab

| Option | What you do with it |
| --- | --- |
| Label address list | Enter the address to print on the labels. |
| Address book icon | Click to choose the address from your address book. |
| Use return address check box | Click to print the only the return address on the labels. |
| New Document button | Click to create a new document with the formats you have specified for the label type. |
| Options button | Choose an item that determines the settings for printing your envelopes. |
| Delivery point barcode check box | Click to print a barcode on the label. This is the code the US Postal service uses to aid in delivery. |
| Print area | Choose an item that determines how many labels you want to print. |
| Label area | View the type of label you chose to print on. Double-click this area to change the type of label. |

# Tools ➤ Letter Wizard

Use this option to use the Letter Wizard to take a lot of the guesswork out of creating letters. This option helps you when you don't have a lot of time to format a formal letter document, but need to produce one quickly. This option will access your address book in Outlook. (For more information, see Tools ➤ Address Book on page 628.)

---

**N O T E**    You can't access the Letter Wizard if your cursor is currently placed inside a table. Make sure your cursor is in standard text before you open the Letter Wizard. ▦

## How You Get Here

✧ Press **Alt+T,Z**              ✧ Choose **Tools** ➤ **Letter Wizard**

## What's In This Dialog Box

Figure 14.15 is a sample of this dialog box and Table 14.14 has a description of the tabs available.

**Figure 14.15**    The Letter Wizard dialog box

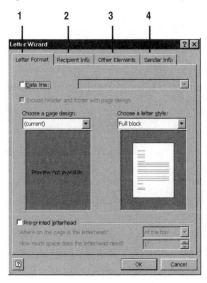

**Table 14.14**   Tabs in the Letter Wizard dialog box

| # | Tab name | What you do with it |
|---|----------|---------------------|
| 1 | Letter Format | Choose an item that determines the placement of the date, page design, letter style, and a pre-printed letterhead. (For a complete description of the options available, see Table 14.15 on page 242.) |
| 2 | Recipient Info tab | Enter the recipient's name, address, and salutation. You may select the name and address from your address book, if it is available. (For a complete description of the options available, see Table 14.16 on page 243.) |
| 3 | Other Elements tab | Enter special instructions regarding a reference line, mailing instructions, attention and subject lines, as well as Cc addressees. (For a complete description of the options available, see Table 14.17 on page 243.) |
| 4 | Sender Info tab | Enter the sender's name, address, and closing. You may select the name and address from your address book, if it is available. (For a complete description of the options available, see Table 14.18 on page 243.) |

The following tables describe the options for the individual tabs in this dialog box:

- Table 14.15 describes the Letter Format tab,
- Table 14.16 describes the Recipient Info tab,
- Table 14.17 describes the Other Elements tab, and
- Table 14.18 describes the Sender Info tab.

**Table 14.15**   Options in the Letter Wizard dialog box Letter Format tab

| Option | What you do with it |
|--------|---------------------|
| Date line check box | Click to include the date in your letter. You should format the date if you have chosen to include the date. |
| Date format drop-down list | Choose an item that determines the format for the date in your letter. |
| Include header and footer check box | Click to place a header and footer with the page design you have chosen. |
| Choose a page design drop-down list and Preview area | Choose an item that determines what kind of page template you want to use for the type of letter you are writing. |
| Choose a letter style drop-down list and Preview area | Choose an item that determines how you want the text of your letter to look like and view the sample. |
| Pre-printed letterhead check box | Click to choose to use your own pre-printed paper letterhead. |
| Where on the page? drop-down list | Choose an item that determines where your pre-printed letterhead will be printed. |
| How much space? list | Click to choose the amount of space your pre-printed letterhead will need when it prints. |

**Table 14.16**   Options in the Letter Wizard dialog box Recipient Info tab

| Option | What you do with it |
| --- | --- |
| Address book icon | Click to choose the recipient's name from your address book. |
| Recipient's name list | Enter or choose the recipient's name from the list. |
| Delivery address area | Enter the address. |
| Salutation area | Choose an item that determines the type of greeting style you are using in your letter. |

**Table 14.17**   Options in the Letter Wizard dialog box Other Elements tab

| Option | What you do with it |
| --- | --- |
| Include area | Choose an item that determines other elements you want to place in your letter. You can choose more elements from the drop-down lists. |
| Courtesy copies area | Enter the address of those you want to send copies to or choose them from your address book. |

**Table 14.18**   Options in the Letter Wizard dialog box Sender Info tab

| Option | What you do with it |
| --- | --- |
| Address book icon | Click to choose an address from your address book. |
| Sender's name list | Enter the sender's name. |
| Return address area | Enter the sender's return address. |
| Omit check box | Click to use a pre-printed return address and not print one. |
| Closing area | Choose an item that determines the types and styles of closing information you want to include in your letter. |
| Preview area | View the sender's closing information. |

# Tools ➤ Macro

Use this option to run Macros, a preset series of keyboard strokes and mouse clicks used to perform frequently performed steps, such as inserting a return address and today's date on a letter. (For more information, see Tools ➤ Macro on page 101.)

## How You Get Here

✦ Press **Alt+T,M**         ✦ Choose **Tools** ➤ **Macro**

# Tools ➤ Templates and Add-Ins

Use this option to apply or add a template (a predetermined set of defaults for fonts, styles, macros, auto text, and auto correct features) to a document. You can choose one of the standard templates shipped with Word or you can create a custom template of your own. (For more information, see File ➤ New on page 122.)

## How You Get Here

❖ Press **Alt+T,I**          ❖ Choose **Tools** ➤ **Templates and Add-Ins**

## What's Different

Figure 14.16 is a sample of this dialog box and Table 14.19 has a description of options that are unique to Word. (For more information, see Tools ➤ Add-Ins on page 106.)

**Figure 14.16**   The Templates and Add-ins dialog box

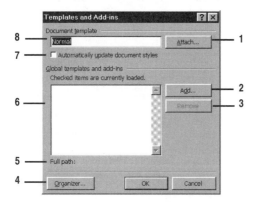

**Table 14.19**   Options in the Templates and Add-ins dialog box

| # | Option | What you do with it |
|---|--------|---------------------|
| 1 | Attach button | Click to attach the highlighted template to the active document. |
| 2 | Add button | Click to add checked items in the Global Template listing to the global template. The checked items will automatically be applied to the global template each time you open a document. |
| 3 | Remove button | Click to remove checked items in the Global Template listing from the global template. The checked items will automatically be removed from the global template each time you open a document. Uncheck the item to remove it from the Word template but leave it on the list. Some default items cannot be unchecked. |
| 4 | Organizer button | Click to open the Organizer dialog box, where you can copy and attach templates and add-ins into other files and documents. |
| 5 | Full Path field | View the location for the highlighted template or add-in. |

**Table 14.19**   Options in the Templates and Add-ins dialog box, continued

| # | Option | What you do with it |
|---|--------|---------------------|
| 6 | Global templates and add-ins listing | View whether listed items are currently attached (checked) or unattached (unchecked). |
| 7 | Automatically update check box | Click to have the template styles automatically attached and updated each time you open the document. |
| 8 | Document template text box | View the template currently attached to the document. To attach another template, enter the template and click the Attach button. |

# Tools ➤ Customize

Use this option to display the Customize window, where you can customize toolbars, keyboard shortcuts, and menu commands. Customizing allows you to create new tools, shortcuts, and commands, and modify existing ones to better suit your individual needs. For example, you may want to create a tool to execute a frequently used option that is usually only available using a menu option. (For more information, see View ➤ Toolbars ➤ Customize on page 76.)

## How You Get Here

◇ Press **Alt+T,C**          ◇ Choose **Tools ➤ Customize**

# Tools ➤ Options

Use this option to modify many elements, such as screen appearance, printing, spelling, etc. This feature is helpful for those who don't mind getting under the hood of the computer, tweaking a few elements, all in the interest of style and efficiency.

---

**N O T E**   These tabs let you customize the settings for the features and are not another method for applying them. ▮

## How You Get Here

◇ Press **Alt+T,O**          ◇ Choose **Tools ➤ Options**

## What's In This Dialog Box

Figure 14.17 is a sample of this dialog box and Table 14.20 has a description of the tabs available.

**Figure 14.17** The Options dialog box

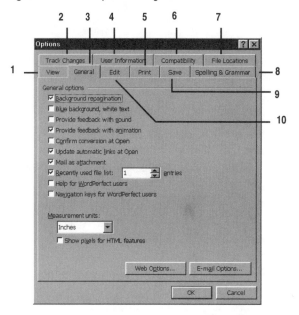

**Table 14.20** Tabs in the Options dialog box

| # | Tab name | What you do with it |
|---|----------|---------------------|
| 1 | View | Click to select technical elements related to the visual display of the screen, such as scroll bars, formatting marks, and print options. (For a complete description of the options available, see Table 14.21 on page 248.) |
| 2 | Track Changes | Click to select technical elements related to tracking changes. (For more information, see Tools ➤ Track Changes on page 233.) (For a complete description of the options available, see Table 14.22 on page 248.) |
| 3 | General | Click to select technical elements related to the layout of the screen, such as background page breaks, measurement units (centimeters or inches), Web options, and email options. (For a complete description of the options available, see Table 14.23 on page 248.) |
| 4 | User Information | Click to enter a user profile name that appears in the yellow hover box when you're tracking changes. (For a complete description of the options available, see Table 14.24 on page 249.) |
| 5 | Print | Click to select technical elements related to printing, such as background printing, reverse print order (last page prints first), printing hidden text, and the default tray. (For a complete description of the options available, see Table 14.25 on page 249.) |

**Table 14.20**   Tabs in the Options dialog box, continued

| # | Tab name | What you do with it |
|---|----------|---------------------|
| 6 | Compatibility | Click to select replacements when certain features, such as some fonts or styles, are not available due to the (in)compatibility to Office 2000 with the operating system you are using. (For a complete description of the options available, see Table 14.26 on page 249.) |
| 7 | File Locations | Click to determine the default file folder location that new files will be saved in if no specific folder is designated. (For a complete description of the options available, see Table 14.27 on page 249.) |
| 8 | Spelling & Grammar | Click to select technical elements related to spelling and grammar. (For more information, see Tools ➤ Spelling and Grammar on page 224.) (For a complete description of the options available, see Table 14.28 on page 250.) |
| 9 | Edit | Click to select technical elements related to editing, such as over striking or inserting options, the default paragraph style, the picture editor, and click and type. (For a complete description of the options available, see Table 14.29 on page 250.) |
| 10 | Save | Click to select technical elements related to saving, such as setting the Auto recovery time (how often it automatically saves a document), passwords, and automatically creating a backup copy. (For a complete description of the options available, see Table 14.30 on page 250.) |

The following tables describe the options for the individual tabs in this dialog box:

- Table 14.21 describes the View tab,
- Table 14.22 describes the Track Changes tab,
- Table 14.23 describes the General tab,
- Table 14.24 describes the User Information tab,
- Table 14.25 describes the Print tab,
- Table 14.26 describes the Compatibility tab,
- Table 14.27 describes the File Locations tab,
- Table 14.28 describes the Spelling & Grammar tab,
- Table 14.29 describes the Edit tab, and
- Table 14.30 describes the Save tab.

**Table 14.21**    Options in the Options dialog box View tab

| Option | What you do with it |
| --- | --- |
| Show area | Choose an item that determines what you want shown as you work. |
| Formatting marks area | Choose an item that determines what formatting markings you want to see as you work. |
| Print and Web layout options area | Choose an item that determines what printing and web layout tools you want displayed onscreen. |
| Outline and Normal options area | Choose an item that determines what part of the Word window displayed onscreen. |

**Table 14.22**    Options in the Options dialog box Track Changes tab

| Option | What you do with it |
| --- | --- |
| Inserted text area | Choose an item that determines the type of mark, color, and view a sample of the new text. |
| Deleted text area | Choose an item that determines the type of mark, color, and view a sample of the deleted mark. |
| Changed formatting area | Choose an item that determines the type of mark, color, and view a sample of the formatting changes. |
| Changed lines area | Choose an item that determines the type of mark, color, and view a sample of the change bars. |

**Table 14.23**    Options in the Options dialog box General tab

| Option | What you do with it |
| --- | --- |
| General options area | Choose an item that determines what options you want to set for Word. |
| Measurement units drop-down list | Click to choose the type of measurement you want to use. |
| Show pixels for HTML features check box | Click to change the measurement default to pixels. |
| Web Options button | Click to set how your document looks and acts when viewed by a Web browser. |
| E-mail Options button | Click to set the email options for sending email from Word. You can set up your signature, choose stationary, and fonts for the messages you send. |

**Table 14.24**  Options in the Options dialog box User Information tab

| Option | What you do with it |
| --- | --- |
| Name text box | Enter your name. This name will appear in letters, memos, and comments. |
| Initials text box | Enter your initials. These are used for comments, letters, and memos. |
| Mailing address text box | Enter your mailing address. This is your default return address for all letters and envelopes. |

**Table 14.25**  Options in the Options dialog box Print tab

| Option | What you do with it |
| --- | --- |
| Printing options area | Choose an item that determines how to print your document. |
| Include with document area | Choose an item that determines what elements are included when you print your document. |
| Options for current document only area | Click to print any online form data for the current document. |
| Default tray drop-down list | Click to choose the tray used to print your document. |

**Table 14.26**  Options in the Options dialog box Compatibility tab

| Option | What you do with it |
| --- | --- |
| Font Substitution button | Click to choose the font type you want used when a document is using one you don't have on your system. |
| Recommended options for drop-down list | Click to choose the application you want to set display options for or choose custom to set your own. |
| Options list | Click to choose the display options for the current document. This is not a permanent change. |

**Table 14.27**  Options in the Options dialog box File Locations tab

| Option | What you do with it |
| --- | --- |
| File types/Location list | Click to choose a file type and set the location where these files are stored. You can double-click a type or choose the **Modify** button to change the location. |
| Modify button | Click to change the location for the selected file type. |

**Table 14.28**    Options in the Options dialog box Spelling and Grammar tab

| Option | What you do with it |
| --- | --- |
| Spelling area | Choose an item that determines the controls for the spell checking option. |
| Custom dictionary drop-down list | Click to choose the dictionary you want to use when running the spell checker. |
| Dictionaries button | Click to display the dictionaries you have installed. You can add, edit, or remove dictionaries. |
| Grammar area | Choose an item that determines the settings used when grammar is being checked. |
| Recheck Document button | Click to run the spell check again. |
| Writing style drop-down list | Click to choose the style you are using when writing your document. |
| Settings button | Click to change the writing style settings. |

**Table 14.29**    Options in the Options dialog box Edit tab

| Option | What you do with it |
| --- | --- |
| Editing options area | Choose an item that determines the type of editing you want to use. |
| Enable click and type check box | Click to set the automatic formatting options you use as you are typing. |
| Default paragraph style drop-down list | Click to choose the style used as a default when you are typing in your document. |

**Table 14.30**    Options in the Options dialog box Save tab

| Option | What you do with it |
| --- | --- |
| Save options area | Click to choose the options to use when you are saving your documents. |
| File Sharing options area | Click to set the passwords for opening and modifying the current document. |
| Read-only recommended check box | Click to display a recommendation for those who open the document to accept it as a read-only document. If the document is opened without accepting this option it will need to be saved with a different name. |

# The Word Table Menu

## In this chapter

# What Is The Table Menu

This menu lists the commands that you'll use create, edit, and format your tables—those wonderful containers for information that needs to line up about properly across your page. This menu also lists the commands for converting information from a table back to text or text to a table and sorting information in a table based on the information stored in a specific column. You can create very simple tables that help you line up information without having to create a bunch of tab markers or you can create very complex tables that have unique borders and shading to emphasize certain aspects of the table.

If a menu option has an ellipsis (three dots) or an arrow beside it, the application "asks" you for additional information before the action takes place. If the menu doesn't have one of these symbols, the action you choose happens immediately. If the action takes place immediately, you won't see a sample screen in this section.

# Table ➤ Draw Table

Use this option to draw a table in your document like you would draw one using a pencil and paper. The cursor changes to a pencil and Word automatically opens the Table and Borders toolbar. Once you draw the outside parameters of the table, you can draw in columns and rows, change the line style or color, and add shading. (For more information, see The Tables and Borders Toolbar on page 252.)

## How You Get Here

✧ Click     ✧ Press **Alt+A,W**    ✧ Choose **Table ➤ Draw Table**

# The Tables and Borders Toolbar

Use this option to display the Tables and Borders toolbar so that you can draw and format a table for your document. When you use the options on this toolbar, you must continue using the draw option to format the table. If you're tired of drawing things one at a time, you can use any of the other options in the Table menu or Format menu to get things done more quickly for larger areas of a table. This toolbar has the most commonly used tools needed to create, edit, and format your tables. You can add more options to the toolbar if you find yourself wishing that you could just do "x" without having to use the menu bar. (For more information, see View ➤ Toolbars ➤ Customize on page 76.)

**TIP**    When you're done drawing your table, click the Draw Table icon  to change your cursor back to the standard cursor so you can work with other options in Word .

## What's In This Toolbar

Figure 15.1 is a sample of this toolbar and Table 15.1 has a description of the icons available.

**Figure 15.1**   The Tables and Borders toolbar

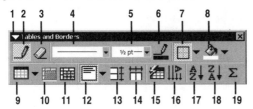

 **T I P**   You can either use the options on this toolbar to format your tables or choose one of the options from the Format menu. If you want to change quite a few options for the table (such as the line style *and* the line weight *and* the border color *and* the shading options), choose **Format ➤ Borders and Shading**. (For more information, see Format ➤ Borders and Shading on page 202.)

**Table 15.1**   Options in the Tables and Borders toolbar

| # | Option | What you do with it |
|---|--------|---------------------|
| 1 | More Buttons button | Click to display the Add or Remove Buttons menu so that you can customize this toolbar to include those buttons you use most often. |
| 2 | Draw Table button | Click to draw an entire table, including the outside dimensions and the appropriate number of rows and columns. If you don't want to draw your table, choose **Table ➤ Insert Table.** (For more information, see Table ➤ Insert ➤ Table on page 255.) |
| 3 | Eraser button | Click to change the pointer to an eraser icon so that you can get rid of a column or row. |
| 4 | Line Style drop-down list | Choose an item that determines what type of lines are used when you draw the border around the table and when you draw the columns and rows in the table. |
| 5 | Line Weight drop-down list | Choose an item that determines how thick the line is when you draw the external and internal borders for your table. |
| 6 | Border Color (Auto) button | Choose an item that determines what color is applied when you draw the external and internal borders for your table. |
| 7 | Outside Border button | Choose an item that determines which sides of your table have a border. |
| 8 | Shading Color button | Choose an item that determines what color is used to fill your rows and columns. |
| 9 | Insert Table button | Click to display the Insert Table dialog box so that you can enter a specific number of columns and rows for your table instead of drawing them one at a time. (For more information, see Table ➤ Insert ➤ Table on page 255.) |
| 10 | Merge Cells button | Click to combine the contents of two or more cells, columns, or rows into one unit. |

**Table 15.1**   Options in the Tables and Borders toolbar, continued

| # | Option | What you do with it |
|---|--------|---------------------|
| 11 | Split Cells button | Click to divide the highlighted cell(s) into multiple rows or columns. |
| 12 | Align button | Choose an item that determines how the contents of the highlighted cells line up between the cell margins. |
| 13 | Distribute Rows Evenly button | Click to make two or more rows the same height. |
| 14 | Distribute Columns Evenly button | Click to change the width of two or more columns so that they're the same width. |
| 15 | Table AutoFormat button | Click to  display the Table AutoFormat dialog box so that you can use one of the predefined formats to format the borders and shading for the highlighted table. (For more information, see Table ➤ Table AutoFormat on page 262.) |
| 16 | Change Text Direction button | Click to change the direction of the text in the highlighted cells. You can rotate text either right or left at a 90 degree angle. |
| 17 | Sort Ascending button | Click to arrange the contents of the highlighted cells starting with the lowest value in the first cell to the highest value in the last cell. |
| 18 | Sort Descending button | Click to arrange the contents of the highlighted cells starting with the highest value in the first cell to the lowest value in the last cell. |
| 19 | AutoSum button | Click to automatically calculate the total of the numbers in a row or column. Word inserts the total in the cell where your cursor was positioned when you chose this option. |

# Table ➤ Insert

Use this option to add a new table to your document or to add columns and rows to an existing table.

## How You Get Here

✦ Click ▦        ✦ Press **Alt+A,I**        ✦ Choose **Ta̲ble ➤ I̲nsert**

## What's In This Flyout Menu

Figure 15.2 is a sample of this flyout menu.

**Figure 15.2**   The Table ➤ Insert flyout menu

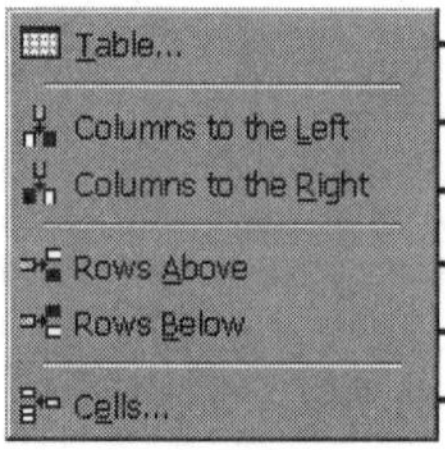

## Table ➤ Insert ➤ Table

Use this option to insert a new table at the current cursor position. This option is similar to the Table ➤ Draw table option; however, with this option you can decide how many rows and columns and the width of the columns *before* you insert the table. You can also choose a predefined format that automatically formats the borders and shading. (For more information, see Table ➤ Table AutoFormat on page 262.)

### How You Get Here

✧ Click      ✧ Press **Alt+A,I,T**     ✧ Choose **Ta̲ble ➤ I̲nsert ➤ T̲able**

### What's In This Dialog Box

Figure 15.3 is a sample of this dialog box and Table 15.2 has a description of the options available.

**Figure 15.3**   The Insert Table dialog box

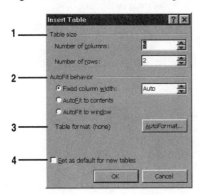

**Table 15.2**   Options in the Insert Table dialog box

| # | Option | What you do with it |
|---|--------|---------------------|
| 1 | Table size area | Enter or choose the number of columns and rows that you want to create when you insert the table. You're not stuck with these values forever—you can always add and delete rows or columns later. |
| 2 | AutoFit behavior area | Choose an item that determines how wide the columns will be when you insert the table.<br>■ Enter a value in the **Fixed column width** text box to create columns that are a specific width.<br>■ Click the **AutoFit contents** radio button to create column widths that are based on the longest line of text in the column.<br>■ Click the **AutoFit window** radio button to force the table to fit the width of the currently displayed window if you're creating a table in a document that will be viewed as a Web page. |

**Table 15.2**    Options in the Insert Table dialog box, continued

| # | Option | What you do with it |
|---|--------|---------------------|
| 3 | Table format/AutoFormat button | Click to display a list of predefined formats that you can use to format the look of your table. (For more information, see Table ➤ Table AutoFormat on page 262.) |
| 4 | Set as default for new tables check box | Click to use the current options as the default for any new tables you insert in your document. |

## Table ➤ Insert ➤ Columns to the Left

Use this option to insert a blank column to the left of the column where the cursor is currently positioned.

### How You Get Here

✧ Press **Alt+A,I,L**            ✧ Choose **Table ➤ Insert ➤ Columns to the Left**

## Table ➤ Insert ➤ Columns to the Right

Use this option to insert a blank column to the *right* of the column where the cursor is currently positioned.

### How You Get Here

✧ Press **Alt+A,I,R**            ✧ Choose **Table ➤ Insert ➤ Columns to the Right**

## Table ➤ Insert ➤ Rows Above

Use this option to insert a blank row *above* the row where the cursor is currently positioned.

### How You Get Here

✧ Press **Alt+A,I,A**            ✧ Choose **Table ➤ Insert ➤ Rows Above**

## Table ➤ Insert ➤ Rows Below

Use this option to insert a blank row *below* the row where the cursor is currently positioned.

### How You Get Here

✧ Press **Alt+A,I,B**            ✧ Choose **Table ➤ Insert ➤ Rows Below**

## Table ➤ Insert ➤ Cells

Use this option to insert blank cells into an existing table.

---

**N O T E**   You must position your cursor in a table for these options to be available. Make sure you get your cursor in the *right* position before using any of these options since Word has its own method for deciding where to put the new cells. ▨

### How You Get Here

✧ Press **Alt+A,I,E**          ✧ Choose **Table ➤ Insert ➤ Cells**

### What's In This Dialog Box

Figure 15.4 is a sample of this dialog box and Table 15.3 has a description of the options available.

**Figure 15.4**   The Insert Cells dialog box

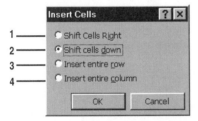

**Table 15.3**   Options in the Insert Cells dialog box

| # | Option | What you do with it |
|---|--------|---------------------|
| 1 | Shift Cells Right radio button | Click to move the existing cells to the *right* after you insert the new cells. |
| 2 | Shift cells down radio button | Click to move the existing cells *down* after you insert the new cells. |
| 3 | Insert entire row radio button | Click to insert a blank row *above* the current cursor position. |
| 4 | Insert entire column radio button | Click to insert a blank column to the *left* of the current cursor position. |

# Table ➤ Delete

Use this option to get rid of an entire table or specific rows, columns or cells within a table.

---

**N O T E**    You must position your cursor in a table for these options to be available.    ■

## How You Get Here

✧ Press **Alt+A,D**          ✧ Choose **Table ➤ Delete**

## What's In This Flyout Menu

Figure 15.5 is a sample of this flyout menu.

**Figure 15.5**    The Table ➤ Delete flyout menu

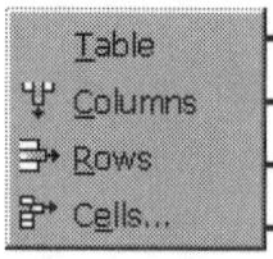

| | |
|---|---|
| ━━━━━ Table ➤ Delete ➤ Table | 258 |
| ━━━━━ Table ➤ Delete ➤ Columns | 258 |
| ━━━━━ Table ➤ Delete ➤ Rows | 258 |
| ━━━━━ Table ➤ Delete ➤ Cells | 259 |

## Table ➤ Delete ➤ Table

Use this option to get rid of the entire table where the cursor is currently positioned.

### How You Get Here

✧ Press **Alt+A,D,T**          ✧ Choose **Table ➤ Delete ➤ Table**

## Table ➤ Delete ➤ Columns

Use this option to get rid of the column where the cursor is currently positioned.

### How You Get Here

✧ Press **Alt+A,D,C**          ✧ Choose **Table ➤ Delete ➤ Columns**

## Table ➤ Delete ➤ Rows

Use this option to get rid of the row where the cursor is currently positioned.

### How You Get Here

✧ Press **Alt+A,D,R**          ✧ Choose **Table ➤ Delete ➤ Rows**

## Table ➤ Delete ➤ Cells

Use this option to get rid of the highlighted cells and decide what happens to the remaining cells or columns after the cells are deleted.

### How You Get Here

✧ Press **Alt+A,D,E**

✧ Choose **Table ➤ Delete ➤ Cells**

### What's In This Dialog Box

Figure 15.6 is a sample of this dialog box and Table 15.4 has a description of the options available.

**Figure 15.6**   The Delete Cells dialog box

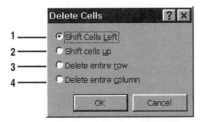

**Table 15.4**   Options in the Delete Cells dialog box

| # | Option | What you do with it |
|---|--------|---------------------|
| 1 | Shift Cells Left radio button | Click to move the existing cells to the *left* after you delete the highlighted cells. |
| 2 | Shift cells up radio button | Click to move the existing cells *up* after you delete the highlighted cells. |
| 3 | Delete entire row radio button | Click to delete the entire row where the cursor is currently positioned. |
| 4 | Delete entire column radio button | Click to delete the entire column where the cursor is currently positioned. |

# Table ➤ Select

Use this option to highlight specific portions of your table so that you can work with it—this can be a lot easier than dragging that darned mouse over what you need (at least for me, I never seem to get the right amount on the first try!). Once you've got the right amount highlighted, you can apply formatting changes or do whatever else you need to do.

### How You Get Here

✧ Press **Alt+A,C**

✧ Choose **Table ➤ Select**

## What's In This Flyout Menu

Figure 15.7 is a sample of this flyout menu.

**Figure 15.7**   The Table ➤ Select flyout menu

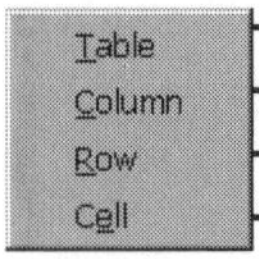

| | |
|---|---|
| Table ➤ Select ➤ Table | 260 |
| Table ➤ Select ➤ Column | 260 |
| Table ➤ Select ➤ Row | 260 |
| Table ➤ Select ➤ Cell | 260 |

## Table ➤ Select ➤ Table

Use this option to highlight the entire table. Changes made to the formatting apply to the entire table.

### How You Get Here

✧ Press **Alt+A,C,T**          ✧ Choose **Table ➤ Select ➤ Table**

## Table ➤ Select ➤ Column

Use this option to highlight the column where the cursor is currently positioned. Changes made to the formatting apply to the entire column.

### How You Get Here

✧ Press **Alt+A,C,C**          ✧ Choose **Table ➤ Select ➤ Column**

## Table ➤ Select ➤ Row

Use this option to highlight the row where the cursor is currently positioned. Changes made to the formatting apply to the entire row.

### How You Get Here

✧ Press **Alt+A,C,R**          ✧ Choose **Table ➤ Select ➤ Row**

## Table ➤ Select ➤ Cell

Use this option to highlight the cell where the cursor is currently positioned. Changes made to the formatting apply to the cell (not just the cell contents).

### How You Get Here

✧ Press **Alt+A,C,E**          ✧ Choose **Table ➤ Select ➤ Cell**

# Table ➤ Merge Cells

Use this option to combine the contents of two or more cells, columns, or rows into one unit.

## How You Get Here

✧ Click     ✧ Press **Alt+A,M**    ✧ Choose **Table ➤ Merge Cells**

**N O T E**   This option is only available when more than one cell is highlighted. ▨

# Table ➤ Split Cells

Use this option to divide the highlighted cells into multiple rows or columns.

## How You Get Here

✧ Click    ✧ Press **Alt+A,P**    ✧ Choose **Table ➤ Split Cells**

## What's In This Dialog Box

Figure 15.8 is a sample of this dialog box and Table 15.5 has a description of the options available.

**Figure 15.8**   The Split Cells dialog box

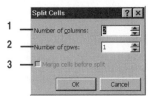

**Table 15.5**   Options in the Split Cells dialog box

| # | Option | What you do with it |
|---|--------|---------------------|
| 1 | Number of columns text box | Enter or choose how many columns you want to divide the highlighted cells into. |
| 2 | Number of rows text box | Enter or choose how many rows you want to divide the highlighted cells into. |
| 3 | Merge cells before split check box | Click to to combine the highlighted cells and then apply the settings in this dialog box to them. Don't turn on this option if you want to individually apply the settings to the highlighted cells. |

# Table ➤ Split Table

Use this option to divide one table into two tables or to add text before a table.

> **TIP** To divide the table, click in the row that will become the first row of the second table. To insert text before a table, click in the first row of the table.

## How You Get Here

❖ Press **Alt+A,T**          ❖ Choose **Table ➤ Split Table**

# Table ➤ Table AutoFormat

Use this option to have Word automatically apply a professionally designed format to the table where the cursor is positioned. You can choose which elements you want to apply or have Word apply all the formats in one pass. This option can save a lot of time and energy when you want to produce professional looking tables.

## How You Get Here

❖ Click       ❖ Press **Alt+A,F**          ❖ Choose **Table ➤ Table AutoFormat**

## What's In This Dialog Box

Figure 15.9 is a sample of this dialog box and Table 15.6 has a description of the options available.

**Figure 15.9**    The Table AutoFormat dialog box

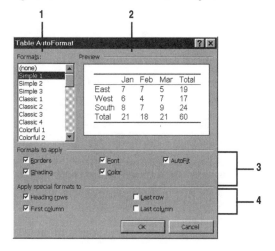

**Table 15.6**   Options in the Table AutoFormat dialog box

| # | Option | What you do with it |
|---|--------|---------------------|
| 1 | Formats list | Choose an item that determines which format is applied to the table where the cursor is positioned. |
| 2 | Preview area | View the highlighted format before you apply it to the table where the cursor is positioned. |
| 3 | Apply special formats to check boxes | Click to choose which rows are included or excluded when you apply the format highlighted in the Formats list. |
| 4 | Formats to apply radio button | Click to choose which formats you want to include or exclude when you apply the format highlighted in the Formats list. |

# Table ➤ AutoFit

Use this option to change the column widths in an existing table.

**N O T E**   You can also choose these options when you're creating a new table.  ▪

## How You Get Here

✧ Press **Alt+A,A**          ✧ Choose **Table ➤ AutoFit**

## What's In This Flyout Menu

Figure 15.10 is a sample of this flyout menu.

**Figure 15.10**   The Table ➤ AutoFit flyout menu

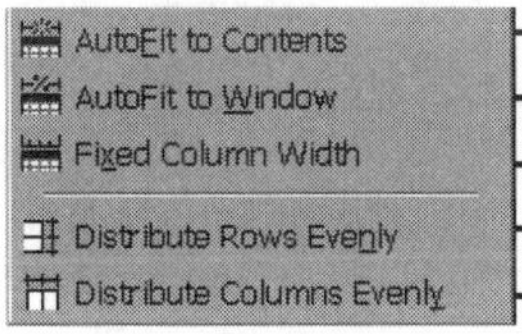

## Table ➤ AutoFit ➤ AutoFit to Contents

Use this option to change the column width based on the length of the longest line in the column where your cursor is positioned (or columns if you want to resize more than one column).

## How You Get Here

✧ Press **Alt+A,A,F**          ✧ Choose **Table ➤ AutoFit ➤ AutoFit to Contents**

### Table ➤ AutoFit ➤ AutoFit to Window

Use this option to automatically resize the highlighted table to fit within the width of the window when you're viewing the document in Web Layout view or if you're viewing the document in a Web browser.

### How You Get Here

❖ Press **Alt+A,A,W**          ❖ Choose **Table ➤ AutoFit ➤ AutoFit to Window**

### Table ➤ AutoFit ➤ Fixed Column Width

Use this option to set all columns to a specific fixed width.

### How You Get Here

❖ Press **Alt+A,A,X**          ❖ Choose **Table ➤ AutoFit ➤ Fixed Column Width**

### Table ➤ AutoFit ➤ Distribute Rows Evenly

Use this option to change the height of two or more rows so that they're the same height.

### How You Get Here

❖ Click [icon]     ❖ Press **Alt+A,A,N**     ❖ Choose **Table ➤ AutoFit ➤ Distribute Rows Evenly**

### Table ➤ AutoFit ➤ Distribute Columns Evenly

Use this option to change the width of two or more columns so that they're the same width.

### How You Get Here

❖ Click [icon]     ❖ Press **Alt+A,A,Y**     ❖ Choose **Table ➤ AutoFit ➤ Distribute Columns Evenly**

## Table ➤ Heading Rows Repeat

Use this option to automatically insert the text of the first row in the table (the column headings) at the top of the table if it spans more than one page.

---

**N O T E**   You can only apply this option to the *first row* in a table. ▪

### How You Get Here

❖ Press **Alt+A,H**          ❖ Choose **Table ➤ Heading Rows Repeat**

# Table ➤ Convert

Use this option to change existing text to a table or to change an existing table to standard, everyday text.

## How You Get Here

✧ Press **Alt+A,V**          ✧ Choose **Table ➤ Convert**

## What's In This Flyout Menu

Figure 15.11 is a sample of this flyout menu.

**Figure 15.11**  The Table ➤ Convert flyout menu

| | |
|---|---|
| Te_xt to Table... | Table ➤ Convert ➤ Text to Table    265 |
| Ta_ble to Text... | Table ➤ Convert ➤ Table to Text    266 |

## Table ➤ Convert ➤ Text to Table

Use this option to display the Text to Table dialog box so that you can convert the highlighted text to a table.

## How You Get Here

✧ Press **Alt+A,V,X**          ✧ Choose **Table ➤ Convert ➤ Text to Table**

## What's In This Dialog Box

Figure 15.12 is a sample of this dialog box and Table 15.7 has a description of the options available.

**Figure 15.12**  The Convert Text to Table dialog box

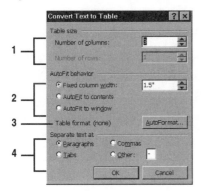

**Table 15.7**    Options in the Convert Text to Table dialog box

| # | Option | What you do with it |
|---|--------|---------------------|
| 1 | Table size area | Enter or choose the number of columns and rows that will be created in the new table. |
| 2 | AutoFit behavior area | Choose an item that determines how wide the columns will be in the new table. If you want all the columns to be a specific width, enter or choose a number in the Fixed column width text box. If you want Word to size the columns based on the width of the longest line in each column, click the **AutoFit contents** radio button. |
| 3 | AutoFormat button | Click to  display the Table AutoFormat dialog box so that you can use one of the predefined formats to format the borders and shading for the new table. (For more information, see Table ➤ Table AutoFormat on page 262.) |
| 4 | Separate text at radio buttons | Choose an item that determines what character Word uses to create the columns for your new table. |
|   |  | **Note**    Try not to click the **Commas** radio button for everyday text since we often use commas in our sentences. This option is typically used with text that comes in from another source, such as a database or spreadsheet. |

## Table ➤ Convert ➤ Table to Text

Use this option to change a table into standard, everyday text (text that isn't stored in neat little cells).

## How You Get Here

✧ Press **Alt+A,V,B**            ✧ Choose **Ta̲ble ➤ Conv̲ert ➤ Ta̲ble to Text**

## What's In This Dialog Box

Figure 15.13 is a sample of this dialog box and Table 15.8 has a description of the options available.

**Figure 15.13**    The Convert Table To Text dialog box

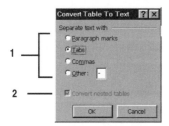

**Table 15.8**   Options in the Convert Table To Text dialog box

| # | Option | What you do with it |
|---|--------|---------------------|
| 1 | Separate text with area | Choose an item that determines what character Word uses to replace the column boundaries. |
| 2 | Convert nested tables check box | Click to convert a table that is stored within another table (a "nested" table) to text. |

# Table ➤ Sort

Use this option to automatically organize the information in the highlighted columns in either ascending (smallest value to largest value) or descending (largest value to smallest value) order.

## How You Get Here

❖ Click [🔼] 　　❖ Press **Alt+A,S** 　　❖ Choose **Table ➤ Sort**

## What's In This Dialog Box

Figure 15.14 is a sample of this dialog box and Table 15.9 has a description of the options available.

**Figure 15.14** ➤ The Sort dialog box

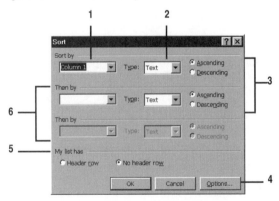

**Table 15.9**   Options in the Sort dialog box

| # | Option | What you do with it |
|---|--------|---------------------|
| 1 | Sort by drop-down list | Enter or choose which column you want to use to sort the information. |
| 2 | Type | Choose an item that determines which sort method you want to use when you sort the information in the columns. |
| 3 | Ascending/Descending radio buttons | Choose an item that determines whether the information in the column chosen in the Sort by drop-down list is sorted starting with the smallest value first (ascending order) or the largest value first (descending order). |

**Table 15.9**    Options in the Sort dialog box

| # | Option | What you do with it |
|---|--------|---------------------|
| 4 | Options button | Click to display the Sort Options dialog box so that you can include additional sorting parameters for your information. |
| 5 | My list has areas | Choose an item that determines whether Word evaluates the information in the first row (header row) when it performs the sort function. Click the **Header Row** radio button it you want Word to *exclude* the first row when it sorts the information. |
| 6 | Then by area | Fill in the information for this area if you also want to sort the information using another column (or columns). You can define up to three sorting rules at one time. |

# Table ➤ Formula

Use this option to use predefined functions to perform mathematical calculations for cells that have numbers in them. There quite a few functions available, but we haven't described every one of them in this book.

## How You Get Here

✧ Press **Alt+A,0**          ✧ Choose **Table ➤ Formula**

## What's In This Dialog Box

Figure 15.15 is a sample of this dialog box and Table 15.10 has a description of the options available.

**Figure 15.15**    The Formula dialog box

**Table 15.10**    Options in the Formula dialog box

| # | Option | What you do with it |
|---|--------|---------------------|
| 1 | Formula text box | Enter the formula you want to use and enter the range of cells you want to use for the calculation. Or, if you're not quite up to remembering the exact order used for everything, choose a function from the **Paste function** drop-down list, then choose an existing bookmark name from the **Paste bookmark** drop-down list. |
| 2 | Number format drop-down list | Choose an item that determines how you want to format the *results* of your calculation. |

**Table 15.10**   Options in the Formula dialog box, continued

| # | Option | What you do with it |
|---|--------|---------------------|
| 3 | Paste function drop-down list | Choose an item that determines what function name is inserted in the Formula text box. |
| 4 | Paste bookmark drop-down list | Choose an item that determines which range of cells you've bookmarked for use in calculations. |
|   |        | **Note** If you know you're going to do a lot of calculations, close this dialog box and then create a bookmark for the range of cells you want to use. This is **much** easier than trying to remember cryptic cell names and getting nasty error messages.  (For more information, see Insert ➤ Bookmark on page 189.) |

# Table ➤ Hide/Show Gridlines

Use this option to hide or display the non-printing lines that surround the table and mark the rows and columns. Remember, borders and gridlines are two different things: borders are actually lines that print in the areas you choose, gridlines are nonprinting lines that help you see the edge of the table and edges of the rows and columns.

---

**N O T E**   When you create a table in a standard document, Word assumes that you want to print a 1/2 point black border around the out side of the table and between the rows and columns (although you can change this to about anything that suits your fancy). On Web pages, however, Word assumes that you *don't want* a border that prints. Therefore, you might want to show the gridlines so that you can see the "shape" of the table . ▨

### How You Get Here

✧ Press **Alt+A,G**          ✧ Choose **Table ➤ Hide/Show Gridlines**

# Table ➤ Properties

Use this option to display the Properties dialog box so that you can customize the table, columns, rows, and the contents of cells.

### How You Get Here

✧ Press **Alt+A,R**          ✧ Choose **Table ➤ Properties**

## What's In This Dialog Box

Figure 15.16 is a sample of this dialog box and Table 15.11 has a description of the tabs available.

**Figure 15.16**   The Table Properties dialog box

**Table 15.11**   Tabs in the Table Properties dialog box

| # | Tab name | What you do with it |
|---|---|---|
| 1 | Table | Click to set the overall parameters for the table where the cursor is currently positioned. (For a complete description of the options available, see Table 15.12 on page 271.) |
| 2 | Row | Click to set the overall parameters for the table where the cursor is currently positioned. You can also step through the other rows in the table by clicking the **Next Row** or **Previous Row** buttons. (For a complete description of the options available, see Table 15.13 on page 271.) |
| 3 | Column | Click to set the overall parameters for the table where the cursor is currently positioned. (For a complete description of the options available, see Table 15.14 on page 272.) |
| 4 | Cell | Click to set the overall parameters for the cell where the cursor is currently positioned. (For a complete description of the options available, see Table 15.15 on page 272.) |

The following tables describe the options for the individual tabs in this dialog box:

- Table 15.12 describes the Table tab,
- Table 15.13 describes the Row tab,
- Table 15.14 describes the Column tab, and
- Table 15.15 describes the Cell tab.

**Table 15.12**   Options in the Table Properties dialog boxTable tab

| Option | What you do with it |
|---|---|
| Size area | Click to set a specific size for the entire table. You can also choose what unit of measure you want to use for the table (e.g., inches or picas). |
| Alignment area | Choose an item that determines where Word aligns the left edge of the table and how far you want the table indented from the left margin. |
| Text wrapping area | Choose an item that determines whether text before and after the table "jumps over" the table or runs around it *when* the table doesn't span the full width of the page. If you click the **Around** icon, the Positioning button is also available. |
| Positioning button | Click to display the Table Positioning dialog box so that you can choose exactly how the text wraps around the table if it doesn't span the full width of the page. This is only available if you click the **Around** icon. |
| Borders and Shading button | Click to display the Borders and Shading dialog box so that you can choose the appropriate lines and shading for your table. (For more information, see Format ➤ Borders and Shading on page 202.) |
| Options button | Click to display the Table Options dialog box so that you can more accurately format the currently highlighted table. |

**Table 15.13**   Options in the Table Properties dialog box Row tab

| Option | What you do with it |
|---|---|
| Size area | Click to set a specific height for the currently highlighted row and choose whether you want to make the row the exact height specified or whether it must always at least the height specified. |
| Options area | Choose an item that determines whether Word is allowed to split the currently highlighted row between pages and whether to repeat this row on every page of a multi-page table.<br><br>**Note**   You can only choose the **Repeat as header row** option if this is the first (header) row in the table. |
| Previous Row button | Click to look at, or change, the current settings for the previous row in the table. |
| Next Row button | Click to look at, or change, the current settings for the next row in the table. |

**Table 15.14**    Options in the Table Properties dialog box Column tab

| Option | What you do with it |
| --- | --- |
| Size area | Click to set a specific width for the currently highlighted column and choose whether you want to make the column the exact width specified or whether it must always be at least the width specified. |
| Previous Column button | Click to look at, or change, the current settings for the previous column in the table. |
| Next Column button | Click to look at, or change, the current settings for the next column in the table. |

**Table 15.15**    Options in the Table Properties dialog box Cell tab

| Option | What you do with it |
| --- | --- |
| Size area | Click to set a specific width for the currently highlighted cell and choose whether you want to make the cell the exact width specified or whether it must always be at least the width specified. |
| Alignment area | Choose an item that determines where Word aligns the text within the cell margins. |
| Options button | Click to display the Cell Options dialog box so that you can enter the margins for the highlighted cell and choose how the text fits within the cell when the text is too long to fit on one line. |

# The Word Window Menu

**In** this chapter

New Window

Arrange All

Split

✓ 1 Document One

# What Is The Window Menu

This menu has options that let you choose how you want to display your files when you have more than one open or compare different files or copy information between them. Most of the actions take place immediately, so you won't see many new windows or screens in this section.

If a menu option has an ellipsis (three dots) or an arrow beside it, the application "asks" you for additional information before the action takes place. If the menu doesn't have one of these symbols, the action you choose happens immediately. If the action takes place immediately, you won't see a sample screen in this section.

# Window ➤ New Window

Use this option to open a new window with the same contents as the active window so that you can display different parts of the same document. The title bar then displays the original document name followed by a number that indicates which window you're working in.

## How You Get Here

✧ Press **Alt+W,N**             ✧ Choose **Window** ➤ **New Window**

# Window ➤ Arrange All

Use this option to display all open windows on the desktop at the same time.

## How You Get Here

✧ Press **Alt+W,A**             ✧ Choose **Window** ➤ **Arrange All**

# Window ➤ Split/Remove Split

Use this option to divide the active window into horizontal panes. As you scroll through the document, all text above the split is frozen and doesn't scroll until you use the scroll bars for that pane. The other pane has its own set of scroll bars, so you can scroll around in different parts of the same document. Choose **Window ➤ Remove Split** to display a single window.

### How You Get Here

✧ Press **Alt+W,S**        ✧ Choose **Window** ➤ **Split or Remove Split**

# Window ➤ (List of Files Currently Open)

Use this option to switch between windows when there is more than one document open or to maximize the display of the selected window.

### How You Get Here

✧ Press **Alt+W,file number**     ✧ Choose **Window** ➤ **file number**

# A Look At Excel

**In this part**

# The Excel File Menu

# What Is The File Menu

This menu lists the commands that you'll use to perform actions that affect the entire file, such as saving the document so that you don't lose your work, printing the document, opening additional documents, or reviewing various information about the active file.

If a menu option has an ellipsis (three dots) or an arrow beside it, the application "asks" you for additional information before the action takes place. If the menu doesn't have one of these symbols, the action you choose happens immediately. If the action takes place immediately, you won't see a sample screen in this section.

# File ➤ New

Use this option to create a new workbook based on an existing workbook (called a "template") or to create a new template that you can use to make life easier in the future. You can choose a template to make creating a workbook a little easier or, if you prefer, you can create new templates and store them in the tabs displayed. If you need some help working with a template, or if you're new to creating workbooks in Excel, you can use a Wizard, which walks you through the process of creating a new workbook one step at a time.

### How You Get Here

✧ Click       ✧ Press **Alt+F,N** or **Ctrl+N**      ✧ Choose **File ➤ New**

---

**N O T E**   If you click  or use a keyboard shortcut to create a new workbook, Excel *assumes* that you want to use the default template (workbook.xls). If you want to create a new workbook using a different template, choose **File ➤ New**. ■

---

**TIP**   If you want to take a quick look at what a template looks like *before* you use the template, click the desired template name then look in the Preview area.

## What's Different

Figure 17.1 is a sample of this dialog box and Table 17.1 has a description of options that are unique to Excel. (For more information, see File ➤ New on page 38.)

**Figure 17.1** The New dialog box

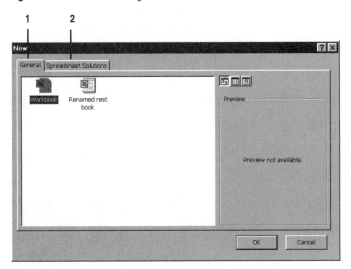

**Table 17.1** Tabs in the New dialog box

| # | Tab name | What you do with it |
|---|----------|---------------------|
| 1 | General | Double-click one of the templates displayed to create a basic workbook. |
| 2 | Spreadsheet Solutions | Double-click one of the templates displayed create a new workbook that has a lot of the work already done for you. |

# File ➤ Open

Use this option to open an existing workbook so that you can take a look at what you've done or add more stuff to your masterpiece. (For more information, see File ➤ Open on page 39.)

**N O T E** File ➤ Open has the same options in all three applications. The only difference is in the Files of type drop-down list; in Excel the types are spreadsheet or database applications. If you open a file of a different type, Excel may open an Import wizard to help you convert the file to the proper format. ▪

## How You Get Here

◆ Click 🖿  ◆ Press **Alt+F,O** or **Ctrl+O**  ◆ Choose **File** ➤ **Open**

# File ➤ Close

Use this option to close the active file and save it in the original file folder (you know, that one you used when you *first* saved the file). If the file has not been saved you'll be asked if you want to save any changes you have made. If you click the **Yes** button so that your most recent changes are saved, the application overwrites the old version of the file. (For more information, see File ➤ Close on page 41.)

## How You Get Here

✧ Click 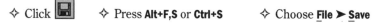 or Double-click     ✧ Press **Alt+F,C** or **Ctrl+W**     ✧ Choose **File ➤ Close**

# File ➤ Save

Use this option to save any changes you've made to a file. (For more information, see File ➤ Save on page 42.)

> **T I P**   Be sure to save your files frequently (you don't want to lose any of the hard work you've done). A good rule of thumb is to save frequently enough that you can easily recover if the system crashes. For example, if you just wrote a great paragraph or created an awesome formula, save your file immediately after finishing the it. My rule is that I don't go any longer than five minutes without saving, which means I can't lose more than five minutes work! Most of the applications also have an automatic save function that can be set to automatically save your files after a specified amount of time.

## How You Get Here

✧ Click      ✧ Press **Alt+F,S** or **Ctrl+S**     ✧ Choose **File ➤ Save**

# File ➤ Save As

save the file for the first time or to save an existing file with a different name or file type. (For more information, see File ➤ Save As on page 42.)

> **T I P**   Be sure you look at where you're storing the file before you click **Save**—don't let "fast fingers" get the better of you. The most frequent reason people can't find a file is because they didn't pay attention to the file folder that was open when they last saved a file.

## How You Get Here

✧ Press **Alt+F,A**       ✧ Choose **File ➤ Save As**

# File ➤ Save as Web Page

Use this option to save an existing file as a Web page, using HTML. Sometimes you'll want to save what you're working on as a Web page, so you can view it yourself later in a browser or send it to someone else to look at. This is helpful if, for example, you want to share your week's schedule with users who don't have Outlook. However, don't expect the Web page to be used as a data source. That is, don't expect your Excel Web page to be usable as an Excel worksheet, for example.

## How You Get Here

✧ Press **Alt+F,G**          ✧ Choose **File ➤ Save as Web Page**

## What's Different

Figure 17.2 is a sample of this dialog box and Table 17.2 has a description of options that are unique to Excel. (For more information, see File ➤ Save as Web Page on page 43.).

**Figure 17.2**   The Save As dialog box

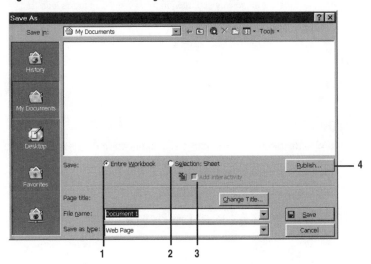

**Table 17.2**   Options in the Save As dialog box

| # | Option | What you do with it |
|---|--------|---------------------|
| 1 | Entire Workbook radio button | Click to include all sheets of the workbook in the web page. |
| 2 | Selection radio button | Click to include only the area selected in the web page. |

**Table 17.2**    Options in the Save As dialog box, continued

| # Option | What you do with it |
| --- | --- |
| 3    Add interactivity check box | Click to choose to let Web page cells act like spreadsheet cells. Values can be changed in the web page and functions will update. |
| 4    Publish button | Click to open a dialog box where you can make decisions about publishing your workbook as a web page. |

# File ➤ Save Workspace

Use this option to save several workbooks as a single file. This option helps when you have several workbooks that you tend to work on at the same time and saves the workbooks and their positions on the screen when you saved the workspace. The Save Worksheet dialog box looks very similar to the Save dialog box and the Open dialog box, but it automatically has the Save as type option set to Workspace. (For more information, see File ➤ Open on page 39.)

> **N O T E**    You open a Workspace file the same way you open in other file. Look for an icon that has multiple worksheets with the Excel icon. ▪

## How You Get Here

✧ Press **Alt+F,W**          ✧ Choose **File** ➤ **Save Workspace**

# File ➤ Web Page Preview

Use this option to see how a file looks as a web page. The application opens your Web browser and displays the active file.

## How You Get Here

✧ Press **Alt+F,B**          ✧ Choose **File** ➤ **Web Page Preview**

# File ➤ Page Setup

Use this option to control the appearance of your printed workbook, including the overall page size, the amount of white space on the page (margins), the space allowed for text at the top of the page (header) and at the bottom of the page (footer), and the paper tray used when you print your documents.

## How You Get Here

✧ Press **Alt+F,U**              ✧ Choose **File** ➤ **Page Setup**

## What's In This Dialog Box

Figure 17.3 is a sample of this dialog box and Table 17.3 has a description of the tabs available.

**Figure 17.3**   The Page Setup dialog box

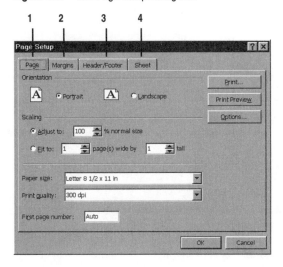

**Table 17.3**   Tabs in the Page Setup dialog box

| # | Tab name | What you do with it |
|---|----------|---------------------|
| 1 | Page | Click to set what size paper you're using and which way the paper is oriented (portrait is up-and-down and landscape is oriented left-to-right). (For a complete description of the options available, see Table 17.4 on page 286.) |
| 2 | Margins | Click to set the amount of white space on the perimeter of your document. (For a complete description of the options available, see Table 17.5 on page 286.) |
| 3 | Header/Footer | Click to create the text that you want to use in a header (text that is at the top of every page) and in a footer (text that is at the bottom of every page). |
| | | **Note**   This tab and it's options are fully covered in the View Menu chapter, the **View ➤ Header/Footer** option. (For a complete description of the options available, see Table 19.6 on page 317.) |
| 4 | Sheet | Click to choose which portions of the workbook you want to print, what types of elements you want to print (e.g., gridlines or no gridlines), or in what order the pages are printed. (For a complete description of the options available, see Table 17.6 on page 287.) |

The following tables describe the options for the individual tabs in this dialog box:

- Table 17.4 describes the Page tab,
- Table 17.5 describes the Margins tab, and
- Table 17.6 describes the Sheet tab.

**Table 17.4**    Options in the Page Setup dialog box Page tab

| Option | What you do with it |
| --- | --- |
| Orientation area | Click to choose which way the paper is oriented (portrait is oriented up-and-down and landscape is oriented left-to-right). |
| Print button | Click to display the Print dialog box where you can set the options for printing the worksheet. (For more information, see File ➤ Print on page 44.) |
| Print Preview button | Click to see how your workbook will look *before* you print it on paper. You can also make changes to your document and send your document to the printer while in Print Preview mode. |
| Options button | Click to display the Options window so that you can set up the specifications for the selected printer. |
| First page number text box | Enter what number you want printed on the first page of the workbook. If you choose **Auto**, Excel automatically assigns the number "1" to the first page and numbers the remaining pages sequentially. You can also enter a different number if you don't want to start with the number "1". |
| Print quality drop-down list | Choose an item that determines how good your printed workbook looks (Print quality is measured in dots per inch and the options displayed depend on the printer you're printing to. The higher the number, the higher the print quality.) |
| Scaling area | Choose whether your workbook prints at full size or at a percentage of the original size.<br>■ Click **Adjust to % of normal size to** enter a specific reduction or enlargement percentage or use the up and down arrows to choose a preset value from the list.<br>■ Click **Fit to pages** to print more than one worksheet on a page at a time. |
| Paper size drop-down list | Choose an item that determines what paper size you plan to print to. |

**Table 17.5**    Options in the Page Setup dialog box Margins tab

| Option | What you do with it |
| --- | --- |
| Top text box | Enter the amount of white space you want at the top of the page. |
| Header text box | Enter the amount of white space from the top page edge to where the header is inserted. |
| Right text box | Enter the amount of white space you want on the right side of the page. |
| Footer text box | Enter the amount of white space from the bottom page edge to where the footer is inserted. |
| Bottom text box | Enter the amount of white space you want at the bottom of the page. |

**Table 17.5**  Options in the Page Setup dialog box Margins tab, continued

| Option | What you do with it |
|---|---|
| Left text box | Enter the amount of white space you want on the left side of the page. |
| Center on page area | Choose an item that determines how the worksheet is center. Click **Horizontally** to center the print area between the left and right margins, click **Vertically to** center the print area between the top and bottom margins. |

**Table 17.6**  Options in the Page Setup dialog box Sheet tab

| Option | What you do with it |
|---|---|
| Print area text box | Enters the cell range automatically as you highlight the area you want to print. |
| Rows to repeat at top | Enters the cell range automatically as you highlight the rows that repeat. |
| Columns to repeat at left | Enters the cell range automatically as you highlight the columns on the left that repeat. |
| Print: Gridlines check box | Prints the cell grid that Excel displays. |
| Print: Row and column headings check box | Prints the Excel row letters and column numbers. |
| Print: Black and white check box | Print formatted text with colors as black and white. |
| Print: Draft quality check box | Prints using low quality printing settings. |
| Comments drop-down list | Choose where you want comments printed. |
| Page order: Down, then over radio button | Print the workbook 1,2,3... to end (down), then A,B,C...to end (across), then next active sheet back, down, across, to end. |
| Page order: Over, then down radio button | Print the workbook pages A,B,C...to end (across), 1,2,3... to end (down), then next active sheet back, across, down, to end. |

# File ➤ Print Area

Use this option to choose which area of the worksheet you want to print.

## How You Get Here

✧ Press **Alt+F,T**    ✧ Choose **File ➤ Print Area**

## What's In This Flyout Menu

Figure 17.4 is a sample of this flyout menu.

**Figure 17.4**    The File ➤ Print Area flyout menu

## File ➤ Print Area ➤ Set Print Area

Use this option to print a specific range of cells to print. This area is saved with the workbook every time you save the workbook or close the workbook.

---

**N O T E**    Once you've set a specific range of cells, Excel "assumes" that you want to print the area instead of the entire worksheet. If you want to print the entire worksheet, either clear the print area or click 🖨 on the Standard toolbar. ▪

## How You Get Here

✧ Press **Alt+F,T,S**        ✧ Choose **F̲ile ➤ Pri̲nt Area ➤ S̲et Print Area**

## File ➤ Print Area ➤ Clear Print Area

Use this option to clear the existing print area so that you can print the entire worksheet.

## How You Get Here

✧ Press **Alt+F,T,C**        ✧ Choose **F̲ile ➤ Pri̲nt Area ➤ C̲lear Print Area**

# File ➤ Print Preview

Use this option to help you get a feel for how your printed document will look *before* you waste your time printing out something that isn't right. You can move through the worksheet, see and change margins, set up the page, and print directly from this window.

## How You Get Here

✧ Click         ✧ Press **Alt+F,V**        ✧ Choose **F̲ile ➤ Print Previe̲w**

## What's In This Window

Figure 17.5 is a sample of this window and Table 17.7 has a description of the options available.

**Figure 17.5**   The Print Preview window

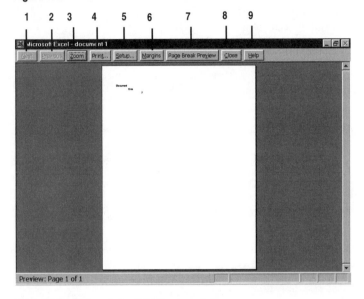

**Table 17.7**   Options in the Print Preview window

| # | Option | What you do with it |
|---|--------|---------------------|
| 1 | Next button | Click to display the next page of the worksheet |
| 2 | Previous button | Click to display the previous page of the worksheet. |
| 3 | Zoom button | Choose an item that determines how much of the document you can see on your screen at one time. |
| 4 | Print button | Click to print the active worksheet. (For more information, see File ➤ Print on page 290.) |
| 5 | Setup button | Click to open the Page Setup dialog box so that you can customize your print settings. (For more information, see File ➤ Page Setup on page 284.) |
| 6 | Margins button | Click to view or change the margins for your worksheet. |
| 7 | Page Break Preview button | Click to view your worksheet divided into the pages that mimic what your worksheet will look like when you actually print it. |
| 8 | Close button | Click to display the Normal view of your worksheet. |
| 9 | Help button | Click to display Excel's online help function. |

# File ➤ Print

Use this option to create a paper copy of the active file. You can send the file to the default printer or you can choose a new printer, as long as it has already been set up for you. If you only want to print a few pages in a file you can choose from the Page range area the pages to print. (For more information, see File ➤ Print on page 44.)

---

**N O T E**    You can also create an electronic "print" file that you can send to a commercial printer or use to generate a portable document format (PDF) file. ■

## How You Get Here

✧ Click 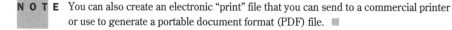          ✧ Press **Alt+F,P** or **Ctrl+P**          ✧ Choose **File** ➤ **Print**

## What's Different

Figure 17.6 is a sample of this dialog box and Table 17.8 has a description of the options that are unique to Excel.

**Figure 17.6**    The Print dialog box

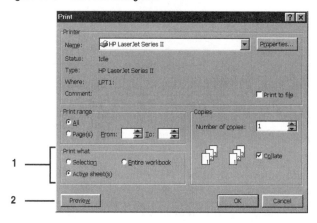

**Table 17.8**    Options in the Print dialog box

| # | Option | What you do with it |
|---|--------|---------------------|
| 1 | Print what area | Choose an item that determines exactly what parts of the file you want to print. |
| 2 | Preview button | Click to see how your printed document looks *before* you print it. (For more information, see File ➤ Print Preview on page 288.) |

# File ➤ Send To

Use this option to send your document, spreadsheet or slide to someone using your email or Internet connection. Generally, any of the options in this flyout menu will use your default email connections or the Outlook application to send an email message. You fill in the information for the recipient like you would for any other email message and then you're ready to send it. This option and the flyout menu options are completely described in the Common File Menu chapter. (For more information, see File ➤ Send To on page 46 or What Is The Outlook Mail Application on page 648.)

## How You Get Here

✧ Press **Alt+F,D**          ✧ Choose **File** ➤ **Send To**

# File ➤ Properties

Use this option to review technical information and record technical information about the active file. (For more information, see File ➤ Properties on page 49.)

## How You Get Here

✧ Press **Alt+F,I**          ✧ Choose **File** ➤ **Properties**

# File ➤ (List of Recently Opened Files)

Use this option to open recently used files, without having to dig through a long list of file folders and drive names to find the file you need.

## How You Get Here

✧ Press **Alt+F,** choose **number of file in list**   ✧ Choose **File** ➤ **number of file**

# File ➤ Exit

Use this option to close all open files *and* the application that you're using.

---

**N O T E**   If you have made changes in any file you'll be asked if you want to save the changes when you exit the application. ▪

## How You Get Here

✧ Click ⊠ or Double-click 🖼      ✧ Press **Alt+F,X**   ✧ Choose **File** ➤ **Exit**

# The Excel Edit Menu

# What Is The Edit Menu

This menu lists the commands that you'll use to copy information from one place to another, delete information from your file, locate specific words or phrases, change information one instance at a time or throughout the entire file, add links to other documents or locations, and change the look of objects.

If a menu option has an ellipsis (three dots) or an arrow beside it, the application "asks" you for additional information before the action takes place. If the menu doesn't have one of these symbols, the action you choose happens immediately. If the action takes place immediately, you won't see a sample screen in this section.

 **T I P**   Many of the commands on the Edit menu are also available on the shortcut menu. If you like to use your mouse, you can right-click, then choose one of the options displayed. Remember, these menus change based on your cursor location and what is highlighted.

# Edit ➤ Undo

Use this option to change your mind and remove one or more changes made to the active file. You can also undo several actions at once *if* you click the drop-down list to the right of the **Undo** button. Although most actions can be "undone", there are some that can't. If you can't undo an action, the Edit menu displays "Can't undo" instead of "Undo".

**N O T E**   A word of caution: the application won't just let you undo an action in the middle of the Undo list. It "assumes" that you want to undo all actions preceding the one you've chosen. For example, let's say that you've deleted five different paragraphs, then decide that you really didn't want to delete the third paragraph. The application kindly keeps a list of those five actions. You quickly click the drop-down list to the right of the **Undo** button and choose the third action. The application, however, "assumes" that you also want to undo actions one and two. ▪

 **T I P**   If you decide you didn't *really* mean to undo an action, choose **Edit ➤ Redo**.

## How You Get Here

✧ Click 🔙     ✧ Press **Alt+E,U** or **Ctrl+Z**   ✧ Choose **E̲dit ➤ U̲ndo**

# Edit ➤ Repeat/Redo

Use this option to either duplicate one or more actions or to change your mind about the last time you chose **Edit ➤ Undo.** You can also repeat/redo several actions at once *if* you click the drop-down list to the right of the Repeat/Redo button. Although most actions can be "repeated" or "redone", there are some that can't. If you can't repeat or redo an action, the Edit menu displays "Can't repeat" or "Can't redo". The name of this menu option changes based on your most recent action.

---

**N O T E**   A word of caution: the application won't just let you choose one action in the middle of the Redo list. It "assumes" that you want to redo all actions preceding the one you've chosen. For example, let's say that you've reinserted three paragraphs using the **Edit ➤ Undo** option. The application kindly keeps a list of those three actions. You quickly click the drop-down list to the right of the Repeat/Redo button and choose the second action. The application, however, "assumes" that you also want to redo action one. ■

---

## How You Get Here

✧ Click 🔁    ✧ Press **Alt+E,R** or **Ctrl+Y**    ✧ Choose **Edit ➤ Redo** or **Edit ➤ Repeat**

# Edit ➤ Cut

Use this option to completely remove highlighted text or objects from the active file. Items that you cut are stored in an area called the "Clipboard" and can be inserted anywhere, in any open file, regardless of the application.

---

**N O T E**   The Clipboard is cleared once you close the application. ■

---

## How You Get Here

✧ Click ✂    ✧ Press **Alt+E,T** or **Ctrl+X**    ✧ Choose **Edit ➤ Cut**

# Edit ➤ Copy

Use this option to leave the highlighted text or objects in their current position and store a copy in a temporary storage area called the "Clipboard". Items that you copy can be inserted anywhere, in any open file, regardless of the application.

### How You Get Here

✧ Click 🖺      ✧ Press **Alt+E,C** or **Ctrl+C**    ✧ Choose **Edit ➤ Copy**

# Edit ➤ Paste

Use this option to insert text or objects that are stored in the Clipboard at the current cursor position. Items that you've cut or copied can be inserted anywhere, in any open file, regardless of the application.

### How You Get Here

✧ Click 🖺      ✧ Press **Alt+P,** or **Ctrl+V**     ✧ Choose **Edit ➤ Paste**

# Edit ➤ Paste Special

Use this option to choose the format of the text or object that you're inserting at the cursor position. This is the option you want to use if you want to link the current file to an external file or if you're copying information between applications and need to control how the information is inserted. For example, you've created a beautiful proposal and want to insert a chart or graph from Excel or a slide from PowerPoint. You also know that this information will change several times before you issue the report. If you choose Paste ➤ Special, you can make your changes to the source file and those changes are reflected in your report. (For more information, see Edit ➤ Paste Special on page 56.)

### How You Get Here

✧ Press **Alt+E,S**              ✧ Choose **Edit ➤ Paste Special**

# Edit ➤ Paste as Hyperlink

Use this option to create a hyperlink for pictures, text, worksheet cells, or a highlighted database object. A hyperlink is an area that is "hot", that is you can click the area so that you automatically jump to a different spot in the current file or in another file.

---

**N O T E**  When you drag text and graphics from one Office program to another one, the application recognizes the location of the information. ▪

### How You Get Here

✧ Press **Alt+E,H**          ✧ Choose **Edit ➤ Paste as Hyperlink**

# Edit ➤ Fill

Use this option to enter numbers and dates into ranges in your worksheet.

### How You Get Here

✧ Press **Alt+E,F**          ✧ Choose **Edit ➤ Fill**

### What's In This Flyout Menu

Figure 18.1 is a sample of this flyout menu.

**Figure 18.1**   The Edit ➤ Fill flyout menu

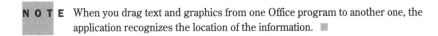

### Edit ➤ Fill ➤ Down

Use this option to enter the same value into a range of cells below the first cell in the selected range. The value entered in the *first cell* is the value repeated.

### How You Get Here

✧ Press **Alt+E,I,D**          ✧ Choose **Edit ➤ Fill ➤ Down**

## Edit ➤ Fill ➤ Right

Use this option to enter the same value into a range of cells to the right of the first cell in the selected range. The value entered in the *first* cell is the value repeated.

### How You Get Here

✦ Press **Alt+E,I,R**        ✦ Choose **Edit ➤ Fill ➤ Right**

## Edit ➤ Fill ➤ Up

Use this option to enter the same value into a range of cells prior to first cell in the selected range. The value entered in the *first cell* is the value repeated.

### How You Get Here

✦ Press **Alt+E,I,U**        ✦ Choose **Edit ➤ Fill ➤ Up**

## Edit ➤ Fill ➤ Left

Use this option to enter the same value into a range of cells to the left of the first cell in the selected range. The value entered in the *first cell* is the value repeated.

### How You Get Here

✦ Press **Alt+E,I,L**        ✦ Choose **Edit ➤ Fill ➤ Left**

## Edit ➤ Fill ➤ Across Worksheets

Use this option to copy the selected range of cells to other worksheets. You can copy just the contents of the selected range, the contents *and* the formatting, or only the formatting.

### How You Get Here

✦ Press **Alt+E,I,A**        ✦ Choose **Edit ➤ Fill ➤ Across Worksheets**

## Edit ➤ Fill ➤ Series

Use this option to enter values that follow a specific pattern in a range of cells that follow a pattern. You can set the pattern to fill columns or rows, express a trend, or enter dates at regular intervals.

### How You Get Here

✦ Press **Alt+E,I,S**        ✦ Choose **Edit ➤ Fill ➤ Series**

## What's In This Dialog Box

Figure 18.2 is a sample of this dialog box and Table 18.1 has a description of the options available.

**Figure 18.2** The Series dialog box

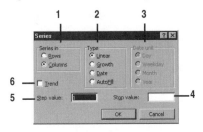

**Table 18.1** Options in the Series dialog box

| # | Option | What you do with it |
|---|--------|---------------------|
| 1 | Series in area | Choose an item that determines whether Excel fills in the data for the selected row(s) or selected column(s). |
| 2 | Type area | Choose an item that determines the types of series you want for the selected cells. |
| 3 | Date unit area | Choose an item that determines how a series of dates will increase in the selected range of cells. This option is only available if you click the **Date** radio button. |
| 4 | Stop value text box | Enter a value at which you want the series to end. This number can be either negative or positive, but you don't have to enter a specific number to fill a series. |
| 5 | Step value text box | Enter the incremental value by which you want the series to increase. This number can be either negative or positive. |
| 6 | Trend check box | Click to calculate a best fit line for a linear series or a geometric curve for a growth series. If you click this radio button, Excel ignores the value in the **Stop** value text box. |

## Edit ➤ Fill ➤ Justify

Use this option to wrap text in the selected cell range to the next line.

---

**N O T E** You can't justify cells that contain numbers or formulas. ▪

## How You Get Here

✧ Press **Alt+E,I,J**          ✧ Choose **E**dit ➤ F**i**ll ➤ **J**ustify

# Edit ➤ Clear

Use this option to permanently clear the contents of selected rows or columns from the active file, *without* storing the information the temporary storage area (the Clipboard).

## How You Get Here

✧ Press **Alt+E,A**          ✧ Choose **Edit ➤ Clear**

## What's In This Flyout Menu

Figure 18.3 is a sample of this flyout menu.

**Figure 18.3**   The Edit ➤ Clear flyout menu

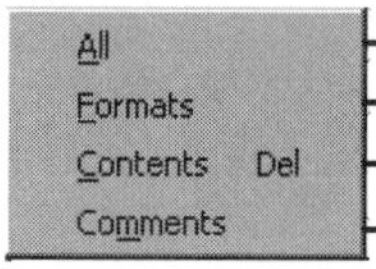

| Menu | Command | Page |
|------|---------|------|
| All | Edit ➤ Clear ➤ All | 300 |
| Formats | Edit ➤ Clear ➤ Formats | 300 |
| Contents   Del | Edit ➤ Clear ➤ Contents | 300 |
| Comments | Edit ➤ Clear ➤ Comments | 301 |

## Edit ➤ Clear ➤ All

Use this option to erase *everything* in a cell or range, including the formatting and contents.

## How You Get Here

✧ Press **Alt+E,A,A**          ✧ Choose **Edit ➤ Clear ➤ All**

## Edit ➤ Clear ➤ Formats

Use this option to remove *only* the formats from the selected range. Numbers, formulas, and text resume their default appearance.

## How You Get Here

✧ Press **Alt+E,A,F**          ✧ Choose **Edit ➤ Clear ➤ Formats**

## Edit ➤ Clear ➤ Contents

Use this option to remove numbers, formulas, and text from the selected range of cells *without* changing the formatting.

## How You Get Here

✧ Press **Alt+E,A,C** or **Del**          ✧ Choose **Edit ➤ Clear ➤ Contents**

### Edit ➤ Clear ➤ Comments

Use this option to remove embedded comments from a cell *without* changing the text, numbers, or formatting in the selected range.

### How You Get Here

✧ Press **Alt+E,A,M**        ✧ Choose **Edit ➤ Clear ➤ Comments**

# Edit ➤ Delete

Use this option to remove everything in the selected range and adjust the position of the remaining cells in the worksheet.

### How You Get Here

✧ Press **Alt+E,D**        ✧ Choose **Edit ➤ Delete**

### What's In This Dialog Box

Figure 18.4 is a sample of this dialog box and Table 18.2 has a description of the options available.

**Figure 18.4**   The Delete dialog box

**Table 18.2**   Options in the Delete dialog box

| # | Option | What you do with it |
|---|--------|---------------------|
| 1 | Shift cells left radio button | Click to move the remaining cells to the *left* after you delete the selected range. |
| 2 | Shift cells up radio button | Click to move the remaining cells *up* after you delete the selected range. |
| 3 | Entire row radio button | Click to remove the entire row where the cursor is positioned. |
| 4 | Entire column radio button | Click to remove the entire column where the cursor is positioned. |

# Edit ➤ Delete Sheet

Use this option to permanently remove an entire worksheet from your workbook. Once you choose this option, you can't use Undo—so think carefully before you click that **OK** button!

### How You Get Here

✧ Press **Alt+E,L**              ✧ Choose **Edit** ➤ **Delete Sheet**

# Edit ➤ Move or Copy Sheet

Use this option to copy a worksheet or move multiple worksheets. You can create a new workbook when you move or copy a worksheet.

### How You Get Here

✧ Press **Alt+E,M**              ✧ Choose **Edit** ➤ **Move or Copy Sheet**

### What's In This Dialog Box

Figure 18.5 is a sample of this dialog box and Table 18.3 has a description of the options available.

**Figure 18.5**    The Move or Copy dialog box

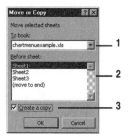

**Table 18.3**    Options in the Move or Copy dialog box

| # | Option | What you do with it |
|---|--------|---------------------|
| 1 | To book drop-down list | Choose an item that determines where you want to place the worksheet. The workbook that you want to copy *to* must be open before choosing this option. You can also choose **New Book** to create a new workbook to hold this worksheet. |
| 2 | Before sheet drop-down list | Choose an item that determines where the worksheet will be inserted. |
| 3 | Create a copy check box | Click to make a duplicate of the worksheet selected before you move it. |

# Edit ➤ Find

Use this option to find text and numbers in the active worksheet.

## How You Get Here

✧ Click 🔍          ✧ Press **Alt+E,F** or **Ctrl+F**     ✧ Choose **Edit ➤ Find**

## What's In This Dialog Box

Figure 18.6 is a sample of this dialog box and Table 18.4 has a description of the options available.

**Figure 18.6**   The Find dialog box

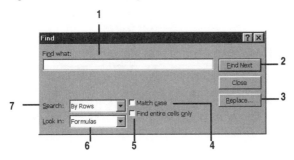

**Table 18.4**   Options in the Find dialog box

| # | Option | What you do with it |
|---|--------|---------------------|
| 1 | Find what text box | Enter the text you want to look for. |
| 2 | Find Next button | Click to begin the search or go to the next occurrence of the information entered in the Find what text box. |
| 3 | Replace button | Click to open the Replace dialog box so that you can enter a replacement for the text in the Find what text box. (For more information, see Edit ➤ Replace on page 304.) |
| 4 | Match case check box | Click to locate *only* text that matches the same pattern of upper-case and lower-case letters entered in the Find what text box. |
| 5 | Find entire cells only check box | Click to *only* find cells that exactly match what you entered in the Find what text box. |
| 6 | Look in drop-down list | Choose an item that determines what worksheet element contains the information you entered in the Find what text box. |
| 7 | Search drop-down list | Choose an item that determines which direction Excel uses to search for the information entered in the Find what text box. Excel either searches *down* through the columns or the *right* across the rows. To search *up* or *left*, press and hold the **Shift** key before you click the **Find Next** button. |

# Edit ➤ Replace

Use this option to change one or more occurrences of the text entered in the Find dialog box to the text entered in the Replace dialog box.

 **TIP**    This is a *really* efficient way to change information quickly and efficiently. For example, you've got the great proposal all done when, OOPS, the boss says he forgot to tell you the markup should be 30%, but it's currently 10%. But...the boss still wants that proposal done in five minutes!

## How You Get Here

✧ Press **Alt+E,E** or **Ctrl+H**    ✧ Choose **Edit ➤ Replace**

## What's In This Dialog Box

Figure 18.7 is a sample of this dialog box and Table 18.5 has a description of the options available.

**NOTE**    Many of the options in the Replace dialog box are the same as the Find dialog box. (For a complete description of the options available, see Table 18.4 on page 303.) ▦

**Figure 18.7**    The Replace dialog box

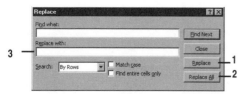

**Table 18.5**    Options in the Replace dialog box

| # | Option | What you do with it |
|---|--------|---------------------|
| 1 | Replace button | Click to change the currently selected text with the text entered in the Replace with text box. |
| 2 | Replace All button | Click to change **all** instances of the text entered in the Find text box to the text entered in the Replace with text box.<br>**Be careful—this is also known as search and** *destroy*. If you aren't careful, you could end up with a real mess. It's usually better to click the **Replace** button to make sure you've got everything just right. |
| 3 | Replace with text box | Enter the text you want to change to. |

# Edit ➤ Go To

Use this option to move quickly from one part of your file to another part.

## How You Get Here

✧ Press **Alt+E,G** or **Ctrl+G**   ✧ Choose **Edit** ➤ **Go To**

## What's In This Dialog Box

Figure 18.8 is a sample of this dialog box and Table 18.6 has a description of the options available.

**Figure 18.8**   The Go To dialog box

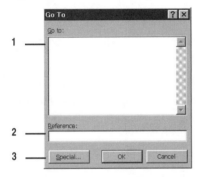

**Table 18.6**   Options in the Go To dialog box

| # | Option | What you do with it |
|---|--------|---------------------|
| 1 | Go to list | Choose an item that determines which named range you jump to or choose any one of the four most recently used Go To commands. |
| 2 | Reference text box | Enter a specific named range or range address. |
| 3 | Special button | Click to display the Go to Special dialog box so that you can choose specific types of information to jump to. |

# Edit ➤ Links

Use this option to open, edit, and maintain the connection ("link") between two files. A link is a way to insert graphics and files into another document so that you can update information if the source is changed. (For more information, see Edit ➤ Links on page 58.)

---

**N O T E**   You can't edit a link until you've inserted one. If you haven't inserted a link, this option is grayed out. ▨

## How You Get Here

✦ Press **Alt+E,K**              ✦ Choose **Edit** ➤ **Links**

# Edit ➤ Object

Use this option to open and edit source files, change the conditions of the links between objects and the files they are linked to, convert objects to different file types, and open them in the appropriate application. When you choose this option, the application "senses" what type of object you've highlighted and changes the menu name to match.

---

**N O T E**   Not all options listed on this flyout menu are available for all object types.

Word, Excel, and PowerPoint have the same options on the flyout menu. (For more information, see Edit ➤ Object on page 60.) ▨

## How You Get Here

✦ Press **Alt+E,O**              ✦ Choose **Edit** ➤ **Object**

# The Excel View Menu

**In this chapter**

Normal
Page Break Preview
Toolbars
Formula Bar
Status Bar
Header and Footer...
Comments
Custom Views...
Full Screen
Zoom...
Sized with Window
Chart Window

# What Is The View Menu

This menu lists the commands that determine what information is displayed for your application. You can choose how the main part of your file is displayed and what toolbars are visible (or, as is sometimes the case, in your way!); take a look at the information that is consistently used at the top and bottom of your file (the header and footer); display an onscreen ruler (so you can make adjustments visually rather than mathematically); change how big or small your display is (great for tired eyes); and just generally customize what you see on the screen. In most cases, the reason for multiple views is so that you can specialize how you see your work. No single view can encompass everyone's needs; if nothing else, the screen would become too cluttered for use.

If a menu option has an ellipsis (three dots) or an arrow beside it, the application "asks" you for additional information before the action takes place. If the menu doesn't have one of these symbols, the action you choose happens immediately. If the action takes place immediately, you won't see a sample screen in this section.

# View ➤ Normal

Use this option to view your worksheet in its "typical" mode, with the standard grid and scroll bars.

## How You Get Here

✧ Press **Alt+V,N**          ✧ Choose **View ➤ Normal**

# View ➤ Page Break Preview

Use this option to view your worksheet divided into the pages that mimic what your worksheet will look like when you actually print it.

## How You Get Here

✧ Press **Alt+V,P**          ✧ Choose **View ➤ Page Break Preview**

# View ➤ Toolbars

Use this option to choose the toolbars you want displayed while you work. Toolbars are collections of icons (or buttons) and are especially handy when doing work that involves repeated tasks. However, if you open lots of toolbars they'll clutter the screen and you can waste more time than you realize by constantly moving them around as you work. You can customize the toolbars to fit your needs. (For more information, see View ➤ Toolbars ➤ Customize on page 76.)

## How You Get Here

✧ Press **Alt+V,T**          ✧ Choose **View ➤ Toolbars**

## What's In This Flyout Menu

Figure 19.1 is a sample of this flyout menu.

**Figure 19.1**   The View ➤ Toolbars flyout menu

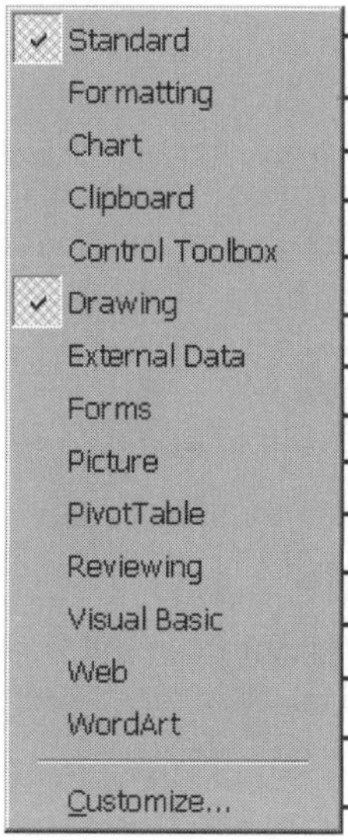

# View ➤ Toolbars ➤ Standard

Use this option to display the Standard toolbar, which has icons for many of your most frequently used options, such as Save, Print, Open, Cut, Paste, and Spellcheck. Although this toolbar displays when you do a standard Office 2000 installation, you can turn it off if you want to see more of your file and less of the icons.

## How You Get Here

❖ Press **Alt+V,T** choose **Standard**   ❖ Choose **View ➤ Toolbars ➤ Standard**

## What's Different

Figure 19.2 is a sample of this toolbar and Table 19.1 has a description of the icons that are unique to Excel.

**Figure 19.2**   The Standard toolbar

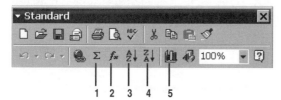

**Table 19.1**   Icons in the Standard toolbar

| # | Icon | What you do with it |
|---|------|---------------------|
| 1 | AutoSum | Click to add up a column of numbers and insert the total in the cell where the cursor was positioned when you clicked this icon. Excel makes its best guess on what range you wanted to add up, but you can always change the range if you want to. |
| 2 | Paste Function | Click to open the Paste Function dialog box so that you can insert a predefined function in the cell where the cursor is positioned. |
| 3 | Sort Ascending | Click to sort the cells *preceding* the currently highlighted cell with the lowest value in the top cell and the highest value in the bottom cell. |
| 4 | Sort Descending | Click to sort the cells *preceding* the currently highlighted cell with the highest value in the top cell and the lowest value in the bottom cell. |
| 5 | Chart Wizard | Click to start the Chart Wizard, which gives you step-by-step instructions for creating or editing a chart. |

## View ➤ Toolbars ➤ Formatting

Use this option to display the Formatting toolbar which has icons for the font used for your text, borders that surround an element, and other icons for changing the look of the elements in your file. (For more information, see The Formatting Toolbar on page 338.)

### How You Get Here

✧ Press **Alt+V,T** choose **Formatting**   ✧ Choose **View** ➤ **Toolbars** ➤ **Formatting**

## View ➤ Toolbars ➤ Chart

Use this option to display a toolbar that has controls for editing a chart that you've inserted in the active worksheet. (For more information, see The Chart Toolbar on page 414.)

### How You Get Here

✧ Press **Alt+V,T** choose **Chart**   ✧ Choose **View** ➤ **Toolbars** ➤ **Chart**

## View ➤ Toolbars ➤ Clipboard

Use this option to display the Clipboard toolbar, which stores up to 12 copied items. This is very helpful when you have copied items from other applications and want to combine them in one document. If you're working in a non-Office application and have an Office application open, all copied items are added to the Clipboard. However, the Clipboard toolbar is only available in an Office application and cannot be customized. (For more information, see View ➤ Toolbars ➤ Clipboard on page 67.)

### How You Get Here

✧ Press **Alt+V,T** choose **Clipboard**   ✧ Choose **View** ➤ **Toolbars** ➤ **Clipboard**

## View ➤ Toolbars ➤ Control Toolbox

Use this option to display the Control Toolbox toolbar so that you create a custom form with ActiveX controls such as radio buttons, text boxes, scroll bars, and other neat stuff that can darn near make your file sing and dance (but that kind of stuff is beyond the scope of this book). These controls are similar to the controls created with a programming language, such as Visual Basic. With an ActiveX control, however, you're actually writing a macro that is stored with the control and it is only available when the file with the control is open. (For more information, see View ➤ Toolbars ➤ Control Toolbox on page 68.)

---

**N O T E** These are the same types of controls you can add using the Visual Basic Editor. For more information try, *Special Edition, Using Visual Basic For Applications 5*, by Paul Sanna, (ISBN: 0789709597). ▪

### How You Get Here

✧ Press **Alt+V,T** choose **Control Toolbox** ✧ Choose **View ➤ Toolbars ➤ Control Toolbox**

## View ➤ Toolbars ➤ Drawing

Use this option to display the Drawing toolbar so that you can create your own drawings, insert shapes, add callouts, and apply color to your masterpiece. (For more information, see View ➤ Toolbars ➤ Drawing on page 69.)

### How You Get Here

✧ Click  ✧ Press **Alt+V,T** choose **Drawing** ✧ Choose **View ➤ Toolbars ➤ Drawing**

## View ➤ Toolbars ➤ External Data

Use this option to a display a toolbar with controls that you can use to define how Excel queries ("talks to") external data sources, such as an Access database. These sources may be on your local hard drive or they may stored on a remote site, such as a network. (For more information, see The External Data Toolbar on page 411.)

### How You Get Here

✧ Press **Alt+V,T** choose **External Data** ✧ Choose **View ➤ Toolbars ➤ External Data**

## View ➤ Toolbars ➤ Forms

Use this option to display the Forms toolbar so that you can create a document with "empty" places to fill in information at a later date (think "IRS"). For instance, you can use a form as a questionnaire with blank spaces for answers or you can use this toolbar along with the Database toolbar to create forms to use on the Web.

---

**N O T E**   The Edit box, Combination List Edit and Combination drop-down list options aren't available in Excel 2000, however, they can be used for Excel 5.0 dialog sheets. ■

## How You Get Here

◇ Press **Alt+V,T** choose **Forms**     ◇ Choose **View** ➤ **Toolbars** ➤ **Forms**

## What's In This Toolbar

Figure 19.3 is a sample of this toolbar and Table 19.2 has a description of the icons available.

**Figure 19.3**   The Forms toolbar

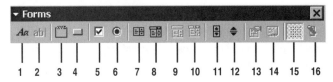

**Table 19.2**   Icons in the Forms toolbar

| # | Icon | What you do with it |
|---|------|---------------------|
| 1 | Label | Click to add text to a worksheet or form to provide descriptive information. |
| 2 | Edit Box | Click to insert a text form field. |
| 3 | Group Box | Click to insert a border and label around related controls. |
| 4 | Button | Click to insert a button that runs a macro. |
| 5 | Check Box | Click to insert a box that toggles items on or off. |
| 6 | Option Button | Click to insert a button that toggles items on or off. |
| 7 | List Box | Click to insert a drop-down list box. |
| 8 | Combo Box | Click to insert a box with scroll bars. |
| 9 | Combination List-Edit | Click to insert a text box that is connected to a drop-down list with a scroll bar. |
| 10 | Combination Drop-down list edit | Click to insert a drop-down list that you can edit information in. |
| 11 | Scroll Bar | Click to insert a scroll bar. |

**Table 19.2**   Icons in the Forms toolbar, continued

| # | Icon | What you do with it |
|---|------|---------------------|
| 12 | Spinner | Click to insert a spinner control. |
| 13 | Control Properties | Click to open the Format Control dialog box. Here you set or review the properties of the highlighted control. |
| 14 | Edit Code | Click to open the Visual Basic editor so that you can create and edit macros. |
| 15 | Toggle Grid | Click to turn the cell grid on and off. |
| 16 | Run Dialog | Click to run the dialog being designed. |

## View ➤ Toolbars ➤ Picture

Use this option to display the Picture toolbar so that you can insert images into your document and control the way they look. (For more information, see Insert ➤ Picture on page 83 or View ➤ Toolbars ➤ Picture on page 71.)

### How You Get Here

✧ Press **Alt+V,T** choose **Picture**       ✧ Choose **View** ➤ **Toolbars** ➤ **Picture**

## View ➤ Toolbars ➤ PivotTable

Use this option to insert an interactive table or list into your worksheet that evaluates or summarizes existing data. You can manipulate the data by dragging it to the location you want.

### How You Get Here

✧ Press **Alt+V,T** choose **PivotTable**   ✧ Choose **View** ➤ **Toolbars** ➤ **PivotTable**

### What's In This Toolbar

Figure 19.4 is a sample of this toolbar and Table 19.3 has a description of the icons available.

**Figure 19.4**   The PivotTable toolbar

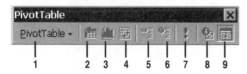

**Table 19.3**   Icons in the PivotTable toolbar

| # | Icon | What you do with it |
|---|------|---------------------|
| 1 | PivotTable | Choose an item that determines which menu PivotTable options you want to use. |
| 2 | Format Report | Click to apply built-in formats to a PivotTable report. |

**Table 19.3**   Icons in the PivotTable toolbar, continued

| # | Icon | What you do with it |
|---|------|---------------------|
| 3 | Chart Wizard | Click to start the Chart Wizard. |
| 4 | PivotTable Wizard | Click to start the Chart Wizard and the PivotTable Wizard. |
| 5 | Hide Detail | Click to hide displayed detail data. On an outlined worksheet, this control turns off the detail rows or columns of highlighted summary row or column. |
| 6 | Show Detail | Click to reveal detail data for the highlighted cell. |
| 7 | Refresh Data | Updates the data in the PivotTable. |
| 8 | Field Settings | Click to change the settings for the highlighted field in the PivotTable or PivotChart report. |
| 9 | Hide Fields | Click to hide fields in a PivotTable. |

## View ➤ Toolbars ➤ Reviewing

Use this option to display the Reviewing toolbar so that you can review existing comments, insert comments, delete existing comments, or accept the changes made to a document. This is a great way keep track of notes, comments, and questions; that way you and other authors can review this information before the text is actually added to the final file. (For more information, see Insert ➤ Comment on page 82 or View ➤ Comments on page 79.)

### How You Get Here

✧ Press **Alt+V,T** choose **Reviewing**   ✧ Choose **View** ➤ **Toolbars** ➤ **Reviewing**

### What's Different

Figure 19.5 is a sample of this toolbar and Table 19.4 has a description of the icons that are unique to Excel. (For more information, see View ➤ Toolbars ➤ Reviewing on page 72.).

**Figure 19.5**   The Reviewing toolbar

**Table 19.4**   Icons in the Reviewing toolbar

| # | Icon | What you do with it |
|---|------|---------------------|
| 1 | Show All Comments | Click to display all the comments in the Comment pane. |
| 2 | Update File | Click to update a read-only file to the most recent version or update changes made by other users to a shared workbook *before* you save your changes. |

## View ➤ Toolbars ➤ Visual Basic

Use this option to display the Visual Basic toolbar so that you can create a new program such as a macro. Macros are small programs that you use for different purposes. You can create macros that do some of the tedious, repetitive work that you would normally do at the keyboard, one step at a time. In fact, you can create a program for almost any task that you need to perform, which is a great way to ensure accuracy and relieve the boredom of doing the same thing over and over again. (For more information, see View ➤ Toolbars ➤ Visual Basic on page 73.)

---

**N O T E**   Although the details of programming with Visual Basic are beyond the scope of this book, you might want to try, *Special Edition, Using Visual Basic For Applications 5*, by Paul Sanna, (ISBN: 0789709597). ■

## How You Get Here

✧ Press **Alt+V,T** choose **Visual Basic**        ✧ Choose **View** ➤ **Toolbars** ➤ **Visual Basic**

## View ➤ Toolbars ➤ Web

Use this option to display the Web toolbar so that you can see and use the icons that are used most frequently in a Web Browser. (For more information, see View ➤ Toolbars ➤ Web on page 74.)

## How You Get Here

✧ Press **Alt+V,T** choose **Web**        ✧ Choose **View** ➤ **Toolbars** ➤ **Web**

## View ➤ Toolbars ➤ WordArt

Use this option to display the WordArt toolbar so that you can insert and format art items so they look just the way you want them to. This toolbar includes icons for moving and resizing your art objects or changing the way your text is aligned or wrapped around the object. (For more information, see Insert ➤ Picture ➤ WordArt on page 87.)

## How You Get Here

✧ Press **Alt+V,T** choose **WordArt**    ✧ Choose **View** ➤ **Toolbars** ➤ **WordArt**

## View ➤ Toolbars ➤ Customize

Use this option to display the Customize window so that you can customize most of the toolbars or menu options. (For more information, see View ➤ Toolbars ➤ Customize on page 76.)

## How You Get Here

✧ Press **Alt+V,T,C**        ✧ Choose **View** ➤ **Toolbars** ➤ **Customize**

# View ➤ Formula Bar

Use this option to toggle (turn on and off) the bar used to add, change, or review the formulas you enter in a cell.

## How You Get Here

❖ Press **Alt+V,F**          ❖ Choose **View ➤ Formula Bar**

## What's In The Formula Bar

Figure 19.6 is a sample of the Formula Bar and Table 19.5 has a description of the options available.

**Figure 19.6**    The Formula Bar

**Table 19.5**    Options in the Formula Bar

| # | Option | What you do with it |
|---|--------|---------------------|
| 1 | Name Box | Click to display the name of the currently highlighted cell. |
| 2 | Cancel button | Click to erase the text being entered into the cell and Formula Bar. |
| 3 | Enter button | Click to place the text entered into the Formula Bar into the cell. |
| 4 | Edit Formula button | Click to edit a cell that has a formula in it. |
| 5 | Formula Bar | Click to add, change, or review the formulas in the cell where the cursor is currently positioned. |

# View ➤ Status Bar

Use this option to toggle (turn on and off) the Status Bar that displays at the bottom of the Excel window. The status bar is a quick check for what's on and what's off, such as the status of Caps Lock, Scroll Lock, and Num Lock.

## How You Get Here

❖ Press **Alt+V,S**          ❖ Choose **View ➤ Status Bar**

# View ➤ Header and Footer

Use this option to open the Page Setup dialog box with the Header and Footer tab highlighted so that you can create or edit the information that appears at the top (header) and bottom (footer) of every page when you print the worksheet.

## How You Get Here

✧ Press **Alt+V,H**        ✧ Choose **View ➤ Header and Footer**

## What's In This Dialog Box

Figure 19.7 is a sample of this dialog box and Table 19.6 has a description of the options available.

**Figure 19.7**   The Page Setup dialog box

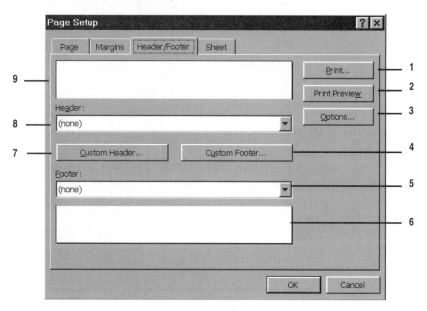

**Table 19.6**   Options in the Page Setup dialog box Header/Footer tab

| # | Option | What you do with it |
|---|--------|---------------------|
| 1 | Print button | Click to display the Print dialog box so that you can print your worksheet. |
| 2 | Print Preview button | Click to see what your worksheet will look like when you actually send it to the printer. |
| 3 | Options button | Click to display the Properties dialog box for your printer so that you can review or change the information for the highlighted printer. |

**Table 19.6**    Options in the Page Setup dialog box Header/Footer tab, continued

| # | Option | What you do with it |
|---|--------|---------------------|
| 4 | Custom Footer button | Click to open the Footer dialog box so that you can add custom text for the left side, center, and right side of your footer. You can insert system information, such as the date or page number, change the font characteristics for the text, and type static text (text that stays the same every time you print the worksheet). |
| 5 | Footer drop-down list | Choose an item that determines which predefined footer text you want to use. |
| 6 | Footer text box | View the text that is printed at the bottom (footer) of every page when you click **Print Preview** or actually send the worksheet to your printer. |
| 7 | Custom Header button | Click to open the Header dialog box so that you can add custom text for the left side, center, and right side of your header. You can insert system information, such as the date or page number, change the font characteristics for the text, and type static text (text that stays the same every time you print the worksheet). |
| 8 | Header drop-down list | Choose an item that determines which predefined header text you want to use. |
| 9 | Header text box | View the text that is printed at the top (header) of every page when you click **Print Preview** or actually send the worksheet to your printer. |

# View ➤ Comments

Use this option to view any comments that have been inserted in the current file. This option opens a pane in the current window which has the comment text in it.

---

**N O T E**    Comments in the current document are indicated by yellow highlighting within the text. ▪

---

**N O T E**    This option only displays information if you, or other authors, have inserted comments using the **Insert ➤ Comments** option. (For more information, see Insert ➤ Comment on page 82.). If there *are* comments in your worksheet, the application automatically displays the comments (which look like sticky notes) and the Reviewing toolbar. (For more information, see View ➤ Toolbars ➤ Reviewing on page 314.) ▪

## How You Get Here

✧ Press **Alt+V,C**          ✧ Choose **View ➤ Comments**

# View ➤ Custom Views

Use this option to open the Custom Views dialog box and choose an existing view or create a custom view of the worksheet. To create a new view, set up the worksheet the way you want it seen later, then open the Custom Views dialog box to "capture" the view as a new custom view.

## How You Get Here

✧ Press **Alt+V,V**          ✧ Choose **View ➤ Custom Views**

## What's In This Dialog Box

Figure 19.8 is a sample of this dialog box and Table 19.7 has a description of the options available.

**Figure 19.8**   The Custom Views dialog box

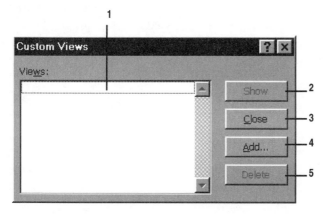

**Table 19.7**   Options in the Custom Views dialog box

| # Option | What you do with it |
|---|---|
| 1 Views list | Choose an item that determines which view you want to work with. |
| 2 Show button | Click to display your worksheet using the currently highlighted view. |
| 3 Close button | Click to close the Custom Views dialog box. |
| 4 Add button | Click to open the Add View dialog box so that you can create new views. |
| 5 Delete button | Click to permanently remove the currently highlighted view. |

# View ➤ Full Screen

Use this option to make the current worksheet take up the full "real estate" available for your monitor. When you choose this option, all the toolbars, and other controls are hidden.

## How You Get Here

✧ Press **Alt+V,U**          ✧ Choose **View ➤ Full Screen**

# View ➤ Zoom

Use this option to set the size of the display for the current file. You can let the application calculate the size or you can set a precise size that suits your needs.

---

**N O T E**   When you choose a larger number, you see a bigger version of your file, but you can't see as much of the file at one time. You'll spend more time scrolling but your eyes won't be so worn out. ▪

## How You Get Here

❖ Press **Alt+V,Z**          ❖ Choose **View** ➤ **Zoom**

## What's Different

Figure 19.9 is a sample of this dialog box and Table 19.8 has a description of the options that are unique to Excel. (For more information, see View ➤ Zoom on page 79.)

**Figure 19.9**   The Zoom dialog box

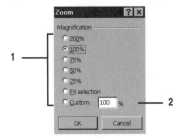

**Table 19.8**   Options in the Zoom dialog box

| # | Option | What you do with it |
|---|--------|---------------------|
| 1 | Magnification area | Choose an item that determines determines how the information displays on your screen. |
| 2 | Custom text box | Enter a specific zoom level for the active worksheet. |

# View ➤ Sized with Window

Use this option to make a chart fit in its *own* window.

---

**N O T E** This option is only available if you have chosen a chart before you choose the View menu. ■

## How You Get Here

✧ Press **Alt+V,W**          ✧ Choose **View ➤ Sized with Window**

# View ➤ Chart Window

Use this option to *display* a chart in its own window.

---

**N O T E** This option is only available if you have selected a chart before you choose the View menu. ■

## How You Get Here

✧ Press **Alt+V,A**          ✧ Choose **View ➤ Chart Window**

# The Excel Insert Menu

## In this chapter

# What Is The Insert Menu

This menu lists the commands that you'll use to add page breaks, page numbers, stored text phrases, comments, pictures, and hyperlinks. Many types of items you want to put in your document are inserted from this menu.

If a menu option has an ellipsis (three dots) or an arrow beside it, the application "asks" you for additional information before the action takes place. If the menu doesn't have one of these symbols, the action you choose happens immediately. If the action takes place immediately, you won't see a sample screen in this section.

# Insert ➤ Cells

Use this option to determine the direction cells will shift when you add new cells. You can also use this option for moving or copying cells. When you choose cells and cut or copy them this option changes to **Insert ➤ Cut Cells** or **Insert ➤ Copied Cells**.

 Excel "assumes" that you want to insert the same number of cells that were selected when you chose this option. For example, if you've highlighted six rows, then choose **Insert ➤ Cells**, Excel obligingly inserts six new rows for you.

## How You Get Here

✧ Press **Alt+I,E**        ✧ Choose **Insert ➤ Cells**

## What's In This Dialog Box

Figure 20.1 is a sample of this dialog box and Table 20.1 has a description of the options available.

**Figure 20.1**    The Insert dialog box

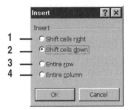

**Table 20.1**    Options in the Insert dialog box

| # | Option | What you do with it |
|---|--------|---------------------|
| 1 | Shift cells right | Click to make cells move to the right of the selected cell(s) as new cells are added. |
| 2 | Shift cells down | Click to make cells move down from the selected cell(s) as a new cells are added. |

**Table 20.1**   Options in the Insert dialog box, continued

| # | Option | What you do with it |
|---|--------|---------------------|
| 3 | Entire row | Click to add an entire row, not just a new cell. |
| 4 | Entire column | Click to add an entire column, not just a new cell. |

# Insert ➤ Rows

Use this option to add blank rows to the worksheet *above* the current cursor position.

The number of rows inserted is based on how many rows are highlighted when you choose this option. That means a quick way to add several new rows is to make sure you highlight the right number of rows *before* you choose this option.

## How You Get Here

✧ Press **Alt+I,R**          ✧ Choose **Insert** ➤ **Rows**

# Insert ➤ Columns

Use this option to add blank columns to the worksheet to the *left* of the current cursor position.

The number of columns inserted is based on how many columns are highlighted when you choose this option. That means a quick way to add several new columns is to make sure you highlight the right number of columns *before* you choose this option.

## How You Get Here

✧ Press **Alt+I,C**          ✧ Choose **Insert** ➤ **Columns**

# Insert ➤ Worksheet

Use this option to add blank worksheets to your workbook.

---

**N O T E**    Remember, a *workbook* is the file where you work with, and store, your data and can have many different *worksheets*. You can store different types of information on different worksheets so that it's nice and organized, but is available for use when you want to analyze your information. ▪

---

**TIP**    You can add several new blank worksheets at once, but you need to decide how many you want to add *before* you choose this option. To add several worksheets, press and hold the **Shift** key and enter the number of worksheets you want to enter, then choose this option.

### How You Get Here

✧ Press **Alt+I,W**          ✧ Choose **Insert ➤ Worksheet**

# Insert ➤ Chart

Use this option to create and format charts to place in your worksheet. This is a nifty wizard that walks you through creating and customizing your charts, step-by-step. Just follow the directions on the wizard to complete your chart. If you change your mind about something in the chart you can cancel or move backwards through the wizard. After you have placed your chart, double-click the chart to display the Format Chart window where you can format the various axes, gridlines, fonts, colors, and properties for your chart. (For more information, see Format ➤ Selected Area on page 356.)

### How You Get Here

✧ Click           ✧ Press **Alt+I,H**          ✧ Choose **Insert ➤ Chart**

# Insert ➤ Page Break

Use this option to force specific cells to start on a new page of paper when you print your workbook, instead of letting Excel make that decision based for you. If you want to break the sheet horizontally choose a heading directly *below* the row where you want it to break. To break vertically choose a heading directly to the *right* of the column beside where you want it to break.

### How You Get Here

✧ Press **Alt+I,B**          ✧ Choose **Insert ➤ Page Break**

# Insert ➤ Function

Use this option to add a predefined formula to the highlighted cell. Excel uses functions to perform calculations on the values in a range of cells. For example, you can use the SUM function to add the values together for a range of cells (no more hand totaling columns of numbers again!). There are a ton of different functions you use to perform everything from basic calculations to complex mathematical operations. Before you start worrying about all these numbers, take heart—once you choose which function you want to insert, Excel displays the Formula Bar and helps you enter the information for your worksheet functions. The Formula Bar displays the name of the function, each of the valid arguments, a description of the function and the arguments, the current result of the function, and the current result of the entire formula.

---

**N O T E**  All functions have a specific order, called the syntax, for the "parts" of the calculation. The syntax is: function name, an opening parenthesis, the arguments (or specific values) separated by commas if there are multiple arguments, and a closing parenthesis. If the function starts a formulas, you must insert an equal sign (=) before the function name. ▇

## How You Get Here

✧ Click   ✧ Press **Alt+I,F**  ✧ Choose **Insert** ➤ **Function**

## What's In This Dialog Box

Figure 20.2 is a sample of this dialog box and Table 20.2 has a description of the options available.

**Figure 20.2**  The Paste Function dialog box

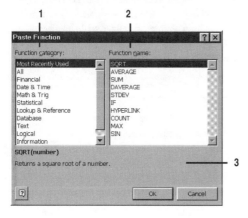

**Table 20.2**   Options in the Paste Function dialog box

| # | Option | What you do with it |
|---|--------|---------------------|
| 1 | Function category list | Choose an item that determines which major group (called a "category") of functions you want to work with. |
| 2 | Function name list | Choose an item that determines the type of operation for the selected category.<br>Choose an item that determines which type of function you want to insert at the current cursor position. The options available change based on which Category you choose. And, when you actually click the **OK** button, Excel inserts the function name and displays the Formula Bar so that you can choose the appropriate information for the highlighted function. |
| 3 | Description area | View a brief summary of the selected field function and what it will do when you insert the function at the current cursor position. |

# Insert ➤ Name

Use this option to give a highlighted area on the worksheet a descriptive, "everyday", name (called a named range) instead of dealing with those convoluted names that Excel is familiar with. You know, the ones that use the column and row labels? Something like =SUM(C20:C30)? Excel does OK with those cell names, but us poor humans usually do a bit better with names. Once you name a specific range of cells, you can use the name in formulas, in functions, or to jump quickly to a specific place in the workbook. You can name plain old ranges or give an understandable name to a really complex formula. Now that formula above could become =SUM(FirstQuarter Sales) instead of =SUM(C20:C30).

---

**N O T E**   These named ranges are available to any sheet in the workbook and can also be used if you're importing information from one workbook to another. Also, names *must* start with a letter and can be up to 255 characters long, with no spaces. Excel isn't case sensitive (that is, it doesn't recognize the difference between uppercase and lowercase), so be careful when you name the highlighted range. ▪

---

**N O T E**   The Name box on the Formula toolbar has a list of the currently named ranges in your workbook. (For more information, see View ➤ Formula Bar on page 316.) ▪

## How You Get Here

✧ Press **Alt+I,N**              ✧ Choose **Insert ➤ Name**

## What's In This Flyout Menu

Figure 20.3 is a sample of this flyout menu.

**Figure 20.3**   The Insert ➤ Name flyout menu

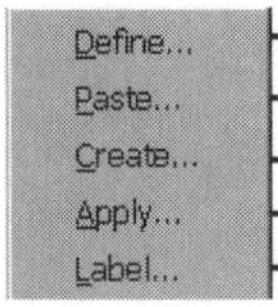

## Insert ➤ Name ➤ Define

Use this option to give the highlighted cells a name you recognize. If you make a mistake you can delete the name and start over again. This option works best if you highlight the desired cell range first, although you can manually type the correct cell values if you are very familiar with your workbook.

---

**N O T E**   You can also click the **Collapse** button to highlight a new range of cells if you aren't in the mood to type complex cell addresses.

## How You Get Here

✧ Press **Alt+I,N,D**          ✧ Choose **Insert ➤ Name ➤ Define**

## What's In This Dialog Box

Figure 20.4 is a sample of this dialog box and Table 20.3 has a description of the options available.

**Figure 20.4**   The Define Name dialog box

**Table 20.3**    Options in the Define Name dialog box

| # | Option | What you do with it |
|---|--------|---------------------|
| 1 | Names in workbook text box | Enter the name for the highlighted range of cells. |
| 2 | Names in workbook list | View the list of named ranges already in your workbook. Choose one of the names if you want to delete it or insert it in a cell. |
| 3 | Refers to text box | View the address of the highlighted range of cells. This box automatically inserts the address for you; if that isn't the address you need, click the **Collapse** button to choose a different range of cells. |

## Insert ➤ Name ➤ Paste

Use this option to place a named range into a formula or in a range of cells.

### How You Get Here

✧ Press **Alt+I,N,P**          ✧ Choose **Insert ➤ Name ➤ Paste**

### What's In This Dialog Box

Figure 20.5 is a sample of this dialog box and Table 20.4 has a description of the options available.

**Figure 20.5**    The Paste Name dialog box

**Table 20.4**    Options in the Paste Name dialog box

| # | Option | What you do with it |
|---|--------|---------------------|
| 1 | Paste name list | Click to choose a name to place into the Formula Bar or into a range of cells. |
| 2 | Paste list button | Click to place the entire list of named references into your worksheet at the current cursor position. |

## Insert ➤ Name ➤ Create

Use this option to create a name using the row or column headings for the highlighted range of cells.

### How You Get Here

✧ Press **Alt+I,N,C**          ✧ Choose **Insert ➤ Name ➤ Create**

## What's In This Dialog Box

Figure 20.6 is a sample of this dialog box and Table 20.5 has a description of the options available.

**Figure 20.6** The Create Names dialog box

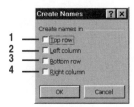

**Table 20.5** Options in the Create Names dialog box

| # | Option | What you do with it |
|---|--------|---------------------|
| 1 | Top row | Click to use the headings in the top row as the name of your named range. |
| 2 | Left column | Click to use the headings in the left column as the name of your named range. |
| 3 | Bottom row | Click to use the headings in the bottom row as the name of your named range. |
| 4 | Right column | Click to use the headings in the right column as the name of your named range. |

## Insert ➤ Name ➤ Apply

Use this option to apply names to formulas you have previously created. You can apply names to formulas in a range of cells, or to the entire worksheet. If you choose a range make sure you choose the row and column headings as well as the cells containing the formulas so that your names are applied to the correct cells.

## How You Get Here

✧ Press **Alt+I,N,A**       ✧ Choose **Insert ➤ Name ➤ Apply**

## What's In This Dialog Box

Figure 20.7 is a sample of this dialog box and Table 20.6 has a description of the options available.

**Figure 20.7**    The Apply Name dialog box

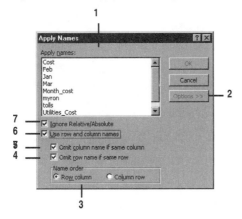

**Table 20.6**    Options in the Apply Name dialog box

| # | Option | What you do with it |
|---|--------|---------------------|
| 1 | Apply names list | Click to choose a name to apply to the highlighted range of cells. |
| 2 | Options button | Click to display more options that you can use when you apply a name to a highlighted range of cells. |
| 3 | Name order radio buttons | Click to assign the order for the column or row names. |
| 4 | Omit row name if same row check box | Click to replace name with a column oriented name. |
| 5 | Omit column name if same column check box | Click to replace name with a row oriented name. |
| 6 | Use row check box | Click to use the names in the row or column headings that refer to the cells if Excel can't find the exact names for the cells. |
| 7 | Ignore Relative/Absolute check box | Click to replace references with names regardless of the reference types of the names or references. If you turn this option off, Excel replaces absolute references with absolute names, relative references with relative names, and mixed references with mixed names. |

## Insert ➤ Name ➤ Label

Use this option to create labels for numbers used in headings. Excel generally uses numbers in cells as your typical everyday number. However, when you create a label for a range this option lets you use a number to define it. For instance, if you have a column heading for the year 1998 Excel converts this name to the Natural Language formula for the range. This means that the label enclosed in parentheses (for a formula) the label is surrounded with single quotes and treats it as if it was text. You can remove any desired label range from this list without removing the name from any cells in your worksheet that contains one.

## How You Get Here

✧ Press **Alt+I,N,L**          ✧ Choose **Insert ➤ Name ➤ Label**

## What's In This Dialog Box

Figure 20.8 is a sample of this dialog box and Table 20.7 has a description of the options available.

**Figure 20.8**   The Label Ranges dialog box

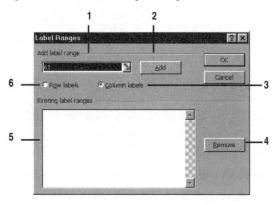

**Table 20.7**   Options in the Label Ranges dialog box

| # | Option | What you do with it |
|---|--------|---------------------|
| 1 | Add label range text box | Enter the range of cells for the label you want to name. |
| 2 | Add button | Click to add the range to the Existing label ranges list. |
| 3 | Column labels radio button | Click to use the column labels as the label name. |
| 4 | Remove button | Click to remove the highlighted range from the Existing label ranges list. |
| 5 | Existing label ranges list | View the currently defined label ranges or highlight a label so that you can delete it. |
| 6 | Row labels radio button | Click to use the row labels as the label name. The highlighted cell range can only be one column wide. |

# Insert ➤ Comment

Use this option to add written or audio notes (if you have a sound card and microphone) to a file that you're editing or reviewing. Be sure you either highlight the text you're making a comment about or click the cursor at the end of the text *before* you choose this command. Once you insert a comment, the text looks like someone used a highlighting marker over the text, which makes it very easy to see where the comments are. (For more information, see Insert ➤ Comment on page 82.)

---

**N O T E**    Several different authors can review the same file and the application keeps track of the comment *and* the name of the person who made the comment. If you place your cursor over a highlighted comment, the reviewer name and comment displays. (For more information, see View ➤ Toolbars ➤ Reviewing on page 72 or View ➤ Comments on page 79.) ▪

## How You Get Here

✧ Press **Alt+I,M**              ✧ Choose **Insert ➤ Comment**

# Insert ➤ Picture

Use this option to insert various types of artwork in your file, including scanned items, the clipart that came with Office 2000, digital pictures, sound clips, and moving pictures. You can embed the artwork (store an actual copy) or create a link to the original file. If you create a link to the original file, you'll always have the latest information, no matter how many times you've edited the original artwork. (For more information, see Insert ➤ Picture on page 83.)

---

**N O T E**    Office 2000 accepts most of the popular graphics formats. Some of the formats, however, require a separate filter before you can bring them into your file. These filters are available on your original Office 2000 CD. So, if you don't have the filter you need, you can use the Office 2000 setup program to add them. ▪

## How You Get Here

✧ Press **Alt+I,P**              ✧ Choose **Insert ➤ Picture**

# Insert ➤ Object

Use this option to place items from other applications into your file or to create new items using another application. Inserting an object differs from inserting a file because you create the object with a source application instead of selecting an existing file from your computer system. These items can be embedded in the document or linked to a source. (For more information, see Insert ➤ Object on page 89.)

 **TIP** This option is primarily for inserting file types that Word doesn't really know how to handle, such as native Portable Document Format (PDF) or Paint Shop Pro (PSP) files. The Insert ➤ File option is primarily for file types that Word already knows about, such as Rich Text Format (RTF) or standard text files created in other applications. (For more information, see Insert ➤ File on page 188.)

### How You Get Here

✧ Press **Alt+I,O**          ✧ Choose **Insert** ➤ **Object**

# Insert ➤ Hyperlink

Use this option to create a connection between two parts of your file, between the active file and another file, or create a connection between the active file and a website address. Once you've inserted the hyperlink, the text changes color and is underlined and you can click on it to quickly jump to the destination specified. (For more information, see Insert ➤ Hyperlink on page 90.) You can use the Web toolbar to work with the hyperlink and you can edit the information stored in the hyperlink after you've inserted it. (For more information, see View ➤ Toolbars ➤ Web on page 74.)

 **TIP** You can also create a screen tip that displays when you place your cursor over the link. If you need to edit the link, highlight it, then right-click to display the shortcut menu.

### How You Get Here

✧ Click           ✧ Press **Alt+I,I** or **Ctrl+K**     ✧ Choose **Insert** ➤ **Hyperlink**

# The Excel Format Menu

In this chapter

# What Is The Format Menu

This menu lists the commands that you'll use to change the "look" of your file. You can choose the typeface for your text (the typeface for this text is Century Old Style), choose the spacing and alignment for your paragraph, and, in general, tweak the look of your file. Generally, any type of format you want to apply to cells can be set somewhere within this menu.

If a menu option has an ellipsis (three dots) or an arrow beside it, the application "asks" you for additional information before the action takes place. If the menu doesn't have one of these symbols, the action you choose happens immediately. If the action takes place immediately, you won't see a sample screen in this section.

---

**N O T E**    Most of the options for this menu are located on the Formatting toolbar for this application. ■

# The Formatting Toolbar

Use this option to quickly perform the formatting tasks in your file. The options described here are the default icons that appear on the toolbar. You can, however, customize this toolbar so that it has all the icons for the tasks you perform most frequently. If you want to apply other formatting options not appearing on this toolbar see the related topic in this chapter for more information.

## How You Get Here

◆ Press **Alt+V,T** choose **Formatting**    ◆ Choose **View** ➤ **Toolbars** ➤ **Formatting**

## What's In This Toolbar

Figure 21.1 is a sample of this toolbar and Table 21.1 has a description of the icons available.

**Figure 21.1**    The Formatting toolbar

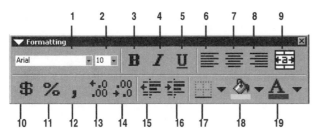

**Table 21.1**    Icons in the Formatting Toolbar

| # | Icon | What you do with it |
|---|------|---------------------|
| 1 | Font | Click to choose the typeface you want to apply to the selected text. |
| 2 | Font Size | Click to choose the size you want to apply to the selected text. |
| 3 | Bold | Click to make the selected text darker than the standard font. |
| 4 | Italic | Click to make the selected text "lean" to the right. |
| 5 | Underline | Click to apply a line under the selected text. |
| 6 | Align Left | Click to align the cell contents on the left side. |
| 7 | Center | Click to align the cell contents around a center point. |
| 8 | Align Right | Click to align the cell contents along the right side. |
| 9 | Merge and Center | Click to center the text in multiple cells across all cells in the selection. |
| 10 | Currency Style | Click to display and print a dollar sign and two decimal positions for the selected cells. |
| 11 | Percent Style | Click to multiple the numbers in the selected cells by 100 and add a percent (%) sign to them. |
| 12 | Comma Style | Click to display and print commas for the thousands placeholders and two decimal positions for the selected cells. |
| 13 | Increase Decimal | Click to increase the number of decimal places that display and print for the selected text. |
| 14 | Decrease Decimal | Click to decrease the number of decimal places that display and print for the selected text. |
| 15 | Decrease Indent | Click to make the space between the text and the cell border smaller. |
| 16 | Increase Indent | Click to make the space between the text and the cell border larger. |
| 17 | Borders drop-down list | Click to display a drop-down menu different border styles. This menu also displays as a toolbar by clicking and dragging the menu bar off the Formatting toolbar. (For more information, see Format ➤ Cells on page 341.) |
| 18 | Fill Color drop-down list | Click to apply a colored background to the selected cells. To display this option as a toolbar, click and drag the menu bar off the Formatting toolbar. |
| 19 | Font Color drop-down list | Click to apply a color to the text in the selected cells. To display this option as a toolbar, click and drag the menu bar off the Formatting toolbar. |

# Formatting Keyboard Shortcuts

The following table lists many of the keyboard shortcuts you can use to quickly format selected cells or text within cells.

 **TIP**    If an effect has already been applied, you can press **Ctrl+Spacebar** to return the formatting to the default value set for the paragraph style.

To see a description of the formatting applied to your text, press **Shift+F1** and click on the text. Once you've looked at the description, press **Esc.**

**Table 21.2**    Keyboard shortcuts for formatting your cells and text

| To do this | Press this |
| --- | --- |
| **Apply font effects** | |
| Bold | **Ctrl+B** |
| Change the font size | **Ctrl+Shift+P**, then **Up or Down arrow** <br> Press **Enter** when the right size displays |
| Change the typeface | **Ctrl+Shift+F**, then **Up or Down arrow** <br> Press **Enter** when the right size displays |
| Italics | **Ctrl+I** |
| Strikethrough | **Ctrl+5** |
| Underline | **Ctrl+U** |
| **Format data** | |
| Apply the General number format | **Ctrl+Shift+~** (tilde) |
| Apply the Currency format with two decimal places (negative numbers appear in parentheses) | **Ctrl+Shift+$** |
| Apply the Percentage format with no decimal places | **Ctrl+Shift+%** |
| Apply the Exponential number format with two decimal places | **Ctrl+Shift+^** |
| Apply the Date format with the day, month, and year | **Ctrl+Shift+#** |
| Apply the Time format with the hour and minute and indicate a.m. or p.m. | **Ctrl+Shift+@** |
| Apply the Number format with two decimal places, thousands separate, and – for negative values | **Ctrl+Shift+!** |
| Apply the Outline border | **Ctrl+Shift+&** |
| Display the Style option | **Alt+'** (Apostrophe) |
| Display the Format Cells option | **Ctrl+1** |
| **Hide/Unhide rows or columns** | |
| Hide columns | **Ctrl+0** (zero) |
| Hide rows | **Ctrl+9** |

**Table 21.2**    Keyboard shortcuts for formatting your cells and text

| To do this | Press this |
|---|---|
| Unhide columns | **Ctrl+Shift+)** |
| Unhide rows | **Ctrl+Shift+(** |

# Format ➤ Cells

Use this option to change the way cell values are formatted, the way text is aligned, what font is used to display and print your worksheet or to add borders and patterns that emphasize specific parts of your worksheet.

**N O T E**    You can't use the Format ➤ Cells option if the worksheet is protected or if the selected range of cells is locked. ▦

## How You Get Here

✧ Press **Alt+O,E** or **Ctrl+1**    ✧ Choose **Format ➤ Cells**

## What's In This Dialog Box

Figure 21.2 is a sample of this dialog box and Table 21.3 has a description of the options available.

**Figure 21.2**    The Format Cells dialog box

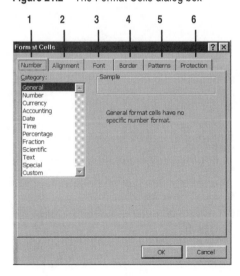

**Table 21.3**    Tabs in the Format Cells dialog box

| # | Tab name | What you do with it |
|---|----------|---------------------|
| 1 | Number | Choose an item that determines how the values for the selected cells are displayed. (For a complete description of the options available, see Table 21.4 on page 342.) |
| 2 | Alignment | Choose an item that determines how the text is aligned in the selected cells. (For a complete description of the options available, see Table 21.5 on page 343.) |
| 3 | Font | Choose an item that determines the typeface and other effects you want to apply to the selected cells. (For a complete description of the options available, see Table 21.6 on page 343.) |
| 4 | Border | Choose an item that determines the type of outlines you want for the selected cells. (For a complete description of the options available, see Table 21.7 on page 344.) |
| 5 | Patterns | Choose an item that determines the type of background you want in the selected cells. (For a complete description of the options available, see Table 21.8 on page 344.) |
| 6 | Protection | Choose an item that determines whether you want to lock and/or hide selected cells in your worksheet. (For a complete description of the options available, see Table 21.9 on page 344.)<br><br>**Note**  You must first protect the worksheet in the Tools menu. (For more information, see Tools ➤ Protection on page 374.) |

The following tables describe the options for the individual tabs in this dialog box:

- Table 21.4 describes the Number tab,
- Table 21.5 describes the Alignment tab,
- Table 21.6 describes the Font tab,
- Table 21.7 describes the Border tab,
- Table 21.8 describes the Patterns tab, and
- Table 21.9 describes the Protection tab.

**Table 21.4**    Options in the Format Cells dialog box Number tab

| # | Option | What you do with it |
|---|--------|---------------------|
| 1 | Category list | Choose an item that determines how the numbers display and print in the selected cells. When you choose an option other than General, related drop-down lists and text boxes are available. |
| 2 | Decimal places text box | Enter a number that determines how many numbers display and print to the right of the decimal point. |
| 3 | Use 1000 Separator (,) check box | Click to display and print commas for the thousands placeholders for the selected cells |

**Table 21.4**   Options in the Format Cells dialog box Number tab, continued

| # | Option | What you do with it |
| --- | --- | --- |
| 4 | Negative numbers list | Choose an item that determines how numbers with a value less than zero display and print in the selected cells. |
| 5 | Sample area | View how your selected format will look in your worksheet. |

**Table 21.5**   Options in the Format Cells dialog box Alignment tab

| # | Option | What you do with it |
| --- | --- | --- |
| 1 | Text alignment area | Choose an item that determines how you want text to line up in the selected cells. You can choose both horizontal and vertical alignment and a specific indent amount. |
| 2 | Orientation area | Enter a value that determines the degree of slant the text has in the selected cells. |
| 3 | Text control area | Click to control how text displays and prints in the selected cells.<br>■ Choose **Wrap text** if you want cells with text that exceeds the current cell width to wrap to additional lines.<br>■ Choose **Shrink to fit** if you want Excel to reduce the font size for cells with text that exceeds the current cell width.<br>■ Choose **Merge cells** if you want to combine two or more cells into the first cell. |

**Table 21.6**   Options in the Format Cells dialog box Font tab

| # | Option | What you do with it |
| --- | --- | --- |
| 1 | Font list | Choose an item that determines the typeface you want for the selected cells. |
| 2 | Font style list | Choose an item that determines the way the font will look. |
| 3 | Size list | Choose or enter a point size for the font. |
| 4 | Underline style drop-down list | Choose an item that determines the style of underline you want for the selected font. |
| 5 | Color drop-down list | Choose an item that determines the color of the font. |
| 6 | Normal font check box | Click to apply settings for the Normal style to the selected cells. |
| 7 | Effects area check boxes | Choose an item that determines the effect you want to apply. |
| 8 | Preview area | View the selected settings before you apply them. |

**Table 21.7**    Options in the Format Cells dialog box Border tab

| # | Option | What you do with it |
|---|--------|---------------------|
| 1 | Presets area | Click to choose the type of preset format you want to apply to the selected cells. |
| 2 | Line area | Click to apply a line style and color to your borders. If you want to change the style of a border you must choose the border in the Border area and then click the type of line style to apply. |
| 3 | Border area | Choose an item that determines the type of border you want to apply to the selected cells. You can also build your own borders in this area. |

**Table 21.8**    Options in the Format Cells dialog box Patterns tab

| # | Option | What you do with it |
|---|--------|---------------------|
| 1 | Color area | Click to choose the color you want to apply to the selected cells. |
| 2 | Pattern drop-down list | Click to display the drop-down list of patterns and colors. Choose an item that determines the type of pattern you want in the selected cells and the color of that pattern. |
| 3 | Sample area | View the selected colors and patterns before you apply them to the selected cells. |

**Table 21.9**    Options in the Format Cells dialog box Protection tab

| # | Option | What you do with it |
|---|--------|---------------------|
| 1 | Locked check box | Click to prevent the contents of the selected cells from being changed in any way. |
| | | **Note**  Locking a cell has no effect unless you first protect the worksheet. (For more information, see Tools ➤ Protection on page 374.) |
| 2 | Hidden check box | Click to prevent formulas from displaying in the Formula bar when a cell with a formula is selected. |
| | | **Note**  Hiding a cell has no effect unless you first protect the worksheet. (For more information, see Tools ➤ Protection on page 374.) |

# Format ➤ Row

Use this option to apply change the height of selected rows or hide/unhide selected rows.

N O T E   You can also change the width of a row by clicking and dragging the row label. The row labels are the numbers at the left of the window. ▦

## How You Get Here

✧ Press **Alt+O,R**          ✧ Choose **Format ➤ Row**

## What's In This Flyout Menu

Figure 21.3 is a sample of this flyout menu.

**Figure 21.3**   The Format ➤ Row flyout menu

| | |
|---|---|
| Format ➤ Row ➤ Height | 345 |
| Format ➤ Row ➤ AutoFit | 345 |
| Format ➤ Row ➤ Hide | 346 |
| Format ➤ Row ➤ Unhide | 346 |

## Format ➤ Row ➤ Height

Use this option to change how tall you want the selected rows. The measurement unit used is points and you can choose sizes anywhere from zero (0) to 409 (zero hides the row.) It's a good idea to make the row height at least two or three points larger than the font size.

**TIP**   You can also position the double-headed mouse pointer between two row headers and drag the mouse to change the row height.

### How You Get Here

✧ Press **Alt+O,R,E**   ✧ Choose **Format ➤ Row ➤ Height**

## What's In This Dialog Box

Figure 21.4 is a sample of this dialog box and has a description of the option available.

**Figure 21.4**   The Row Height dialog box

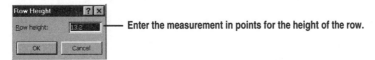

Enter the measurement in points for the height of the row.

## Format ➤ Row ➤ AutoFit

Use this option to let the height of the tallest entry in the selected rows determine the height of each row.

**TIP**   You can also position the double-headed mouse pointer between two row headers and double-click to change the height to the tallest entry.

### How You Get Here

✧ Press **Alt+O,R,A**   ✧ Choose **Format ➤ Row ➤ Autofit**

## Format ➤ Row ➤ Hide

Use this option to conceal the rows you've highlighted.

 You can also highlight the desired rows and press **Ctrl+9** or drag the white plus mouse pointer on row headers, right-click the selection, then choose **Hide**.

### How You Get Here

✧ Press **Alt+O,R,H** or **Ctrl+9**        ✧ Choose **Format ➤ Row ➤ Hide**

## Format ➤ Row ➤ Unhide

Use this option to reveal hidden rows. If the header row numbers aren't continuous, you have hidden rows. If you have deselected the hidden row, drag the cursor across several adjacent rows and choose the Unhide option.

 You can also highlight the hidden rows and press **Ctrl+Shift+(** or right-click and choose **Unhide**.

### How You Get Here

✧ Press **Alt+O,R,U** or **Ctrl+Shift+(**        ✧ Choose **Format ➤ Row ➤ Unhide**

# Format ➤ Column

Use this option to apply change the width of selected columns or hide/unhide selected columns.

**N O T E**    You can also change the height of a column by clicking and dragging the column label. The column labels are the numbers at the top of the window. ▮

### How You Get Here

✧ Press **Alt+O,C**        ✧ Choose **Format ➤ Column**

## What's In This Flyout Menu

Figure 21.5 is a sample of this flyout menu.

**Figure 21.5**   The Format ➤ Column flyout menu

| | | |
|---|---|---|
| Format ➤ Column ➤ Width | 347 |
| Format ➤ Column ➤ AutoFit Selection | 347 |
| Format ➤ Column ➤ Hide | 348 |
| Format ➤ Column ➤ Unhide | 348 |
| Format ➤ Column ➤ Standard Width | 348 |

## Format ➤ Column ➤ Width

Use this option to change how wide you want the selected columns or to make several columns the same width at one time.

 **TIP**   You can also position the double-headed mouse pointer between two column headers and drag to change the column width or right-click a column header and choose **Column Width**.

## How You Get Here

✧ Press **Alt+O,C,W**   ✧ Choose **Format ➤ Column ➤ Width**

## What's In This Dialog Box

Figure 21.6 is a sample of this dialog box and a description of the only option available.

**Figure 21.6**   The Column Width dialog box

Enter the size in points for the column width.

## Format ➤ Column ➤ AutoFit Selection

Use this option to let the width of the widest entry in the selected columns determine the width of each column.

**TIP**   You can also position the double-headed mouse pointer between two column headers and double-click to change the width to the widest entry.

## How You Get Here

✧ Press **Alt+O,C,A**   ✧ Choose **Format ➤ Column ➤ AutoFit Selection**

## Format ➤ Column ➤ Hide

Use this option to conceal the highlighted columns.

> **TIP** You can also highlight the desired columns and press **Ctrl+0** or drag the white plus mouse pointer on column headers, right-click the selection, then choose **Hide**.

### How You Get Here

✧ Press **Alt+O,C,H**  ✧ Choose **Format ➤ Column ➤ Hide**

## Format ➤ Column ➤ Unhide

Use this option to reveal hidden columns. If the header column letters aren't continuous, you have hidden columns.

> **TIP** You can also highlight the hidden columns and press **Ctrl+Shift+)** or right-click and choose **Unhide**.

### How You Get Here

✧ Press **Alt+O,C,U**  ✧ Choose **Format ➤ Column ➤ Unhide**

## Format ➤ Column ➤ Standard Width

Use this option to make the highlighted columns the same width. You can enter the standard size number you want for the worksheet.

### How You Get Here

✧ Press **Alt+O,C,S**  ✧ Choose **Format ➤ Column ➤ Standard Width**

### What's In This Dialog Box

Figure 21.7 is a sample of this dialog box and has a description of the only option available.

**Figure 21.7**    The Standard Width dialog box

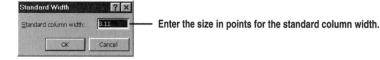

Enter the size in points for the standard column width.

# Format ➤ Sheet

Use this option to change the name of a worksheet, hide or unhide a worksheet, or display a picture in the background of the worksheet.

## How You Get Here

✧ Press **Alt+O,H**    ✧ Choose **Format ➤ Sheet**

## What's In This Flyout Menu

Figure 21.8 is a sample of this flyout menu.

**Figure 21.8**   The Format ➤ Sheet flyout menu

| | |
|---|---|
| Format ➤ Sheet ➤ Rename | 349 |
| Format ➤ Sheet ➤ Hide | 349 |
| Format ➤ Sheet ➤ Unhide | 349 |
| Format ➤ Sheet ➤ Background | 350 |

## Format ➤ Sheet ➤ Rename

Use this option to change the name of the selected sheet. This option highlights the sheet name tab at the bottom of the window.

> **TIP** You can also double-click the sheet name and type a new name or right-click the sheet name and choose **Rename**. Be sure to press **Enter** after you've typed the new name.

## How You Get Here

✧ Press **Alt+O,H,R**  ✧ Choose **Format ➤ Sheet ➤ Rename**

## Format ➤ Sheet ➤ Hide

Use this option to conceal the current sheet so that no one can make changes to it.

## How You Get Here

✧ Press **Alt+O,H,H**  ✧ Choose **Format ➤ Sheet ➤ Hide**

## Format ➤ Sheet ➤ Unhide

Use this option to reveal a hidden sheet. You can choose which sheet to you want to reveal.

## How You Get Here

✧ Press **Alt+O,H,U**  ✧ Choose **Format ➤ Sheet ➤ Unhide**

## Format ➤ Sheet ➤ Background

Use this option to place a graphic into the background of the sheet. This background pattern doesn't print unless you're using Excel to build a Web page. If you want to insert graphics that will print as a background, see Insert ➤ Picture on page 334.

### How You Get Here

✧ Press **Alt+O,H,B**    ✧ Choose **Format** ➤ **Sheet** ➤ **Background**

# Format ➤ AutoFormat

Use this option to have Excel evaluate the selected cells or PivotTable and automatically apply formatting to specific elements in the worksheet.

### How You Get Here

✧ Press **Alt+O,A**            ✧ Choose **Format** ➤ **AutoFormat**

### What's In This Dialog Box

Figure 21.9 is a sample of this dialog box and Table 21.10 has a description of the options available.

**Figure 21.9**    The AutoFormat dialog box

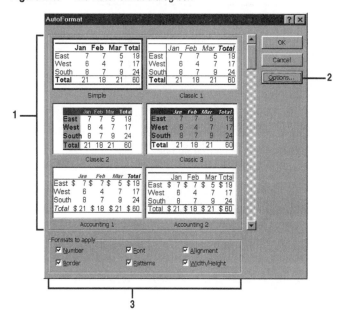

**Table 21.10**  Options in the AutoFormat dialog box

| # | Option | What you do with it |
|---|--------|---------------------|
| 1 | Style preview area | Choose an item that determines the type of format you want to apply. |
| 2 | Options button | Click to display the Formats to apply area so that you can choose the specific formats Excel applies or doesn't apply. |
| 3 | Formats to apply area | Click to apply the elements of the selected format. |

# Format ➤ Conditional Formatting

Use this option to highlight cells that contain formula results you want to keep track of. For instance, you might want to keep track of values that fall below a certain range. You can change the color of a cells contents to make it show up more readily and, if the value in the cell doesn't meet the specified condition, Excel suppresses the formats and the cells contents don't display.

**N O T E**  You can apply only one Conditional Format to a cell at a time. However, you may choose to have up to three different types of conditions in one format. ■

## How You Get Here

✧ Press **Alt+O,D**          ✧ Choose **Format ➤ Conditional Formatting**

## What's In This Dialog Box

Figure 21.10 is a sample of this dialog box and Table 21.11 has a description of the options available.

**Figure 21.10**  Options in the Conditional Formatting dialog box

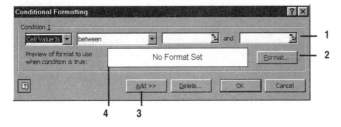

**Table 21.11**    Options in the Conditional Formatting dialog box

| # | Option | What you do with it |
|---|--------|---------------------|
| 1 | Condition 1 area | Choose an item that determines the conditions you want to apply to your worksheet. (There are two other condition areas that have the same options as Condition 1.) |
| 2 | Format button | Click to choose the elements you want to change, such as fonts, borders, or patterns. |
| 3 | Add button | Click to add more types of conditions to this Conditional Format. |
| 4 | Preview area | View how the format displays if the condition is true. |

# Format ➤ Style

Use this option to create or apply a predetermined set of formats to the cells selected. Styles help you consistently format your worksheet—you make all the decisions about what a specific element (such as a title) should look like *once*, then you store that definition in a style. When you're ready to format a specific element, you apply the style and off you go. Now everything can look consistent without you having to remember what you did the last time! You can define new styles, redefine Excel's standard styles, or just use the styles that are stored with your template.

**N O T E**    You cannot modify styles in a shared or locked worksheet. If you have locked your worksheet, you must unlock it before the changes take effect. ■

## How You Get Here

✧ Press **Alt+O,S**          ✧ Choose **Format ➤ Style**

## What's In This Dialog Box

Figure 21.11 is a sample of this dialog box and Table 21.12 has a description of the options available.

**Figure 21.11**   The Style dialog box

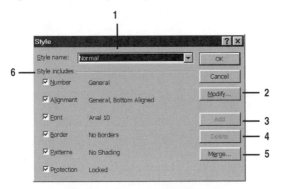

**Table 21.12**   Options in the Style dialog box

| # | Option | What you do with it |
|---|--------|---------------------|
| 1 | Style name drop-down list | Choose an item that determines which style you want to apply or change. |
| 2 | Modify button | Click to display the Format Cells dialog box so that you can change the preset elements for the style you selected. (For more information, see Format ➤ Cells on page 341.) |
| 3 | Add button | Click to create a new style with the settings selected in the Style includes area. |
| 4 | Delete button | Click to delete the currently selected style. (You can delete all styles except Normal.) |
| 5 | Merge button | Click to copy styles from one open worksheet to another. |
| 6 | Style includes area | Click to choose which elements you want to apply when you apply the selected style. |

# The Excel Chart Format Menu

**In this chapter**

# What Is The Chart Format Menu

This menu is only active if you have inserted and highlighted a chart. It lists the commands that you'll use to change what your chart looks like on screen and when you print it. Charts contain areas that reflect information you have placed in a worksheet, such as totals for first quarter sales. Different charts can be formatted using options available for that type of chart. For instance, if you want to change the overlapping distance on a bar or column chart you  can. But this option doesn't work for the pie chart.

If a menu option has an ellipsis (three dots) or an arrow beside it, the application "asks" you for additional information before the action takes place. If the menu doesn't have one of these symbols, the action you choose happens immediately. If the action takes place immediately, you won't see a sample screen in this section.

---

**N O T E**   Most of the options for this menu are located on the Chart toolbar for this application. (For more information, see The Chart Toolbar on page 414.) You can also double-click an area to display the formatting windows. ■

# Format ➤ Selected Area

Use this option to customize the various areas on a chart. The various areas on a chart are called axis, chart, data labels, walls, floor, gridlines, categories, data series, plot, and legend. These areas can be formatted with color, font, line pattern and placement, just to name a few. The windows that display when you choose an area on a chart correspond to that type of area. For instance, if you have a data series highlighted, the menu displays **Selected Data Series**.

---

**N O T E**   Several of these windows contain the same tabs and options so only the Format Axis and Format Data Series dialog boxes are described in this chapter. ■

## How You Get Here

◇ Press **Alt+O,E** or **Ctrl+1**   ◇ Choose **Format ➤ Selected Area**

## What's In This Dialog Box

Figure 22.1 is a sample of this dialog box and Table 22.1 has a description of the tabs available.

**Figure 22.1**   The Format Axis dialog box

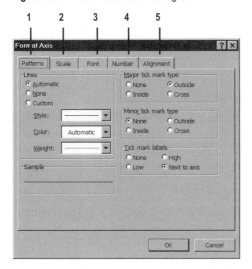

**Table 22.1**   Tabs in the Format Axis dialog box

| # Tab name | What you do with it |
|---|---|
| 1  Patterns | Choose an item that determines the lines/borders style and colors. You can also format the tick marks on the axis in the chart. (For a complete description of the options available, see Table 22.2 on page 358.) |
| 2  Scale | Choose an item that determines the way the axis values are displayed. (For a complete description of the options available, see Table 22.3 on page 358.) |
| 3  Font | Choose an item that determines the font, font style, size and other special characteristics for the text in the chart. (For a complete description of the options available, see Table 22.4 on page 358.) |
| 4  Number | Choose an item that determines the type of number format you want to display in the axis. (For a complete description of the options available, see Table 22.5 on page 359.) |
| 5  Alignment | Choose an item that determines the way the text will align in the chart. (For a complete description of the options available, see Table 22.6 on page 359.) |

The following tables describe the options for the individual tabs in this dialog box:

- Table 22.2 describes the Patterns tab,
- Table 22.3 describes the Scale tab,
- Table 22.4 describes the Font tab,
- Table 22.5 describes the Number tab, and
- Table 22.6 describes the Alignment tab.

**Table 22.2**   Options in the Format Axis dialog box Patterns tab

| Option | What you do with it |
| --- | --- |
| Border/Lines area | Choose an item that determines the style for the borders and lines in your chart. You can choose the thickness, color and style, and apply shadows. You can also use the default settings by choosing **Automatic**. |
| Color Area | Choose an item that determines the colors you want to use for the highlighted series. You can choose a custom color or keep the default colors. |
| Sample view area | View the colors before you apply them. |

**Table 22.3**   Options in the Format Axis dialog box Scale tab

| Option | What you do with it |
| --- | --- |
| Auto area | Choose an item that determines the values that display on the axis. |
| Display units list | Click to choose the units to display on the chart. |
| Show display units check box | Click to display the individual units on the chart. |
| Logarithmic scale check box | Click to change the powers of the axis to 10. |
| Values in reverse order check box | Click to order the categories in reverse. |
| Category axis check box | Click to take the largest value and add change it to the x axis. |

**Table 22.4**   Options in the Format Axis dialog box Font tab

| Option | What you do with it |
| --- | --- |
| Font list | Choose an item that determines the typeface you want to use for the highlighted cells. |
| Font style list | Choose an item that determines the way the font will look. |
| Size list | Choose or enter a point size for the font. |
| Underline style drop-down list | Choose an item that determines the style of underline you want for the highlighte text. |
| Font Color drop-down list | Choose an item that determines the color of the font. |
| Normal font check box | Click to apply settings for the Normal style to the highlighted cells. |
| Effects area check boxes | Choose an item that determines the effect you want to apply. |

**Table 22.4**   Options in the Format Axis dialog box Font tab, continued

| Option | What you do with it |
| --- | --- |
| Auto scale check box | Click to scale text automatically whenever the chart size changes so it stays the same size relative to the overall size of the chart. |
| Preview area | View the settings before you apply them. |

**Table 22.5**   Options in the Format Axis dialog box Number tab

| Option | What you do with it |
| --- | --- |
| Category list | Choose an item that determines how the numbers display and print in the highlighted cells. When you choose an option other than General, related drop-down lists and text boxes are available. |
| Sample area | View how your currently defined format will look in your worksheet. |
| Linked to source check box | Click to link to the source text. |

**Table 22.6**   Options in the Format Axis dialog box Alignment tab

| Option | What you do with it |
| --- | --- |
| Orientation area | Enter a value that determines the degree of slant the text has in the highlighted cells. |

## What's In This Dialog Box

Figure 22.2 is a sample of this dialog box and Table 22.7 has a description of the tabs available.

**N O T E**   The options change depending on what type of chart you've highlighted before choosing this option. We have chosen a few chart types to describe here. ▪

**Figure 22.2**    The Format Data Series dialog box

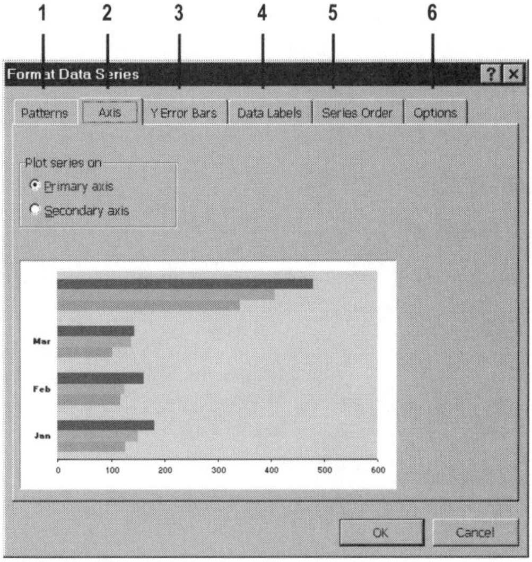

**Table 22.7**    Tabs in the Format Data Series dialog box

| # | Tab name | What you do with it |
|---|----------|---------------------|
| 1 | Patterns | (For a complete description of the options available, see Table 22.2.) |
| 2 | Axis | Choose an item that determines which axis to plot the series on. (For a complete description of the options available, see Table 22.8 on page 361.) |
| 3 | Y/X Error Bars | Choose an item that determines the value for a range you want to display. (For a complete description of the options available, see Table 22.9 on page 361.) |
| 4 | Data Labels | Choose an item that determines the labels you want to display. (For a complete description of the options available, see Table 22.10 on page 361.) |
| 5 | Series Order | Choose an item that determines the order of the bars/columns in your chart. (For a complete description of the options available, see Table 22.11 on page 361.) |
| 6 | Options | Choose an item that determines placement, line thickness and starting points, to name a few, for the elements in the chart. (For a complete description of the options available, see Table 22.12 on page 361.) |

The following tables describe the options for the individual tabs in this dialog box:

- Table 22.8 describes the Axis tab,
- Table 22.9 describes the Y Error Bars tab,
- Table 22.10 describes the Data Labels,
- Table 22.11 describes the Series Order tab, and
- Table 22.12 describes the Options tab.

**Table 22.8**   Options in the Format Data Series dialog box Axis tab

| Option | What you do with it |
| --- | --- |
| Plot series on area | Click to choose the axis you want to plot for the chart. |
| Sample view area | View the options you have chosen before they are applied. |

**Table 22.9**   Options in the Format Data Series dialog box Y Error Bars tab

| Option | What you do with it |
| --- | --- |
| Display area | Click to choose the value to display. |
| Error amount area | Click to choose the amount of error measurement for the chart. |

**Table 22.10**   Options in the Format Data Series dialog box Data Labels tab

| Option | What you do with it |
| --- | --- |
| Data Labels area | Choose an item that determines the labels you want to display on the chart. |
| Show Legend key check box | Click to display the legend markers in the chart. |

**Table 22.11**   Options in the Format Data Series dialog box Series Order tab

| Option | What you do with it |
| --- | --- |
| Series Order list | Click to choose the series you want to reorder. |
| Move up button | Click to move the highlighted series up in the chart. |
| Move down button | Click to move the highlighted series down in the chart. |
| Sample view area | View the highlighted series movements before you apply them. |

**Table 22.12**   Options in the Format Data Series dialog box Options tab

| Option | What you do with it |
| --- | --- |
| Overlap list | Click to change the amount of overlap within a category. |
| Gap width list | Click to change the spacing between categories. |
| Series lines check box | Click to add lines between categories on the series in the chart. |
| Vary colors by point check box | Click to change the color of the data points in the chart. |
| Sample view area | View the new placement for the highlighted element. |

## What's In This Dialog Box

Figure 22.3 is a sample of this dialog box and has a description of the options available.

**Figure 22.3**   Format Legend dialog box Placement tab

Click to choose
where you want to
place the legend in
the chart.

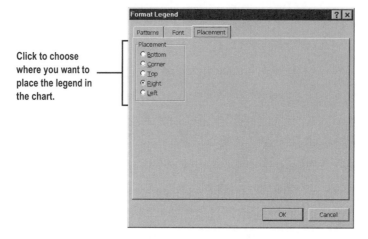

## What's In This Dialog Box

Figure 22.4 is a sample of this dialog box and Table 22.13 has a description of the options available.

**Figure 22.4**   The Format Chart Area dialog box Properties tab

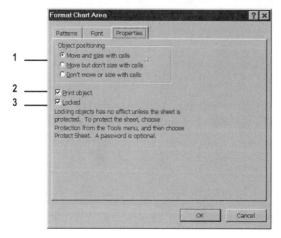

**Table 22.13**  Options in the Format Chart Area dialog box Properties tab

| # | Option | What you do with it |
|---|--------|---------------------|
| 1 | Object positioning area | Click to choose where you want the chart to display. |
| 2 | Print object check box | Click to print the chart whenever you print the worksheet. |
| 3 | Locked check box | Click to prevent the chart from being changed if the worksheet is locked. |

# Format ➤ Sheet

Use this option to change the name of a worksheet, display or hide a worksheet, or display a picture in the background of the worksheet.

## How You Get Here

◇ Press **Alt+O,H**  ◇ Choose **Format** ➤ **Sheet**

## What's In This Flyout Menu

Figure 22.5 is a sample of this flyout menu.

**Figure 22.5**  The Format ➤ Sheet flyout menu

| | |
|---|---|
| Rename | Format ➤ Sheet ➤ Rename — 363 |
| Hide | Format ➤ Sheet ➤ Hide — 363 |
| Unhide... | Format ➤ Sheet ➤ Unhide — 364 |
| Background... | Format ➤ Sheet ➤ Background — 364 |

## Format ➤ Sheet ➤ Rename

Use this option to change the name of the chosen sheet. This option highlights the sheet name tab at the bottom of the window. (For more information, see Format ➤ Sheet ➤ Rename on page 349.)

 **TIP**   You can also double-click the sheet name and type a new name or right-click the sheet name and choose **Rename**. Be sure to press **Enter** after you've typed the new name.

## How You Get Here

◇ Press **Alt+O,H,R**  ◇ Choose **Format** ➤ **Sheet** ➤ **Rename**

## Format ➤ Sheet ➤ Hide

Use this option to conceal the current sheet so that no one can make changes to it. (For more information, see Format ➤ Sheet ➤ Hide on page 349.)

## How You Get Here

◇ Press **Alt+O,H,H**  ◇ Choose **Format** ➤ **Sheet** ➤ **Hide**

## Format ➤ Sheet ➤ Unhide

Use this option to reveal a hidden sheet. You can choose which sheet to you want to reveal. (For more information, see Format ➤ Sheet ➤ Unhide on page 349.)

### How You Get Here

◇ Press **Alt+O,H,U**    ◇ Choose **Format ➤ Sheet ➤ Unhide**

## Format ➤ Sheet ➤ Background

Use this option to place a graphic into the background of the sheet. This background pattern doesn't print unless you're using Excel to build a Web page. (For more information, see Format ➤ Sheet ➤ Background on page 350.)

### How You Get Here

◇ Press **Alt+O,H,B**    ◇ Choose **Format ➤ Sheet ➤ Background**

# The Excel Tools Menu

# What Is The Tools Menu

This menu includes options that make using your application easier and more efficient. Some of the more popular tools include spellcheck, AutoCorrect, and macros. This menu also includes options for customizing your application, such as changing the default ("assumed") location for storing files or selecting whether you want the scroll bars to show on your screen.

If a menu option has an ellipsis (three dots) or an arrow beside it, the application "asks" you for additional information before the action takes place. If the menu doesn't have one of these symbols, the action you choose happens immediately. If the action takes place immediately, you won't see a sample screen in this section.

# Tools ➤ Spelling

Use this option to look for words that may be misspelled. The application automatically flags any word it doesn't recognize, even if the word is spelled correctly for *your* environment For example, a proper name, such as the name of a lake, might be spelled correctly but the application flags it because it isn't in the dictionary. You can choose one of the options displayed, skip over the flagged word, add a word to a dictionary so that the word isn't flagged again, or type in your own replacement. (For more information, see Tools ➤ Spelling on page 94.)

**TIP** You can check the spelling of a specific word, sentence, or paragraph by selecting it and choosing **Tools ➤ Spelling**.

You should always visually proofread your document because the application only flags words not found in the standard dictionary. So if you accidentally type 'form" when you should have typed "from," the application doesn't consider it an error and skips over it.

Excel assumes that you want to spellcheck the current worksheet. If you want to check a cell (or range of cells) or several worksheets, choose the appropriate areas first, then choose **Tools ➤ Spelling**.

## How You Get Here

◇ Click     ◇ Press **Alt+T,S** or **F7**    ◇ Choose **Tools ➤ Spelling**

## What's Different

Figure 23.1 is a sample of this dialog box and Table 23.1 has a description of the options unique to Excel.

**Figure 23.1**    The Spelling dialog box

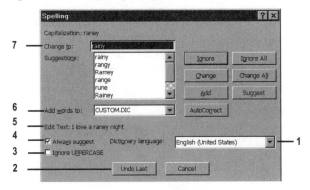

**Table 23.1**    Options in the Spelling dialog box

| # | Option | What you do with it |
|---|--------|---------------------|
| 1 | Dictionary language drop-down list | Choose an item that determines what language you are spell checking for. |
| 2 | Undo Last button | Click to reverse the previous action. |
| 3 | Ignore UPPERCASE check box | Click to skip words that are all uppercase when the spell checker is running. |
| 4 | Always suggest check box | Click to get suggestions on misspelled words. |
| 5 | Edit Text/Cell Value field | View the value of the text/cell being highlighted. |
| 6 | Add words to drop-down list | Choose an item that determines what dictionary you are using. |
| 7 | Change to text box | Enter the correct spelling for the word. If the spell checker has a suggested word it will display in this text box. |

# Tools ➤ AutoCorrect

Use this option to add text so that you can automatically correct or replace frequently (mis)typed words. For example, you can tell Excel to replace "Febuary" with "February" if you always mistype this word. You can also use this option to automatically replace certain abbreviated keystrokes with an extended version. For example, you can have Excel automatically replace "AKA" with the phrase "also known as" whenever you type the abbreviation. (For more information, see Tools ➤ AutoCorrect on page 96.)

## How You Get Here

◇ Press **Alt+T,A**          ◇ Choose **Tools** ➤ **AutoCorrect**

# Tools ➤ Share Workbook

Use this option to identify workbooks that you want to share with other users for review or editing. Sharing a workbook opens a copy of the workbook on a network where several authorized users can make changes to it simultaneously.

---

**N O T E**   You must be connected to a network, LAN, the Internet, or an intranet, to use this option. ▨

## How You Get Here

◇ Press **Alt+T,H**            ◇ Choose **Tools ➤ Share Workbook**

## What's In This Dialog Box

Figure 23.2 is a sample of this dialog box and Table 23.2 has a description of the tabs available.

**Figure 23.2**   The Share Workbook dialog box

**Table 23.2**   Tabs in the Share Workbook dialog box

| # Tab name | What you do with it |
|---|---|
| 1   Editing | Add or remove authorized users to the shared workbook, and allow workbook merging (more than one user making changes at the same time). (For a complete description of the options available, see Table 23.3 on page 369.) |
| 2   Advanced | Click to choose options related how frequently the file is updated, how long changes are tracked (number of days), and how to resolve conflicts when two or more users each make different changes to the same cell. (For a complete description of the options available, see Table 23.4 on page 369.) |

The following tables describe the options for the individual tabs in this dialog box:

- Table 23.3 describes the Editing tab, and
- Table 23.4 describes the Advanced tab.

**Table 23.3**   Options in the Share Workbook dialog box Editing tab

| Option | What you do with it |
|---|---|
| Allow changes...check box | Click to let more than one person edit the same workbook at the same time. |
| Who has this workbook open now list | View the list of users for this file and the date and time they opened it. |
| Remove user button | Click to break the connection of the selected user. You must choose the user from the Who has this workbook open now list before you click this button.<br><br>**Note**   Use with caution! A user working on this file could lose their work if you remove them while they are still editing in the workbook. |

**Table 23.4**   Options in the Share Workbook dialog box Advanced tab

| Option | What you do with it |
|---|---|
| Track changes area | Click to keep a record of changes made to the workbook. You can then review the changes made and merge them as you want. |
| Update changes area | Click to set the time span when other user's work will be saved and whether you will see their changes. |
| Conflicting changes area | Click to get a message when changes made by multiple users conflict. You will be asked which changes you want to save. |
| Include in personal view area | Click to set your own independently saved printing and filtering settings for the shared workbook. |

# Tools ➤ Track Changes

Use this option to display a flyout menu containing the three options: Highlight Changes, Accept or Reject Changes, and Compare Documents. This option lets you make changes to an original document and then see exactly where these changes were made (they appear in a different color of your choice), who made these changes and when (a yellow hover box indicates the computer profile name and date the changes were made. Several editors can work on the same document, with each editor having a different profile, each represented with a different color text. This is helpful when you're editing a co-workers report. Your co-worker can see exactly what you've done and accept or reject your edits as appropriate.

N O T E    See **Tool ➤ Options ➤ General** tab to change profile name.

    You must choose this option *before* you start making changes or the changes aren't marked.

## How You Get Here

◇ Press **Alt+T,T**                    ◇ Choose **Tools ➤ Track Changes**

## What's In This Flyout Menu

Figure 23.3 is a sample of this flyout menu.

**Figure 23.3**    The Tools ➤ Track Changes flyout menu

| | |
|---|---|
| Highlight Changes... | ————Tools ➤ Track Changes ➤ Highlight Changes        370 |
| Accept or Reject Changes... | ————Tools ➤ Track Changes ➤ Accept or Reject Changes   372 |

## Tools ➤ Track Changes ➤ Highlight Changes

Use this option to specify where changes are going to be highlighted. You can choose to highlight changes on the screen, in the printed document or in both places. When changes are highlighted you can also choose the color and style of the highlight. For instance, you may want to place a double underline beneath the text and make the text red for easy visibility.

N O T E    You need a color printer to print tracked changes.

## How You Get Here

◇ Press **Alt+T,T,H**          ◇ Choose **Tools ➤ Track Changes ➤ Highlight Changes**

## What's In This Dialog Box

Figure 23.4 is a sample of this dialog box and Table 23.5 has a description of the options available.

**Figure 23.4** The Highlight Changes dialog box

**Table 23.5** Options in the Highlight Changes dialog box

| # | Option | What you do with it |
|---|--------|---------------------|
| 1 | Track changes while editing check box | Click to automatically share the workbook and show history of changes. Clearing this box removes the workbook from a shared domain, and removes all history of changes. |
| 2 | When text box | Enter or choose a range of time (since I last saved, since date, all) when changes are to be displayed with your chosen highlights. |
| 3 | Who text box | Enter or choose name of users whose changes you want displayed with your chosen highlights. This is helpful when more than one person is authorized to make changes. |
| 4 | Where text box | Enter a specific range of cells to be used in reviewing changes. This is helpful if you want to only check a portion of the worksheet instead of the whole worksheet. |
| 5 | Highlight changes on screen check box | Click to show changes made onscreen. To view the details of the changes made hover the cursor over the highlighted cell. |
| 6 | List changes on a new sheet check box | Click to display changes on a separate History worksheet. This option is only available after you have saved the workbook as a shared file. |

## Tools ➤ Track Changes ➤ Accept or Reject Changes

Use this option to search an edited document for changes and review each one to accept or reject it in the revised document. This process converts edited text into "real" text, which no longer appears highlighted.

---

**N O T E**   Excel always brings up a window stating that it must save the document and make a shared copy before all of the Accept or Reject Changes processes. ■

### How You Get Here

◇ Press **Alt+T,T,A**

◇ Choose **Tools** ➤ **Track Changes** ➤ **Accept or Reject Changes**

### What's In This Dialog Box

Figure 23.5 is a sample of this dialog box and Table 23.6 has a description of the options available.

**Figure 23.5**   The Select Changes to Accept or Reject dialog box

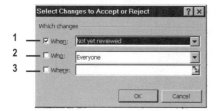

**Table 23.6**   Options in the Select Changes to Accept or Reject dialog box

| # | Option | What you do with it |
|---|--------|---------------------|
| 1 | When text box | Enter or choose a range of time (since I last saved, since date, all) when changes are to be reviewed. |
| 2 | Who text box | Enter or choose name of users whose changes you want to review. This is helpful when more than one person is authorized to make changes. |
| 3 | Where text box | Enter a specific range of cells to be used in reviewing changes. This is helpful if you want to only check a portion of the worksheet instead of the whole worksheet. |

# Tools ➤ Merge Workbooks

Use this option to place changes tracked in the active document into a document selected from the Select File to Merge dialog box. (Use this option when you want to keep a copy of the original—just in case.) You can make changes to a *copy* of the original, review the changes and accept or reject them, *then* merge the changes into the original document.

---

**N O T E**  You can only merge documents from a shared workbook, so you don't have to do a **File ➤ Save As** like you do for Word. ▦

## How You Get Here

◇ Press **Alt+T,W**          ◇ Choose **Tools ➤ Merge Workbooks**

## What's In This Dialog Box

Figure 23.6 is a sample of this dialog box and has a description of the options available.

**Figure 23.6**   The Select Files to Merge Into Current Workbook dialog box

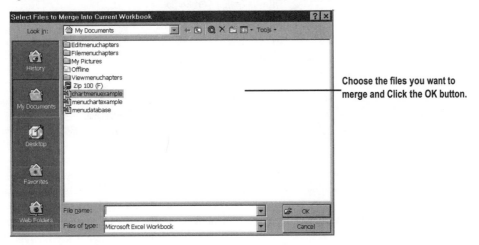

Choose the files you want to merge and Click the OK button.

# Tools ➤ Protection

Use this option to password-protect your document and keep unauthorized users from making changes to it. When you protect a document you, or authorized users, must use a password to access the document and choose **Unprotect Document** before changes are made. This is helpful when you have several people sharing a computer, sharing a file, or working together on a particular project, and you want to be sure that any changes made are made by those authorized to do so. If you've already protected the file, the menu displays the Unprotect option. Selecting this automatically unprotects the worksheet or workbook, without bringing up any additional windows.With all protection windows, Excel uses an optional password system. Only the people who know the password can make a change to the worksheet or workbook. And passwords can only be added if the original workbook is unshared.

 **T I P**   You can leave specific cells unprotected if you want to be able to change them without unprotecting the worksheet. To do this, choose the cells, then turn off the locked feature on the Protection tab in the Format Cells dialog box.

## How You Get Here

◇ Press **Alt+T,P**          ◇ Choose **Tools** ➤ **Protection**

## What's In This Flyout Menu

Figure 23.7 is a sample of this flyout menu.

**Figure 23.7**   The Tools ➤ Protection flyout menu

| | |
|---|---|
| Protect Sheet... | Tools ➤ Protection ➤ Protect Sheet — 374 |
| Protect Workbook... | Tools ➤ Protection ➤ Protect Workbook — 375 |
| Protect and Share Workbook... | Tools ➤ Protection ➤ Protect and Share Workbook — 376 |

## Tools ➤ Protection ➤ Protect Sheet

Use this option to prevent someone from making changes to cells, objects, or scenarios in a specific worksheet. You can also choose a password to use when you have several people sharing a worksheet, and you want to be sure that the sheet is protected from anyone making changes to the protection you have set.

## How You Get Here

◇ Press **Alt+T,P,P**          ◇ Choose **Tools** ➤ **Protection** ➤ **Protect Sheet**

 **T I P**   If you have complex formulas, you might want to unprotect the data entry cells (choose the cells, the choose **Format** ➤ **Cells**, Protection tab and make sure the Locked option is not turned on), then protect the workbook. That way a user can't accidentally overwrite any of your formulas.

## What's In This Dialog Box

Figure 23.8 is a sample of this dialog box and Table 23.7 has a description of the options available.

**Figure 23.8**  The Protect Sheet dialog box

**Table 23.7**  Options in the Protect Sheet dialog box

| # | Option | What you do with it |
|---|--------|---------------------|
| 1 | Contents check box | Click to prevent an unauthorized user from making changes to the contents of a cell. |
|   |  | **Note**  If you do not specify a password anyone can change the protection for the worksheet. |
| 2 | Objects check box | Click to prevent an unauthorized user from making changes to graphic objects (charts and tables) embedded in the worksheet. |
|   |  | **Note**  If you do not specify a password anyone can change the protection for the worksheet. |
| 3 | Scenarios check box | Click to prevent an unauthorized user from making changes to the scenarios of a cell. |
|   |  | **Note**  If you do not specify a password anyone can change the protection for the worksheet. |
| 4 | Password text box | Enter a password assigned to authorized users. Only those entering the correct password can enable or disabled protections. |

## Tools ➤ Protection ➤ Protect Workbook

Use this option to prevent someone from making changes to the structure or windows in a workbook. You can also choose a password to use when you have several people sharing a workbook, and you want to be sure that the sheet is protected from anyone making changes to the protection you have set.

## How You Get Here

◇ Press **Alt+T,P,W**

◇ Choose **Tools ➤ Protection ➤ Protect Workbook**

## What's In This Dialog Box

Figure 23.9 is a sample of this dialog box and Table 23.8 has a description of the options available.

**Figure 23.9**   The Protect Workbook dialog box

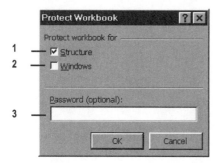

**Table 23.8**   Options in the Protect Workbook dialog box

| # | Option | What you do with it |
|---|--------|---------------------|
| 1 | Structure check box | Click to protect the workbook from an unauthorized user from making changes to the structure of the workbook, which includes inserting, deleting, hiding or renaming sheets. |
| | | **Note**  If you do not specify a password anyone can change the protection for the workbook. |
| 2 | Windows check box | Click to protect the workbook from an unauthorized user from making changes to the windows in the workbook, which includes moving, resizing, hiding or closing them. |
| | | **Note**  If you do not specify a password anyone can change the protection for the workbook. |
| 3 | Password text box | Enter a password assigned to authorized users. Only those entering the correct password can enable or disabled protections. |

## Tools ➤ Protection ➤ Protect and Share Workbook

Use this option to protect the structure and windows of a shared workbook. If the selected workbook is not currently shared, Excel displays a window asking if you would like to designate that workbook as a shared workbook.

## How You Get Here

◇ Press **Alt+T,P,S**    ◇ Choose **Tools** ➤ **Protection** ➤ **Protect and Share Workbook**

## What's In This Dialog Box

Figure 23.10 is a sample of this dialog box and Table 23.9 has a description of the options available.

**Figure 23.10**   The Protect Shared Workbook dialog box

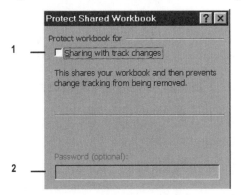

**Table 23.9**   Options in the Protect Shared Workbook dialog box

| # | Option | What you do with it |
|---|--------|---------------------|
| 1 | Sharing with track changes check box | Click to share your workbook and keep someone from turning off the change tracking option. |
|   |  | **Note**  If you do not specify a password anyone can change the protection for the workbook. |
| 2 | Password text box | Enter a password assigned to authorized users. Only those entering the correct password can enable or disabled protections. |

# Tools ➤ Online Collaboration

Use this option to conduct a conversation online, similar to making a multiple-party telephone call. You will be collaborating with other people on one file at the same time. Those people who are participating will be able to edit and chat using the server that you specify. As host you will control the meeting, setting up who and how participants will interact during the meeting. In order for someone to join a meeting they all must have access to the same Internet or intranet (an inter-office network) and have Microsoft Netmeeting installed on their computer or network. However, they don't have to have the application you are working from to chat with you or edit your file online. This option works with your default email server and accesses your address book there. (For more information, see What Is The Outlook Mail Application on page 647.) This can be pretty complex, especially if you are having a Web discussion. You must first set up a server, then open the presentation you want to have the discussion about, then give the command. Most people would rather email the presentation around for comments rather than have a "live" discussion/collaboration about it.

### How You Get Here

◇ Press **Alt+T,N**                    ◇ Choose **Tools ➤ Online Collaboration**

# Tools ➤ Goal Seek

Use this option to change the value of an independent cell until a target value in a dependent cell is reached. For example, if you have a formula in cell F12 that indicates a profitability percentage and you want to know the maximum number of defective products (stored in cell G3) without compromising profitability, you can enter the percentage you are looking in F12 and adjust the value in cell G3 until the target value (in F12) is reached.

### How You Get Here

◇ Press **Alt+T,G**                    ◇ Choose **Tools ➤ Goal Seek**

### What's In This Dialog Box

Figure 23.11 is a sample of this dialog box and Table 23.10 has a description of the options available.

**Figure 23.11**   The Goal Seek dialog box

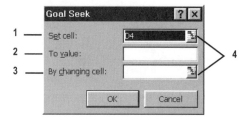

**Table 23.10**   Options in the Goal Seek dialog box

| # | Option | What you do with it |
|---|--------|---------------------|
| 1 | Set cell text box | Enter the cell name that contains the formula that needs a specific value (the goal or target value). |
| 2 | To value text box | Enter the value that needs to appear in the cell identified in the Set cell text box. |
| 3 | By changing cell text box | Enter the cell whose value will be changed to achieve the target "To value" in the cell identified above. This cell must be referenced in the formula in the cell containing the target value. |
| 4 | Collapse button | Click to temporarily collapse the dialog box, so you can see the full view of the spreadsheet while goal-seeking. Once you've collapsed this dialog box, click this button again to restore the dialog box to the original size. |

# Tools ➤ Scenarios

Use this option to view data using a "what if" condition. For example, you could look at a spreadsheet containing the breakdown of your mortgage payment schedule, showing for each payment the amount paid in interest, the amount paid to principle and the remaining balance. You could run a "what if" scenario to see what this schedule would look like if you paid an additional $100 each month.

## How You Get Here

◇ Press **Alt+T,E**          ◇ Choose **Tools ➤ Scenarios**

## What's In This Dialog Box

Figure 23.12 is a sample of this dialog box and Table 23.11 has a description of the options available.

**Figure 23.12**   The Scenario Manager dialog box

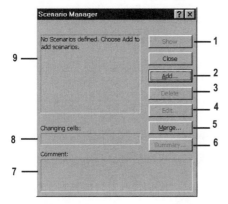

**Table 23.11**   Options in the Scenario Manager dialog box

| # | Option | What you do with it |
|---|--------|---------------------|
| 1 | Show button | Click to display the changes to the scenarios you have chosen on the worksheet. |
| 2 | Add button | Click to display the Add Scenarios window, where you can define and apply scenarios. |
| 3 | Delete button | Click to delete the selected scenario. |
| 4 | Edit button | Click to display the Edit Scenario window, where you can make changes to the name, the reference cells, and the values of the selected scenario. |
| 5 | Merge button | Click to display the Merge Scenarios window, where you can identify the workbook into which you want the selected scenario merged. |
| 6 | Summary button | Click to display the Summary window, where you can create a separate tab in the worksheet that displays the scenario values. |

**Table 23.11**   Options in the Scenario Manager dialog box, continued

| # | Option | What you do with it |
|---|--------|---------------------|
| 7 | Comments text box | View information on the creator of the scenario and comments regarding its function. |
| 8 | Changing Cells text box | View a list of the cells whose values are saved under the current scenario. |
| 9 | Scenario text box | View a list of all active scenarios for the active worksheet. |

# Tools ➤ Auditing

Use this option to trace the cells referenced in a formula. Each of the options in the flyout menu happens as soon as you choose the option. For example, if you have a formula that refers to a cell in another worksheet, you can find exactly where that cell is. This is helpful when troubleshooting; you may have deleted a worksheet that carried a reference cell, and now a formula displays #REF! as a value. The auditing features help you trace the missing reference cell and fix the problem.

**N O T E**   This action happens immediately; there are no other warnings.  ▪

## How You Get Here

◇ Press **Alt+T,U**         ◇ Choose **Tools ➤ Auditing**

## What's In This Flyout Menu

Figure 23.13 is a sample of this flyout menu and Table 23.12 has a description of the options available.

**Figure 23.13**   The Tools ➤ Auditing flyout menu

10 —— Trace Precedents
11 —— Trace Dependents
12 —— Trace Error
13 —— Remove All Arrows
14 —— Show Auditing Toolbar

**Table 23.12**   Options in the Tools ➤ Auditing flyout menu

| # | Option | Keyboard shortcut | What you do with it |
|---|--------|-------------------|---------------------|
| 10 | Trace Precedents | Press **Alt+T,U,T** | Display an arrow that goes *from the cells that supply values* directly to the formula in the active cell. Blue arrows show cells that are dependent on the selected cell. Red arrows show cells that produce errors. |
| 11 | Trace Dependents | Press **Alt+T,U,D** | Display an arrow that goes from *to the active cell* from formulas that depend on the value in the active cell. Blue arrows show cells that are dependent on the selected cell. Red arrows show cells that produce errors. |
| 12 | Trace Error | Press **Alt+T,U,E** | Display a red arrow that points to the cells responsible for the formula error in the active cell. |
| 13 | Remove All Arrows | Press **Alt+T,U,A** | Remove the auditing arrows from the screen. |
| 14 | Show Auditing Toolbar | Press **Alt+T,U,S** | Display the Auditing toolbar on the screen. |

# The Auditing Toolbar

Use this option to display the toolbar you use when you are auditing a worksheet.

## How You Get Here

◇ Press **Alt+T,U,S**          ◇ Choose **Tools** ➤ **Auditing** ➤ **Show Auditing Toolbar**

## What's In This Toolbar

Figure 23.14 is a sample of this toolbar and Table 23.13 has a description of the icons available.

**Figure 23.14**   The Auditing toolbar

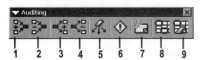

**Table 23.13**   Icons in the Auditing toolbar

| # | Icon | What you do with it |
|---|------|---------------------|
| 1 | Trace Precedents | Click to display an arrow that goes *from the cells that supply values* directly to the formula in the active cell. Blue arrows show cells that are dependent on the selected cell. Red arrows show cells that produce errors. |
| 2 | Remove Precedents Arrows | Click to remove one level of dependent arrows. |
| 3 | Trace Dependents | Click to display an arrow that goes from *to the active cell* from formulas that depend on the value in the active cell. Blue arrows show cells that are dependent on the selected cell. Red arrows show cells that produce errors. |

**Table 23.13**    Icons in the Auditing toolbar, continued

| # | Icon | What you do with it |
|---|------|---------------------|
| 4 | Remove Dependents Arrows | Click to remove one level of precedents arrows. |
| 5 | Remove All Arrows | Click to remove the auditing arrows from the screen. |
| 6 | Trace Error | Click to display a red arrow that points to the cells responsible for the formula error in the active cell. |
| 7 | New Comment | Click to enter a comment. |
| 8 | Circle Invalid Data | Click to circle the cells containing values that are above the limit you set for Validation. (For more information, see Data ➤ Validation on page 397.) |
| 9 | Clear Validation Circles | Click to hide the circles around the cells containing values that are above the limit you set for Validation. (For more information, see Data ➤ Validation on page 397.) |

# Tools ➤ Macro

Use this option to choose one of several activities related to macros, such as record, playback, stop, and erase. Macros are a series of steps that you program in a set order and are helpful when you need to perform the same series of steps over and over. In fact, macros are a great way to "replace yourself" at the keyboard when you do the same tasks over and over again. (Never thought you'd be given permission to be lazy, did you?) (For more information, see Tools ➤ Macro on page 101.)

**TIP**    Macros can save you a lot of time—if you have a repetitive task that is more than four or five keystrokes, you should create a macro.

## How You Get Here

◇ Press **Alt+T,M**              ◇ Choose **Tools ➤ Macro**

# Tools ➤ Add-Ins

Use this option to apply or add a feature that is not common enough to be loaded with the general application, but may be helpful to some of the users. Add-ins are programs that add optional commands and features to Microsoft Excel. Before you can use an add-in, you must load it into Microsoft Excel.

**N O T E**    Applying an add-in to a workbook uses some memory, so only load those add-ins you use. Clearing (unchecking) an add-in simply frees up memory in the workbook; it doesn't delete the add-in from the library. ■

## How You Get Here

◇ Press **Alt+T,I**    ◇ Choose **Tools ➤ Add-Ins**

## What's In This Dialog Box

Figure 23.15 is a sample of this dialog box and Table 23.14 has a description of options that are unique to Excel.

**Figure 23.15**    The Add-Ins dialog box

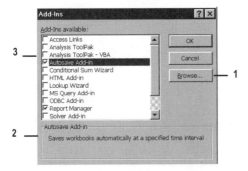

**Table 23.14**    Options in the Add-Ins dialog box

| # | Option | What you do with it |
|---|--------|---------------------|
| 1 | Browse button | Click to display the Browse window, where you can load add-ins from other programs, or add-ins that you have created. |
| 2 | Access Links text box | View information on the add-in you chose in the list above. |
| 3 | Add-Ins available list | Click to choose which add-ins you want automatically available in the active workbook. |

# Tools ➤ Customize

Use this option to display the Customize window, where you can customize toolbars, keyboard shortcuts, and menu commands. Customizing allows you to create new tools, shortcuts, and commands, and modify existing ones to better suit your individual needs. (For example, you may want to create a tool to execute a frequently used option that is usually only available using a menu option). (For more information, see Tools ➤ Customize on page 107.)

## How You Get Here

◇ Press **Alt+T,C**    ◇ Choose **Tools ➤ Customize**

# Tools ➤ Options

Use this option to modify many elements, such as screen appearance, printing, spelling, etc. This feature is helpful for those who don't mind getting under the hood of the computer, tweaking a few elements, all in the interest of style and efficiency.

---

**N O T E**   These tabs let you customize the settings for the features and are not another method for applying them. ■

## How You Get Here

◇ Press **Alt+T,O**

◇ Choose **Tools** ➤ **Options**

## What's In This Dialog Box

Figure 23.16 is a sample of this dialog box and Table 23.15 has a description of the tabs available.

**Figure 23.16**   The Options dialog box

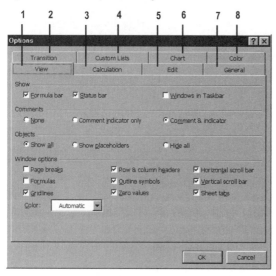

**Table 23.15**   Tabs in the Options dialog box

| # | Tab name | What you do with it |
|---|----------|---------------------|
| 1 | View | Click to choose technical elements related to the visual display of the screen, such as formula bars, comments, and objects. (For a complete description of the options available, see Table 23.16 on page 385.) |
| 2 | Transition | Click to set the transition options for the workbook. (For a complete description of the options available, see Table 23.17 on page 386.) |
| 3 | Calculation | Click to specify how calculations are performed and shown in a workbook. (For a complete description of the options available, see Table 23.18 on page 386.) |
| 4 | Custom Lists | Click to create and import lists in a workbook. (For a complete description of the options available, see Table 23.19 on page 386.) |
| 5 | Edit | Click to choose technical elements related to editing, such as over striking or inserting options, the default paragraph style, the picture editor, and click and type.(For a complete description of the options available, see Table 23.20 on page 386.) |
| 6 | Chart | Click to change the settings for the charts in the workbook. (For a complete description of the options available, see Table 23.21 on page 387.) |
| 7 | General | Click to choose technical elements related to the layout of the screen, such as background page breaks, measurement units (centimeters or inches), Web options, and email options. (For a complete description of the options available, see Table 23.22 on page 387.) |
| 8 | Color | Click to choose more colors for the workbook items. (For a complete description of the options available, see Table 23.23 on page 387.) |

The following tables describe the options for the individual tabs in this dialog box:

- Table 23.16 describes the View tab,
- Table 23.17 describes the Transition tab,
- Table 23.18 describes the Calculation tab,
- Table 23.19 describes the Custom Lists tab,
- Table 23.20 describes the Edit tab,
- Table 23.21 describes the Chart tab,
- Table 23.22 describes the General tab, and
- Table 23.23 describes the Color tab.

**Table 23.16**   Options in the Options dialog box View tab

| Option | What you do with it |
|--------|---------------------|
| Show area | Click to display the formula and status bars. If you want the open file displayed on the Windows taskbar you can set that option here. |
| Comments area | Choose an item that determines how comments are displayed. |

**Table 23.16**   Options in the Options dialog box View tab, continued

| Option | What you do with it |
| --- | --- |
| Objects area | Choose an item that determines how objects are displayed. |
| Window options area | Choose an item that determines how the various elements are displayed. For instance, you may not want the gridlines displayed in your workbooks. |

**Table 23.17**   Options in the Options dialog box Transition tab

| Option | What you do with it |
| --- | --- |
| Save Excel files as drop-down list | Choose an item that determines the default file type when you save in Excel. |
| Settings area | Choose an item that determines the settings for display, viewing, and opening the workbook. |
| Sheet Options area | Choose an item that determines how you want formulas converted between Lotus 1-2-3 and Excel. |

**Table 23.18**   Options in the Options dialog box Calculation tab

| Option | What you do with it |
| --- | --- |
| Calculation area | Choose an item that determines how you want the calculations performed in the workbooks. |
| Iteration check box | Click to set the repetitions for goal seeking or circular references. |
| Maximum iterations text box | Enter the highest number of repetitions you want. |
| Maximum change text box | Enter the number for the changes below this number. |
| Workbook options area | Choose an item that determines the calculation options effecting the entire workbook. |

**Table 23.19**   Options in the Options dialog box Custom Lists tab

| Option | What you do with it |
| --- | --- |
| Custom lists listing | Click to choose a list. |
| List entries listing | Enter the list items. |
| Import list from cells text box | Enter the cell range for the list you are importing from. |
| Import button | Click to start the import. |

**Table 23.20**   Options in the Options dialog box Edit tab

| Option | What you do with it |
| --- | --- |
| Settings area | Choose an item that determines how your edits will display in the workbook. |

**Table 23.21**   Options in the Options dialog box Chart tab

| Option | What you do with it |
| --- | --- |
| Active chart area | Choose an item that determines the display options for the charts in the workbook. |
| Chart tips area | Click to show the tips for the chart items. This is where you hover over an item in a chart and a tip displays containing a description of the item. |

**Table 23.22**   Options in the Options dialog box General tab

| Option | What you do with it |
| --- | --- |
| Settings area | Click to set the viewing, display, and opening options for Excel. |
| Web Options button | Click to set how your workbook looks and acts when viewed by a Web browser. |
| Sheets in new workbook list | Enter the number of sheets you want to start with whenever you create a new workbook. |
| Standard font drop-down lists | Click to choose the default font for all new workbooks. Choose the size for the default font. |
| Default file location text box | Enter the full path name for the location for the default working folder. |
| Alternate startup file location text box | Enter the full path location for the file you want opened automatically whenever you start Excel. |
| User name text box | Enter your name. |

**Table 23.23**   Options in the Options dialog box Color tab

| Option | What you do with it |
| --- | --- |
| Standard colors list | Click to choose a color for the workbook. |
| Modify button | Click to display additional color options. |
| Reset button | Click to restore the color to the default. |
| Chart fills list | Click to choose a color for the chart background. |
| Chart lines list | Click to choose a color for the lines in a chart. |
| Copy colors from drop-down list | Click to copy the colors from one open workbook to another. |

# The Excel Data Menu

# What Is The Data Menu

This menu lists the commands that you'll use to perform actions that affect data, such as sorting columns of numbers, applying a filter so that you can look at specific information, and specifying the type of data you want entered in a worksheet.

> **N O T E**   Several of the text fields have a **Collapse** button  which lets you reduce the size of dialog box so that you can use your mouse to choose a cell, or range of cells instead of having to type the information manually. Once you've chosen the range, click the **Collapse** button again to redisplay the dialog box. ▪

If a menu option has an ellipsis (three dots) or an arrow beside it, the application "asks" you for additional information before the action takes place. If the menu doesn't have one of these symbols, the action you choose happens immediately. If the action takes place immediately, you won't see a sample screen in this section.

# Data ➤ Sort

Use this option to sort a selected range of columns or rows alphabetically, numerically, or by date based on the information in a specific field. Sorting is extremely helpful in organizing your data to make it more meaningful. You can also perform second and third level (secondary and tertiary) sorts; for example you can sort first by state, then by zip code, and finally, by last name.

> **N O T E**   Excel may display a warning indicating that the range selected may need to be expanded. This warning is likely to come up, for example, if you've selected a single column containing names, but not an adjoining column with the phone numbers. If you sort *without* expanding the range, the names are alphabetized, but the phone numbers won't move and won't be lined up correctly. ▪

## How You Get Here

◇ Click 🔽   ◇ Press **Alt+D,S**   ◇ Choose **Data** ➤ **Sort**

## What's In This Dialog Box

Figure 24.1 is a sample of this dialog box and Table 24.1 has a description of the options available.

**Figure 24.1**   The Sort dialog box

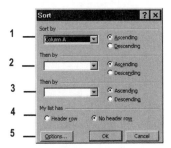

**Table 24.1**   Options in the Sort dialog box

| # | Option | What you do with it |
|---|--------|---------------------|
| 1 | Sort by area | Choose an item that determines which column or row Excel should use for the primary sort (the listing includes the headings of your selected columns or rows). Click the **Ascending** radio button to sort the selected data from the lowest to the highest value. Click the **Descending** radio button to sort from the highest to lowest value. |
| 2 | Then by area 1 | Choose an item that determines which column or row Excel should use for the secondary sort (the listing includes the available headings of your selected columns or rows). Click the **Ascending** radio button to sort the selected data from the lowest to the highest value. Click the **Descending** radio button to sort from the highest to lowest value. |
| 3 | Then by area 2 | Choose an item that determines which column or row Excel should use for the tertiary sort (the listing includes the available headings of your selected columns or rows). Click the **Ascending** radio button to sort the selected data from the lowest to the highest value. Click the **Descending** radio button to sort from the highest to lowest value. |
| 4 | My list has area | Click to tell Excel whether to exclude the first (header) row from the sort or that there isn't a header row at all. Click the **Header row** radio button when your first row has labels that shouldn't be sorted. |
| 5 | Options button | Click to display the Options dialog box so that you can identify a sort other than "normal," such as a sorting by days of the week or months of the year. "Normal" sorts these labels alphabetically. You can also choose a left-to-right sort, when sorting rows. |

# Data ➤ Filter

Use this option to look at specific information in your worksheet. For example, you may want to see a list of only those clients that ordered a product in the last six months. Or you might want to see only those employees in the Accounting department.

## How You Get Here

◇ Press **Alt+D,F**   ◇ Choose **Data** ➤ **Filter**

## What's In This Flyout Menu

Figure 24.2 is a sample of this flyout menu.

**Figure 24.2**   The Data ➤ Filter flyout menu

| | |
|---|---|
| Data ➤ Filter ➤ AutoFilter | 392 |
| Data ➤ Filter ➤ Show All | 393 |
| Data ➤ Filter ➤ Advanced Filter | 393 |

## Data ➤ Filter ➤ AutoFilter

Use this option to quickly query your worksheet for specific information. The worksheet contracts to show you just the information you requested—records that don't match the query criteria are automatically hidden from view, but aren't deleted from the worksheet. When you choose AutoFilter, Excel adds a drop-down list to the first row of each column (the field names) so that you can choose which entries you want displayed. Click the **All** option to redisplay all the records. Click the menu option to deselect AutoFilter and the drop-down lists disappear.

> **TIP** Besides listing a single item from that column (for example, in a State column, a list of states in the column appears), the list gives you two additional options: top ten and custom. The top ten option is very useful for number columns. You can choose the top ten, bottom 10, top 5, top 3, top 10 percent, etc. The custom options lets you display on the records that meet operations-based (less than, greater than, etc.) criteria. You can't choose more than one filter in any one column.

> **N O T E**   When filtering data, all records (the entire row) that don't have the criteria of the selected field (column) are filtered out. The entire row is affected; you can't manipulate the data in the column only. ■

## How You Get Here

◇ Press **Alt+D,F,F**   ◇ Choose **Data** ➤ **Filter** ➤ **AutoFilter**

## Data ➤ Filter ➤ Show All

Use this option to display all rows in a filtered list. Although you can apply multiple filters (only one per row though), this option displays all records no matter how many filters have been used.

### How You Get Here

◇ Press **Alt+D,F,S**   ◇ Choose **Data** ➤ **Filter** ➤ **Show All**

## Data ➤ Filter ➤ Advanced Filter

Use this option to define the criteria used to display a choose group of records. The result is very similar to AutoFilter, but you can more closely define the filtering criteria. This option is helpful for those who have unique criteria that cannot be met using AutoFilter.

◇ Press **Alt+D,F,A**   ◇ Choose **Data** ➤ **Filter** ➤ **Advanced Filter**

### What's In This Dialog Box

Figure 24.3 is a sample of this dialog box and Table 24.2 has a description of the options that are available.

**Figure 24.3**   The Advanced Filter dialog box

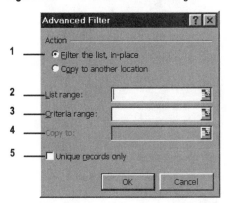

**Table 24.2**   Options in the Advanced Filter dialog box

| # | Option | What you do with it |
|---|--------|---------------------|
| 1 | Action radio button | Click to display filter results within the list (which means the worksheet contracts, just like an AutoFilter) or to display the filter results on a separate *section* of the worksheet. You can't display the filter results on a separate worksheet. |
| 2 | List range text box | Enter the range of cells you want filtered. As long as your cellpointer was in any cell in the database when you choose this option, the correct range of cells should already be in the box. |

**Table 24.2**    Options in the Advanced Filter dialog box, continued

| # Option | What you do with it |
| --- | --- |
| 3   List criteria text box | Enter the range of cells that hold the criteria. You always choose at least two rows—the header row for the criteria (field names) and at least one criteria row. You can have multiple criteria row if you want OR conditions to apply. You can type in the range or you can highlight the range on your worksheet. |
| 4   Copy to text box | Enter the range of cells to which you want the filtered list copied. This option is only available when you click the **Copy to another location** radio button. |
| 5   Unique records only check box | Click to eliminate duplicate records. A duplicate record is defined as a record, or records, that have exactly the same information in each field. The filter only displays only one occurrence of the record. |

# Data ➤ Form

Use this option to display a data entry form so that you can enter a new record in your worksheet. Once you fill out the form, Excel adds the record to the active worksheet. The form gets it's information from the active worksheet: the title bar is the worksheet label, the field names are the same as the first row (the heading row).

 **TIP**    Use the scrollbars to the right of the fields to move among adjacent records.

 **N O T E**    Excel may display a warning indicating that the range selected doesn't have a readily distinguishable header row. To accept the first row as the header row (where the field names are derived), click the **OK** button. ▨

## How You Get Here

◇ Press **Alt+D,O**          ◇ Choose **Data ➤ Form**

## What's In This Dialog Box

Figure 24.4 is a sample of this dialog box and Table 24.3 has a description of the options available.

**Figure 24.4**   The Sheet # dialog box

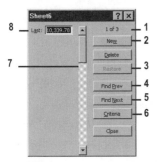

**Table 24.3**   Options in the Sheet # dialog box

| # | Option | What you do with it |
|---|--------|---------------------|
| 1 | Record Number field | View the number of the selected record. If the field says "New Record", this record is added to the existing list. |
| 2 | New button | Click to bring up a blank form. The data you enter in this form becomes a new record and is added to end of the worksheet. |
| 3 | Restore button | Click to undo all entries made to the record and return it to its original state. You must click this button *before* you click the **Enter** button or scroll to the next record or the changes are made and you'll have to edit the entry again. |
| 4 | Find Prev button | Click to move to the previous record. If you have selected a criteria (done by clicking the **Criteria** button), Excel moves to the previous record that matches that criteria. |
| 5 | Find Next button | Click to move to the next record. If you have selected a criteria (done by clicking the **Criteria** button), Excel moves to the next record that matches that criteria. |
| 6 | Criteria button/ Form button | Click to change the form to a Criteria form so that you can set specific parameters for looking up records. When you have set your criteria, click the **Form** button to return to a normal form. To turn off the criteria, click the **Criteria** button and delete the criteria. |
| 7 | Record scroll bar | Scroll to the next record. |
| 8 | Record text box | Enter a new value. |

**TIP**   Text criteria is letter based, so a criteria of "Pres" finds President, Vice President, Presiding Manager—any entry that has the letters "pres". You can use the operators like less (<) than or greater than (>). You can use the asterisk wildcard (*) to represent "all other letters." For example: S* finds all entries that begins with S. You can use the question mark (?) wildcard to represent "any one letter". For example: S?? finds SAM, SAP, or SOS, but not SAMMY, SAMANTHA, or SAPPY.

# Data ➤ Subtotals

Use this option to quickly create subtotals of the numerical data in your database. You tell Excel what field you want to subtotal in your database and Excel creates the subtotals for you. You have to sort your database first so that all the data is correctly grouped before you execute this command. You can also add a summary to the end of the subtotals.

**TIP**   Be sure you sort your database *before* you use this option so that the data is correctly grouped when Excel calculates the subtotal.

## How You Get Here

◇ Press **Alt+D,B**          ◇ Choose **Data** ➤ **Subtotal**

## What's In This Dialog Box

Figure 24.5 is a sample of this dialog box and Table 24.4 has a description of the options available.

**Figure 24.5**   The Subtotal dialog box

**Table 24.4**  Options in the Subtotal dialog box

| # | Option | What you do with it |
|---|--------|---------------------|
| 1 | At each change in drop-down list | Choose an item that determines what field Excel uses to create the subtotal groups. For example, you might group by JobTitles to subtotal on the Salary field. |
| 2 | Use function drop-down list | Choose an item that determines what mathematical calculation you want to use for creating your subtotals. |
| 3 | Add subtotal to drop-down list | Choose an item that determines what field is subtotaled. At each break in the field chosen, Excel inserts a new row that displays the subtotal. |
| 4 | Replace current subtotals check box | Click to recalculate an existing subtotal and overwrite the existing value. If you don't click this button, Excel inserts a new row with the new calculations. |
| 5 | Page Break between groups check box | Click to insert a page break between each group that is being calculated. |
| 6 | Summary below data check box | Click to put a Grand Total as the last line of the subtotaled worksheet. |
| 7 | Remove All button | Click to remove all subtotals from the worksheet. |

# Data ➤ Validation

Use this option to establish criteria for valid entries into a specific field or range of cells. For example, you may want to keep people from entering more than nine digits in the zip code field. Once you set up the criteria, you'll get an error message if you try to enter unacceptable information. (You can customize the error message.)

---

**N O T E**  Be sure you choose the cell or range or cells you want validated *before* you choose this option since the value entered *only* applies to the currently selected range.  ▩

## How You Get Here

◇ Press **Alt+D,L**          ◇ Choose **D**ata ➤ **Va**l**i**dation

## What's In This Dialog Box

Figure 24.6 is a sample of this dialog box and Table 24.5 has a description of the tabs available.

**Figure 24.6**    The Data Validation dialog box

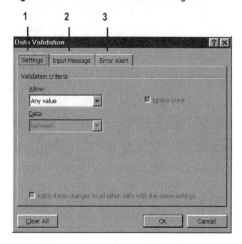

**Table 24.5**    Tabs in the Data Validation dialog box

| # | Tab name | What you do with it |
|---|----------|---------------------|
| 1 | Settings | Click to choose what information you can enter in a given cell or range of cells. (For a complete description of the options available, see Table 24.6 on page 399.) |
| 2 | Input Message | Click to enter the title and message you wish to appear when a specific cell is selected. (For a complete description of the options available, see Table 24.6 on page 399.) |
| 3 | Error Alert | Click to enter the specific type of error and the error message to display when someone tries to enter invalid data. (For a complete description of the options available, see Table 24.6 on page 399.) |

The following tables describe the options for the individual tabs in this dialog box:

- Table 24.6 describes the Settings tab,
- Table 24.7 describes the Input Message tab, and
- Table 24.8 describes the Error Alert tab.

**Table 24.6**    Options in the Data Validation dialog box Settings tab

| Option | What you do with it |
| --- | --- |
| Allow drop-down list | Click to restrict the data to be entered in the selected cells to a specific type. |
| Ignore blank check box | Click to prevent an error message displaying whenever a restricted cell is blank. |
| Data drop-down list | Click to choose the type of comparison operator you want to use based on the type of data you allowed entered. |
| Apply these changes...check box | Click to apply these same restriction settings to all other cells in the worksheet with the same validation settings. |
| Clear All button | Click to cancel all the settings in this dialog box. |

**Table 24.7**    Options in the Data Validation dialog box Input Message tab

| Option | What you do with it |
| --- | --- |
| Show input message check box | Click to display a prompt message when a restricted cell is selected. |
| Title text box | Enter an optional title for the prompt message. |
| Input message text box | Enter the prompt message. |

**Table 24.8**    Options in the Data Validation dialog box Input Error Alert tab

| Option | What you do with it |
| --- | --- |
| Show error alert check box | Click to display an error message when invalid data is entered in a restricted cell. |
| Style drop-down list | Click to choose the type of error message you want displayed. The error options displayed for continuing are different based on the style you choose. |
| Title text box | Enter the optional title for the error message. |
| Error message text box | Enter the error message. |

# Data ➤ Table

Use this option to forecast values using what-if analysis on selected cell ranges in your worksheet. You will see how changing certain values in formulas can affect results. If you are calculating more than one version of an operation Data Tables gives you a way to do this easily. When you have finished the calculations you can view and compare the results of them all on your worksheet. The data table requires either one or two variables to perform the analysis based on the input cell(s) and whether the values are listed across a row or down a column.

## How You Get Here

◇ Press **Alt+D,O**          ◇ Choose **D**ata ➤ **T**able

## What's In This Dialog Box

Figure 24.7 is a sample of this dialog box and Table 24.9 has a description of the options available.

**Figure 24.7**    The Table dialog box

**Table 24.9**    Options in the Table dialog box

| # | Option | What you do with it |
|---|--------|---------------------|
| 1 | Row input cell text box | Enter the cell reference for the row input cell. |
| 2 | Column input cell text box | Enter the cell reference for the column input cell. |

# Data ➤ Text to Columns

Use this option to copy text created in another program (such as Microsoft Word) into a worksheet and convert that text into individual cells. Once you choose this option, Excel opens the Convert Text to Columns Wizard and walks you through the process of converting the text.

**N O T E**    You can only convert one column at a time, but that column can have as many rows as you need. ▓

**T I P**    Microsoft has provided several wizards to walk you through some of the more complex processes step-by-step. This Wizard has some instructions, but they may still seem cryptic to the novice user. You may need to play around with the different selections to gain more confidence in the outcome.

## How You Get Here

◇ Press **Alt+D,E**    ◇ Choose **Data ➤ Text to Columns**

## What's In This Dialog Box

Figure 24.8 is a sample of the wizard and has a description of options available.

**Figure 24.8**   The Convert Text to Columns wizard

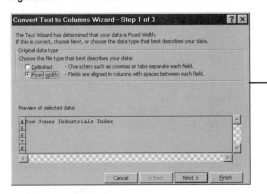

Follow the instructions in the Wizard to complete the conversion of text to columns. If you don't like the options you picked you can back up and change them, or cancel and start over. But you can only do that if you don't click the finish button first.

# Data ➤ Consolidate

Use this option to identify criteria for consolidating data from one or more sources (including data from other workbooks or data embedded in other applications). Once consolidated, the summary data is displayed in a table, which is a great way to combine information for a management summary report.

**N O T E**   You can consolidate up to 255 source areas. ▓

## How You Get Here

✧ Press **Alt+D,N**          ✧ Choose **Data ➤ Consolidate**

## What's In This Dialog Box

Figure 24.9 is a sample of this dialog box and Table 24.9 has a description of the options available.

**Figure 24.9**   The Consolidate dialog box

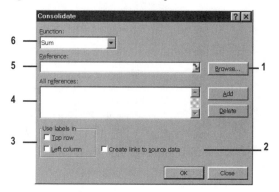

**Table 24.10**   Options in the Consolidate dialog box

| # | Option | What you do with it |
|---|--------|---------------------|
| 1 | Browse button | Click to locate other files that have information that you want to consolidate. |
| 2 | Create links to source data check box | Click to automatically update the consolidation data if the source data changes. |
| 3 | Use labels in area | Click to use the labels from your source area when you consolidate by category. This option only works if you selected the selected the row with the labels when you entered the range. Don't use this option if you want to consolidate by position or if the information is arranged similarly, but has different labels. |
| 4 | All references list | View the list of ranges that will be consolidated when you click the **OK** button. |
| 5 | Reference text box | Enter the range you want to consolidate. Once the correct range is in the text box, click the **Add** button to add this range to the All references list. |
| 6 | Function drop-down list | Choose an item that determines what mathematical function Excel uses to consolidate the data. |

# Data ➤ Group and Outline

Use this option to outline your spreadsheet (yes, this is typically a word processing function, but this option *really* helps you manage a large worksheet). You can show different "views" of your information based on what you hide or show or just show columns with summaries, etc.

## How You Get Here

  ◇ Press **Alt+D,G**          ◇ Choose **Data ➤ Group and Outline**

## What's In This Flyout Menu

Figure 24.10 is a sample of this flyout menu.

**Figure 24.10**   The Data ➤ Group and Outline flyout menu

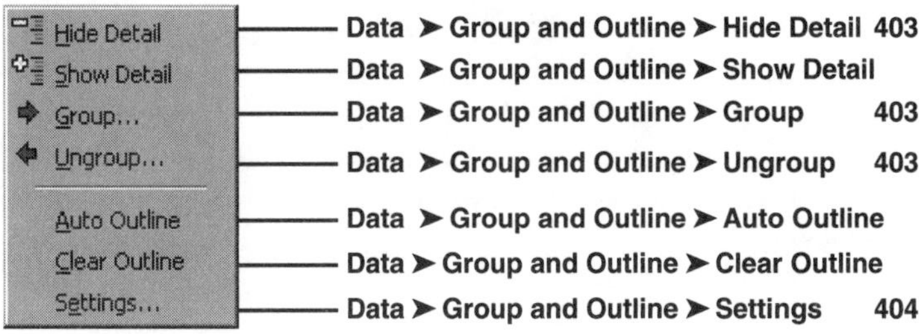

| Menu item | Path | Page |
|---|---|---|
| Hide Detail | Data ➤ Group and Outline ➤ Hide Detail | 403 |
| Show Detail | Data ➤ Group and Outline ➤ Show Detail | |
| Group... | Data ➤ Group and Outline ➤ Group | 403 |
| Ungroup... | Data ➤ Group and Outline ➤ Ungroup | 403 |
| Auto Outline | Data ➤ Group and Outline ➤ Auto Outline | |
| Clear Outline | Data ➤ Group and Outline ➤ Clear Outline | |
| Settings... | Data ➤ Group and Outline ➤ Settings | 404 |

# Data ➤ Group and Outline ➤ Hide Detail

Use this option to hide all the background details for PivotTables, PivotCharts, and outlines so that you can concentrate on the summary information in the report.

## How You Get Here

✧ Press **Alt+D,G,H**          ✧ Choose **Data ➤ Group and Outline ➤ Hide Detail**

# Data ➤ Group and Outline ➤ Show Detail

Use this option to redisplay all the background details for your PivotTables, PivotCharts, and outlines.

## How You Get Here

✧ Press **Alt+D,G,S**          ✧ Choose **Data ➤ Group and Outline ➤ Show Detail**

# Data ➤ Group and Outline ➤ Group

Use this option to combine either row data or column data to create outline levels based on formulas in your worksheet.

## How You Get Here

✧ Press **Alt+D,G,G**          ✧ Choose **Data ➤ Group and Outline ➤ Group**

# Data ➤ Group and Outline ➤ Ungroup

Use this option to choose the rows and columns whose data you want ungrouped from a single line of an outline.

## How You Get Here

✧ Press **Alt+D,G,U**          ✧ Choose **Data** ➤ **Group and Outline** ➤ **Ungroup**

## Data ➤ Group and Outline ➤ Auto Outline

Use this option to automatically apply an outline format to the selected range of cells or to the worksheet (if you haven't selected a range) based on formulas and references. The outline displays in a pane on the left side of the worksheet. Excel automatically groups the data based on how the data is organized: for example, if your worksheet has months of the year and then the totals, Excel creates a totals group.

## How You Get Here

✧ Press **Alt+D,G,A**          ✧ Choose **Data** ➤ **Group and Outline** ➤ **Auto Outline**

## Data ➤ Group and Outline ➤ Clear Outline

Use this option to remove an outline created with Data ➤ Group and Outline ➤ Auto Outline.

## How You Get Here

✧ Press **Alt+D,G,C**          ✧ Choose **Data** ➤ **Group and Outline** ➤ **Clear Outline**

## Data ➤ Group and Outline ➤ Settings

Use this option to choose the location for your summary rows (or columns) if you apply a summary option such as Data ➤ Group and Outline ➤ Group or Data ➤ Group and Outline ➤ Auto Outline. You can also automatically format the summary rows and columns by applying Excel's built-in styles.

## How You Get Here

✧ Press **Alt+D,G,E**          ✧ Choose **Data** ➤ **Group and Outline** ➤ **Settings**

### What's In This Dialog Box

Figure 24.11 is a sample of this drop down list and Table 24.11 has a description of options available.

**Figure 24.11**   The Settings dialog box

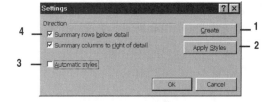

**Table 24.11**   Options in the Settings dialog box

| # | Option | What you do with it |
|---|--------|---------------------|
| 1 | Create button | Click to create an outline or summary report from selected cells based on settings established in this dialog box. |
| 2 | Apply Styles button | Click to apply Excel's built in styles to an existing summary or outline. |
| 3 | Automatic Styles check box | Click to apply an automatic outline or summary style (such as Row Level 1, Column Level 1, etc.) to the summary. |
| 4 | Direction area | Click to indicate where you want Excel to put the summary rows or columns. |

# Data ➤ PivotTable and PivotChart Report

Use this option to display the PivotTable and PivotChart Wizard, which walks you through creating a PivotTable and PivotChart. A PivotTable report lets you compare related totals in an interactive table. This report displayed in various ways for instance, you can filter the data, display just the details for certain areas, or rotate the rows and columns to view the source data's summaries. For a graphical view of the PivotTable report you can create a PivotChart report where you can view charts of the results from the related PivotTable report.

## How You Get Here

✧ Click      ✧ Press **Alt+D,P**          ✧ Choose **Data** ➤ **PivotTable and PivotChart Report**

## What's In This Dialog Box

Figure 24.12 is a sample of the wizard and has a description of the options available.

**Figure 24.12**   The PivotTable and PivotChart wizard

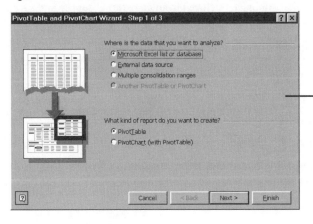

Follow the instructions on the wizard to create your PivotTable or PivotChart. If you don't like the options you picked you can back up and change them, or cancel and start over. But you can only do that if you don't click the finish button first.

# Data ➤ Get External Data

Use this option to pull information from other applications or locations (such as the Internet or an intranet) and place them into your worksheet. When you choose this option you can access Web pages, relational databases, and Excel lists for use in your workbook. This data can be stored within your workbook or you can save the data as separate query files for sharing with other workbooks.

## How You Get Here

✧ Press **Alt+D,D**              ✧ Choose **Data** ➤ **Get External Data**

## What's In This Flyout Menu

Figure 24.13 is a sample of this flyout menu.

**Figure 24.13**    The Data ➤ Get External Data flyout menu

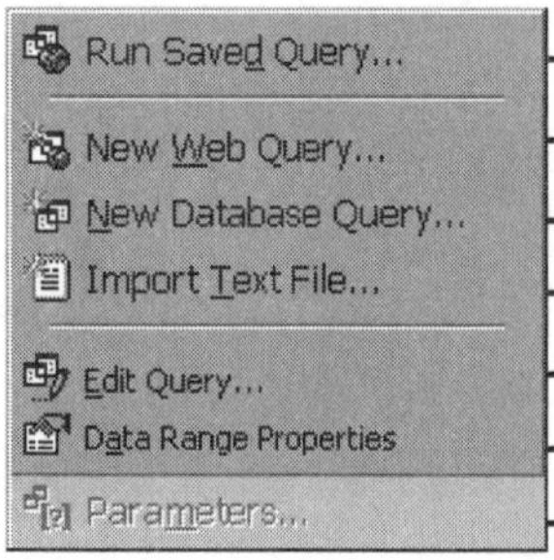

| | |
|---|---|
| Run Saved Query... | —— Data ➤ Get External Data ➤ **Run Saved Query**          406 |
| New Web Query... | —— Data ➤ Get External Data ➤ **New Web Query**          406 |
| New Database Query... | —— Data ➤ Get External Data ➤ **New Database Query**          407 |
| Import Text File... | —— Data ➤ Get External Data ➤ **Import Text File**          408 |
| Edit Query... | —— Data ➤ Get External Data ➤ **Edit Query**          408 |
| Data Range Properties | —— Data ➤ Get External Data ➤ **Data Range Properties**          409 |
| Parameters... | —— Data ➤ Get External Data ➤ **Parameters**          410 |

## Data ➤ Get External Data ➤ Run Saved Query

Use this option to run a query that you have retrieved from an external source and saved onto either a floppy disk or your hard drive. The Run Query dialog box should look a bit familiar—it's the same basic dialog box you see when you choose **File** ➤ **Open**. (For more information, see File ➤ Open on page 39.)

## How You Get Here

✧ Press **Alt+D,D,D**              ✧ Choose **Data** ➤ **Get External Data** ➤ **Run Saved Query**

## Data ➤ Get External Data ➤ New Web Query

Use this option to create a new query from a Web page. You can specify what parts of the Web page you want to keep and the formatting you want to save it with.

## How You Get Here

✧ Press **Alt+D, D,W**              ✧ Choose **Data** ➤ **Get External Data** ➤ **New Web Query**

## What's In This Dialog Box

Figure 24.14 is a sample of this dialog box and Table 24.12 has a description of the options available.

**Figure 24.14**   The New Web Query dialog box

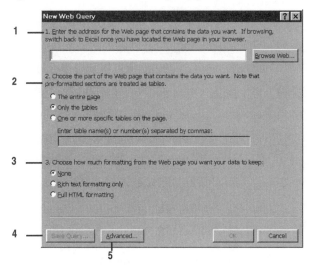

**Table 24.12**   Options in the New Web Query dialog box

| # | Option | What you do with it |
|---|--------|---------------------|
| 1 | Enter the address text box | Enter the address of the web page. |
| 2 | Choose web page part radio buttons | Click to choose the part of the web page you want to save. |
| 3 | Choose the formatting radio buttons | Click to choose how much formatting you want to save with the query. |
| 4 | Save Query button | Click to save as a separate query file so it can be used in other workbooks. |
| 5 | Advanced button | Click to set more options for the saved query. |

## Data ➤ Get External Data ➤ New Database Query

Use this option to create a new query for a database. You can create the query using any type of existing database file. When you have created the query you will use the Microsoft Query application for customizing and recording the query.

### How You Get Here

✧ Press **Alt+D,D,N**            ✧ Choose **Data ➤ Get External Data ➤ New Database Query**

## What's In This Dialog Box

Figure 24.15 is a sample of this dialog box and has a description of the options available.

**Figure 24.15**    The Choose Data Source dialog box

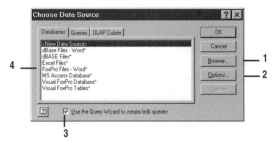

**Table 24.13**    Options in the Choose Data Source dialog box

| # | Option | What you do with it |
|---|--------|---------------------|
| 1 | Browse button | Click to search for additional data sources. |
| 2 | Options button | Click to display the Data Source Options dialog box where you can search the default locations for data sources. |
| 3 | Use the Query Wizard...check box | Click to display the Query Wizard that will walk you through creating and editing your queries. If you want you can opt to use Microsoft Query to create your queries by removing the checkmark in the check box. |
| 4 | Data source list | Choose an item that determines what type of data source you want to query. |

## Data ➤ Get External Data ➤ Import Text File

Use this option to import text files into your Excel worksheets. You can choose any text file you have saved previously.

### How You Get Here

✧ Press **Alt+D,D,T**          ✧ Choose **Data ➤ Get External Data ➤ Import Text File**

## Data ➤ Get External Data ➤ Edit Query

Use this option to change the queries you have saved previously. You can set the parameters for the query and change the properties.

### How You Get Here

✧ Press **Alt+D,D,E**          ✧ Choose **Data ➤ Get External Data ➤ Edit Query**

## What's In This Dialog Box

Figure 24.16 is a sample of this dialog box and has a description of options available.

**Figure 24.16**   The Edit Web Query dialog box

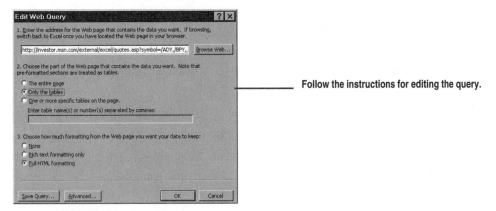

Follow the instructions for editing the query.

## Data ➤ Get External Data ➤ Data Range Properties

Use this option to set the various formatting, refreshing and password properties for the selected external data range.

### How You Get Here

✦ Press **Alt+D,D,A**          ✦ Choose **Data ➤ Get External Data ➤ Data Range Properties**

## What's In This Dialog Box

Figure 24.17 is a sample of this dialog box and Table 24.14 has a description of the options available.

**Figure 24.17**   The External Data Range Properties dialog box

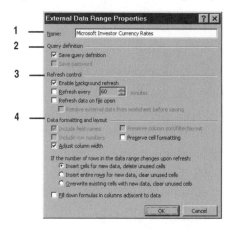

**Table 24.14**   Options in the External Data Range Properties dialog box

| # | Option | What you do with it |
|---|--------|---------------------|
| 1 | Name text box | Enter the name of the query database. |
| 2 | Query definition area | Click to specify a password for the external data range. |
| 3 | Refresh control area | Click to choose the options for refreshing the external data. |
| 4 | Data formatting and layout area | Click to choose the formatting and layout options for the external data range. |

## Data ➤ Get External Data ➤ Parameters

Use this option to create a message that prompts you for the query you want in the workbook. This is only for the current session and cannot be used to retrieve data from OLAP databases.

## How You Get Here

✧ Press **Alt+D,D,M**          ✧ Choose **Data ➤ Get External Data ➤ Parameters**

## What's In This Dialog Box

Figure 24.18 is a sample of this dialog box and Table 24.15 has a description of the options available.

**Figure 24.18**    The Parameters dialog box

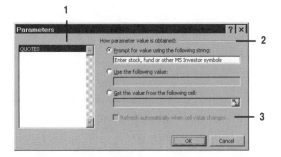

**Table 24.15**    Options in the Parameters dialog box

| # | Option | What you do with it |
|---|--------|---------------------|
| 1 | Parameters list | Click to choose the parameter you want to change. |
| 2 | How parameter value is obtained area | Choose an item that determines the text or value you want to display in the prompt for this parameter. |
| 3 | Refresh automatically check box | Click to use the new prompt and save it. |

# The External Data Toolbar

Use this option to a display a toolbar with controls that you can use to define how Excel queries ("talks to") external data sources, such as an Access database. These sources may be on your local hard drive or they may stored on a remote site, such as a network.

## How You Get Here

✧ Press **Alt+V,T** choose **External Data**    ✧ Choose **View** ➤ **Toolbars** ➤ **External Data**

## What's In This Toolbar

Figure 24.19 is a sample of this toolbar and Table 24.16 has a description of the icons available.

**Figure 24.19**    The External Data Toolbar

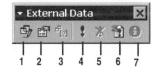

**Table 24.16**    Icons in the External Data Toolbar

| # | Icon | What you do with it |
|---|------|---------------------|
| 1 | Edit Query | Click to edit an existing query. |
| 2 | Data Range Properties | Click to set or review data range properties. |
| 3 | Query Parameters | Click to set query parameters. |
| 4 | Refresh Data | Click to update the data from the data source. |
| 5 | Cancel Refresh | Click to cancel the data update. |
| 6 | Refresh All | Click to update all existing queries. |
| 7 | Refresh Status | Click to view update status. |

# Data ➤ Refresh Data

Use this option to make sure that you're working with the most current edition of the external data. It updates the data from the source so you have current stuff in your workbook.

## How You Get Here

✧ Press **Alt+D,R**

✧ Choose **Data** ➤ **Refresh Data**

# The Excel Chart Menu

## In this chapter

# What Is The Chart Menu

This menu lists the commands that you'll use to perform actions that affect a *chart*, such as editing a chart, changing the type of chart you're working with, creating new chart types, and manually adding data to an existing chart. Charts are graphical representations of information you have placed in a worksheet, such as totals for the first quarter sales. (For more information, see What Is The Chart Format Menu on page 356.)

---

**N O T E**   You must first insert a chart, then choose it for this menu to be active. (For more information, see Insert ➤ Chart on page 326.) When you have a chart selected the options on the Insert Menu and the Format Menu change. The Insert Menu only has the Picture, Worksheet, Chart and Hyperlink options. The Format menu changes according to the object on the chart you have selected. For instance, if you have the axis selected, the Format menu displays Selected Axis. When you choose this option the Format Axis window displays. (For more information, see Format ➤ Selected Area on page 356.) ■

---

If a menu option has an ellipsis (three dots) or an arrow beside it, the application "asks" you for additional information before the action takes place. If the menu doesn't have one of these symbols, the action you choose happens immediately. If the action takes place immediately, you won't see a sample screen in this section.

# The Chart Toolbar

Use this option to display the chart toolbar that has controls for creating or editing a chart that you've inserted in the active worksheet. You can use this toolbar or double-click on the part of the chart you want to format to display the window containing the options for formatting. (For more information, see Format ➤ Selected Area on page 356.)

## How You Get Here

✧ Press **Alt+V,T** choose **Chart**      ✧ Choose **View** ➤ **Toolbars** ➤ **Chart**

## What's In This Toolbar

Figure 25.1 is a sample of this toolbar and Table 25.1 has a description of the icons available.

**Figure 25.1**   The Chart toolbar

**Table 25.1**   Icons in the Chart toolbar

| # | Icon | What you do with it |
|---|------|---------------------|
| 1 | Chart Objects | Choose an item that determines what chart area or characteristic is to be edited. If nothing is selected, this is grayed out. |
| 2 | Format Chart Area | Click to open a formatting dialog box that's suitable for the chart object selected. |
| 3 | Chart Type | |
| 4 | Legend | Click to place or remove a legend from the selected chart. |
| 5 | Data Table | Click to place or remove a data table from the selected chart. |
| 6 | By Row | Click to display the chart by row. |
| 7 | By Column | Click to display the chart by column. |
| 8 | Angle Text Downward | Click to make the selected chart text angle downward. |
| 9 | Angle Text Upward | Click to make the selected chart text angle upward. |

# Chart ➤ Chart Type

Use this option to open the Chart Type dialog box and choose a chart type. The "chart type" refers to the physical format and display properties for the selected chart. You can choose chart types that display as a three dimensional (3-D) chart or as a flat one dimensional chart. Different data is displayed to its best advantage in different kinds of charts. For example, pie charts are an excellent way to illustrate percentages of a whole, but bar charts are better for comparing two or more quantities.

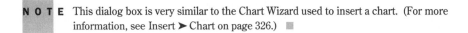

**N O T E**   This dialog box is very similar to the Chart Wizard used to insert a chart.  (For more information, see Insert ➤ Chart on page 326.)  ■

   **T I P**   You can also change the chart type by clicking the drop-down list beside the Chart Type button on the Chart toolbar.

## How You Get Here

✧ Press **Alt+C,T**          ✧ Choose **Chart** ➤ **Chart Type**

## What's In This Dialog Box

Figure 25.2 is a sample of this dialog box and Table 25.2 has a description of the tabs available.

**Figure 25.2**   The Chart Type dialog box

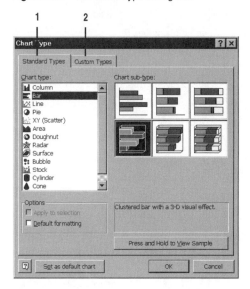

**Table 25.2**   Tabs in the Chart Type dialog box

| # | Tab name | What you do with it |
|---|----------|---------------------|
| 1 | Standard Types | Choose an item that determines how the data series displays. This tab includes the most commonly used chart types. (For a complete description of the options available, see Table 25.3 on page 416.) |
| 2 | Custom Types | Choose from a number of specialized or more emphatic chart types or create a new type based on the currently selected chart. (For a complete description of the options available, see Table 25.4 on page 417.) |

The following tables describe the options for the individual tabs in this dialog box:

- Table 25.3 describes the Standard Types tab, and
- Table 25.4 describes the Custom Types tab.

**Table 25.3**   Options in the Chart Type dialog box Standard Types tab

| Option | What you do with it |
|--------|---------------------|
| Chart type list | Choose an item that determines the general chart type for the selected chart. |
| Apply to selection check box | Click to apply the selected chart type to the currently selected data series. If a single data series isn't selected, this check box is grayed out. |

**Table 25.3** Options in the Chart Type dialog box Standard Types tab, continued

| Option | What you do with it |
| --- | --- |
| Default formatting check box | Click to remove the formatting chosen and return the chart to its default appearance. |
| Chart sub-type: area | Choose an item that determines the specific sub-type of chart. The sub-type determines how the selected chart type actually displays and prints. |
| Press and Hold to View Sample button | Click to see how the selected chart will look if you apply the options to the selected data series. |
| Set as default chart button | Click to set the chosen chart type and sub-type as the default type for all charts you create in the future. |

**Table 25.4** Options in the Chart Type dialog box Custom Types tab

| Option | What you do with it |
| --- | --- |
| Chart type list | Choose an item that determines the custom chart type to be applied to the current chart. |
| User-defined radio button | Click to choose from a list of user-defined chart types. When this radio button is clicked, the Add and Delete buttons are available. |
| Built-in radio button | Click to choose from a list of pre-defined chart types. When this radio button is clicked, the Add and Delete buttons aren't available. |
| Add button | Click to open the Add Custom Chart Type dialog box and enter a name and description for the new chart type. The new type is defined based on how the currently selected chart is defined. This button displays only when the User-defined radio button is clicked. |
| Delete button | Click to delete a user-defined chart type. This button displays only when the User-defined radio button is clicked. |
| Sample area | View a sample of how the chosen chart type will look if you apply it to the selected data series. |

# Chart ➤ Source Data

Use this option to open the Source Data dialog box and choose one or more data series and data range functions. You can add or remove values, x-axis labels, or y-axis labels in the Source Data dialog box.

## How You Get Here

✧ Press **Alt+C,S**           ✧ Choose **Chart** ➤ **Source Data**

## What's In This Dialog Box

Figure 25.3 is a sample of this dialog box and Table 25.5 has a description of the tabs **available**.

**Figure 25.3**    The Source Data dialog box

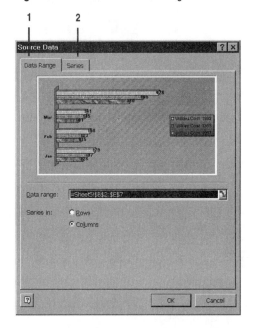

**Table 25.5**    Tabs in the Source Data dialog box

| # | Tab name | What you do with it |
|---|----------|---------------------|
| 1 | Data Range | View and highlight the cell data ranges for the selected chart.  (For a complete description of the options available, see Table 25.6 on page 419.) |
| 2 | Series | View and highlight available data series and create a new series.  (For a complete description of the options available, see Table 25.7 on page 419.) |

The following tables describe the options for the individual tabs in this dialog box:

- Table 25.6 describes the Data Range tab, and
- Table 25.7 describes the Series tab.

**Table 25.6**   Options in the Source Data dialog box Data Range tab

| Option | What you do with it |
| --- | --- |
| Data Range view area | View how the options chosen will affect the selected chart. |
| Data range text box | Enter the cell range for the data to plot on the selected chart. If the range was already selected before opening this window, the range should be displayed here. |
| Series in Rows radio button | Click to specify that the data is being defined in rows. |
| Series in columns radio button | Click to specify that the data is being defined in columns. |

**Table 25.7**   Options in the Source Data dialog box Series tab

| Option | What you do with it |
| --- | --- |
| Series view area | View how the options chosen will affect the selected chart. |
| Series list | Choose an item that determines which series is to be used. Adding or deleting series in this box doesn't affect the *data* already in the selected table. |
| Add button | Click to add a new data series. Before clicking, enter a name and value in the Name and Value text boxes. |
| Remove button | Click to delete the highlighted series. |
| Name text box | Enter the name for a new series. |
| Values text box | Enter a range of cells for the new series. |
| Category (X) axis labels text box | Enter a range of cells to be used as category labels. |

# Chart ➤ Chart Options

Use this option to open the Chart Options window and set the appearance of the selected chart. You can add text, axes, gridlines, legends, data labels, and a data table or modify the look and position of these options.

 **N O T E**   The options available change based on the type of chart selected when you choose this menu option. ▨

## How You Get Here

✧ Press **Alt+C,O**          ✧ Choose **Chart** ➤ **Chart Options**

## What's In This Dialog Box

Figure 25.4 is a sample of this dialog box and Table 25.8 has a description of the tabs available.

**Figure 25.4**    The Chart Options dialog box

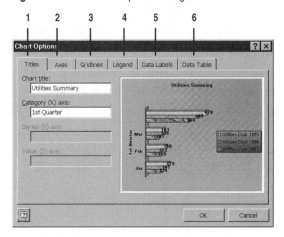

**Table 25.8**    Tabs in the Chart Options dialog box

| # | Tab name | What you do with it |
|---|----------|---------------------|
| 1 | Titles | View and enter titles for the overall chart and for specific chart components. The text can either float or be assigned to the chart title or an axis. (For a complete description of the options available, see Table 25.9 on page 421.) |
| 2 | Axes | View and set how axes are displayed or hide a selected axis. (For a complete description of the options available, see Table 25.10 on page 421.) |
| 3 | Gridlines | Turn gridlines (lines going up and down or across the chart) on and off and set gridline size. (For a complete description of the options available, see Table 25.11 on page 422.) |
| 4 | Legend | Set whether to include a legend (key) in the selected chart and set its position on the chart. The legend describes what each bar, line, or pie slice means. (For a complete description of the options available, see Table 25.12 on page 422.) |
| 5 | Data Labels | Set whether a data label (a label that displays with each data point) is used and set what type of label it is. (For a complete description of the options available, see Table 25.13 on page 422.) |
| 6 | Data Table | Set whether to display the chart data as both a table and a chart. (For a complete description of the options available, see Table 25.14 on page 423.) |

The following tables describe the options for the individual tabs in this dialog box:

- Table 25.9 describes the Titles tab,
- Table 25.10 describes the Axes tab,
- Table 25.11 describes the Gridlines tab,
- Table 25.12 describes the Legend tab,
- Table 25.13 describes the Data Labels tab, and
- Table 25.14 describes the Data Table tab.

**Table 25.9**  Options in the Chart Options dialog box Titles tab

| Option | What you do with it |
| --- | --- |
| Chart title text box | Enter the name of the you want to display at the top of the chart. (This can also be the axis title.) |
| Category (X) axis text box | Enter the name of the X axis title. This can also be chart title, if there is no chart title already entered. The X axis is the horizontal axis, except for Bar charts. |
| Value (Y) axis text box | Enter the name of the Y axis title. The Y axis is the vertical axis. |
| Secondary category (X) axis text box | Enter the axis text for the secondary X axis, which is often found on mixed charts (such as Line and Bar charts). If there is no secondary X axis, this option is grayed out. |
| Secondary value (Y) axis text box | Enter the axis text for the secondary Y axis, which is often found on mixed charts (such as Line and Bar charts). If there is no secondary Y axis, this option is grayed out. |
| Title view area | View how the selected chart will look if you apply the currently selected values. |

**Table 25.10**  Options in the Chart Options dialog box Axes tab

| Option | What you do with it |
| --- | --- |
| Category (X) axis check box | Click to show or hide the category X axis text typically found below the chart. |
| Automatic radio button | Click to set the X axis to display a time scale, if the axis data is already formatted for dates. If the data is not formatted for dates, the X axis is displayed as the default category. |
| Category radio button | Click to set the X axis to display as the default category. |
| Time-scale radio button | Click to set the X axis to display as a time scale, even if the data is not formatted for date. The category axis displays tick marks evenly spaced based on major and minor units of time. |
| Value (Y) axis check box | Click to show or hide the Y axis text typically found on the left side of the chart. |
| Axes view area | View how the selected chart will look if you apply the currently selected values. |

**Table 25.11**    Options in the Chart Options dialog box Gridline tab

| Option | What you do with it |
| --- | --- |
| Category (X) axis Major gridlines check box | Click to show or hide the X axis major gridlines on the selected chart. |
| Category (X) axis Minor gridlines check box | Click to show or hide the X axis minor gridlines on the selected chart. |
| Value (Y) axis Major gridlines check box | Click to show or hide the Y axis major gridlines on the selected chart. |
| Value (Y) axis Minor gridlines check box | Click to show or hide the Y axis minor gridlines on the selected chart. |
| Gridlines view box | View how the selected chart will look if you apply the currently selected values. |

**Table 25.12**    Options in the Chart Options dialog box Legend tab

| Option | What you do with it |
| --- | --- |
| Show legend check box | Click to show or hide the legend on the selected chart. |
| Placement radio buttons | Click to choose a placement position for the legend on the selected chart. (You can also drag the legend to the desired position.) These options are grayed out if the Show legend check box hasn't been checked. |
| Legend view area | View how the selected chart will look if you apply the currently selected values. |

**Table 25.13**    Options in the Chart Options dialog box Data Labels tab

| Option | What you do with it |
| --- | --- |
| None radio button | Click to hide all data labels on the selected chart. |
| Show value radio button | Click to show or hide labels that reflect the data value. |
| Show percent radio button | Click to show or hide, in pie and doughnut charts, labels that reflect percentage of the whole. |
| Show label radio button | Click to show or hide the category or series labels. |
| Show label and percent radio button | Click to show or hide, in pie and doughnut charts, labels that reflect both percentage and category. |
| Show bubble sizes radio button | Click to show or hide, in bubble charts, labels reflecting bubble sizes. |
| Legend key check box | Click to show or hide the legend key next to the labels in the selected chart. |
| Data label view area | View how the selected chart will look if you apply the currently selected values. |

**Table 25.14**   Options in the Chart Options dialog box Data Table tab

| Option | What you do with it |
| --- | --- |
| Show data table check box | Click to show or hide the data table with the selected chart. |
| Show legend keys check box | Click to show or hide the legend keys. This option is available only if the Show data table check box is checked. |
| Data table view area | View how the selected chart will look if you apply the currently selected values. |

# Chart ➤ Location

Use this option to open the Chart Location dialog box and pick a specific location for the selected chart. The chart can be placed on a chart sheet or as an object on an existing sheet. If you choose the chart sheet location this places just the chart as its own sheet in the workbook. You can also click and drag the chart to the desired location on a sheet.

## How You Get Here

✧ Press **Alt+C,L**        ✧ Choose **C**hart ➤ **L**ocation

## What's In This Dialog Box

Figure 25.5 is a sample of this dialog box and Table 25.15 has a description of the options available.

**Figure 25.5**   The Chart Location dialog box

**Table 25.15**   Options in the Chart Location dialog box

| # | Option | What you do with it |
| --- | --- | --- |
| 1 | As new sheet radio button | Click to make the chart display on a new sheet. |
| 2 | As new sheet text box | Enter a name for the new sheet. |
| 3 | As object in drop-down list | Choose an item that determines what sheet the chart is placed on. |
| 4 | As object in radio button | Click to make the chart appear on an existing sheet. |

# Chart ➤ Add Data

Use this option to open the Add Data dialog box and manually add data to the selected chart.

---

**N O T E**    You must first type the data in the appropriate row or column on your worksheet.  ▓

## How You Get Here

✧ Press **Alt+C,A**          ✧ Choose **Chart ➤ Add Data**

## What's In This Dialog Box

Figure 25.6 is a sample of this dialog box and has a description of the only option available.

**Figure 25.6**    The Add Data dialog box

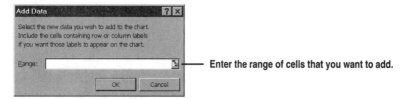

Enter the range of cells that you want to add.

# Chart ➤ Add Trendline

Use this option to use a trendline to smooth out the fluctuations in your data or to make predictions based on the selected data. This option displays the Add Trendline dialog box so that you can choose the trendline characteristics for the selected data. If your chart is a 3-D type this option is grayed out. To make this option available you must change the chart type to something other than a 3-D-type chart. (For more information, see Chart ➤ Chart Type on page 415.)

## How You Get Here

✧ Press **Alt+C,R**          ✧ Choose **Chart ➤ Add Trendline**

## What's In This Dialog Box

Figure 25.7 is a sample of this dialog box and Table 25.16 has a description of the tabs available.

**Figure 25.7**    The Add Trendline dialog box

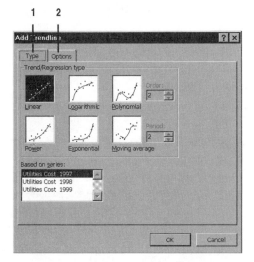

**Table 25.16**    Tabs in the Add Trendline dialog box

| # | Tab name | What you do with it |
|---|----------|---------------------|
| 1 | Type | Choose a trend/regression type of trendline and the order, period, and series. (For a complete description of the options available, see Table 25.17 on page 425.) |
| 2 | Options | Choose a trendline name and set other trendline characteristics. (For a complete description of the options available, see Table 25.18 on page 426.) |

The following tables describe the options for the individual tabs in this dialog box:

- Table 25.17 describes the Type tab, and
- Table 25.18 describes the Options tab.

**Table 25.17**    Options in the Add Trendline dialog box Type tab

| Option | What you do with it |
|--------|---------------------|
| Trend/Regression type list | Click to choose a specific trend/regression type for the selected data |
| Order text box | Enter or choose an order that determines the highest polynomial order. This option is available only when Polynomial has been selected. |

**Table 25.17**    Options in the Add Trendline dialog box Type tab, continued

| Option | What you do with it |
|---|---|
| Period text box | Enter or choose the number of periods to use when calculating the moving average. This option is available only when you've chosen Moving average. |
| Based on series list | Choose an item that determines which series you want to use for creating the trendline. |

**Table 25.18**    Options in the Add Trendline dialog box Options tab

| Option | What you do with it |
|---|---|
| Automatic radio button | Click to give the trendline the same name as the series you selected. The proposed name is displayed to the right of the radio button. |
| Custom radio button | Click to enter a specific name for the trendline. The name is entered in the text box to the right of the radio button. |
| Forward text box | Enter a time value, in periods, for the trendline to be plotted past the existing data. |
| Backward text box | Enter a time value, in periods, for the trendline to be plotted before the existing data. |
| Set intercept check box | Click to set the value where the trendline crosses the y-axis instead of being based on the data. The intercept point is set in the text box to the right of the check box. |
| Display equation on chart check box | Click to display the equation for the trendline in the trendline label for the selected chart. |
| Display R-squared value on chart check box | Click to display an r-squared value for the trendline in the trendline label for the selected chart. (The r-squared value gives you an idea of how close the trendline matches the data points.) |

# Chart ➤ 3-D View

Use this option to open the 3-D View dialog box and set the characteristics of 3-D charts, such as how it is tilted or rotated on your worksheet. This option is only available if the chart is a 3-D type; if the chart isn't 3-D, this option is grayed out. To make it a 3-D type choose the Chart Type option on the Chart menu and choose a 3-D type from the chart list. (For more information, see Chart ➤ Chart Type on page 415.)

## How You Get Here

✧ Press **Alt+C,V**          ✧ Choose **Chart** ➤ **3-D View**

## What's In This Dialog Box

Figure 25.8 is a sample of this dialog box and Table 25.19 has a description of the options available.

**Figure 25.8**   The 3-D View dialog box

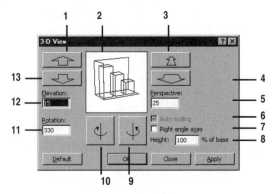

**Table 25.19**   Options in the 3-D View dialog box

| # | Option | What you do with it |
|---|--------|---------------------|
| 1 | Increase elevation button | Click to increase the elevation of the view in increments of 5 degrees (you can choose a value from -90 to 90 degrees for most charts, 10-80 degrees for pie charts). |
| 2 | Sample view area | View how the chart will look if you apply the current values to the selected chart. |
| 3 | Increase perspective button | Click to increase the depth of the chart (you can choose a value between 0-100). This option is not available when the Right Angle axes check box is selected or for 3-D bar charts. |
| 4 | Decrease perspective button | Click to decrease the depth of the chart (you can choose a value between 0-100). This option is not available when the Right Angle axes check box is selected or for 3-D bar charts. |
| 5 | Perspective text box | Enter a specific value for the perspective (you can choose a value between 0-100). This option is not available when the Right Angle axes check box is selected or for 3-D bar charts. |
| 6 | Auto scaling check box | Click to make Excel automatically scale the 3-D chart so that it is close to a 2-D chart in size. This option is available only when the Right angle axes check box is checked. |
| 7 | Right angle axes check box | Click to make the 3-D chart show only right-angle axes, eliminating true 3-D perspective. When this check box is clicked, the perspective controls in this dialog box disappear. |
| 8 | Height text box | Enter a value for the height of the z axis, which is calculated as a percentage of the x-length. |

**Table 25.19**   Options in the 3-D View dialog box, continued

| # | Option | What you do with it |
|---|--------|---------------------|
| 9 | Rotate plot counterclockwise button | Click to rotate the viewing angle counterclockwise (you can choose a value from 0-360 degrees). |
| 10 | Rotate plot clockwise button | Click to rotate the viewing angle clockwise (you can choose a value from 0-360 degrees). |
| 11 | Rotation text box | Enter a value of horizontal degrees from which to view the chart. |
| 12 | Elevation text box | Enter a specific value of vertical degrees from which to view the chart (you can choose a value from -90 to 90 degrees for most charts, 10-80 degrees for pie charts). |
| 13 | Decrease elevation button | Click to decrease the elevation of the view in increments of 5 degrees (you can choose a value from -90 to 90 degrees for most charts, 10-80 degrees for pie charts). |

# The Excel Window Menu

## In this chapter

# What Is The Window Menu

This menu has options that let you choose how you want to display your files when you have more than one open or compare different files or copy information between them. Most of the actions take place immediately, so you won't see many new windows or screens in this section.

If a menu option has an ellipsis (three dots) or an arrow beside it, the application "asks" you for additional information before the action takes place. If the menu doesn't have one of these symbols, the action you choose happens immediately. If the action takes place immediately, you won't see a sample screen in this section.

# Window ➤ New Window

Use this option to open a new window with the same contents as the active window so that you can display different parts of the same document. The title bar then displays the original document name followed by a number that indicates which window you're working in.

## How You Get Here

✧ Press **Alt+W,N**          ✧ Choose **Window ➤ New Window**

# Window ➤ Arrange

Use this option to display all open windows on the desktop at the same time.

## How You Get Here

✧ Press **Alt+W,A**          ✧ Choose **Window ➤ Arrange**

## What's In This Dialog Box

Figure 26.1 is a sample of this dialog box and Table 26.1 has a description of the options available.

**Figure 26.1**   The Arrange Windows dialog box

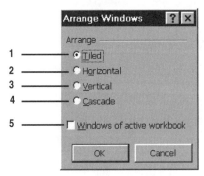

**Table 26.1**    Options in the Arrange Windows dialog box

| # | Option | What you do with it |
|---|--------|---------------------|
| 1 | Tiled radio button | Click to display the open windows as a grid-style layout. |
| 2 | Horizontal radio button | Click to display the open windows across your screen. |
| 3 | Vertical radio button | Click to display the open windows up and down your screen. |
| 4 | Cascade radio button | Click to display the opened windows in a stacked layout, with the top left corner and the title bar showing. |
| 5 | Windows of active workbook check box | Click to arrange *just* the windows in the active workbook. If this option is turned off, the application arranges *all* your open workbooks. |

# Window ➤ Hide

Use this option to prevent the display of one or more open windows. The window is still open, but it isn't displayed on your Open Files list and you can't use **Ctrl+F6** to switch to it.

### How You Get Here

✧ Press **Alt+W,H**　　　✧ Choose **Window ➤ Hide**

# Window ➤ Unhide

Use this option to open the Unhide dialog box so that you can redisplay hidden windows.

---

**N O T E**　 This option is only available if you have hidden at least one window. ▨

### How You Get Here

✧ Press **Alt+W,U**　　　✧ Choose **Window ➤ Unhide**

# Window ➤ Split/Remove Split

Use this option to divide the active window into horizontal panes. As you scroll through the document, all text above the split is frozen and doesn't scroll until you use the scroll bars for that pane. The other pane has its own set of scroll bars, so you can scroll around in different parts of the same document. Choose **Window ➤ Remove Split** to display a single window.

### How You Get Here

✧ Press **Alt+W,S**　　　✧ Choose **Window ➤ Split or Remove Split**

# Window ➤ Freeze/Unfreeze Panes

Use this option to divide the active window into horizontal and vertical panes after you've got the right information at the top and left sides of the worksheet. This is great for large worksheets with labels identifying the columns or rows—once you freeze an area it stays on the screen no matter where you move your cursor.

 **TIP**  You can also click and drag on each Freeze line to move it to the row or column you want to freeze. Choose **Window ➤ Unfreeze Panes** to return to a single window display.

## How You Get Here

✧ Press **Alt+W,F**     ✧ Choose **Window ➤ Freeze Panes** or **Unfreeze Panes**

# Window ➤ (List of Files Currently Open)

Use this option to switch between windows when there is more than one document open or to maximize the display of the selected window.

## How You Get Here

✧ Press **Alt+W,file number**    ✧ Choose **Window ➤ file number**

# A Look At PowerPoint

**In this part**

# The PowerPoint File Menu

## In this chapter

## What Is The File Menu

This menu lists the commands that you'll use to perform actions that affect the entire file, such as saving the document so that you don't lose your work, printing the document, opening additional documents, or reviewing various information about the active file.

If a menu option has an ellipsis (three dots) or an arrow beside it, the application "asks" you for additional information before the action takes place. If the menu doesn't have one of these symbols, the action you choose happens immediately. If the action takes place immediately, you won't see a sample screen in this section.

## File ➤ New

Use this option to create a new presentation based on an existing presentation (called a "template") or to create a new template that you can use to make life easier in the future. You can choose a template to make creating a presentation a little easier or, if you prefer, you can create new templates and store them in the tabs displayed. There are two basic types of templates, Design and Content. The design templates contain elements that are predefined that you can apply to any presentation. The content templates contain predefined elements just like design templates. They also have slides containing suggestions for specific subjects. Any of these templates can be customized. If you need some help working with a template, or if you're new to creating presentations in PowerPoint, you can use a Wizard, which walks you through the process of creating a new presentation one step at a time.

### How You Get Here

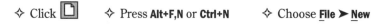

✧ Click 🗋     ✧ Press **Alt+F,N** or **Ctrl+N**     ✧ Choose **File ➤ New**

---

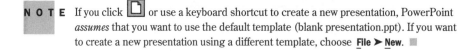

**N O T E**   If you click 🗋 or use a keyboard shortcut to create a new presentation, PowerPoint *assumes* that you want to use the default template (blank presentation.ppt). If you want to create a new presentation using a different template, choose **File ➤ New**. ▪

---

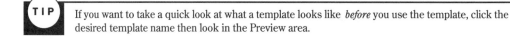

**T I P**   If you want to take a quick look at what a template looks like *before* you use the template, click the desired template name then look in the Preview area.

## What's In This Dialog Box

Figure 27.1 is a sample of this dialog box and Table 27.1 has a description of the options that are unique to PowerPoint. (For more information, see File ➤ New on page 38.)

**Figure 27.1**   The New Presentation dialog box

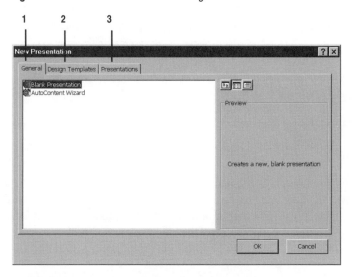

**Table 27.1**   Tabs in the New Presentation dialog box

| # | Tab name | What you do with it |
|---|----------|---------------------|
| 1 | General | Double-click one of the templates displayed to build your own presentation or double-click the AutoContent Wizard to get some help building a presentation. |
| 2 | Design Templates | Double-click one of the templates displayed to work with a professionally designed template with some of the text already included. |
| 3 | Presentations | Double-click one of the templates displayed to create a new presentation based on a professionally designed template. |

# File ➤ Open

Use this option to open an existing presentation so that you can take a look at what you've done or add more stuff to your masterpiece. (For more information, see File ➤ Open on page 39.)

---

**N O T E**   File ➤ Open has the same options in all three applications. The only difference is in the Files of type drop-down list; in PowerPoint the types are presentations, presentation templates, outlines, and HTML files. ▪

## How You Get Here

✧ Click    ✧ Press **Alt+F,O** or **Ctrl+O**   ✧ Choose **File** ➤ **Open**

# File ➤ Close

Use this option to close the active file and save it in the original file folder (you know, that one you used when you *first* saved the file). If the file has not been saved you'll be asked if you want to save any changes you have made. If you click the **Yes** button so that your most recent changes are saved, the application overwrites the old version of the file. (For more information, see File ➤ Close on page 41.)

## How You Get Here

✧ Click  or Double-click    ✧ Press **Alt+F,C** or **Ctrl+W**   ✧ Choose **File** ➤ **Close**

# File ➤ Save

Use this option to save any changes you've made to a file. (For more information, see File ➤ Save on page 42.)

---

**TIP**   Be sure to save your files frequently (you don't want to lose any of the hard work you've done). A good rule of thumb is to save frequently enough that you can easily recover if the system crashes. For example, if you just wrote a great paragraph or created an awesome formula, save your file immediately after finishing the it. My rule is that I don't go any longer than five minutes without saving, which means I can't lose more than five minutes work!

## How You Get Here

✧ Click    ✧ Press **Alt+F,S** or **Ctrl+S**   ✧ Choose **File** ➤ **Save**

# File ➤ Save As

Use this option to save the file for the first time or to save an existing file with a different name or file type. (For more information, see File ➤ Save As on page 42.)

**TIP** Be sure you look at where you're storing the file before you click **Save**—don't let "fast fingers" get the better of you. The most frequent reason people can't find a file is because they didn't pay attention to the file folder that was open when they last saved a file.

## How You Get Here

✧ Press **Alt+F,A**          ✧ Choose **File ➤ Save As**

# File ➤ Save as Web Page

Use this option to save an existing file as a Web page, using HTML. Sometimes you'll want to save what you're working on as a Web page, so you can view it yourself later in a browser or send it to someone else to look at.

## How You Get Here

✧ Press **Alt+F,G**          ✧ Choose **File ➤ Save as Web Page**

## What's Different

Figure 27.2 is a portion of this dialog box and Table 27.2 has a description of options that are unique to PowerPoint. (For more information, see File ➤ Save as Web Page on page 43.)

**Figure 27.2**   The Save As dialog box

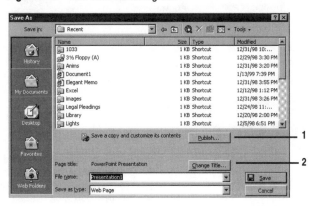

**Table 27.2**   Options in the Save As dialog box

| # | Option | What you do with it |
|---|--------|---------------------|
| 1 | Publish button | Click to open a dialog box where you can make decisions about publishing your workbook as a web page. |
| 2 | Change Title button | Rename the file for online purposes. This title will appear on the web page's title bar. |

# File ➤ Pack and Go

Use this option to pull together all the pieces of your presentation so that you can run your slide show on another computer. Choosing this option starts the Pack and Go Wizard, which walks you through the steps for gathering all the files and fonts used in your presentation. You can also include a copy of the PowerPoint viewer if the target computer doesn't have PowerPoint installed.

**N O T E**   You can package linked files and any TrueType fonts used in the presentation.   ■

**T I P**   If you make changes to your presentation, be sure you choose **File ➤ Pack and Go** to make sure you get all the latest and greatest for your presentation.

## How You Get Here

❖ Press **Alt+F,K**          ❖ Choose **File ➤ Pack and Go**

## What's In This Dialog Box

Figure 27.3 is a sample of this wizard.

**Figure 27.3**   The Pack and Go wizard

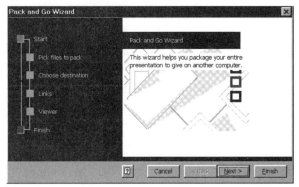

Follow the instructions in the Wizard to complete this option. If you picked the wrong thing you can go back and change it or cancel and start over. Just make sure you don't click the finish button first.

# File ➤ Web Page Preview

Use this option to see how a file looks as a web page. The application opens your Web browser and displays the active file.

## How You Get Here

✧ Press **Alt+F,B**      ✧ Choose **File ➤ Web Page Preview**

# File ➤ Page Setup

Use this option to control how your final presentation looks, including the overall slide size, the way your paper is oriented for slides (portrait is up-and-down and landscape is oriented left-to-right), the way your paper is oriented for notes and handouts, and what number is assigned to the first slide.

## How You Get Here

✧ Press **Alt+F,U**      ✧ Choose **File ➤ Page Setup**

## What's In This Dialog Box

Figure 27.4 is a sample of this dialog box and Table 27.3 has a description of the options available.

**Figure 27.4**    The Page Setup dialog box

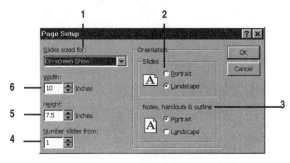

**Table 27.3**    Options in the Page Setup dialog box

| # | Option | What you do with it |
|---|--------|---------------------|
| 1 | Slides sized to drop-down list | Choose an item that determines standard page size for your slides. |
| 2 | Orientation: Slides area | Click to choose which way the slides are oriented (portrait is up-and-down and landscape is left-to-right). |
| 3 | Orientation: Notes, handouts & outline area | Click to choose which way the notes, handouts, and outlines are oriented (portrait is up-and-down and landscape is left-to-right). |
| 4 | Number slides from text box | Enter the number you want assigned to the first slide of the presentation. |

**Table 27.3**   Options in the Page Setup dialog box, continued

| # Option | What you do with it |
|---|---|
| 5  Height text box | Displays the vertical measure of the slide based on the item selected from the Slides sized for drop-down list. You can also enter or choose a custom size. |
| 6  Width text box | Displays the horizontal measure of the slide based on the item selected from the Slides sized for drop-down list. You can also enter or choose a custom size. |

# File ➤ Print

Use this option to create a paper copy of the active file. You can send the file to the default printer or you can choose a new printer, as long as it has already been set up for you. If you only want to print a few pages in a file you can choose from the Page range area the pages to print. (For more information, see File ➤ Print on page 44.)

---

**N O T E**   You can also create an electronic "print" file that you can send to a commercial printer or use to generate a PDF (Portable Document Format) file. ■

## How You Get Here

✧ Click 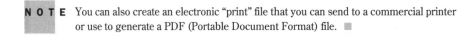       ✧ Press **Alt+F,P** or **Ctrl+P**       ✧ Choose **File** ➤ **Print**

## What's Different

Figure 27.5 is a sample of this dialog box and Table 27.4 has a description of the options that are unique to PowerPoint.

**Figure 27.5** The Print dialog box

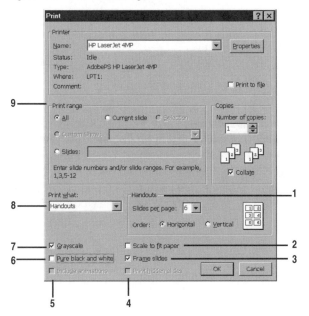

**Table 27.4** Options in the Print dialog box

| # | Option | What you do with it |
|---|--------|---------------------|
| 1 | Handouts area | Enter the number of slides you want printed on one page and in what order you want them printed. This option is only available if you choose to print handouts or notes pages. |
| 2 | Scale to fit paper check box | Click to reduce or enlarge the text on the slide so that it fills the entire page. This option only affects the printed presentation; it doesn't change how the slides are stored in the electronic file. |
| 3 | Frame slides check box | Click to add a border around printed slides, handouts, and notes pages. |
| 4 | Print hidden slides check box | Click to print all slides, even if they've been hidden while you're working on the presentation. |
| 5 | Include animations check box | Click to print any animated areas as an icon. |
| 6 | Pure black and white check box | Click to print the entire presentation in black and white. This may make some items unreadable if you've used color or grayscale options in your presentation. |
| 7 | Grayscale check box | Click to print the entire presentation in shades of gray. This may make some items unreadable if you've layered colors. |

**Table 27.4**   Options in the Print dialog box, continued

| # | Option | What you do with it |
|---|--------|---------------------|
| 8 | Print what drop-down list | Choose an item that determines exactly what parts of the presentation you're going to print. |
| 9 | Print range area | Click to choose which slide (or slides) you want to print. |

# File ➤ Send To

Use this option to send your document, spreadsheet or slide to someone using your email or Internet connection. Generally, any of the options in this flyout menu will use your default email connections or the Outlook application to send an email message. You fill in the information for the recipient like you would for any other email message and then you're ready to send it. This option and the flyout menu options are completely described in the Common File Menu chapter. (For more information, see File ➤ Send To on page 46 or What Is The Outlook Mail Application on page 648.)

## How You Get Here

✧ Press **Alt+F,D**         ✧ Choose **F**il**e** ➤ **Sen**d **to**

## What's Different

Figure 27.6 is a sample of this flyout menu.

**Figure 27.6**   The File ➤ Send To flyout menu

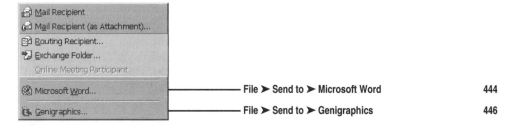

| | |
|---|---|
| File ➤ Send to ➤ Microsoft Word | 444 |
| File ➤ Send to ➤ Genigraphics | 446 |

## File ➤ Send to ➤ Microsoft Word

Use this option to copy your presentation as a Microsoft Word document. You can choose how your presentation's slides and text will appear in a Word document.

## How You Get Here

✧ Press **Alt+F,D,W**         ✧ Choose **F**il**e** ➤ **Sen**d **to** ➤ **Microsoft** **W**ord

## What's In This Dialog Box

Figure 27.7 shows the options in this dialog box and Table 27.5 has a description of the options available.

**Figure 27.7**  The Write-Up dialog box

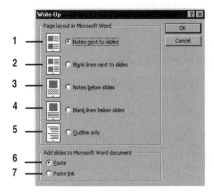

**Table 27.5**  Options in the Write-Up dialog box

| # | Option | What you do with it |
|---|--------|---------------------|
| 1 | Notes next to slides radio button | Places your presentation notes below the slides. |
| 2 | Blank lines next to slides radio button | Places lines for handwritten notes beside the side. |
| 3 | Notes below slides radio button | Places your presentation notes below the slides. |
| 4 | Blank lines below slides radio button | Places lines for handwritten notes below the side. |
| 5 | Outline only radio button | Sends Word only the text outline of the presentation. |
| 6 | Add slides: Paste radio button | Copies the slide "as is" into the Word document. |
| 7 | Add slides: Paste link radio button | Links the picture in the Word file to slides in the PowerPoint presentation. Pictures in the Word document are updated to reflect changes in the PowerPoint presentation slides. |

### File ➤ Send to ➤ Genigraphics

Use this option to order presentation materials from a third party vendor. The Genigraphics Wizard opens where you can send presentation materials to Genigraphics for processing. They are a vendor of presentation materials and services that can provide supplies for meetings, conferences and presentations.

### How You Get Here

✧ Press **Alt+F,D,G**          ✧ Choose **File ➤ Send to ➤ Genigraphics**

### What's In This Dialog Box

Figure 27.8 is a sample of the Genigraphics Wizard.

**Figure 27.8**   The Genigraphics wizard

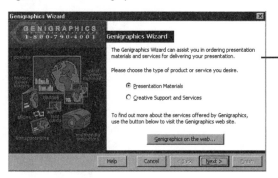

Follow the instructions in the Wizard to complete this option. If you picked the wrong thing you can go back and change it or cancel and start over. Just make sure you don't click the finish button first.

## File ➤ Properties

Use this option to review technical information and record technical information about the active file. (For more information, see File ➤ Properties on page 49.)

### How You Get Here

✧ Press **Alt+F,I**          ✧ Choose **File ➤ Properties**

## File ➤ (List of Recently Opened Files)

Use this option to open recently used files, without having to dig through a long list of file folders and drive names to find the file you need. (For more information, see File ➤ (List of Recently Opened Files) on page 52.)

### How You Get Here

✧ Press **Alt+F,** choose **number of file in list**   ✧ Choose **File ➤ number of file**

# File ➤ Exit

Use this option to close all open files *and* the application that you're using. (For more information, see File ➤ Exit on page 52.)

---

**N O T E**   If you have made changes in any file you'll be asked if you want to save the changes when you exit the application. ■

## How You Get Here

✧ Click ☒ or Double-click 🔲         ✧ Press **Alt+F,X**     ✧ Choose F̲ile ➤ E̲xit

# The PowerPoint Edit Menu

## In this chapter

# What Is The Edit Menu

This menu lists the commands that you'll use to copy information from one place to another, delete information from your file, locate specific words or phrases, change information one instance at a time or throughout the entire file, add links to other documents or locations, and change the look of objects.

If a menu option has an ellipsis (three dots) or an arrow beside it, the application "asks" you for additional information before the action takes place. If the menu doesn't have one of these symbols, the action you choose happens immediately. If the action takes place immediately, you won't see a sample screen in this section.

 Many of the commands on the Edit menu are also available on the shortcut menu. If you like to use your mouse, you can right-click, then choose one of the options displayed. Remember, these menus change based on your cursor location and what is highlighted.

# Edit ➤ Undo

Use this option to change your mind and remove one or more changes made to the active file. You can also undo several actions at once *if* you click the drop-down list to the right of the **Undo** button. Although most actions can be "undone", there are some that can't. If you can't undo an action, the Edit menu displays "Can't undo" instead of "Undo".

**N O T E**   A word of caution: the application won't just let you undo an action in the middle of the Undo list. It "assumes" that you want to undo all actions preceding the one you've chosen. For example, let's say that you've deleted five different paragraphs, then decide that you really didn't want to delete the third paragraph. The application kindly keeps a list of those five actions. You quickly click the drop-down list to the right of the **Undo** button and choose the third action. The application, however, "assumes" that you also want to undo actions one and two. ▨

 If you decide you didn't *really* mean to undo an action, choose **Edit ➤ Redo**.

## How You Get Here

✧ Click      ✧ Press **Alt+E,U** or **Ctrl+Z**     ✧ Choose **E̲dit ➤ U̲ndo**

# Edit ➤ Repeat/Redo

Use this option to either duplicate one or more actions or to change your mind about the last time you chose **Edit ➤ Undo.** You can also repeat/redo several actions at once *if* you click the drop-down list to the right of the Repeat/Redo button. Although most actions can be "repeated" or "redone", there are some that can't. If you can't repeat or redo an action, the Edit menu displays "Can't repeat" or "Can't redo". The name of this menu option changes based on your most recent action.

---

**N O T E**   A word of caution: the application won't just let you choose one action in the middle of the Redo list. It "assumes" that you want to redo all actions preceding the one you've chosen. For example, let's say that you've reinserted three paragraphs using the **Edit ➤ Undo** option. The application kindly keeps a list of those three actions. You quickly click the drop-down list to the right of the Repeat/Redo button and choose the second action. The application, however, "assumes" that you also want to redo action one.  ▪

## How You Get Here

✧ Click 🔁     ✧ Press **Alt+E,R** or **Ctrl+Y**    ✧ Choose **Edit ➤ Redo** or **Edit ➤ Repeat**

# Edit ➤ Cut

Use this option to completely remove highlighted text or objects from the active file. Items that you cut are stored in an area called the "Clipboard" and can be inserted anywhere, in any open file, regardless of the application.

---

**N O T E**   The Clipboard is cleared once you close the application.  ▪

## How You Get Here

✧ Click ✂     ✧ Press **Alt+E,T** or **Ctrl+X**    ✧ Choose **Edit ➤ Cut**

# Edit ➤ Copy

Use this option to leave the highlighted text or objects in their current position **and** store a copy in a temporary storage area called the "Clipboard". Items that you copy can be inserted anywhere, in any open file, regardless of the application.

## How You Get Here

✧ Click     ✧ Press **Alt+E,C** or **Ctrl+C**    ✧ Choose **E̲dit** ➤ **C̲opy**

# Edit ➤ Paste

Use this option to insert text or objects that are stored in the Clipboard at the current cursor position. Items that you've cut or copied can be inserted anywhere, in any open file, regardless of the application.

## How You Get Here

✧ Click     ✧ Press **Alt+P**, or **Ctrl+V**    ✧ Choose **E̲dit** ➤ **P̲aste**

# Edit ➤ Paste Special

Use this option to choose the format of the text or object that you're inserting at the cursor position. This is the option you want to use if you want to link the current file to an external file or if you're copying information between applications and need to control how the information is inserted. For example, you've created a beautiful proposal and want to insert a chart or graph from Excel or a slide from PowerPoint. You also know that this information will change several times before you issue the report. If you choose Paste ➤ Special, you can make your changes to the source file and those changes are reflected in your report. (For more information, see Edit ➤ Paste Special on page 56.)

## How You Get Here

✧ Press **Alt+E,S**    ✧ Choose **E̲dit** ➤ **Paste S̲pecial**

# Edit ➤ Paste as Hyperlink

Use this option to create a hyperlink for pictures, text, worksheet cells, or a highlighted database object. A hyperlink is an area that is "hot", that is you can click the area so that you automatically jump to a different spot in the current file or in another file. When you drag text and graphics from one Office program to another one, the application recognizes the location of the information.

## How You Get Here

✧ Press **Alt+E,H**    ✧ Choose **E̲dit** ➤ **Paste as H̲yperlink**

# Edit ➤ Clear

Use this option to permanently delete text or objects from the active file, *without* storing the information in the temporary storage area known as the "Clipboard".

## How You Get Here

✧ Press **Alt+E,A** or **Delete**    ✧ Choose **Edit ➤ Clear**

# Edit ➤ Select All

Use this option to highlight everything in the active file.

## How You Get Here

✧ Press **Alt+E,L** or **Ctrl+A**    ✧ Choose **Edit ➤ Select All**

# Edit ➤ Duplicate

Use this option to make a copy of an object so that you can put a copy of it in any open presentation.

## How You Get Here

✧ Press **Alt+E,I** or **Ctrl+D**    ✧ Choose **Edit ➤ Duplicate**

# Edit ➤ Delete Slide

Use this option to remove the selected slide from your presentation. (And yes, Undo works for this one!)

## How You Get Here

✧ Press **Alt+E,D**    ✧ Choose **Edit ➤ Delete Slide**

# Edit ➤ Find

Use this option to find text or formats in the active presentation.

## How You Get Here

✧ Click 🔍    ✧ Press **Alt+E,F** or **Ctrl+F**    ✧ Choose **Edit ➤ Find**

## What's In This Dialog Box

Figure 28.1 is a sample of this dialog box and Table 28.1 has a description of the options available.

**Figure 28.1**   The Find dialog box

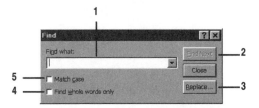

**Table 28.1**   Options in the Find dialog box

| # | Option | What you do with it |
|---|--------|---------------------|
| 1 | Find what text box | Enter the text you want to look for. |
| 2 | Find Next button | Click to begin the search or go to the next occurrence of the information entered in the Find what text box. |
| 3 | Replace button | Click to open the Replace dialog box so that you can enter replacement for the text in the Find what text box. (For more information, see Edit ➤ Replace on page 454.) |
| 4 | Find whole words only check box | Click to *only* find the text in the Find what text box if it is a entire word, not part of another word. |
| 5 | Match case check box | Click to locate *only* text that matches the same pattern of upper-case and lower-case letters entered in the Find what text box. |

# Edit ➤ Replace

Use this option to change text entered in the Find what text box to the text you want it replaced with that you entered in the Replace with text box. You can use this to search for more than one occurrence of the text you want to change.

## How You Get Here

✧ Press **Alt+E,E** or **Ctrl+H**      ✧ Choose **Edit ➤ Replace**

## What's In This Dialog Box

Figure 28.2 is a sample of this dialog box and Table 28.2 has a description of the options available.

---

**N O T E**   Many of the options in the Replace dialog box are the same as the Find dialog box. (For a complete description of the options available, see Table 28.1 on page 454.) ▪

**Figure 28.2**    The Replace dialog box

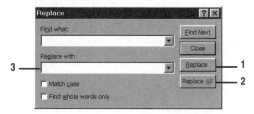

**Table 28.2**    Options in the Replace dialog box

| # | Option | What you do with it |
|---|--------|---------------------|
| 1 | Replace button | Click to change the currently selected text with the text entered in the Replace with text box. |
| 2 | Replace All button | Click to change **all** instances of the text entered in the Find text box to the text entered in the Replace with text box.<br>**Be careful—this is also known as search and** *destroy*. If you aren't careful, you could end up with a real mess. It's usually better to click the **Replace** button to make sure you've got everything just right. |
| 3 | Replace with text box | Enter the text you want to change to. |

# Edit ➤ Go to Property

Use this option to quickly jump to a predefined area in your presentation. You must create this link first using the options on the Custom tab in the **File ➤ Properties** dialog box.

## How You Get Here

✧ Press **Alt+E,G**          ✧ Choose **Edit ➤ Go To**

# Edit ➤ Links

Use this option to open, edit, and maintain the connection ("link") between two files. A link is a way to insert graphics and files into another document so that you can update information if the source is changed. (For more information, see Edit ➤ Links on page 58.)

---

**N O T E**    If you haven't inserted a link, this option is grayed out.

## How You Get Here

✧ Press **Alt+E,K**          ✧ Choose **Edit ➤ Links**

## What's Different

Figure 28.3 is a sample of this dialog box and describes the option unique to PowerPoint.

**Figure 28.3**   The Links dialog box

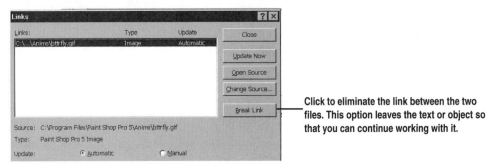

Click to eliminate the link between the two files. This option leaves the text or object so that you can continue working with it.

# Edit ➤ Object

Use this option to open and edit source files, change the conditions of the links between objects and the files they are linked to, convert objects to different file types, and open them in the appropriate application. When you choose this option, the application "senses" what type of object you've highlighted and changes the menu name to match. (For more information, see Edit ➤ Object on page 60.)

---

**N O T E**   Not all options listed on this flyout menu are available for all object types. Word, Excel, and PowerPoint have the same options on the Edit menu.

## How You Get Here

✧ Press **Alt+E,O**          ✧ Choose **Edit** ➤ **Object**

# The PowerPoint View Menu

# What Is The View Menu

This menu lists the commands that determine what information is displayed for your application. You can choose how the main part of your file is displayed and what toolbars are visible (or, as is sometimes the case, in your way!); take a look at the information that is consistently used at the top and bottom of your file (the header and footer); display an onscreen ruler (so you can make adjustments visually rather than mathematically); change how big or small your display is (great for tired eyes); and just generally customize what you see on the screen. In most cases, the reason for multiple views is so that you can specialize how you see your work. No single view can encompass everyone's needs; if nothing else, the screen would become too cluttered for use.

If a menu option has an ellipsis (three dots) or an arrow beside it, the application "asks" you for additional information before the action takes place. If the menu doesn't have one of these symbols, the action you choose happens immediately. If the action takes place immediately, you won't see a sample screen in this section.

# View ➤ Normal

Use this option to view slides in the default window configuration. Normal view has three panes: the Slide pane, the Outline pane, and the Notes pane.

## How You Get Here

✧ Click 🖽       ✧ Press **Alt+V,N**          ✧ Choose **View ➤ Normal**

# View ➤ Slide Sorter

Use this option to view your presentation as a series of miniature slides.

## How You Get Here

✧ Click 🖽       ✧ Press **Alt+V,D**          ✧ Choose **View ➤ Slide Sorter**

# View ➤ Notes Page

Use this option to view or edit the standard page used to store speaker's notes. You can add drawing objects, insert the page number, and resize the box that displays a small version of the slide.

## How You Get Here

✧ Press **Alt+V,P**              ✧ Choose **View ➤ Notes Page**

# View ➤ Slide Show

Use this option to view your slides as a series, just as they will display during the presentation and when you print the slides.

## How You Get Here

✧ Click 🖵    ✧ Press **Alt+V,W** or **F5**    ✧ Choose **View** ➤ **Slide Show**

# View ➤ Master

Use this option to see the various slide masters, which are slides or pages whose contents will be used on every slide or page in the presentation. This allows you to set up titles, graphics, logos, text, or other repeating elements by placing them only once.

## How You Get Here

✧ Press **Alt+V,M**    ✧ Choose **View** ➤ **Master**

## What's In This Flyout Menu

Figure 29.1 is a sample of this flyout menu.

**Figure 29.1**    The View ➤ Master flyout menu

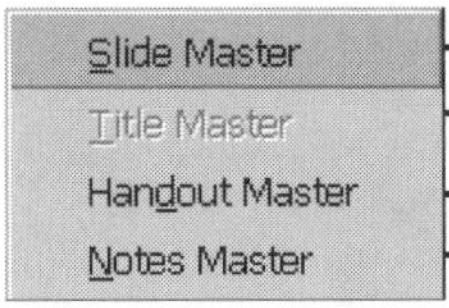

| | |
|---|---|
| Slide Master | ————— View ➤ Master ➤ Slide Master 459 |
| Title Master | ————— View ➤ Master ➤ Title Master 460 |
| Handout Master | ————— View ➤ Master ➤ Handout Master 460 |
| Notes Master | ————— View ➤ Master ➤ Notes Master 460 |

## View ➤ Master ➤ Slide Master

Use this option to display the master slide that determines the overall look of every slide in your presentation. You can put all that fancy stuff that makes your presentation look really professional (you know, those neat looking colors and stuff?) on this master and then you don't have to worry about that stuff again. Choose the color scheme, add your corporate logo and slide numbers, and "bam", all your slides are formatted consistently and you can get down to the real work of putting the words together before you're due to leave for vacation.

## How You Get Here

✧ Press **Alt+V,M,S**    ✧ Choose **View** ➤ **Master** ➤ **Slide Master**

### View ➤ Master ➤ Title Master

Use this option to display the master slide that determines what elements display on every *title slide* in your presentation. This master can have different elements on it so that you can emphasize your main topics or the title of your presentation.

---

**N O T E**   If there is no title master slide, this option is grayed out.   ■

### How You Get Here

✧ Press **Alt+V,M,T**   ✧ Choose **View ➤ Master ➤ Title Master**

### View ➤ Master ➤ Handout Master

Use this option to display the master used to format the handouts you give to all those eager attendees at your presentation. You can print multiple slides on one page and leave the attendees room to write down those pearls of wisdom you didn't want to put on the actual slide.

### How You Get Here

✧ Press **Alt+V,M,D**   ✧ Choose **View ➤ Master ➤ Handout Master**

### View ➤ Master ➤ Notes Master

Use this option to display the master used to format the notes you write to yourself to keep everything running smoothly during your presentation. You can also insert text, graphics, or other elements that display on every printed notes page.

### How You Get Here

✧ Press **Alt+V,M,N**   ✧ Choose **View ➤ Master ➤ Notes Master**

## View ➤ Black and White

Use this option to view all colors on a slide as black and white, including text, graphics, and comments. To see a color representation while black and white view is turned on, choose **View ➤ Slide Miniature**.

### How You Get Here

✧ Click 🖿   ✧ Press **Alt+V,B**   ✧ Choose **View ➤ Black and White**

# View ➤ Slide Miniature

Use this option to open a new window with a small version of the slide where the cursor is currently positioned.

---

**N O T E** This is only available when black and white view is turned on and displays a duplicate version of the current slide in color. ■

### How You Get Here

❖ Press **Alt+V,I**      ❖ Choose **View** ➤ **Slide Miniature**

# View ➤ Toolbars

Use this option to choose the toolbars you want displayed while you work. Toolbars are collections of icons (or buttons) and are especially handy when doing work that involves repeated tasks. However, if you open lots of toolbars they'll clutter the screen and you can waste more time than you realize by constantly moving them around as you work.

---

**N O T E** You can customize many of the toolbars to fit your needs. (For more information, see View ➤ Toolbars ➤ Customize on page 76.) ■

### How You Get Here

❖ Right-click any **Toolbar**   ❖ Press **Alt+V,T**   ❖ Choose **View** ➤ **Toolbars**

## What's In This Flyout Menu

Figure 29.2 is a sample of this flyout menu.

**Figure 29.2**    The View ➤ Toolbars flyout menu

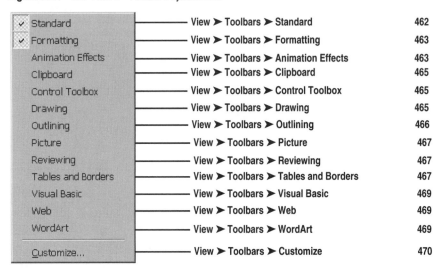

## View ➤ Toolbars ➤ Standard

Use this option to display the Standard toolbar, which has icons for many of your most frequently used options, such as Save, Print, Open, Cut, Paste, and Spellcheck. Although this toolbar displays when you do a standard Office 2000 installation, you can turn it off if you want to see more of your file and less of the icons.

## How You Get Here

✧ Press **Alt+V,T** choose **Standard**    ✧ Choose **View ➤ Toolbars ➤ Standard**

## What's Different

Figure 29.3 is a sample of this toolbar and Table 29.1 has a description of the icons that are unique to PowerPoint. (For more information, see View ➤ Toolbars ➤ Standard on page 65.)

**Figure 29.3**    The Standard toolbar

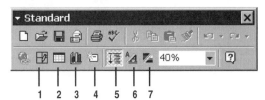

**Table 29.1**   Icons in the Standard toolbar

| # | Icon | What you do with it |
|---|------|---------------------|
| 1 | Tables and Borders | Click to open the Tables and Borders toolbar. (For more information, see The Tables and Borders Toolbar on page 252.) |
| 2 | Insert Table | Click to open a drop-down list for defining a table to be inserted at the cursor position. (For more information, see Table ➤ Insert on page 254.) |
| 3 | Insert Chart | Click to open a window so that you can create a chart for your data. This option uses the same approach as you use when you create a chart in Excel. (For more information, see The Excel Chart Menu on page 413.) |
| 4 | New Slide | Click to display the New Slide dialog box so that you can choose which master you want to use for the new slide. Once you click the **OK** button, PowerPoint inserts a new slide *after* the slide where the cursor is currently positioned. |
| 5 | Expand All | Click to show all levels of text headings on the current slide in the outline pane. |
| 6 | Show Formatting | Click to show or hide graphics and formatting. |
| 7 | Grayscale Preview | Click to display the current presentation in black and white. |

## View ➤ Toolbars ➤ Formatting

Use this option to display the Formatting toolbar which has icons for the font used for your text, borders that surround an element, and other icons for changing the look of the elements in your file. (For more information, see The Formatting Toolbar on page 492.)

### How You Get Here

✧ Press **Alt+V,T** choose **Formatting**   ✧ Choose **View** ➤ **Toolbars** ➤ **Formatting**

## View ➤ Toolbars ➤ Animation Effects

Use this option to display the Animation Effects toolbar, which has controls for making titles and body text appear on the slides in unusual ways. For example, you can have text "fly in" from either side of the screen when you're giving a presentation. (This is one way to keep your audience from falling asleep while you're reviewing those production numbers!)

### How You Get Here

✧ Press **Alt+V,T** choose **Animation Effects**  ✧ Choose **View** ➤ **Toolbars** ➤ **Animation Effects**

## What's In This Toolbar

Figure 29.4 is a sample of this toolbar and Table 29.2 has a description of the icons available.

**Figure 29.4**   The Animation Effects toolbar

**Table 29.2**   Icons in the Animation Effects toolbar

| # | Icon | What you do with it |
|---|------|---------------------|
| 1 | Animate Title | Click to turn on the animation function for the title of your slide. Once you've turned on this option, you can choose various effects to make the title "move" when you display the slides in Slide Show view. |
| 2 | Animate Slide Text | Click to turn on the animation function for the text of your slide. Once you've turned on this option, you can choose various effects to make the text "move" when you display the slides in Slide Show view. |
| 3 | Drive-In Effect | Click to make the highlighted text fly in from the right when you display the slides in Slide Show view. |
| 4 | Flying Effect | Click to make the highlighted text fly in from the left when you display the slides in Slide Show view. |
| 5 | Camera Effect | Click to make the highlighted text appear from its own center outward when you display the slides in Slide Show view. |
| 6 | Flash Once | Click to make the highlighted text flash off, then on again, when you display the slides in Slide Show view. |
| 7 | Laser Text Effect | Click to make the highlighted text appear letter-by-letter, as if it was being "etched" by a series of objects from the side of the slide when you display the slides in Slide Show view. |
| 8 | Typewriter Text Effect | Click to make the highlighted text appear letter-by-letter, as though typed in place when you display the slides in Slide Show view. |
| 9 | Reverse Text Order Effect | Click to make the highlighted text appear in the reverse order in which it was entered when you display the slides in Slide Show view. |
| 10 | Drop-In Text Effect | Click to make the highlighted text appear as a single block, dropping in from the top of the slide when you display the slides in Slide Show view. |
| 11 | Animation Order drop-down list | Choose an item that determines the order in which the animation actions will take place on the current slide when you display the slides in Slide Show view. |
| 12 | Custom Animation | Click to open the Custom Animation dialog box so that you can set a fuller range of animation effects. |
| 13 | Animation Preview | Click to open an animation window that acts out the animation actions in sequence. |

## View ➤ Toolbars ➤ Clipboard

Use this option to display the Clipboard toolbar, which stores up to 12 copied items. This is very helpful when you have copied items from other applications and want to combine them in one document. If you're working in a non-Office application and have an Office application open, all copied items are added to the Clipboard. However, the Clipboard toolbar is only available in an Office application. (For more information, see View ➤ Toolbars ➤ Clipboard on page 67.)

---

**N O T E**   You can't customize this toolbar. ▨

## How You Get Here

✧ Press **Alt+V,T** choose **Clipboard**   ✧ Choose **View** ➤ **Toolbars** ➤ **Clipboard**

## View ➤ Toolbars ➤ Control Toolbox

Use this option to display the Control Toolbox toolbar so that you create a custom form with ActiveX controls such as radio buttons, text boxes, scroll bars, and other neat stuff that can darn near make your file sing and dance (but that kind of stuff is beyond the scope of this book). These controls are similar to the controls created with a programming language, such as Visual Basic. With an ActiveX control, however, you're actually writing a macro that is stored with the control and it is only available when the file with the control is open. (For more information, see View ➤ Toolbars ➤ Control Toolbox on page 68.)

---

**N O T E**   These are the same types of controls you can add using the Visual Basic Editor. For more information try, *Special Edition, Using Visual Basic For Applications 5*, by Paul Sanna, (ISBN: 0789709597). ▨

## How You Get Here

✧ Press **Alt+V,T** choose **Control Toolbox**   ✧ Choose **View** ➤ **Toolbars** ➤ **Control Toolbox**

## View ➤ Toolbars ➤ Drawing

Use this option to display the Drawing toolbar so that you can create your own drawings, insert shapes, add callouts, and apply color to your masterpiece. (For more information, see View ➤ Toolbars ➤ Drawing on page 69.)

## How You Get Here

✧ Click       ✧ Press **Alt+V,T** choose **Drawing**   ✧ Choose **View** ➤ **Toolbars** ➤ **Drawing**

## View ➤ Toolbars ➤ Outlining

Use this option to move text around on the slides. You can make the text move **up, down, right or left**. Just as you make an outline for your presentation, you can use these controls to manipulate text to form your outline.

### How You Get Here

✧ Press **Alt+V,T** choose **Outlining**          ✧ Choose **View ➤ Toolbars ➤ Outlining**

### What's In This Toolbar

Figure 29.5 is a sample of this toolbar and Table 29.3 has a description of the icons available.

**Figure 29.5**    The Outlining toolbar

**Table 29.3**    Icons in the Outlining toolbar

| # | Icon | What you do with it |
|---|------|---------------------|
| 1 | Promote | Click to move the text where the cursor is positioned one level higher in the slide hierarchy. The level in the hierarchy is determined by what level is currently assigned to the text. For example, if you promote the first bullet in a list, that text becomes a slide title. |
| 2 | Demote | Click to move the text where the cursor is positioned one level lower in the slide hierarchy. The level in the hierarchy is determined by what level is currently assigned to the text. For example, if you demote a slide title, that text becomes part of the body text for the slide. |
| 3 | Move Up | Click to move the text where the cursor is positioned up one level in the text order. For example, if you move the first bullet in a list up, that item becomes the last item on the previous slide. |
| 4 | Move Down | Click to move the text where the cursor is positioned down one level in the text order. For example, if you move the slide title down, the entire slide moves to the next position in the slide order. |
| 5 | Collapse | Click to show only the highest heading level for the slide where the cursor is positioned. |
| 6 | Expand | Click to show everything on the slide where the cursor is positioned. |
| 7 | Collapse All | Click to show only the highest heading level for all the slides in the presentation. |
| 8 | Expand All | Click to show everything for all the slides in the presentation. |

**Table 29.3** Icons in the Outlining toolbar, continued

| # Icon | What you do with it |
|---|---|
| 9 Summary Slide | Click to create a new slide that has the titles of the slides that are currently highlighted. The summary slide is inserted in front the first slide highlighted and displays a bulleted list of the slide titles. |
| | Note This is an easy way to create a slide that gives the agenda for your presentation. |
| 10 Show Formatting | Click to show or hide graphics and formatting that are used when you print your presentation or view the presentation on a computer. |
| | Note The default outline view doesn't show all the fancy formatting which means it also displays information more quickly as you scroll through your presentation. |

## View ➤ Toolbars ➤ Picture

Use this option to display the Picture toolbar so that you can insert images into your document and control the way they look. (For more information, see Insert ➤ Picture on page 83.) (For more information, see View ➤ Toolbars ➤ Picture on page 71.)

### How You Get Here

✧ Press **Alt+V,T** choose **Picture**     ✧ Choose **View ➤ Toolbars ➤ Picture**

## View ➤ Toolbars ➤ Reviewing

Use this option to display the Reviewing toolbar so that you can review existing comments, insert comments, delete existing comments, or accept the changes made to a document. (For more information, see View ➤ Toolbars ➤ Reviewing on page 72.) This is a great way keep track of notes, comments, and questions; that way you and other authors can review this information before the text is actually added to the final file. (For more information, see Insert ➤ Comment on page 82 or View ➤ Comments on page 79.)

### How You Get Here

✧ Press **Alt+V,T** choose **Reviewing**  ✧ Choose **View ➤ Toolbars ➤ Reviewing**

## View ➤ Toolbars ➤ Tables and Borders

Use this option to display the Tables and Borders toolbar so that you can insert tables and change the way tables and borders look in your file.

### How You Get Here.

✧ Click      ✧ Press **Alt+V,T** choose **Tables and Borders**      ✧ Choose **View ➤ Toolbars ➤ Tables and Borders**

## What's In This Toolbar

Figure 29.6 is a sample of this toolbar and Table 29.4 has a description of the icons available.

**Figure 29.6**   The Tables and Borders toolbar

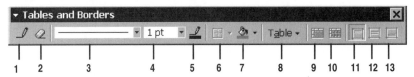

**Table 29.4**   Icons in the Tables and Borders toolbar

| # | Icon | What you do with it |
|---|------|---------------------|
| 1 | Draw Table | Click to change pointer to pencil icon, then click and drag the outline of the table. Click inside the table to establish rows and columns.Click draw an entire table, including the outside dimensions and the appropriate number of rows and columns. If you don't want to draw your table, choose **Insert Microsoft Table** from the Standard toolbar. (For more information, see Table ➤ Insert on page 254.) |
| 2 | Eraser | Click to change the pointer to an eraser icon so that you can get rid of a column or row. |
| 3 | Border Style drop-down list | Choose an item that determines what type of lines are used when you draw the border around the table and when you draw the columns and rows in the table. |
| 4 | Border Width drop-down list | Choose an item that determines how thick the line is when you draw the border around the table and when you draw the columns and rows in the table. |
| 5 | Border Color | Choose an item that determines what color is applied when you draw the border around the table and when you draw the columns and rows in the table. |
| 6 | Outside Borders | Choose an item that determines which side (or sides) of your table have a border. |
| 7 | Fill Color | Choose an item that determines what color is used to fill a solid object. |
| 8 | Insert Table drop-down list | Click to display Insert Table dialog box so that you can add a table to your slide. |
| 9 | Merge Cells | Click to merge highlighted cells. |
| 10 | Split Cell | Click to split one cell into several rows and/or columns. |
| 11 | Align Top | Click to line the text at the top of the cell. |
| 12 | Center Vertically | Click to line the text in the center of the cell. |
| 13 | Align Bottom | Click to line the text at the bottom of the cell. |

## View ➤ Toolbars ➤ Visual Basic

Use this option to display the Visual Basic toolbar so that you can create a new program such as a macro. Macros are small programs that you use for different purposes. You can create macros that do some of the tedious, repetitive work that you would normally do at the keyboard, one step at a time. In fact, you can create a program for almost any task that you need to perform, which is a great way to ensure accuracy and relieve the boredom of doing the same thing over and over again. (For more information, see View ➤ Toolbars ➤ Visual Basic on page 73.)

---

**N O T E**  Although the details of programming with Visual Basic are beyond the scope of this book, you might want to try, *Special Edition, Using Visual Basic For Applications 5*, by Paul Sanna, (ISBN: 0789709597). ▓

### How You Get Here

❖ Press **Alt+V,T** choose **Visual Basic**     ❖ Choose **View ➤ Toolbars ➤ Visual Basic**

## View ➤ Toolbars ➤ Web

Use this option to display the Web toolbar so that you can see and use the icons that are used most frequently in a Web Browser. (For more information, see View ➤ Toolbars ➤ Web on page 74.)

### How You Get Here

❖ Press **Alt+V,T** choose **Web**     ❖ Choose **View ➤ Toolbars ➤ Web**

## View ➤ Toolbars ➤ WordArt

Use this option to display the WordArt toolbar so that you can insert and format art items so they look just the way you want them to. (For more information, see View ➤ Toolbars ➤ WordArt on page 75.) This toolbar includes icons for moving and resizing your art objects or changing the way your text is aligned or wrapped around the object. (For more information, see Insert ➤ Picture ➤ WordArt on page 87.)

### How You Get Here

❖ Press **Alt+V,T** choose **WordArt**     ❖ Choose **View ➤ Toolbars ➤ WordArt**

### View ➤ Toolbars ➤ Customize

Use this option to display the Customize window so that you can customize most of the toolbars or menu options. (For more information, see View ➤ Toolbars ➤ Customize on page 76.)

### How You Get Here

✧ Press **Alt+V,T,C**

✧ Choose **View ➤ Toolbars ➤ Customize**

# View ➤ Ruler

Use this option to turn the ruler on and off so that you can place or size items in your presentation. The ruler displays the position of elements within the current document, including graphics and tabs.

**N O T E**   The ruler only displays in the slide pane. ▨

### How You Get Here

✧ Press **Alt+V,R**

✧ Choose **View ➤ Ruler**

# View ➤ Guides

Use this option to turn on and off a set of crosshairs that can be moved to precisely measure an element's position on the slide.

### How You Get Here

✧ Press **Alt+V,G**

✧ Choose **View ➤ Guides**

# View ➤ Header and Footer

Use this option to display the Header and Footer dialog box. You can create headers and footers for notes pages and handouts. Footers can also be placed on slides.

**N O T E**   Slides do not have headers, although both notes and handouts do. ▨

### How You Get Here

✧ Press **Alt+V,H**

✧ Choose **View ➤ Header and Footer**

## What's In This Dialog Box

Figure 29.7 is a sample of this dialog box and Table 29.5 has a description of the tabs available.

**Figure 29.7**   The Header and Footer dialog box

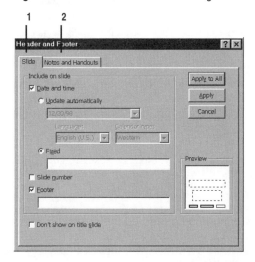

**Table 29.5**   Tabs in the Header and Footer dialog box

| # | Tab name | What you do with it |
|---|----------|---------------------|
| 1 | Slide | Click to set or review the current settings for the slide footer. (For a complete description of the options available, see Table 29.6 on page 471.) |
| 2 | Notes and Handouts | Set or review headers and footers for notes and handouts. (For a complete description of the options available, see Table 29.7 on page 472.) |

The following tables describe the options for the individual tabs in this dialog box:

- Table 29.6 describes the Slide tab, and
- Table 29.7 describes the Notes and Handouts tab.

**Table 29.6**   Options in the Header and Footer dialog box Slide tab

| Option | What you do with it |
|--------|---------------------|
| Date and time check box | Click to insert the current date and time in the slide footer. |
| Update automatically radio button | Click to make sure the date is updated automatically to reflect the current date. |
| Update automatically drop-down list | Choose an item that determines how the date is displayed when it's inserted in the slide footer. |
| Language drop-down list | Choose an item that determines what language to use for the date field that you've inserted in the slide footer. |

**Table 29.6**   Options in the Header and Footer dialog box Slide tab, continued

| Option | What you do with it |
| --- | --- |
| Calendar type drop-down list | Choose an item that determines what calendar convention to use for the date field when it's inserted in the slide footer. |
| Fixed radio button | Click to put a specific date in the footer and prevent the date from being automatically updated every time you open the presentation. |
| Fixed text box | Enter the fixed text that you want to appear in the slide footer. |
| Slide number check box | Click to have PowerPoint insert the appropriate slide number in the slide footer. |
| Footer check box | Click to enable the text in the text box to appear in the slide footer. |
| Footer text box | Enter the text that will display in the slide footer. |
| Preview area | View how the slides will look with the currently defined footer text. |
| Apply to All button | Click to apply the footer to *all* slides in the presentation. |
| Apply button | Click to apply the footer *only* to the current slide. |
| Don't show on title slide | Click to disable the header and footer appearing on the title slide. |

**Table 29.7**   Options in the Header and Footer dialog box Notes and Handouts tab

| Option | What you do with it |
| --- | --- |
| Date and time check box | Click to insert the current date and time in the header for Notes and Handouts pages. |
| Update automatically radio button | Click to make sure the date and time is updated automatically to reflect the current date and time. |
| Update automatically drop-down list | Choose an item that determines how the date is displayed when it's inserted in the Notes and Handouts pages |
| Language: drop-down list | Choose an item that determines what language to use for the date field when it's inserted in the Notes and Handouts pages |
| Calendar type: drop-down list | Choose an item that determines what calendar convention to use for the date field when it's inserted in the Notes and Handouts pages. |
| Fixed radio button | Click to put a specific date in the Notes and Handouts pages and prevent the date from being automatically updated every time you open the presentation. |
| Fixed text box | Enter the fixed text that you want to appear in Notes and Handouts pages. |
| Header check box | Click to enable the text in the text box to appear in the note/handout header. |
| Header text box | Enter the text that will appear in the note/handout header. |
| Page number check box | Click to have PowerPoint insert the appropriate page number on the Notes and Handouts pages. |
| Footer check box | Click to enable the text in the text box to appear in the note/handout footer. |

**Table 29.7**  Options in the Header and Footer dialog box Notes and Handouts tab, continued

| Option | What you do with it |
|---|---|
| Footer text box | Enter the text that will display at the bottom of every page or slide. |
| Preview area | View how the Notes and Handouts pages will look with the currently defined header and footer text. |
| Apply to All button | Click to apply the header and footer to all Notes and Handouts pages in the presentation. |

# View ➤ Comments

Use this option to view any comments that have been inserted in the current file. This option opens a pane in the current window which has the comment text in it. (For more information, see View ➤ Toolbars ➤ Reviewing on page 467.)

**N O T E**  Comments in the current document are indicated by yellow highlighting within the text. ▪

## How You Get Here

✧ Press **Alt+V,0**       ✧ Choose **View ➤ Comments**

# View ➤ Zoom

Use this option to set the size of the display for the current file. You can let the application calculate the size or you can set a precise size that suits your needs. (For more information, see View ➤ Zoom on page 79.)

**N O T E**  When you choose a larger number, you see a bigger version of your file, but you can't see as much of the file at one time. You'll spend more time scrolling but your eyes won't be so worn out. ▪

## How You Get Here

✧ Press **Alt+V,Z**       ✧ Choose **View ➤ Zoom**

# The PowerPoint Insert Menu

# What Is The Insert Menu

This menu lists the commands that you'll use to add page breaks, page numbers, stored text phrases, comments, pictures, and hyperlinks. Many types of items you want to put in your document are inserted from this menu.

If a menu option has an ellipsis (three dots) or an arrow beside it, the application "asks" you for additional information before the action takes place. If the menu doesn't have one of these symbols, the action you choose happens immediately. If the action takes place immediately, you won't see a sample screen in this section.

# Insert ➤ New Slide

Use this option to add a blank slide after the slide where the cursor is currently positioned. You can use one of the predefined slides for your template or insert a blank slide and customize the layout. If you choose the **Don't show this dialog box again** check box, the next new slide you insert uses the layout of the last new slide.

## How You Get Here

✧ Click 🖾    ✧ Press **Alt+I,N** or **Ctrl+M**    ✧ Choose **Insert ➤ New Slide**

## What's In This Dialog Box

Figure 30.1 is a sample of this dialog box and Table 30.1 has a description of the options available.

**Figure 30.1**    The New Slide dialog box

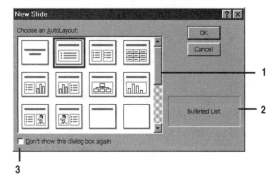

**Table 30.1**    Options in the New Slide dialog box

| # | Option | What you do with it |
|---|--------|---------------------|
| 1 | Choose an AutoLayout list | Click to choose one of the predefined slide layout formats for your new slide. |

**Table 30.1** Options in the New Slide dialog box, continued

| # | Option | What you do with it |
|---|--------|---------------------|
| 2 | Description area | View a description of the typical use for the highlighted layout. |
| 3 | Don't show this dialog box again button | Click to avoid seeing this dialog box the next time you insert a new slide. If this option is turned on PowerPoint uses the currently highlighted format for any new slides you add. |

# Insert ➤ Duplicate Slide

Use this option to add a copy of a slide after the slide where the cursor is currently positioned. The new slide includes all the text and formatting of the slide you copy from—so make sure you pay attention to where your cursor is placed *before* you use this option.

## How You Get Here

✧ Press **Alt+I,D** or **Ctrl+Shift+D**   ✧ Choose **Insert ➤ Duplicate Slide**

# Insert ➤ Slide Number

Use this option to add the number of the slide where you have placed your cursor. If you want to place numbers on all slides it is better to use the Header and Footer command to control the placement and formatting for the slide number.(For more information, see View ➤ Header and Footer on page 470.)

## How You Get Here

✧ Press **Alt+I,U**         ✧ Choose **Insert ➤ Slide Number**

# Insert ➤ Date and Time

Use this option to place the current date, the current time, or the current date *and* time at the current cursor position. You can choose several different formats and automatically update this information every time you open the file. You can insert this information in the body of your file or insert in the header or footer so that it displays on every page. ▪

**TIP**   If you want to have the application update this information every time you open the file, be sure to click the **Update automatically** check box. Be careful with this one—it really does update the date every time you open the file, not just when you make changes to the file.

## How You Get Here

✧ Press **Alt+I,T**         ✧ Choose **Insert ➤ Date and Time**

## What's In This Dialog Box

Figure 30.2 is a sample of this dialog box and Table 30.2 has a description of the options available.

**Figure 30.2**    The Date and Time dialog box

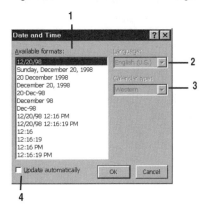

**Table 30.2**    Options in the Date and Time dialog box

| # | Option | What you do with it |
|---|--------|---------------------|
| 1 | Available formats list | Choose an item that determines what the date/time will look like when you insert it in your presentation. |
| 2 | Language drop-down list | Choose an item that determines what language is applied to the date/time when you insert it in your document. The default language is the one you've set up for PowerPoint. |
| 3 | Calendar type drop-down list | Click to choose to whether you want PowerPoint to update the date and time *every* time you open the document. |
| 4 | Update automatically check box | Click to store the currently highlighted format as the new formatting style. |

# Insert ➤ Symbol

Use this option to place special characters, such as a trademark or copyright symbol, in your document. When the Symbol dialog box displays, you can change the font or assign a keyboard shortcut sequence if you think you'll use a symbol frequently.

## How You Get Here

✧ Press **Alt+I,S**          ✧ Choose **Insert ➤ Symbol**

## What's In This Dialog Box

Figure 30.3 is a sample of this dialog box and Table 30.3 has a description of the options available.

**Figure 30.3**   The Symbol dialog box

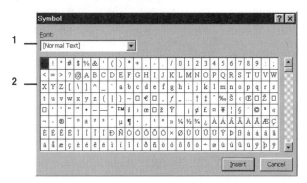

**Table 30.3**   Options in the Symbol dialog box

| # | Option | What you do with it |
|---|--------|---------------------|
| 1 | Font drop-down list | Choose an item that determines which font has the symbol or letter you want to insert. |
| 2 | Symbols list | View the symbols or letters available for the font you've chosen. Click to highlight a specific symbol or letter. To insert the highlighted character at the current cursor position, double-click it or click the **Insert** button. |

# Insert ➤ Comment

Use this option to add written comments to a file that you're editing or reviewing. Be sure you either highlight the text you're making a comment about or click the cursor at the end of the text *before* you choose this command. Once you insert a comment, the text looks like a little yellow sticky note (you know, those ones that you couldn't live without?) (For more information, see Insert ➤ Comment on page 82 or View ➤ Toolbars ➤ Reviewing on page 72.)

## How You Get Here

✧ Press **Alt+I,M**          ✧ Choose **Insert ➤ Comment**

# Insert ➤ Slides from Files

Use this option to place one or more slides from another presentations *after* the highlighted slide in the active presentation. Can't remember what the slides look like or only want to insert a few slides? No problem. You can preview the slides before you insert them, either with or without the titles and then pick just the right slides or pick all of the slides if you're trying to combine two presentations into one presentation.

> **N O T E**   When you insert slides from another presentation, they take on the format of the active presentation. So be sure you review each slide to make sure the information still fits on the slide properly. ▪

## How You Get Here

❖ Press **Alt+I,F**            ❖ Choose **Insert ➤ Slides from Files**

## What's In This Dialog Box

Figure 30.4 is a sample of this dialog box and Table 30.4 has a description of the tabs available.

**Figure 30.4**   The Slide Finder dialog box

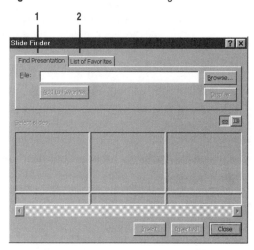

**Table 30.4**   Tabs in the Slide Finder dialog box

| # | Tab name | What you do with it |
|---|----------|---------------------|
| 1 | Find Presentation | Click to find the presentation that has the slides you're looking for.  (For a complete description of the options available, see Table 30.5 on page 481.) |
| 2 | List of Favorites | Click to review a list of presentations that you use frequently. (For a complete description of the options available, see Table 30.5 on page 481.) |

The following table describes the options for *both* tabs in this dialog box:

■ Table 30.5 describes the Find Presentation *and* List of Favorites tab.

**Table 30.5**  Options in the Slide Finder dialog box Find Presentation *and* List of Favorites tabs

| Option | What you do with it |
| --- | --- |
| File text box | Enter the name of the file that has the slides you want to insert. |
| Add to Favorites button | Click to add the presentation listed in the File text box to a list of frequently accessed presentations. If you use a specific presentation frequently, adding the file to your Favorites list saves you time because you don't have to go looking for it every time you need it.<br><br>**Note**  This button is available only on the Find Presentation tab. |
| Browse button | Click to display the folders on any drive you have access to so that you can find the presentation you need. |
| Display button | Click to view the slides in the presentation listed in the File text box. |
| Slide Display button | Click to display a minature version of each slide in the presentation listed in the File text box. |
| Slide List Display button | Click to display the titles of each slide in the presentation listed in the File text box. (This displays a simple list, but not of the fancy stuff.) |
| Select slides area | Click to choose the slides that you want to insert in your presentation. If you want to insert *all* of the slides, click the **Insert All** button. |
| Insert button | Click to insert the highlighted slides in your active presentation. |
| Insert All button | Click to insert all slides in the active presentation. |

# Insert ➤ Slides from Outline

Use this option to create new slides from an outline created in another application. PowerPoint recognizes quite a few file types, including Rich Text Format (RTF), ASCII (plain old text) and Hypertext Markup Language (HTML). You'll get the best results if the outline has been formatted using styles or tags to indicate heading levels. If this information is stored in the outline, PowerPoint uses each major heading to create a new slide, which can save you a bunch of time!

---

**N O T E**  This dialog box is the same basic dialog box displayed when you choose **File ➤ Open**. Choose the file location, name, and type, then decide whether you want to insert a copy of the picture in your file or create a link to the source file. (For more information, see File ➤ Open on page 39.) ■

## How You Get Here

✧ Press **Alt+I,L**          ✧ Choose **Insert ➤ Slides from Outline**

# Insert ➤ Picture

Use this option to insert various types of artwork in your file, including scanned items, the clipart that came with Office 2000, digital pictures, sound clips, and moving pictures. You can embed the artwork (store an actual copy) or create a link to the original file. If you create a link to the original file, you'll always have the latest information, no matter how many times you've edited the original artwork. (For more information, see Insert ➤ Picture on page 83.)

---

**N O T E**   Office 2000 accepts most of the popular graphics formats. Some of the formats, however, require a separate filter before you can bring them into your file. These filters are available on your original Office 2000 CD. So, if you don't have the filter you need, you can use the Office 2000 setup program to add them. ■

## How You Get Here

✧ Press **Alt+I,P**          ✧ Choose **Insert** ➤ **Picture**

## What's In This Flyout Menu

Figure 30.5 is a sample of this flyout menu.

**Figure 30.5**   The Insert ➤ Picture flyout menu

——————— Insert ➤ Picture ➤ Organization Chart          482

——————— Insert ➤ Picture ➤ Microsoft Word Table          483

## Insert ➤ Picture ➤ Organization Chart

Use this option to add an organizational charts to your presentation using the separate application included with Office 2000 (which is loaded when you choose this option). Office 2000 provides a set of predefined charts that you can use to create professional looking organizational charts. All you have to do is fill in the blanks on the outline. If needed, you can add more boxes. Choose the box type from the toolbar and then click the location on the chart where you want it to appear. ■

## How You Get Here

✧ Press **Alt+I,P,O**          ✧ Choose **Insert** ➤ **Picture** ➤ **Organization Chart**

## What's In This Window

Figure 30.6 is a sample of this window.

**Figure 30.6** The Microsoft Organization Chart window

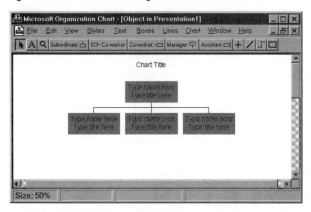

## Insert ➤ Picture ➤ Microsoft Word Table

Use this option to create a table on the currently highlighted slide. With this option, you have full access to all the features in Word's table editor. (For more information, see The Word Table Menu on page 251.)

### How You Get Here

✧ Press **Alt+I,P,T**

✧ Choose **Insert ➤ Picture ➤ Microsoft Word Table**

### What's In This Dialog Box

Figure 30.7 is a sample of this dialog box and Table 30.6 has a description of the options available.

**Figure 30.7** The Insert Table dialog box

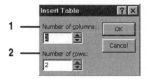

**Table 30.6** Options in the Insert Table dialog box

| # | Option | What you do with it |
|---|--------|---------------------|
| 1 | Number of columns text box | Enter the number of columns you want created for the table you're inserting. |
| 2 | Number of rows text box | Enter the number of rows you wanted created for the table you're inserting. |

# Insert ➤ Text Box

Use this option to draw a box around the currently highlighted text or insert a new text box if no text is currently highlighted. If no text is highlighted, the cursor changes to a plus (+) and you can draw the text box by dragging your mouse across the document. Once you've inserted a text box, you change change the properties by displaying the shortcut menu and choosing **Edit Text Box.**

---

**N O T E**    You can also link a series of text boxes so that the text automatically moves to the next linked box as the amount of text expands. ▪

## How You Get Here

❖ Press **Alt+I,X**           ❖ Choose **Insert ➤ Text Box**

# Insert ➤ Movies and Sounds

Use this option to place animation and audio in your presentation. When you run the slide show the animations and sounds play where you've inserted them. For the most part this is similar to inserting pictures or clip art in a presentation. (For more information, see Insert ➤ Picture on page 83.)

## How You Get Here

❖ Press **Alt+I,V**           ❖ Choose **Insert ➤ Movies and Sounds**

## What's In This Flyout Menu

Figure 30.8 is a sample of this flyout menu.

**Figure 30.8**    The Insert ➤ Movies and Sounds flyout menu

| Menu item | Path | Page |
|---|---|---|
| Movie from Gallery... | Insert ➤ Movies and Sounds ➤ Movie from Gallery | 484 |
| Movie from File... | Insert ➤ Movies and Sounds ➤ Movie from File | 485 |
| Sound from Gallery... | Insert ➤ Movies and Sounds ➤ Sound from Gallery | 485 |
| Sound from File... | Insert ➤ Movies and Sounds ➤ Sound from File | 485 |
| Play CD Audio Track... | Insert ➤ Movies and Sounds ➤ Play CD Audio Track | 485 |
| Record Sound | Insert ➤ Movies and Sounds ➤ Record Sound | 486 |

## Insert ➤ Movies and Sounds ➤ Movie from Gallery

Use this option to insert movies from the predefined gallery you have installed on your system. (For more information, see Insert ➤ Picture on page 83.)

## How You Get Here

❖ Press **Alt+I,V,M**     ❖ Choose **Insert ➤ Movies and Sounds ➤ Movie from Gallery**

## Insert ➤ Movies and Sounds ➤ Movie from File

Use this option to insert movies from files created in other applications. (For more information, see Insert ➤ Picture on page 83.)

### How You Get Here

✧ Press **Alt+I,V,F**     ✧ Choose **Insert ➤ Movies and Sounds ➤ Movie from File**

## Insert ➤ Movies and Sounds ➤ Sound from Gallery

Use this option to insert audio from the predefined gallery installed on your system. (For more information, see Insert ➤ Picture on page 83.)

### How You Get Here

✧ Press **Alt+I,V,S**   ✧ Choose **Insert ➤ Movies and Sounds ➤ Sound from Gallery**

## Insert ➤ Movies and Sounds ➤ Sound from File

Use this option to insert audio from files created from other applications. (For more information, see Insert ➤ Picture on page 83.)

### How You Get Here

✧ Press **Alt+I,V,U**   ✧ Choose **Insert ➤ Movies and Sounds ➤ Sound from File**

## Insert ➤ Movies and Sounds ➤ Play CD Audio Track

Use this option to insert audio from a selected CD track.(For more information, see Insert ➤ Picture on page 83.)

### How You Get Here

✧ Press **Alt+I,V,C**   ✧ Choose **Insert ➤ Movies and Sounds ➤ Play CD Audio Track**

## What's In This Dialog Box

Figure 30.9 is a sample of this dialog box and Table 30.7 has a description of the options available.

**Figure 30.9**    The Movies and Sound Options dialog box

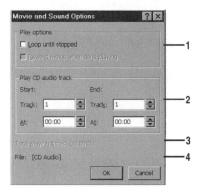

**Table 30.7**    Options in the Movies and Sound Options dialog box

| # | Option | What you do with it |
|---|--------|---------------------|
| 1 | Play options area | Choose an item that determines whether you want to stop playing automatically or manually or rewind a movie when it is finished playing. |
| 2 | Play CD audio track area | Enter the exact location of the audio track you're inserting, including track number and the start and stop time. |
| 3 | Total playing time area | View the total play time for the selected CD track. |
| 4 | File description area | View the information for the selected CD track. |

## Insert ➤ Movies and Sounds ➤ Record Sound

Use this option to record your own audio for the highlighted slide. Use the buttons in this dialog box like you would a standard tape recorder. (For more information, see Insert ➤ Picture on page 83.)

---

**N O T E**    PowerPoint embeds the sound on the selected slide and adds the filename to the sounds list on the Custom Animation dialog box. ▦

## How You Get Here

✧ Press **Alt+I,V,R**      ✧ Choose **Insert ➤ Movies and Sounds ➤ Record Sound**

## What's In This Dialog Box

Figure 30.10 is a sample of this dialog box and Table 30.8 has a description of the options available.

**Figure 30.10** The Record Sound dialog box

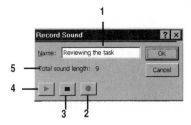

**Table 30.8** Options in the Record Sound dialog box

| # | Option | What you do with it |
|---|--------|---------------------|
| 1 | Name text box | Enter the file name for the sound you are recording. |
| 2 | Begin recording button | Click to start recording the sound. |
| 3 | Stop recording button | Click to stop recording the sound. |
| 4 | Play sound button | Click to playback the recorded sound. |
| 5 | Total sound length area | View the length of the sound recorded. |

# Insert ➤ Chart

Use this option to create and format charts to place in your worksheet. This is a nifty wizard that walks you through creating and customizing your charts, step-by-step. Just follow the directions on the wizard to complete your chart. If you change your mind about something in the chart you can cancel or move backwards through the wizard. After you have placed your chart, double-click the chart to display the Format Chart window where you can format the various axes, gridlines, fonts, colors, and properties for your chart. (For more information, see Format ➤ Selected Area on page 356.)

## How You Get Here

✧ Click      ✧ Press **Alt+I,H**          ✧ Choose **Insert ➤ Chart**

# Insert ➤ Table

Use this option to place a basic table in your presentation. Choose the number of columns and rows for the table you are creating. When you click the **OK** button the Tables and Borders toolbar displays so you can use the controls to customize your table. (For more information, see View ➤ Toolbars ➤ Tables and Borders on page 467.)

---

**N O T E**   This option is different from the **Insert ➤ Picture ➤ Microsoft Word Table** option. With **Insert ➤ Table** you won't get all the menu options and features for Word tables used by the **Insert ➤ Picture ➤ Microsoft Word Table** option. So if you only want a basic table this is the option to use. ▪

## How You Get Here

✧ Press **Alt+I,B**          ✧ Choose **Insert ➤ Table**

## What's In This Dialog Box

Figure 30.11 is a sample of this dialog box and Table 30.9 has a description of the options available.

**Figure 30.11**   The Insert Table dialog box

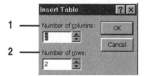

**Table 30.9**   Options in the Insert Table dialog box

| # | Option | What you do with it |
|---|--------|---------------------|
| 1 | Number of columns list | Enter the number of columns you want created for the table you're inserting. |
| 2 | Number of rows list | Enter the number of rows you wanted created for the table you're inserting. |

# Insert ➤ Object

Use this option to place items from other applications into your file or to create new items using another application. Inserting an object differs from inserting a file because you create the object with a source application instead of selecting an existing file from your computer system. These items can be embedded in the document or linked to a source. (For more information, see Insert ➤ Object on page 89.)

 This option is primarily for inserting file types that Word doesn't really know how to handle, such as native Portable Document Format (PDF) or Paint Shop Pro (PSP) files. The Insert ➤ File option is primarily for file types that Word already knows about, such as Rich Text Format (RTF) or standard text files created in other applications. (For more information, see Insert ➤ File on page 188.)

## How You Get Here

✧ Press **Alt+I,O**          ✧ Choose **Insert ➤ Object**

# Insert ➤ Hyperlink

Use this option to create a connection between two parts of your file, between the active file and another file, or create a connection between the active file and a website address. Once you've inserted the hyperlink, the text changes color and is underlined and you can click on it to quickly jump to the destination specified. (For more information, see Insert ➤ Hyperlink on page 90.) You can use the Web toolbar to work with the hyperlink and you can edit the information stored in the hyperlink after you've inserted it. (For more information, see View ➤ Toolbars ➤ Web on page 74.)

 You can also create a screen tip that displays when you place your cursor over the link. If you need to edit the link, highlight it, then right-click to display the shortcut menu.

## How You Get Here

✧ Click           ✧ Press **Alt+I,I** or **Ctrl+K**          ✧ Choose **Insert ➤ Hyperlink**

# The PowerPoint Format Menu

# What Is The Format Menu

This menu lists the commands that you'll use to change the "look" of your file. You can choose the typeface for your text (the typeface for this text is Century Old Style), define bullets or numbering, set tab markers, choose the spacing and alignment for your paragraph (or paragraph styles), and, in general, tweak the look of your file. Generally, any type of style you want to apply to the text can be set somewhere within this menu.

If a menu option has an ellipsis (three dots) or an arrow beside it, the application "asks" you for additional information before the action takes place. If the menu doesn't have one of these symbols, the action you choose happens immediately. If the action takes place immediately, you won't see a sample screen in this section.

---

**N O T E**   Most of the options for this menu are located on the Formatting toolbar for this application. ▪

# The Formatting Toolbar

Use this option to quickly perform the formatting tasks in your file. The options described here are the default icons that appear on the toolbar. You can, however, customize this toolbar so that it has all the icons for the tasks you perform most frequently. If you want to apply other formatting options not appearing on this toolbar see the related topic in this chapter for more information.

## How You Get Here

✧ Press **Alt+V,T** choose **Formatting**     ✧ Choose **View ➤ Toolbars ➤ Formatting**

## What's In This Toolbar

Figure 31.1 is a sample of this toolbar and Table 31.1 has a description of the icons available.

**Figure 31.1**   The Formatting toolbar

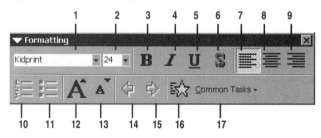

**Table 31.1**   Icons in the Formatting toolbar

| # | Icon | What you do with it |
|---|------|---------------------|
| 1 | Font | Click to choose the typeface you want to apply to the highlighted text. |
| 2 | Font Size | Click to choose the size you want to apply to the highlighted text. |
| 3 | Bold | Click to make the highlighted text darker than the standard font. |
| 4 | Italic | Click to make the highlighted text "lean" to the right. |
| 5 | Underline | Click to apply a line under the highlighted text. |
| 6 | Text Shadow | Click to apply dropped letter effect to highlighted text. |
| 7 | Align Left | Click to align the text lines on the left side. |
| 8 | Center | Click to align the text lines around a center point. |
| 9 | Align Right | Click to align the text lines on the right side. |
| 10 | Numbering | Click to sequentially number the highlighted text. |
| 11 | Bullets | Click to apply bullets to the highlighted text. |
| 12 | Increase Font Size | Click to make the font one size larger than the current size. |
| 13 | Decrease Font Size | Click to make the font one size smaller than the current size. |
| 14 | Promote | Click to make the space between the text and the margins larger. You can also press **Tab** to increase indents. |
| 15 | Demote | Click to make the space between the text and the margins smaller. You can press **Shift+Tab** to decrease an indent. |
| 16 | Animation Effects | Click to display the Animation Effects toolbar so that you can choose the type of effect you want to apply. You can preview the effect by clicking the **Preview** button. (For more information, see Slide Show ➤ Preset Animation on page 530.) |
| 17 | Common Tasks | Click to display a drop-down menu of frequently performed tasks. You can also display this menu as a toolbar by clicking and dragging the menu bar off the Formatting toolbar. <br> (For more information, see Format ➤ Slide Layout on page 501.) <br> (For more information, see Format ➤ Apply Design Template on page 505.) |

# Formatting Keyboard Shortcuts

See Table 31.2 on page 494 for a list of keyboard shortcuts you can use to quickly format highlighted text.

> **TIP**
>
> If an effect has already been applied, you can press **Ctrl+Spacebar** to return the formatting to the default value set for the paragraph style.
>
> To see a description of the formatting applied to your text, press **Shift+F1** and click on the text. Once you've looked at the description, press **Esc.**

**Table 31.2**   Keyboard shortcuts for formatting your text

| To do this | Press this |
| --- | --- |
| **Change Alignment** | |
| Left | **Ctrl+L** |
| Center | **Ctrl+E** |
| Justify | **Ctrl+J** |
| Right | **Ctrl+R** |
| **Apply font effects** | |
| Bold | **Ctrl+B** |
| Change the font size | **Ctrl+Shift+P**, then **Up or Down arrow** <br> Press **Enter** when the right size displays |
| Change the typeface | **Ctrl+Shift+F**, then **Up or Down arrow** <br> Press **Enter** when the right size displays |
| Italics | **Ctrl+I** |
| Subscript | **Ctrl+=** |
| Superscript | **Ctrl+Shift+=** |
| Underline | **Ctrl+U** |
| **Change case** | |
| Change case (cycle through uppercase, title case and lowercase) | **Shift+F3** |
| **Increase/decrease font size** | |
| Decrease the font size in preset increments | **Ctrl+Shift+<** |
| Increase the font size in preset increments | **Ctrl+Shift+>** |
| **Change indents** | |
| Move the text one level higher | **Shift+Tab** |
| Move the text one level lower | **Tab** |

# Format ➤ Font

Use this option to define how you want your text to display and print, including the typeface, size and weight plus a variety of special effects such as superscript, subscript, and shadowing. You can also determine how close or far apart your characters are and whether characters are animated.

## How You Get Here

✧ Press **Alt+O,F** or **Ctrl+D**     ✧ Choose **Format ➤ Font**

## What's In This Dialog Box

Figure 31.2 is a sample of this dialog box and Table 31.3 has a description of the options available.

**Figure 31.2**   The Font dialog box

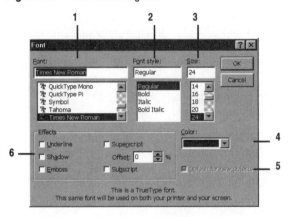

**Table 31.3**   Options in the Font dialog box

| # | Option | What you do with it |
|---|--------|---------------------|
| 1 | Font list | Choose an item that determines the typeface you want. |
| 2 | Font style list | Choose an item that determines the way the font will look. |
| 3 | Size list | Choose or enter a point size for the font. |
| 4 | Color drop-down list | Choose an item that determines the color of the font. |
| 5 | Default for new objects check box | Click to use the current font information for new default settings. |
| 6 | Effects area check boxes | Choose an item that determines the effect you want to apply. |

# Format ➤ Bullets and Numbering

Use this option to format a list of items in your document. You can choose different numbering styles and bullet characters to customize the look of your lists.

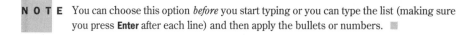

**N O T E**    You can choose this option *before* you start typing or you can type the list (making sure you press **Enter** after each line) and then apply the bullets or numbers.  ■

## How You Get Here

✧ Click  or          ✧ Press **Alt+0,B**          ✧ Choose **Format ➤ Bullets and Numbering**

## What's In This Dialog Box

Figure 31.3 is a sample of this dialog box and Table 31.4 has a description of the tabs available.

**Figure 31.3**    The Bullets and Numbering dialog box

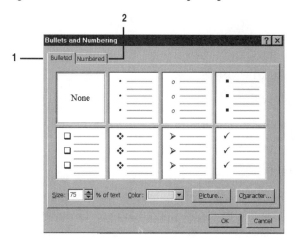

**Table 31.4**    Tabs in the Bullets and Numbering dialog box

| # | Tab name | What you do with it |
|---|----------|---------------------|
| 1 | Bulleted | Choose an item that determines what bullet character is used for the highlighted paragraphs. (For a complete description of the options available, see Table 31.5 on page 497.) |
| 2 | Numbered | Choose an item that determines the style. Click to apply the style of numbered list you want. (For a complete description of the options available, see Table 31.6 on page 497.) |

The following tables describe the options for the individual tabs in this dialog box:

■ Table 31.5 describes the Bulleted tab, and
■ Table 31.6 describes the Numbered tab.

**Table 31.5** Options in the Bullets and Numbering dialog box Bulleted tab

| Option | What you do with it |
| --- | --- |
| Bullet format buttons | Click to choose the desired type of bullet format. |
| Picture button | Click to display the Picture bullets dialog box so that you can use a graphic element that is stored in another file as a bullet character for your list. You can also insert a bullet character that is animated. (For more information, see Insert ➤ Picture on page 482.) |
| Character button | Click to display the Bullet character dialog box so that you can choose the specific character you want to use for the bullets. |
| Color button | Click to choose the color for the bullet. |
| Size list | Enter the size of the bullet relative to the size of the text font. |

**Table 31.6** Options in the Bullets and Numbering dialog box Numbered tab

| Option | What you do with it |
| --- | --- |
| Number format buttons | Click to choose the desired type of number format. |
| Start at list | Click to choose the starting number or letter for a list. |
| Color button | Click to choose the color for the numbers or letters in a list. |
| Size list | Enter the size of the bullet relative to the size of the text font. |

# Format ➤ Alignment

Use this option to set where the text or highlighted item lines up in relation to the margins of the slide or text box.

## How You Get Here

✧ Press **Alt+O,A**     ✧ Choose **Format** ➤ **Alignment**

## What's In This Flyout Menu

Figure 31.4 is a sample of this flyout menu.

**Figure 31.4** The Format ➤ Alignment flyout menu

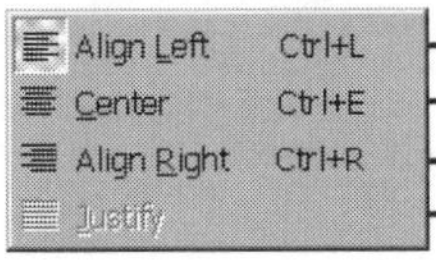

| | | | |
| --- | --- | --- | --- |
| ☰ Align Left | Ctrl+L | Format ➤ Alignment ➤ Align Left | 498 |
| ☰ Center | Ctrl+E | Format ➤ Alignment ➤ Center | 498 |
| ☰ Align Right | Ctrl+R | Format ➤ Alignment ➤ Align Right | 498 |
| ☰ Justify | | Format ➤ Alignment ➤ Justify | 498 |

### Format ➤ Alignment ➤ Align Left

Use this option to line text up on the left side of the highlighted slide or text box.

### How You Get Here

✦ Click [icon]      ✦ Press **Alt+O,A,L** or **Ctrl+L**   ✦ Choose **Format ➤ Alignment ➤ Align Left**

### Format ➤ Alignment ➤ Center

Use this option to line text up evenly around a center point on the highlighted slide or text box.

### How You Get Here

✦ Click [icon]      ✦ Press **Alt+O,A,C** or **Ctrl+E**   ✦ Choose **Format ➤ Alignment ➤ Center**

### Format ➤ Alignment ➤ Align Right

Use this option to line text up on the right side of the highlighted slide or text box.

### How You Get Here

✦ Click [icon]      ✦ Press **Alt+O,A,R** or **Ctrl+R**   ✦ Choose **Format ➤ Alignment ➤ Align Right**

### Format ➤ Alignment ➤ Justify

Use this option to line text up on both the right and left sides of the highlighted slide or text box. This option only works if you've got multiple lines in the paragraph.

### How You Get Here

✦ Click [icon]      ✦ Press **Alt+O,A,J** or **Ctrl+J**   ✦ Choose **Format ➤ Alignment ➤ Justify**

## Format ➤ Line Spacing

Use this option to define the distance between each line of text in a paragraph or the distance between multiple paragraphs.

---

**N O T E**   You can choose the line spacing for individual slides or Notes and Handouts pages or for the entire presentation. The units can either be lines or points.  (For more information, see View ➤ Master on page 459.) ▪

### How You Get Here

✦ Press **Alt+O,S**              ✦ Choose **Format ➤ Line Spacing**

## What's In This Dialog Box

Figure 31.5 is a sample of this dialog box and Table 31.7 has a description of the options available.

**Figure 31.5**   The Line Spacing dialog box

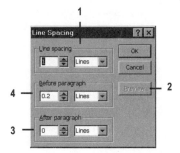

**Table 31.7**   Options in the Line Spacing dialog box

| # | Option | What you do with it |
|---|--------|---------------------|
| 1 | Line spacing list | Click to adjust the amount of space between each line of the highlighted text. You can enter the amount or use the arrows to choose a number of lines or points. |
| 2 | Preview button | View what the text will look like when you apply the highlighted values. |
| 3 | After paragraph list | Click to adjust the spacing below a paragraph. You can enter the amount or use the arrows to choose a specific value. |
| 4 | Before paragraph list | Click to adjust the spacing above a paragraph. You can enter the amount or use the arrows to choose a specific value. |

# Format ➤ Change Case

Use this option to change the capitalization of the highlighter letters in your file.

## How You Get Here

◇ Press **Alt+O,E**          ◇ Choose **Format ➤ Change Case**

## What's In This Dialog Box

Figure 31.6 is a sample of this dialog box and Table 31.8 has a description of the options available.

**Figure 31.6**   The Change Case dialog box

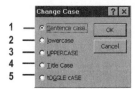

**Table 31.8**   Options in the Change Case dialog box

| # | Option | What you do with it |
|---|--------|---------------------|
| 1 | Sentence case radio button | Click to capitalize the first letter in the first word in a sentence. |
| 2 | lowercase radio button | Click to eliminate all capitalization in the highlighted text. |
| 3 | UPPERCASE radio button | Click to make *all* letters in the highlighted text capitalized. |
| 4 | Title Case radio button | Click to capitalize the first letter of each word in the highlighted text. |
| 5 | tOGGLE cASE radio button | Click to reverse the capitalization of each word in the highlighted text. If the text is currently capitalized, it switches to lowercase and vice versa. |

# Format ➤ Replace Fonts

Use this option to change your current typeface to the one chosen in this dialog box.

## How You Get Here

◇ Press **Alt+O,R**        ◇ Choose **Format ➤ Replace Fonts**

## What's In This Dialog Box

Figure 31.7 is a sample of this dialog box and Table 31.9 has a description of the options available.

**Figure 31.7**   The Replace Font dialog box

**Table 31.9**   Options in the Replace Font dialog box

| # | Option | What you do with it |
|---|--------|---------------------|
| 1 | Replace button | Click to apply the highlighted font to your entire presentation. |
| 2 | With drop-down list | Click to choose which font you want to change to. |
| 3 | Replace drop-down list | Click to choose the font you want to change. |

# Format ➤ Slide Layout

Use this option to apply a preset format to the currently highlighted slide. For instance, you can change the format of an existing slide to rearrange the information or change the number of text boxes that are available. If you have changed a slide, you can also reapply the original format with all the master elements available on that master.

**TIP**  To change the master slide layout for several slides at one time, choose **Slide Sorter** view, hold down **Shift** while you highlight the slides, then choose **Format ➤ Slide Layout**.

## How You Get Here

◇ Press **Alt+O,L**         ◇ Choose **Format ➤ Slide Layout**

## What's In This Dialog Box

Figure 31.8 is a sample of this dialog box and Table 31.10 has a description of the options available.

**Figure 31.8**   The Slide Layout dialog box

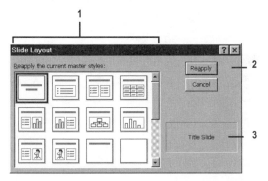

**Table 31.10**   Options in the Slide Layout dialog box

| # | Option | What you do with it |
|---|--------|---------------------|
| 1 | Change/Reapply the current master styles area | Click to choose which style you want to apply to the currently highlighted slides. |
| 2 | Apply/Reapply button | Click to apply the highlighted style to your slide. |
| 3 | Layout title area | View the name and a brief description of the slide master. |

# Format ➤ Slide Color Scheme

Use this option to change the color of your text objects, graphic objects, and background for either the highlighted slides or the entire presentation. There are eight kinds of objects on a slide that you can change using the Custom tab options or you can use the options on the Standard tab to choose a preset color scheme. Choose **View ➤ Slide Sorter** to highlight the slides you want to change and then make your changes. (For more information, see View ➤ Slide Sorter on page 458.)

**TIP**   To change the color scheme for several slides at one time, choose **Slide Sorter** view, hold down **Shift** while you choose the slides, then choose **Format ➤ Slide Color Scheme**.

## How You Get Here

◇ Press **Alt+O,C**          ◇ Choose **Format ➤ Slide Color Scheme**

## What's In This Dialog Box

Figure 31.9 is a sample of this dialog box and Table 31.11 has a description of the tabs available.

**Figure 31.9**   The Color Scheme dialog box

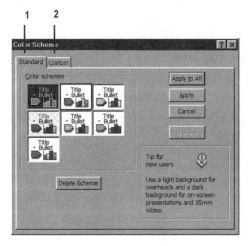

**Table 31.11**  Tabs in the Color Scheme dialog box

| # Tab name | What you do with it |
|---|---|
| 1 Standard | Choose an item that determines the preset color scheme you want to use. (For a complete description of the options available, see Table 31.12 on page 503.) |
| 2 Custom | Choose an item that determines which items you want to change. (For a complete description of the options available, see Table 31.13 on page 503.) |

The following tables describe the options for the individual tabs in this dialog box:

- Table 31.12 describes the Standard tab, and
- Table 31.13 describes the Custom tab.

**Table 31.12**  Options in the Color Scheme dialog box Standard tab

| Option | What you do with it |
|---|---|
| Color schemes buttons | Click to choose which preset color scheme you want to apply. |
| Apply to All button | Click to apply the preset color scheme to the entire presentation *and* the master slide. |
| Apply button | Click to apply the preset color scheme to the highlighted slides. |
| Preview button | Click to see what the slides will look like if you apply the currently highlighted color scheme. |
| Tips area | View suggestions that may help you create a more professional presentation. |
| Delete Scheme | Click to remove the highlighted color scheme. If you want to restore this scheme click the **Undo** button. |

**Table 31.13**  Options in the Color Scheme dialog box Custom tab

| Option | What you do with it |
|---|---|
| Scheme colors check boxes | Click to choose which slide element you want to change. |
| Change Color button | Click to choose the color for the highlighted slide element. You can choose a standard color or create one of your own. |
| Apply to All button | Click to apply the customized color scheme to the entire presentation *and* the master slide. |
| Apply button | Click to apply the customized color scheme to the highlighted elements on the highlighted slides. |
| Preview button | Click to see what the slides will look like if you apply the currently highlighted color scheme. |

**Table 31.13**   Options in the Color Scheme dialog box Custom tab, continued

| Option | What you do with it |
|---|---|
| Preview area | View what the currently highlighted color scheme will look like if you apply it to the slides. |
| Add as Standard Color Scheme button | Click to add the customized color scheme to the ones that display on the Standard tab. |

# Format ➤ Background

Use this option to set up the background for a presentation, including colors, gradients, patterns, and textures. You can also add a graphic that serves as the background.

## How You Get Here

◇ Press **Alt+O,K**          ◇ Choose **Format ➤ Background**

## What's In This Dialog Box

Figure 31.10 is a sample of this dialog box and Table 31.14 has a description of the options available.

**Figure 31.10**   The Background dialog box

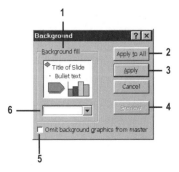

**Table 31.14**   Options in the Background dialog box

| # | Option | What you do with it |
|---|---|---|
| 1 | Background fill preview area | View what your slide will look like if you apply the currently highlighted background color. |
| 2 | Apply to All button | Click to apply the customized background to the entire presentation *and* the master slide. |
| 3 | Apply button | Click to apply the current settings to the highlighted slides. |
| 4 | Preview button | View what the currently highlighted background color scheme will look like if you apply it to the slides. |

**Table 31.14**   Options in the Background dialog box, continued

| # | Option | What you do with it |
|---|--------|---------------------|
| 5 | Omit background graphics from master check box | Click to choose whether you want the graphics from the master template to display on a slide. For instance, if you want to omit a company logo from a highlighted slide you would make this check box active. |
| 6 | Background drop-down list | Click to choose a color for the slide background. You can also choose colors from the Colors dialog box by choosing the More Colors option on the flyout menu. (For more information, see Format ➤ Background ➤ More Colors on page 210.) |
| | | **Note**   You can also apply a fill effects by choosing it from the flyout menu and displaying the Fill Effects dialog box. (For more information, see Format ➤ Background ➤ Fill Effects on page 211.) |

# Format ➤ Apply Design Template

Use this option to apply a color scheme and master templates from a template file or another PowerPoint presentation that you've saved to this location. You can see a sample of any template in the preview area by clicking the filename.

**N O T E**   The files of type drop-down list displays Design Templates. This dialog box is the same as the Open dialog box. (For more information, see File ‰ Open on page 39.) ▪

## How You Get Here

◇ Press **Alt+O,Y**        ◇ Choose **Format ➤ Apply Design Template**

# Format ➤ Colors and Lines

Use this option to choose the style of the lines or borders for the highlighted item. You can choose from a background color, arrow style, or a line style or color to customize your presentation. (For a complete description of the options available, see Table 31.16 on page 507.)

## How You Get Here

◇ Press **Alt+O,N**        ◇ Choose **Format ➤ Colors and Lines**

# Format ➤ Placeholder/Object

Use this option to customize graphics, shapes, or text boxes that you've inserted in your presentation. The menu option displayed is specific to the action. For instance, if you highlight text, the menu option displays **Placeholder**.

---

**N O T E**   This menu option is active only if you've highlighted an existing graphic or text. (For more information, see Insert ➤ Picture on page 482.) ▣

## How You Get Here

◇ Press **Alt+0,0**        ◇ Choose **Format ➤ Placeholder** or **Object**

## What's In This Dialog Box

Figure 31.11 is a sample of this dialog box and Table 31.15 has a description of the tabs available.

---

**N O T E**   On the Web tab you enter a description of the highlighted text in the Alternative text area and this displays while the Web page is loading. ▣

**Figure 31.11**   The Format AutoShape dialog box

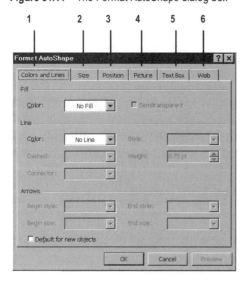

**Table 31.15**    Tabs in the Format AutoShape dialog box

| # | Tab name | What you do with it |
|---|---|---|
| 1 | Colors and Lines | Choose an item that determines how you want the colors and lines to display. (For a complete description of the options available, see Table 31.16 on page 507.) |
| 2 | Size | Choose an item that determines the width and height of the highlighted item. (For a complete description of the options available, see Table 31.17 on page 508.) |
| 3 | Layout | Choose an item that determines where you want the highlighted item in relation to the text of your document. (For a complete description of the options available, see Table 31.18 on page 508.) |
| 4 | Picture | Choose an item that determines how you will control the way a picture displays. (For a complete description of the options available, see Table 31.19 on page 508.) |
| 5 | Text Box | Choose an item that determines the spacing of the text from the edge of the frame. (For a complete description of the options available, see Table 31.20 on page 508.) |
| 6 | Web | Choose an item that determines the text that will display while a graphic is loading on a web page. |

The following tables describe the options for the individual tabs in this dialog box:

- Table 31.16 describes the Colors and Lines tab,
- Table 31.17 describes the Size tab,
- Table 31.18 describes the Layout tab,
- Table 31.19 describes the Picture tab, and
- Table 31.20 describes the Text Box tab.

**Table 31.16**    Options in the Format AutoShape dialog box Colors and Lines tab

| Option | What you do with it |
|---|---|
| Fill area | Click to choose the color that fills the inside of a picture. |
| Lines area | Click to choose the color and type of line style for your document. |
| Arrows area | Click to choose the type of arrow style for your document. |
| Preview button | View what the presentation will look like if you accept the settings. |
| Default for new objects check box | Click to use the currently set options as the default for any new shapes or graphics. |

**Table 31.17**   Options in the Format AutoShape dialog box Size tab

| Option | What you do with it |
|---|---|
| Size and rotate area | Click to choose the width and height of the picture or text box. You can also rotate a picture by degrees. |
| Scale area | Click to size a picture by a percentage value of its original size. |
| Original size area | View the height and width of the picture as it was originally created. |
| Reset button | Click to return the highlighted picture to its original size. |

**Table 31.18**   Options in the Format AutoShape dialog box Position tab

| Option | What you do with it |
|---|---|
| Position on slide area | Click to choose where you want to place the highlighted item. |

**Table 31.19**   Options in the Format AutoShape dialog box Picture tab

| Option | What you do with it |
|---|---|
| Crop from area | Click to cut the picture size down to the desired size. |
| Image control area | Click to set the color and related settings for the picture. |
| Reset button | Click to change the settings to how they were originally. |
| Recolor button | Click to change any of the colors in the object. |

**Table 31.20**   Options in the Format AutoShape dialog box Text Box tab

| Option | What you do with it |
|---|---|
| Text anchor point | Click to place the anchor for the text box. |
| Internal margin area | Click to define the margin size *inside* the highlighted text box. |

# The PowerPoint Tools Menu

# What Is The Tools Menu

This menu includes options that make using your application easier and more efficient. Some of the more popular tools include spellcheck, AutoCorrect, and macros. This menu also includes options for customizing your application, such as changing the default ("assumed") location for storing files or selecting whether you want the scroll bars to show on your screen.

If a menu option has an ellipsis (three dots) or an arrow beside it, the application "asks" you for additional information before the action takes place. If the menu doesn't have one of these symbols, the action you choose happens immediately. If the action takes place immediately, you won't see a sample screen in this section.

# Tools ➤ Spelling

Use this option to look for words that may be misspelled. The application automatically flags any word it doesn't recognize, even if the word is spelled correctly for *your* environment For example, a proper name, such as the name of a lake, might be spelled correctly but the application flags it because it isn't in the dictionary. You can choose one of the options displayed, skip over the flagged word, add a word to a dictionary so that the word isn't flagged again, or type in your own replacement. The dictionary is shared by all the Office 2000 applications, so if you add a word to the dictionary while using Excel, that word isn't flagged in any other Office application. (For more information, see Tools ➤ Spelling on page 94.)

 **T I P**   You can check the spelling of a specific word, sentence, or paragraph by selecting it and choosing **Tools ➤ Spelling**.

You should always visually proofread your document because the application only flags words not found in the standard dictionary. So if you accidentally type 'form' when you should have typed "from," the application doesn't consider it an error and skips over it.

PowerPoint assumes that you want to spellcheck every slide in your presentation. If you want to check specific words or phrases, highlight the appropriate areas first, then choose **Tools ➤ Spelling**.

## How You Get Here

◇ Click    ◇ Press **Alt+T,S** or **F7**   ◇ Choose **Tools ➤ Spelling**

# Tools ➤ Language

Use this option to determine which language is used for the spell check, when the presentation contains more than one language. If the presentation contains more than one language, foreign words and grammar may appear as errors. You must first choose the text with the other language and use this option to mark that text so the spell checker will use the correct dictionary when it checks your presentation.

---

**N O T E**   When setting a language to something other than the default language, PowerPoint may display a dialog box asking you to install the multi-language pack. PowerPoint does not load all dictionaries by default, in the interest of saving space on your hard drive. Insert your CD and install the desired language packs on your computer system.

## How You Get Here

◇ Press **Alt+T,L**          ◇ Choose **Tools ➤ Language**

## What's In This Dialog Box

Figure 32.1 is a sample of this dialog box and has a description of the only option available.

**Figure 32.1**   The Language dialog box

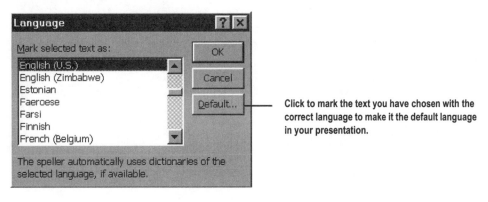

Click to mark the text you have chosen with the correct language to make it the default language in your presentation.

# Tools ➤ AutoCorrect

Use this option to add text so that you automatically correct or replace frequently (mis)typed words. For example, you can tell PowerPoint to replace "Febuary" with "February" if you always mistype this word. You can also use this option to automatically replace certain abbreviated keystrokes with an extended version. For example, you can have PowerPoint automatically replace "ASAP" with the phrase "as soon as possible" whenever you type the abbreviation.

## How You Get Here

◇ Press **Alt+T,A**   ◇ Choose **Tools ➤ AutoCorrect**

# Tools ➤ Online Collaboration

Use this option to conduct a conversation online, similar to making a multiple-party telephone call. You will be collaborating with other people on one file at the same time. Those people who are participating will be able to edit and chat using the server that you specify. As host you will control the meeting, setting up who and how participants will interact during the meeting. In order for someone to join a meeting they all must have access to the same Internet or intranet (an inter-office network) and have Microsoft Netmeeting installed on their computer or network. However, they don't have to have the application you are working from to chat with you or edit your file online. This option works with your default email server and accesses your address book there. (For more information, see What Is The Outlook Mail Application on page 647.) (For more information, see Tools ➤ Online Collaboration on page 97.)

---

**N O T E**   This can be pretty complex, especially if you are having a Web discussion. You must first set up a server, then open the presentation you want to have the discussion about, then give the command. Most people would rather email the presentation around for comments rather than have a "live" discussion/collaboration about it.  ▪

## How You Get Here

◇ Press **Alt+T,N**   ◇ Choose **Tools ➤ Online Collaboration**

# Tools ➤ Meeting Minder

Use this option to take minutes, record action items, and add to your notes pages during a slide show. These notes can then be presented as either Meeting Minutes or Action Items on an additional slide for presentation or as a printout. Action items appear on a new slide at the end of your slide show and you can post the action items to Microsoft Outlook or transfer the minutes and action items to a new Word document and print it. (For more information, see What About Calendar's Forms on page 706.)

---

**N O T E**   If you take notes during a presentation, the Meeting Minder appears only on your screen—other participants see only the slide show. ▨

## How You Get Here

◇ Press **Alt+T,T**        ◇ Choose **Tools ➤ Meeting Minder**

## What's In This Dialog Box

Figure 32.1 is a sample of this dialog box and Table 32.1 has a description of the tabs available.

**Figure 32.2**   The Meeting Minder dialog box

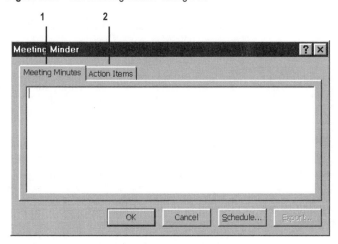

**Table 32.1**   Tabs in the Meeting Minder dialog box

| # | Option | What you do with it |
|---|--------|---------------------|
| 1 | Meeting Minutes tab | Enter notes to be presented on the Meeting Minutes slide of the presentation.(For a complete description of the options available, see Table 32.2.) |
| 2 | Action Items tab | Enter items to be presented on the Action Items slide of the presentation. (For a complete description of the options available, see Table 32.3.) |

The following tables describe the options for the individual tabs in this dialog box:

- Table 32.2 describes the Meeting Minutes tab, and
- Table 32.3 describes the Action Items tab.

**Table 32.2**   Options in the Meeting Minder dialog box Meeting Minutes tab

| Option | What you do with it |
|--------|---------------------|
| Schedule button | Click to schedule a meeting in Outlook. The appointment dialog box from Outlook is displayed. (For more information, see What About Calendar's Forms on page 706.) This button is only available if you have Outlook installed. |
| Export button | Click to send meeting minutes to Word or post action items to Outlook. |

**Table 32.3**   Options in the Meeting Minder dialog box Action Items tab

| Option | What you do with it |
|--------|---------------------|
| Description text box | Enter a description of the action item. |
| Assigned To text box | Enter the name of the person you are assigning the action item to. |
| Due Date text box | Enter the date. |
| Action Item text box | Enter the action items. |
| Schedule button | Click to schedule a meeting in Outlook. The appointment dialog box from Outlook is displayed. (For more information, see What About Calendar's Forms on page 706.) This button is only available if you have Outlook installed. |
| Export button | Click to send meeting minutes to Word or post action items to Outlook. |

# Tools ➤ Macro

Use this option to choose one of several activities related to macros, such as record, playback, stop, and erase. Macros are a series of steps that you program in a set order and are helpful when you need to perform the same series of steps over and over. In fact, macros are a great way to "replace yourself" at the keyboard when you do the same tasks over and over again. (Never thought you'd be given permission to be lazy, did you?) (For more information, see Tools ➤ Macro on page 101.)

 **TIP**   Macros can save you a lot of time—if you have a repetitive task that is more than four or five keystrokes, you should create a macro.

## How You Get Here

◇ Press **Alt+T,M**              ◇ Choose **Tools** ➤ **Macro**

# Tools ➤ Add-Ins

Use this option to apply or add a feature that isn't a standard option in the general application, but may be useful. Add-ins are programs that add optional commands and features to PowerPoint. However, before you can use an add-in, you must load it into PowerPoint or create your own add-in and then add it to the library.

**N O T E**  Selecting an add-in for your presentation uses some memory, so load only those add-ins you use. Clearing (unchecking) an add-in simply frees up memory in the workbook; it doesn't delete the add-in from the library. ■

## How You Get Here

◇ Press **Alt+T,I**          ◇ Choose **Tools ➤ Add-Ins**

## What's Different

Figure 32.3 is a sample of this dialog box and Table 32.4 has a description of options that are unique to PowerPoint. (For more information, see Tools ➤ Add-Ins on page 106.)

**Figure 32.3**  The Add-Ins dialog box

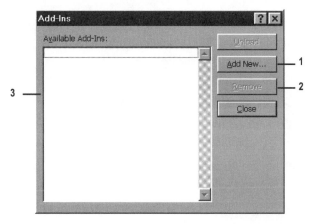

**Table 32.4**  Options in the Add-Ins dialog box

| # | Option | What you do with it |
|---|--------|---------------------|
| 1 | Add New button | Click to display the Add New Add-Ins window, where you can load add-ins from other programs or add-ins that you have created. |
| 2 | Remove button | Click to remove the selected add-ins. |
| 3 | Available Add-Ins list | Choose an item that determines which add-ins you want automatically available in the active presentation. |

# Tools ➤ Customize

Use this option to display the Customize window, where you can customize toolbars, keyboard shortcuts, and menu commands. Customizing allows you to create new tools, shortcuts, and commands, and modify existing ones to better suit your individual needs. (For example, you may want to create a tool to execute a frequently used option that is usually only available using a menu option). (For more information, see Tools ➤ Customize on page 107.)

## How You Get Here

◇ Press **Alt+T,C**          ◇ Choose **Tools** ➤ **Customize**

# Tools ➤ Options

Use this option to modify many elements, such as screen appearance, printing, spelling, etc. This feature is helpful for those who don't mind getting under the hood of the computer, tweaking a few elements, all in the interest of style and efficiency.

## How You Get Here

◇ Press **Alt+T,O**          ◇ Choose **Tools** ➤ **Options**

## What's In This Dialog Box

Figure 32.4 is a sample of this dialog box and Table 32.5 has a description of the tabs available.

**Figure 32.4**    The Options dialog box

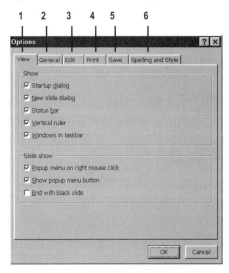

**Table 32.5**   Tabs in the Options dialog box

| # | Tab name | What you do with it |
|---|----------|---------------------|
| 1 | View | Click to choose technical elements related to the visual display of the screen, such as status bars, vertical ruler, and slide show popup menus. (For a complete description of the options available, see Table 32.6 on page 517.) |
| 2 | General | Click to choose technical elements related to the layout of the screen, such as sound feedback, user information, and Web options. (For a complete description of the options available, see Table 32.7 on page 518.) |
| 3 | Edit | Click to choose technical elements related to editing, such as replacing straight quotes with smart quotes, drag-and-drop text editing, setting the default font for inserted charts, and a maximum number of undos. (For a complete description of the options available, see Table 32.8 on page 518.) |
| 4 | Print | Click to choose technical elements related to printing, such as background printing, printing hidden slides, and the default print settings. (For a complete description of the options available, see Table 32.9 on page 518.) |
| 5 | Save | Click to choose technical elements related to saving, such as setting the Auto recovery time (how often it automatically saves a presentation), default file location, and what kind of files you are saving. (For a complete description of the options available, see Table 32.10 on page 518.) |
| 6 | Spelling & Style | Click to choose technical elements related to spelling and style. (For more information, see Tools ➤ Spelling on page 510.) (For a complete description of the options available, see Table 32.11 on page 518.) |

The following tables describe the options for the individual tabs in this dialog box:

- Table 32.6 describes the View tab,
- Table 32.7 describes the General tab,
- Table 32.8 describes the Edit tab,
- Table 32.9 describes the Print tab,
- Table 32.10 describes the Save tab, and
- Table 32.11 describes the Spelling & Style tab.

**Table 32.6**   Options in the Options dialog box View tab

| Option | What you do with it |
|--------|---------------------|
| Show area | Choose an item that determines what you want shown as you work. |
| Slide show area | Choose an item that determines how you want the popup menus displayed on your slide show and if you want to end with a black slide. |

**Table 32.7**  Options in the Options dialog box General tab

| Option | What you do with it |
| --- | --- |
| General options area | Choose an item that determines what options you want to set for PowerPoint. |
| User information area | Enter the PowerPoint user information. This information is used for comments and tracking changes. |
| Web Options button | Click to set how your presentation looks and acts when viewed by a Web browser. |

**Table 32.8**  Options in the Options dialog box Edit tab

| Option | What you do with it |
| --- | --- |
| Text area | Choose an item that determines the type of editing you want to use. |
| New charts take on PowerPoint font check box | Click to set the font options for newly inserted charts. |
| Maximum number of undos list | Click to choose the highest number of undos you want. |

**Table 32.9**  Options in the Options dialog box Print tab

| Option | What you do with it |
| --- | --- |
| Printing options area | Choose an item that determines how to print your presentation. |
| Options for current document only area | Click to set the print options for the current presentation. |

**Table 32.10**  Options in the Options dialog box Save tab

| Option | What you do with it |
| --- | --- |
| Save options area | Click to choose the options to use when you are saving your presentation. Specify what type of file to save as and the default file location where you want to save those files. |

**Table 32.11**  Options in the Options dialog box Spelling and Style tab

| Option | What you do with it |
| --- | --- |
| Spelling area | Choose an item that determines the controls for the spell checking option. |
| Check style check box | Click to check the style according to the style options you have set. |
| Style Options button | Click to set the options for the style in your presentation. |

# The PowerPoint Slide Show Menu

# What Is The Slide Show Menu

This menu contains options for setting up and running your presentation on a computer or projector. You can insert animation effects in the slides, record narration to customize your presentations, and set up an online presentation for viewing by others on a network. The various bells and whistles that make a slide show interesting are all here.

If a menu option has an ellipsis (three dots) or an arrow beside it, the application "asks" you for additional information before the action takes place. If the menu doesn't have one of these symbols, the action you choose happens immediately. If the action takes place immediately, you won't see a sample screen in this section.

 **N O T E** If you are only going to print out your presentation you can skip this menu. ■

 **T I P** The (right-click) shortcut menu is great to use when you are running your show. It has options for the most frequently used actions like moving to the next the slide, printing the current slide, and ending the slide show.

# Using the Slide Show Options

When you're ready to set up your slide show presentation it's easier if you go about it in a specific order. Even though you can perform any of the other options on this menu first, we believe it is better to get some basic set up done first. Here's some help to get you started.

1. Decide how you're going to use the slide show (choose **Slide Show ➤ Set Up Show**).
   There are a few questions that you need to answer before you start. Will a speaker be presenting the slide show or does the audience go through it at their own pace? Do you want to show with or without animation or narration? Will you advance the slides manually? Are you going to use a projector? Answering these questions first will help you design a spectacular slide show.

2. Decide how you to display the when you move from one slide to the next (choose **Slide Show ➤ Slide Transition**).
   You can apply a variety of different effects to keep your presentation interesting. Beware, though, too much movement can be distracting.

3. Place controls on the slides so you can move around the presentation (choose **Slide Show ➤ Action Buttons**).
   You can add "movement" buttons to one or more slides so that you can control how you get around in your presentation. For example, you can add a button that takes you to the last slide, the first slide, or even a specific slide when you click it.

4. Decide what special effects you want for individual slides within your slide show (choose either **Slide Show ➤ Preset Animation** or **Slide Show ➤ Custom Animation).**
   Now you can get really fancy! You can control how the individual elements on a slide are "presented". Want to make sure the audience focuses on one point at a time? You can tell PowerPoint to "paint" the text of one bullet, then the next, then next. As with other options, less is more. If you use too much animation your audience will get overwhelmed.

5. Record the words you want to include in your slide show (choose **Slide Show ➤ Record Narration**).
   You'll need a good quality microphone and a sound board before you can do this. Once you've got the proper hardware, run some tests to make sure everything is working well before you spend hours recording your comments. You can record comments for specific slides or record something for every slide—great for when you can't be there.

6. Rehearse, rehearse, rehearse (choose **Slide Show ➤ Rehearse Timings**).
   With this built-in feature, you can see how long it takes for you to discuss a particular point or get through an entire presentation. And you can store the information and let the computer move to the next slide while you concentrate on wowing your audience.

These are a few of the options we think will get your presentation off in good order. Of course, you can perform any one of these options in the order you choose. We have tried to give you some sort of order to help you more effectively set up the various components in a slide show presentation.

## Slide Show ➤ View Show

Use this option to see the presentation as it runs through the slide show. The screen immediately changes to the Slide Show View and starts running. What you see on screen and how you advance through the show will depend on how you set it up. (For more information, see Slide Show ➤ Set Up Show on page 525.)

 **TIP** To stop viewing your slide show, right-click, then choose **End Show**.

### How You Get Here

◇ Click     ◇ Press **Alt+D,V** or **F5**    ◇ Choose **Slide Show ➤ View Show**

# Slide Show ➤ Rehearse Timings

Use this option to practice presenting your slide show, allowing time for the audience to read what is on the slide and listen to the narration you've provided. When you are finished rehearsing, you can choose to accept the time or not. If it isn't right you can always rehearse again.

## How You Get Here

◇ Press **Alt+D,R**     ◇ Choose **Sli̲de Show ➤ R̲ehearse Timings**

## What's In This Toolbar

Figure 33.1 is a sample of this toolbar and Table 33.1 has a description of the icons available.

**Figure 33.1**   The Rehearsal toolbar

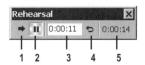

**Table 33.1**   Icons in the Rehearsal toolbar

| # | Icon | What you do with it |
|---|------|---------------------|
| 1 | Next | Click to move forward one slide at a time. |
| 2 | Pause | Click to temporarily stop timing your presentation. |
| 3 | Slide Time | View the accumulated time for the elements on the slide. |
| 4 | Repeat | Click to start the timing over at 0:00:00. |
| 5 | Time Display area | View the accumulated time for the entire slide show. |

# Slide Show ➤ Record Narration

Use this option to use your computer like a tape recorder. You can set the level and the quality of the recording, save the narration as a separate file, or embed the narration in the slide show.

## How You Get Here

◇ Press **Alt+D,N**     ◇ Choose **Sli̲de Show ➤ Record N̲arration**

## What's In This Dialog Box

Figure 33.2 is a sample of this dialog box and Table 33.2 has a description of the options available.

**Figure 33.2**   The Record Narration dialog box

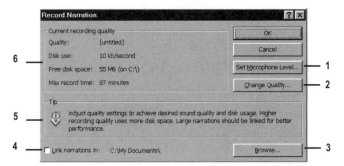

**Table 33.2**   Options in the Record Narration dialog box

| # | Option | What you do with it |
|---|--------|---------------------|
| 1 | Set Microphone Level button | Click to make sure that the volume is correct for your recording and that your microphone is working properly. |
| 2 | Change Quality button | Click to change the sound quality for the sound file. |
| 3 | Browse button | Click to store the narration as a separate file. |
| 4 | Link narrations in check box | Click to link the separate narration file to the presentation. If this box is unchecked PowerPoint embeds the narration in the presentation. |
| 5 | Tip Description area | View various tips for creating nicely done recording. |
| 6 | Current recording quality area | View the information for the narration you are recording. |

# Slide Show ➤ Online Broadcast

Use this option to set, schedule, and begin broadcasting your slide show on your network. This is a very effective way to give a presentation to different people in different geographic locations. They can sit back and watch using their own computers, view your notes, and even send you feedback by email. After the broadcast is finished and has been archived others can review it using the Lobby page. The Lobby page is the page in the web browser that contains the information on the slide show.

---

**N O T E**   You must have a sound card installed on your computer and your audience must have a web browser. If you're using live video, you'll also ned a NetShow server. ▪

## How You Get Here

◇ Press **Alt+D,0**            ◇ Choose **Sli̲de Show** ➤ **O̲nline Broadcast**

## What's In This Flyout Menu

Figure 33.3 is a sample of this flyout menu.

**Figure 33.3**    The Slide Show ➤ Online Broadcast flyout menu

## Slide Show ➤ Online Broadcast ➤ Set Up and Schedule

Use this option to establish the date and time when others will view your slide show.

---

**N O T E**    You must know where your shared folder is located to complete this option. If you have questions regarding how your system is set up, contact your system administrator for help. ▪

## How You Get Here

◇ Press **Alt+D,O,S**          ◇ Choose **Sli̲de Show ➤ O̲nline Broadcast ➤ S̲et Up and Schedule**

## What's In This Dialog Box

Figure 33.4 is a sample of this dialog box and Table 33.3 has a description of the options available.

**Figure 33.4**    The Broadcast Schedule dialog box

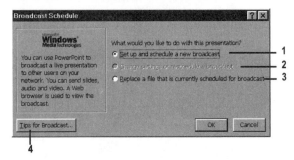

**Table 33.3**    Options in the Broadcast Schedule dialog box

| # | Option | What you do with it |
|---|--------|---------------------|
| 1 | Set up radio button | Click to set up the new broadcast, including the time and date. |
| 2 | Change settings radio button | Click to edit the settings for a previously scheduled broadcast. |
| 3 | Replace a file radio button | Click to change the presentation file that will be used for a scheduled broadcast. |
| 4 | Tips for Broadcast button | Click to activate the help menu with the information regarding broadcasting. |

## Slide Show ➤ Online Broadcast ➤ Begin Broadcast

Use this option to actually start broadcasting your slide show. You can practice running the broadcast before your actual scheduled time, which might be a good idea. If you have another computer close by you can watch the broadcast to see exactly what your audience will see.

### How You Get Here

◇ Press **Alt+D,O,B**          ◇ Choose **Sli̱de Show ➤ O̱nline Broadcast ➤ Begin Broadcast**

# Slide Show ➤ Set Up Show

Use this option to set how your slide show will be viewed by the audience. It lets you control how the audience will advance through the show and whether they will have audio and video as it runs. You can choose to set up all your slides or a few at a time. There is an option to set up a projector if you are using overheads for the show. You also have the ability to choose the pen color for any illustrations or notes you may want to write onscreen as the show runs.

 **TIP**   We think it's better to get all this information set up before you use the other options—there's no law that says you have to, but we find that this way is a little more efficient.

### How You Get Here

◇ Press **Alt+D,S**          ◇ Choose **Sli̱de Show ➤ S̱et Up Show**

### What's In This Dialog Box

Figure 33.5 is a sample of this dialog box and Table 33.4 has a description of the options available.

**Figure 33.5**    The Set Up Show dialog box

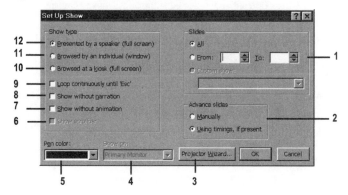

**Table 33.4**   Options in the Set Up Show dialog box

| # | Option | What you do with it |
|---|--------|---------------------|
| 1 | Slides area | Click to choose the slides you want included in the slide show. |
| 2 | Advance slides area | Click to choose how you want to move from slide to slide.<br>■ If you want to choose when to move to the next slide, click the **Manually** radio button. This means that PowerPoint ignores any timing information stored with the slide show and that you'll need to use the keyboard or mouse to move to the next slide.<br>■ If you want to put your slide show on "autopilot", click the **Using timings, if present** radio button<br>**Note**   You must record the time for each slide before this option will work. |
| 3 | Projector Wizard button | Click to match the settings in your computer to the projector system you plan to use when you run your slide show. |
| 4 | Show on drop-down list | Click to choose the monitor you will use for the slide show.<br>**Note**   This option is available only if you have Windows 98 or Windows NT 5.0 on your system. |
| 5 | Pen color drop-down list | Click to choose the color for the pen you will use if you decide to write notes on your slides while you're giving a presentation. |
| 6 | Show scrollbar check box | Click to have the Web toolbar display on the slide show.<br>**Note**   This option is available only if you choose the **Browse by an individual** radio button. |
| 7 | Show without animation check box | Click to make the slide show act as if there where no animation effects chosen. Great for when others will be browsing the show individually. |
| 8 | Show without narration check box | Click to run the show without narration. |
| 9 | Loop continuously until Esc check box | Click to run the slide show continuously until someone presses the **Esc** key. This option is selected automatically if you choose the **Browse at a kiosk** radio button. |
| 10 | Browsed at a kiosk radio button | Click to set the slide show to run, then automatically start again if there has been no activity for five minutes. The audience can use specific commands (such as buttons inserted on a slide) to move through the show or jump to other slides. |
| 11 | Browsed by an individual radio button | Click to give the audience individual control over the slide show. This lets them use all the commands available for running a show. |
| 12 | Presented by a speaker radio button | Click to run the show with the standard full screen view and movement commands. |

# Slide Show ➤ Action Buttons

Use this option to place buttons that control the various actions in your slide show. You can decide where you want to put the button and choose a specific size and color for each one.

**N O T E** Once you place a button, the Action Settings dialog box displays so that you can get really specific about what happens when someone clicks the new button. (For more information, see Slide Show ➤ Action Settings on page 529.) ▪

**T I P** You can drag this option off the Slide Show menu and display it as a toolbar, which is how we display it below.

## How You Get Here

◇ Press **Alt+D,I**          ◇ Choose **Slide Show ➤ Action Buttons**

## What's In This Toolbar

Figure 33.6 is a sample of this toolbar and Table 33.5 has a description of the options available.

**N O T E** These buttons have a "preset" action that was chosen by Microsoft's developers. You can, however, most of these options can be modified after you've inserted the button. (For more information, see Slide Show ➤ Action Settings on page 529.) ▪

**Figure 33.6** The Action Buttons toolbar

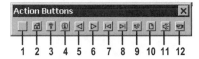

**Table 33.5** Icons in the Action Buttons toolbar

| # | Icon | What you do with it |
|---|------|---------------------|
| 1 | Custom | Click to create your own special action button on a slide. One you let go of the mouse, the Action Settings dialog box displays so that you can pick what happens when you use this button during your slide show. |
| 2 | Home | Click to choose this action button to drag or click on the slide where you want to place the button. The Action Settings dialog box displays where you set up the action for this button. |

**Table 33.5**   Icons in the Action Buttons toolbar, continued

| #  | Icon | What you do with it |
|----|------|---------------------|
| 3  | Help | Click to choose this action button to drag or click on the slide where you want to place the button. The Action Settings dialog box displays where you set up the action for this button. |
| 4  | Information | Click to choose this action button to drag or click on the slide where you want to place the button. The Action Settings dialog box displays where you set up the action for this button. |
| 5  | Back or Previous | Click to choose this action button to drag or click on the slide where you want to place the button. The Action Settings dialog box displays where you set up the action for this button. |
| 6  | Forward or Next | Click to choose this action button to drag or click on the slide where you want to place the button. The Action Settings dialog box displays where you set up the action for this button. |
| 7  | Beginning | Click to choose this action button to drag or click on the slide where you want to place the button. The Action Settings dialog box displays where you set up the action for this button. |
| 8  | End | Click to choose this action button to drag or click on the slide where you want to place the button. The Action Settings dialog box displays where you set up the action for this button. |
| 9  | Return | Click to choose this action button to drag or click on the slide where you want to place the button. The Action Settings dialog box displays where you set up the action for this button. |
| 10 | Document | Click to choose this action button to drag or click on the slide where you want to place the button. The Action Settings dialog box displays where you set up the action for this button. |
| 11 | Sound | Click to choose this action button to drag or click on the slide where you want to place the button. The Action Settings dialog box displays where you set up the action for this button. |
| 12 | Movie | Click to choose this action button to drag or click on the slide where you want to place the button. The Action Settings dialog box displays where you set up the action for this button. |

# Slide Show ➤ Action Settings

Use this option to set or change how a *previously inserted* button behaves when you use it during a slide show. You can link a slide to another slide in the same presentation, link to another file, link to a website, run other programs, or even play a soundbite—the options available depend on which button you've inserted.

---

**N O T E**  Both tabs in the Action Settings dialog box have the same actions, the only difference is in how you activate the button. The options in the Mouse Over tab let you activate a button by hovering the mouse cursor over it and the options in the Mouse Click tab let you activate the button by pressing the left mouse button. ▥

## How You Get Here

◇ Press **Alt+D,A**          ◇ Choose **Sli̲de Show ➤ A̲ction Settings**

## What's In This Dialog Box

Figure 33.7 is a sample of this dialog box and Table 33.6 has a description of the options available.

---

**N O T E**  Since the options on each tab are the same we're only going to describe the options for the Mouse Click tab. ▥

**Figure 33.7**  The Action Settings dialog box

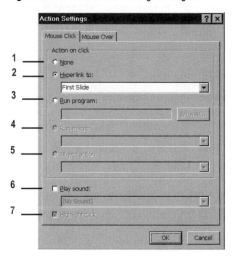

**Table 33.6**   Options in the Action Settings dialog box

| # | Option | What you do with it |
|---|--------|---------------------|
| 1 | None radio button | Click to remove the click or hover action from the button. |
| 2 | Hyperlink to: radio button and drop-down list | Choose an item that determines what you want PowerPoint to display when you click the button during a slide show. |
| 3 | Run program radio button and drop-down list | Choose an item that determines what program you want to run when you click the button during a slide show.<br>**Note**   You can either enter the program name and location or click the **Browse** button to choose a program on your computer system. |
| 4 | Run macro radio button and drop-down list | Choose an item that determines what macro you want to run when you click the button during a slide show. |
| 5 | Object action radio button and drop-down list | Choose an item that determines what action takes place (e.g., open, edit, or play) when you click the button during a slide show. |
| 6 | Play sound check box and drop-down list | Choose an item that determines what soundbite or narration file is played when you click the button during a slide show. |
| 7 | Highlight click check box | Click to change the button to reverse video when you click it or hover over it during a slide show.<br>**Note**   You can't choose this option if you've got text highlighted. |

# Slide Show ➤ Preset Animation

Use this option to use of variety of stored actions to emphasize or control how the objects on your slide appear when you're doing a slide show. You can have objects fly around, come in from one side or another, make the bullets appear one at a time and, in general, dazzle your audience.

**TIP**   If you want more control over the animation, choose **Slide Show ➤ Custom Animation.** (For more information, see Slide Show ➤ Custom Animation on page 531.)

## How You Get Here

◇ Press **Alt+D,P**          ◇ Choose **Slide Show ➤ Preset Animation**

## What's In This Flyout Menu

Figure 33.8 is a sample of this flyout menu and has a description of the options available.

**Figure 33.8**   The Slide Show ➤ Preset Animation flyout menu

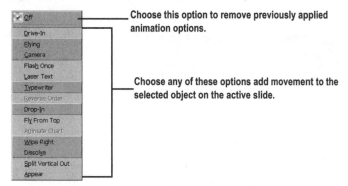

Choose this option to remove previously applied animation options.

Choose any of these options add movement to the selected object on the active slide.

# Slide Show ➤ Custom Animation

Use this option to completely control the special effects (such as sounds or movements) applied to the objects on a slide. The preset animation options are neat, but with this option, you can choose timing options, add a sound effect as the object is added to the slide, dim specific objects as new objects are added, control what happens when you use sound effects—and just plain drive yourself nuts fiddling with the options.

## How You Get Here

◇ Press **Alt+D,M**

◇ Choose **Slide Show ➤ Custom Animation**

## What's In This Dialog Box

Figure 33.9 is a sample of this dialog box and Table 33.7 has a description of the options available.

**Figure 33.9**    The Custom Animation dialog box

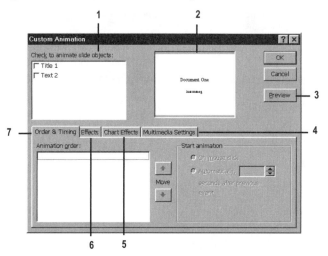

**Table 33.7**    Options in the Custom Animation dialog box

| # | Option | What you do with it |
|---|--------|---------------------|
| 1 | Check to animate area | Choose an item that determines which slide objects you want to animate. |
| 2 | Preview area | View the slide with the effects you have chosen before you apply them. |
| 3 | Preview button | Click to see what the highlighted animation will look like when you're doing a slide show. |
| 4 | Multimedia Settings tab | Click to display the Multimedia Settings tab so that you can choose how multimedia effects (either movies, sounds, or OLE objects) are displayed during your slide show. (For a complete description of the options available, see Table 33.8 on page 533.) |
| 5 | Chart Effects tab | Click to display the Chart Effects tab so that you can choose how you your charts or graphs are animated (you know, that stuff like sound and movement) during your slide show. These options are active only when a chart or graph is selected. (For a complete description of the options available, see Table 33.9 on page 533.) |
| 6 | Effects tab | Click to display the Effects tab so that you can choose get *very specific* how what effects are used for the highlighted object. (For a complete description of the options available, see Table 33.10 on page 533.) |
| 7 | Order & Timing tab | Click to display the Order & Timing tab so that you can decide how long it takes to display an object and in what order the objects appear during your slide show. (For a complete description of the options available, see Table 33.11 on page 534.) |

The following tables describe the options for the individual tabs in this dialog box:

■ Table 33.8 describes the Multimedia tab,
■ Table 33.9 describes the Chart Effects tab,
■ Table 33.10 describes the Effects tab, and
■ Table 33.11 describes the Order & Timing tab.

**Table 33.8**   Options in the Custom Animation dialog box Multimedia tab

| Option | What you do with it |
| --- | --- |
| Play using animation order check box | Click to play the movie or sound *before* playing any other animation effects for the current slide. |
| While playing radio buttons | Choose an item that determines how you want the multimedia object to interact with the slide while it is running (for example, you can have the slide show stop while the sound is played). |
| After playing radio buttons | Choose an item that determines how you want the object to act when the multimedia option is done. |
| More Options button | Click to set the options for the movie, sound, or OLE objects CD track and rewinding actions. |
| Object action drop-down list | Choose an item that determines the action (don't play, edit, or open) for the highlighted object. |
| Hide while not playing check box | Click to hide the object after it is finished playing. |

**Table 33.9**   Options in the Custom Animation dialog box Chart Effects tab

| Option | What you do with it |
| --- | --- |
| Introduce chart elements area | Choose an item that determines how the chart elements are placed on a slide (such as by Series or by category) during your slide show. |
| Entry animation and sound area | Choose an item that determines what effects are used when the slide is the first displayed during your slide show. |
| After animation area | Choose an item that determines how text is placed on a slide (such as letter by letter or word by word) during your slide show. |

**Table 33.10**   Options in the Custom Animation dialog box Effects tab

| Option | What you do with it |
| --- | --- |
| Entry animation and sound area | Choose an item that determines what effects are used when the slide is the first displayed during your slide show. |
| After animation area | Choose an item that determines what effects are used when you're done using the current slide during your slide show. |
| Introduce text area | Choose an item that determines how text is placed on a slide (such as letter by letter or word by word) during your slide show. |

**Table 33.11**    Options in the Custom Animation dialog box Order & Timing tab

| Option | What you do with it |
| --- | --- |
| Animation order list | Click to choose which object you want to work with. |
| Move up and down buttons | Click to move the highlighted object to a higher or lower position in the list. |
| Start animation area | Choose an item that determines how the animation effects will display during your slide show. |

# Slide Show ➤ Animation Preview

Use this option to view the selected animation for the active slide. This is a great way to see what will happen for a particular slide without running through the show to see it. Click in the preview window to repeat the animation effect.

## How You Get Here

◇ Press **Alt+D,E**          ◇ Choose **Slide Show ➤ Animation Preview**

## What's In This Window

Figure 33.10 is a sample of this window.

**Figure 33.10**    The Animation Preview window

# Slide Show ➤ Slide Transition

Use this option to control what happens when you move from one slide to the next during a slide show. You can use special animation options when you display the next slide, choose how fast (or slow) the transition is done, add sound effects that are played when you display the next slide, and choose whether you manually move to the next slide or automatically display the next slide after a certain time period.

## How You Get Here

◇ Press **Alt+D,T**          ◇ Choose **Slide Show ➤ Slide Transition**

## What's In This Dialog Box

Figure 33.11 is a sample of this dialog box and Table 33.12 has a description of the options available.

**Figure 33.11**    The Slide Transition dialog box

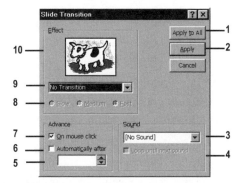

**Table 33.12**    Options in the Slide Transition dialog box

| # | Option | What you do with it |
|---|--------|---------------------|
| 1 | Apply to All button | Click to apply the highlighted effect to all the slides in the slide show and to the master slide. |
| 2 | Apply button | Click to apply the highlighted effect to the selected slides. |
| 3 | Sound drop-down list | Choose an item that determines what sound effect is played when the slide is displayed during your slide show. |
| 4 | Loop until next sound check box | Click to play the highlighted sound continuously until the next sound starts. |
| 5 | Advance automatically after list | Enter the length of time you want to wait before the next slide displays during your slide show. |
| 6 | Advance automatically after check box | Click to have the slide advance after a specified time. You can click both this and the On mouse click check boxes if you want the option of either type of advancing. |
| 7 | Advance on mouse click check box | Click to have the slide advance only when you click it. <br> **Note**   You can click both the On mouse click check box and the Automatically after check box. |
| 8 | Effect speed radio buttons | Click to choose how quickly the next slide is displayed during your slide show. |
| 9 | Effect transition drop-down list | Choose an item that determines which effect is used when you move to the next slide during your presentation. You can apply a different effect to each slide or use the same effect for all of the slides in your slide show. |
| 10 | Effect preview area | View the effect of the slide transition before you apply it. |

# Slide Show ➤ Hide Slide

Use this option to hide the selected slide from view when you run the slide show. Make sure you are on the slide you want to hide because this action takes place immediately. Choose the option again to display the slide again.

## How You Get Here

◇ Press **Alt+D,H**        ◇ Choose **Slide Show ➤ Hide Slide**

# Slide Show ➤ Custom Shows

Use this option to create variations of the active presentation. This is an efficient way to use the same basic set of slides over and over again, but to pick which slides you want to use for a specific audience. For example, let's say you have 75 slides describing how great you are. But you only need 50 of those slides for the top brass and 25 slides for your immediate boss. You can store all 75 slides in one file, then create two custom shows—one with 50 slides for the top brass and one with 25 slides for your immediate boss without storing, copying, cutting, and pasting slides all over the place (and trying to remember where you stored them).

**TIP** This is a great way to store commonly used slides in one place and then reuse the same slides over and over again. When you need to make edits, you only have to go to one place, not several.

## How You Get Here

◇ Press **Alt+D,C**        ◇ Choose **Slide Show ➤ Custom Shows**

## What's In This Dialog Box

Figure 33.12 is a sample of this dialog box and Table 33.13 has a description of the options available.

**Figure 33.12**   The Custom Shows dialog box

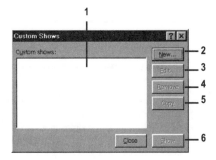

**Table 33.13**   Options in the Custom Shows dialog box

| # | Option | What you do with it |
|---|--------|---------------------|
| 1 | Custom shows list | View the list of previously defined custom slide shows. |
| 2 | New button | Click to display the Define Custom Show dialog box so that you give the custom slide show a name you'll recognize later and pick which slides go in this slide show. |
| 3 | Edit button | Click to display the Define Custom Show dialog box so that you can add or remove slides from the highlighted custom slide show. |
|   |   | **Note**   This option is only available if you've previously defined a custom slide show. |
| 4 | Remove button | Click to delete the highlighted slide show from the Custom shows list. |
|   |   | **Note**   This doesn't delete the entire file, just the custom view of the file. |
| 5 | Copy button | Click to make a copy of the highlighted slide show. |
| 6 | Show button | Click to see what the highlighted slide show will look like as a "real" slide show. |

# The PowerPoint Window Menu

## In this chapter

# What Is The Window Menu

This menu has options that let you choose how you want to display your files when you have more than one open or compare different files or copy information between them. Most of the actions take place immediately, so you won't see many new windows or screens in this section.

If a menu option has an ellipsis (three dots) or an arrow beside it, the application "asks" you for additional information before the action takes place. If the menu doesn't have one of these symbols, the action you choose happens immediately. If the action takes place immediately, you won't see a sample screen in this section.

# Window ➤ New Window

Use this option to open a new window with the same contents as the active window so that you can display different parts of the same document. The title bar then displays the original document name followed by a number that indicates which window you're working in.

## How You Get Here

◇ Press **Alt+W,N**          ◇ Choose **Window** ➤ **New Window**

# Window ➤ Arrange All

Use this option to display all open windows on the desktop at the same time.

## How You Get Here

◇ Press **Alt+W,A**          ◇ Choose **Window** ➤ **Arrange All**

# Window ➤ Fit to Page

Use this option to put each presentation its own window, with its own title bar, scroll bars, etc.

## How You Get Here

◇ Press **Alt+W,F**          ◇ Choose **Window** ➤ **Fit to Page**

# Window ➤ Cascade

Use this option to organize all of the open presentations in a stack with the upper left corner and title bar in view.

## How You Get Here

◇ Press **Alt+W,C**          ◇ Choose **Window** ➤ **Cascade**

# Window ➤ Next Pane

Use this option to move to the next pane on the active presentation screen. However, this option is only available when you're working in one presentation screen.

## How You Get Here

◇ Press **Alt+W,P** or **F6**   ◇ Choose **Window** ➤ **Next Pane**

# Window ➤ (List of Files Currently Open)

Use this option to switch between windows when there is more than one document open or to maximize the display of the selected window.

## How You Get Here

◇ Press **Alt+W,file number**   ◇ Choose **Window** ➤ **file number**

# A Look At Outlook

# Before You Dive Into Outlook

# What Is Outlook

Outlook, is, well, a different beast. It's more like command central than your typical application like Microsoft Word that does one thing. In fact, it's really a series of applications conveniently accessed from one place, the Outlook Desktop. Outlook acts as an office management program by giving us a quick way to monitor our daily activities, check our email, look up information about clients and other contacts. In short, it helps us keep track of the stuff we do every day.

Like the other Microsoft applications covered in this book, the Outlook applications work easily with one another and with Word, Excel, and PowerPoint. Oh, and in case you're wondering, Outlook also works closely with Access, even though it isn't discussed in this book.

---

**N O T E**   Due to the three basic ways of installing Outlook some menu options may not be included in this manual. We have given you the options we considered most important. ■

---

The following table gives you a quick idea of what applications are included in Outlook. Calendar, Inbox, and Contacts are the most complex of the Outlook applications and these applications are where you'll probably spend the majority of your time and effort.

**Table 35.1**   Applications in Outlook

| Outlook application | Icon | What you do with it | Associated Items |
|---|---|---|---|
| Calendar | | Use this application to make appointments (one-time only and recurring), set up meetings with other Outlook users, even set an audio alarm prior to an appointment. Sound a little bit familiar? You're right, this is an electronic version of the datebook you carry with you. | ■ Appointments<br>■ Meeting Requests<br>■ Events |
| Mail | | Use this application to create, send, receive, forward, and delete email messages. This application includes your Inbox, where you receive incoming mail, your Sent Items (where copies of outgoing mail are stored), Drafts (which holds messages that have been written, but not sent), and an Outbox (which holds messages that you've "sent" but haven't actually cross the electronic chasm yet). Even though there are a set of default folders for different types of messages, you can create more folders to organize your work any way you want. | ■ Mail Messages<br>■ Fax Messages<br>■ Discussions |
| Notes | | Use this application to jot down notes that would normally be written on a small yellow sticky note and then stuck on some other piece of paper. In fact, each note actually looks like the familiar yellow sticky notes. | Notes |

**Table 35.1**    Applications in Outlook, continued

| Outlook application | Icon | What you do with it | Associated Items |
|---|---|---|---|
| Contacts | | Use this application to create and maintain an electronic version of your standard card file, including names, addresses, and other types of contact information. This application is used most often with other applications, such as when you're choosing participants for a meeting that you're putting in your electronic calendar or choosing recipients for an email message. | ■ Contacts<br>■ Distribution Lists |
| Tasks | | Use this application to create and maintain an electronic "to do list". This can be your own private list or you can have other Outlook users use this list. | ■ Tasks<br>■ Task Requests |
| Journal | | Use this application to automatically view and update the history of projects, reports, and other documents created in Outlook. | Journal Entries |

# What Is The Outlook Desktop

As previously mentioned, Outlook is a series of applications accessed from one place: the *Outlook Desktop*. Think of your physical desktop—you know the one with all the various piles, pictures, and general stuff sitting around on it? Gets a little crowded doesn't it?

Well, the Outlook Desktop follows the same basic concept. Each application, such as the Calendar, has it's own window. It's own special menu items. It's own special everything, sort of. There is a bit of overlap between some of the menu items and functionality. But, all in all, the desktop can be a bit scary because there is so much going on.

Don't let it get to you too much. Just think of it as a central staging area for all the Outlook applications and folders, and as a way you can get to other applications on your system. We've tried to make the Outlook Desktop a little bit less scary by organizing the information in this part by the menu options that are common to all of the applications and then by the individual application's unique functionality.

## What's In This Window

Figure 35.1 is a sample of this window and Table 35.2 has a description of the options available.

---

**N O T E**    We used the Outlook Today pane as a starting point for the following graphic. The default setup for Office 2000 typically displays the Inbox window first.

Oh, and by the way, the specific options listed for the menu bar and toolbars change depending on which application you're working with. ■

**Figure 35.1**   Options in the Outlook Desktop

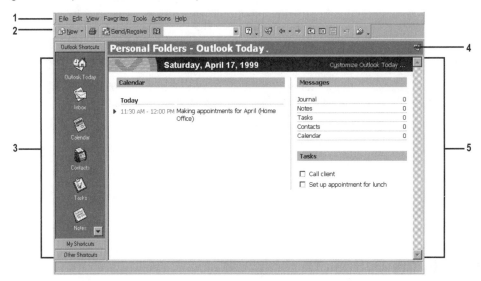

**Table 35.2**   Options in the Outlook Desktop

| # | Option | What you do with it |
|---|--------|---------------------|
| 1 | Menu bar | Click to display the submenus for a specific group of commands. |
| 2 | Toolbar | Click to perform a specific command. |
| 3 | Outlook Shortcuts bar | Click to open the application or folder that you want to work with. |
| 4 | Folder Banner | View the name of the active application. |
|   |  | **Note**   You can also click the Folder Banner arrow to display a list of your personal folders. |
| 5 | Application window | Perform the activities associated with the active application. In some applications, several panes may be open within this window. |

# What Are Items

An *item* in Outlook is a basically a specific activity that you work with in an application. These activities are what you're going to use most often to get your work done. You probably don't care about the application name as much as you'll care about making that appointment to pick up your lottery money, or sending that email telling your boss what a great job you did, or creating a to-do list that keeps a project moving forward at light speed. Although the term "item" may throw you a bit, don't panic. It's just a way to give names to the things you do in a normal day. By the way, these items are stored in folders. There are several items associated with Outlook, each of which is stored in its related folder. These items include:

| | | | |
|---|---|---|---|
| ■ | Appointments | ■ | Journal Entries |
| ■ | Contacts | ■ | Meeting Requests |
| ■ | Discussions | ■ | Mail Messages |
| ■ | Distribution Lists | ■ | Notes |
| ■ | Events | ■ | Tasks |
| ■ | Fax Messages | ■ | Task Requests |

# What Are Folders

*Folders* are Outlook's way of helping you keep everything organized. And, just like those folders you keep in your desk drawer (or on your desk, for that matter), you can put folders *inside* other folders so that you can be even more organized. In fact, Outlook is kind of nice to you: it automatically creates a file folder for each of the applications (such as Inbox or Calendar) and then creates a series of folders to hold the *items* (a meeting notice, an email message, a to-do item) for each application. There are three basic types of folders:

■ Application Folders,
■ Personal Folders, and
■ Item Folders.

---

**N O T E**   You can have multiple applications and folders open at one time, but only one *window* can be active. Open, but inactive items, are shown on the Taskbar at the bottom of your Outlook Desktop. ■

## Application Folders

These folders hold all the relevant files for the applications within Outlook. You'll rarely be messing around in these folders since Outlook also creates a shortcut to the application for you and puts it in a rather visible place: the Outlook Shortcuts bar.

## Personal Folders

When Outlook is installed, it creates something called a *Personal Folder* on your own computer so that it has a place to store the various items (messages, meetings, tasks, etc.) that you create during a typical day. Although Outlook makes some assumptions about where these items should be stored, you can change the defaults or even make additional personal folders that make more sense to you.

Confused? I'm not surprised. I was too. But it's basically like this. When you install Outlook, it creates:

- a folder for each application;
- a folder called a Personal Folder; and
- a series of folders *within* the Personal Folder for different items, such as sent messages, meeting notices, and tasks.

You can take a look at what's in your Personal Folders (we've included a sample below).

**Figure 35.2**   The Personal File Folder list

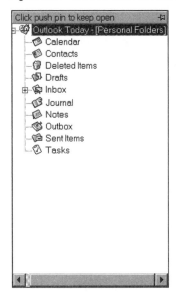

## Personal Folder Files

A personal folder file is a file that is located on your own computer (not somewhere out there on someone else's computer). Personal folder files contain folders, messages, forms, and files and show up in Outlook as the "Personal Folder". You work with a personal folder file as you would with any other file, and you can save, copy, and move a .pst file to another location on your hard disk, to a floppy disk, or to a server. You can also designate a personal folder file as the delivery location for your incoming messages.

**N O T E** Personal folders are saved with the extension .pst, and the folder items remain on your computer, not on the server. If you use another computer, you won't be able to see items stored in personal folders. ■

## The Folder Shortcut Menu

The Folder Shortcut Menu gives you access to commands that you can use to control the folders. You display the shortcut menu by right-mouse clicking while hovering over the folder you want. As with all right-click shortcut menus the options available will depend on what you are hovering over at the time you right-click.

**N O T E** This menu also displays when you right-click while hovering over an icon in the Outlook Shortcuts bar. ■

## What's In This Menu

Figure 35.3 is a sample of this menu and Table 35.3 has a description of the options available.

**Figure 35.3** The Folder shortcut menu

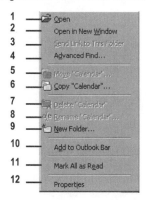

**Table 35.3** Options in the Folder shortcut menu

| # | Option | What you do with it |
|---|--------|---------------------|
| 1 | Open | Click to display the contents of the folder or the application. |
| 2 | Open in New Window | Click to open the item in a new window, which lies on top of the Outlook desktop. |
| 3 | Send Link to this Folder | Click to apply a previously selected link to this folder. This option is only available if you have previously selected a link. (For more information, see File ➤ Folder ➤ Send Link to This Folder on page 564.) |

**Table 35.3**    Options in the Folder shortcut menu, continued

| # Option | What you do with it |
|---|---|
| 4  Advanced Find | Click to display the Advanced Find dialog box, which has many search parameters and characteristics that let you precisely target what you're looking for. |
| 5  Move "Name of Folder" | Click to display the Move folder dialog box, where you can choose the folder (in folder tree view) to which you want the item moved. (For more information, see File ➤ Folder ➤ Move "Folder Name" on page 564.) |
| 6  Copy "Name of Folder" | Click to display the Copy folder dialog box, where you can choose the folder (in folder tree view) to which you want the item copied. (For more information, see File ➤ Folder ➤ Copy "Folder Name" on page 565.) |
| 7  Delete "Name of Folder" | Click to move the selected folder to the Deleted folder. Outlook displays a warning box to ensure you want to do this. (For more information, see File ➤ Folder ➤ Delete "Folder Name" on page 566.) |
| 8  Rename "Name of Folder" | Click to change the name to a text box, where you can enter the new name of the folder. (For more information, see File ➤ Folder ➤ Rename "Folder Name" on page 567.) |
| 9  New Folder | Click to create a new folder within the currently highlighted folder. (For more information, see File ➤ Folder ➤ New Folder on page 563.) |
| 10  Add to/Remove from Outlook bar | Click to move the selected folder into the current view displayed on the Outlook bar. (For more information, see Shortcuts Menu ➤ Outlook Bar Shortcut on page 604.) |
| 11  Mark All as Read | Click to remove the bold from all items within the highlighted folders. (For more information, see Edit ➤ Mark All as Read on page 591.) |
| 12  Properties | Click to display the Properties menu so that you can view or change information about the highlighted folder. (For more information, see File ➤ Folder ➤ Properties for "Folder Name" on page 567.) |

# What Are Shortcuts

*Shortcuts* are just that—a quick way to open something, such as an application, by clicking an icon. Outlook has shortcuts for lots of things, such as applications, folders, items, etc. It also creates groups of like things that you can reorganize if they aren't working very well for you.

**N O T E**    Outlook organizes the shortcuts by groups, but you can reorganize the shortcuts if you don't like the defaults.

# What Is Outlook Today

Let's see if we can confuse you a bit more—we had to really think about this one.

Remember when we told you that there were six different applications within Outlook? Well, the Outlook Today window isn't a separate application, although it does have its own icon on the Outlook Shortcuts bar. What it is a really neat way to look at what is going on in the other Outlook applications. Kind of a summary of what's going on today, if you will.

As with every other Windows application, there are default settings. But you can change those: you can pick which applications you want to know about in the Outlook Today window and you can pick which items are displayed. Now how's that for being able to quickly see what's on for today? With one quick glance, you can check your appointments, see how many email messages are waiting for you in your Inbox, and see what you're supposed to get done before the midnight hour strikes.

## How You Get Here

◇ Click      ◇ Press **Alt+V,G,K**   ◇ Choose **View** ➤ **Go To** ➤ **Outlook Today**

## What's In This Window

Figure 35.4 is a sample of this window and Table 35.4 has a description of the options available.

**Figure 35.4**   The Outlook Today window

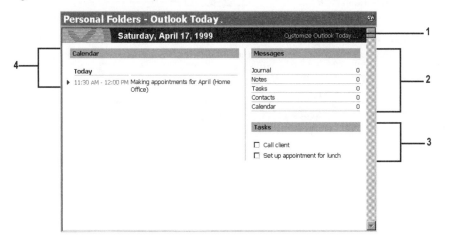

**Table 35.4**   Options in the Outlook Today window

| #   | Option                          | What you do with it |
|-----|---------------------------------|---------------------|
| 1   | Customize Outlook Today button  | Click to display the Customize Outlook Today window so that you can choose what information displays in this window. |
| 2   | Messages area                   | View a summary of how many things are going on for each time of Item you've included in your Outlook Today window. |
| 3   | Tasks area                      | View a list of your to-do list items tasks and check off tasks you've completed. |
| 4   | Calendar area                   | View a list of upcoming appointments, meetings, and events. |

**TIP**   Remember, this is a summary of the items you've chosen to display. Double-click an item if you want to look at it in more detail.

# Customize The Outlook Today Window

Use this option to make changes regarding what types of information display when you open the Outlook Today window.

## How You Get Here

◇ Click **Customize Outlook Today**   ◇ Press **Alt+U,**then **Enter**

## What's In This Dialog Box

Figure 35.5 is a sample of this dialog box and Table 35.5 has a description of the options available.

**Figure 35.5**   The Outlook Today Options dialog box

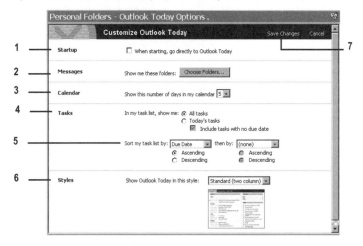

**Table 35.5**   Options in the Outlook Today Options dialog box

| # | Option | What you do with it |
|---|--------|---------------------|
| 1 | Startup check box | Click to display the Outlook Today window when you first open Outlook. |
| 2 | Messages | Click to choose those folders whose unread messages you want listed in the Outlook Today window. |
| 3 | Calendar | Click to choose how many days worth of calendar events are displayed in the Outlook Today window. You can display up to seven days. |
| 4 | In my task list, show me radio button | Choose an item that determines which tasks are displayed in the Outlook Today window. |
| 5 | Sort my task list by area | Choose an item that determines how the tasks are sorted when they're displayed in the Outlook Today window. You can sort these items based on a maximum of two criteria and choose whether the information is displayed in ascending (lowest to highest) or descending (highest to lowest) order. |
| 6 | Styles | Click to choose how you want the various items you've chosen displayed when you're viewing the Outlook Today window. |
| 7 | Save Changes button | Click to accept changes you've made and return to the Outlook Today window. |

# The Common File Menu Options

# What Is The File Menu

This menu lists the commands that you'll use to perform actions that affect the entire item or document in an application. These commands include saving your items so that you don't lose your work, printing an item, creating new items, creating shortcuts, choosing forms, and opening personal file folders.

If a menu option has an ellipsis (three dots) or an arrow beside it, the application "asks" you for additional information before the action takes place. If the menu doesn't have one of these symbols, the action you choose happens immediately. If the action takes place immediately, you won't see a sample screen in this section.

---

**N O T E**   Most of the options on the File menu are the same regardless of which application you're using. ▨

# File ➤ New

Use this option to create any type of item from any of the six applications. For example, let's say you're working in the Calendar application and suddenly remember that you need to send an email message to your boss. You start to open the Inbox, then remember that you don't have to do that! You can stay right there in the Calendar application and choose **File ➤ New ➤ Mail Message**. Up pops the Message form, you create and send your message, and Outlook returns you to the Calendar application.

---

**N O T E**   New items are created in a special type of window called a form. Want to take a guess at where it got its name? You're right. Because these onscreen forms look just like the old fashioned forms we used to fill out with pen and paper. You've even got special fields and everything. By the way, each item has its own form, which is covered in depth in the related application chapter. ▨

### How You Get Here

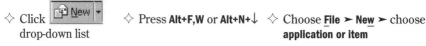

◇ Click    ▣ New ▾    ◇ Press **Alt+F,W** or **Alt+N+↓**    ◇ Choose **File ➤ New ➤** choose
     drop-down list                                                       **application or item**

### What's In This Flyout Menu

Figure 36.1 is a sample of this flyout menu and Table 36.1 has a description of the options available.

**N O T E** Most of these options are also available from one of the main menu options, so we've put a cross-reference to the place where you can find more details. ▪

**Figure 36.1** The File ➤ New flyout menu

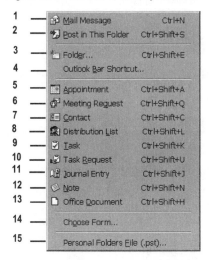

**Table 36.1** Options in the File ➤ New flyout menu

| # | Option | What you do with it |
|---|--------|---------------------|
| 1 | Mail Message | Click to start entering information for a new email message in a blank Message form. (For more information, see A Look At Outlook Mail's Forms on page 671.) |
| 2 | Post in This Folder | Click to open an untitled discussion form. Discussions are conversations that occur via email, often among several participants. One person starts a "thread" by clicking this option and filling out and posting a discussion form. Others on the network put in their comments, and after a time that thread dies and a new one is submitted by one of the group's members. If you've been on UseNet on the Internet, you'll recognize Outlook's discussions. Post in This Folder opens a form that lets you start a new discussion. |
| 3 | Folder | Click to display the Create New Folder dialog box, where you create and name a subfolder of the selected folder. (For more information, see File ➤ Folder on page 562.) |
| 4 | Outlook Bar Shortcut | Click to display the Add to Outlook Bar dialog box so that you can choose which folders or items you want to add to the Outlook Shortcuts bar.(For more information, see The Outlook Shortcuts Bar Shortcut Menu on page 602.) |

**Table 36.1**   Options in the File ➤ New flyout menu, continued

| # Option | What you do with it |
|---|---|
| 5 Appointment | Click to open an untitled Appointment form, where you can enter information such as the date, time, and place of an appointment. (For more information, see A Look At Calendar's Forms on page 705.) |
| 6 Meeting Request | Click to open an untitled Meeting Request form, which is identical to an appointment form, with the addition of a To: text box (for the email address) and a Send option under the Tools menu. (For more information, see A Look At Calendar's Forms on page 705.) |
| 7 Contact | Click to open an untitled Contact form, where you can enter personal and business related information, such as phone numbers, and addresses, of persons you contact using Outlook. (For more information, see A Look At The Contact Form on page 739.) |
| 8 Distribution List | Click to open an untitled Distribution List form, where you can group existing contacts into specific lists, or create new groups with new contacts. (For more information, see A Look At The Contact Form on page 739.) |
| 9 Task | Click to open an untitled Task form, where you can enter information such as subjects and due dates for ongoing tasks. (For more information, see A Look At The Task Form on page 783.) |
| 10 Task Request | Click to open an untitled Task Request form, which is identical to the Task form, with the addition of a To: text box (for the email address) and a Send option under the Tools menu. (For more information, see A Look At The Task Form on page 783.) |
| 11 Journal Entry | Click to open an untitled Journal Entry, where you can manually enter information relating to business or personal activities within any of the Microsoft Office applications (Journal Entries can be easily programmed to record automatically). (For more information, see A Look At The Journal Entry Form on page 765.) |
| 12 Note | Click to display an untitled Note form, which is the electronic equivalent of the sticky notes that are so popular for jotting down little reminders. (For more information, see A Look At The Notes Form on page 803.) |
| 13 Office Document | Click to choose any of the other Office applications (Word, Excel, etc.) and create a new file document within the active application. This is no different than using the typical Office application. Check the individual commands for more details on this subject. |
| 14 Choose Form | Click to choose from all available forms (Notes, Appointment, etc.). This dialog box offers a description area, where you can easily view the functions of all forms listed. (For more information, see Tools ➤ Forms on page 633.) |
| 15 Personal Folders File (.pst) | Click to create a new folder for the Personal Folder List. This is different than creating a sub-folder for one of the existing Personal File Folders. Folders at this level can be encrypted, and can contain passwords. |

# File ➤ Open

Use this option to display existing items in the appropriate application window.

## How You Get Here

◇ Press **Alt+F,O** or **Ctrl+O**    ◇ Choose **File ➤ Open**

## What's In This Flyout Menu

Figure 36.2 is a sample of this flyout menu.

**Figure 36.2**    File ➤ Open flyout menu

| | | |
|---|---|---|
| Selected Items    Ctrl+O | ———— File ➤ Open ➤ Selected Items | 561 |
| Other User's Folder… | ———— File ➤ Open ➤ Other User's Folder | 561 |
| Personal Folders File (.pst)… | ———— File ➤ Open ➤ Personal Folders File (.pst) | 561 |

## File ➤ Open ➤ Selected Items

Use this option to open a highlighted item in its appropriate application. For example, you can highlight a mail message and click this option to open the message in the mail reader. You can accomplish the same thing by double-clicking on the item.

### How You Get Here

◇ Press **Alt+F,O,S** or **Ctrl+O**    ◇ Choose **File ➤ Open ➤ Selected Items**

## File ➤ Open ➤ Other User's Folder

Use this option to access the folder file of another user within an interoffice network. You can access this option only if you are connected to an intranet system and you can only access items to which you have authorization. This dialog box has the same options as the standard Open dialog box. (For a complete description of the options available, see Table 3.2 on page 40.)

### How You Get Here

◇ Press **Alt+F,O,O**    ◇ Choose **File ➤ Open ➤ Other User's Folder**

## File ➤ Open ➤ Personal Folders File (.pst)

Use this option to open the selected folder from your personal folder file, using the Select a Folder dialog box. This dialog box has the same options as the standard Open dialog box. (For a complete description of the options available, see Table 3.2 on page 40.)

### How You Get Here

◇ Press **Alt+F,O,P**    ◇ Choose **File ➤ Open ➤ Personal Folder File (.pst)**

# File ➤ Close All Items

Use this option to close all open items, regardless of their applications.

## How You Get Here

◇ Press **Alt+F,E**        ◇ Choose **File ➤ Close All Items**

# File ➤ Save As

Use this option to save the item for the first time or to save an existing item with a different name or file type. This dialog box has the same options as the standard Open dialog box and Save As dialog box. (For a complete description of the options available, see Table 3.2 on page 40.)

Be sure you look at where you're storing the item before you click **Save**—don't let "fast fingers" get the better of you. The most frequent reason people can't find a file is because they didn't pay attention to the file folder that was open when they last saved a file.

## How You Get Here

◇ Press **Alt+F,A**        ◇ Choose **File ➤ Save As**

# File ➤ Save Attachments

Use this option to save attachments that are sent to you with your email messages. "Attachments" are usually files that are carried along into your computer with email messages, and may be almost anything: spreadsheets, memos, jokes, software. Be sure to save attachments before you delete your email messages, because the attachments will go into oblivion with them.

## How You Get Here

◇ Press **Alt+F,N**        ◇ Choose **File ➤ Save Attachments**

# File ➤ Folder

Use this option to create a new folder and copy, move, or rename the highlighted folder. You can also specify properties for the highlighted folder, such as how long the folder should be archived, and enter a description of the folder's contents. The options in this flyout menu are also located on the shortcut menu that displays when you right-click on a folder in the personal folder list. The shortcut menu has other options which you may find on other menus.

## How You Get Here

◇ Press **Alt+F,F**        ◇ Choose **File ➤ Folder**

## What's In This Flyout Menu

Figure 36.3 is a sample of this flyout menu.

**Figure 36.3**   The File ➤ Folder flyout menu

## File ➤ Folder ➤ New Folder

Use this option to create a new, unnamed file folder that you can use to organize your items.

> **N O T E**   You not only get to give this new folder a name that fits the contents (or at least a name that you'll recognize), you get to pick where you want to store the actual folder. ▤

## How You Get Here

◇ Press **Alt+F,F,N** or **Ctrl+Shift+E**          ◇ Choose **File** ➤ **Folder** ➤ **New Folder**

## What's In This Dialog Box

Figure 36.4 is a sample of this dialog box and Table 36.2 has a description of the options available.

**Figure 36.4**   The Create New Folder dialog box

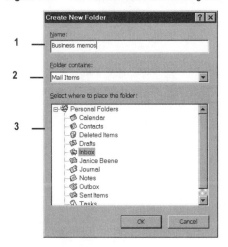

**Table 36.2**    Options in the Create New Folder dialog box

| # | Option | What you do with it |
|---|--------|---------------------|
| 1 | Name text box | Enter the name you want to give this file folder. Remember, this is the name that appears in any list of file folders in Outlook. |
| 2 | Folder contains drop-down list | Choose an item that determines what type of items (such as Tasks or Appointments) you plan to store in the highlighted folder. |
| 3 | Select where to place the folder list | Choose an item that determines where the new folder will be stored in your current hierarchy of folders. |

## File ➤ Folder ➤ Send Link to This Folder

Use this option to provide a link to your folder, so that others on the network can access it more conveniently. Instead of an Internet address, the link appears as the drive and folder address. When the viewer clicks on the link, the document or item opens.

---

**N O T E**    You must be connected to a network to access this option. ▪

## How You Get Here

◇ Press **Alt+F,F,S**          ◇ Choose **File** ➤ **Folder** ➤ **Send Link to This Folder**

## File ➤ Folder ➤ Move "Folder Name"

Use this option to move the highlighted folder from it's current position to another location in your folder hierarchy. Remember, this is a *move*, not a copy. So when you get done, you've moved the folder and the contents to another location. If you want to keep the folder in both places, choose **File** ➤ **Folder** ➤ **Copy "Folder"**. (For more information, see File ➤ Folder ➤ Copy "Folder Name" on page 565.)

## How You Get Here

◇ Press **Alt+F,F,V**          ◇ Choose **File** ➤ **Folder** ➤ **Move**

## What's In This Dialog Box

Figure 36.5 is a sample of this dialog box and Table 36.3 has a description of the options available.

**Figure 36.5**   The Move Folder dialog box

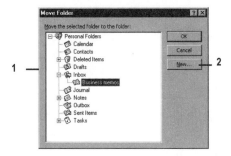

**Table 36.3**   Options in the Move Folder dialog box

| # | Option | What you do with it |
|---|--------|---------------------|
| 1 | Move the selected folder list | Click to choose the folder into which the highlighted folder is placed. |
| 2 | New button | Click to display the Create a New Folder dialog box so that you create a new folder before you actually move the highlighted folder. This is helpful if you want to move the folder into a folder you realize you haven't yet created. (For a complete description of the options available, see Table 36.2.) |

## File ➤ Folder ➤ Copy "Folder Name"

Use this option to make a duplicate copy of the highlighted folder so that you can keep one copy in the original place and put another copy in another location in your folder hierarchy. If you want to move the highlighted item from one place to another, choose **File ➤ Folder ➤ Move "Folder"**. (For more information, see File ➤ Folder ➤ Move "Folder Name" on page 564.)

> **TIP**   For those of you using internal networks, the "move" option is probably the better choice for your sanity. Most of the system administrators I've known get pretty testy when you start using up lots and lots of disk space. So you might want to think twice between using **Edit ➤ Copy to Folder.**

## How You Get Here

◇ Press **Alt+F,F,C**          ◇ Choose **File ➤ Folder ➤ Copy**

## What's In This Dialog Box

Figure 36.6 is a sample of this dialog box and Table 36.4 has a description of the options available.

**Figure 36.6**    The Copy Folder dialog box

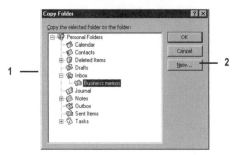

**Table 36.4**    Options in the Copy Folder dialog box

| # | Option | What you do with it |
|---|--------|---------------------|
| 1 | Copy the selected folder list | Click to choose the folder into which a copy of the selected folder is placed. |
| 2 | New button | Click to display the Create a New Folder dialog box so that you create a new folder before you actually copy the highlighted folder. This is helpful if you want to copy the folder into a folder you realize you haven't yet created. (For a complete description of the options available, see Table 36.2.) |

## File ➤ Folder ➤ Delete "Folder Name"

Use this option to get rid of the highlighted or currently open folder. Outlook displays a warning box to ensure you want to delete the folder. The folder is moved to the Deleted Items folder, unless you have otherwise customized this process. There it will remain until you delete it again. Shortcuts to the folder aren't automatically be deleted; they have to be manually deleted.

## How You Get Here

◇ Press **Alt+F,F,D**          ◇ Choose **F**ile ➤ **F**older ➤ **D**elete

## File ➤ Folder ➤ Rename "Folder Name"

Use this option to change the name of the highlighted folder.

---

**N O T E**   Once you've entered the new folder name, you must press the **Enter** key before anything really happens. Just thought you might like to know so that you not sitting there wondering what went wrong. ▇

### How You Get Here

◇ Press **Alt+F,F,R**      ◇ Choose **File** ➤ **Folder** ➤ **Rename**

## File ➤ Folder ➤ Properties for "Folder Name"

Use this option to display the Properties dialog box, where you can view and edit information related to the selected folder, such as its location, type, and a description. You can also make modifications to the AutoArchive features of this folder.

---

**N O T E**   Figure 36.7 shows most of the tabs I found while working with Outlook. However, the tabs displayed may vary based on the particular folder you have open. ▇

### How You Get Here

◇ Press **Alt+F,F,I**      ◇ Choose **File** ➤ **Folder** ➤ **Properties for**

### What's In This Dialog Box

Figure 36.7 is a sample of this dialog box and Table 36.5 has a description of the tabs available.

**Figure 36.7**   The "Folder Name" Properties dialog box

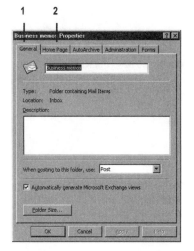

**Table 36.5**   Tabs in the "Folder Name" Properties dialog box

| # | Tab name | What you do with it |
|---|----------|---------------------|
| 1 | General | Click to view and edit information relating to the name, type, location, and size of the highlighted folder. (For a complete description of the options available, see Table 36.6 on page 568.) |
| 2 | Home Page | Click to view and edit information related to the Web page address given to this folder (if it has one). (For a complete description of the options available, see Table 36.7 on page 569.) |

The following tables describe the options for the individual tabs in this dialog box:

- Table 36.6 describes the General tab, which is available in all applications,
- Table 36.7 describes the Home Page tab, which is available in all applications,
- Table 36.8 describes the AutoArchive tab, which is available in all applications except Contacts,
- Table 36.9 describes the Outlook Address Book tab, which is available in Contacts,
- Table 36.10 describes the Activities tab, which is available in Contacts, and
- Table 36.11 describes the Sharing tab, which is available in Tasks.

**Table 36.6**   Options in the "Folder Name" Properties dialog box General tab

| Option | What you do with it |
|--------|---------------------|
| Folder name text box | Enter a new name, if necessary, for the folder. |
| Description text box | Enter a description of the items contained within the folder. |

**Table 36.6**  Options in the "Folder Name" Properties dialog box General tab, continued

| Option | What you do with it |
|---|---|
| When posting drop-down list | Choose an item that determines which type of item or form is used when posting to this folder. |
| Automatically generate check box | Click to allow items created to have views that can be displayed in Microsoft Exchange as well as in Outlook. |
| Folder Size button | Click to display the Folder Size dialog box, where you can view the adequacy of the folder size. |

**Table 36.7**  Options in the "Folder Name" Properties dialog box Home Page tab

| Option | What you do with it |
|---|---|
| Show home page check box | Click to display the web page address for this folder when you're viewing the folder. Leave unchecked to view the contents instead. |
| Address text box | Enter the Web page address (URL) or the document path name associated with the highlighted folder. This text box is filled in automatically if you choose a home page with the Browse button. |
| Browse button | Click to display the Find Web Files dialog box, where you can search for the URL or Home Page that you want displayed when this folder is opened. |
| Restore Defaults button | Click to remove any changes you have made to the settings and restore them to the default values. |

**Table 36.8**  Options in the "Folder Name" Properties dialog box AutoArchive tab

| Option | What you do with it |
|---|---|
| Clean out items older than check box | Click to enable the Clean Out options list and let Outlook automatically move items that are older than the age specified to the designated location. |
| Clean out items older than list | Choose an item that determines the age at which items are moved from the folder to the designated location. |
| Clean out items older than drop-down list | Choose an item that determines the span of time in months, weeks, or days. |
| Move old items to radio button Move old items to text box | Click to turn on the move option and enter the name of the folder where Outlook should move "old" items. |
| Browse button | Click to display the Find Personal Folders dialog box so that you can search through the entire list to find the folder you want to use for the Move old items to text box. |
| Permanently delete old items radio button | Click to remove designated items permanently from the folder list. They are not sent to Deleted Items. |

**Table 36.9** Options in the "Folder Name" Properties dialog box Outlook Address Book tab

| Option | What you do with it |
|---|---|
| Show this folder as an e-mail Address Book check box | Click to enable Outlook to display the current folder in the form of an address book. |
| Name of the address book text box | Enter the name of the address book that Outlook displays. |

**Table 36.10** Options in the "Folder Name" Properties dialog box Activities tab

| Option | What you do with it |
|---|---|
| Folder Groups area | View the available folder groups currently defined. |
| Copy button | Click to make a copy of the currently selected folder group. |
| Reset button | Click to restore the defaults to all groups. This means that Outlook-defined groups are restored to their original states, while user-defined groups are deleted. |
| New button | Click to create a new folder group. |
| Default activities view drop-down list | Specifies the default action type view associated with all contacts. |

**Table 36.11** Options in the "Folder Name" Properties dialog box Sharing tab

| Option | What you do with it |
|---|---|
| Owner and name area | View the folder's name and its administrator. |
| Net folder description text box | Enter the description that will accompany the folder on other user's systems. |
| Updates will be sent out every drop-down list | Choose an item that determines how often your changes to the net folder will be sent to subscribers as updates. |
| Verify contents of member folders every radio buttons | Choose an item that determines whether you verify your subscribers' contents never, or at regular intervals. |
| Update size cannot exceed drop-down list | Choose an item that determines the maximum permissible size of the update you'll send. Many network administrators assign upper limits to file transfer sizes. |
| Journal events for this folder check box | Click to record all events for this folder in your journal. This is helpful for revision control, or just covering your behind when questions are asked. |
| Send Updates Now button | Click to send updates immediately, regardless of when they were last sent or how often you've set the interval for. An update won't be sent if it's bigger than your set maximum. |
| Stop Sharing This Folder button | Click to remove all privileges and connections to this folder. A message is sent to its subscribers informing them of the disconnection. |

# File ➤ Share

Use this option to give other users are access to your folders across a network. This helps you arrange meetings that fit everyone's schedule, share your list of contacts (See Contacts), and keep track of tasks handled by a team of people. Note, though, that when you share a folder, you're giving others access to *your folders* and not getting access to someone else's. To get access to someone else's goodies, you have to ask them to give you permission.

 **N O T E**   You must be connected to a network to access this option. ▨

## How You Get Here

◇ Press **Alt+F,H**          ◇ Choose **File ➤ Share**

## What's In This Flyout Menu

Figure 36.8 is a sample of this flyout menu.

**Figure 36.8**   The File ➤ Share flyout menu

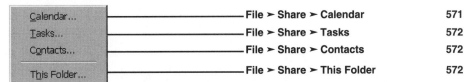

| | |
|---|---|
| Calendar... —— File ➤ Share ➤ Calendar | 571 |
| Tasks... —— File ➤ Share ➤ Tasks | 572 |
| Contacts... —— File ➤ Share ➤ Contacts | 572 |
| This Folder... —— File ➤ Share ➤ This Folder | 572 |

## File ➤ Share ➤ Calendar

Use this option to identify the users who are allowed to access your Calendar data.

## How You Get Here

◇ Press **Alt+F,H,C**          ◇ Choose **File ➤ Share ➤ Calendar**

## What's In This Dialog Box

Figure 36.9 is a sample of this wizard.

**Figure 36.9**   The Net Folder wizard

Follow the instructions for sharing folders.
This wizard displays for all options on the
Share flyout menu.

## File ➤ Share ➤ Tasks

Use this option to identify the users who are allowed to access your Task data.

### How You Get Here

◇ Press **Alt+F,H,T**          ◇ Choose **File ➤ Share ➤ Tasks**

## File ➤ Share ➤ Contacts

Use this option to identify the users who are allowed to access your Contacts data.

### How You Get Here

◇ Press **Alt+F,H,O**          ◇ Choose **File ➤ Share ➤ Contacts**

## File ➤ Share ➤ This Folder

Use this option to identify users who are allowed to access information stored in the highlighted
folder.

### How You Get Here

◇ Press **Alt+F,H,H**          ◇ Choose **File ➤ Share ➤ This Folder**

# File ➤ Import and Export

Use this option to display the Import and Export Wizard, which takes you step-by-step through the process of importing files from other programs or files, such as Act! and Lotus Organizer.

## How You Get Here

◇ Press **Alt+F,T**

◇ Choose **File ➤ Import and Export**

## What's In This Dialog Box

Figure 36.10 is a sample of this wizard.

**Figure 36.10** The File ➤ Import and Export wizard

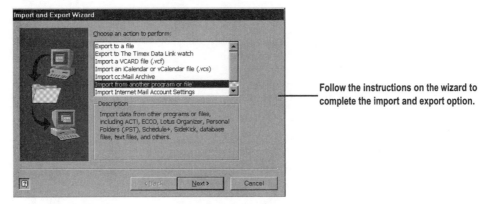

Follow the instructions on the wizard to complete the import and export option.

# File ➤ Archive

Use this option to set up how Outlook saves backup copies somewhere other than where you're actively working. You can choose folders and items to archive, as well as archival properties such as how long to wait before archiving, whether or not to hold the archived items in an archive folder, and whether to delete the items.

 **TIP** Archiving is helpful in that it keeps your active folders from becoming cluttered with old items you didn't want to throw away, "just in case." You can tell Outlook to remove any items older than three months (or any other period of time), and hold them in an archive folder. If you really want to clean house, you can tell Outlook to discard these items, and they will be permanently deleted.

## How You Get Here

◇ Press **Alt+F,R**

◇ Choose **File ➤ Archive**

## What's In This Dialog Box

Figure 36.11 is a sample of this dialog box and Table 36.12 has a description of the options available.

**Figure 36.11**    The Archive dialog box

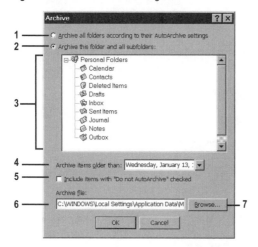

**Table 36.12**    Options in the Archive dialog box

| # | Option | What you do with it |
|---|--------|---------------------|
| 1 | Archive all folders according to their AutoArchive settings radio button | Click to maintain the original settings as they are entered in the properties tab of the specific folder. |
| 2 | Archive this folder and all subfolders radio button | Click to move items from the highlighted folder, and its subfolders, into the designated folders according to the age specifications. |
| 3 | Folder list | Choose an item that determines which folders you want AutoArchived according to the specified ages. |
| 4 | Archive items older than list | Choose an item that determines the age at which items are AutoArchived. |
| 5 | Include items check box | Click to override those items with the Do Not AutoArchive feature turned on. |
| 6 | Archive file text box | Enter the path name of the file you want archived items moves to. |
| 7 | Browse button | Click to display the Open Personal Folders, from which you choose the folder you want opened. |

# File ➤ Page Setup

Use this option to view and make changes to the default print styles applied to the current item. This includes changes to the paper size, the format, and the header and footer text. Page Setup provides a myriad of styles, depending on which application you are in. The common options for all applications are a Table style and a Memo style.

**N O T E**  The page set up relates directly to the print styles, that is, how what you're seeing on the screen looks when printed on paper. Changes to the print style don't affect how the information displays on your computer screen. ▦

## How You Get Here

◇ Press **Alt+F,U**          ◇ Choose **File ➤ Page Setup**

## What's In This Flyout Menu

Table 36.19 is a sample of this flyout menu.

**Figure 36.12**   The File ➤ Page Setup flyout menu

| | |
|---|---|
| Table Style ————————— File ➤ Page Setup ➤ Table Style | 575 |
| Memo Style ————————— File ➤ Page Setup ➤ Memo Style | 578 |
| Define Print Styles... ————— File ➤ Page Setup ➤ Define Print Styles | 579 |

## File ➤ Page Setup ➤ Table Style

Use this option to make changes to a page displayed in table view. This is helpful when you want to print out a listing of all items within a folder. Options unique to the table view appear in the Format tab, where you can apply different fonts and font sizes to column headings and row text.

## How You Get Here

◇ Press **Alt+F,U,** choose **Table Style**    ◇ Choose **File ➤ Page Setup ➤ Table Style**

## What's In This Dialog Box

Figure 36.13 is a sample of this dialog box and Table 36.13 has a description of the options available.

**Figure 36.13**   The Page Setup: Table Style dialog box

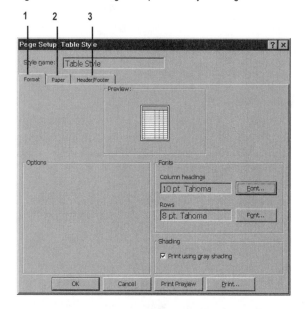

**Table 36.13**   Tabs in the Page Setup: Table Style dialog box

| # | Tab name | What you do with it |
|---|----------|---------------------|
| 1 | Format | View a preview, and make changes to fonts and shading. (For a complete description of the options available, see Table 36.13 on page 576.) |
| 2 | Paper | View and make changes to the paper type, size, orientation, and margins. (For a complete description of the options available, see Table 36.14 on page 577.) |
| 3 | Header/Footer | View and make changes to headers and footers. (For a complete description of the options available, see Table 36.15 on page 577.) |

The following tables describe the options for the individual tabs in this dialog box:

- Table 36.13 describes the Format tab,
- Table 36.14 describes the Paper tab, and
- Table 36.15 describes the Header/Footer tab.

**Table 36.14**   Options in the Page Setup: Table Style dialog box Format tab

| Option | What you do with it |
|---|---|
| Preview area | View a thumbnail image of what the text will look like when it's printed (*before* you have to run down three flights of stairs to see that you picked the wrong options). |
| Options area | View the specified layout options, if any. |
| Fonts area | View and make changes to the fonts for the column headings and the row text (they don't have to be the same). |
| Shading area | Click to automatically apply a gray shading to column headings, dates, and other specified elements. If you are going to fax the document, don't' turn on this option since it makes it darn near impossible to read the information. |
| Print Preview button | Click to take a closer look at exactly how the document will look when you print it. |
| Print button | Click to open the Print dialog box, where you can define print elements, such as the number of pages, the page range, page style, and identify the printer. |

**Table 36.15**   Options in the Page Setup: Table Style dialog box Paper tab

| Option | What you do with it |
|---|---|
| Paper area | View and make changes to the type, dimensions, and source of the paper. |
| Margins area | View and make changes to the top, bottom, left, and right margins. |
| Page area | View and make changes to the size and dimensions of the printed page area. (Your printed page may take two pieces of paper, as is the case in some spreadsheets). |
| Orientation area | Choose an item that determines whether the item is printed top-to-bottom (portrait) or left-to-right (landscape). |
| Print Preview button | Click to look at the item the same way it will look when you actually print it to the physical printer. |
| Print button | Click to open the Print dialog box so that you can define print elements, such as the number of pages, the page range, page style, and identify the printer. |

**Table 36.16**   Options in the Page Setup: Table Style dialog box Header/Footer tab

| Option | What you do with it |
|---|---|
| Header area | Enter information in any or all of the left, center, or right justified text boxes so that the same information prints in the same position at the top of every page. |
| Header area Font button | View and make changes to the font for the active header (left, center, or right justified). |

**Table 36.16**   Options in the Page Setup: Table Style dialog box Header/Footer tab, continued

| Option | What you do with it |
| --- | --- |
| Footer area | Enter information in any or all of the left, center, or right justified text boxes so that the same information prints in the same position at the bottom of every page. |
| Footer area Font button | View and make changes to the font for the active footer (left, center, or right justified). |
| Insert toolbar | Click any or all buttons to insert page numbers, date and time stamps, etc. at the top or bottom of your pages. |
| Reverse on even pages check box | Check to reverse the left and right headers and footers on even and odd pages. If you check this option, Outlook puts the page number on the outside edges of each page: on the left side for even numbered pages and on the right side for odd numbered pages. |

## File ➤ Page Setup ➤ Memo Style

Use this option to make changes to a page you want to print in Memo view. This is helpful when you want to relay the contents of a folder (a list or a contact profile) within the format of a memo. Options unique to the Memo view appear in the Format tab, where you can apply different fonts and font sizes to the title and fields in the heading for the memo.

### How You Get Here

◇ Press **Alt+F,U,** choose **Memo Style**   ◇ Choose **File** ➤ **Page Setup** ➤ **Memo Style**

### What's In This Dialog Box

Figure 36.14 is a sample of this dialog box and Table 36.17 has a description of the options available.

**Figure 36.14**   The Page Setup: Memo Style dialog box

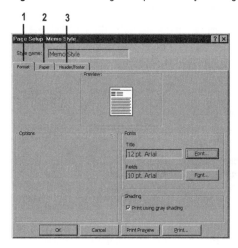

**N O T E**  This dialog box has the same tabs and basic functionality as the Table Style dialog box. ▣

The following tables describe the options for the individual tabs in this dialog box:

■   Table 36.13 describes the Format tab,
■   Table 36.14 describes the Paper tab, and
■   Table 36.15 describes the Header/Footer tab.

**Table 36.17**   Tabs in the Page Setup: Memo Style dialog box

| # Tab name | What you do with it |
|---|---|
| 1   Format | View a preview, and make changes to fonts and shading. (For a complete description of the options available, see Table 36.13 on page 576.) |
| 2   Paper | View and make changes to the paper type, size, orientation, and margins. (For a complete description of the options available, see Table 36.14 on page 577.) |
| 3   Header/Footer | View and make changes to headers and footers. (For a complete description of the options available, see Table 36.15 on page 577.) |

## File ➤ Page Setup ➤ Define Print Styles

Use this option to create, modify, and remove predefined rules for printing different types of documents, such as tables or memos.

**N O T E**  Applications with alternate displays, such as Calendar, have additional print styles. ▣

### How You Get Here

◇ Press **Alt+F,U,S**            ◇ Choose **File ➤ Page Setup ➤ Define Print Styles**

## What's In This Dialog Box

Figure 36.15 is a sample of this dialog box and Table 36.18 has a description of the options available.

**Figure 36.15**    The Define Print Styles dialog box

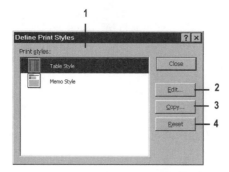

**Table 36.18**    Options in the Define Print Styles dialog box

| # | Option | What you do with it |
|---|--------|---------------------|
| 1 | Print styles list | Choose an item that determines the print style you wish to define. |
| 2 | Edit button | Click to open the Page Set Up dialog box so that you can make changes to the Format, Paper, and Header/Footer text. (For more information, see File ➤ Page Setup on page 575.) |
| 3 | Copy button | Click to make a copy of the highlighted style so that you can make a few changes rather than having to start from scratch to define a new style. |
| 4 | Reset button | Click to remove all changes made and restore the settings back to those loaded when you installed Outlook. |

# File ➤ Print Preview

Use this option to see how your document will look *before* you print the document on paper. With this option, you can display full pages or thumbnails (multiple pages of your document in a reduced view) so that you can quickly scan your document for layout errors. You can also make changes to your document and send your document to the printer while in Print Preview mode.

## How You Get Here

◇ Press **Alt+F,V**        ◇ Choose **File** ➤ **Print Preview**

## What's In This Dialog Box

Figure 36.16 is a sample of this dialog box and Table 36.19 has a description of the options available.

**Figure 36.16**   The Print Preview dialog box

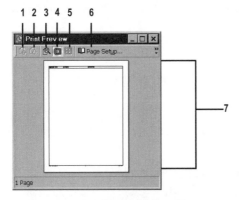

**Table 36.19**   Options in the Print Preview dialog box

| # | Option | What you do with it |
|---|--------|---------------------|
| 1 | Page Up icon | Click to move the insertion point and what is displayed to the previous page. This option is only available on pages two or above in a multi-page document. |
| 2 | Page Down icon | Click to move the insertion point and what is displayed to the next page. This option is only available on a multi-page document. |
| 3 | Actual Size icon | Click to display the document in its actual size. In this view, you need to use the scroll bars to view the entire page. |
| 4 | One Page icon | Click to size the page so that you can see an entire page within the viewing screen. |
| 5 | Multiple Pages icon | Click to size the pages so you can see many pages at one time on the viewing screen. |
| 6 | Page Setup icon | Click to open the Page Set Up dialog box, where you can make changes to the Format, Paper, and Header/Footer text. (For more information, see File ➤ Page Setup on page 575.) |
| 7 | View Page area | View the document. The pointer becomes a magnifying glass when hovering over the document. Click to enlarge the view, click again to return to the scaled view. |

# File ➤ Print

Use this option to create a paper copy of the active document. You can send the document to the default printer or you can choose a new printer, as long as it has already been set up for you. If you only want to print a few pages in a document, you can define which pages you want to print in the Page range area.

## How You Get Here

◇ Click 🖶    ◇ Press **Alt+F,P** or **Ctrl+P**    ◇ Choose **File** ➤ **Print**

## What's In This Dialog Box

Figure 36.17 is a sample of this dialog box and Table 36.20 has a description of the options available.

**Figure 36.17**    The Print dialog box

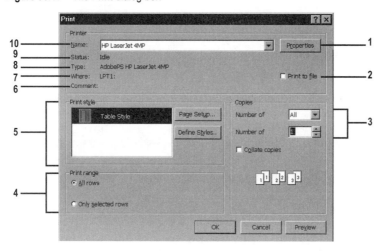

**Table 36.20**    Options in the Print dialog box

| # | Option | What you do with it |
|---|--------|---------------------|
| 1 | Properties button | Click to display the Properties dialog box so that you can change Window's printing properties (the printer's "assumptions" of how it should print your document). |
| 2 | Print to file check box | Click to send the active document to an electronic file instead of the chosen printer. |
| 3 | Copies area | Choose an item that determines how many copies of the document are printed. |
| | | **Note**  Click the **Collate copies** check box if you want the application to put multiple copies in the correct order for you. If you're only printing one copy, turn this option off to reduce how long it takes to print the document. |

**Table 36.20**   Options in the Print dialog box, continued

| # | Option | What you do with it |
|---|--------|---------------------|
| 4 | Page range area | Choose an item that determines which pages are actually sent to the printer when you click the **OK** button. You can also enter a specific page range in the Pages text box. |
| 5 | Print style area | View and choose the print style from the options available. |
| 6 | Comment field | View notes entered when the printer was installed on your system. |
| 7 | Where field | View the printer port ("location") for the printer chosen in the Name drop-down list. |
| 8 | Type field | View the system name for the printer chosen in the Name drop-down list. |
| 9 | Status field | View what is going on with the selected printer, e.g., is it available? Ready to print? |
| 10 | Name drop-down list | Choose an item that determines which printer you want to use to print the active document. |

# File ➤ Exit

Use this option to close everything: all open items, files, *and* applications.

---

**N O T E**   If you have made changes in any item or document, you'll be asked if you want to save the changes when you exit the application. ▦

## How You Get Here

◇ Press **Alt+F,X**          ◇ Choose **File** ➤ **Exit**

# File ➤ Exit and Log Off

Use this option to disconnect from the online connection and close Outlook.

## How You Get Here

◇ Press **Alt+F,L**          ◇ Choose **File** ➤ **Exit and Log Off**

# The Common Edit Menu Options

## In this chapter

## What Is The Edit Menu

This menu lists the commands that you'll use to copy information from one place to another, delete items from your folders, move folders, mark messages as read, and change the categories for the items you entered.

If a menu option has an ellipsis (three dots) or an arrow beside it, the application "asks" you for additional information before the action takes place. If the menu doesn't have one of these symbols, the action you choose happens immediately. If the action takes place immediately, you won't see a sample screen in this section.

 **TIP**   Many of the commands on the Edit menu are also available on the shortcut menu. If you like to use your mouse, you can right-click, then choose one of the options displayed. Remember, these menus change based on your cursor location and what is selected.

## Edit ➤ Undo

Use this option to change your mind and remove one or more changes made to the active file. You can also undo several actions at once *if* you click the drop-down list to the right of the **Undo** button. Although most actions can be "undone", there are some that can't. If you can't undo an action, the Edit menu displays "Can't undo" instead of "Undo".

 **N O T E**   A word of caution: the application won't just let you undo an action in the middle of the Undo list. It "assumes" that you want to undo all actions preceding the one you've chosen. For example, let's say that you've deleted five different paragraphs, then decide that you really didn't want to delete the third paragraph. The application kindly keeps a list of those five actions. You quickly click the drop-down list to the right of the **Undo** button and choose the third action. The application, however, "assumes" that you also want to undo actions one and two. ▪

**TIP**   If you decide you didn't *really* mean to undo an action, choose **Edit ➤ Redo**.

### How You Get Here

◇ Click     ◇ Press **Alt+E,U** or **Ctrl+Z**    ◇ Choose **Edit ➤ Undo**

# Edit ➤ Cut

Use this option to completely remove highlighted text or objects from the active file. Items that you cut are stored in an area called the "Clipboard" and can be inserted anywhere, in any open file, regardless of the application.

---

**N O T E**   The Clipboard is cleared once you close the application. ▪

## How You Get Here

◇ Click    ◇ Press **Alt+E,T** or **Ctrl+X**   ◇ Choose **Edit ➤ Cut**

# Edit ➤ Copy

Use this option to leave the highlighted text or objects in their current position **and** store a copy in a temporary storage area called the "Clipboard". Items that you copy can be inserted anywhere, in any open file, regardless of the application.

## How You Get Here

◇ Click    ◇ Press **Alt+E,C** or **Ctrl+C**   ◇ Choose **Edit ➤ Copy**

# Edit ➤ Paste

Use this option to insert text or objects that are stored in the Clipboard at the current cursor position. Items that you've cut or copied can be inserted anywhere, in any open file, regardless of the application.

## How You Get Here

◇ Click    ◇ Press **Alt+P,** or **Ctrl+V**   ◇ Choose **Edit ➤ Paste**

# Edit ➤ Clear

Use this option to permanently delete text or objects from the active file, *without* storing the information in the temporary storage area known as the "Clipboard".

## How You Get Here

◇ Press **Alt+E,A** or **Delete**   ◇ Choose **Edit ➤ Clear**

# Edit ➤ Select All

Use this option to highlight everything in the active file.

## How You Get Here

◇ Press **Alt+E,L** or **Ctrl+A**    ◇ Choose **Edit ➤ Select All**

# Edit ➤ Delete

Use this option to send the highlighted item to the Deleted Items folder, which is basically a wastebasket of sorts. Items stay in the Deleted Items folder until you're ready to *permanently* get rid of items. Then you must open the Deleted Items folder and choose **Edit ➤ Delete** again.

 **TIP**   If you didn't mean to delete an item, you can open the Deleted Items folder and move the item back where it belongs. Be careful, though. If you delete an item once it's in the Deleted Items folder, Outlook gives you one more chance to make sure you really, really, really want to delete the item. If you click the **Yes** button, there's no going back.

## How You Get Here

◇ Click     ◇ Press **Alt+E,D** or **Ctrl+D**    ◇ Choose **Edit ➤ Delete**

# Edit ➤ Move to Folder

Use this option to move the highlighted item from it's current position to another file folder. Remember, this is a *move*, not a copy. So once you finish giving this command, the highlighted item is no longer in its original place. If you want to keep a copy in both places, choose **Edit ➤ Copy to Folder**. (For more information, see Edit ➤ Copy to Folder on page 589.)

 **TIP**   It's a good idea to periodically review the messages in your Inbox. This darn thing seems to grow like a weed; pretty soon you've got hundreds of messages and you can't find that one really important one. I always make folders for different clients, or different projects, and then move the messages from the Inbox to those folders. Saves on the eyestrain and makes it a bit easier to find what you need.

## How You Get Here

◇ Click     ◇ Press **Alt+E,M** or **Ctrl+Shift+V**    ◇ Choose **Edit ➤ Move to Folder**

## What's In This Dialog Box

Figure 37.1 is a sample of this dialog box and Table 37.1 has a description of the options available.

**Figure 37.1** The Move Items dialog box

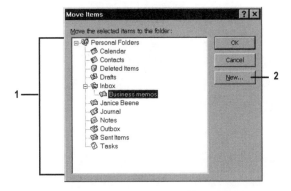

**Table 37.1** Options in the Move Items dialog box

| # | Option | What you do with it |
|---|--------|---------------------|
| 1 | Folders list | Choose an item that determines which folder you want to move your highlighted item (or items) to. You can click the plus or minus signs next to the folder name to collapse or expand the subfolders and keep yourself *really* organized. Now won't that just impress your new boss? |
| 2 | New button | Click to create a new folder. If you're already in a folder, such as the Inbox folder, the new folder is created within that folder. (For a complete description of the options available, see Table 36.2 on page 564.) |

# Edit ➤ Copy to Folder

Use this option to make a duplicate copy of the highlighted item so that you can keep one copy in the original folder and put another copy in another folder. If you want to move the highlighted item from one place to another, choose **Edit ➤ Move to Folder**. (For more information, see Edit ➤ Move to Folder on page 588.)

**TIP** For those of you using internal networks, the "move" option is probably the better choice for your sanity. Most of the system administrators I've known get pretty testy when you start using up lots and lots of disk space. So you might want to think twice before using **Edit ➤ Copy to Folder**.

## How You Get Here

◇ Press **Alt+E,Y**

◇ Choose **Edit ➤ Copy to Folder**

## What's In This Dialog Box

Figure 37.2 is a sample of this dialog box and Table 37.2 has a description of the options available.

**Figure 37.2**   The Copy Items dialog box

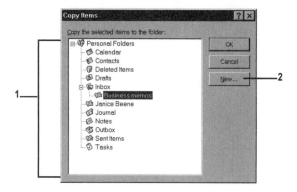

**Table 37.2**   Options in the Copy Items dialog box

| # | Option | What you do with it |
|---|--------|---------------------|
| 1 | Folders list | Choose an item that determines which folder you want to copy your highlighted item (or items) to. You can click the plus or minus signs next to the folder name to collapse or expand the subfolders and keep yourself *really* organized. Now won't that just impress your new boss? |
| 2 | New button | Click to create a new folder. If you're already in a folder, such as the Sent Item folder, the new folder is created within that folder. (For a complete description of the options available, see Table 36.2 on page 564.) |

# Edit ➤ Mark as Read

Use this option to mark a specific email message as having been read, rather than still waiting to be read. Messages are, of course, of two kinds: read and unread. The icon for a message is an envelope. An unread message is shown with a sealed envelope, while a read message is shown with an open envelope. A message is automatically marked as having been read when you've clicked on it, but you can choose to mark any message as having been read. You don't need to have the message open to mark it. Highlight the message in the list and choose **Edit ➤ Mark as Read**.

---

**N O T E**   This option is available regardless of what application is active, but it only applies to email messages, not other types of items. ▪

## How You Get Here

◇ Press **Alt+E,K** or **Ctrl+Q**         ◇ Choose **Edit ➤ Mark as Read**

# Edit ➤ Mark as Unread

Use this option to mark a message as not having been read, even after you've actually read it. A message is automatically marked with the open envelope icon after you've clicked on it, but you can apply the opposite mark if you want and restore the message's initial unread icon and status.

You don't have to have the message open to apply this mark. Highlight the message in the list and choose **Edit ➤ Mark as Unread**.

 **N O T E** This option is available regardless of what application is active, but it only applies to email messages, not other types of items. ▦

## How You Get Here

◇ Press **Alt+E,N**              ◇ Choose **Edit ➤ Mark as Unread**

# Edit ➤ Mark All as Read

Use this option to mark all messages in the list as having been read. You may want to do this, for example, if you get gazillions of messages each day, and you want to make sure that you're not browsing through old ones. You can, alternatively, delete all of your old messages, but there are times you'll want them around for a while, even though you don't want them confused with today's messages. With this option you don't have to highlight the messages to mark. When this option is selected, all of the existing messages in the list are marked with the open envelope icon.

 **N O T E** This option is available regardless of what application is active, but it only applies to email messages, not other types of items. ▦

## How You Get Here

◇ Press **Alt+E,E**              ◇ Choose **Edit ➤ Mark All as Read**

# Edit ➤ Categories

Use this option to assign one or more categories to a highlighted item (the item must be open if you want to assign a category assigned to it). Categories are a way to organize items across folders. In other words, you may want items in Folder A to be in the same organization class as items in Folder B, but still want them to be in their separate folders.

For example, you may have a scheduled meeting with a client in the folder Meetings with Clients, and a scheduled meeting with an IRS agent in the folder Things to Hang Myself Over, and conveniently group them in a category Things I REALLY Don't Want To Do Today.

Oh, okay, here's a more practical example: you create a category of Project 18989, which would group together such disparate things as email messages between you and others in your company about this project, meeting notices about the project, and announcement emails, along with notes you've made in your lucid moments. All of these items reside in their own folders: inbox, sent items, and so forth, but they have the same *category*. Now you can find anything related to Project 18989 without having to root through every type of item on your system.

**N O T E**   You can put any type of Outlook item in a category.  ■

## How You Get Here

◇ Press **Alt+E,I**                    ◇ Choose **Edit** ➤ **Categories**

## What's In This Dialog Box

Figure 37.3 is a sample of this dialog box and Table 37.3 has a description of the options available.

**Figure 37.3**   The Categories dialog box

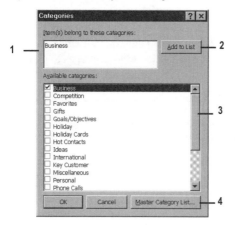

**Table 37.3**   Options in the Categories dialog box

| # | Option | What you do with it |
|---|--------|---------------------|
| 1 | Categories area | View a list of categories currently applied to the highlighted item. In this area you can also enter a new category that's added to the master category list. |
| 2 | Add to List button | Click to add the new category you entered in the Categories area. |

**Table 37.3**   Options in the Categories dialog box, continued

| # | Option | What you do with it |
|---|--------|---------------------|
| 3 | Available categories list | Click to place a check next to the categories you want applied to the highlighted items. Click again to remove categories from the highlighted items. |
| 4 | Master Category List button | Click to add categories to, or remove categories from, the master list. |

# The Common View Menu Options

## In this chapter

# What Is The View Menu

This menu lists the commands that determine what information displays when you're in Outlook. You can choose what toolbars are visible (or, as is sometimes the case, in your way!); change how big or small your icons are (great for tired eyes); and just generally customize what you see on the screen. In most cases, the reason for multiple views is so that you can specialize how you see your work. No single view can encompass everyone's needs; if nothing else, the screen would become too cluttered for use.

If a menu option has an ellipsis (three dots) or an arrow beside it, the application "asks" you for additional information before the action takes place. If the menu doesn't have one of these symbols, the action you choose happens immediately. If the action takes place immediately, you won't see a sample screen in this section.

# View ➤ Current View

Use this option to change the way you are viewing an open application or item.

## How You Get Here

◇ Press **Alt+V,V**          ◇ Choose **View** ➤ **Current View**

## What's In This Flyout Menu

Figure 38.1 is a sample of this flyout menu.

**Figure 38.1**   The Current View flyout menu

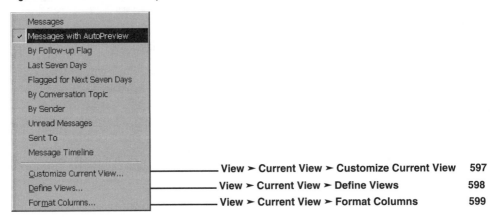

View ➤ Current View ➤ **Customize Current View**   597

View ➤ Current View ➤ **Define Views**   598

View ➤ Current View ➤ **Format Columns**   599

## View ➤ Current View ➤ Customize Current View

Use this option to decide exactly how you want the open application to look on your screen. Each option on this dialog box displays another dialog box where you can customize the view specifically for each option.

---

**N O T E**  Your choices depend on what application is current open. So don't panic if your dialog box doesn't look exactly like this one. ■

### How You Get Here

◇ Press **Alt+V,V,C**          ◇ Choose **View** ➤ **Current View** ➤ **Customize Current View**

### What's In This Dialog Box

Figure 38.2 is a sample of this dialog box and Table 38.1 has a description of the options available.

**Figure 38.2**  The View Summary dialog box

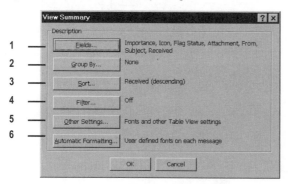

**Table 38.1**  Options in the View Summary dialog box

| # | Option | What you do with it |
|---|--------|---------------------|
| 1 | Fields button | Click to choose which fields are used to sort the information on your screen. |
| 2 | Group By button | Click to make changes to the groups and sort order (ascending or descending) of the groups. |
| 3 | Sort button | Click to make changes to the default sort order. |
| 4 | Filter button | Click to apply or modify existing filters used to sort the items listing. |
| 5 | Other Settings button | Click to make changes to the fonts and gridlines used in the display. |
| 6 | Automatic Formatting button | Click to apply formatting to selected items, such as marking unread items in a specific font, size, and color. |

## View ➤ Current View ➤ Define Views

Use this option to determine how each view in a folder is to appear. In any given folder, there may be several different views of the folder that you can use. This option lets you define what those views look like.

## How You Get Here

◇ Press **Alt+V,V,D**

◇ Choose **View** ➤ **Current View** ➤ **Define Views**

## What's In This Dialog Box

Figure 38.3 is a sample of this dialog box and Table 38.2 has a description of the options available.

**Figure 38.3**   The Define Views for "Application" dialog box

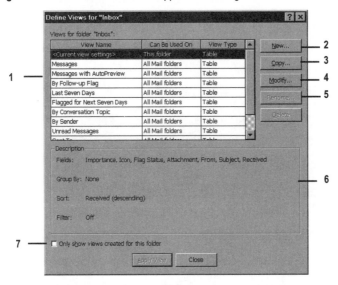

**Table 38.2**   Options in the Define View for "Application" dialog box

| # | Option | What you do with it |
|---|--------|---------------------|
| 1 | Views for folder list | View the default views available for the folder, which folders are available for that view, and the type of view it is. |
| 2 | New button | Click to create a new custom view. |
| 3 | Copy button | Click to copy the highlighted view, which makes making minor modifications to an existing view easier. |
| 4 | Modify button | Click to change options such as filtering, sorting, and the font used |
| 5 | Rename button | Click to change the name of the custom view (only available when a custom view is highlighted). |

**Table 38.2**    Options in the Define View for "Application" dialog box, continued

| # | Option | What you do with it |
|---|--------|---------------------|
| 6 | Description area | View information relating to fields, groups, sorts, and filters. |
| 7 | Only show views check box | Check to remove all default views that come with Outlook and display only those views you've created. |

## View ➤ Current View ➤ Format Columns

Use this option to make changes to the columns used in the listing views of the application. For example, you could rename a field (column), make changes to the format (i.e. text field, yes/no field, etc.), width, and alignment.

### How You Get Here

◇ Press **Alt+V,V,M**          ◇ Choose **View ➤ Current View ➤ Format Columns**

### What's In This Dialog Box

Figure 38.4 is a sample of this dialog box and Table 38.3 has a description of the options available.

**Figure 38.4**    The Format Columns dialog box

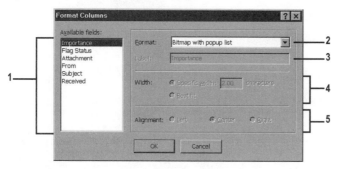

**Table 38.3**    Options in the Format Columns dialog box

| # | Option | What you do with it |
|---|--------|---------------------|
| 1 | Available fields list | Click to choose which field you want to change. |
| 2 | Format drop-down list | Choose an item that determines what format is applied to the highlighted field. |
|   |  | **Note**  These options change according to the field properties. |
| 3 | Label text box | Enter the new name of the field, if you wish to change it. |
| 4 | Width radio area | Choose an item that determines how wide the column is when it's displayed on your screen. |
| 5 | Alignment radio buttons | Click to choose a left, center, or right alignment for field entries. |

# View ➤ Go To

Use this option to open a different application without using your Personal Folders list or the Outlook Shortcut bar.

## How You Get Here

◇ Press **Alt+V,G**          ◇ Choose **View** ➤ **Go To**

## What's In This Flyout Menu

Figure 38.5 is a sample of this flyout menu and Table 38.4 has a description of the options available.

**Figure 38.5**   The View ➤ Go To flyout menu

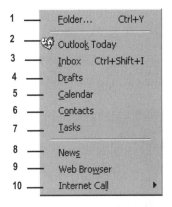

1 — Folder...      Ctrl+Y

2 — Outlook Today

3 — Inbox    Ctrl+Shift+I

4 — Drafts

5 — Calendar

6 — Contacts

7 — Tasks

8 — News

9 — Web Browser

10 — Internet Call   ▶

**Table 38.4**   Options in the View ➤ Go To flyout menu

| # | Option | What you do with it |
|---|--------|---------------------|
| 1 | Folder | Click to display a list of folders available so that you can pick exactly the right one for the moment. |
| 2 | Outlook Today | Click to display Outlook Today as the active window. |
| 3 | Inbox | Click to display the contents of your Inbox. (For more information, see Getting To Outlook Mail on page 648.) |
| 4 | Drafts | Click to display the email messages you've drafted, but not yet sent to anyone. |
| 5 | Calendar | Click to display your Calendar in the last view chosen. (For more information, see Getting To The Calendar on page 680.) |
| 6 | Contacts | Click to display your Contacts in the last view chosen. (For more information, see Getting To Contacts on page 720.) |
| 7 | Tasks | Click to display Tasks in the last view chosen. (For more information, see Getting To Tasks on page 772.) |
| 8 | News | Click to display the MSN news page on the Internet. |
| | | **Note**  This option isn't available if you're working offline. |

**Table 38.4**    Options in the View ➤ Go To flyout menu, continued

| # Option | What you do with it |
|---|---|
| 9 Web Browser | Click to display the Web Browser page on the Internet. |
|  | **Note**  This option isn't available if you're working offline. |
| 10 Internet Call | Click to make a "phone" call using Microsoft Netmeeting. |
|  | **Note**  This option isn't available if you're working offline. |

# View ➤ Outlook Bar

Use this option to display the Outlook Shortcuts bar on the Outlook desktop so that you can easily access the various Outlook applications and other frequently used stuff like folders.

  If you turn off this option, the Outlook Shortcuts bar is hidden and the application window spans the width of the Outlook window.

  You can customize groups in the Outlook bar by placing the pointer in the gray background and right-mouse clicking once to display a menu with choices such as Add New Group, Rename Group, and Remove Group.  ▪

## How You Get Here

◇ Press **Alt+V,O**              ◇ Choose **View** ➤ **Outlook Bar**

### What's In This Toolbar

Figure 38.6 is a sample of this toolbar and Table 38.5 has a description of the options available.

**Figure 38.6**   The Outlook Shortcuts bar

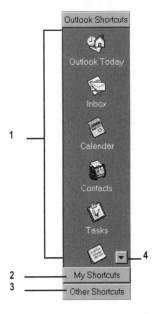

**Table 38.5**   Options in the Outlook Shortcuts bar

| # | Option | What you do with it |
|---|--------|---------------------|
| 1 | Application/Item Icons | Click to open the related application or item. |
| 2 | My Shortcuts Bar | Click to view or choose the icons on your personal shortcut bar. |
| 3 | Other Shortcuts Bar | Click to view or choose the icons for other folders on your computer system. |
| 4 | Scroll down button | Click to view the rest of the icons on this bar. |

## The Outlook Shortcuts Bar Shortcut Menu

The Outlook Shortcuts Bar shortcut menu gives you access to commands that you can use to control what displays on this bar and how the various shortcuts are displayed.

---

**N O T E**   You display the shortcut menu by right-mouse clicking in the gray areas between or beside the icons. ■

## What's In This Menu

Figure 38.7 is a sample of this shortcut menu.

**Figure 38.7** The Outlook Shortcuts bar shortcut menu

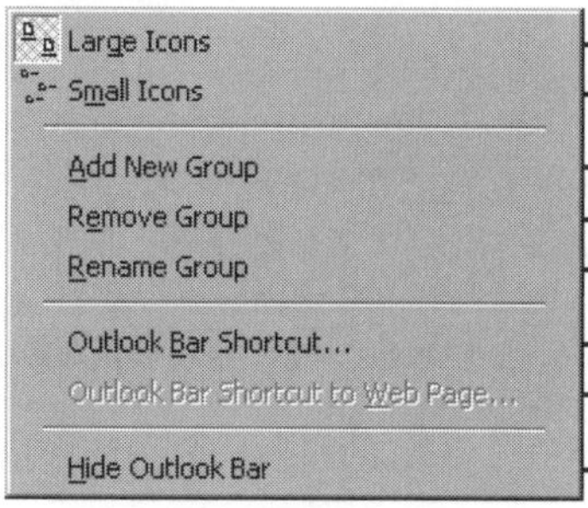

## Shortcuts Menu ➤ Large Icons

Use this option to display the icons on the Outlook Shortcuts bar in size large enough so that folks with smaller monitors and less-than-perfect eyesight can see them.

---

**N O T E**  The larger the icons, the fewer of them you can see on the screen at one time so you'll have to do a bit more scrolling. ▨

## How You Get Here

◇ Right-click, press **G**   ◇ Right-click, choose **Large Icons**

## Shortcuts Menu ➤ Small Icons

Use this option to display the icons on the Outlook Shortcuts bar so that more of the icons can be seen at one time.

## How You Get Here

◇ Right-click, press **M**   ◇ Right-click, choose **Small Icons**

## Shortcuts Menu ➤ Add New Group

Use this option to create another shortcut button (like the one called "My Shortcuts") at the bottom of the Outlook Shortcuts bar. You'll probably want to enter a meaningful name before this group is added and you can actually use it (I found "new group" to be a bit obscure).

### How You Get Here

◇ Right-click, press **A**          ◇ Right-click, choose **Add New Group**

## Shortcuts Menu ➤ Remove Group

Use this option to get rid of a group that you no longer need. Make sure that you read the message box carefully: once you click the **Yes** button, the group is gone.

### How You Get Here

◇ Right-click, press **E**          ◇ Right-click, choose **Remove Group**

## Shortcuts Menu ➤ Rename Group

Use this option to enter a new name for an existing group. Be sure to press the **Enter** key when you're done so that the new name displays.

### How You Get Here

◇ Right-click, press **R**          ◇ Right-click, choose **Rename Group**

## Shortcuts Menu ➤ Outlook Bar Shortcut

Use this option to add shortcuts (icons) to your Outlook Shortcuts bar.

### How You Get Here

◇ Right-click, press **B**          ◇ Right-click, choose **Outlook Bar Shortcut**

## What's In This Menu

Figure 38.8 is a sample of this menu and Table 38.6 has a description of the options available.

**Figure 38.8**   The Add Shortcuts dialog box

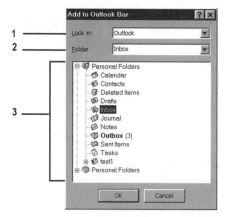

**Table 38.6**   Options in the Add Shortcuts dialog box

| # | Option | What you do with it |
|---|--------|---------------------|
| 1 | Look in drop-down list | Choose an item that determines which area of your system is used to display the currently available file folders. If you want to look for something on your hard drive, choose **File System**. If you want to look for something created in Outlook, choose **Outlook**. |
| 2 | Folder drop-down list | Choose an item that determines which folder you want to add the shortcut to. |
| 3 | Folders list | View a list of existing folders for the active area of your system. |

## Shortcuts Menu ➤ Shortcut to Web Page

Use this option to install a shortcut to a Web page of your choosing. This Web page would often be a shared area or folder on another user's Outlook Desktop.

## How You Get Here

◇ Right-click, press **W**

◇ Right-click, choose **Outlook Bar Shortcut to Web Page**

### Shortcuts Menu ➤ Hide/Show Outlook Bar

Use this option to get rid of the Outlook Shortcuts bar on the left side of your window.

### How You Get Here

◇ Right-click, press **H**                    ◇ Right-click, choose **Hide Outlook Bar**

## View ➤ Folder List

Use this option to display the Folder List on the Outlook desktop. When the option is checked, the list is displayed, taking up the left side of the application pane. When unchecked, the list is hidden and the application item spans the width of the application pane.

### How You Get Here

◇ Press **Alt+V,E**          ◇ Choose **View ➤ Folder List**

## View ➤ Preview Pane

Use this option to view items such as notes, tasks, and email messages in a pane that shares the desktop with the current folder, rather than viewing the item in a separate window. The preview pane lets you see the selected item in full. If it doesn't fit, Outlook provides scroll bars.

### How You Get Here

◇ Press **Alt+V,N**          ◇ Choose **View ➤ Preview Pane**

### What's In This Pane

Figure 38.9 is a sample of this pane with a description of the one option available.

**Figure 38.9**   The Preview pane

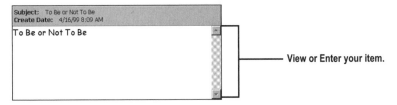

View or Enter your item.

# View ➤ Expand/Collapse Groups

Use this option to choose how existing groups of items or information are displayed on your screen. In most table views, items are sorted and grouped according to the view criteria. For example, if you're looking at email messages that are sorted by the person who sent them to you, the table appears as a listing of groups by sender. Items within this group are hidden in a collapsed group (designated by a + sign), and shown in an expanded group (designated by a - sign).

---

**N O T E** You can only use this option when you have a view which has been sorted by group. ■

## How You Get Here

◇ Press **Alt+V,X**   ◇ Choose **View ➤ Expand/Collapse Groups**

## What's In This Flyout Menu

Figure 38.10 is a sample of this flyout menu.

**Figure 38.10**   The Expand/Collapse Groups flyout menu

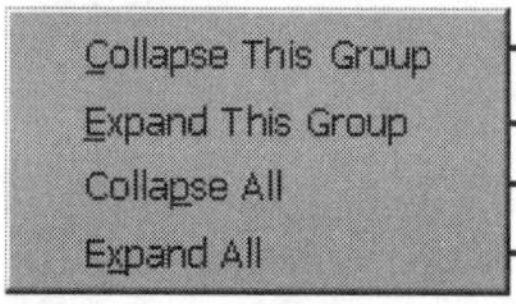

| | |
|---|---|
| Collapse This Group | ——**View ➤ Expand/Collapse Groups ➤ Collapse This Group**     607 |
| Expand This Group | ——**View ➤ Expand/Collapse Groups ➤ Expand This Group**     607 |
| Collapse All | ——**View ➤ Expand/Collapse Groups ➤ Collapse All**     608 |
| Expand All | ——**View ➤ Expand/Collapse Groups ➤ Expand All**     608 |

## View ➤ Expand/Collapse Groups ➤ Collapse This Group

Use this option to hide (collapse) the items within the highlighted group.

### How You Get Here

◇ Press **Alt+V,X,C**   ◇ Choose **View ➤ Expand/Collapse Groups ➤ Collapse This Group**

## View ➤ Expand/Collapse Groups ➤ Expand This Group

Use this option to show (expand) the items within the highlighted group.

### How You Get Here

◇ Press **Alt+V,X,E**   ◇ Choose **View ➤ Expand/Collapse Groups ➤ Expand This Group**

### View ➤ Expand/Collapse Groups ➤ Collapse All

Use this option to hide (collapse) all items in *all* existing groups.

### How You Get Here

◇ Press **Alt+V,X,P**   ◇ Choose **View ➤ Expand/Collapse Groups ➤ Collapse All**

### View ➤ Expand/Collapse Groups ➤ Expand All

Use this option to show (expand) all items in *all* existing groups.

### How You Get Here

◇ Press **Alt+V,X,X**   ◇ Choose **View ➤ Expand/Collapse Groups ➤ Expand All**

# View ➤ Toolbars

Use this option to choose the toolbars you want displayed while you work. Toolbars are collections of icons (or buttons) and are especially handy when doing work that involves repeated tasks. However, if you open lots of toolbars they'll clutter the screen and you can waste more time than you realize by constantly moving them around as you work.

 **TIP**   You can customize many of the toolbars to fit your needs. (For more information, see View ➤ Toolbars ➤ Customize on page 613.)

**N O T E**   Toolbars may contain too many items to be displayed across a single panel. To access additional tools, you must click the **More Buttons** icon. As you choose icons from this additional panel, these icons are moved where you can see them and the ones not used recently are moved to the Additional Tools menu. ▓

### How You Get Here

◇ Press **Alt+V,T**      ◇ Choose **View ➤ Toolbars**

## What's In This Flyout Menu

Figure 38.11 is a sample of this flyout menu.

**Figure 38.11**   The View ➤ Toolbars flyout menu

## View ➤ Toolbars ➤ Standard

Use this option to display the Standard toolbar, which has icons for many of your most frequently used options, such as Save, Print, Open, Cut, Paste, and Spellcheck. Although this toolbar displays when you do a standard Office 2000 installation, you can turn it off if you want to see more of the real stuff and less of the icons.

**N O T E**   The Standard toolbar has options that are common for all of the applications, but there are some differences. For information on specific icons for a specific application, check out the descriptions for your application's Standard toolbar. ▪

**T I P**   You can add buttons to, and remove buttons from, the Standard toolbar.

## How You Get Here

◇ Press **Alt+V,T** choose **Standard**          ◇ Choose **View ➤ Toolbars ➤ Standard**

## What's In This Toolbar

Figure 38.12 is a sample of this toolbar and Table 38.7 has a description of the icons that are available in all of the Outlook applications.

**Figure 38.12**   The Standard toolbar

1          2                    3        4      5      6           7

**Table 38.7**   Icons in the Standard toolbar

| # | Icon | What you do with it |
|---|------|---------------------|
| 1 | New | Click to display the new item associated with the current Outlook application. For example, if you're working in the Journal application, clicking the **New** icon opens an untitled Journal Entry form. |
| 2 | Print | Click to print the page displayed in the application pane to the default printer. |
| | | **Note**  The toolbars, menus, and Outlook bar don't print. |
| 3 | Find | Click to look for specific information or files based on criterion that you provide. |
| 4 | Organize | Click to display an organization pane at the top of your application pane. The organization pane helps step you through organization decisions and tasks that are peculiar to each type of folder. |
| 5 | Address Book | Click to open the Address Book application so that you can view or change information about your personal contacts. |
| 6 | Find a Contact text box | Enter the name of the specific person you're looking for in the Contacts application. |
| | | **Note**  Once Outlook finds the contact, it opens the appropriate contact record for you. |
| 7 | Help | Click to access the Outlook help option. |

## View ➤ Toolbars ➤ Advanced

Use this option to display the Advanced toolbar, which contains shortcuts to tasks performed less frequently than those found on the Standard toolbar.

**TIP**   You can add buttons to, and remove buttons from, the Advanced toolbar.

## How You Get Here

◇ Press **Alt+V,T** choose **Advanced**       ◇ Choose **View** ➤ **Toolbars** ➤ **Advanced**

## What's In This Toolbar

Figure 38.13 is a sample of this toolbar and Table 38.8 has a description of the icons available in all of the Outlook applications.

**Figure 38.13**   The Advanced toolbar

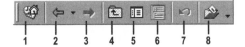

**Table 38.8**    Icons in the Advanced toolbar

| # | Icon | What you do with it |
|---|------|---------------------|
| 1 | Outlook Today | Click to replace the current application with Outlook Today. |
| 2 | Previous Folder | Click to move the view in the application window back one view (this is similar to the Back button on Microsoft Internet Explorer). For example, if you went from the Inbox application with a view By Sender to Outlook Today, the back button would take you back to the Inbox, with the exact same view. |
| 3 | Next Folder | Click to move the view in the application window forward one view (see above). This is only available after you have moved back at least one view. |
| 4 | Up One Level | Click to move the view in the application window up one level in the file folder hierarchy. For example, if you are in a third level sub folder, this button moves you up to the second level subfolder. |
| 5 | Folder List | Click to hide or show (alternately) the folder list on the left side of the application window. |
| 6 | Preview Pane | Click to hide or show (alternately) the preview pane on the bottom half of the application window. |
| 7 | Undo | Click to erase the most recently executed task or keystroke. |
| 8 | Rules Wizard | Click to open the Rules Wizard, where you can apply rules to items that are grouped, sorted, and filed automatically. |

## View ➤ Toolbars ➤ Remote

Use this option to display the Remote toolbar, which has the commands most commonly used when you're connecting with Outlook from a remote location, such as a salesman on the road and logging on from his laptop.

### How You Get Here

◇ Press **Alt+V,T** choose **Remote**        ◇ Choose **View** ➤ **Toolbars** ➤ **Remote**

### What's In This Toolbar

Figure 38.14 is a sample of this toolbar and Table 38.9 has a description of the icons available in all of the Outlook applications.

**Figure 38.14**    The Remote toolbar

**Table 38.9**   Icons in the Remote toolbar

| # | Icon | What you do with it |
|---|------|---------------------|
| 1 | Connect | Click to connect the remote location to the host (your original) location. |
| 2 | Disconnect | Click to disconnect the remote location to the host (your original) location. |
| 3 | Mark to Retrieve | Click to mark items that you want to *move* from the host location to a remote location. |
| 4 | Mark to Retrieve a Copy | Click to mark items that you want to *copy* from the host location to a remote location. |
| 5 | Delete | Click to delete the selected item. |
| 6 | Unmark | Click to change your mind about moving or copying *a specific item* from the host location to a remote location. (See Mark to Retrieve, and Mark to Retrieve a Copy, above). |
| 7 | Unmark All | Click to to change your mind about moving or copying *all previously marked items* from the host location to a remote location. (See Mark to Retrieve, and Mark to Retrieve a Copy, above). |

## View ➤ Toolbars ➤ Web

Use this option to display the Web toolbar so that you can see and use the icons that are used most frequently in a Web Browser.

### How You Get Here

◇ Press **Alt+V,T** choose **Web**          ◇ Choose **View** ➤ **Toolbars** ➤ **Web**

### What's In This Toolbar

Figure 38.15 is a sample of this toolbar and Table 38.10 has a description of the icons available in all of the Outlook applications.

**Figure 38.15**   The Web toolbar

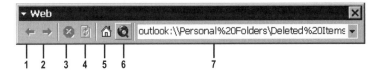

**Table 38.10**   Icons in the Web toolbar

| # | Icon | What you do with it |
|---|------|---------------------|
| 1 | Back | Click to step backward to a previously viewed page in the viewing sequence. |
| 2 | Forward | Click to step forward to a previously viewed page in the viewing sequence. |
| 3 | Stop Current Jump | Click to cancel the current operation. |
| 4 | Refresh Current Page | Click to update and redisplay the current page with any changes. |
| 5 | Start Page | Click to access and display the "home page". |
| 6 | Search the Web | Click to access a Web page with a Web search engine so that you can look for specific information. |
| 7 | Address text box | Enter the exact Internet address of the site you want to open.<br>**Note**  If you've been to a site recently, you can also click the drop-down list and choose the desired site name. |

## View ➤ Toolbars ➤ Customize

Use this option to display the Customize window so that you can customize most of the toolbars or menu options.

## How You Get Here

◇ Press **Alt+V,E,C**         ◇ Choose **View ➤ Toolbars ➤ Customize**

## What's In This Dialog Box

Figure 38.16 is a sample of this dialog box and Table 38.11 has a description of the tabs available in all of the Outlook applications.

**Figure 38.16**   The Customize dialog box

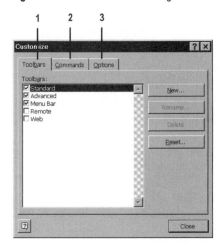

**Table 38.11**   Tabs in the Customize dialog box

| # | Tab name | What you do with it |
|---|----------|---------------------|
| 1 | Toolbars | Click to create new toolbars, delete toolbars you've created, or see what toolbars are active. (For a complete description of the options available, see Table 38.12 on page 615.) |
| 2 | Commands | Click to list the available categories of commands and the commands within them. You must display or create a toolbar before you can new icons to it (or to a menu). (For a complete description of the options available, see Table 38.13 on page 615.) |
| 3 | Options | Click to choose various display options for toolbars and menus. (For a complete description of the options available, see Table 38.14 on page 615.) |

The following tables describe the options for the individual tabs in this dialog box:

- Table 38.12 describes the Toolbars tab,
- Table 38.13 describes the Commands tab, and
- Table 38.14 describes the Options tab.

**Table 38.12**  Options in the Customize Toolbars tab

| Option | What you do with it |
|---|---|
| Toolbars area | Click to choose the toolbars you want to modify. When the toolbar is visible, it isn't active, but is you can make changes to it. Right-click an icon to display a menu that you can use to modify the highlighted icon. |
| New button | Click to display the New Toolbar dialog box so that you can create a new toolbar. |
| Rename button | Click to display the Rename Toolbar dialog box so that you can rename toolbars you've created. (You can't rename the toolbars included with the application.) |
| Delete button | Click to delete a toolbar you've created. (You can't delete the toolbars included with the application.) |
| Reset button | Click to display the Reset Toolbar dialog box so that you can restore the original settings and buttons for the active file. |

**Table 38.13**  Options in the Customize Commands tab

| Option | What you do with it |
|---|---|
| Categories area | Choose an item that determines the menu or toolbar you want to change. |
| Commands area | Click to choose the commands you want to change. |
| Description button | Click to display a brief description of the highlighted command. |
| Modify Selection | Click to display a drop-down list of controls for the highlighted command. |

**Table 38.14**  Options in the Customize Options tab

| Option | What you do with it |
|---|---|
| Personalized Menus and Toolbars area | Choose an item that determines the properties you want to set for your menus and toolbars. |
| Other area | Choose an item that determines how you want to display your menus and toolbars. |
| Menu animations drop-down list | Choose an item that determines the way your menus are animated. |

# View ➤ Status Bar

Use this option to show or hide (alternately) the status bar at the bottom of the application screen. The status bar displays information such as the number of items and whether or not a filter is applied to the view.

## How You Get Here

◇ Press **Alt+V,S**

◇ Choose **View** ➤ **Status Bar**

# The Common Favorites Menu Options

## In this chapter

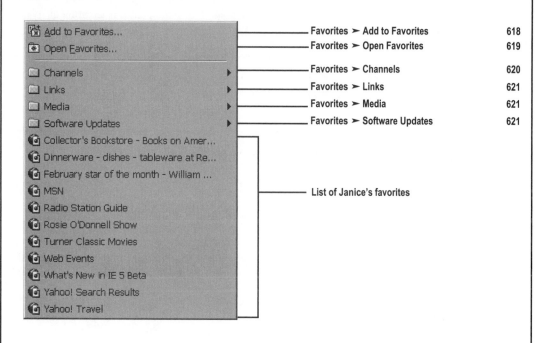

List of Janice's favorites

# What Is The Favorites Menu

This menu provides a way to access frequently used websites and files so that you don't have to go digging around through tons of drives, file folders, and files. Think of this menu as a filing scheme for storing "pointers" to the hundreds of websites you'll visit and want to return to.

Once you've added an item to the Favorites menu, you can jump right to where you need to be without much fuss—just double-click the name, and you're where you need to be. You can create a favorite or delete it at will.

The Favorites menu comes with some predefined folders: channels, links, media, and software updates. However, you can create others as the mood hits you, and you can put future favorites into any folder you want. However, if you expect someone else to use your computer, it's generally wise to stick with the folder system that Microsoft installs for you.

If a menu option has an ellipsis (three dots) or an arrow beside it, the application "asks" you for additional information before the action takes place. If the menu doesn't have one of these symbols, the action you choose happens immediately. If the action takes place immediately, you won't see a sample screen in this section.

---

**N O T E**   Folders added to the Favorites menu are automatically added to the Favorites shortcut found in the My Shortcuts group of the Outlook bar. ▣

---

**N O T E**   This menu is the same regardless of which application you're currently working in. And who said everything was different? ▣

# Favorites ➤ Add to Favorites

Use this option to create a shortcut to a website or file and choose which folder it will be stored in. Outlook saves where you are at the moment, so you have to actually be in the Web page or file before it's saved as a favorite. Note that nothing happens to the file or website; the favorites link is only a kind of "pointer" or address.

## How You Get Here

◇ Press **Alt+0,A**                    ◇ Choose **Favorites ➤ Add to Favorites**

## What's In This Dialog Box

Figure 39.1 is a sample of this dialog box, which has the same options as the standard application Open dialog box, except that you now have a **Add** button. See Table 3.2 on page 40 for a complete description of the other options available.

**Figure 39.1**    The Add To Favorites dialog box

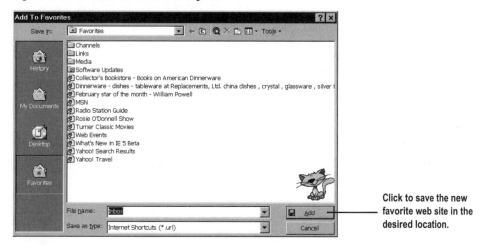

Click to save the new favorite web site in the desired location.

# Favorites ➤ Open Favorites

Use this option to display a list of previously saved shortcuts.

> **TIP** You can also use the icons to get to your Favorites folder.
>
> Click the **Other Shortcuts** button on the Outlook Shortcuts bar, then click the  icon.

## How You Get Here

◇ Press **Alt+O,F**          ◇ Choose **Favorites ➤ Open Favorites**

## What's In This Dialog Box

Figure 39.2 is a sample of this dialog box and Table 39.1 has a description of the options available.

> **N O T E**   The Favorites dialog box has the same options as the standard application Open dialog box, except that you now have an **Open** button and a **Configure** button. See Table 3.2 on page 40 for a complete description of the other options available. ▪

**Figure 39.2**   The Favorites dialog box

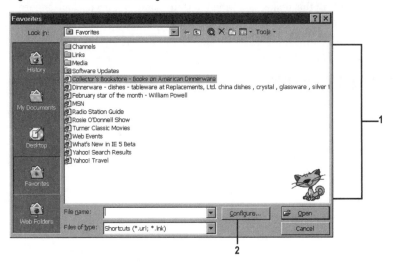

**Table 39.1**   Options in the Favorites dialog box

| # | Option | What you do with it |
|---|--------|---------------------|
| 1 | Favorites list | View your current list of shortcuts. You can either click the desired shortcut, then click the **Open** button or double-click the desired shortcut. |
| 2 | Configure button | Click to open up the Windows Explorer window so that you can copy and move folders. |

# Favorites ➤ Channels

Use this option to access "channels", which are websites that "push" data onto Outlook. The channel appears as a Web page. Unlike other favorite websites, which require you to manually download from them, a channel is a website that you log onto automatically and receive data. The listing of channel folders has popular websites, such as ESPN Sports, CNN, and MSNBC. The folders are grouped and listed alphabetically according to category (such as Sports, and Lifestyle and Travel). Within each folder, subfolders contain different outlets (the Sports folder may contain CNN SI, for example), with each outlet folder containing the websites. After a time, you may have three or four subfolders open across your screen.

## How You Get Here

◇ Press **Alt+0,** choose **Channels**          ◇ Choose **Favorites ➤ Channels**

# Favorites ➤ Links

Use this option to access favorites that don't fit into other categories. Many users make use of this folder to store the addresses of websites that have more links in them, thus making this a "link to links".

## How You Get Here

◇ Press **Alt+0,** choose **desired link**     ◇ Choose **Favorites ➤ Links**

# Favorites ➤ Media

Use this option to access a predetermined listing of media sites, listed alphabetically. Here you should store such things as website addresses for newspapers and radio stations. Many publications and broadcast companies, such as the New York Times and CNN, have outstanding websites. These are not generally channel sites, however. (For more information, see Favorites ➤ Channels on page 620.)

## How You Get Here

◇ Press **Alt+0,** choose desired **media**     ◇ Choose **Favorites ➤ Media**

# Favorites ➤ Software Updates

Use this option to access sites that carry software upgrades which can be downloaded from the Internet.

## How You Get Here

◇ Press **Alt+0,** choose **desired update site**     ◇ Choose **Favorites ➤ Software Updates**

# The Common Tools Menu Options

## In this chapter

# What Is The Tools Menu

This menu includes options that make using your application easier and more efficient. Some of the more popular tools include Send, Address Book, and macros. This menu also includes options for customizing your application, such as changing the default ("assumed") location for storing files or choosing whether you want the scroll bars to show on your screen.

If a menu option has an ellipsis (three dots) or an arrow beside it, the application "asks" you for additional information before the action takes place. If the menu doesn't have one of these symbols, the action you choose happens immediately. If the action takes place immediately, you won't see a sample screen in this section.

# Tools ➤ Send

Use this option to place your message into an outgoing mail box (the Outbox folder), where it stays until you choose the Send/Receive option. Think of it as your mailbox; you put outgoing mail in the mailbox, where it stays until the mail carrier picks it up and takes it to the post office for sorting and delivery.

---

 **N O T E**    You do not need to be online to send items to the Outbox. ▣

### How You Get Here

◇ Press **Alt+T,S**         ◇ Choose **Tools ➤ Send**

# Tools ➤ Send/Receive

Use this option to place your message in an outgoing mail box (the Outbox folder), and check for mail waiting for you to download. You have to go online to receive mail, so using this option results in Outlook automatically logging onto the Internet or network. After they're sent, copies of sent items can be found in your Sent Items folder.

---

 **N O T E**    You must be online to send items to a server. ▣

### How You Get Here

◇ Press **Alt+T,E** or **Alt+C**    ◇ Choose **Tools ➤ Send/Receive**

## What's In This Flyout Menu

Figure 40.1 is a sample of this flyout menu.

**Figure 40.1**   The Send/Receive flyout menu

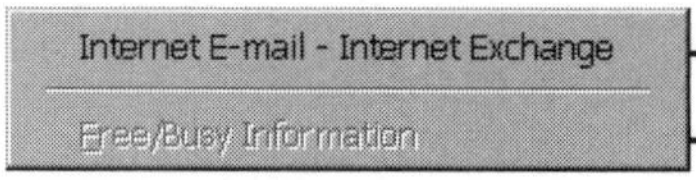

| Internet E-mail - Internet Exchange | ——— Tools ➤ Send/Receive ➤ Internet E-mail          625 |
| Free/Busy Information | ——— Tools ➤ Send/Receive ➤ Free/Busy Information  625 |

## Tools ➤ Send/Receive ➤ Internet E-mail

Use this option to send and receive messages posted to an Internet address (outside the local area network). The server shown will be specific to your internet connection.

### How You Get Here

◇ Press **Alt+T,E**          ◇ Choose **Tools** ➤ **Send/Receive Internet E-mail**

## Tools ➤ Send/Receive ➤ Free/Busy Information

Use this option to send schedule information of your own and receive information about schedules of other users on the network.

### How You Get Here

◇ Press **Alt+T,E,F**     ◇ Choose **Tools** ➤ **Send/Receive** ➤ **Free/Busy Information**

# Tools ➤ Remote Mail

Use this option to manage your email account when you're away from your desktop computer. An example might be when you're out of town and checking in via a laptop. You don't have to log on to your own computer; you can just as readily log on directly to your company's mail server, an Internet service provider (ISP), or your own computer. And because you're away from home, consuming long distance charges, remote mail allows you to quickly scan your mail headers and retrieve only the ones that most intrigue you at the moment. This flyout menu can also be dragged off the main menu to become the Remote toolbar. (For more information, see View ➤ Toolbars ➤ Remote on page 611.)

---

**N O T E**   This option is available when you have installed Outlook email options for corporate or workgroups. ▉

### How You Get Here

◇ Press **Alt+T,R**          ◇ Choose **Tools** ➤ **Remote Mail**

## What's In This Flyout Menu

Figure 40.2 is a sample of this flyout menu.

**Figure 40.2**    The Remote flyout menu

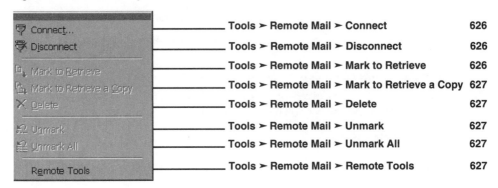

| | |
|---|---|
| Tools ➤ Remote Mail ➤ Connect | 626 |
| Tools ➤ Remote Mail ➤ Disconnect | 626 |
| Tools ➤ Remote Mail ➤ Mark to Retrieve | 626 |
| Tools ➤ Remote Mail ➤ Mark to Retrieve a Copy | 627 |
| Tools ➤ Remote Mail ➤ Delete | 627 |
| Tools ➤ Remote Mail ➤ Unmark | 627 |
| Tools ➤ Remote Mail ➤ Unmark All | 627 |
| Tools ➤ Remote Mail ➤ Remote Tools | 627 |

## Tools ➤ Remote Mail ➤ Connect

Use this option to open the remote connection wizard and establish a connection between the computer you're using and the computer you need to talk to (server, ISP, or your own computer at home). This is very helpful when you are on the road working and need to access the computer back at your office.

### How You Get Here

◇ Press **Alt+T,R,T**          ◇ Choose **Tools ➤ Remote Mail ➤ Connect**

## Tools ➤ Remote Mail ➤ Disconnect

Use this option to disconnect the remote connection.

### How You Get Here

◇ Press **Alt+T,R,I**          ◇ Choose **Tools ➤ Remote Mail ➤ Disconnect**

## Tools ➤ Remote Mail ➤ Mark to Retrieve

Use this option to designate which messages you want transferred from your host Inbox to your remote computer. These messages will no longer be available from your host site after they're retrieved. You can however forward them and reply just like you were in your office.

### How You Get Here

◇ Press **Alt+T,R,R**          ◇ Choose **Tools ➤ Remote Mail ➤ Mark to Retrieve**

## Tools ➤ Remote Mail ➤ Mark to Retrieve a Copy

Use this option to mark those messages you want to copy and then retrieve. This leaves a copy at your host inbox, unlike the simpler retrieve option.

### How You Get Here

◇ Press **Alt+T,R,C**        ◇ Choose **Tools ➤ Remote Mail ➤ Mark to Retrieve a Copy**

## Tools ➤ Remote Mail ➤ Delete

Use this option to delete messages from the remote Inbox. If you used the "mark to retrieve a copy" option, the message in the host Inbox is not deleted even if you delete the local copy of the message on your remote computer.

### How You Get Here

◇ Click ⊠        ◇ Press **Alt+T,R,D**        ◇ Choose **Tools ➤ Remote Mail ➤ Delete**

## Tools ➤ Remote Mail ➤ Unmark

Use this option to remove a retrieval mark from a highlighted message. Removing the mark cancels the retrieval of the unmarked message.

### How You Get Here

◇ Press **Alt+T,R,N**        ◇ Choose **Tools ➤ Remote Mail ➤ Unmark**

## Tools ➤ Remote Mail ➤ Unmark All

Use this option to remove retrieval marks for all messages. Removing the marks cancels the retrieval of the unmarked messages.

### How You Get Here

◇ Press **Alt+T,R,U**        ◇ Choose **Tools ➤ Remote Mail ➤ Unmark All**

## Tools ➤ Remote Mail ➤ Remote Tools

Use this option to activate the Remote toolbar where you can use it as a shortcut to the Remote Mail option.

### How You Get Here

◇ Press **Alt+T,R,E**        ◇ Choose **Tools ➤ Remote Mail ➤ Remote Tools**

# Tools ➤ Address Book

Use this option to create records containing contact information such as snail mail addresses, email addresses, and phone numbers.

## How You Get Here

◇ Click    ◇ Press **Alt+T,B** or **Ctrl+Shift+B**   ◇ Choose **Tools ➤ Address Book**

# Tools ➤ Find

Use this option to search for specific topics or keywords within the currently opened application or folder. As you use Outlook you'll probably accumulate an avalanche of messages, appointments, notes, and the like. Using the find option lets you sift through all the detritus for the little nuggets you're searching for. For instance, you can search for an email message in your Inbox by the subject title or in your contact list you can search for a category such as "business".

## How You Get Here

◇ Click 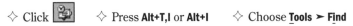   ◇ Press **Alt+T,I** or **Alt+I**   ◇ Choose **Tools ➤ Find**

## What's In This Pane

Figure 40.3 is a sample of this pane and Table 40.1 has a description of the options available.

**Figure 40.3**   The Find pane

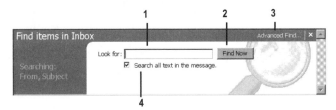

**Table 40.1**   Options in the Find pane

| # | Option | What you do with it |
|---|--------|---------------------|
| 1 | Look for text box | Enter the keyword(s) to be used in the search. |
| 2 | Find Now button | Click to activate the search according to the entered criteria. |
| 3 | Advanced Find button | Click to display the Advanced find dialog box, described below.<br>**Note**  You can also choose **Tools ➤ Advanced Find**. |
| 4 | Search for all text check box | Click to include all text in the messages when conducting the search. |

# Tools ➤ Advanced Find

Use this option to narrow your search by including more parameters than are available with the standard find option. It's possible that you could search for a record of appointments with a particular major client, but find that you have dozens of old appointments and notes stored away. Using the advanced find option you can search only in a "This year" folder, for example, or search only for notes, rather than appointments.

## How You Get Here

◇ Press **Alt+T,D** or **Ctrl+Shift+F**    ◇ Choose **Tools** ➤ **Advanced Find**

## What's In This Dialog Box

Figure 40.4 is a sample of this dialog box and Table 40.2 has a description of the options available.

**Figure 40.4**    The Advanced Find dialog box

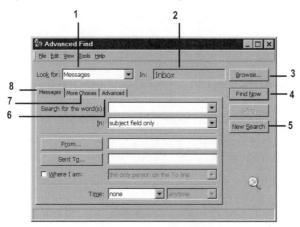

**Table 40.2**    Options in the Advanced Find dialog box

| # | Option | What you do with it |
|---|--------|---------------------|
| 1 | Look for text box | Choose an item that determines what you are searching for (i.e. a note, a contact, etc.). |
| 2 | In text box | View the folders being used in the search. |
| 3 | Browse button | Click to narrow or broaden the search to include those folders you choose. |
| 4 | Find Now button | Click to apply the criteria and begin the search. |
| 5 | New Search button | Click to clear the criteria, and re-enter new criteria for a new search. |
| 6 | Advanced tab | Click to enter advanced filters, such as the subcategory of the highlighted item. |

**Table 40.2**   Options in the Advanced Find dialog box, continued

| # | Option | What you do with it |
|---|--------|---------------------|
| 7 | More Choices tab | Click to enter information in more detailed filters, such as categories, levels of importance, or marked as read. |
| 8 | Messages tab | Click to enter the key words, delimiters, and time span for the message(s) you're searching for. You can search by date the item was created or last modified. |

# Tools ➤ Organize

Use this option to change how the information in an open application or folder is organized. A pane opens above the current application window, giving you a way to step through organization tasks for the currently open application.

**N O T E**   Each application has a different Organizer pane and "wizard".  ▓

## How You Get Here

◇ Click 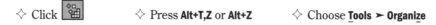  ◇ Press **Alt+T,Z** or **Alt+Z**   ◇ Choose **Tools** ➤ **Organize**

## What's In This Pane

Figure 40.5 is a sample of this dialog box and Table 40.3 has a description of the options available.

**Figure 40.5**   The Organize pane for the Inbox

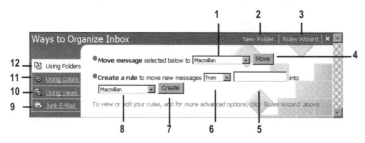

**Table 40.3**   Options in the Organize pane

| # | Option | What you do with it |
|---|--------|---------------------|
| 1 | Move message to drop-down list | Choose an item that determines the folder that you want to move the item into. |
| 2 | New Folder button | Click to create a new, unnamed folder. |
| 3 | Rules Wizard button | Click to open the Rules Wizard dialog box. |

**Table 40.3**  Options in the Organize pane, continued

| # | Option | What you do with it |
|---|--------|---------------------|
| 4 | Move button | Click to activate the designated move (move the highlighted item into the chosen folder). |
| 5 | Create a rule location drop-down list | Choose an item that determines the location to which you want the highlighted addressee's items (sent to or sent from) automatically moved. |
| 6 | Create a rule from drop-down list | Choose an item that determines whether you want items sent from, or to, the highlighted addressee moved into the chosen folder. |
| 7 | Create button | Click to establish the rule as you have designated (to or from addressee into a specified folder). |
| 8 | Create a rule destination text box | View the status of the move (i.e. done!). |
| 9 | Junk E-Mail link | Click to display a form for identifying and managing junk mail (which you must define by sender each time you receive junk mail from a new sender). |
| 10 | Using Views link | Choose an item that determines which view option you want to use. |
| 11 | Using Colors link | Click to display a form for applying a color code to specific addressees. |
| 12 | Using Folders link | Choose an item that determines what folder you want to move the highlighted item into. |

# Tools ➤ Rules Wizard

Use this option to automate the processing of mail items. For example, you can create a rule that automatically places all mail items from a specific sender into a folder marked "useless stuff from a twit".

## How You Get Here

◇ Press **Alt+T,L**

◇ Choose **Tools** ➤ **Rules Wizard**

## What's In This Dialog Box

Figure 40.6 is a sample of this dialog box and Table 40.4 has a description of the options available.

**Figure 40.6**   The Rules Wizard dialog box

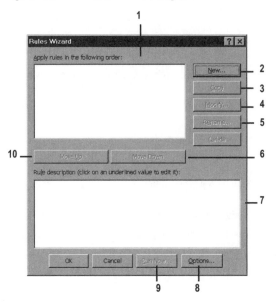

**Table 40.4**   Options in the Rules Wizard dialog box

| # | Option | What you do with it |
|---|--------|---------------------|
| 1 | Apply rules order list | View the order of the rules, and click to choose a rule to copy, modify, or delete. |
| 2 | New button | Click to create a new rule. |
| 3 | Copy button | Click to make a copy of the highlighted rule. Use this button if you need a rule similar to another rule, but with a few modifications. |
| 4 | Modify button | Click to change the highlighted rule. |
| 5 | Rename button | Click to change the name of the highlighted rule. |
| 6 | Move Down button | Click to move the highlighted rule down one level in the order. |
| 7 | Rule description area | Enter a description of the rule. Click on underlined sections to modify the rules used. |
| 8 | Options button | Click to update the rules for the server and import and export rules from other files. |
| 9 | Run Now button | Click to display the Run Rules Now dialog box so that you can choose specifications for which folders and which items apply to the rule. |
| 10 | Move Up button | Click to move the highlighted rule up one level in the order. |

# Tools ➤ Empty "Deleted Items" Folder

Use this option to empty the contents (permanently delete) of the Deleted Items folder. Outlook displays a warning box to ask you if you really, really, really want to empty the Deleted Items folder.

---

 **N O T E** Items deleted from an application or folder are not permanently deleted. Instead, it goes into a "deleted items" folder, so you can retrieve it later if you have a change of heart.

Not all items go into this folder when they're deleted. Some are permanently deleted, but Outlook always warns you before any item is permanently deleted. ▪

### How You Get Here

◇ Press **Alt+T,Y**          ◇ Choose **Tools ➤ Empty "Deleted Items" Folder**

# Tools ➤ Forms

Use this option to choose, edit, and create custom forms for Outlook.

### How You Get Here

◇ Press **Alt+T,F**          ◇ Choose **Tools ➤ Forms**

### What's In This Flyout Menu

Figure 40.7 is a sample of this flyout menu.

**Figure 40.7**   The Tools ➤ Forms flyout menu

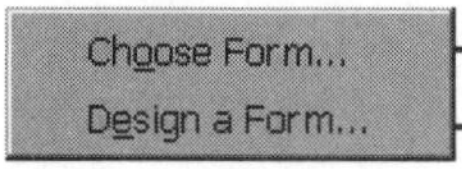

| | | |
|---|---|---|
| Choose Form... | Tools ➤ Forms ➤ Choose Form | 633 |
| Design a Form... | Tools ➤ Forms ➤ Design a Form | 634 |

### Tools ➤ Forms ➤ Choose Form

Use this option to choose a default form (such as a mail message form, or an appointment form), or to choose a custom designed form. This option allows you to access custom designed forms.

### How You Get Here

◇ Press **Alt+T,F,O**          ◇ Choose **Tools ➤ Forms ➤ Choose Form**

### Tools ➤ Forms ➤ Design a Form

Use this option to customize a form. You'll actually modify the form in additional tabs that are added to the default form design.

### How You Get Here

◇ Press **Alt+T,F,E**          ◇ Choose **Tools ➤ Forms ➤ Design a Form**

## Tools ➤ Macro

Use this option to create, edit, or run a macro. Macros are recorded steps of application operations. You'd usually record a macro to perform frequently performed tasks, reducing dozens or even hundreds of steps to a single click. Recording a macro works a lot like running a tape recorder; You choose "record," execute the task (undoing any mistakes you might make), then choose "stop recording." You name the macro and save it. It can then be run from a macro list, from a menu, or from a button you put on a toolbar. Macros are ideal for multi-step processes which cannot be simplified with keystroke shortcuts.

### How You Get Here

◇ Press **Alt+T,M**          ◇ Choose **Tools ➤ Macro**

### What's In This Flyout Menu

Figure 40.8 is a sample of this flyout menu.

**Figure 40.8**    The Tools ➤ Macro flyout menu

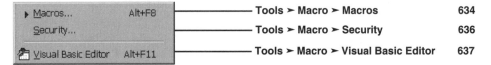

| | |
|---|---|
| Tools ➤ Macro ➤ Macros | 634 |
| Tools ➤ Macro ➤ Security | 636 |
| Tools ➤ Macro ➤ Visual Basic Editor | 637 |

### Tools ➤ Macro ➤ Macros

Use this option to choose the macro that you want to run or to modify an existing macro.

---

**N O T E**    Office 2000 provides the ability to create and edit macros using Visual Basic Editor. ▦

### How You Get Here

◇ Press **Alt+T,M,M** or **Alt+F8**          ◇ Choose **Tools ➤ Macro ➤ Macros**

## What's In This Dialog Box

Figure 40.9 is a sample of this dialog box and Table 40.5 has a description of the options available.

**Figure 40.9** The Macro dialog box

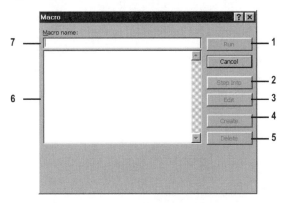

**Table 40.5** Options in the Macro dialog box

| # | Option | What you do with it |
|---|--------|---------------------|
| 1 | Run button | Click to run the macro you have highlighted. |
| 2 | Step Into button | Click to run the macro in Visual Basic Editor, one step at a time, pausing at each step. |
| 3 | Edit button | Click to open the Visual Basic and the Editing windows to edit the macro using the Visual Basic for Applications programming language. |
| 4 | Create button | Click to open the Visual Basic and Create windows to create a macro using the Visual Basic for Applications programming language. |
| 5 | Delete button | Click to delete the macro currently highlighted. Outlooks warns you before deleting. |
| 6 | Macros list | Click to choose an available macro. |
| 7 | Description text box | Enter comments that describe a new macro or view the description of an existing macro. |

**TIP** Try to give your macro a name that describes what it does and be sure to take a few extra minutes to enter a description in the Description text box. This helps you remember what the macro does and is a great help if you plan to share the macro with someone else.

## Tools ➤ Macro ➤ Security

Use this option to have Outlook let you know when you receive a file from someone else that has macros embedded in it. Macros can be used to write computer viruses, so a security notice gives you a *little* piece of mind and one more level of protection for your data.

### How You Get Here

◇ Press **Alt+T,M,S**          ◇ Choose **Tools** ➤ **Macro** ➤ **Security**

### What's In This Dialog Box

Figure 40.10 is a sample of this dialog box and Table 40.6 has a description of the tabs available.

**Figure 40.10**   The Security dialog box

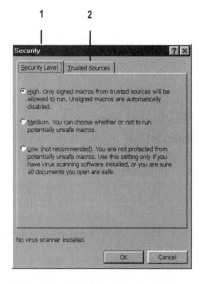

**Table 40.6**   Tabs in the Security dialog box

| # | Option | What you do with it |
|---|--------|---------------------|
| 1 | Security Level | Click to assign a security level that is used to screen macros that you receive from other sources. |
| 2 | Trusted Sources | Click to enter information about sources whose documents are considered safe and whose macros don't need to be identified or disabled. |

## Tools ➤ Macro ➤ Visual Basic Editor

Use this option to create or edit macros using the Visual Basic programming language.

---

**N O T E**  This option isn't for the faint or heart or for those unfamiliar with this language. If you're interesting in learning more about programming with Visual Basic, check out *Special Edition: Using Visual Basic For Applications 5,* by Paul Sanna (ISBN: 0789709597). ▇

### How You Get Here

◇ Press **Alt+T,M,V** or **Alt+F11**     ◇ Choose **Tools** ➤ **Macro** ➤ **Visual Basic Editor**

# Tools ➤ Customize

Use this option to change the toolbars and menus to suit how you work, not how somebody "out there" thought you should work. Any changes made here affect all the menus and toolbars in Outlook no matter what you're doing.

### How You Get Here

◇ Press **Alt+T,C**     ◇ Choose **Tools** ➤ **Customize**

### What's In This Dialog Box

Figure 40.11 is a sample of this dialog box and Table 40.7 has a description of the tabs available.

**Figure 40.11**   The Customize dialog box

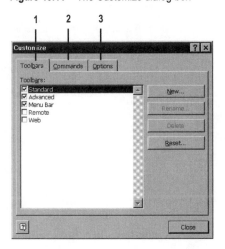

**Table 40.7**   Tabs in the Customize dialog box

| # | Tab name | What you do with it |
|---|----------|---------------------|
| 1 | Toolbars | Click to create a new toolbar, to delete toolbars you've created, or to see what toolbars are active. (For a complete description of the options available, see Table 40.8 on page 638.) |
| 2 | Commands | Click to list the available categories of commands and the commands within them. You must display or create a toolbar before you can add new icons to it. (For a complete description of the options available, see Table 40.9 on page 638.) |
| 3 | Options | Click to choose display options for toolbars and menus. (For a complete description of the options available, see Table 40.10 on page 639.) |

The following tables describe the options for the individual tabs in this dialog box:

- Table 40.8 describes the Customize Toolbars tab,
- Table 40.9 describes the Commands tab, and
- Table 40.10 describes the Option tab.

**Table 40.8**   Options in the Customize Toolbars tab

| Option | What you do with it |
|--------|---------------------|
| Toolbars area | Click to choose the toolbar you want to modify. During modification the toolbar is visible, but it isn't active, so you can make changes to it. Right-click on an icon to display a menu that you can use to modify the highlighted icon. |
| New button | Click to display the New Toolbar dialog box, which has options for creating a new toolbar. |
| Rename button | Click to display the Rename Toolbar dialog box, which lets you rename your custom toolbars. You can't rename the toolbars that come with Outlook. |
| Delete button | Click to delete a toolbar you've created. You can't delete the toolbars that come with Outlook. |
| Reset button | Click to display the Reset Toolbar dialog box, which allows you to restore the original settings and buttons. |

**Table 40.9**   Options in the Customize Commands tab

| Option | What you do with it |
|--------|---------------------|
| Categories area | Click to choose the menu or toolbar you want to change. |
| Commands area | Click to choose the commands you want to change. |
| Description button | Click to display a brief description of the highlighted command. |
| Modify Selection drop-down list | Click to display a drop-down list of controls for the highlighted command. |

**Table 40.10**   Options in the Customize Options tab

| Option | What you do with it |
| --- | --- |
| Personalized Menus and Toolbars area | Click to choose the properties you want to set for your menus and toolbars. |
| Other area | Click to choose how you want to display your menus and toolbars. |
| Menu animations drop-down list | Choose an item that determines the way your menus are animated. |

# Tools ➤ Options

Use this option to set the default preferences for each of the Outlook applications, such as establishing which server is used, how your spellchecker functions, and what type of security options are used to help protect you and your system.

## How You Get Here

◇ Press **Alt+T,O**          ◇ Choose **Tools ➤ Options**

## What's In This Dialog Box

Figure 40.12 is a sample of this dialog box and Table 40.11 has a description of the tabs available.

**Figure 40.12**   The Options dialog box

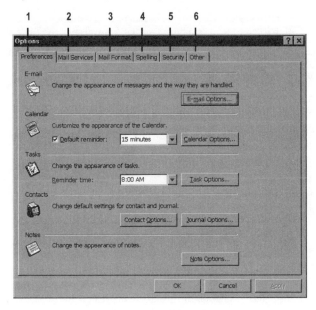

**Table 40.11**   Tabs in the Options dialog box

| # | Tab name | What you do with it |
|---|----------|---------------------|
| 1 | Preferences tab | Click to make changes to the default options of the Outlook applications. (For a complete description of the options available, see Table 40.12 on page 640.) |
| 2 | Mail Services tab | Click to make changes to the default options related to email delivery, such as the accounts manager, the mail account options, and the dial-up options. (For a complete description of the options available, see Table 40.13 on page 641.) |
| 3 | Mail Format tab | Click to make changes to the default settings for how email messages are sent and received. For example, you can choose an HTML or plain text format and what signature information is automatically included in your messages.(For a complete description of the options available, see Table 40.14 on page 642.) |
| 4 | Spelling tab | Click to make changes to the default options for spell check. (For a complete description of the options available, see Table 40.15 on page 643.) |
| 5 | Security tab | Click to make changes to the default options for your email account, web sites and other Internet addresses, and digital IDs. (For a complete description of the options available, see Table 40.16 on page 643.) |
| 6 | Other tab | Click to make changes to the default options for miscellaneous features. (For a complete description of the options available, see Table 40.17 on page 643.) |

The following tables describe the options for the individual tabs in this dialog box:

- Table 40.12 describes the Preferences tab,
- Table 40.13 describes the Mail Services tab,
- Table 40.14  describes the Mail Format tab,
- Table 40.15 describes the Spelling tab,
- Table 40.16 describes the Security tab, and
- Table 40.17 describes the Other tab.

**Table 40.12**   Options in the Options dialog box Preferences tab

| Option | What you do with it |
|--------|---------------------|
| E-Mail Options button | Click to display the E-mail options dialog box, where you can change the way messages appear, and how they are handled. |
| Calendar Options button | Click to display the Calendar options dialog box, where you can change the default display for the first day of the year, of the week, and the beginning and ending times on the appointment pane. You can also choose the time zone and add holidays automatically. |

**Table 40.12**  Options in the Options dialog box Preferences tab, continued

| Option | What you do with it |
|---|---|
| Calendar Default reminder check box | Click to set the default time for a reminder that appears a set number of minutes prior to every appointment. |
| Task Option button | Click to display the Task Options dialog box, where you can change the default colors assigned to completed and overdue tasks. |
| Task Reminder time drop-down list | Choose an item that determines the time of day when you want to be reminded of tasks due that day. |
| Contact Options button | Click to display the Contact Options dialog box, where you can make changes to the default Full Name order and File As order. |
| Journal Options button | Click to display the Journal Options dialog box, where you can check which items and which contacts are automatically recorded in your journal. In the same dialog box you can choose what double clicking on a journal item does, and establish the parameters for AutoArchiving journal entries. |
| Note Options button | Click to display the Note Options dialog box, where you can set the default options for the appearance of notes, including the size, color, and font. |

**Table 40.13**  Options in the Options dialog box Mail Services tab

| Option | What you do with it |
|---|---|
| Accounts button | Click to display the Internet Accounts dialog box, where you can make changes to the Mail and Internet servers. |
| Send messages immediately when connected check box | Click to have messages in your outbox sent immediately after connecting to the Internet. Leave unchecked to use the Send/Receive option to send messages. |
| Check for new messages every check box/list | Click to have Outlook retrieve messages from the server at the designated time interval. Enter or choose the interval at which you want Outlook to retrieve messages from the server. This option is available only when the "Check for new messages" check box is checked. |
| Warn before switching dial-up connection check box | Click to display a confirmation message before Outlook switches the dial-up connection. |
| Hang up when finished sending, receiving, or updating check box | Click to automatically disconnect after sending and retrieving messages. If you are not connected and you click on Send/Receive, Outlook automatically establishes a connection to send and retrieve messages. Once the transfer is completed, Outlook automatically disconnects you from the server. |
| Automatically dial when checking for new messages check box | Click to automatically dial the connection number for the mail server when you click on any control that checks for new messages. |
| Don't download messages larger than check box/list | Click to prevent Outlook from downloading messages larger than the size indicated in the accompanying list. |

**Table 40.13**   Options in the Options dialog box Mail Services tab, continued

| Option | What you do with it |
| --- | --- |
| Reconfigure Mail Support button | Click to open the Start Up dialog box, where you can reset servers and accounts. |
| Apply button | Click to apply the changes you have made. This option is only available when you have made changes, and must be chosen before Reconfiguring Mail Support, or those changes are lost. |

**Table 40.14**   Options in the Options dialog box Mail Format tab

| Option | What you do with it |
| --- | --- |
| Send in this message format drop-down list | Choose an item that determines which format you want to be the default format for outgoing mail messages. |
| Use Microsoft Word check box | Click to use Microsoft Word to edit email items. Leave unchecked to use the Outlook editor. |
| Settings button | Click to display the Settings dialog box for the chosen format. Options include when to wrap text and several encoding options. This dialog box is not available when Rich Text format is highlighted. |
| International Options button | Click to apply options for the language to use in headings and encoding for outgoing messages. |
| Use this stationery drop-down list | Choose an item that determines which stationery you want as the default background for all outgoing mail messages. You can choose "none" if you don't want to use this type of background or if your system doesn't support this option. |
| Fonts button | Click to establish default settings for message fonts and stationery fonts (if the message was sent using a stationary background and you are replying to it) for outgoing messages. |
| Stationery Picker button | Click to choose and make changes to the stationary available to you. You can also view a sample of the stationery. |
| Use this signature by default drop-down list | Choose an item that determines the signature you want to appear on all outgoing messages. You can always delete your signature from any message that doesn't require a signature. |
| Don't use when replying check box | Check to leave the signature out when replying to or forwarding messages. |
| Signature Picker button | Click to open the Signature Picker dialog box, where you can create new signatures and edit or delete existing ones. |

**Table 40.15**   Options in the Options dialog box Spelling tab

| Option | What you do with it |
| --- | --- |
| General Options area check boxes | Click to choose which default options you want applied for spell check. You can choose more than one option. |
| Edit button | Click to add, edit, or remove items in your custom dictionary. Changes made here are not applied to currently open items. |
| Language drop-down list | Choose an item that determines the default language used in the spell check. |

**Table 40.16**   Options in the Options dialog box Security tab

| Option | What you do with it |
| --- | --- |
| Encrypt contents check box | Click to encrypt messages so that only the recipient can read them. |
| Add digital signature check box | Click to apply a digital signature, which assures the recipient that you were the sender and the message was not altered. |
| Send clear text check box | Click to ensure that those recipients who are not set up to receive digital signatures can bypass this and read the message. |
| Default Security Setting drop-down list | Choose an item that determines the security setting you want applied to all mail items. |
| Set up Secure E-Mail button | Click to make changes to the security settings and their options. |
| Zone drop-down list | Choose an item that determines the zone to which you want HTML messages to be assigned. Zones include Internet, restricted, trusted, and local intranet. |
| Zone Settings button | Click to make changes or specify the security level for each of the available zones. |
| Attachment Security button | Click to specify the level of security applied to attached items and files. This protects against virus-infected attachments. |
| Import/Export Digital ID button | Click to import or export a digital ID from another source. This procedure requires the use of a password. |
| Get Digital ID button | Click to download a digital ID from the Internet. You must be online to access this option. |

**Table 40.17**   Options in the Options dialog box Other tab

| Option | What you do with it |
| --- | --- |
| Empty Deleted Items check box | Click to have Outlook automatically clear the Deleted Items folder of all items each time you exit Outlook. |
| Advanced Options button | Click to make choices regarding which warnings you'll receive *before* you delete startup folder and what appearance options apply to your system. |

**Table 40.17**   Options in the Options dialog box Other tab, continued

| Option | What you do with it |
|---|---|
| AutoArchive button | Click to apply default settings for AutoArchive features, such as the time interval for archiving, and what to do with deleted items. |
| Preview Pane button | Click to apply default settings for the appearance of the preview pane, such as the header font, and whether messages are marked as read in the preview pane. |

# A Look At The Outlook Mail Application

**In this part**

# What Is The Outlook Mail Application

**In this chapter**

# What Is The Outlook Mail Application

Outlook Mail is your central location for communicating electronically with other people. It's where all those messages you send and receive are stored, where you go to look up those little tidbits you just know you saw in some message or another, and where you go when you want to forward a message you've received to someone else. This is also where the messages are stored when you advise people of an upcoming meeting that you want them to attend.

Strangely, the icon on the Outlook Shortcuts bar calls this the Inbox, even though it manages more than just your incoming mail. Go figure! Actually there are four folders created by Outlook to hold various types of messages.

■ The Inbox folder holds all incoming messages that have not yet been filed in another folder and is what you'll see when open this application.
■ The Outbox folder holds all sent messages, which have not yet gone to the server.
■ The Drafts folder holds all messages that have been closed without being sent.
■ The Sent Items folder holds a copy of the messages that have been sent to the server.

---

**N O T E**  Outlook lets you create an message and close it without sending it (calling it a "draft"). You can send the item to the Outbox (your electronic mailbox) without being online. Once online, you can click the Send/Receive button (or choose **Tools ➤ Send/Receive**) to send all Outbox items to the server. Once this is done, copies of these items are automatically retained in the Sent Items folder. ▦

# Getting To Outlook Mail

There are several ways to get to Outlook Mail, the most common being to:

■ Click the ▦ icon on the Outlook Shortcuts bar,
■ **Alt+F,W,M** or **Ctrl+Shift+M**, or
■ Choose **File ➤ New ➤ Mail Message.**

# How Outlook Mail Is Organized

Figure 41.1 shows what the typical Inbox looks like. This is where you'll see a list of your incoming messages and do most of your everyday work. From here, you can reply to a message, forward a message to someone else, review messages that you've received, create new folders to hold different types of messages ("all the better to keep this area clutter-free." said the big bad wolf).

**Figure 41.1**   The Outlook Mail application—Inbox view

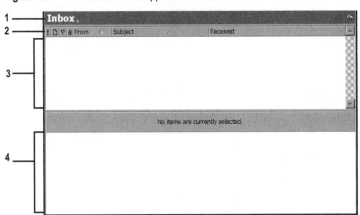

> **N O T E**   We've used the Inbox to show you the main components of the Outlook Message window. However, all four folders created when you install Outlook look and act very much the same as this one. ■

The main parts of this window are as follows.

1. **Title bar**
   This tells you the name of the folder you're currently displaying.

2. **Sort By bar**
   The information in this bar provides a quick summary of the currently highlighted message, including whether there are attachments, who sent the message, the subject of the message, and who received the message. Each of these columns can be resized to show more, or less, of a particular type of information. You can also quickly resort your messages by clicking on the appropriate column title. (For more information, see What's In The Sort By Bar on page 650.)

3. **Message pane**
   This pane lists the messages that are in the active folder.

4. **Message Text pane**
   This area includes the actual text of the currently highlighted message. You can scroll up and down to view different parts of the message.

# What's In The Sort By Bar

The Sort By bar is just that: it let's you organize (sort) your messages based on specific criteria about your messages in either ascending or descending order. Figure 41.1 is a sample of a Sort By bar from the Inbox folder and Table 41.2 describes the options available.

**Figure 41.2**   The Sort By bar

**Table 41.1**   Options in the Sort By bar

| # | Option | What you do with it |
|---|--------|---------------------|
| 1 | Importance | Click to sort your messages based on the importance assigned by the sender. |
| 2 | Icon | Click to sort your messages by their read status. The most common icons are Read and Unread. |
| 3 | Flagged | Click to sort your messages based on whether you've flagged a message for later attention, whether the message has no flag, or whether the message flag has already been dealt with. |
| 4 | Attachment | Click to sort your messages based on whether a message does, or does not, have a file attached to it. |
| 5 | From | Click to sort your messages in alphabetical order based on the name of the person who sent the message. |
| 6 | Sort Order arrow | View which field is being used to sort your messages and whether the messages are being displayed in ascending order (up arrow) or descending order (down arrow). |
| 7 | Subject | Click to sort your messages in alphabetical order based on the subject line included with the message. |
| 8 | Received | Click to sort your messages in alphabetical order based on the date you received the message in your Inbox folder. |
| | | **Note**  The item may have been sent weeks ago, but if you were on vacation, and just opened Outlook Mail and clicked on "Send/ Receive," the receive date will be today. |

# Getting Around In The Calendar

Keyboardists beware! You *can* use the keyboard to get around Outlook Mail, but it isn't intuitive or easy. You might want to pick up that mouse and give it a try. Mousers: you'll be in heaven since the Outlook Mail is tailor-made for mousing around.

- Mousers: In the Appointment pane and the Date Navigator pane, just click on the month, day, and time in which you want to add, edit, or delete appointment information. Use the arrows to move to another month or click on the name of the month and choose a new month from the drop down list.
- Keyboardists: The left and right arrows move you back and forth through the days in the Date Navigator, and the up and down arrows move you up and down the times listed in the Appointment pane.
- Mousers and keyboardists: There is a shortcut menu that has a list of the most commonly used options from the standard menu bar. Just right-click and choose the option you need.

# What's Different in Outlook Mail's Toolbars

The Inbox standard and advanced toolbars by default contain shortcuts commonly used in the Inbox application. These toolbars can be customized by showing and hiding buttons from the listing found under the More Buttons tool.

A majority of the icons on both the Standard and Advanced toolbars were discussed in the chapter on common View menu options. (For more information, see View ➤ Toolbars on page 608.) There are only a few differences that you need to learn about for the Calendar application.

- For more information about the Standard toolbar, see Differences in Outlook Mail's Standard Toolbar on page 651.
- For more information about the Advanced toolbar, see Differences in Outlook Mail's Advanced Toolbar on page 652.

## Differences in Outlook Mail's Standard Toolbar

Use this toolbar as a shortcut for commonly performed tasks, such as Send/Receive, Reply, Forward, and creating a new message.

## How You Get Here

◇ Press **Alt+V,T** choose **Standard**     ◇ Choose **View** ➤ **Toolbars** ➤ **Standard**

## What's Different

Figure 41.3 is a sample of this toolbar and Table 41.2 has a description of the icons that are unique to Outlook Mail.

**Figure 41.3**   Outlook Mail's Standard toolbar

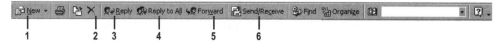

**Table 41.2**   Icons in Outlook Mail's Standard toolbar

| # | Icon | What you do with it |
|---|------|---------------------|
| 1 | New | Click to open an untitled Mail Message form so that you can create a new message. |
| 2 | Delete | Click to move the highlighted messages to the Deleted Items folder. |
| 3 | Reply | Click to open a new Mail Message form with the sender's address filled in for you. The default Outlook settings also include a copy of the original message in the Message Text pane. |
| 4 | Reply to All | Click to open a new Mail Message form with the sender's address and the address of all the recipients who got the original message filled in for you. The default Outlook settings also include a copy of the original message in the Message Text pane. |
| 5 | Forward | Click to open a new Mail Message form with a copy of the original text in the Message Text pane. You'll need to fill in the appropriate email address and add any comments that you feel are appropriate before clicking the **Send** icon. |
| 6 | Send/Receive | Click to tell Outlook mail to check for any new messages and move all messages in the Outbox to the server. You must be online to do this. |

## Differences in Outlook Mail's Advanced Toolbar

Use this toolbar as a shortcut to some of the less frequently used tasks, such as Group by box, Rules Wizard, and Print Preview.

## How You Get Here

◇ Press **Alt+V,T** choose **Advanced**      ◇ Choose **View** ➤ **Toolbars** ➤ **Advanced**

## What's Different

Figure 41.4 is a sample of this toolbar and Table 41.3 has a description of the icons that are unique to Outlook Mail.

**Figure 41.4**   The Outlook Mail Advanced toolbar

**Table 41.3**   Icons in Outlook Mail's Advanced toolbar

| # | Icon | What you do with it |
|---|------|---------------------|
| 1 | Print Preview | Click to display a view of what the message will look like if you send it to a printer. |
| 2 | Current View | Choose an item that determines how your messages are displayed on your screen. |
| 3 | Group By Box | Click to arrange the table view according to predefined groups. This can also be found on the right mouse menu when clicking in the table view. |
| 4 | Field Chooser | Click to choose which fields are used when sorting items in table view. This can also be found on the right mouse menu when clicking in the table view. |
| 5 | AutoPreview | Click to change the table view to alternately hide or show the first few lines of the message. |

# The Outlook Mail View Menu

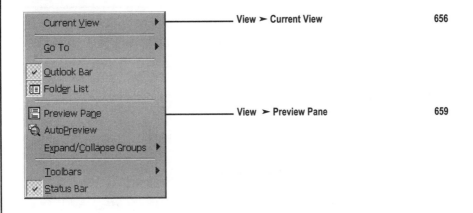

# What's Different In Outlook Mail's View Menu

The Outlook Mail's View menu is like any other View menu in a Microsoft application: it provides different ways for you to look the same information. It just depends on what you need at any given time. You can sort the messages in any of the folders associated with Outlook Mail by sender, flag, unread messages, subject, sender, and more. There are two types of views in this application: a table view and a timeline view.

- Table views sort the messages according to the designated criteria, such as a listing of messages received in the last seven days.
- Timeline view marks messages along a time line.

If a menu option has an ellipsis (three dots) or an arrow beside it, the application "asks" you for additional information before the action takes place. If the menu doesn't have one of these symbols, the action you choose happens immediately. If the action takes place immediately, you won't see a sample screen in this section.

---

**N O T E**    Most of the options in this menu were described earlier in this book. (For more information, see The Common View Menu Options on page 595.) ■

# View ➤ Current View

Use this option to change the way you are viewing the application or item.

## How You Get Here

◇ Press **Alt+V,V**          ◇ Choose **View** ➤ **Current View**

## What's In This Flyout Menu

Figure 42.1 is a sample of this flyout menu.

**Figure 42.1**    The View ➤ Current View flyout menu

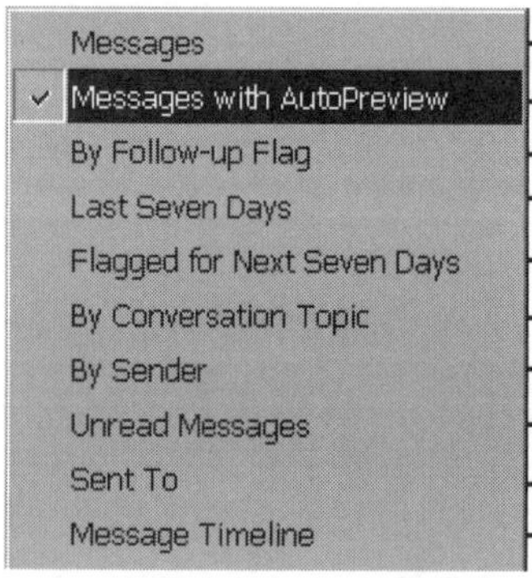

## View ➤ Current View ➤ Messages

Use this option to view all messages stored in the currently displayed Outlook Mail folder.

### How You Get Here

◇ Press **Alt+V,V** choose **Messages**  ◇ Choose **View** ➤ **Current View** ➤ **Messages**

## View ➤ Current View ➤ Messages with AutoPreview

Use this option to display the first few lines of the message below the message heading.

### How You Get Here

◇ Press **Alt+V,V** choose **Messages with AutoPreview**  ◇ Choose **View** ➤ **Current View** ➤ **Messages with AutoPreview**

## View ➤ Current View ➤ By Follow-up Flag

Use this option to display only those messages in the currently displayed Outlook Mail folder that have a follow-up flag.

### How You Get Here

◇ Press **Alt+V,V** choose **By Follow-up Flag**  ◇ Choose **View** ➤ **Current View** ➤ **By Follow-up Flag**

## View ➤ Current View ➤ Last Seven Days

Use this option to display only those messages in the currently displayed Outlook Mail folder that were received within the last seven days.

### How You Get Here

◇ Press **Alt+V,V** choose **Last Seven Days**  ◇ Choose **View** ➤ **Current View** ➤ **Last Seven Days**

## View ➤ Current View ➤ Flagged for Next Seven Days

Use this option to display only those messages in the currently displayed Outlook Mail folder that have a flag with a due date in the next seven days.

### How You Get Here

◇ Press **Alt+V,V** choose **Flagged for Next Seven Days**  ◇ Choose **View** ➤ **Current View** ➤ **Flagged for Next Seven Days**

## View ➤ Current View ➤ By Conversation Topic

Use this option to display the messages in the currently displayed Outlook Mail folder sorted by the text in the Subject line.

### How You Get Here

◇ Press **Alt+V,V**
choose **By Conversation Topic**

◇ Choose **View** ➤ **Current View** ➤ **By Conversation Topic**

## View ➤ Current View ➤ By Sender

Use this option to display the messages in the currently displayed Outlook Mail folder sorted by the sender's address.

### How You Get Here

◇ Press **Alt+V,V** choose **By Sender**

◇ Choose **View** ➤ **Current View** ➤ **By Sender**

## View ➤ Current View ➤ Unread Messages

Use this option to display only those messages in the currently displayed Outlook Mail folder that have not yet been read.

### How You Get Here

◇ Press **Alt+V,V** choose **Unread Messages**

◇ Choose **View** ➤ **Current View** ➤ **Unread Messages**

## View ➤ Current View ➤ Sent To

Use this option to display the messages in the currently displayed Outlook Mail folder sorted by who the message was sent to.

### How You Get Here

◇ Press **Alt+V,V** choose **Sent To**

◇ Choose **View** ➤ **Current View** ➤ **Sent To**

## View ➤ Current View ➤ Message Timeline

Use this option to view all messages on a timeline background. You can move along the timeline using the scroll bars.

### How You Get Here

◇ Press **Alt+V,V** choose **Message Timeline**

◇ Choose **View** ➤ **Current View** ➤ **Message Timeline**

# View ➤ Preview Pane

Use this option to view all messages in the currently displayed Outlook Mail folder with a split pane. The bottom pane contains the contents of the highlighted message. See Figure 41.1 on page 649 for a sample of the Preview Pane.

## How You Get Here

◇ Press **Alt+V,N**

◇ Choose **View ➤ Preview Pane**

# The Outlook Mail Actions Menu

## In this chapter

# What Is The Actions Menu

This menu lists the commands that you'll use to initiate any new activity related to creating new mail messages, forwarding messages you've received, and replying to messages you've received. Other Microsoft applications work with documents (or files) and most are created using the New menu.  Outlook applications, however, are usually relational.  That is, they involve actions such as sending an email message, or scheduling a meeting with co-workers. Initiating these activities is done with the Actions menu. The New menu still exists, but is used to create new folders, etc.

If a menu option has an ellipsis (three dots) or an arrow beside it, the application "asks" you for additional information before the action takes place. If the menu doesn't have one of these symbols, the action you choose happens immediately. If the action takes place immediately, you won't see a sample screen in this section.

---

**N O T E**   You'll use one basic form (the Events form) to enter your appointments and meetings so we've lumped that information into another chapter. (For more information, see A Look At Calendar's Forms on page 705.) ▪

# Actions ➤ New Mail Message

Use this option to create and send messages to those in your Contacts list or to any valid email address. (For more information, see A Look At Outlook Mail's Forms on page 671.).

## How You Get Here

◇ Click    ◇ Press **Alt+A,N** or **Ctrl+N**   ◇ Choose **Actions ➤ New Mail Message**

# Actions ➤ New Mail Message Using

Use this option to a create message using a specific format such as HTML, Microsoft Word, or Rich Text Format (RTF). Create a new message using this option if you're sending a message to someone who has to have a specific format or they won't be able to read your message.

## How You Get Here

◇ Press **Alt+A,M**   ◇ Choose **Actions ➤ New Mail Message Using**

## What's In This Flyout Menu

Figure 43.1 is a sample of this flyout menu.

**Figure 43.1** The Actions ➤ New Mail Message Using flyout menu

## Actions ➤ New Mail Message Using ➤ More Stationery

Use this option to choose a specific default or custom stationery format for the background of your messages. When using stationery on your email the download time for those receiving your messages will be somewhat longer than usual. So if your messages are large in size (with attachments and so on) you may want to skip the stationery for those particular messages.

### How You Get Here

◇ Press **Alt+A,M,M**      ◇ Choose **Actions ➤ New Mail Message Using ➤ More Stationery**

### What's In This Dialog Box

Figure 43.2 is a sample of this dialog box and Table 43.1 has a description of the options available.

**Figure 43.2** The Select a Stationery dialog box

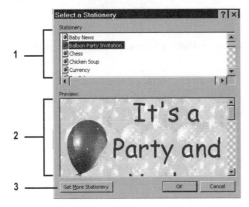

**Table 43.1**   Options in the Select a Stationery dialog box

| # | Option | What you do with it |
|---|--------|---------------------|
| 1 | Stationery list | Choose an item that determines which stationary is used for your messages. |
| 2 | Preview area | View the stationery highlighted in the Stationery list. |
| 3 | Get More Stationery button | Click to add more stationery options to your list. |

## Actions ➤ New Mail Message Using ➤ Microsoft Word

Use this option to create the message using Microsoft Word. Using Word provides more options and flexibility, including an expanded format menu and the ability to incorporate graphs.

**N O T E**   Most people just attach a Microsoft Word document. ■

### How You Get Here

◇ Press **Alt+A,M,W**          ◇ Choose **Actions ➤ New Mail Message Using ➤ Microsoft Word**

## Actions ➤ New Mail Message Using ➤ Microsoft Outlook

Use this option to create the message using any one of the Microsoft Office applications, including Excel and PowerPoint. Using these applications provides more options and flexibility, including an expanded format menu and the ability to incorporate graphs.

### How You Get Here

◇ Press **Alt+A,M,O**          ◇ Choose **Actions ➤ New Mail Message Using ➤ Microsoft Outlook**

### What's In This Flyout Menu

Figure 43.3 is a sample of this flyout menu and Table 43.2 has a description of the options available.

**Figure 43.3**   The New Mail Message Using ➤ Microsoft Office flyout menu

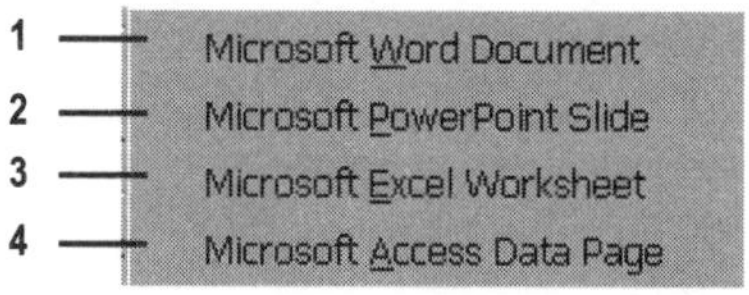

1 —— Microsoft Word Document
2 —— Microsoft PowerPoint Slide
3 —— Microsoft Excel Worksheet
4 —— Microsoft Access Data Page

**Table 43.2**   Options in the New Mail Message Using ➤ Microsoft Office flyout menu

| # | Option | What you do with it |
|---|--------|---------------------|
| 1 | Microsoft Word Document | Click to create the new message using Microsoft Word as the creation tool. |
| 2 | Microsoft PowerPoint Slide | Click to create the new message using Microsoft PowerPoint as the creation tool. |
| 3 | Microsoft Excel Worksheet | Click to create the new message using Microsoft Excel as the creation tool. |
| 4 | Microsoft Access Data Page | Click to create the new message using Microsoft Access as the creation tool. |

## Actions ➤ New Mail Message Using ➤ Plain Text

Use this option to create the body of your message in plain text, a format that is readable by most of the email systems currently in use. When using this option, you can't do any fancy formatting or include things such as pictures or graphs.

### How You Get Here

◇ Press **Alt+A,M,P**            ◇ Choose **Actions** ➤ **New Mail Message Using** ➤ **Plain Text**

## Actions ➤ New Mail Message Using ➤ Microsoft Office Rich Text

Use this option to apply a format more complex than the plain text format. Rich text format can carry over detailed text formatting, but you can't use many of the graphic format options available.

### How You Get Here

◇ Press **Alt+A,M,O**   ◇ Choose **Actions** ➤ **New Mail Message Using** ➤ **Microsoft Office Rich Text**

## Actions ➤ New Mail Message Using ➤ HTML (No Stationery)

Use this option to apply the HTML format, which allows you to use a wide variety of fonts, colors, graphics, photographs, anything that HTML supports. Recipients can actually view your email in a browser, or in Windows 98 windows.

---

**N O T E**   Many people can't read messages with an HTML format or can't view them as you originally intended. If the receiver's system won't handle HTML, the message will have a ton of tags embedded in the actual text of the message, making it pretty darned hard to read the message. Go lightly on this one unless you know for sure the receiver can also read the HTML formatting.

**TIP** Wanna do something nice for people who read a lot of messages from one of the listserves out there? Don't use HTML to format messages that are posted to the list. Simple readers can't display HTML. People can get irritated.

## How You Get Here

◇ Press **Alt+A,M,H**    ◇ Choose **Actions ➤ New Mail Message Using ➤ HTML (No Stationery)**

# Actions ➤ Flag for Follow Up

Use this option to designate what type of follow up is required for the message, such as a reply, or even "no response necessary". Flags are reminders that there is something more to be done with the item. Flagged items have a red flag icon in their table view, and the flag is noted in a yellow banner on the opened item.

**TIP** In a table view, you can sort messages by flag.

**N O T E** You can only assign one follow up action at a time to a message. ▨

## How You Get Here

◇ Press **Alt+A,F** or **Ctrl+Shift+G**    ◇ Choose **Actions ➤ Flag for Follow Up**

## What's In This Dialog Box

Figure 43.4 is a sample of this dialog box and Table 43.3 has a description of the options available.

**Figure 43.4**    The Flag for Follow Up dialog box

**Table 43.3**   Options in the Flag for Follow Up dialog box

| # | Option | What you do with it |
|---|--------|---------------------|
| 1 | Flag To drop-down list | Choose an item that determines the what type of follow up flag should be assigned to the currently highlighted message. Options include: Follow up, For your information, Forward, No response necessary, Read, Reply, Reply to all, and Review. |
| 2 | Due By drop-down list | Click to choose the date by which you want to complete the action for the highlighted message. |
| 3 | Completed check box | Click to mark when the follow up action has been completed. (Completed items flags become gray). |
| 4 | Clear Flag button | Click to remove all flags from the message. |

# Actions ➤ Find All

Use this option to look for messages that meet a specific criterion, such as all related messages or all messages from a specific sender.

## How You Get Here

◇ Press **Alt+A,I**          ◇ Choose **Actions** ➤ **Find All**

## What's In This Flyout Menu

Figure 43.5 is a sample of this flyout menu.

**Figure 43.5**   The Find All flyout menu

Related Messages...          Actions ➤ Find All ➤ Related Messages          667

Messages from Sender...     Actions ➤ Find All ➤ Messages from Sender     668

## Actions ➤ Find All ➤ Related Messages

Use this option to find all messages that have the same topic as that in the Subject text box.

---

**N O T E**   This option opens the Advanced Find dialog box so that you can be very specific about what messages you want to look for. (For more information, see Tools ➤ Advanced Find on page 629.) ▮

## How You Get Here

◇ Press **Alt+A,I,R**          ◇ Choose **Actions** ➤ **Find All** ➤ **Related Messages**

## Actions ➤ Find All ➤ Messages from Sender

Use this option to find all messages that you've received from a specific person.

---

**N O T E**   This option opens the Advanced Find dialog box so that you can be very specific about what messages you want to look for. (For more information, see Tools ➤ Advanced Find on page 629.) ▮

### How You Get Here

◇ Press **Alt+A,I,M**          ◇ Choose **Actions ➤ Find All ➤ Messages from Sender**

# Actions ➤ Junk E-mail

Use this option to organize email you don't want cluttering up the Inbox. Junk email is redirected into another folder, usually the Junk Mail folder. Basically, you are taking the organize option, in which you designate files sent to or from a specific sender, and tell Outlook to automatically file them in a designated folder.

---

**N O T E**   You must turn on the Junk Mail option first in the Organize window of Outlook Mail. (For more information, see Tools ➤ Organize on page 630.) ▮

### How You Get Here

◇ Press **Alt+A,J**          ◇ Choose **Actions ➤ Junk E-mail**

### What's In This Flyout Menu

Figure 43.6 is a sample of this flyout menu.

**Figure 43.6**   The Actions ➤ Junk E-mail flyout menu

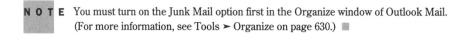

| | |
|---|---|
| ┌ Actions ➤ Junk E-mail ➤ Add to Junk Senders list | 669 |
| └ Actions ➤ Junk E-mail ➤ Add to Adult Content Senders list | 669 |

### Actions ➤ Junk E-mail ➤ Add to Junk Senders list

Use this option to identify the a specific sender as a Junk Sender. This option works in conjunction with the Junk E-mail tab on the Organize window, where you choose a color code to apply to all items identified as Junk E-mail. (For more information, see Tools ➤ Organize on page 630.)

#### How You Get Here

◇ Press **Alt+A,J,J**    ◇ Choose **Actions ➤ Junk E-mail ➤ Add to Junk Senders list**

### Actions ➤ Junk E-mail ➤ Add to Adult Content Senders list

Use this option to identify a specific sender as sending messages that contain adult content. This option works in conjunction with the Junk E-mail tab on the Organize window, where you choose a color code to apply to all items identified as containing adult content. (For more information, see Tools ➤ Organize on page 630.)

#### How You Get Here

◇ Press **Alt+A,J,A**    ◇ Choose **Actions ➤ Junk E-mail ➤ Add to Adult Content Senders list**

## Actions ➤ Reply

Use this option to open a new Mail Message form with the sender's address filled in for you. The default Outlook settings also include a copy of the original message in the Message Text pane.

### How You Get Here

◇ Click     ◇ Press **Alt+A,R or Ctrl+R**    ◇ Choose **Actions ➤ Reply**

## Actions ➤ Reply to All

Use this option to open a new Mail Message form with the sender's address and the address of all the recipients who got the original message filled in for you. The default Outlook settings also include a copy of the original message in the Message Text pane.

### How You Get Here

◇ Click     ◇ Press **Alt+A,L or Ctrl+Shift+R**    ◇ Choose **Actions ➤ Reply to All**

# Actions ➤ Forward

Use this option to open a new Mail Message form with a copy of the item as an attachment. You'll need to fill in the appropriate email address and add any comments that you feel are appropriate before clicking the **Send** icon.

## How You Get Here

◇ Click         ◇ Press **Alt+A,W** or **Ctrl+F**    ◇ Choose **Actions ➤ Forward**

# A Look At Outlook Mail's Forms

## In this chapter

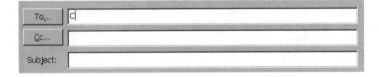

# What About Outlook Mail's Forms

Wow, we got lucky. Although there are a few different incarnations of the Message form, we couldn't find too many real differences. There are some changes in title bars (for example, when you're replying to a message the title bar says "reply to" instead of "new message).

Remember, you're filling in an electronic form. You're used to a lot of other forms, so you'll do just fine. Start at the top and fill in the blanks, click the **Send** button and you're off to the races (or at least your message is). This form, like all the other forms in Outlook, has its own set of menus, buttons, and all the other paraphernalia, although most of the options available should look pretty familiar—you've seen them in various places in the Office 2000 applications.

A few notes about messages.

- Messages can be sent immediately, or saved and sent later.
- Saved items that aren't sent are automatically stored in the Drafts folder.
- Mail items can be sorted according to six filters.
- Messages are sorted by the presence of a flag, not by the type of reminder on the mail item itself.
- Messages can be designated (by the sender only) as being of High, Normal, or Low importance.
- When you receive a message you can flag it to remind yourself to do some follow up work when you get a minute or two. This follow up (read and replay, read only, forward, etc.) appears in a yellow banner at the top of the mail item.

# Getting To The Forms

There are several ways to get to Outlook Mail's forms.

To create a new message you could:

- Click the **New** icon on the Standard toolbar and choose **New Message**,
- Press **Alt+F,W,M** or **Ctrl+N+Enter**, or
- Choose **File** ➤ **New** ➤ **Mail Message**.

To reply to a message you could:

- Click the **Reply** icon,
- Press **Alt+A,R** or **Ctrl+R**, or
- Choose **Actions** ➤ **Reply**.

To forward a message you could:

- Click the **Forward** icon,
- Press **Alt+A,W** or **Ctrl+F**, or
- Choose **Actions** ➤ **Forward**.

# A Look At Outlook Mail's Forms

There are several forms used when you're working with Outlook Mail, but they all have the same options as the Message form, so we've only included one sample. (Figure 44.1 is a sample of the form used to create a new message and Table 44.1 has a description of the options available.)

**Figure 44.1** The Message form

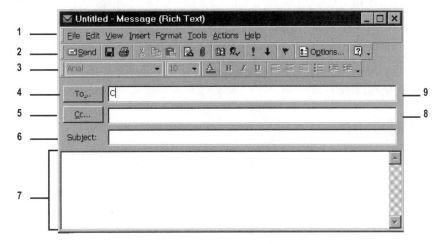

**Table 44.1** Options in the Message form

| # | Option | What you do with it |
|---|--------|---------------------|
| 1 | Message menu | Click to display the submenus for a specific group of commands. |
| 2 | Message Standard toolbar | Click to perform a specific command using a toolbar rather than a menu item. (For a complete description of the options available, see Table 44.2 on page 674.) |
| 3 | Formatting toolbar | Click to format the body of your appointment, meeting, or event message. (For a complete description of the options available, see Table 44.3 on page 675.) |
| 4 | To button | Click to choose names from your Address Book instead of typing the address in the To text box. |
| 5 | Cc button | Click to choose names from your Address Book instead of typing the address in the Cc text box. |
| 6 | Subject text box | Enter a description of the message contents that will give the recipients a quick idea of what to expect in the message. |
| 7 | Message pane | Enter the text of the message. |
| 8 | Cc text box | Enter the email address of the additional people who will receive a copy of this message. |
| 9 | To text box | Enter the email address of the people who will receive this message. |

# What's Different In Outlook Mail's Forms Toolbars

The Outlook Mail Message Standard and Formatting toolbars by default contain shortcuts commonly used when you are creating a new message. These toolbars can be customized, by showing and hiding buttons from the listing found under the More Buttons tool.

## Differences In Outlook Mail's Forms Standard Toolbar

Use this toolbar as a shortcut for perform common tasks, such as adding your signature to a message, copying, and setting the importance of your message.

### How You Get Here

◇ Press **Alt+V,T** choose **Standard**     ◇ Choose **View** ➤ **Toolbars** ➤ **Standard**

### What's Different

Figure 44.2 is a sample of this toolbar and Table 44.2 has a description of the icons available.

**Figure 44.2**   The Outlook Mail Forms Standard toolbar

**Table 44.2**   Icons in the Outlook Mail Forms Standard toolbar

| #  | Icon            | What you do with it                                                              |
|----|-----------------|---------------------------------------------------------------------------------|
| 1  | Send            | Click to send your message.                                                     |
| 2  | Save            | Click to save the message.                                                      |
| 3  | Cut             | Click to delete the highlighted text.                                           |
| 4  | Copy            | Click to send the highlighted text to the Clipboard.                            |
| 5  | Paste           | Click to copy the text you placed on the Clipboard into the desired location.   |
| 6  | Signature       | Click to insert or create a new signature that you can place in your message.   |
| 7  | Insert File     | Click to attach a file to this message.                                         |
| 8  | Check Names     | Click to make sure your message is addressed correctly.                         |
| 9  | Importance: High| Click to mark your message as very urgent.                                      |
| 10 | Importance: Low | Click to mark your message as not very urgent.                                  |
| 11 | Flag for Follow Up | Click to mark your message to be followed up later.                          |
| 12 | Options         | Click to display a list of additional options for your message.                 |

## Outlook Mail Forms Formatting Toolbar

Use the icons on this toolbar to determine what the text of your message looks like. You can choose the font size, color, and whether you want special effects such as underlining and bullets.

### How You Get Here

◇ Press **Alt+V,T** choose **Formatting**   ◇ Choose **View** ➤ **Toolbars** ➤ **Formatting**

### What's In This Toolbar

Figure 44.3 is a sample of this toolbar and Table 44.3 has a description of the icons available.

**Figure 44.3**   The Outlook Mail Forms Formatting toolbar

**Table 44.3**   Icons in the Outlook Mail Forms Formatting toolbar

| # | Icon | What you do with it |
|---|------|---------------------|
| 1 | Font | Click to choose the typeface you want to apply to the highlighted text. |
| 2 | Font Size | Click to choose the size you want to apply to the highlighted text. |
| 3 | Font Color | Click to apply a color to the highlighted text. |
| 4 | Bold | Click to make the highlighted text bold. |
| 5 | Italic | Click to make the highlighted text italic. |
| 6 | Underline | Click to underline the highlighted text. |
| 7 | Align Left | Click to align the text lines on the left side. |
| 8 | Center | Click to align the text lines around a center point. |
| 9 | Align Right | Click to align the text lines on the right side. |
| 10 | Bullet | Click to apply bullets to the highlighted text. |
| 11 | Decrease Indent | Click to make the space between the text and the margins smaller. You can press **Shift+Tab** to decrease the indent. |
| 12 | Increase Indent | Click to make the space between the text and the margins larger. You can also press **Tab** to increase indents. |

# A Look At The Calendar Application

# What Is The Calendar Application

## What Is The Calendar

The Calendar is used just like you would use any other calendar, only it happens to be electronic. You can use it to schedule your typical appointments (like the doctor's appointment you need to remember) or to schedule meetings with other people in your company. If your company has set up an intranet, or uses another form of networking, you may also be able to review meeting participants' calendars to find the best time to hold that project meeting or see when everyone is free to celebrate all of those July birthdays. You can also look at the same appointments several different ways: for example, you can look at just today's appointments to get a quick idea of what you need to be doing and then look at your calendar for an entire week (just to see if you're going to have time to see that wonderful show at the Ritz).

The basic things you'll do when you're working with the Calendar are:

- Entering appointments using the Event form,
- Scheduling a meeting using the Event form,
- Changing existing appointments or meetings,
- Reviewing to-do list activities,
- Changing existing information in one of the above categories, and
- Reviewing current or future events by displaying different views of the information you've entered.

## Getting To The Calendar

There are several ways to get to the Calendar, the most common being to:

- Click the ▣ icon on the Outlook Shortcuts bar,
- Press **Alt+V,G,C**, or
- Choose **View** ➤ **Go To** ➤ **Calendar**.

# How The Calendar Is Organized

Figure 45.1 shows one example of what your calendar can look like. Although you can look at different information in a bunch of different ways, there are only three basic parts to the application window (these are called "panes" in Windows-speak).

**Figure 45.1**   The Calendar application

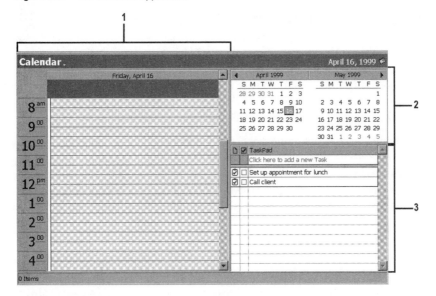

The three parts are:

**1.** The Appointments Pane

This pane displays your appointments, although the way the appointments are displayed depends on what view you're using at any given moment. You might be looking at one day's appointments or an entire month's appointments. No matter what view you're using, existing appointments are shown here. You can also enter or edit information about a specific appointment from this pane by double-clicking the appropriate entry. (For more information, see The Calendar Actions Menu on page 699.)

**2.** The Date Navigator Pane

The pane displays a monthly calendar with the current day emphasized with a gray box. Outlook assumes that you want to look at the current month and the following month, although you can display any months you need to by clicking the left or right arrow above the calendar.

**3.** The TaskPad Pane

This pane displays a lists of tasks you've entered into your electronic to-do list and indicates whether or not you've completed the tasks. You can add more tasks, change the status of existing tasks, or delete tasks from this pane just by double-clicking the appropriate entry. (For more information, see What Is The Tasks Application on page 771.)

# What, Exactly, Are Appointments

Calendar doesn't necessarily look at appointments the same way you do (or at least how I do). For me, if it goes on my calendar, it's an appointment. It may be a meeting with a client, a doctor's appointment, or a federal holiday. To me, they're all appointments. They're all appointments to Calendar, too. In fact, the form that you use to add these things to your calendar (the *Event Form)* looks pretty much the same regardless of which event you're adding. Calendar, however, makes a distinction between a basic appointment, and events and meetings:

- Appointments are occurrences that take place at a specific time and place. These are often such things as doctor's appointments.
- Events are appointments that last all day. They should be add to your calendar by choosing **Actions ➤ New All Day Event.** Events can be off-site all-day meetings, holidays, or sick days. Events have no start or end time, because they're presumed to take up the entire day.
- Meetings are appointments with somebody else. For many people, meetings are the most common kind of appointment.

# Getting Around In The Calendar

Keyboardists beware! You *can* use the keyboard to get around the Calendar, but it isn't intuitive or easy. You might want to pick up that mouse and give it a try. Mousers: you'll be in heaven since the Calendar is tailor-made for mousing around.

- Mousers: In the Appointment pane and the Date Navigator pane, just click on the month, day, and time in which you want to add, edit, or delete appointment information.  Use the arrows to move to another month or click on the name of the month and choose a new month from the drop down list.
- Keyboardists: The left and right arrows move you back and forth through the days in the Date Navigator, and the up and down arrows move you up and down the times listed in the Appointment pane.
- Mousers and keyboardists: There is a shortcut menu that has a list of the most commonly used options from the standard menu bar. Just right-click and choose the option you need.

---

**N O T E**    The most common answer I give regarding questions about Outlook is "it depends". In this case, what you see depends on what view you're working with, on which pane is active, and on what you just did. So once again, the answer to the question "What menus and toolbars are available?" is "it depends". We've tried to cover the majority of the options, but don't be surprised if you find a new one. ■

# What's Different In Calendar's Toolbars

A majority of the icons on both the Standard and Advanced toolbars were discussed in the chapter on common View menu options. (For more information, see View ➤ Toolbars on page 608.) There are only a few differences that you need to learn about for the Calendar application.

- For more information about the Standard toolbar, see Differences In Calendar's Standard Toolbar on page 683.
- For more information about the Advanced toolbar, see Differences In Calendar's Advanced Toolbar on page 684

## Differences In Calendar's Standard Toolbar

Use this toolbar as a shortcut for commonly performed tasks, such as Go To Today, Work Week, and other viewing options.

### How You Get Here

◇ Press **Alt+V,T** choose **Standard**   ◇ Choose **View ➤ Toolbars ➤ Standard**

### What's Different

Figure 45.1 is a sample of this toolbar and Table 45.1 has a description of the icons unique to the Calendar. (For more information, see View ➤ Toolbars ➤ Standard on page 609.)

**Figure 45.2**   The Calendar's Standard toolbar

**Table 45.1**   Icons in the Calendar's Standard toolbar

| # | Icon | What you do with it |
|---|------|---------------------|
| 1 | Go to Today | Click to display the appointments for today in the Appointment pane. |
| 2 | Day | Click to view a time span of one day in the appointment pane. |
| 3 | Work Week | Click to view a time span of the five work days in the appointment pane. |
| 4 | Week | Click to view a time span of one week in the appointment pane. |
| 5 | Month | Click to view a time span of one month in the appointment pane. |

## Differences In Calendar's Advanced Toolbar

Use this toolbar as a shortcut to some of the less frequently used tasks, such as the shortcut for planning a meeting. (For more information, see View ➤ Toolbars ➤ Advanced on page 610.)

## How You Get Here

◇ Press **Alt+V,T** choose **Advanced**    ◇ Choose **View** ➤ **Toolbars** ➤ **Advanced**

## What's In This Toolbar

Figure 45.3 is a sample of this toolbar and has a description of the one icon that is unique to the Calendar.

**Figure 45.3**    The Calendar's Advanced toolbar

Plan a Meeting—Click to enter information for a meeting. The Plan a Meeting dialog box is basically the same as the Attendee Availability tab on the Event window.

# The Calendar File Menu

## In this chapter

## What's Different In The Calendar File Menu

This menu lists the commands that you'll use to perform actions that affect the entire item or document in an application. These commands include saving your items so that you don't lose your work, printing an item, creating new items, creating shortcuts, choosing forms, and opening personal file folders.

If a menu option has an ellipsis (three dots) or an arrow beside it, the application "asks" you for additional information before the action takes place. If the menu doesn't have one of these symbols, the action you choose happens immediately. If the action takes place immediately, you won't see a sample screen in this section.

---

**N O T E**   Calendar's File menu has only one different option—File ➤ Save as Web Page, so don't be too surprised at how short this chapter is. (Yes, you can blame me for forcing that consistency thang!)

---

**T I P**   For information on the other options in the File menu, check out The Common File Menu Options on page 557.

---

## File ➤ Save as Web Page

Use this option to save an existing file as a Web page, using HTML. Sometimes you'll want to save what you're working on as a Web page, so you can view it yourself later in a browser or send it to someone else to look at. This is helpful if, for example, you want to share your week's schedule with users who don't have Outlook. However, don't expect the Web page to be used as a data source. That is, don't expect your Excel Web page to be usable as an Excel worksheet, for example.

### How You Get Here

◇ Press **Alt+F,G**                    ◇ Choose <u>File</u> ➤ **Save as Web Page**

## What's In This Dialog Box

Figure 46.1 is a sample of this dialog box and has a description of the options available.

**Figure 46.1**   The Save as Web Page dialog box

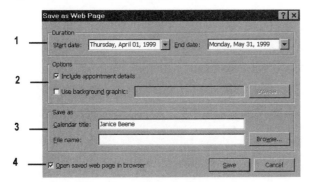

**Table 46.1**   Options in the Save as Web Page dialog box

| # | Option | What you do with it |
|---|--------|---------------------|
| 1 | Duration area | Choose an item that determines what interval of dates you want to save as a web page. |
| 2 | Options area | Choose an item that determines the details and graphics you want to include. You can use the **Browse** button to search for a specific file containing the desired graphic. |
| 3 | Save as area | Enter the title for this web page and the filename. You can use the **Browse** button to search for a specific file. |
| 4 | Open saved web page in browser check box | Click to automatically open the saved page in an Internet browser whenever someone opens the file. |

# The Calendar View Menu

**In this chapter**

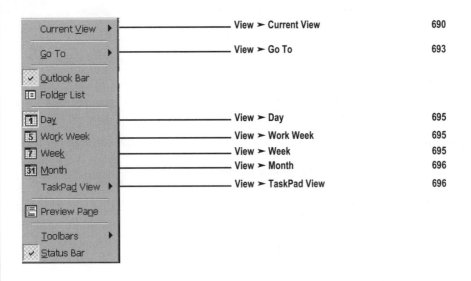

# What's Different In Calendar's View Menu

The Calendar's View menu is like any other View menu in a Microsoft application: it provides different ways for you to look the same information. It just depends on what you need at any given time. You can look at your appointments and meetings as one big list or you can look at something that resembles the more familiar datebook that you carry with you in your car. Instead of weeding through a ton of appointments and meetings to find the ones you want to look at, you can tell the Calendar you only want to look at ones that meet a specific criteria. For example, maybe you only want to look at meetings for a given month or with a given person.

If a menu option has an ellipsis (three dots) or an arrow beside it, the application "asks" you for additional information before the action takes place. If the menu doesn't have one of these symbols, the action you choose happens immediately. If the action takes place immediately, you won't see a sample screen in this section.

---

**N O T E**    Most of the options in this menu were described earlier in this book. (For more information, see The Common View Menu Options on page 595.) ■

# View ➤ Current View

Use this option to change the way you are viewing the Calendar or specific appointments and meetings already entered in your electronic calendar.

## How You Get Here

◇ Press **Alt+V,V**          ◇ Choose **View** ➤ **Current View**

## What's In This Flyout Menu

Figure 47.1 is a sample of this flyout menu.

**Figure 47.1**    The View ➤ Current View flyout menu

## View ➤ Current View ➤ Day/Week/Month

Use this option to view your calendar on a daily, weekly, or monthly basis (and add icons that match these increments on the Standard toolbar). This view is used to choose days and times to make appointments, and is considered the default view (when you start or reboot your computer, and first open Calendar, this is the view you get).

 **N O T E** Once you change views and close Outlook, re-opening Outlook and opening Calendar displays the most recent view selected. ▪

 **T I P** If you want to view two or three days, click and drag across those days in the Navigator pane.

### How You Get Here

◇ Press **Alt+V,V** choose **Day/Week/Month**     ◇ Choose **View** ➤ **Current View** ➤ **Day/Week/Month**

## View ➤ Current View ➤ Day Week/Month with AutoPreview

Use this option to automatically show the first few lines of comments you type into your appointments. These lines appear directly underneath the appointment entry, rather than in a separate pane.

### How You Get Here

◇ Press **Alt+V,V** choose **Day/Week/Month with AutoPreview**     ◇ Choose **View** ➤ **Current View** ➤ **Day/Week/Month with AutoPreview**

## View ➤ Current View ➤ Active Appointments

Use this view to display a listing of all future appointments recorded in the Calendar.

 **T I P** In this and the following lists, you can sort according to a column by clicking on the column title. If you keep clicking the column title, the information switches between ascending and descending order.

### How You Get Here

◇ Press **Alt+V,V** choose **Active Appointments**     ◇ Choose **View** ➤ **Current View** ➤ **Active Appointments**

## View ➤ Current View ➤ Events

Use this option to display a list of all the events scheduled in the Calendar.

---

**N O T E**   An event is a Calendar item that lasts all day, such as a company holiday or the company picnic held every Monday during the summer.  ▪

### How You Get Here

◇ Press **Alt+V,V** choose
   **Events**

◇ Choose **View** ➤ **Current View** ➤ **Events**

## View ➤ Current View ➤ Annual Events

Use this option to display a list of those events that happen only once a year.

---

**N O T E**   This list is actually a subset of the Events list and may be something personal, like a friend's birthday, or something business-related, like a national holiday.  ▪

### How You Get Here

◇ Press **Alt+V,V** choose
   **Annual Events**

◇ Choose **View** ➤ **Current View** ➤ **Annual Events**

## View ➤ Current View ➤ Recurring Appointments

Use this option to display only those appointments that you've marked as happening on a regular basis (which is where the term "recurring" comes from).

---

**N O T E**   This is a way to quickly enter appointments that happen in a set pattern, such as the weekly team meeting or the monthly outing. You have to mark an appointment or meeting as recurring when you enter it into your Calendar—Outlook won't do that for you.  ▪

### How You Get Here

◇ Press **Alt+V,V** choose
   **Recurring Appointments**

◇ Choose **View** ➤ **Current View** ➤ **Recurring Appointments**

## View ➤ Current View ➤ By Category

Use this option to display the appointments and meetings you've entered in your calendar based on a specific grouping ("category"). You do have to assign a category to the appointment or meeting (Outlook hasn't the foggiest idea what categories you want so it assigns a category of "none" unless you tell it otherwise).

---

**N O T E** Categories help you create a hierarchy of information and then group it together. For example, if you've got a big project you're working on (called it Project Update) and want to mark all meetings and appointments based on this project. You can enter the category "Project Update" and then look at all the meetings and appointments for just this project. This is a way to enter appointments that happen in a set pattern, such as the weekly team meeting or the monthly outing. You have to mark an appointment or meeting as recurring when you enter it into your Calendar—Outlook won't do that for you. ■

### How You Get Here

◇ Press **Alt+V,V** choose **By Category**    ◇ Choose **View ➤ Current View ➤ By Category**

# View ➤ Go To

Use this option to move quickly from one part of Outlook to another. This is an alternate method to using the Outlook Shortcuts bar or the Folder List. (For more information, see View ➤ Go To on page 600.)

### How You Get Here

◇ Press **Alt+V,G**    ◇ Choose **View ➤ Go To**

## What's In This Flyout Menu

Figure 47.2 is a sample of this flyout menu.

**Figure 47.2**   The View ➤ Go To flyout menu

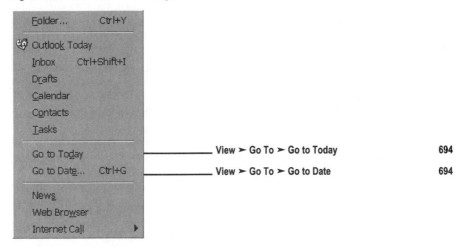

## View ➤ Go To ➤ Go to Today

Use this option to display the appointments for today in the Appointment pane.

> **N O T E**   This option is only available in the tri-pane view (the one that displays when you choose **View ➤ Current View ➤ Day/Week/Month**). ▨

### How You Get Here

◇ Press **Alt+V,G,D**          ◇ Choose **View ➤ Go To ➤ Go to Today**

## View ➤ Go To ➤ Go to Date

Use this option to display the Calendar information for a specific date. This is an alternate approach to using the Date Navigator.

> **N O T E**   This option is only available in the tri-pane view (the one that displays when you choose **View ➤ Current View ➤ Day/Week/Month**). ▨

### How You Get Here

◇ Press **Alt+V,G,E** or **Ctrl+G**   ◇ Choose **View ➤ Go To ➤ Date**

### What's In This Dialog Box

Figure 47.3 is a sample of this dialog box and Table 47.1 has a description of the options available.

**Figure 47.3** The Go To Date dialog box

**Table 47.1** Options in the Go To Date dialog box

| # | Option | What you do with it |
|---|--------|---------------------|
| 1 | Date drop-down list | Choose an item that determines what date you want to jump to. |
| 2 | Show in drop-down list | Choose an item that determines what view of your calendar you want to look at while reviewing the information available for the date specified in the Date drop-down list. |

# View ➤ Day

Use this option to display one day's worth of information in the Appointment pane.

### How You Get Here

◇ Click    ◇ Press **Alt+V,Y**   ◇ Choose **View ➤ Day**

# View ➤ Work Week

Use this option to display five days worth of information (a work week) in the Appointment pane.

### How You Get Here

◇ Click    ◇ Press **Alt+V,R**   ◇ Choose **View ➤ Work Week**

# View ➤ Week

Use this option to display seven days worth of information in the Appointment pane.

### How You Get Here

◇ Click    ◇ Press **Alt+V,K**   ◇ Choose **View ➤ Week**

# View ➤ Month

Use this option to display an entire month's worth of information in the Appointment pane.

## How You Get Here

◇ Click    ◇ Press **Alt+V,O**   ◇ Choose **View ➤ Month**

# View ➤ TaskPad View

Use this option to display the information in your Taskpad in a way that suits your current needs.

## How You Get Here

◇ Press **Alt+V,D**   ◇ Choose **View ➤ TaskPad View**

## What's In This Flyout Menu

Figure 47.4 is a sample of this flyout menu.

**Figure 47.4**   The TaskPad View flyout menu

### View ➤ TaskPad View ➤ All Tasks

Use this option to display all currently defined tasks in a table view.

#### How You Get Here

◇ Press **Alt+V,D,A**   ◇ Choose **View ➤ TaskPad View ➤ All Tasks**

### View ➤ TaskPad View ➤ Today's Tasks

Use this option to display only those tasks that are due to be completed today.

#### How You Get Here

◇ Press **Alt+V,D,T**   ◇ Choose **View ➤ TaskPad View ➤ Today's Tasks**

### View ➤ TaskPad View ➤ Active Tasks for Selected Days

Use this option to display only those tasks that match the date(s) highlighted in the Date Navigator pane. You will probably use this view frequently for quickly reviewing your tasks.

#### How You Get Here

✧ Press **Alt+V,D,C**     ✧ Choose **View** ➤ **TaskPad View** ➤ **Active Tasks for Selected Days**

### View ➤ TaskPad View ➤ Tasks for Next Seven Days

Use this option to display only those tasks that are current for the next seven days.

#### How You Get Here

✧ Press **Alt+V,D,S**     ✧ Choose **View** ➤ **TaskPad View** ➤ **Tasks for Next Seven Days**

### View ➤ TaskPad View ➤ Overdue Tasks

Use this option to apply a filter to display only those tasks whose due date has passed.

#### How You Get Here

✧ Press **Alt+V,D,O**     ✧ Choose **View** ➤ **TaskPad View** ➤ **Overdue Tasks**

### View ➤ TaskPad View ➤ Tasks Completed on Selected Days

Use this option to display only those tasks which were marked as complete on the on the day(s) highlighted in the Date Navigator.

#### How You Get Here

✧ Press **Alt+V,D,K**     ✧ Choose **View** ➤ **TaskPad View** ➤ **Tasks Completed on Selected Days**

### View ➤ TaskPad View ➤ Include Tasks With No Due Date

Use this option to view all tasks that don't have a specific due date.

---

**N O T E**   This option works in any view. ▮

#### How You Get Here

✧ Press **Alt+V,D,D**     ✧ Choose **View** ➤ **TaskPad View** ➤ **Include Tasks With No Due Date**

# The Calendar Actions Menu

## In this chapter

# What Is The Actions Menu

This menu lists the commands that you'll use to initiate any new activity related to setting appointments and setting up meetings. Other Microsoft applications work with documents (or files) and most are created using the New menu. Outlook applications, however, are usually relational. That is, they involve actions such as sending an email message, or scheduling a meeting with coworkers. Initiating these activities is done with the options in the Actions menu. The New menu still exists, but is used to create new folders, etc.

If a menu option has an ellipsis (three dots) or an arrow beside it, the application "asks" you for additional information before the action takes place. If the menu doesn't have one of these symbols, the action you choose happens immediately. If the action takes place immediately, you won't see a sample screen in this section.

N O T E   You'll use one basic form (the Events form) to enter your appointments and meetings so we've lumped that information into another chapter. (For more information, see A Look At Calendar's Forms on page 705.) ▦

# Actions ➤ New Appointment

Use this option to fill in the Event form and add an appointment to your calendar. Once you've added an appointment, you can change it or delete it or even forward it to the people who should be meeting with you.

## How You Get Here

✧ Click      ✧ Press **Alt+A,0** or **Ctrl+N**   ✧ Choose **Actions ➤ New Appointment**

# Actions ➤ New All Day Event

Use this option to create an event (which is basically an appointment or meeting that lasts an entire day). This is functionally identical to the standard Event form used to enter a new appointment. The Calendar just goes ahead and turns on the All Day Event check box for you.

T I P   Choosing **Actions ➤ New All Day Event** saves you a little time and keeps you from forgetting to click the **All Day Event** check box when you're adding a new event. You can, however, choose **Actions ➤ New Appointment** and then click the **All Day Event** check box.

## How You Get Here

✧ Press **Alt+A,E**           ✧ Choose **Actions ➤ New All Day Event**

# Actions ➤ New Meeting Request

Use this option to invite other people to a meeting that you want to hold. You can enter the email addresses of those invited to the meeting and automatically send an email message to advise people of the meeting.

### How You Get Here

◇ Press **Alt+A,Q or Ctrl+Shift+Q**   ◇ Choose **Actions ➤ New Meeting Request**

# Actions ➤ Plan a Meeting

Use this option to invite other people to a meeting *and* check the attendees' calendars to see if the time slot you want is actually open. How well this works depends on whether everyone involved enters the information on their electronic calendars.

---

**N O T E**   This dialog box is functionally identical to the Attendee Availability tab of the Event form, with the exception of the Make a Meeting and Close buttons. (For more information, see What's In The Attendee Availability Tab on page 713.) ▮

### How You Get Here

◇ Press **Alt+A,P**                    ◇ Choose **Actions ➤ Plan a Meeting**

### What's Different

Figure 48.1 is a sample of this dialog box and has a description of the options available.

**Figure 48.1**   The Plan a Meeting dialog box

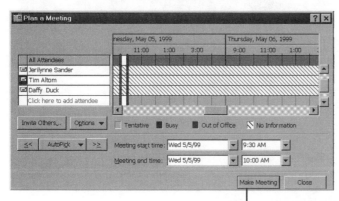

Click to open an Event form where you can complete the details of your meeting.

# Actions ➤ New Recurring Appointment

Use this option to add a recurring appointment to your calendar. A recurring appointment is one that you attend on a regular basis at the same time. You can choose how long the appointment lasts, how often the appointment occurs, and how long this appointment should show up on your calendar. Once you've entered a recurring appointment, you don't have to worry about it again. The system automatically inserts the appointment information in your calendar at the appropriate times.

**TIP**   This option is great for those appointments that tend to get left off of your calendar because you just *know* you'll remember them. You know the ones like "work out at 6:00 p.m." three nights a week?

## How You Get Here

◇ Press **Alt+A,A**         ◇ Choose **Actions ➤ New Recurring Appointment**

## What's In This Dialog Box

Figure 48.2 is a sample of this dialog box and Table 48.1 has a description of the options available.

**Figure 48.2**   The Appointment Recurrence dialog box

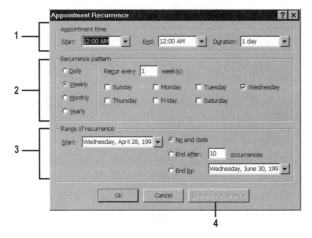

**Table 48.1** Options in the Appointment Recurrence dialog box

| # | Option | What you do with it |
|---|--------|---------------------|
| 1 | Appointment time area text boxes. | Enter the start and end times, or the start time and duration, from the drop down lists. You can also manually enter this text. |
| 2 | Recurrence pattern area | Choose an item that determines how frequently this appointment occur and enter a number that determines how frequently this appointment shows up on your calendar. The options to the right change according to the pattern selected. |
| 3 | Range of recurrence area | Enter a start date and enter the length of time you wish to continue seeing this appointment on your calendar. (for 10 occurrences, for one year, etc.). |
| 4 | Remove Recurrence button | Click to indicate that this appointment is no longer a recurring appointment. |

# Actions ➤ New Recurring Meeting

Use this option to create an item on your schedule for a meeting that occurs on a regular basis. Like the Actions ➤ New Recurring Appointment option, this saves you a lot of time and mental energy since you don't have to manually enter the appointment into your Calendar. (For a complete description of the options available, see Table 48.1 on page 703.)

## How You Get Here

◇ Press **Alt+A,C**   ◇ Choose **Actions ➤ New Recurring Meeting**

# Actions ➤ Add or Remove Attendees

Use this option to change who you want to attend a meeting or to respond to someone who is unable to attend. This dialog box contains a listing of your contacts. Those you choose are added to the attendee list, and should now appear on the Attendee Availability tab of the Event form.

---

**N O T E**   This option is available only when you have chosen to review a meeting entry that has attendees. ■

## How You Get Here

◇ Press **Alt+A,V**   ◇ Choose **Actions ➤ Add or Remove Attendees**

# Actions ➤ Forward as iCalendar

Use this option to save the highlighted item and attach it to an email message so that someone else can look at your calendar.

## How You Get Here

◇ Press **Alt+A,L**      ◇ Choose **Actions ➤ Forward as iCalendar**

## What's In This Dialog Box

Figure 48.3 is a sample of this dialog box and has a description of the options available

**Figure 48.3**   The FW: Message dialog box

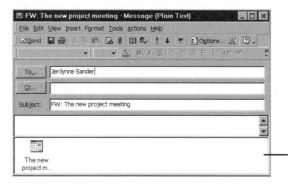

The attached calendar displays in this pane on an New Mail Message window.

# Actions ➤ Forward

Use this option to send a message you've received on to someone else. When you choose this option the Mail Message window displays so you can enter your message and choose whom you want to send the message to. This option is also found on the Standard toolbar for email.

## How You Get Here

◇ Click       ◇ Press **Alt+A,W** or **Ctrl+F**   ◇ Choose **Actions ➤ Forward**

# CHAPTER 49

# A Look At Calendar's Forms

## In this chapter

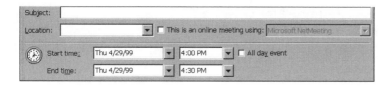

# What About Calendar's Forms

There are several forms that you'll use when you decide to work with the Calendar. Although they have different names, the forms look quite a bit alike and have many of the same options. Sounds pretty easy. And, basically, it is. You fill in the form just like you would fill in a form at your doctor's office or for the IRS. You, in essence, just answer the "questions". This form, like all the other forms in Outlook, has it's own set of menus, buttons, and all the other paraphernalia, although most of the options available should look pretty familiar—you've seen them in various places in the Office 2000 applications.

# Getting To The Forms

There are several ways to get to Calendar forms, depending on what you need to do.

- To display the Appointment form so that you can add a new appointment:

  - Click the **New** icon on the Standard toolbar and choose **Appointment,**
  - Press **Alt+F,W,A** or **Ctrl+N** or **Ctrl+Shift+A**, or
  - Choose **File** ➤ **New** ➤ **Appointment**.
- To display the Meeting form so that you add a new meeting:

  - Click the **New** icon on the Standard toolbar and choose **Meeting Request,**
  - Press **Alt+F,W,Q** or **Ctrl+Shift+Q**, or
  - Choose **File** ➤ **New** ➤ **Meeting Request**.
- To display the Event form so that you can add the information for a new event, press **Alt+A,W, E**

# A Look At Calendar's Forms

There are three forms used when you're working with Calendar:

- An Appointment form,
- A Meeting form, and
- An Event form.

## The Appointment Form

Figure 49.2 is a sample of the form that you'll use when you want to add something to your own calendar and Table 49.1 has a description of the options available.

**Figure 49.1**    The Appointment form

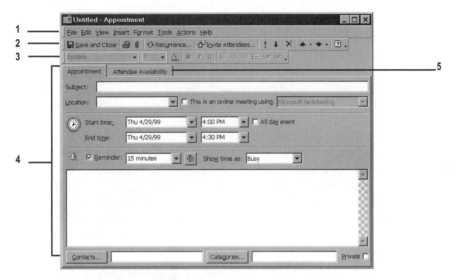

**Table 49.1**    Options in the Appointment form

| # | Option | What you do with it |
|---|--------|---------------------|
| 1 | Appointment menus | Click to display the submenus for a specific group of commands. |
|   |  | **Note**  Most of these menu options are the same as those found on the Outlook menu bar. However, there are a few commands that apply specifically to adding or changing appointments. |
| 2 | Appointments Standard toolbar | Click to perform a specific command using a toolbar rather than a menu item. (For more information, see Differences In Calendar's Forms Standard Toolbar on page 714.) |
| 3 | Formatting toolbar | Click to format the body of your appointment, meeting, or event message. (For more information, see The Calendar Forms Formatting Toolbar on page 715.) |

**Table 49.1**   Options in the Appointment form, continued

| # Option | What you do with it |
|---|---|
| 4   Appointments tab | Click to fill in (or change) the information about a specific appointment. Since most of these items are the same for all three Calendar forms, they're described in their own section. (For a complete description of the options available, see Table 49.4 on page 712.) |
| 5   Attendee Availability Tab | Fill in (or change) the information about the schedules and availability of people that you're inviting to a meeting. You can check attendee availability only if the attendees are using Outlook and are connected to the same network that you're connected to. (For a complete description of the options available, see Table 49.5 on page 714.) |
| | **Note**   Technically, any appointment with attendees is considered a *meeting*. |

## The Meeting Form

Figure 49.2 is a sample of the form that you'll use when you're scheduling meetings with other people that have electronic calendars or when you want to automatically notify attendees of an upcoming meeting. In addition to the options you'll see on the Appointment form, this one has a place for you to enter email addresses so that you can let everybody know that you're trying to schedule a meeting. Table 49.2 has a description of the options available.

**Figure 49.2**   The Meeting form

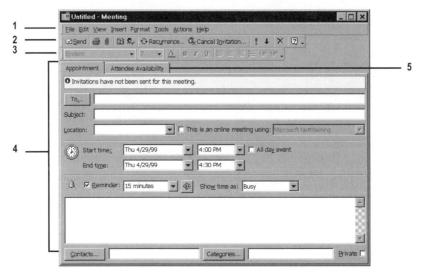

**Table 49.2**  Options in the Meeting form

| # | Option | What you do with it |
|---|--------|---------------------|
| 1 | Meeting menus | Click to display the submenus for a specific group of commands. |
|   |   | **Note**  Most of these menu options are the same as those found on the Outlook menu bar. However, there are a few commands that apply specifically to adding or changing appointments. |
| 2 | Meeting Standard toolbar | Click to perform a specific command using a toolbar rather than a menu item. (For more information, see Differences In Calendar's Forms Standard Toolbar on page 714.) |
| 3 | Formatting toolbar | This toolbar contains the tools you need for formatting the body of your appointment message. |
| 4 | Appointments tab | Fill in (or change) the information about a specific appointment. Since most of these items are the same for all three Calendar forms, they're described in their own section. (For a complete description of the options available, see Table 49.4 on page 712.) |
| 5 | Attendee Availability Tab | Fill in (or change) the information about the schedules and availability of people that you're inviting to a meeting. You can check attendee availability only if the attendees are using Outlook and are connected to the same network that you're connected to. (For a complete description of the options available, see Table 49.5 on page 714.) |
|   |   | **Note**  Technically, Outlook sees any appointment with attendees as a *meeting*. |

## The Event Form

Figure 49.3 is a sample of the form that you'll use when you're ready to add a new event to your calendar (remember, events are those all day appointments like a national holiday).Table 49.3 has a description of the options available.

**Figure 49.3**   The Event form

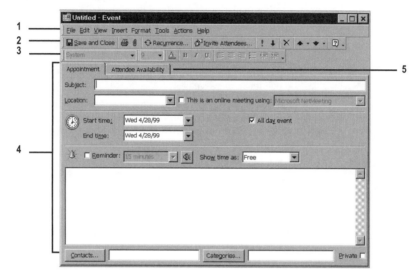

**Table 49.3**   Options in the Event form

| # | Option | What you do with it |
|---|--------|---------------------|
| 1 | Event menus | Click to display the submenus for a specific group of commands. |
|   |  | **Note**   Most of these menu options are the same as those found on the Outlook menu bar. However, there are a few commands that apply specifically to adding or changing appointments. |
| 2 | Event Standard toolbar | Click to perform a specific command using a toolbar rather than a menu item. (For more information, see Differences In Calendar's Forms Standard Toolbar on page 714.) |
| 3 | Formatting toolbar | This toolbar contains the tools you need for formatting the body of your appointment. |

**Table 49.3**   Options in the Event form, continued

| # | Option | What you do with it |
|---|--------|---------------------|
| 4 | Appointments tab | Fill in (or change) the information about a specific appointment. Since most of these items are the same for all three Calendar forms, they're described in their own section. (For a complete description of the options available, see Table 49.4 on page 712.) |
| 5 | Attendee Availability Tab | Fill in (or change) the information about the schedules and availability of people that you're inviting to a meeting. You can only check attendee availability if the attendees are using Outlook and are connected to the same network. (For a complete description of the options available, see Table 49.5 on page 714.) |
| | | Note   Technically, any appointment with attendees is considered a *meeting*. |

# What's In The Appointment Tab

Use the options in this tab to set up specific criteria (such as the date, time, location) for the different types of appointments that you create and maintain. Figure 49.4 is a sample of this tab' and Table 49.4 has a description of the options available. (And yes, I know that we promised to be consistent when we wrote this manual, but I just couldn't see putting a description of this tab in a bunch of times with the same information over and over again!)

---

**N O T E**   Once you've used one of the Calendar forms, the others shouldn't be too bad since there are only a couple of differences between the forms. ■

**Figure 49.4**   The Appointment tab

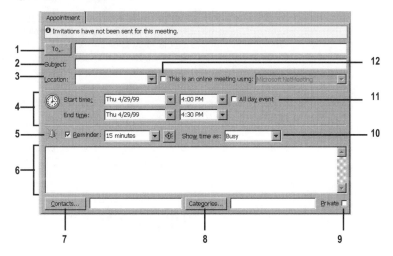

**Table 49.4**    Options in the Appointment tab

| # | Option | What you do with it |
|---|--------|---------------------|
| 1 | To button and text box | Click to choose the attendees for your meeting. You can also enter the email addresses in the text box if you happen to know them. |
|   |  | **Note**  This option displays whenever you are entering a meeting request or when you click the **Invite Attendees** icon on the Standard toolbar. You won't see this option if you're working with the Appointments or Event forms. |
| 2 | Subject text box | Enter the subject of the appointment, meeting or event. You might want to make sure this is something that helps you remember the purpose of the meeting since it displays in the various Calendar views. |
| 3 | Location drop-down list and text box | Choose an item that determines where you have to go (or be) for this appointment, meeting, or event. You can also enter a location name. This information displays in the various Calendar views. |
| 4 | Time area | Choose an item that determines the date and time when your appointment or meeting will be held. |
|   |  | **Note**  This option changes a bit when you're working with an Event. When you turn on the All day Event option, the time drop-down lists go away—this is, after all, an *all day event!* You don't need a start or stop time for that, right? |
| 5 | Reminder check box and drop-down list | Check to set an audible alarm that reminds you about your upcoming appointment, meeting, or event. Once you've turned on this option, you can choose how much notice you want to receive from the Reminder drop-down list. |
| 6 | Notes text box | Enter additional notes about the appointment, meeting, or event. |
| 7 | Contacts button/text box | Click to display a list so that you can choose the attendees for this appointment, meeting, or event from your existing list of contacts (the ones entered in the Contacts application). Or, if you prefer, you can enter the names manually in the text box. |
| 8 | Categories button/text box | Click to display the Categories dialog box so that you can choose an existing group for this appointment, meeting, or event. Although this may not seem particularly relevant, it helps when you're trying to sort information later. You can also enter these categories manually by separating each category with a comma. |
| 9 | Private check box | Click to hide the current appointment, meeting, or event from other people that have access to your calendar. |
| 10 | Show time as drop-down list | Choose an item that determines how you want the time frame for this appointment, meeting, or event blocked out on your calendar. |

**Table 49.4**   Options in the Appointment tab, continued

| # Option | What you do with it |
|---|---|
| 11 All day event check box | Click to indicate that this is an all day event. Once you turn on this option, the time drop-down lists disappear and the Calendar inserts and end date for the event. |
| | **Note**  This option is already turned on for you if you choose **Add New All Day Event** instead of **Add New Appointment**. |
| 12 This is an online meeting check box and drop-down list | Click to let your system know that you'll be "attending" this meeting using electronic media. Once you've turned on this option, you need to choose the server that will be used to conduct the meeting. |

## What's In The Attendee Availability Tab

Use the options in this tab to fill in or change the information about the schedules and availability of people that you're inviting to a meeting. This tab shows up on all three of the Calendar forms and the options are available on all three. No matter what you intended or believed when you set up a form, once you use the functions on this tab, the Calendar figures you're setting up a meeting. Figure 49.5 is a sample of this tab and Table 49.5 has a description of the options available. (Yup, you caught me again. I'm not using the menus for the main levels. But doggone it, it just wasn't working since they changed so frequently.)

---

**N O T E**    Once you've used one of the Calendar forms, the others shouldn't be too bad since there are only a couple of differences between the forms. ■

**Figure 49.5**   The Attendee Availability tab

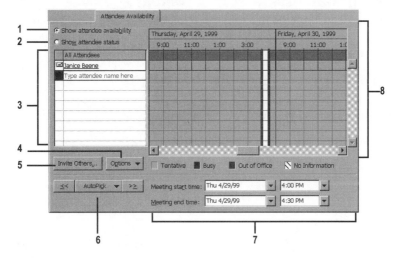

**Table 49.5**   Options in the Attendee Availability tab

| # | Option | What you do with it |
|---|--------|---------------------|
| 1 | Show attendee availability radio button | Click to display a matrix of the meeting attendees or invitees, and a version of their calendars with "busy" times blocked out. |
| 2 | Show Attendee status radio button | Click to display a matrix of the attendees who have responded to your request for a meeting and their actual response (can't attend, etc.). |
| 3 | All attendees text boxes | Enter names of attendees for the meeting. |
| 4 | Options button | Click to display a drop down list, where you can choose how you want the attendees schedule displayed in the matrix (i.e. Show only working hours). |
| 5 | Invite Others button | Click to display the Contacts list so that you choose more attendees for your meeting. These names are automatically placed on the All Attendees list. |
| 6 | AutoPick button | Choose an item that determines the next available free time for all designated attendees. |
|   |   | **Note**   Use the Back arrow to choose a date and time earlier than currently shown, and the Forward arrow to choose a date and time later than currently shown. |
| 7 | Time area | Choose an item that determines the date and time when your meeting will be held. |
| 8 | Availability Matrix | View the availability of each attendee, based on the information stored in their calendars. Check the color-coded legend below the matrix for a definition of what each color means.  The green (begin time) and red (end time) bar is the indicates the meeting time indicated in the Time area. |

# What's Different In Calendar's Forms Toolbars

The Calendar Event form standard and formatting toolbars by default contain shortcuts commonly used when you are creating a new event. These toolbars can be customized, by showing and hiding buttons from the listing found under the More Buttons tool.

## Differences In Calendar's Forms Standard Toolbar

Use this toolbar as a shortcut for commonly performed tasks, such as attaching a file, inviting attendees to meetings, and saving a copy of your appointment, meeting, or event.

---

**N O T E**   The Appointment form and Event form toolbars are exactly the same. The Standard toolbar for the Meeting form has a **Send** icon instead of a **Save and Close** icon.  ▓

## How You Get Here

◇ Press **Alt+V,T** choose **Standard**     ◇ Choose **View** ➤ **Toolbars** ➤ **Standard**

## What's Different

Figure 49.6 is a sample of this toolbar and Table 49.6 has a description of the icons unique to the Forms Standard toolbar.

**Figure 49.6**   The Calendar Forms Standard toolbar

**Table 49.6**   Icons in the Calendar Forms Standard toolbar

| # | Icon | What you do with it |
|---|------|---------------------|
| 1 | Save and Close | Click to save this event and close the event window. |
|   |   | **Note**  If you are planning a meeting or inviting people to this appointment this icon changes to the **Send** icon so that you can send email message to the people you're inviting to the meeting. |
| 2 | Insert File | Click to attach a file to this appointment. |
| 3 | Recurrence | Click to set up a event that you will routinely attend. |
| 4 | Invite Attendees | Click to activate the To button and text box where you can enter or choose the attendees for your event. |
|   |   | **Note**  When you choose this icon it changes to read Cancel Invitation. |
| 5 | Importance: High | Click to mark your message as very urgent and tell the system to send it as quickly as possible. |
| 6 | Importance: Low | Click to mark your message as not very urgent and tell the system to send it as soon as it gets a chance. |
| 7 | Previous Item | Click to move to a previous item. |
| 8 | Next Item | Click to move to the next item. |

## The Calendar Forms Formatting Toolbar

Use the icons on this toolbar to determine what the text of your appointment, meeting, or event looks like. You can choose the font size, color, and whether you want special effects such as underlining and bullets.

---

**N O T E**   This toolbar is the same for all of the forms used in the various applications. (For more information, see Outlook Mail Forms Formatting Toolbar on page 675.) ▦

# A Look At The Contacts Application

# CHAPTER 50

# What Is The Contacts Application

## In this chapter

# What Is The Contacts Application

Outlook Contacts is the glue that holds many of Outlooks components together.  It manages all of the email addresses used when you contact people to set up a meeting (Calendar), send an email message or fax (Outlook Mail), or forward any other Outlook item, such as notes, tasks, and even journal items. Contacts manages much more than just the email addresses; it also can hold just about everything you need to know about that person, including the names of the spouse and children, the business phone number, the company he or she works for and his or her title, even birthdays and company anniversaries.

# Getting To Contacts

There are several ways to get to the Calendar, the most common being to:

■   Click the 🖼 icon on the Outlook Shortcuts bar,
■   Press **Alt+F,W,C** or **Ctrl+Shift+C** or **Alt+N+↓+C,** or
■   Choose F̲ile ➤ Ne̲w ➤ **Contacts.**

# How Contacts Desktop Is Organized

The default view is Address Cards and looks like a phone book or card file (Figure 50.1 gives you a quick look at a couple of contact records in this view). Although you can look at different information in a bunch of different ways, there is still a basic set of information that you'll see in most views: the contact record and the alphabetical indicators. The exceptions are category view (if a contact isn't in a category) and if Contacts is viewed as a Web page (if it isn't set up properly yet).

**Figure 50.1**   The Contacts Application

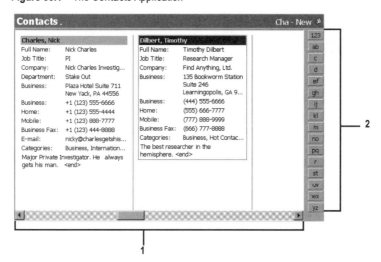

The two parts are:

1. **The Contact record pane**
   This pane displays the information about as many contacts as can be displayed on your screen at one time. You can use the scroll bars to move back and forth through the list to find the record you need. If you're using a table view, the items are sorted based on the criteria you choose. If you're using the Address Record view, the contact information is sorted alphabetically.

2. **The Alphabet Sort pane**
   The pane displays a set of tabbed dividers that you can use to quickly jump to a specific part of the alphabet.

# What's Different In Contacts' Toolbars

A good majority of the icons on both the Standard and Advanced toolbars were discussed in the chapter on common View menu options.(For more information, see View ➤ Toolbars on page 608.) There are only a few differences that you need to learn about for the Calendar application.

## Differences in Contacts' Standard Toolbar

Use this toolbar as a shortcut for commonly performed tasks, such as creating a new message for a contact and automatically dialing a contact's telephone number.

## How You Get Here

◇ Press **Alt+V,T** choose **Standard**  ◇ Choose **View ➤ Toolbars ➤ Standard**

## What's Different

Figure 50.2 is a sample of this toolbar and Table 50.1 has a description of the icons unique to Contacts. (For more information, see View ➤ Toolbars ➤ Standard on page 609.)

**Figure 50.2**  The Contacts' Standard toolbar

**Table 50.1**  Icons in the Contacts' Standard toolbar

| # | Icon | What you do with it |
|---|------|---------------------|
| 1 | Flag for Follow Up | Click to apply a flag and designate what follow-up action is intended. |
| 2 | New Message to Contact | Click to open a new Message form with the current contact as the addressee. |
| 3 | AutoDialer | Click to automatically dial the phone number of a designated contact. <br> **Note**  You must have a modem to use this option. |

## Differences in Contacts' Advanced Toolbar

Use this toolbar as a shortcut to some of the less frequently used tasks, such as the shortcut for creating a meeting request for the currently displayed contact. (For more information, see View ➤ Toolbars ➤ Advanced on page 610.)

## How You Get Here

◇ Press **Alt+V,T** choose **Advanced**    ◇ Choose **View** ➤ **Toolbars** ➤ **Advanced**

## What's Different

Figure 50.3 is a sample of this toolbar and Table 50.2 has a description of the icons that are unique to Contacts.

**Figure 50.3**    The Contacts' Advanced toolbar

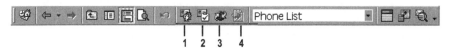

**Table 50.2**    Icons in the Contacts' Advanced toolbar

| # | Icon | What you do with it |
|---|------|---------------------|
| 1 | New Meeting Request to Contact | Click to open a Meeting Request form addressed to the current contact(s). |
| 2 | New Task for Contact | Click to open a Task Request form addressed to the current contact(s). |
| 3 | Call Using NetMeeting | Click to start a conference using NetMeeting. NetMeeting must be installed to access this option. |
|   |  | Note  Since we haven't discussed NetMeeting in this book, we thought you might like to know where to get some more information. Try *Windows 98 Multimedia: Lights! Camera! Action!* by Adam Vujic (this is published by Que and the ISBN is 078971857X). |
| 4 | Explore Web Page | Click to open the Web Page listed for the highlighted contact. You must be online to access this option. |

# The Contacts View Menu

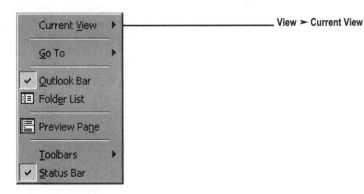

# What's Different In Contact's View Menu

The Contacts view menu provides options for displaying the information about the contacts you've added to your Contacts database. You can look at the information the same way you would look at your physical card file (the Address Card view) or you can view the contacts as a table sorted by the information you need most at any given time. When you view the information about your contacts in Address Card view, the names are in alphabetical order. When you view the information as a table, you can choose how the information is organized.

If a menu option has an ellipsis (three dots) or an arrow beside it, the application "asks" you for additional information before the action takes place. If the menu doesn't have one of these symbols, the action you choose happens immediately. If the action takes place immediately, you won't see a sample screen in this section.

---

**N O T E**    Most of the options in this menu were described earlier in this book. (For more information, see The Common View Menu Options on page 595.) ■

# View ➤ Current View

Use this option to change the way you are viewing the application or item.

## How You Get Here

◇ Press **Alt+V,V**           ◇ Choose **View ➤ Current View**

## What's In This Flyout Menu

Figure 51.1 is a sample of this flyout menu.

**Figure 51.1**    The View ➤ Current View flyout menu

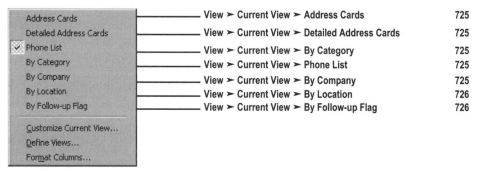

| | |
|---|---|
| View ➤ Current View ➤ Address Cards | 725 |
| View ➤ Current View ➤ Detailed Address Cards | 725 |
| View ➤ Current View ➤ By Category | 725 |
| View ➤ Current View ➤ Phone List | 725 |
| View ➤ Current View ➤ By Company | 725 |
| View ➤ Current View ➤ By Location | 726 |
| View ➤ Current View ➤ By Follow-up Flag | 726 |

## View ➤ Current View ➤ Address Cards

Use this option to display information about your contacts in a view that looks very similar to the old, familiar business card file. Distribution lists are shown first, followed by individual contacts.

### How You Get Here

◇ Press **Alt+V,V** choose **Address Cards**      ◇ Choose **View** ➤ **Current View** ➤ **Address Cards**

## View ➤ Current View ➤ Detailed Address Cards

Use this option to display your contacts in Address Card format, with more detailed information included.

### How You Get Here

◇ Press **Alt+V,V**
  choose **Detailed Address Cards**      ◇ Choose **View** ➤ **Current View** ➤ **Detailed Address Cards**

## View ➤ Current View ➤ Phone List

Use this option to display a list of contacts in a table, sorted by the phone number. Other information, such as company, is also displayed.

### How You Get Here

◇ Press **Alt+V,V** choose **Phone List**      ◇ Choose **View** ➤ **Current View** ➤ **Phone List**

## View ➤ Current View ➤ By Category

Use this option to display a list of contacts in a table, sorted by the category assigned to the contact. If no category has been assigned, the display indicates (none).

### How You Get Here

◇ Press **Alt+V,V** choose **By Category**      ◇ Choose **View** ➤ **Current View** ➤ **By Category**

## View ➤ Current View ➤ By Company

Use this option to display a list of contacts in a table, sorted by the company name.

### How You Get Here

◇ Press **Alt+V,V** choose **By Company**      ◇ Choose **View** ➤ **Current View** ➤ **By Company**

## View ➤ Current View ➤ By Location

Use this option to display a list of your contacts in a table, sorted by the country where the contact does business.

### How You Get Here

◇ Press **Alt+V,V** choose **By Location**     ◇ Choose **View** ➤ **Current View** ➤ **By Location**

## View ➤ Current View ➤ By Follow-up Flag

Use this option to displays a list of your contacts in table, sorted by the presence of a follow-up flag. They aren't sorted according to the follow-up action indicated under the flag heading of the item.

### How You Get Here

◇ Press **Alt+V,V** choose **By Follow-up Flag**   ◇ Choose **View** ➤ **Current View** ➤ **By Follow-up Flag**

# The Contacts Tools Menu

**In this chapter**

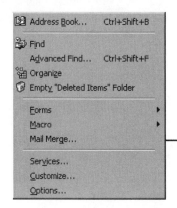

# What Is The Contacts Tools Menu

This menu includes options that make using your application easier and more efficient. This chapter contains one option that is unique to the Contacts Application. (For more information, see The Common Tools Menu Options on page 623.)

If a menu option has an ellipsis (three dots) or an arrow beside it, the application "asks" you for additional information before the action takes place. If the menu doesn't have one of these symbols, the action you choose happens immediately. If the action takes place immediately, you won't see a sample screen in this section.

# Tools ➤ Mail Merge

Use this option to create a file from your list of contacts so that you can send a specific group of contacts the same message, print mailing labels for hardcopy mailings, or put the contact information into a form letter. You can filter your contacts using different types of views to narrow the list of names you want to include in the mail merge. For instance, if you want to email your competition regarding a great new contract you've won, you can search by category view for all those categorized as competition! You could also create a personal list of birthdays of your favorite people to help remind you to send cards or flowers.

## How You Get Here

◇ Press **Alt+T,G**          ◇ Choose **Tools ➤ Mail Merge**

## What's In This Dialog Box

Figure 52.1 is a sample of this dialog box and Table 52.1 has a description of the options available.

**Figure 52.1**   The Mail Merge Contacts dialog box

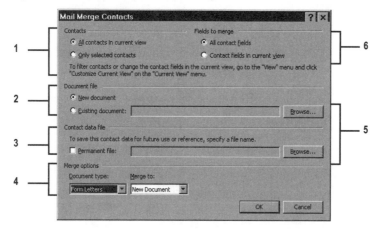

**Table 52.1**   Options in the Mail Merge Contacts dialog box

| # | Option | What you do with it |
|---|--------|---------------------|
| 1 | Contacts area | Choose an item that determines which contacts you want to use for this mailing or mail merge function. |
| 2 | Document file area | Choose an item that determines whether you want use an existing document as the source for the common information or whether you want to create a new one. |
| 3 | Contact data file area | Choose an item that determines whether you want to keep a permanent record of the particular merge function you're working on right now. |
| 4 | Merge options area | Choose an item that determines what type of document you're creating and whether you want to merge the new information to a different file. |
| 5 | Browse buttons | Click to search for the desired file using the standard Windows Explore functions. |
| 6 | Fields to merge area | Click to choose the individual fields containing the contact information you want to include in the merge. |

# The Contacts Actions Menu

## In this chapter

# What Is The Actions Menu

This menu lists the commands that you'll use to initiate any new activity related to working with your contacts. For example, creating a Meeting Request form for a specific contact or sending an email message to the currently displayed contact—without even having to fill in the address information. Other Microsoft applications work with documents (or files) and most are created using the New menu. Outlook applications, however, are usually relational. That is, they involve actions such as sending an email message, or scheduling a meeting with coworkers. Initiating these activities is done with the options in the Actions menu. The New menu still exists, but is used to create new folders, etc.

If a menu option has an ellipsis (three dots) or an arrow beside it, the application "asks" you for additional information before the action takes place. If the menu doesn't have one of these symbols, the action you choose happens immediately. If the action takes place immediately, you won't see a sample screen in this section.

# Actions ➤ New Contact

Use this option to add a new contact to your contacts database.

## How You Get Here

◇ Click 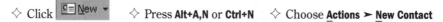   ◇ Press **Alt+A,N** or **Ctrl+N**   ◇ Choose **Actions ➤ New Contact**

# Actions ➤ New Contact from Same Company

Use this option to add a new contact to your contacts database. This option opens a New Contact form, with the current company information automatically entered in the Company Name field.

## How You Get Here

◇ Press **Alt+A,C**        ◇ Choose **Actions ➤ New Contact from Same Company**

# Actions ➤ New Distribution List

Use this option to create a new distribution list.

## How You Get Here

◇ Press **Alt+A,D** or **Ctrl+Shift+L**  ◇ Choose **Actions ➤ New Distribution List**

# Actions ➤ New Message to Contact

Use this option to create an email message for the current contact. The New Message form opens with the email address already completed for you.

## How You Get Here

◇ Press **Alt+A,M**          ◇ Choose **Actions** ➤ **New Message to Contact**

# Actions ➤ New Letter to Contact

Use this option to open the Letter Wizard, with the contact information automatically entered into the designated headings (address, first name, etc.).

## How You Get Here

◇ Press **Alt+A,L**          ◇ Choose **Actions** ➤ **New Letter to Contact**

# Actions ➤ New Meeting Request to Contact

Use this option to create a Meeting Request for the current contact. The Meeting Request form opens with the appropriate address information already completed for you.

## How You Get Here

◇ Press **Alt+A,G**          ◇ Choose **Actions** ➤ **New Meeting Request to Contact**

# Actions ➤ New Appointment with Contact

Use this option to create an Appointment form with the current contact information already completed for you.

## How You Get Here

◇ Press **Alt+A,P**          ◇ Choose **Actions** ➤ **New Appointment with Contact**

# Actions ➤ New Task for Contact

Use this option to create a Task form with the current contact information already completed for you.

## How You Get Here

◇ Press **Alt+A,T**          ◇ Choose **Actions** ➤ **New Task for Contact**

# Actions ➤ New Journal Entry for Contact

Use this option to create a Journal Entry form with the current contact information already completed for you.

### How You Get Here

◇ Press **Alt+A,J**          ◇ Choose **Actions ➤ New Journal Entry for Contact**

# Actions ➤ Link

Use this option to establish a link between the current contact and an item (in Outlook) or the current contact and a specific file (in Microsoft Windows Explorer). Links are used when more than one person (contact) shares information and updates made by one are automatically updated in the linked contact's item or file as well.

### How You Get Here

◇ Press **Alt+A,I**          ◇ Choose **Actions ➤ Link**

### What's In This Flyout Menu

Figure 53.2 is a sample of this flyout menu.

**Figure 53.1**   The Actions ➤ Link flyout menu

| | | |
|---|---|---|
| Items... | Actions ➤ Link ➤ Items | 734 |
| File... | Actions ➤ Link ➤ File | 734 |

### Actions ➤ Link ➤ Items

Use this option to establish a link between the current contact and an Outlook item chosen from Personal Folder File.

### How You Get Here

◇ Press **Alt+A,I,I**          ◇ Choose **Actions ➤ Link ➤ Items**

### Actions ➤ Link ➤ File

Use this option to establish a link between your contact and a file from another application, such as Word or Excel.

### How You Get Here

◇ Press **Alt+A,I,F**          ◇ Choose **Actions ➤ Link ➤ File**

# Actions ➤ Call Contact

Use this option to place a call using AutoDial to the phone number entered for the selected contact.

---

**N O T E**  You must be connected to a modem to access this option. ▣

## How You Get Here

◇ Press **Alt+A,A**    ◇ Choose **Actions ➤ Call Contact**

## What's In This Flyout Menu

Figure 53.2 is a sample of this flyout menu.

**Figure 53.2**   The Actions ➤ Call Contact flyout menu

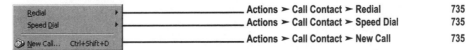

| | |
|---|---|
| Actions ➤ Call Contact ➤ Redial | 735 |
| Actions ➤ Call Contact ➤ Speed Dial | 735 |
| Actions ➤ Call Contact ➤ New Call | 735 |

## Actions ➤ Call Contact ➤ Redial

Use this option to redial the designated number. This is used, for example, when the line was busy or if you've just hung up, but forgotten to tell the contact the piece of information that prompted you to call him or her the first time.

## How You Get Here

◇ Press **Alt+A,A,R**    ◇ Choose **Actions ➤ Call Contact ➤ Redial**

## Actions ➤ Call Contact ➤ Speed Dial

Use this option to use the speed dial options pre-set for this contact. The flyout menu indicated (none) if there have been none designated.

## How You Get Here

◇ Press **Alt+A,A,D**    ◇ Choose **Actions ➤ Call Contact ➤ Speed Dial**

## Actions ➤ Call Contact ➤ New Call

Use this option to automatically dial the number of any contact designated in the New Call dialog box.

## How You Get Here

◇ Press **Alt+A,A,N** or **Ctrl+Shift+D**    ◇ Choose **Actions ➤ Call Contact ➤ New Call**

## What's In This Dialog Box

Figure 53.3 is a sample of this dialog box and Table 53.1 has a description of the options available.

**Figure 53.3**   The New Call dialog box

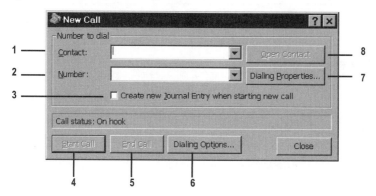

**Table 53.1**   Options in the New Call dialog box

| # | Option | What you do with it |
|---|--------|---------------------|
| 1 | Contact text box/drop-down list | Choose an item that determines the name of the contact you want to call, or enter the contact manually. |
| 2 | Number text box/drop-down list | Choose an item that determines the phone number of the contact you want to call (he or she may have more than one phone number). You may also enter the telephone number manually. |
| 3 | Create new Journal Entry when starting new call check box | Click to automatically start a Journal entry for this call. This records the stop and start time of the call and other standard Journal information. |
| 4 | Start Call button | Click to dial the number as displayed in the Number text box. |
| 5 | End Call button | Click to disconnect the call. |
| 6 | Dialing Options button | Click to set up Speed Dialing options, and establish dialing properties and line properties. |
| 7 | Dialing Properties button | Click to display the properties associated with this phone call, including the location of your modem, whether you're using pulse or tone dialing, and whether call waiting is enabled or disabled. |
| 8 | Open Contact button | Click to display the full Contact form for the highlighted contact. |

# Actions ➤ Call using NetMeeting

Use this option to place a phone call using NetMeeting. You must have NetMeeting installed to access this option.

---

**N O T E**   Although we haven't discussed NetMeeting in this book, you can get some more information about this really cool way to hold an online meeting. Check out *Windows 98 Multimedia: Lights! Camera! Action!* by Adam Vujic (this is published by Que and the ISBN is 078971857X). ■

## How You Get Here

◇ Press **Alt+A,E**          ◇ Choose **Actions ➤ Call using NetMeeting**

# Actions ➤ Flag for Follow Up

Use this option to designate what type of follow up is required for the current Contact, such as a reply or even "no response necessary". Flags are reminders that there is something more to be done with the item. (I don't know about you, but I can use all the reminders I can get!) Flagged items have a red flag icon in their listing view and the flag is noted in a yellow banner on the opened item.

## How You Get Here

◇ Press **Alt+A,F** or **Ctrl+Shift+G**     ◇ Choose **Actions ➤ Flag for Follow Up**

# Actions ➤ Forward as vCard

Use this option to send the Contact form as an email attachment to another contact or to a different email address.

## How You Get Here

◇ Press **Alt+A,V**          ◇ Choose **Actions ➤ Forward as vCard**

# Actions ➤ Forward

Use this option to open a new Mail Message form with a copy of the item as an attachment. You'll need to fill in the appropriate email address and add any comments that you feel are appropriate before clicking the **Send** icon.

## How You Get Here

◇ Press **Alt+A,W** or **Ctrl+F**    ◇ Choose **Actions ➤ Forward**

# A Look At The Contact Form

## In this chapter

| | | | | |
|---|---|---|---|---|
| Full Name... | Nick Charles | Business | ▼ | +1 (123) 555-6666 |
| Job title: | PI | Home | ▼ | +1 (123) 555-4444 |
| Company: | Nick Charles Investigations Extro | Business Fax | ▼ | +1 (123) 444-8888 |
| File as: | Charles, Nick ▼ | Mobile | ▼ | +1 (123) 888-7777 |

## What About The Contact Form

Use this option to enter information regarding a person you frequently contact, including co-workers who share an intranet system, and outside contacts on the Contact form. The amount of information stored within each contact is quite extensive, and is available to all Outlook applications. For example, Outlook Calendar automatically notes in its master calendar the birthday you have entered in the Contact form.

## Getting To The Contact Form

There are several ways to get to the Contact form:

- Click the **New** icon on the Standard toolbar and choose **New Contact**,
- Press **Alt+F,W,C** or **Ctrl+N** or **Ctrl+Shift+C**, or
- Choose **File** ➤ **New** ➤ **Contact**.

## A Look At The Contact Form

Figure 54.1 is a sample of the form that you'll use when you want to add a contact to your database and Table 54.1 has a description of the options available.

**Figure 54.1**    The New Contact form

**This window is shown split in half so we can add the numbers to the graphic.**

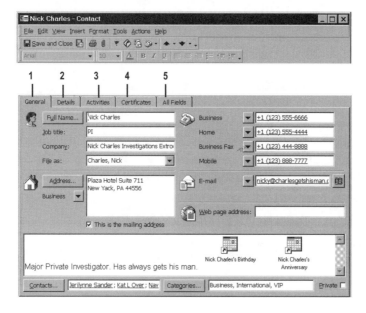

**Table 54.1**   Options in the Contact form

| # | Option | What you do with it |
|---|--------|---------------------|
| 1 | General tab | Use this tab to enter commonly accessed information, such as name, address, phone number, and email address. (For a complete description of the options available, see Table 54.2 on page 742.) |
| 2 | Details tab | Use this tab to enter more detailed information, such as the names of the boss, the assistant, the wife, and a Web page. (For a complete description of the options available, see Table 54.3 on page 743.) |
| 3 | Activities tab | Use this tab to see in table view all activities (items) linked to the contact. (For a complete description of the options available, see Table 54.4 on page 744.) |
| 4 | Certificates tab | Use this tab to designate certificates, or digital IDs, which enable you to send encrypted messages to the contact. Only those having the certificate can decode the message. (For a complete description of the options available, see Table 54.5 on page 745.) |
| 5 | All Fields tab | Use this tab to create a customized table using only those fields you designate. (For a complete description of the options available, see Table 54.6 on page 746.) |

# What's In The General Tab

Use the options in this tab to enter and maintain detailed information about the contact's name, title, phone numbers, address, and electronic contact information. Figure 54.2 is a sample of this tab and Table 54.2 has a description of the options available.

**Figure 54.2**   The General tab

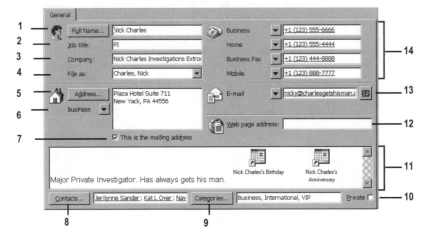

**Table 54.2**   Options in the General tab

| # | Option | What you do with it |
|---|--------|---------------------|
| 1 | Full Name button/text box | Click to display the Check Full Name dialog box, where you can enter each part of the name (Last, First, Middle, etc.) in a separate text box, or enter the full name of the contact. This is not necessarily how the name will appear on the Contact list. |
| 2 | Job Title text box | Enter the contact's job title. |
| 3 | Company text box | Enter the company the contact works for. |
| 4 | File as text box | Contact's name is entered with last name first. You can change the name entered here if you want to organize your contacts differently. |
| 5 | Address button/text box | Click to enter each part of the address (Street, City, State, etc.) into a separate text box, or enter the address manually into the text box. |
| 6 | Business drop-down list | Click to choose one of three types of addresses: Business, Home, and other. All three addresses can be stored in this form, but only one is displayed at a time. |
| 7 | This is the mailing address check box | Check if you want the address displayed to be used in other programs, such as printing labels in Word. |
| 8 | Contacts button/text box | Click to add related contacts to this contact's information. |
| 9 | Categories button/text box | Click to add categories to this contact's information. |
| 10 | Private check box | Click to hide this item from others with access to this folder. |
| 11 | Notes text box | Enter any notes you want to be related to this contact. |
| 12 | Web page Address text box | Enter the web page address of the contact. |
| 13 | E-mail text box | Enter an email address or choose one from your contacts list by clicking on the **Address book** icon. The email drop-down arrow contains three email numbers, only one of which is displayed. |
| 14 | Phone text boxes | Choose an item that determines which type of phone numbers you are entering (business, fax, etc). Enter the appropriate phone number in the text box. You can store up to 19 different types of numbers for each contact, but only four can be displayed at any given time. |

# What's In The Details Tab

Use the options in this tab to enter and maintain information about the contact, such as the department he or she works in, a birthday, a spouse's name, or the anniversary date. Figure 54.3 is a sample of this dialog box and Table 54.3 has a description of the options available.

**Figure 54.3**   The Details tab

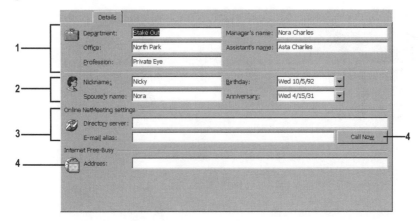

**Table 54.3**   Options in the Details tab

| # | Option | What you do with it |
|---|--------|---------------------|
| 1 | Work details area | Enter information related to the contact's work, including the department, the office, the profession, the manager's name, and the assistant's name. |
| 2 | Personal details area | Enter information related to a nickname, spouse's name, and birthdays and anniversaries (which can be chosen from a drop down date navigator). |
| 3 | Online NetMeeting Settings area | Enter the name of the server designated for NetMeetings with this contact and the email alias (typically the email address of the contact). |
| 4 | Internet Free-Busy area | Enter the URL or server path name for your Free/Busy file. A Free/Busy file contains information regarding your schedule (are you free or busy for a given date and time?) which can be shared by authorized users of the file. |
| 5 | Call Now button | Click to dial the phone number of the contact for an online meeting. You must be connected to a modem to use this option. |

# What's In The Activities Tab

Use the options in this tab to review information about activities that you have scheduled with this contact. Figure 54.4 is a sample of this dialog box and Table 54.4 has a description of the options available.

**Figure 54.4**    The Activities tab

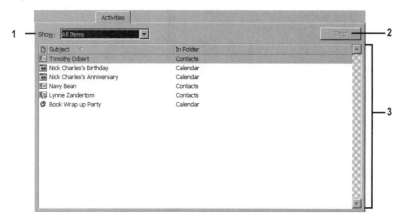

**Table 54.4**    Options in the Activities tab

| # | Option | What you do with it |
|---|--------|---------------------|
| 1 | Show drop-down list | Choose an item that determines which types of activities you want displayed. You can choose one type(such as email messages) or choose **All Types** to look at absolutely everything, regardless of what type of item it is. |
| 2 | Stop button | Click to stop the search for items indicated in the Show: text box. |
| 3 | Items area | View items linked to the contact through the Contacts text box. To view more details about an item, click on it. |

# What's In The Certificates Tab

Use the options in this tab to control create a digital signature for this contact. Figure 54.5 is a sample of this dialog box and Table 54.5 has a description of the options available.

**Figure 54.5**   The Certificates tab

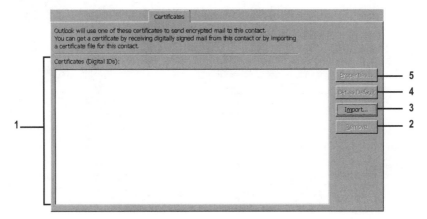

**Table 54.5**   Options in the Certificates tab

| # | Option | What you do with it |
|---|--------|---------------------|
| 1 | Certificates pane | View the certificates for the contact. |
| 2 | Remove button | Click to remove the highlighted certificate from the list. |
| 3 | Import button | Click to import a certificate from another source, such as a Windows folder. |
| 4 | Set as Default button | Click to establish a default certificate to be automatically applied when sending messages to the current contact. This button is available only when the contact has two or more certificates. |
| 5 | Properties button | Click to display the settings for the certificate, including who issued the certificate, when it expires, and the trust settings. |

# What's In The All Fields Tab

Use the options in this tab to customize your views of the contact information you've entered. Figure 54.6 is a sample of this dialog box and Table 54.6 has a description of the options available.

**Figure 54.6** The All Fields tab

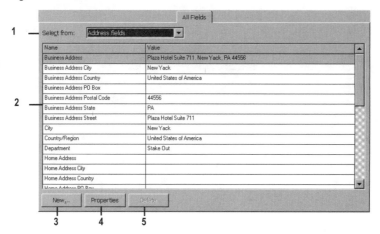

**Table 54.6** Options in the All Fields tab

| Option | What you do with it |
| --- | --- |
| 1 Select from drop-down list | Choose an item that determines which field heading you want to include in this custom table view. |
| 2 Fields list | View a table view of all fields and entries chosen in the Select From drop down list. Click on a field to make modifications to the entry. |
| 3 New button | Click to add a new field to the table view. The Select From automatically changes to User Defined Fields in Folder. |
| 4 Properties button | Click to view the properties (such as when created and what type of entry it is) associated with the chosen field. |
| 5 Delete button | Click to delete the highlighted field. You can only delete fields you have created yourself. |

# What's Different In The Contact Form Toolbars

The Contact form toolbars contain shortcuts commonly used in the Contact application. These toolbars can be customized by showing and hiding buttons from the listing found under the More Buttons tool.

## Differences In The Contact Form Standard Toolbar

Use this toolbar as a shortcut for commonly performed tasks, such as saving the information about a contact and automatically dialing the contact's telephone number.

## How You Get Here

◇ Press **Alt+V,T** choose **Standard**    ◇ Choose **View** ➤ **Toolbars** ➤ **Standard**

## What's Different

Figure 54.7 is a sample of this toolbar and Table 54.7 has a description of the icons available. (For more information, see View ➤ Toolbars ➤ Standard on page 609.)

**Figure 54.7**    The Contacts form Standard toolbar

**Table 54.7**    Icons in the Contacts form Standard toolbar

| # | Icon | What you do with it |
|---|------|---------------------|
| 1 | Save and New | Click to save the current Contacts form and open a blank Contacts form. |
| 2 | Display Map of Address | Click to display a map of the contact's indicated address, using Microsoft Internet Explorer. You must be online to access this option. |
| 3 | New Message to Contact | Click to open an untitled Message form addressed to the current contact. |
| 4 | AutoDialer | Click to dial a connection to any designated contact. You must be connected to a modem to access this option. |

## The Contact Form Formatting Toolbar

Use the icons on this toolbar to determine what the text of your message looks like. You can choose the font size, color, and whether you want special effects such as underlining and bullets.

---

**N O T E**    This toolbar is the same for all of the forms used in the various applications. (For more information, see Outlook Mail Forms Formatting Toolbar on page 675.) ■

# What Is The Distribution List

Use this option to identify members of a specific group, to whom you regularly distribute email messages and other electronic correspondences. This window contains its own menus and toolbars whose different options are described here. Once you've created a distribution list, you can use the list name in email messages and meeting requests (beats the dickens out of typing those nasty old email addresses over and over again).

## How You Get Here

◇ Press **Alt+F,W,L** or **Ctrl+Shift+L**    ◇ Choose **File** ➤ **New** ➤ **Distribution List**

## What's In This Window

Figure 54.8 is a sample of this window and Table 54.8 has a description of the options available.

**Figure 54.8**   The Distribution List window Members tab

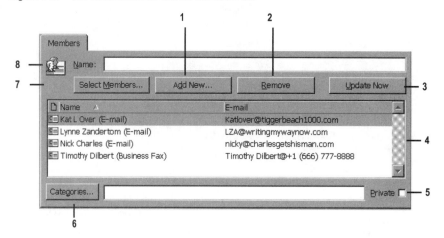

**Table 54.8**   Options in the Distribution List window Members tab

| Option | What you do with it |
|---|---|
| 1   Add new button | Click to enter the name and email address of new members you wish to appear on the list. |
| 2   Remove button | Click to delete chosen members from the list. |
| 3   Update Now button | Click to automatically update the list with any changes you have just made. |
| 4   Distribution list | Click to choose a member. View the list of members you have added to the distribution list. |
| 5   Private check box | Click to hide this item from other people who may have access to the distribution lists. |

**Table 54.8** Options in the Distribution List window Members tab, continued

| Option | What you do with it |
| --- | --- |
| 6 Categories button/text box | Click to assign a category to this distribution list. |
| 7 Select Members button | Click to display the Select members dialog box, where you can enter or choose names from your existing contact list. |
| 8 Name text box | Enter the name of list (i.e. Marketing Department) as you plan to use it. |

## What's In This Dialog Box

Figure 54.9 is a sample of this dialog box and has a description of the options available.

**Figure 54.9** The Distribution List window Notes tab

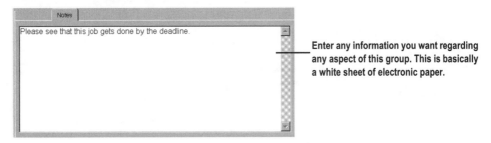

Enter any information you want regarding any aspect of this group. This is basically a white sheet of electronic paper.

# The Distribution List Standard Toolbar

Use this option to for commands to control your distribution list. You can send messages to contacts from here, copy and paste into your notes tab and move to a previous list item.

## What's Different

Figure 54.10 is a sample of this toolbar and Table 54.9 has a description of the icons available.

**Figure 54.10** The Distribution List Standard toolbar

**Table 54.9**   Icons in the Distribution List Standard toolbar

| # | Icon | What you do with it |
|---|------|---------------------|
| 1 | Cut | Click to cut chosen text or objects, to be added to the clipboard and pasted later. |
| 2 | Copy | Click to copy chosen text or objects, to be added to the clipboard and pasted later. |
| 3 | Paste | Click to open the Clipboard window, and choose which cut or copied items you want to paste at the insertion point. |
| 4 | New Message to Contact | Click to open an untitled Mail Message form, addressed to all members of the distribution list. |

# A Look At The Journal Application

**In this part**

# CHAPTER 55

# What Is The Journal Application

**In this chapter**

# What Is The Journal Application

The Outlook Journal can help you keep track of the tasks you perform in Outlook. You can choose which items are automatically tracked and which contacts in your contact database include tracking information. With the Journal application, you'll be able to automatically track the task date, the start and stop time for the task, and the file name you were working with. You can also manually enter a Journal Entry for something that you forgot to set up or that you just want to track this one time. The Journal can even create a Journal Entry each time you use one of the Office or Office-compatible applications to work with a file.

---

**N O T E**    You can tell Outlook which tasks you want automatically recorded by choosing **Tools ➤ Options** and clicking the **Journal Options** button. ▦

---

 A Journal entry helps you maintain an accurate business history of your projects and tasks. This is especially beneficial for billing purposes, as you can keep accurate time on a business call, using the Start/Stop time features on this form.

# Getting To The Journal

There are several ways to get to the Journal application and the Journal Entry form. Here are a few of them.

- To open the Journal application without opening a form, click the  icon on the Outlook Shortcuts bar.
- To open a blank form:
  - Press **Alt+F,W,J** or **Ctrl+Shift+J** or
  - Choose **File ➤ New ➤ Journal Entry.**

# How The Journal Is Organized

Figure 55.1 shows what the Journal looks like in the default view. Although you can look at different information in a bunch of different ways, each view shows the same basic information: the actual entry and the date the entry was made.

**Figure 55.1**   The Journal application

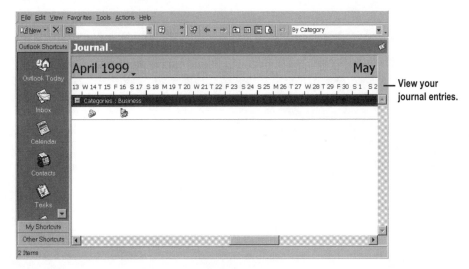

— View your
journal entries.

# What's Different In Journal's Toolbars

The Journal's toolbars may look pretty familiar if you've been working with the Calendar. If you're not sure what the various icons do, check out the information on the Calendar application. (For more information, see What's Different In Calendar's Toolbars on page 683.)

# The Journal View Menu

## In this chapter

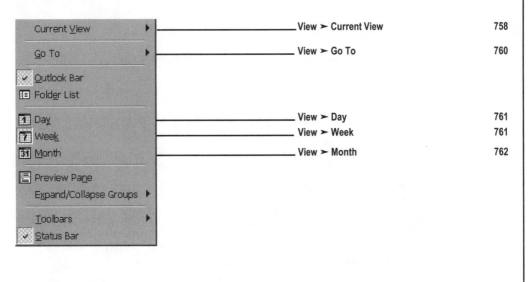

# What's Different In Journal's View Menu

The options in this menu let you look at your Journal Entries in different ways to suit different needs. In Journal, there are two types of views: Timeline views, and listings. Timeline views display Journal entries using a traditional line with time breaks which can span one day, one week, or one month.

If a menu option has an ellipsis (three dots) or an arrow beside it, the application "asks" you for additional information before the action takes place. If the menu doesn't have one of these symbols, the action you choose happens immediately. If the action takes place immediately, you won't see a sample screen in this section.

---

**N O T E**   Most of the options in this menu were described earlier in this book. (For more information, see The Common View Menu Options on page 595.) ▓

# View ➤ Current View

Use this option to change the way you are viewing the application or item.

## How You Get Here

◇ Press **Alt+V,V**

◇ Choose **View** ➤ **Current View**

## What's In This Flyout Menu

Figure 56.1 is a sample of this flyout menu.

**Figure 56.1**   The View ➤ Current View flyout menu

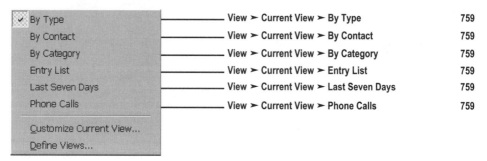

## View ➤ Current View ➤ By Type

Use this option to display your Journal Entries sorted by the type of entry created, such as a document or a phone call.

### How You Get Here

◇ Press **Alt+V,V** choose **By Type**    ◇ Choose **View** ➤ **Current View** ➤ **By Type**

## View ➤ Current View ➤ By Contact

Use this option to display your Journal Entries based on the contact name (for contacts) or the sender name (for mail messages).

### How You Get Here

◇ Press **Alt+V,V** choose **By Contact**    ◇ Choose **View** ➤ **Current View** ➤ **By Contact**

## View ➤ Current View ➤ By Category

Use this view to display your Journal Entries sorted by the category you have assigned to them.

### How You Get Here

◇ Press **Alt+V,V** choose **By Category**    ◇ Choose **View** ➤ **Current View** ➤ **By Category**

## View ➤ Current View ➤ Entry List

Use this option to display the Journal Entries in a table view so that you can sort them according the field names (by type, by date started, by date due, etc.).

### How You Get Here

◇ Press **Alt+V,V** choose **Entry List**    ◇ Choose **View** ➤ **Current View** ➤ **Entry List**

## View ➤ Current View ➤ Last Seven Days

Use this option to display a list of Journal Entries created within the last seven days.

### How You Get Here

◇ Press **Alt+V,V** choose **Last Seven Days**    ◇ Choose **View** ➤ **Current View** ➤ **Last Seven Days**

## View ➤ Current View ➤ Phone Calls

Use this option to display a list of Journal Entries that recorded phone call activities.

### How You Get Here

◇ Press **Alt+V,V** choose **Phone Calls**    ◇ Choose **View** ➤ **Current View** ➤ **Phone Calls**

# View ➤ Go To

Use this option to move quickly from one part of Outlook to another or viewing a journal entry for a specific date. This is an alternate method to using the Outlook Shortcuts bar or the Folder List. (For more information, see View ➤ Go To on page 600.)

## How You Get Here

✧ Press **Alt+V,G**          ✧ Choose **View ➤ Go To**

## What's In This Flyout Menu

Figure 56.2 is a sample of this flyout menu.

**Figure 56.2**   The View ➤ Go To flyout menu

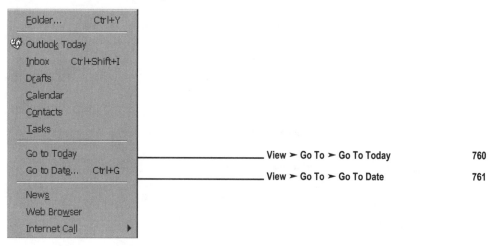

## View ➤ Go To ➤ Go To Today

Use this option to move the timeline view to show today's date.

---

**N O T E**   This option is available only in a timeline view. ▪

## How You Get Here

✧ Press **Alt+V,G,D**          ✧ Choose **View ➤ Go To ➤ Go To Today**

## View ➤ Go To ➤ Go To Date

Use this option to move the timeline view to a date specified in the Go To Date dialog box.

---

**N O T E** This option is available only in a timeline view. ▨

### How You Get Here

◇ Press **Alt+V,G,E** or **Ctrl+G** ◇ Choose **View** ➤ **Go To** ➤ **Go To Date**

### What's In This Dialog Box

Figure 56.3 is a sample of this dialog box and has a description of the options available.

**Figure 56.3** The Go To Date dialog box

Enter the date for the
Journal Entries you want
to view.

# View ➤ Day

Use this option to display a time span of one day in the timeline view.

---

**N O T E** This option is available only in a timeline view. ▨

### How You Get Here

◇ Click  Day ◇ Press **Alt+V,Y** ◇ Choose **View** ➤ **Day**

# View ➤ Week

Use this option to display a time span on one week in the timeline view.

---

**N O T E** This option is available only in a timeline view. ▨

### How You Get Here

◇ Click [7 Week]    ◇ Press **Alt+V,K**    ◇ Choose **View ➤ Week**

# View ➤ Month

Use this option to display a time span on one month in the timeline view.

---

**N O T E**    This option is available only in a timeline view. ▦

### How You Get Here

◇ Click [31 Month]    ◇ Press **Alt+V,O**    ◇ Choose **View ➤ Month**

# The Journal Actions Menu

## In this chapter

## What Is The Journal Actions Menu

This menu lists the commands that you'll use to create or manipulate Journal Entries. Journal items may be unfamiliar to you, even if you've used lots of other Microsoft products. Other Microsoft applications work with documents (or files) and most are created using the New menu. Outlook applications, however, are usually relational. That is, they involve actions such as sending an email message, or scheduling a meeting with coworkers. Initiating these activities is done with the options in the Actions menu. The New menu still exists, but is used to create new folders and the like.

If a menu option has an ellipsis (three dots) or an arrow beside it, the application "asks" you for additional information before the action takes place. If the menu doesn't have one of these symbols, the action you choose happens immediately. If the action takes place immediately, you won't see a sample screen in this section.

## Actions ➤ New Journal Entry

Use this option to create a new Journal Entry manually instead of waiting for Outlook to do it for you. (For more information, see What About The Journal Entry Form on page 766.)

### How You Get Here

◇ Click  ◇ Press **Alt+A,N** or **Ctrl+N**   ◇ Choose **Actions ➤ New Journal Entry**

## Actions ➤ Forward

Use this option to open a new Mail Message form with a copy of the item as an attachment. You'll need to fill in the appropriate email address and add any comments that you feel are appropriate before clicking the **Send** icon.

### How You Get Here

◇ Press **Alt+A,W** or **Ctrl+F**   ◇ Choose **Actions ➤ Forward**

# A Look At The Journal Entry Form

## In this chapter

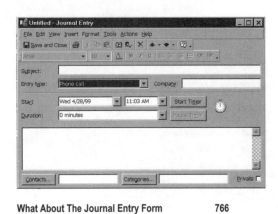

# What About The Journal Entry Form

Use this form to enter tracking information about a specific Outlook task. enter information regarding a person you frequently contact, including co-workers who share an intranet system, and outside contacts on the Contact form. The amount of information stored within each contact is quite extensive, and is available to all Outlook applications. For example, Outlook Calendar automatically notes in its master calendar the birthday you have entered in the Contact form.

# Getting To The Journal Entry Form

There are several ways to get to the Journal Entry form:

■   Click the **New** icon on the Standard toolbar and choose **New Journal Entry**,

■   Press **Alt+F,W,J** or **Ctrl+N** or **Ctrl+Shift+J**, or

■   Choose **File ➤ New ➤ Journal Entry**.

# A Look At The Journal Entry Form

Figure 58.1 is a sample of the form that you'll use when you want to add a Journal Entry to Outlook and Table 58.1 has a description of the options available.

**Figure 58.1**   The Journal Entry form

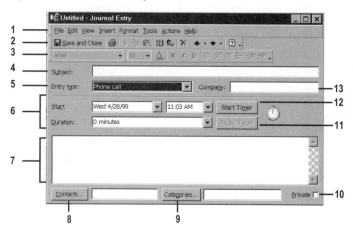

**Table 58.1**   Options in the Journal Entry form

| # | Option | What you do with it |
|---|--------|---------------------|
| 1 | Journal Entry menu | Click to display the submenus for a specific group of commands. |
| 2 | Journal Entry Standard toolbar | Click to perform a specific command using a toolbar rather than a menu item. |
|   |   | **Note**   The Journal Entry form uses the same Standard toolbar as that used for the Calendar forms. (For more information, see Differences In Calendar's Standard Toolbar on page 683 or View ➤ Toolbars on page 608.) |
| 3 | Formatting toolbar | Click to format the body of your appointment, meeting, or event message. (For more information, see Outlook Mail Forms Formatting Toolbar on page 675.) |
| 4 | Subject text box | Enter a unique and descriptive subject title for the activity being documented. |
| 5 | Entry type drop-down list | Choose an item that determines which type of activity (phone call, email, etc.) is being documented. |
| 6 | Time area | Manually enter the date and time you start the activity, or click on the arrows to display a drop down calendar/times listing, where you can scroll to the desired month and click on the desired date/time. |
| 7 | Notes area | Enter a description that you can use to help you remember why you were performing this task or why you wanted to keep a recrd of this task. |
| 8 | Contacts button and text box | Choose an item that determines which contact record the Journal Entry is attached to. You can also manually enter enter the contact name(s) in the text box, separating each contact name with a comma. |
| 9 | Categories button and text box | Choose an item that determines which category name is assigned to the current Journal Entry. You can also manually enter the category(ies) in the text box, separating each category name with a comma. |
| 10 | Private check box | Check to prevent others with access to this application from viewing this Journal Entry. |
| 11 | Pause Timer button | Click to temporarily stop the timer for this Journal Entry. |
| 12 | Start Timer button | Click to start timing the task you're document with this Journal Entry. |
| 13 | Company text box | Enter the name of the company. |

# What's Different In Journal's Toolbars

Well, there isn't anything that's different than what you've used if you've worked with the Calendar forms toolbars. If you need to take a peak at what those cute little pictures mean, check out the information on the Calendar. (For more information, see What's Different In Calendar's Forms Toolbars on page 714.)

# A Look At The Tasks Application

**In this part**

# What Is The Tasks Application

## In this chapter

# What Is The Tasks Application

What is a task? Well, in everyday terms a "task" is one of those things you gotta get done—and boy do there seem to be a lot of them these days! And, since there are so many of the darn things, Outlook provides a way to keep an electronic "to-do" list that helps you keep track of them and helps you feel good when you get to mark one of them as done. You can set start dates and due dates, indicate how high a priority a specific task should have, and even categorize tasks so that you can sort out the really important stuff (like your spouse's dry cleaning) from the truly mundane (like asking your boss for a raise). Or are those backward? Um, have to give that some thought.

# Getting To Tasks

There are several ways to get to the Tasks application and the forms. Here are a few of them.

■    To open the Task application without opening a form, click the 🖎 icon on the Outlook Shortcuts bar.

■    To open a blank form:

■    Press **Alt+F,W,T** or **Ctrl+N** or **Ctrl+Shift+K** or

■    Choose **File** ➤ **New** ➤ **Task.**

# How Tasks Is Organized

You can look at your tasks in several ways, depending on what is important to you at any given time. Figure 59.1 gives you a look at the default view of the Tasks application window.

**Figure 59.1**    The Tasks application window

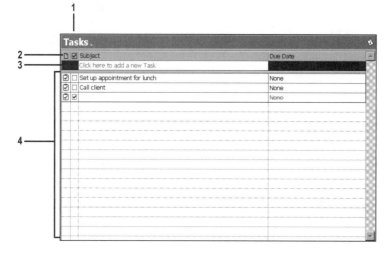

The parts of this window are:

1. **The Title bar**
   This tells you the name of the folder you're currently displaying.

2. **The Sort By bar**
   The information in this bar provides a quick summary of the currently highlighted task, including the description entered in the Subject text box and the date by which the task is supposed to be completed. Each of these columns can be resized to show more, or less, of a particular type of information. You can also quickly resort your tasks by clicking on the appropriate column title. (For more information, see What's In The Sort By Bar on page 773.)

3. **The New Task row**
   This is where you can add a new task to your to-do list. (Just what you needed, eh? Another thing to get done today.)

4. **The Task pane**
   This pane is list of the tasks already on your list. You can click a specific task and edit it from this list or open the Task form if that fits your style a bit better.

## What's In The Sort By Bar

The Sort By bar is just that: it let's you organize (sort) your tasks in either ascending or descending order, based on specific criteria about your tasks. Figure 59.2 is a sample of a Sort By from the Tasks application and Table 59.1 describes the options available.

**Figure 59.2**  The Sort By bar

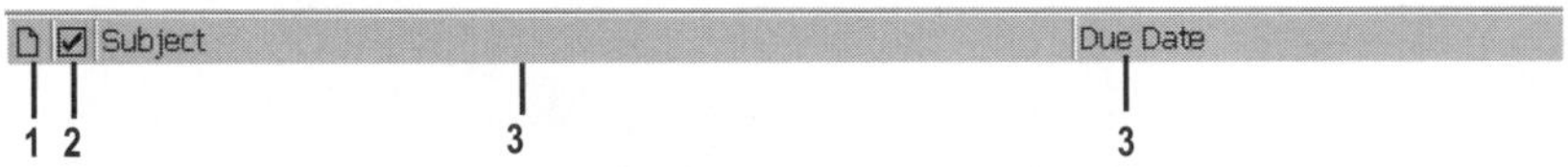

**Table 59.1**  Options in the Sort By bar

| # | Option | What you do with it |
|---|--------|---------------------|
| 1 | Priority | Click to sort your tasks based on how important you rate them. You have to assign a priority to each task if you want to sort tasks by priority. |
| 2 | Status | Click to sort your tasks based on their status (completed or not completed.) |
| 3 | Subject | Click to sort your tasks in alphabetical order based on the subject line included with the task. |
| 4 | Due Date | Click to sort your tasks in based on when the tasks is supposed to be completed. |

## What's Different In Tasks' Toolbars

Quite frankly, nothing is different in the Tasks' toolbars. They are the same standard and advanced toolbars you can find in the calendar or inbox folders. If you need a quick refresher on what all the options are, check out the information in the chapter on the common View options. (For more information, see View ➤ Toolbars ➤ Standard on page 609 or View ➤ Toolbars ➤ Advanced on page 610.)

# The Tasks View Menu

## In this chapter

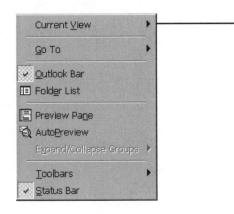

# What's Different In Tasks' View Menu

The options in this menu let you look at your tasks in different ways to suit different needs. You can display your tasks on a linear timeline or as lists that you can customize using specific criteria.

If a menu option has an ellipsis (three dots) or an arrow beside it, the application "asks" you for additional information before the action takes place. If the menu doesn't have one of these symbols, the action you choose happens immediately. If the action takes place immediately, you won't see a sample screen in this section.

---

**N O T E**   Most of the options in this menu were described earlier in this book. (For more information, see The Common View Menu Options on page 595.) ■

# View ➤ Current View

Use this option to change the way you are viewing the application or item.

## How You Get Here

◇ Press **Alt+V,V**          ◇ Choose **View ➤ Current View**

## What's In This Flyout Menu

Figure 60.1 is a sample of this flyout menu.

**Figure 60.1**   The View ➤ Current View flyout menu

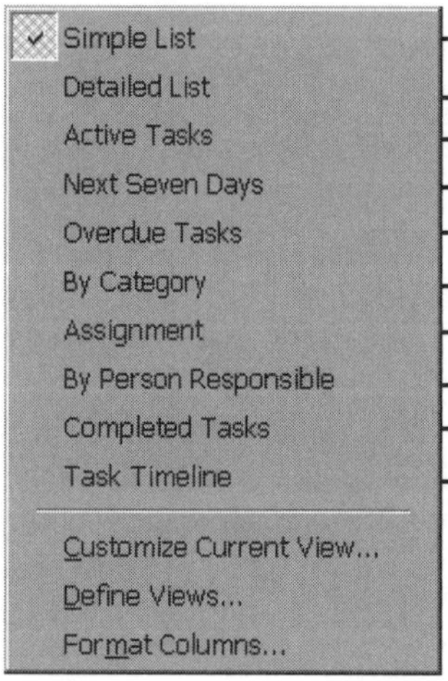

The flyout menu shows the following options:

Simple List
Detailed List
Active Tasks
Next Seven Days
Overdue Tasks
By Category
Assignment
By Person Responsible
Completed Tasks
Task Timeline

Customize Current View...
Define Views...
Format Columns...

## View ➤ Current View ➤ Simple List

Use this option to display a list of your tasks by heading only.

### How You Get Here

◇ Press **Alt+V,V** choose **Simple List**    ◇ Choose **View** ➤ **Current View** ➤ **Simple List**

## View ➤ Current View ➤ Detailed List

Use this option to display a list of all your tasks, with additional field headings such as the task importance and attachments.

### How You Get Here

◇ Press **Alt+V,V** choose **Detailed List**    ◇ Choose **View** ➤ **Current View** ➤ **Detailed List**

## View ➤ Current View ➤ Active Tasks

Use this option to display a list of tasks that have not yet been marked as completed.

### How You Get Here

◇ Press **Alt+V,V** choose **Active Tasks**    ◇ Choose **View** ➤ **Current View** ➤ **Active Tasks**

## View ➤ Current View ➤ Next Seven Days

Use this option to display a list of only those tasks that are due within the next seven days.

### How You Get Here

◇ Press **Alt+V,V** choose **Next Seven Days**   ◇ Choose **View** ➤ **Current View** ➤ **Next Seven Days**

## View ➤ Current View ➤ Overdue Tasks

Use this option to display a list of those tasks that have a due date that has already passed. (In other words, of list of those things you're supposed to get done, but haven't.)

### How You Get Here

◇ Press **Alt+V,V** choose **Overdue Tasks**    ◇ Choose **View** ➤ **Current View** ➤ **Overdue Tasks**

## View ➤ Current View ➤ By Category

Use this view to display a list of all tasks sorted by the category assigned when you created the task. Those given no category are labeled as (none).

### How You Get Here

◇ Press **Alt+V,V** choose **By Category**    ◇ Choose **View** ➤ **Current View** ➤ **By Category**

### View ➤ Current View ➤ Assignment

Use this option to to display a list of those tasks which have been assigned to others.

### How You Get Here

◇ Press **Alt+V,V** choose **Assignment**        ◇ Choose **View** ➤ **Current View** ➤ **Assignment**

### View ➤ Current View ➤ By Person Responsible

Use this option to display a list of all tasks, sorted by the person who was assigned responsibility for getting the task done. This criterion is only available on forms where more than one person shares the task.

### How You Get Here

◇ Press **Alt+V,V**
   choose **By Person Responsible**

◇ Choose **View** ➤ **Current View** ➤ **By Person Responsible**

### View ➤ Current View ➤ Completed Tasks

Use this option to to display a list of those tasks that have been marked complete.

### How You Get Here

◇ Press **Alt+V,V** choose **Completed Tasks**    ◇ Choose **View** ➤ **Current View** ➤ **Completed Tasks**

### View ➤ Current View ➤ Task Timeline

Use this option to display all tasks along a linear calendar. Note that the toolbar changes in this view and that you can adjust the calendar range from one day to one month.

### How You Get Here

◇ Press **Alt+V,V** choose **Task TImeline**     ◇ Choose **View** ➤ **Current View** ➤ **Task Timeline**

# The Tasks Actions Menu

## In this chapter

# What Is The Tasks Actions Menu

This menu lists the commands that you'll use for any new activity related to creating new tasks (such as adding a new task to your to-do list or creating a task request). Other Microsoft applications work with documents (or files) and most are created using the New menu. Outlook applications, however, are usually relational. That is, they involve actions such as sending an email message, or scheduling a meeting with co-workers. Initiating these activities is done with the options in the Actions menu. The New menu still exists, but is used to create new folders and the like.

If a menu option has an ellipsis (three dots) or an arrow beside it, the application "asks" you for additional information before the action takes place. If the menu doesn't have one of these symbols, the action you choose happens immediately. If the action takes place immediately, you won't see a sample screen in this section.

# Actions ➤ New Task

Use this option to open a blank Task form so that you can enter the appropriate information for this task, such as the start date, due date, and level of importance. (For more information, see A Look At The Task Form on page 783.)

### How You Get Here

◇ Click 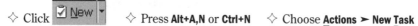   ◇ Press **Alt+A,N** or **Ctrl+N**   ◇ Choose **Actions** ➤ **New Task**

# Actions ➤ New Task Request

Use this option to open a blank Task Request form, which is identical to the new Task form, with the addition of a To: text box and a Send option on the toolbar so that you can have *someone else* get to work on this task. (For more information, see A Look At The Task Form on page 783.)

### How You Get Here

◇ Press **Alt+A,Q** or **Ctrl+Shift+U**   ◇ Choose **Actions** ➤ **New Task Request**

# Actions ➤ Save Task Order

Use this option to save the current order of the tasks (which you may have modified by sorting the information according to the field headers).

### How You Get Here

◇ Press **Alt+A,S**        ◇ Choose **Actions** ➤ **Save Task Order**

# Actions ➤ Forward

Use this option to open a new Mail Message form with a copy of the item as an attachment. You'll need to fill in the appropriate email address and add any comments that you feel are appropriate before clicking the **Send** icon.

## How You Get Here

◇ Press **Alt+A,W** or **Ctrl+F**    ◇ Choose **Actions** ➤ **Forward**

# A Look At The Task Form

## In this chapter

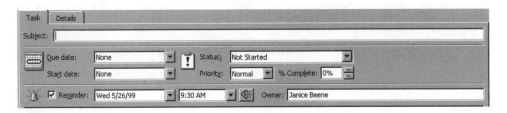

## What About The Task Form

There are two forms used for the Task application: a Task form and a Task Request form. Visually, they're almost identical and there is only one functional difference between the two forms. The Task Request form has a place for you to add an email address so that you can assign this task to someone else. You can add a subject line that lets you know what this task is about, add a deadline, mark it as a priority item, and just plain manage all those bunches of things you've got to get done.

## Getting To The Task Form

There are several ways to get to the Task forms.

To get to the New Task form:

- Click the **New** icon on the Standard toolbar and choose **New Task**,
- Press **Alt+F,W,T** or **Ctrl+N** or **Ctrl+Shift+K**, or
- Choose **File** ➤ **New** ➤ **Task**.

To get to the New Task Request form:

- Click the **New** icon on the Standard toolbar and choose **New Task Request**,
- Press **Alt+F,W,R** or **Ctrl+Shift+U**, or
- Choose **File** ➤ **New** ➤ **Task Request**.

# A Look At The Task Form

Figure 62.1 is a sample of the New Task form that you'll use when you just can't wait to add another item to your to-do list and Table 62.1 has a description of the options available.

**Figure 62.1**  The Task form

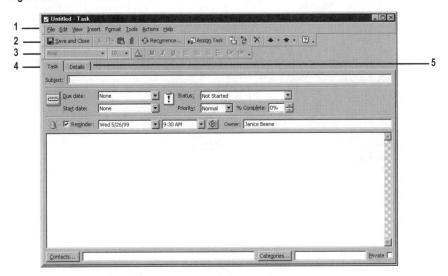

**Table 62.1**  Options in the Task form

| # | Option | What you do with it |
|---|--------|---------------------|
| 1 | Task menus | Click to display the submenus for a specific group of commands. |
| | | **Note**  Most of these menu options are the same as those found on the Outlook menu bar. However, there are a few commands that apply specifically to working with tasks. |
| 2 | Tasks Standard toolbar | Click to perform a specific command using a toolbar rather than a menu item. (For more information, see Differences In Outlook Mail's Forms Standard Toolbar on page 674.) |
| 3 | Formatting toolbar | Click to format the body of your appointment, meeting, or event message. (For more information, see Outlook Mail Forms Formatting Toolbar on page 675.) |
| 4 | Task tab | Enter all the gory details about this task. (For a complete description of the options available, see Table 62.2 on page 786.) |
| 5 | Details tab | Enter the task details such as the time it takes to complete the task, billing information, and mark the task as completed. (For a complete description of the options available, see Table 62.3 on page 788.) |

# What's In The Task Tab

Use the options in this tab to set up specific criteria (such as the due date, when you're supposed to start working on the task, and whether you want an audible alarm to remind you that the task is due) for the different types of tasks that you create and maintain. Figure 62.2 is a sample of this tab and Table 62.2 has a description of the options available. And yes, this book usually shows you the name of the menu, but that structure just wasn't cutting the mustard with Outlook. It's different, for sure.

**Figure 62.2**   The Task tab

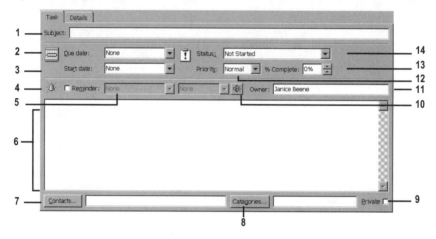

**Table 62.2**   Options in the Task tab

| # | Option | What you do with it |
|---|--------|---------------------|
| 1 | Subject text box | Enter the subject of the task. |
| 2 | Due date drop-down calendar | Enter the date when the task is due to be completed or click on the arrow to display a drop down calendar so that you can scroll to the desired month and click the desired date. |
| 3 | Start date drop-down calendar | Enter the date when the task is due to be started or click on the arrow to display a drop down calendar so that you can scroll to the desired month and click the desired date. |
| 4 | Reminder check box | Click to set an audible alarm that reminds you that this task is supposed to be finished soon. |
| 5 | Reminder date/time text boxes | Manually enter the date and time you wish the alarm to sound or click on the arrow to display a drop down calendar so that you can scroll to the desired month and click the desired date. |
| 6 | Notes pane | Enter the a description of the task you want it to appear in any task pane. |
| 7 | Contacts button/text box | Click to display the Select Contacts dialog box, where you can select from a list of contacts or enter the contact name(s) in the text box, separating each name with a comma. |

**Table 62.2**   Options in the Task tab, continued

| # | Option | What you do with it |
|---|--------|---------------------|
| 8 | Categories button/text box | Click to display the Categories dialog box, where you can select one or more of the listed categories for future filing, or enter the category(ies) in the text box, separating each category with a comma. |
| 9 | Private check box | Check to prevent others with access to this application from viewing this item. |
| 10 | Sound icon | Click to display the Reminder Sound dialog box, where you can select a sound from those available on your system. |
| 11 | Owner text box | View the name of the person who created this task. Enter a name if desired (the default is the name of who owns this copy of Outlook 2000. |
| 12 | Priority drop-down list | Choose an item that determines the priority (high, normal, low) level assigned to this task. |
| 13 | % complete list | Click on the up/down arrows to select a % complete, in increments of 25 (0, 25, 50, 75, and 100). |
| 14 | Status drop-down list | Choose an item that determines the status (not yet started, completed, etc.) of this task. |

## What's In The Details Tab

Use the options in this tab to fill in or change the information about when the task was completed, how long the task took, and other information that describes this task. Figure 62.3 is a sample of this tab and Table 62.3 has a description of the options available.

**Figure 62.3**   The Details tab

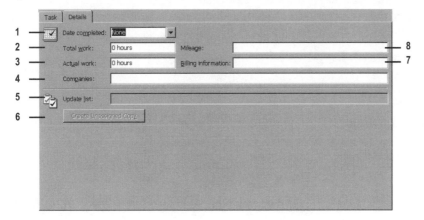

**Table 62.3**   Options in the Tasks Item form Details tab

| # | Option | What you do with it |
|---|---|---|
| 1 | Date completed drop-down calendar | Enter the date when the task was completed or choose a date from the drop-down calendar. |
|   |   | **Note**   Whenever you enter a date here, the status of this task changes to "Completed". |
| 2 | Total work text box | Enter the amount of time you think it will take to complete the task. |
| 3 | Actual work text box | Enter the total time it actually took to complete the task. |
| 4 | Companies text box | Enter the company you have associated with the task. |
| 5 | Update list text box | Create a list of people who need to be notified whenever changes are made to the task. |
| 6 | Create Unassigned Copy button | Click to send a new copy of this task to a new recipient. |
| 7 | Billing information text box | Enter the information regarding this task that will assist you for billing purposes. |
| 8 | Mileage text box | Enter the total mileage driven to complete this task. |

# What's Different In Tasks' Toolbars

The Tasks form standard and formatting toolbars by default contain shortcuts commonly used when you are creating a new event. These toolbars can be customized by showing and hiding buttons from the listing found under the More Buttons tool.

## Differences In The New Task Standard Toolbar

Use this toolbar to perform tasks related to working with tasks, such as assigning a task to a specific individual, moving to a previous item, and saving and closing the Task form.

## How You Get Here

◇ Press **Alt+V,T** choose **Standard**      ◇ Choose <u>V</u>iew ➤ <u>T</u>oolbars ➤ **Standard**

## What's Different

Figure 62.4 is a sample of this toolbar and Table 62.4 has a description of the icons that are unique to the Forms toolbar.

**Figure 62.4**   The Tasks form Standard toolbar

**Table 62.4**  Icons in the Tasks form Standard toolbar

| # | Icon | What you do with it |
|---|------|---------------------|
| 1 | Save and Close | Click to close the task item, while saving the changes you have made. |
| 2 | Recurrence | Click to enter information related to a recurring task, such as the pattern, frequency, the range (start and end dates). |
| 3 | Assign Task | Click to change the Task form to a Task Request form, which contains a To: text box, so you can send the task to a contact. The Assign Task tool toggles to a Cancel Assignment tool. |
| 4 | Send Status Report | Click to send a message regarding this task. The Mail message dialog box displays so that you can address your email message and enter a note regarding the tasks' status. |
| 5 | Mark Complete | Click to mark this task as finished. |

## Differences In The New Task Request Form Standard Toolbar

Use this toolbar to perform commands related to sending a new task request to someone.

## What's Different

Figure 62.5 is a sample of this toolbar and has a description of the only new icon available. The rest of the icons are the same as that displayed for the New Task form. (For more information, see Differences In The New Task Standard Toolbar on page 788.)

**Figure 62.5**  The Task Request form Standard toolbar

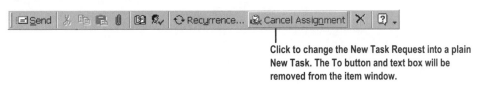

Click to change the New Task Request into a plain New Task. The To button and text box will be removed from the item window.

## Differences In Tasks Formatting Toolbar

Use the icons on this toolbar to determine what the text of your task looks like. You can choose the font size, color, and whether you want special effects such as underlining and bullets.

**N O T E**  This toolbar is the same for all of the forms used in the various applications. (For more information, see Outlook Mail Forms Formatting Toolbar on page 675.) ■

# A Look At The Notes Application

**In this part**

# What Is The Notes Application

**In this chapter**

# What Is The Notes Application

Outlook Notes is the electronic version of those colorful sticky notes that are so popular in today's office. Outlook Notes has a view that actually looks like a noteboard, and the notes themselves come in five stock colors, so you can color code your notes to make it easier to see, at a glance, what's most important. Best of all, you can actually export Notes to other places such as another item or file created in a Microsoft application other than Outlook). When you export the Notes, they're displayed in the target wherever stuck to wherever your pointer happened to be.

**TIP**   Really important notes can be stuck to the Windows desktop, so that when you close everything and get ready to shut down, you'll see the note reminding you to pick up the dry cleaning on the way home.

## Getting To Notes

There are several ways to get to the Notes application and the forms. Here are a few of them.

■   To open the Notes application without opening a form, click the ▨ icon on the Outlook Shortcuts bar.

■   To open a blank form:
   ■   Press **Alt+F,W,N** or **Ctrl+N** or **Ctrl+Shift+N** or
   ■   Choose **File** ➤ **New** ➤ **Note**.

## How Notes Is Organized

The Notes application is the simplest one in Outlook. It consists solely of the noteboard, in which the notes are displayed. These notes can be displayed differently by changing the type of view. Figure 63.1 is a sample of the default view for the Notes application.

**TIP**   You can apply a category by highlighting the note, then selecting **Edit** ➤ **Categories** or by using the shortcut menu.

**NOTE**   Changing the view to sort or filter by a given criterion takes away from the visual organization of notes; the display becomes a list view, and viewing by color means you see a list of the notes with the color indicated in the color field. ▨

**Figure 63.1** The Notes application

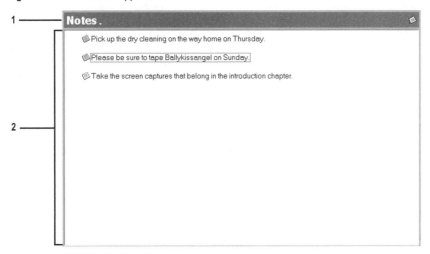

The parts of this window are:

1. **The Title bar**
   This tells you the name of the folder you're currently displaying.

2. **The Notes pane**
   This pane is list of the notes that you've already created. You can double-click a specific note to look at it in more detail.

# What's Different In Notes' Toolbars

A majority of the icons on both the Standard and Advanced toolbars were discussed in the chapter on common View menu options. (For more information, see View ➤ Toolbars on page 608.) There are no differences in the Advanced toolbar and only a few differences in the Standard toolbar.

## Differences In Notes' Standard Toolbar

Use this toolbar as a shortcut for commonly performed tasks, such as creating displaying your notes as large icons or as a list.

## How You Get Here.

◇ Press **Alt+V,T** choose **Standard**        ◇ Choose **View** ➤ **Toolbars** ➤ **Standard**

## What's Different

Figure 63.2 is a sample of this toolbar and Table 63.1 has a description of the icons icons that are unique to Notes.

**Figure 63.2**   The Notes Standard toolbar

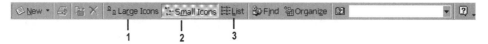

**Table 63.1**   Icons in the Notes Standard toolbar

| # | Icon | What you do with it |
|---|------|---------------------|
| 1 | Large Icons | Click to increase the size of your note icons as they are displayed on the desktop. |
| 2 | Small Icons | Click to decrease the size of your note icons as they are displayed on the desktop. |
| 3 | List | Click to display your notes as a list. |

# The Notes View Menu

**In** this chapter

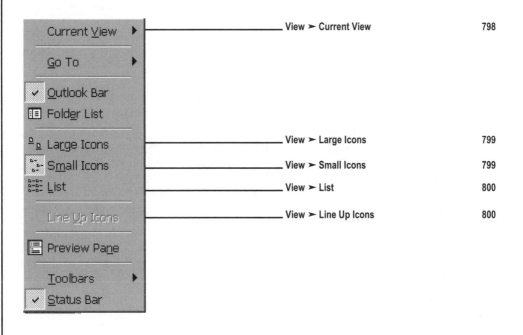

# What's Different In Notes' View Menu

The options in this menu let you look at your notes in different ways to suit different needs. There are three types of views in Notes: icons, lists, and table views. Icons display one or two words in the note; a list is beneficial if you have several notes you need to scan; and table view lets you sort the notes based on specific criteria.

If a menu option has an ellipsis (three dots) or an arrow beside it, the application "asks" you for additional information before the action takes place. If the menu doesn't have one of these symbols, the action you choose happens immediately. If the action takes place immediately, you won't see a sample screen in this section.

# View ➤ Current View

Use this option to change the way you are viewing the application or item.

### How You Get Here

◇ Press **Alt+V,V**

◇ Choose **View ➤ Current View**

### What's In This Flyout Menu

Figure 64.1 is a sample of this flyout menu.

**Figure 64.1**   The View ➤ Current View flyout menu

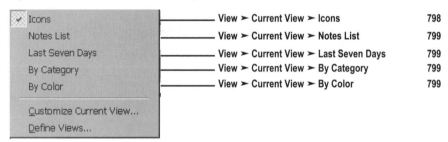

| | | |
|---|---|---|
| View ➤ Current View ➤ Icons | 798 |
| View ➤ Current View ➤ Notes List | 799 |
| View ➤ Current View ➤ Last Seven Days | 799 |
| View ➤ Current View ➤ By Category | 799 |
| View ➤ Current View ➤ By Color | 799 |

## View ➤ Current View ➤ Icons

Use this option to display your notes as pictures on your screen. You choose either small icons that don't take up much screen real estate or large ones that are easier on the eyes.

### How You Get Here

◇ Press **Alt+V,V** choose **Icons**

◇ Choose **View ➤ Current View ➤ Icons**

### View ➤ Current View ➤ Notes List

Use this option to display your notes as one big list with no field names in the header.

#### How You Get Here

◇ Press **Alt+V,V** choose **Notes List**　　◇ Choose **View** ➤ **Current View** ➤ **Notes List**

### View ➤ Current View ➤ Last Seven Days

Use this option to display a list of notes created within the last seven days.

#### How You Get Here

◇ Press **Alt+V,V** choose **Last Seven Days**　◇ Choose **View** ➤ **Current View** ➤ **Last Seven Days**

### View ➤ Current View ➤ By Category

Use this view to display your notes sorted by the category assigned when you created them.

#### How You Get Here

◇ Press **Alt+V,V** choose **By Category**　　◇ Choose **View** ➤ **Current View** ➤ **By Category**

### View ➤ Current View ➤ By Color

Use this option to display your notes sorted by the color assigned when you created them.

#### How You Get Here

◇ Press **Alt+V,V** choose **By Color**　　◇ Choose **View** ➤ **Current View** ➤ **By Color**

## View ➤ Large Icons

Use this option to display your notes as large (well, relatively large) pictures. This option is available only in icon view.

### How You Get Here

◇ Click [Large Icons]　　◇ Press **Alt+V,R**　◇ Choose **View** ➤ **Large Icons**

## View ➤ Small Icons

Use this option to display your notes as small pictures. This option is available only in icon view.

### How You Get Here

◇ Click [Small Icons]　　◇ Press **Alt+V,M**　◇ Choose **View** ➤ **Small Icons**

# View ➤ List

Use this option to display your notes as one big long list. This option is available only in icon view.

## How You Get Here

◇ Click ▦ List          ◇ Press **Alt+V,L**    ◇ Choose **View** ➤ **List**

# View ➤ Line Up Icons

Use this option to align the icons according to a grid pattern. You can click and drag icons to any position on the screen, and this option takes the repositioned note and places it squarely on the grid nearest to it's most recent placement. This option is available only in icon view and after a note has been clicked and dragged to a new position that is not exactly squared up.

## How You Get Here

◇ Press **Alt+V,U**          ◇ Choose **View** ➤ **Line Up Icons**

# The Notes Actions Menu

## In this chapter

# What Is The Notes Actions Menu

This menu lists the commands that you'll use to initiate any new activity related to creating Notes. Other Microsoft applications work with documents (or files) and most are created using the New menu. Outlook applications, however, are usually relational. That is, they involve actions such as sending an email message, or scheduling a meeting with coworkers. Initiating these activities is done with the options in the Actions menu. The New menu still exists, but is used to create new folders and the like.

If a menu option has an ellipsis (three dots) or an arrow beside it, the application "asks" you for additional information before the action takes place. If the menu doesn't have one of these symbols, the action you choose happens immediately. If the action takes place immediately, you won't see a sample screen in this section.

# Actions ➤ New Note

Use this option to open a blank Note form so that you can enter the information you want stored in it. (For more information, see What About The Notes Form on page 804.)

## How You Get Here

◇ Click 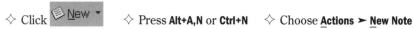 New ▾     ◇ Press **Alt+A,N** or **Ctrl+N**    ◇ Choose **Actions ➤ New Note**

# Actions ➤ Forward

Use this option to open a new Mail Message form with a copy of the item as an attachment. You'll need to fill in the appropriate email address and add any comments that you feel are appropriate before clicking the **Send** icon.

## How You Get Here

◇ Press **Alt+A,W** or **Ctrl+F**    ◇ Choose **Actions ➤ Forward**

# A Look At The Notes Form

**In this chapter**

Please be sure to tape
Ballykissangel on
Sunday.

5/3/99 1:46 PM

## What About The Notes Form

Use this form to create an electronic version of a sticky note, complete with five color options and several possible categories, including those you create.  These help keep you organized, and you can post these notes onto any Outlook, or other file created with a Microsoft application. There are no fancy forms, just the ability to choose one of three sizes, the color, and the category using some of the Note drop down menu options.

---

**N O T E**    Unlike the other Outlook applications, there are no menus or toolbars associated with the Notes form. To use a command, you must choose the it from the Notes application menu bar or toolbars.

## Getting To The Notes Form

There are several ways to get to the Notes form:

■    Click the **New** icon on the Standard toolbar and choose **New Note**,

■    Press **Alt+F,W,N** or **Ctrl+N** or **Ctrl+Shift+N**, or

■    Choose **File** ➤ **New** ➤ **Note.**

## A Look At The Notes Form

Figure 66.1 is a sample of the form that you'll use when you're ready to add a new note. You'll notice that there is only one option: a place to type the text of your note.

**Figure 66.1**    The Notes window

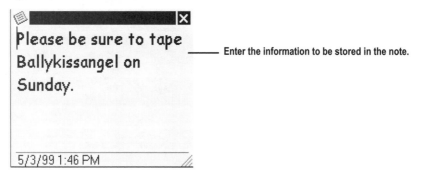

——— Enter the information to be stored in the note.

# Index

# E

# G